THEORIES OF PSYCHOTHERAPY

FIFTH EDITION

C. H. PATTERSON
University of North Carolina at Greensboro

C. EDWARD WATKINS, JR.
University of North Texas

HarperCollinsCollegePublishers

ACQUISITIONS EDITOR: Catherine Woods
PROJECT COORDINATION AND TEXT DESIGN: York Production Services
COVER DESIGN: Kay Petronio
COVER ILLUSTRATION: Eric Dinyer/Graphis Stock
ELECTRONIC PRODUCTION MANAGER: Mike Kemper
MANUFACTURING MANAGER: Helene G. Landers
ELECTRONIC PAGE MAKEUP: York Production Services
PRINTER AND BINDER: R. R. Donnelly & Sons Company
COVER PRINTER: The New England Book Components, Inc.

Theories of Psychotherapy, Fifth Edition

Library of Congress Cataloging-in-Publication Data

Patterson, C. H. (Cecil Holden), 1912–
  Theories of psychotherapy / C. H. Patterson,
C. Edward Watkins, Jr. — 5th ed.
    p. cm.
  Includes bibliographical references and index.
  ISBN 0-673-99103-2
  1. Psychotherapy.   2. Counseling.   I. Watkins, C. Edward
RC480.P38   1996
616.89'14—dc20   95-17191
                                                                 CIP

96 97 98 9 8 7 6 5 4 3 2

To Frances
To Amelia and Grant

CONTENTS

PART THREE: COGNITIVE APPROACHES   193

13. CLIENT-CENTERED THERAPY: ROGERS   385

PART FIVE: EXISTENTIAL PSYCHOTHERAPY   429

14. LOGOTHERAPY: FRANKL   439

PART SIX: CONCLUSION: DIVERGENCE AND CONVERGENCE IN PSYCHOTHERAPY   469

15. DIVERGENCE   471

16.   CONVERGENCE   489

PREFACE

"Theories of Counseling and Psychotherapy" was conceived at a lunch in the Well of the Sea restaurant in the Sherman Hotel in Chicago, during the 1960 meeting of the American Psychological Association. George Middendorf, psychology editor of Harper asked the first author if he could suggest someone who could write a book on theories of psychotherapy similar to that of Hilgard on theories of learning (Hilgard, 1948) and Hall and Lindzey's theories of personality (Hall & Lindzey, 1957). After thinking about it for a brief time (a few weeks), I recommended myself. I had published two books with Harper (*Counseling the Emotionally Disturbed,* 1958 and *Counseling and Psychotherapy: Theory and Practice,* 1959); although neither was a best seller, George offered me a contract.

With each of the first four editions of this text, discussions of various theories were either added or dropped to reflect their importance at the time of publication.[1] For this edition Raimy, Kanfer and Phillips, Rotter's "Social Learning Approach," Hart, and Thorne's "Eclectic System of Clinical Practice" have been dropped. New in this edition are Jung's "Analytical Psychotherapy," Adler's "Individual Psychology," and "Object Relations Theory and Therapy." Of the fourteen theories included here, only six were in the first edition: Dollard and Miller's "Reinforcement Theory and Psychoanalytic Therapy," Wolpe's "Behavior Therapy," Ellis' "Rational Emotive Therapy," Kellys' "Psychology of Personal Constructs," Rogers' "Client-Centered Therapy," and Frankl's "Logotherapy."

For this edition as for previous editions, deciding which theories to drop and which to add was difficult. Many more theories could be included. Consultations with colleagues did not lead to complete agreement. The final choices are those of the authors. Instructors

---

[1]The first edition (Patterson, 1966) included fifteen chapters. In the second edition (Patterson, 1973), three of these chapters were dropped: Salter's "Conditioned Reflex Therapy," the Pepinskys' "Reinforcement Theory of Counseling," and E. L. Phillips' "Interference Theory." Two theories were added, for a total of 14: Kanfer and Phillips' "Learning Foundations of Behavior Therapy" and Perls' "Gestalt Therapy." In the third edition (Patterson, 1980), Grinker's "Transactional Approach" was dropped; Meichenbaum's "Cognitive Behavior Therapy" and Berne's "Transactional Analysis" were added. The fourth edition (Patterson, 1986) saw two of the chapters in the preceding editions dropped: Williamson's "Minnesota Point of View" and Bordin's "Psychoanalytic Counseling." Four new chapters were included: Freud's "Psychoanalysis," Beck's "Cognitive Therapy," Hart's "Functional Eclectic Psychotherapy," and Raimy's "Cognitive Therapy and the Misconception Hypothesis."

who wish their students to study a theory that was included in previous editions will find these editions in a library.

No single criterion can be used as a basis for including a theory. The major criterion, as stated in the fourth edition (Patterson, 1986, p. xiv), is that the approach has a substantial conceptual or theoretical foundation. Significance for the field of psychotherapy—as judged by the authors—is a second criterion. Historical importance is included here, though some of the theories dropped might be considered of historical importance—those of Williamson and Thorne, for example. Popularity is not a criterion, nor is the extent to which a theory is practiced by adherents. Most of the theories, however, are either widely practiced in some form or studied by students of psychotherapy.

Students in psychotherapy should be exposed early in their preparation to the major approaches or points of view. To expect them to read the original sources of even a half dozen of these approaches would be unrealistic. But the thumbnail sketches included in introductory textbooks are inadequate. What is needed is a source book that presents comprehensive and accurate summaries in enough detail to give students a grasp of the structure and the organization of the theories, so that they can compare them and use them as a basis for later reading of original sources for at least some of the theories.

There are a number of ways in which a book such as this may be approached. It is difficult for a single person, with the biases that he or she has, to present various points of view accurately and fairly. One way of minimizing this bias would be to have collaborators representing differing views. The writing of such a book would be difficult, however, and numerous collaborators would be necessary or desirable. A second approach, derived from this difficulty, would be to have a general editor, as well as acknowledged representatives of the various theories, who would present them. Such a book presents problems, however, with regard to bias on the part of the proponents of each theory and the consistency of presentation. Evaluations by people other than the representatives or the editor would be desirable. A third approach would be to have a single person present the various theories, who would then have the pertinent chapters read and critiqued by appropriate colleagues or representatives of the theories presented.

The third approach is the one taken in this book. Two variations of this approach are possible. In the first, the theories could be summarized from the writer's point of view, that is, in an expository or openly critical or evaluative manner. In the second, the writer would attempt to present nonevaluative summaries of the theories as they are propounded by their originators or representatives. A critique or evaluation could follow each presentation. It is the second variation that we have used.

In each chapter, we have described a given approach, not based on our views of the approach but from the point of view of an adherent. We have attempted to be nonevaluative in the presentation of each approach, and we have aimed at comprehensiveness, completeness, and accuracy in each presentation. In some cases, we have reorganized the original theorists' presentations in the interest of clarity. In each case, we immersed ourselves in the writings of the theorist, and in the process, we found ourselves identifying with the theory; as a result, most, if not all, of the theories are presented in a rather favorable light. Overall we have strived for accuracy and clarity.

Evidence that we have been at least fairly successful in avoiding biased presentations is the fact that the summaries have been accepted by the authors or developers of each approach in cases in which they were read by the original author or a person identified closely with the approach. This was done for each theory included in the first edition, and suggestions by readers were incorporated in each summary. The following persons read the chapters in the first edition, which are also included here, and I am indebted to them for reading and commenting on the presentations and in some cases for permitting me to reprint case summaries or typescripts: Albert Ellis, Viktor E. Frankl, George A. Kelly, Neal E. Miller, Carl R. Rogers, Joseph Wolpe, and Donald Meichenbaum. Erving Polster read the chapter on Gestalt therapy. We also would like to thank the following reviewers for their input in the fifth edition: Dr. Al Adams, Regent University; Dr. Roseann Cappella, East Stroudsburg State University; Dr. Helen Cogburn, Auburn University at Montgomery; Dr. James B. Council, North Dakota State University; Dr. Herb Cross, Washington State University; Dr. Richard Dunlop, University of Missouri; Dr. Jon B. Ellis, East Tennessee State University; Dr. Charles Frederickson, Centenary College; Dr. Sandra Jenkins, Pacific University; Dr. Robert Rosenbaum, California Institute of Integral Studies; Dr. Vance Rhoades, Brewton-Parker College; Dr. Carolyn Thomas, Auburn University at Montgomery; and Dr. David Weiss, University of Akron. We believe we have succeeded in being fair in our presentations, perhaps in some cases presenting the theory more clearly, and in a better light, than the original.

Some reviewers and critics have not seemed to be aware that these chapters (and other chapters in earlier editions) were accepted by the theorists (or a representative) as being clear and accurate summaries. Possibly they were reacting to the evaluation sections at the end of the chapters. These evaluations represent the views of the authors—as well as other reviewers and critics who are cited.

New to this edition are three additions to the evaluation sections: (1) statements by and references to other contributors to the theories, (2) brief summaries or evaluations of the research support for the theories, and (3) consideration of future directions. All chapters have been updated; a length and limitations section has also been added to most theory chapters.

The final section of the book—on Divergence and Convergence in Psychotherapy—is also the work of the authors. Instructors who might question or disagree with these chapters should find them a foil for their own views or a stimulus for student discussion.

Two other points should be made:

1. We have retained the designation "client-centered" for Rogers' approach. This is in spite of the claim by Rice and Greenberg (1992) that Rogers decided, after his move to California, "that client-centered therapy should be renamed 'person-centered therapy'" (p. 201). Zimring and Raskin (1992) title their chapter "Carl Rogers and Client/Person-Centered Therapy." They note that it was in the 1970s that "the phrase *person-centered approach* becomes meaningful and appropriate in the phase of the development of the client-centered movement, as client-centered principles are applied to education, industry and other human relations contexts" (p. 643).

Rogers (1986) uses two terms: *client-centered therapy* and the *person-centered approach*. Later, in an article titled "Client-centered? Person-centered?" Rogers states he would like "a term to describe what I do when I am endeavoring to be facilitative in a group of persons who are not my clients." That term is *person-centered*. *Client-centered* is the term used with clients, in therapy.

2. We have deleted the word *counseling* from the title of this edition. The reason is simple: there are no theories of counseling apart from theories of psychotherapy. Mahrer (1992), writing on the future of psychotherapy, said:

> There are entrenched factions straining to differentiate the overlapping boundaries of words such as psychotherapy, psychoanalysis, counseling, guidance, psychological treatment, case work, rehabilitation and related words (e.g., Belkin, 1975; Hamilton, 1977; Hewer, 1972; Manning & Cates, 1972; Pallone, 1977; Wrenn, 1972). The proposal is to accept psychotherapy as the generic word for it, and to recognize meaningful subtypes such as rational-emotive and psychoanalytic psychotherapy, child psychotherapy, and family psychotherapy. (p. 104)

However, the present authors would not equate counseling with psychotherapy—as the first author has done in the past (e.g., Patterson, 1974). The term *counseling* is now applied to a wide range of activities, including information giving, teaching—individual instruction, tutoring—and other educational activities.

The impetus for this fifth edition came from Rod Goodyear, who also expressed an interest in working on the text. Unfortunately, however, he was unable to do so. With this edition, Ed Watkins becomes my co-author. I am pleased to have him join me.

C. H. Patterson

References

Belkin, G. (1975). *Practical counseling in schools.* Dubuque, IA: W. C. Brown.

Hamilton, M. (1977). Graduate training and professional identity. *The Counseling Psychologist,* 7, 26–29.

Hall, C. S., & Lindzey, G. (1957). *Theories of personality.* New York: Wiley.

Hewer, V. (1972). Identity and the psychological practitioner. *Professional Psychology, 3,* 241–250.

Hilgard, E. R. (1948). *Theories of learning.* New York: Appleton-Century-Crofts.

Mahrer, A. R. (1992). Shaping the future of psychotherapy by making changes in the present. *Psychotherapy, 29,* 104–108.

Manning, T., & Cates, J. (1972). Specialization within psychology. *American Psychologist,* 27, 462–467.

Pallone, N. (1977). Counseling psychology: Toward an empirical definition. *The Counseling Psychologist, 7*(2), 29–32.

Patterson, C. H. (1958). *Counseling the emotionally disturbed.* New York: Harper & Brothers.

Patterson, C. H. (1959). *Counseling and psychotherapy: Theory and practice.* New York: Harper & Row.

Patterson, C. H. (1966). *Theories of counseling and psychotherapy.* New York: Harper & Row.

Patterson, C. H. (1973). *Theories of counseling and psychotherapy* (2nd ed.). New York: Harper & Row.

Patterson, C. H. (1974). Distinctions and commonalities between counseling and psychotherapy. In G. F. Farwell, N. R. Gamsky & P. Mathiew-Coughlan (Eds.). *The counselor's handbook.* New York: Intext.

Patterson, C. H. (1980). *Theories of counseling and psychotherapy* (3rd ed.). New York: Harper & Row.

Patterson, C. H. (1986). *Theories of counseling and psychotherapy* (4th ed.). New York: Harper & Row.

Rice, L. M., & Greenberg, L. S. (1992). Humanistic approaches to psychotherapy. In D. K. Freedheim (Ed.). *History of psychotherapy* (pp. 197–224). Washington, DC: American Psychological Association.

Rogers, C. R. (1986). Carl Rogers on the development of the person-centered approach. *Person-Centered Review, 1*, 257–259.

Rogers, C. R. (1987). Client-centered? Person-centered? *Person-Centered Review, 2*, 11–13.

Wrenn, C. G. (1977). Landmarks and the growing edge. *The Counseling Psychologist, 7*(2), 10–13.

Zimring, F. M., & Raskin, N. J. (1992). Carl Rogers and client/person-centered therapy. In D. K. Freedheim (Ed.). *History of psychotherapy* (pp. 629–656). Washington, DC: American Psychological Association.

INTRODUCTION

THE NATURE OF THEORY

What constitutes a theory of psychotherapy? How many theories are there? A theory is more than an opinion, a speculation, a statement of position, or a point of view. It is more than a collection of principles, methods, or techniques. It is more than a summary of knowledge, principles, or methods derived from experience or research.

A theory is an attempt to organize and integrate knowledge and to answer the question "Why?" A theory organizes, interprets, and states in the form of laws or principles the facts and knowledge in an area or a field. This organization or arrangement of what we know makes possible a systematic description from which explanations and predictions can be derived that can then be systematically tested. Theories are invented or constructed for these purposes; they do not exist by themselves somewhere waiting to be discovered. Practice may be based on empirical knowledge. An explanatory theory gives a sense of understanding, direction, and rationality to practice. It provides a guide to application, extension, extrapolation, and modification in new or different situations.

A formal theory has certain characteristics. First, it consists of a set of stated *postulates* or *assumptions*. (Assumptions are sometimes distinguished from postulates; the difference is in the degree of presumption of their being true. Postulates are more tentative.) These state the premises of the field with which the theory is concerned. They are the givens that are accepted and for which proof is not required. They must be internally consistent. Second, there is a set of *definitions* of the terms or concepts in the theory. These definitions relate the concepts to observational data or to operations and thus make possible the study of the concepts in research and experimentation. Third, the terms or concepts bear certain *relationships* to one another; these relationships derive from a set of rules, usually rules of logic. They include cause-and-effect relationships. Fourth, from these assumptions, definitions, and relationships, *hypotheses* are constructed or deduced. These are essentially predictions of what should be true if the assumptions, definitions, relationships, and the reasoning involved in the deductions are true, that is, if the theory is valid. Given certain assumptions, definitions, and relationships, certain things should follow or be true. Hypotheses state in a form that allows for

1

testing what these things are. The testing of hypotheses leads to new knowledge. If hypotheses are not supported by adequate observation and experiment, the theory must be corrected or revised and new hypotheses must be deduced and tested. Theory thus directs research by providing hypotheses to be tested and by directing observation and experiment.

Theory not only predicts new facts and relations, but also organizes and integrates what is known in a meaningful framework. Whether this organization of existing knowledge comes with the formulation of the theory or follows its formulation is not always clear; some writers appear to think of organization as a late development or as a result of a theory. However, the assumptions or postulates of a theory do not arise out of thin air or apart from reality and experience. They are derived or developed from observation and experience or from empirical research; that is, existing facts and knowledge are the bases for the assumptions and definitions of a theory. The process of theory construction, testing, modification or reconstruction, and further testing is a continual process.

Theories cannot be evaluated as to their correctness or validity until they are tested. A theory may be good without being totally correct; in fact, few, if any, theories, even after considerable testing, can be accepted as valid in any complete or absolute sense. A good theory, however, is more likely to be true than a poor one. Certain formal criteria have been proposed for evaluating a theory (Aiken, 1993; Cloninger, 1993; Hall & Lindzey, 1970; Maddi, 1968; Ryckman, 1993; Stefflre & Matheney, 1968)

1. *Importance.* A theory should not be trivial but should be significant. It should be applicable to more than a limited, restricted situation, such as the behavior of rats in a T maze or the learning of nonsense syllables. It should have some relevance to life or to real behavior. Importance is very difficult to evaluate, however, since the criteria are vague or subjective. Acceptance by competent professionals or recognition and persistence in the professional literature may be indicative of importance. Also, if a theory meets other formal criteria, it is probably important.

2. *Preciseness and clarity.* A theory should be understandable, internally consistent, and free from ambiguities. Clarity may be tested by the ease of relating the theory to data or to practice, or the ease of developing hypotheses or making predictions from it and specifying methods of testing them.

3. *Parsimony or simplicity.* Parsimony has long been accepted as a characteristic of a good theory. This means that the theory contains a minimum of complexity and few assumptions. Maddi (1968) questioned this criterion, however, and suggested that one cannot determine which of two theories is most parsimonious until everything is known about the area to which the theory applies. He also questioned its value on the grounds that the most parsimonious theory on the basis of current data might not be the best theory: "It is distinctly possible that a theory which looks parsimonious in explaining today's facts may be actually such an oversimplification in terms of explaining all human functioning as to be wholly inadequate to cope with tomorrow's facts without major overhaul" (p. 456).

Nevertheless, it might be maintained that the phenomena of the world and of nature are relatively simple in terms of basic principles. The law of parsimony appears to be the most widely violated in theory construction. This may be because of the stage of knowledge we have reached, where diversity and complexity are more apparent than are the underlying unity and consistency. Hall and Lindzey (1970) proposed that parsimony is important only after the criteria of comprehensiveness and verifiability have been met. "It becomes an issue only under circumstances where two theories generate exactly the same consequences" (p. 13).

4. *Comprehensiveness.* A theory should be complete, covering the area of interest and including all known data in the field. The area of interest, however, can be restricted.

5. *Operationality.* A theory should be capable of being reduced to procedures for testing its propositions or predictions. Its concepts must be precise enough to be measurable. A strict operationalism can be restrictive, however, as Maddi (1968, p. 454) points out, when a concept is defined by a restricted or limited measurement operation. A current lack of measurement to operationalize a concept should not rule out the use of a concept that is essential for a theory. The concept first should be defined and then a method of measurement chosen or developed. Not all the concepts of a theory need to be operational; concepts may be used to indicate relationships and organization among concepts.

6. *Empirical validity or verifiability.* The preceding criteria are rational in nature and do not directly relate to the correctness or validity of a theory. Eventually, however, a theory must be supported by experience and experiments that confirm it; that is, in addition to its consistency with or ability to account for what is already known, it must generate new knowledge. However, a theory that is disconfirmed by experiment may lead indirectly to new knowledge by stimulating the development of a better theory.

7. *Fruitfulness.* The capacity of a theory to lead to predictions that can be tested, thus leading to the development of new knowledge, has often been referred to as its fruitfulness. But a theory can be fruitful even if it is not capable of leading to specific predictions. It may provoke thinking and the development of new ideas or theories, sometimes because it leads to disbelief or resistance in others.

8. *Practicality.* There is a final criterion of a good theory, which is seldom mentioned or recognized; that is, it should be useful to practitioners in organizing their thinking and practice by providing a conceptual framework for practice. A theory allows the practitioner to move beyond the empirical level of trial-and-error application of techniques to the rational application of principles. Practitioners too often think of theory as something that is irrelevant to what they do, unrelated to practice or to real life. Yet, as Lewin (1944), the developer of topological psychology, is reputed to have said, "there is nothing as practical as a good theory." Operating on the basis of a theory is the difference between being a technician and being a professional.

If we looked for a theory of psychotherapy that met all these criteria, we probably would not find one. Nor would we find such a theory of personality, or of learning. Existing theories are at a primitive stage, and the criteria constitute goals toward which theorists should strive. Most theories of psychotherapy are not cast in a formal form, although some are attempts at formulation in terms of a set of related postulates or assumptions, with their corollaries. In many instances, theoretical concepts are implicit rather than explicit. Explicit statements of points of view in psychotherapy vary from specific statements concerned with only one aspect or element of the therapeutic process or relationship to very general expositions. Frank (1961) wrote that

> some formulations [of psychotherapy] try to encompass all its aspects. Many of these have been immensely insightful and stimulating and have illuminated many fields of knowledge. To achieve all-inclusiveness, however, they have resorted to metaphor, have left major ambiguities unresolved, and have formulated their hypotheses in terms that cannot be subjected to experimental test.
>
> The opposite approach has been to try to conceptualize small segments of the field with sufficient precision to permit experimental tests of the hypotheses, but these formulations run the risk of achieving rigor at the expense of significance. The researcher is faced with the problem of delimiting an aspect of psychotherapy that is amenable to experimental study and at the same time includes the major determinants of the problem under consideration. He finds himself in the predicament of the Norse god Thor, who tried to drain a small goblet only to discover that it was connected with the sea. Under these circumstances there is an inevitable tendency to guide the choice of research problems more by the ease with which they can be investigated than by their importance. One is reminded of the familiar story of the drunkard who lost his keys in a dark alley but looked for them under the lamppost because the light was better there. This has led to a considerable amount of precise but trivial research. (pp. 227–228)

It appears that psychotherapists have been so engrossed in practice that little attention has been given to the development of formal theories. Nevertheless, although not formally stated, there are, in every practice or approach to psychotherapy, implicit assumptions. They often are not clearly stated or perhaps not stated at all, but they are there. Theoretical discussions of psychotherapy frequently allude to assumptions and hypotheses, sometimes confusing the two. Many of these theoretical discussions are in a sense after-the-fact explanations or rationalizations and have not been developed formally for research. Thus they usually are not clearly or systematically stated. Nevertheless, they are embryo theories and should be capable of being explicitly formulated as formal theories.

It is not the purpose of this book to attempt to formulate such theories on the basis of the literature. Its purpose is rather to present existing theories in the forms in which they occur. Thus, the word *theory* is used rather loosely, as it must be if the book is to have any content at all. The phrase *point of view* is probably more appropriate.

THE POINTS OF VIEW AND THEIR ORGANIZATION

Once the concession is made to include points of view or approaches to psychotherapy rather than formalized theories, the candidates for inclusion become numerous. We might attempt either to reduce all theories or approaches to a few central ones or to deal with only the major theories. The Pepinskys (1954) classified theories into five major categories: (1) the trait-and-factor–centered approach, (2) the communications approach, (3) self-theory, (4) the psychoanalytic approach, and (5) the neobehavioral approach. It is perhaps possible to subsume most of the major approaches under these rubrics. The various learning theory approaches of Dollard and Miller and Wolpe, for example, might be included under the neobehavioral category, and the various neoanalytic theories might be included under the psychoanalytic approach.

To some extent, this is the procedure adopted here; that is, the various approaches have been grouped into categories that have some similarity to those of the Pepinskys, but the organization of the approaches, or their ordering, presents a problem. Is it possible to impose any organization on the various approaches? Or are they too heterogeneous to order in any way? One possible manner of organization would be to arrange them on the commonly used continuum of directiveness, from highly directive to highly permissive approaches. There are other bases for organization. One such basis, probably not entirely independent of the directive-permissive continuum, is a continuum from highly rational to highly affective approaches, from theories that are highly cognitive to those that are highly conative in their emphases. Bordin (1948) suggested such a continuum, from an "emphasis on an intellectual process of reasoning out the problem" to "the emphasis upon stimulating the client to further and deeper expression of his attitudes through such methods as accepting and clarifying responses."

At the cognitive end of such a continuum are theories or approaches to psychotherapy that are rational, logical, or intellectual in nature. Perhaps the most extreme example of this would be the rational psychotherapy of Ellis. Farther along the continuum would fall the more psychological approaches, the learning theory and conditioned response theories of Dollard and Miller, Salter, and Wolpe. Still farther along would be the various analytic approaches. Toward the other extreme would be the self-theories or phenomenological approaches, with existentialism perhaps at the most extreme end of the continuum.

Any attempt to group or classify approaches to psychotherapy must result in arbitrary assignments in some cases. It might thus be questioned whether it is necessary or desirable to group the approaches at all. We have to some extent followed the rational-affective continuum, except that we have placed the psychoanalytic approaches first in deference to their historical priority.

A question arises as to how many points of view, or variants of a point of view, should be included. There are, of course, necessary limitations of space. We have attempted to include positions that are dealt with in an extended manner (usually at book length) in the literature of the field. Thus students are introduced to most of the current writers in psychotherapy. Obviously, every book dealing with psychotherapy could not be represented here. The criterion for selection was whether the authors presented either what might be considered a systematic point of view or a significant variant of a particular approach. Even so, it is obvious that we have neglected to include every possible point of view or variant.

RELATION TO OTHER PSYCHOLOGICAL THEORIES

Theories of psychotherapy cannot be clearly separated from theories of learning, theories of personality, or general theories of behavior. All theories of learning and of personality have, explictly or implicitly, related theories of psychopathology and psychotherapy. Psychotherapists work with clients who exhibit behavior and personality disturbances. The goal of psychotherapy is the changing of behavior or personality in some respect or to some extent. Different approaches vary in the specific nature and extent of behavior change toward which they are directed, but they all accept behavior change of some kind, including changes in attitudes, feelings, perceptions, values, or goals, as the objective of therapy. Since learning may be defined broadly as change in behavior, therapy is, of course, concerned with learning and thus with theories of learning.

In fact, it is difficult to distinguish among theories of learning, theories of personality, and theories of psychotherapy. All are concerned with behavior and are thus theories of behavior. Hall and Lindzey (1970) differentiate between theories that deal with any behavioral event of significance to the human organism (general theories of behavior) and those that are limited to certain aspects of human behavior (single-domain theories). It is difficult, however, to make the separation clearly. Hall and Lindzey state that personality theories are general theories of behavior, and they admit that theories of learning may also be considered theories of behavior but so may theories of psychotherapy. Even theories of perception may be theories of behavior, since perception is central to all behavior. Behavior, in short, is all of one piece, and any theory dealing with a major aspect of behavior is or must become a general behavior theory. Theories concerned with the various aspects must be consistent among themselves and together must constitute a general theory of behavior. Eventually, a theory of learning, a theory of personality, a theory of perception, and a theory of psychotherapy must all be parts of a general theory of behavior.

The discussion of theories of psychotherapy, therefore, inevitably involves the areas of personality and learning. Thus, every theory of psychotherapy has, and must have, a theory of personality and of learning behind it. Usually, the related theories of personality and learning are implicit rather than explicit. When they are explicit, they usually have developed from the theory of psychotherapy, as in the case of client-centered therapy, although it may, of course, be the case that a theory of psychotherapy is consistent with an independently developed theory of personality. At any rate, theories of personality and theories of psychotherapy are interrelated.

Thus, insofar as the authors of the various approaches presented deal with personality theory, it will be included as a part of the summary of the approach. There will be no attempt, however, on our part to provide a personality theory to accompany an approach that is lacking in an explicit theory. It is not the purpose of this book to go beyond what has been developed by those concerned with the various approaches to psychotherapy.

PHILOSOPHICAL IMPLICATIONS

Allport (1961) notes that "theories of learning (like much else in psychology) rest on the investigator's conception of the nature of man. In other words, every learning theorist is a philosopher, though he may not know it" (p. 84). This applies perhaps even more forcefully to psychotherapy theorists. Therefore, it is necessary to include in our discussions the philosophical bases that are implicit or explicit in the various counseling theories. Again, no elaborate philosophical formulation will be developed for each theory considered, but it does seem to be necessary to consider the assumptions regarding human nature underlying the various theories, as well as the goals or objectives of psychotherapy that are accepted or advocated by them. In many cases, of course, very little formal consideration was given in the original presentation of the approach, and this will be reflected in the summaries in this book.

NATURE OF THE PRESENTATIONS

It seems desirable that in the discussion of the various theories, some common method or outline should be followed. It is difficult, however, to develop a detailed outline that would be appropriate for all theories. The categories selected are, therefore, few, broad, and general.

The general procedure is to identify the theory in terms of its major proponents, giving some background or orientation to the approach. Then the major concepts, or the essential elements, of the approach are discussed. These include the philosophical background or implications and the related theories of personality and learning or of behavior and its change. Next, the goals of therapy and the therapy process are considered, followed by consideration of the techniques or the behavior of the therapist, who implements the concepts in the process. Then, when possible, one or more illustrative examples of the approach are presented. Finally, a summary and a general evaluation concludes the discussion.

The evaluations are not full-scale critiques of the theories but summaries of the major contributions of each approach and considerations of some of the major objections or criticisms that have been or might be raised against them.

The presentations are intended to be descriptive rather than polemic. We have, like Hilgard (1948, p.v), "approached the task with the desire to be friendly to each of the positions represented, on the assumption that each of them has been proposed by an intelligent and sincere person or group of persons, and that there must be something which each of them can teach us." The purpose of the book is not to present a critique or comparison of the various theories or to attempt to develop a single theory by integrating aspects of various approaches. The purpose is to present in a relatively brief, objective form various current points of view in psychotherapy. This is difficult to do without danger of misrepresentation because of brevity, possible misunderstandings, or biased perceptions. It is hoped that this danger has been minimized by having the presentations read in many cases by representatives of the various approaches. We do, however, accept the responsibility for what appears in the following chapters.

References

Aiken, L. R. (1993). *Personality: Theories, research, and applications.* Englewood Cliffs, NJ: Prentice-Hall.

Allport, G. W. (1961). *Patterns of growth in personality.* New York: Holt, Rinehart and Winston.

Bordin, E. S. (1948). Dimensions of the counseling process. *Journal of Clinical Psychology, 4,* 240–244.

Cloninger, S. C. (1993). *Theories of personality: Understanding persons.* Englewood Cliffs, NJ: Prentice-Hall.

Frank, J. D. (1961). *Persuasion and healing*. Baltimore: Johns Hopkins University Press.

Hall, C. S., & Lindzey, G. (1970). *Theories of personality* (2nd ed.). New York: Wiley.

Hilgard, E. R. (1948). *Theories of learning*. Englewood Cliffs, NJ: Prentice-Hall.

Lewin, K. (1944). Science, power and education. In G. W. Lewin (Ed.). *Studies in topological and vector psychology*. New York: Harper & Brothers.

Maddi, S. R. (1968). *Personality theories: A comparative analysis*. Homewood, IL: Dorsey Press.

Pepinsky, H. B., & Pepinsky, P. (1954). *Counseling: Theory and practice*. New York: Ronald Press.

Ryckman, R. M. (1993). *Theories of personality* (5th ed.). Pacific Grove, CA: Brooks/Cole.

Stefflre, B., & Matheny, K. (1968). *The function of counseling theory*. Boston: Houghton Mifflin.

part one

PSYCHOANALYTIC AND NEOANALYTIC APPROACHES

Psychoanalysis and its offshoots—the various psychoanalytic and neoanalytic theories—have long been considered *the* psychodynamic or depth psychotherapies. With the advent of client-centered therapy in the 1940s and 1950s and of behavior therapy in the 1960s, the psychoanalytic therapies declined. But psychoanalytic therapy, if not orthodox psychoanalysis (that is, strict adherence to Freud and the use of the couch in daily sessions) is far from dead. Indeed, during the past 15 years, there has been a great revival of interest in psychoanalytic thought and its applications, with a flood of books on psychoanalysis being published, with the foundation (in 1982) of a publishing house specifically for books and journals in this area (The Analytic Press), and with the establishment (in 1983) of a journal to review material on psychoanalysis (*Review of Psychoanalytic Books,* International Universities Press). The Division of Psychoanalysis became the thirty-ninth division of the American Psychological Association in 1980 and has grown rapidly since its inception.

Psychoanalytic psychotherapy is not a single, unified approach. There were early dissenters from Freud's theories (summarized by Freud [1929, 1933, 1935] in his later publications): Adler (1927), Fromm (1941), Horney (1937), Jung (1954), Rank (1947), and Sullivan (1938). More recently, psychoanalytically trained and oriented writers—Hartmann

(1958), Erikson (1950), Rapaport (1959), and Kohut (1971)—have recognized the importance of the ego, or the self, in human development and its disorders.

In what follows, you will find chapters on Freud, Jung, Adler, and the object relations viewpoint to psychotherapy. Freud, Jung, and Adler, being the originators of major analytic or neoanalytic schools of thought, continue to have an impact on psychotherapy practice. Object relations theories, while being indebted to the work of Freud, Jung, and Adler, deserve separate attention, so we have devoted a chapter to them. These theorists moved psychoanalytic theory from a focus on intrapersonal pathology and treatment to interpersonal pathology and treatment. Concurrently, Sullivan was developing his theory of interpersonal psychiatry (Sullivan, 1938).

The task of summarizing Freud's voluminous writings, with changes over time, is formidable. Fortunately, much of the work already had been done by a colleague in England, Dr. Richard Nelson-Jones, in a chapter in his book *The Theory and Practice of Counselling Psychology* (1982). The Freud summary is an extensive expansion and revision of Nelson-Jones's chapter, with permission of the publisher.

REFERENCES

Adler, A. (1927). *The practice and theory of individual psychology.* New York: Harcourt Brace Jovanovich.

Erikson, E. H. (1950). *Childhood and society.* New York: Norton.

Freud. S. (1929). *Introductory lectures on psychoanalysis.* London: Allen & Unwin.

Freud. S. (1933). *New introductory lectures on psychoanalysis.* New York: Norton.

Freud, S. (1935). *A general introduction to psychoanalysis.* New York: Liveright.

Fromm, E. (1941). *Escape from freedom.* New York: Holt, Rinehart and Winston.

Hartmann, H. (1958). *Ego psychology and the problem of adaptation.* New York: International Universities Press. (Originally published, 1939.)

Horney, K. (1937). *The neurotic personality of our time.* New York: Norton.

Jung, C. G. (1954). *Collected works: Vol. 16. The practice of psychotherapy.* New York: Pantheon.

Kohut, H. (1971). *The analysis of the self.* New York: International Universities Press.

Nelson-Jones, R. (1982). *The theory and practice of counselling psychology.* London: Holt, Rinehart and Winston.

Rank, O. (1947). *Will therapy and truth and reality.* New York: Knopf.

Rapaport, D. (1959). A historical survey of psychoanalytic ego psychology. [Monograph no. 1]. *Psychological issues.* New York: International Universities Press.

Sullivan, H. S. (1938). Psychiatry: Introduction to the study of interpersonal reactions, I. *Psychiatry, 1,* 121–134. (Reprinted in Mullahy, P. (Ed.). (1949). *A study of interpersonal relations.* New York: Science House.)

chapter 1

Psychoanalysis: Freud

Sigmund Freud (1856–1939) was born in Freiberg, Moravia, a small town in what is now Czechoslovakia. He was the eldest of eight children (five girls, three boys) of his father's second wife. His father, a wool merchant, moved his family to Vienna when Freud was 4. At age 9, he entered Sperl Gymnasium (high school) where he was at the top of his class, graduating with distinction at 17.

His interests were not then in medicine, but he wrote that "it was hearing Goethe's beautiful essay on nature read aloud by Professor Carl Bruhl just before I left school that decided me to become a medical student" (Freud, 1935, p. 14). He enrolled in medicine at the University of Vienna in 1873. From 1876 to 1882, he worked in Ernst Brucke's physiological laboratory, focusing on the histology of nerve cells. In 1881, he passed the final examinations with a grade of "excellent" and received his M.D. degree.

In 1882, Freud began the practice of medicine. But his research interests led him to enter the General Hospital of Vienna, where he engaged in research at the Institute of Cerebral Anatomy. He wanted to study nervous diseases, but found that he had to become his own teacher. In October 1885, he went to Paris on a traveling fellowship and stayed until February 1886, studying at the Salpetrière (a hospital for nervous diseases) under Charcot. It was here that he became interested in hysteria, which Charcot was investigating.

On his return to Vienna, Freud married Martha Bernays and set up a private practice as a specialist in nervous diseases. The youngest of his six children was Anna, who followed her father's calling, becoming a well-known child analyst. His "therapeutic arsenal contained only two weapons, electrotherapy and hypnotism" (Freud, 1935, p. 26). He soon dropped electrotherapy (not to be confused with electroshock) and began to realize the limitations of hypnosis.

In the early 1880s, Freud had developed a close relationship with Josef Breuer, a prominent Viennese physician who, between 1880 and 1882, had successfully treated a young girl with hysterical symptoms by hypnotizing her deeply and encouraging her to verbalize her memories of early emotional situations. Freud began using this method with his patients in the late 1880s, being aware "of the possibility that there could be powerful mental processes which nevertheless remain hidden from the consciousness of man" (Freud, 1935, p. 29). In 1893, Freud and Breuer wrote a paper on the cathartic method (unrestrained and undirected emotional outpouring), and two years later, they published *Studies on Hysteria* (1895).

During the 1890s, Freud suffered from neurotic symptoms, including depression, apathy, and anxiety attacks. Cocaine appeared to calm the agitation and ease the depression; Freud did research on cocaine. It was during this period that he did his most original work. He developed a close friendship with Wilhelm Fliess, a nose and throat specialist, who regarded sexual problems as central in his own work and was the only physician who encouraged Freud in his exposition of his theories of psychosexual development.

Freud abandoned both hypnosis and the technique of placing his hands on the patient's head and exerting pressure, which he sometimes used with hypnosis, but continued the practice of sitting behind the patient, who lay on a sofa. (It appears that this position was not chosen for theoretical or empirical reasons, but because Freud was uncomfortable under the gaze of his patients, whose appointments often totaled up to 12 hours a day.) Freud wrote that "I cannot bear to be gazed at for eight hours a day (or more) 6 days a week" (in Rieff, 1965, p. 146). Freud undertook his self-analysis, which provided material for *The Interpretation of Dreams* (1900/1913), his first major book, and revealed his love for his mother and jealousy of his father, representing a condition that he considered universal and that he termed the "Oedipus complex." Another major work, *Three Contributions to the Theory of Sex* (1905/1962), traces the development of sexuality from its earliest childhood beginnings.

Neuroses that developed in soldiers who had fought in the first World War raised questions about Freud's theories of the relation of psychosexual development and neurosis. He began to develop a theory of the total personality, including the idea that aggression as well as sex could be an important repressed impulse. In the 1920s, he turned to an attempt to understand society, but from a biological basis that neglected cultural influences. "He became increasingly pessimistic, and his final paper on therapy, 'Analysis Terminable and Interminable' (published in 1937), brought his biological thinking to its logical dead end" (Thompson, 1957, p. 14).

Three months after the Nazis overran Austria in 1938, Freud, a Jew, left Vienna and went to London. Freud habitually smoked 20 cigars a day and, in 1923, he learned that he had cancer of the jaw. For the rest of his life he lived in pain, having 33 operations on his jaw. He died in London on September 23, 1939.

Toward the end of his life, Freud (1935) evaluated his work: "Looking back, then, over the patchwork of my life's labours, I can say that I have made many beginnings and thrown out many suggestions. Something will come of them in the future, though I cannot myself tell whether it will be much or little. I can, however, express a hope that I have opened up a pathway for an important advance in our knowledge" (pp. 129–130).

BACKGROUND AND DEVELOPMENT

Freud spent more than 40 years developing his theory of personality. His writings are voluminous, and it is not possible to summarize all the various and changing aspects of his theory.

Thompson (1957) divides the years from 1895 to 1939 into four periods. The first period, from about 1895 to 1900, were the years of Freud's collaboration with Breuer. It saw the beginnings of his theories of unconscious motivation, repression, resistance, transference, anxiety, and the etiology of the neuroses, which derived from his work with patients using hypnosis and free association or catharsis. These methods formed the basis of psychoanalysis. Thompson (1957) notes, "In my opinion, this was the period of Freud's greatest creativeness. No theories he later developed can compare with the brilliance of the early discoveries" (p. 5).

The second period, from 1900 to about 1910, saw the development of Freud's sexual theory from the idea that neurosis is caused by sexual traumas to the concept that sexual development is all important in etiology—the first instinct theory, or libido theory. Sex (procreation or preservation of the species) and self-preservation are the two great drives. After a long, difficult relationship involving Freud's rejection of hypnosis, Breuer broke with Freud at the beginning of this period.

The third period, from 1910 to the early 1920s, began with Adler's attack on Freud's sexual theory and with Jung's defection in 1913. The recognition of the importance of aggression as a drive laid the foundation for a second theory of instincts, which finally was presented in the early 1920s. Aggression and the drive toward repetition are related to Thanatos, the death instinct, while the libido and self-preservation are parts of Eros, the life instinct. This period also saw the emergence of a theory about the total personality (id, ego, and superego). Little change in the method of therapy occurred.

The fourth period, from the mid-1920s to 1939, were the years of Freud's focusing on methods of therapy and extending the therapy. No new methods were developed, however. Freud's interests turned from therapy to society, and in his writings, he expounded his theories rather than developing new theories. Changes in the methods of therapy were introduced, however, by Freud's followers: Rank, Ferenczi, Reich, Sullivan, Horney, and Fromm, the last three of whom incorporated social and cultural elements into the theory and practice of psychoanalysis.

PHILOSOPHY AND CONCEPTS

Freud's orientation was biological, a natural result of his medical training and of the period in which he began to work. His theories of the instincts reflect this biological focus.

The Instincts.   Psychic energy is no different from physical energy. Each may be transformed into the other. Instincts constitute psychic energy, representing the transformation of physical energy into psychic energy. The binding of the energy in an action or image to satisfy an instinct constitutes an *object-cathexis*. Instincts drive and direct behavior, the goal of which is the satisfaction of needs derived from the instincts. Needs create tension, and behavior is directed toward reduction of the tension. Tension is unpleasant; its reduction is pleasurable. This concept of needs is the *pleasure principle,* the attempt to keep excitation or tension as low as possible.

> In the theory of psychoanalysis we have no hesitation in assuming that the course taken by mental events is automatically regulated by the pleasure principle. We believe, that is to say, that the course of those events is invariably set in motion by an unpleasurable tension, and that it takes a direction such that its final outcome coincides with a lowering of that tension—that is with an avoidance of unpleasure or a production of pleasure. (Freud, 1920/1950, p. 1)

The dominance of the pleasure principle is qualified, since other forces oppose it, and the final outcome does not always fulfill the tendency toward pleasure.

There are many instincts, but they are grouped into two basic ones: *Eros* and *Thanatos.* Eros is the life instinct—the preservation of the self and of the species, ego love, and object love. Its energy is called *libido.* The erotic instincts "seek to combine more and more living substance into even greater unities," while the death instincts "oppose this effort and lead what is living back to an inorganic state" (Freud, 1933, p. 140). Thanatos is the death and destructive instinct; it includes aggression and the *repetition compulsion,* which is the automatic repetition of earlier situations in order to master or control them and which may be stronger than the pleasure principle. The death instinct is the compulsion to repeat the earlier inorganic state before living things originated. "The goal of all life is death" (Freud, 1920/1950, p. 38). Aggression is primarily directed toward the self; it is turned outward toward others in self-preservation.

Instincts, the source of energy in behavior, constitute the dynamics of personality. The basic instincts may either work together or oppose each other. The evolution of civilization represents the struggle between Eros and Thanatos in the human species. The question is whether Eros will assert itself. "But who can foresee with what success and what results?" (Freud, 1930/1962, p. 92)

The Unconscious and Consciousness.   Part of a person's life goes on outside awareness. The unconscious influences experience and behavior and includes some material or experiences that are inadmissible to consciousness and some that can relatively easily become conscious. The inadmissible material has been dissociated from conscious thinking, either by never having been admitted to consciousness or by having been repressed from consciousness. The admissible material is in a part of the unconscious called the *"preconscious."* Material may remain in the preconscious without causing problems and usually becomes conscious without therapy. The preconscious may be viewed as a screen between the conscious and the unconscious. Unconscious material may be modified and appear in consciousness in a distorted form, as in dreams.

Consciousness has the function of a sense organ for the perception of psychic qualities. Unlike the two kinds of the unconscious, consciousness has no memory, and a state of consciousness is very transitory. Material becomes conscious, or flows into the consciousness sense organ, from two directions: the external world and inner excitations. Speech enables such internal events as sequences of ideas and intellectual processes to become conscious (Freud, 1923/1962, 1949).

The unconscious is a figure of speech and cannot be located in any bodily area. Yet "the word *unconscious* has more and more been made to mean a mental province rather than a quality which mental things have" (Freud, 1933, pp. 104–105).

The Structure of the Personality

The personality consists of three major systems: the id, the ego, and the superego. Although each has its own functions, operating principles, dynamisms, and mechanisms, the three interact closely. Behavior is usually the result of an interaction among the systems.

The Id. The *id* is the original system, from which the ego and the superego become differentiated. It consists of everything that is inherited and constitutional, including the instincts, which provide the energy for the operation of the other two systems. It strives to bring about the satisfaction of instinctual needs on the basis of the pleasure principle. The id is the "true psychic reality," since it represents the inner world of experience and has no knowledge of objective reality. Its psychic processes are *primary processes*—undirected attempts at immediate satisfaction—which provide the individual with mental images of the objects required for the satisfactions of needs or for *wish fulfillment.* The hallucinations and visions of the psychotic are examples of primary processes. The id is "a chaos, a cauldron full of seething excitement," which "knows no values, no good and evil, no morality" (Freud, 1933, pp. 106–107). It is not governed by logic; it contains contradictory yet coexistent impulses. It is the individual's primary subjective reality at the unconscious level. The id is the seat of the unconscious.

The Ego. The *ego* is a portion of the id that has undergone a modification through the influence of the external world. It develops from the id because of the organism's need to cope with reality for the satisfaction of its instinctual requirements. Although it seeks pleasure and the avoidance of unpleasure, the ego is under the influence of the *reality principle,* which is the delay of immediate gratification in recognition of social requirements. It operates by means of *secondary processes*—perception, problem solving, and repression—that is, realistic, logical thinking and *reality testing.*

The ego is the executive of the personality, mediating and reconciling the demands of the id, the superego, and the outside world. With the aid of the superego, the ego transforms strong id demands into weaker ones that are acceptable to the ego by forming sublimations and reaction formations from them. The ego, however, derives its power from the id, cannot exist apart from or independently of the id, and functions to serve the id, not to frustrate it. Most of the ego is unconscious most of the time; some of it is preconscious, so that it easily can be brought into consciousness.

The Superego. The *superego* is a portion of the ego that has incorporated standards from society, mainly through the influence of the parents in early childhood. The superego also includes later, nonparental influences and the person's own ideals. *Conscience* is one subsystem of the superego; the person's *ego ideal* is the other. The incorporation of parental and social standards is called *introjection.* "The superego is the representative for us of every moral restriction, the advocate of a striving for perfection—it is, in short, as much as we have been able to grasp psychologically of what is described as the higher side of human life" (Freud, 1933, p. 98).

The superego works to inhibit the id's impulses (especially those that are sexual or aggressive), to persuade the ego to substitute moralistic for realistic goals, and to strive for perfection. It opposes both the id and the ego. It is nonrational, however, attempting to block rather than simply to control the instincts. The primary struggle of human beings is with their instincts. Much of the superego is unconscious.

The Development of Personality

The child progresses through a series of stages of development, which are sexual. The term *sexual* refers to a broad range of behaviors, including both affectionate impulses, often called love, and pleasure from the erogenous zones of the body. The sexual impulse is the sexual aspect of the libido. The term *genital* refers to sexual behavior whose aim is reproduction. Sexual life starts soon after birth; sexual behavior does not suddenly emerge at puberty. There are four stages of sexual or personality development. The first three are pregenital, and the fourth is genital. Between the pregenital and genital stages is the latency period.

Persons of both sexes have elements of the opposite sex, so that all individuals are bisexual; a degree of homosexuality thus is congenital, with the final determination of sexual behavior being the result of the intensity of constitutional predisposition and of life experiences and restrictions in one or the other direction. Both females and males develop from children with bisexual inclinations.

The Oral Stage.   The infant's first source of pleasure is oral, deriving from the mouth. The oral stage begins with the ingestion of food by sucking. Fixation at the sucking phase results in such traits as passivity, trust, optimism, and interest in the acquisition of knowledge or possessions—the oral-receptive character. The biting and chewing phase later develops. Fixation at the biting phase leads to such traits as aggressiveness, exploitative behavior, argumentativeness, and sarcasm—the oral-sadistic character.

The Anal Stage.   During the second year, cathexes (instinctual energies seeking discharge) and countercathexes (energies blocking such discharge) develop around the eliminative functions, which lead to the child's first experiences with external regulation of an instinctual impulse, involving the postponement of the pleasures from relieving anal tensions. Strict toilet training may lead to the development of such traits as obstinacy and stinginess—the retentive character. Or the child may vent rage by inappropriate expulsion, which may lead to such traits as cruelty, hostility, and destructiveness. If expulsion is praised and given high importance by the mother, the ground may be laid for productivity and creativity in later life.

The Phallic Stage.   During the phallic stage the sexual and aggressive feelings related to the genital organs develop, including masturbation. The *Oedipus complex* or *Electra complex* appears: the boy develops an object cathexis for his mother and jealousy and hostility toward his father, while the opposite occurs in the girl. The boy develops a fear of castration by his father, and the girl believes that she has been castrated and blames her mother. The boy represses his desire for his mother and hostility toward his father, with whom he identifies; the superego reaches its final development. The girl transfers her early love for her mother to her father although her love is tinged with envy because he has what she lacks. Her Electra complex is not repressed but is modified by reality and weakens with time.

The Oedipus situation is often more complex because of the child's bisexual inclination. The child's feelings for the parent of the same sex may be ambivalent. "In both sexes the relative strength of the masculine and feminine sexual dispositions is what determines whether the outcome of the Oedipus situation shall be an identification with the father or with the mother" (Freud, 1923/1962, p. 23).

The Latency Period.   During the latency period, from about age five or six to puberty, sexual impulses are repressed, and sexual inhibitions develop. Sublimation of sexual impulses occurs.

The Genital Stage.   Puberty reactivates pregenital impulses; if these impulses are displaced and sublimated by the ego, the person passes into the mature genital stage. The genital zones are primary. The narcissism of the pregenital stages becomes channeled into object choices. The adolescent begins to love others altruistically. Sexual attraction, socialization, group activities, vocational planning, and preparation for marriage and a family develop. The person changes from a narcissistic pleasure-seeking child into a reality-oriented socialized adult. There are no sharp divisions between one stage and the next, and the final outcome includes contributions from the earlier stages.

Personality Dynamics: Vicissitudes of the Instincts

Normal development involves a continuous clash between instinctual impulses, which seek immediate gratification, and the restraining forces of a moralistic society and the realities of a physical world. There are four sources of tension: physiological growth processes, frustrations, conflicts, and threats. The individual is forced to learn methods of reducing tension and responds in various ways, some normal and some abnormal. The processes by which instinctual tensions are handled include identification, displacement, sublimation, and anxiety and its defenses, involving defense mechanisms.

Identification.   Identification involves incorporating features of another person into the self, including modeling one's behavior after that of another. It is the method by which energy from the id is diverted into processes of the ego. The id does not distinguish between subjective imagery and reality, but since imagery cannot satisfy a need, the individual must learn to recognize the differences between an image and perception of a real object and to match them by means of the secondary processes.

The child first identifies with the parents and, in so doing, introjects their morals and ideals. Their ideals become the child's ego ideals, and the energy for the superego is provided. Identification also may be a regressive substitute for a libidinous object tie, by means of introjection, so that the ego assumes the characteristics of the object.

Displacement.   Displacement is the transfer of psychic energy, or cathexis, from an original but inaccessible object choice of an instinct to another but similar object choice. If this second choice is blocked, displacement to another choice occurs—and so on until an object is found that can reduce the tension. For example, anger toward a person as an object may be displaced to a door, a wall, or a cat, which is struck instead of the person. A series of displacements constitutes much of personality development. The source and aim of the instinct remain stable, while its object varies. Substitute objects are not as satisfying or as tension reducing as is the original object; each successive object is less satisfying. As a result, over a sequence of displacements there accumulates a pool of undischarged tension, which becomes a permanent motivation for behavior. New and better ways of reducing tension are sought, leading to variability and diversity in behavior. The complex personality is made possible by displacement.

Sublimation.   Sublimation is a form of displacement in which instinctual sexual impulses are diverted to more socially acceptable and creative channels. Thus Leonardo da Vinci's drive to paint Madonnas was a sublimation of his wish for intimacy with his mother, from whom he had been separated at an early age (Freud, 1910/1947). Sublimation does not result in complete satisfaction but leaves some residual tension—a nervousness or restlessness that is the price paid by human beings for civilization (Freud, 1908/1924).

Anxiety.   Anxiety is a specific state of unpleasure that is accompanied by motor discharge along definite pathways. Anxiety is the universal reaction to danger; the ego is the sole seat of anxiety. Danger may be actual or may be anticipated or perceived as impending. There are three kinds of anxiety.

1.   *Realistic anxiety* results from real dangers in the external world.
2.   *Moral anxiety* is fear of the conscience and results from conflict with the superego.
3.   *Neurotic anxiety* is the fear that the id's instinctual impulses will get out of control. It involves fear of the punishment that will ensue.

Anxiety is a warning of danger, informing the ego that something must be done. If anxiety cannot be avoided or dealt with effectively, it is traumatic. When the ego cannot deal with anxiety by rational methods, it resorts to unrealistic methods—the defense mechanisms. Repression, for example, is a result of anxiety, not the reverse (as Freud thought early on).

Defense Mechanisms

When the ego observes that an emerging instinctual demand may place it in danger, it utilizes defense mechanisms to cope with the sources of anxiety, selecting some among the several available, which then become fixated in the ego. The development of defense mechanisms begins with the child's struggle against its sexuality during the first five years of life. Defense mechanisms deny, falsify, or distort reality. They operate unconsciously and may impede realistic behavior long after they have outlived their usefulness. There are numerous defense mechanisms, including repression, regression, reaction formation, projection, introjection, isolation, undoing, turning against the self, reversal, denial, rationalization, compromise, and sublimation. (Only the more common and most important ones are considered here.)

Repression.   There are two kinds of repression. The first consists of making an experience unconscious; that is, material in the preconscious that is inadmissible to consciousness is pushed back into the unconscious. The second consists of forbidding material to enter the preconscious; that is, it remains in the unconscious. Painful memories are thus shut off from consciousness. Sometimes only part of an experience may be repressed; memory of it may remain in consciousness, but feelings are not attached to it. Repressed experiences seek expression in dreams and slips of the tongue. Repressions occur before the age of six. Once formed, they are difficult to overcome.

> The process of repression is not to be regarded as something which takes place once and for all, the results of which are permanent, as when one living thing has been killed and from that time on is dead; on the contrary, repression demands a constant expenditure of energy, and if this were discontinued the success of the repression would be jeopardized, so that a fresh act of repression would be necessary. (Freud, 1915/1925)

Fixation.   Fixations arise when for traumatic or constitutional reasons, one phase in the course of development is emphasized, with a strong binding of libido to that phase and with some libido remaining at that phase. Later, when the forward movement of the libido meets a certain degree of frustration, it reverts to the point of fixation. Fixation at the oral or the anal stages leads to the development of the oral character or the anal character. Fixation may involve arrested development, in which the individual is fixated at an immature level, or it may involve manifestation of habits related to a particular defense mechanism, which may be represented in the character—for example, the oral character or the anal character.

Regression.   Regression is the movement back to the point of fixation. The individual does not necessarily revert completely to the earlier phase; the personality develops infantilisms and manifests childish conduct when frustrated. When a behavior is blocked or frustrated, the individual substitutes another behavior, one that was strongly established at an earlier phase of development.

Reaction Formation.   Reaction formation is the defense against an anxiety-producing impulse by replacing it with its opposite. Compared with a natural expression of behavior, it is showy, compulsive, and extreme. As an example, some overzealous reformers may actually be warding off the anxiety resulting from an attraction to the behavior against which they are crusading. Reaction formation and sublimation are sources of various types of character (anal, oral, and their variants).

Projection.   In projection, the ego deals with the threat of an unacceptable instinctual impulse by externalizing it. Thus, the individual, instead of being aware of libidinous and aggressive impulses, may be sensitive to and aware of such characteristics in others and even attribute them incorrectly to others. Anxiety is reduced by substituting a lesser, external danger for the inner one, and impulses can be expressed under the cover of defending one-self against others.

Defense mechanisms are utilized by normal persons when faced with threats and frustrations. They do not in themselves necessarily constitute abnormal behavior or neurosis.

The Neuroses

Biological, phylogenetic, and psychological factors contribute to neurosis. The human animal is born biologically unfinished and undergoes a long period of helplessness and dependence. This helplessness creates the initial situation of danger and the consequent fear of object loss, which in turn creates the human's need to be loved, which never disappears.

The phylogenetic factor arises from the interruption in human sexual development by the latency period, whereas sexual maturation in related animals proceeds uninterrupted. Following the Lamarckian view of evolution, this must be the result of a momentous occurrence in the history of the human species; its pathogenic importance is evident in the fact that most of the demands of infantile sexuality are regarded by the ego as dangers against which to be guarded. There is also the danger that the sexual impulses of puberty will follow their infantile prototypes into repression.

The psychological factor involves three elements, which comprise the pathogenic neurotic conflict. The first is the frustration of libidinous impulses by the ego, resulting in the damming up of the sexual instinct. Repressions occur in infancy and in early childhood, when the ego is still underdeveloped and relatively weak in relation to the sexual impulses. "We recognize the essential precondition of the neuroses in this lagging of ego development behind libidinal development" (Freud, 1949, p. 113). Repression takes place in reaction to anxiety; the ego anticipates that satisfaction of the emerging sexual drive will lead to danger and represses the dangerous impulse. By the act of repression, however, the ego renounces a part of its organization, and the repressed impulse remains inaccessible to its influence.

The second psychological element in the neurotic conflict is the possible transformation of the frustrated, although not quiescent, sexual impulses into neurotic symptoms, which are the substitute satisfactions for the frustrated sexual instincts. Repression does not always result in symptom formation, however. In the successful resolution of the Oedipus complex, the repressed impulses may be destroyed, with their libidinous energy being transferred to other uses.

The third psychological element is the potential inadequacy of repression with the reawakening and intensification of the sexual instincts at menarche and puberty, following its effectiveness during childhood and the latency period. The individual then experiences an intense neurotic conflict. Without assistance in undoing the repression, the ego will have little or no influence over the transformed instincts of the repressed id. There may also be an alliance of the id with the superego against the ego.

A comparison of normal and neurotic development is given in the story of the caretaker's and the landlord's daughters (Freud, 1933). When they were young, the two girls played games with sexual elements, including stimulating each other's genitals. These experiences awakened sexual impulses that later found expression in masturbation. The caretaker's daughter regarded this sexual activity as natural and harmless, and, unscarred by it, she eventually took a lover and became a mother. The landlord's daughter, however, while still young and as a result of education, became an intelligent, high-minded young woman who renounced her sexuality and whose subsequent neurosis precluded her from marrying. While consciously unaware of her sexual impulses, she was unconsciously still fixated on her early experiences. Because of the higher moral and intellectual development of her ego, she came into conflict with the demands of her sexuality.

Neuroses originate in childhood (up to the age of six), although the symptoms may not appear until much later, when precipitated by mainly or particularly sexual stress or crisis. The stressful situation corresponds to an early repressed disturbance or its effect, which is reactivated and, attempting to return to consciousness, produces symptoms. "The child is father of the man" (Freud, 1949). The neurosis is perpetuated because the repression is unconscious, and the ego does not have access to the repressed material to resolve the conflict. As long as the repression continues, the conditions for the formation of neurotic symptoms exist through the rechanneling of frustrated libidinous impulses. Actual sexual experiences are not necessarily involved, only a disturbance in the sexual processes, "of those organic processes which determine the development and form of expression of the sexual craving" (Freud, 1908/1924, p. 282). Patients' reports of childhood seduction or assault are often fantasies, defenses against memories of their sexual activities when children. (Freud earlier espoused the seduction theory—that all neuroses were caused by actual sexual seductions in childhood. He abandoned this view in 1896.)

In a broad sense, perpetuation of neuroses results from the unsatisfactory way in which society regulates sexual matters. Morality, or the group superego, requires a greater sacrifice of libidinous impulses than is necessary or desirable.

Major Neuroses

Hysteria.   In hysteria, repression involves pushing experiences and their memory out of the mind, rather than forbidding the rise into consciousness of material that had never been in consciousness. The repressed memory remains permanently outside of awareness unless a special event or life situation succeeds in disturbing it. Then it erupts in the form of a hysterical symptom, which represents the point or organ at which the early blocked sexual energy became bound. The intolerable ideas connected with sexual experiences are made innocuous by the transmutation into a physical form of the excitation attached to them, a process of *conversion*. The symptom expresses in a symbolic way the forgotten and repressed memory. A person may develop a hysterical paralysis while remaining otherwise "normal." Regression in hysteria is to the phallic stage of development.

Obsessive Neurosis.   As with all the neuroses, the origin of obsessive neuroses is in a disturbance of the early sexual life, with the immediate cause being disturbance in the "nervous economy." In obsessions, only part of the sexual experience is repressed; the memory remains in consciousness, but with no feelings attached to it. The intolerable ideas become associated with other neutral or innocuous ideas; the obsession acts as a surrogate for the unbearable sexual ideas, taking their place in consciousness. "The detachment of the sexual idea from its affect, and the connection of the latter with another idea, are processes which occur outside consciousness—they may be presumed, but they cannot be proved by any clinical analysis" (Freud, 1908/1924, p. 282). Regression in obsessive neurosis is to the anal stage of development.

Minor Neuroses

Phobias.   Phobias are similar to obsessions. The internal danger of sexual impulses is projected onto an external object.

Neurasthenia.   The source of neurasthenia is similar to that of hysteria, obsessive neurosis, and anxiety neuroses; it involves the present sexual life. Instead of being manifested by specific symptoms, neurasthenia consists of vague symptoms, mainly chronic fatigue and weakness.

Traumatic Neuroses.   Traumatic neuroses are precipitated by a traumatic situation, such as war. Repetitive dreams of the traumatic situation represent attempts to master the emotions aroused by the experience.

PSYCHOANALYSIS: THE THERAPY

Objectives

The aim of life is to be able to love and to work. The neurotic is handicapped in or prevented from a life of enjoyment and efficiency in love or work. If an individual is to live efficiently, the ego must have the energy of the libido at its disposal rather than wasting energy in warding off libidinous impulses through repression. The individual's superego must allow the expression of the libido and the efficient use of the ego. Thus, the objectives of psychoanalysis are (1) the freeing of healthy impulses; (2) the strengthening of reality-based ego functioning, including widening the perceptions of the ego, so that it approves more of the id; and (3) the altering of the contents of the superego, so that it represents humane rather than punitive moral standards.

Psychoanalysis involves the process of reeducating the ego. Repressions were instituted when the ego was weak; now it is stronger and has an ally in the therapist. The pathogenic conflicts of neurotics are different from normal mental conflicts because of the weakness of the ego relative to the id and the superego. Psychoanalysis attempts to remove the cause of the neuroses rather than simply removing symptoms.

Psychoanalysis is appropriate for the treatment of the major neuroses, in which the ego has a minimum of coherence and reality orientation. This is not to be expected in the psychoses, for which psychoanalysis is not indicated (Freud, 1949).

In psychoanalysis, the patient lies on a couch, with the analyst behind the head of the couch, out of the line of vision of the patient. The patient is seen six times a week for one hour a day, in order to focus the patient on his or her problems; the analysis thus essentially involves the patient's whole life. (Freud sometimes saw patients for fewer than six hours a week, and most psychoanalysts now see patients for three to five hours a week.)

Implementation

Freud never presented a systematic statement of the practice of psychoanalysis but discussed techniques in many of his writings. There are five major elements in the process of psychoanalysis.

Free Association.   The basic rule of psychoanalysis is that the patient engages in free association—that is, let the mind wander and report everything that comes to mind, agreeable or disagreeable, meaningful or meaningless, logical or illogical. Censorship and self-criticism must not intervene. Although the patient's productions may appear to have no relation to one another, each association is related in a meaningful way to the preceding one, in a continuous chain of associations. There may be digressions and blockings, but the chain will reveal the patient's mental history and the present organization of the mind.

Dream Analysis.   Patients spontaneously relate their dreams in the process of free association and give free associations to them. During sleep, the ego reduces its repression, and unconscious material thus becomes conscious in the form of dreams. Dreams represent wish fulfillments, being disguised fulfillment of repressed wishes. Even in sleep, the ego retains some censorship, and the latent dream thoughts are distorted in order to make the manifest dream content less threatening. Dreams represent compromises between the repressed impulses of the id and the defensive operations of the ego. The interpretation of a dream involves understanding the latent dream thoughts, which are disguised in the process of dreamwork. Elements of dreamwork involve condensing the latent thoughts into much smaller dream content, displacing the psychic intensity among the elements, and using symbolism. "The interpretation of dreams is the royal road to a knowledge of the unconscious activities of the mind" (Freud, 1900/1913, p. 769).

Transference.   Transference is an aspect of the repetition compulsion. In therapy, it is the repetition of earlier life situations in relation to the therapist; that is, attitudes toward the parents during the Oedipus stage are transferred to the therapist. Female patients try to win the love of a male analyst, while male patients become hostile to and competitive with the analyst. The patient reacts as though he or she were a small child and the analyst were an authority figure, reliving a situation at the time of the original repression.

Therapy begins with the patient having friendly feelings, even love and affection, for the therapist—the positive transference. But as therapy proceeds, negative, hostile feelings develop—the negative transference. The transference thus represents the childhood ambivalence toward the parents, now being relived with the therapist as the parent substitute. The patient's neurosis manifests itself in the therapy situation, constituting the "transference neurosis." Therapy becomes an analysis of the transference in order to show the patient that his or her feelings are not pertinent in the relationship with the analyst but are related to an earlier time. It involves a reliving of the original situation with its affect. The analysis of the transference constitutes a major part of the psychoanalysis and is an important source of insight when the patient is able to see its significance in his or her life.

The analyst maintains an attitude of neutrality during treatment. By doing so, the transference is allowed to emerge naturally. "The . . . [therapist] should be impenetrable to the patient, and, like a mirror reflect nothing but what is shown to him" (Freud, 1959a,

p. 331). If that neutral, mirror stance is compromised, problems can be expected to result. "The loosening of the transference . . . is made more difficult by too intimate an attitude on the part of the doctor . . . " (p. 331). Thus, the analyst does nothing to prevent the transference from occurring naturally. However, the analytic situation, in which the analyst is hardly a real person (being out of sight of the patient and impersonal), contributes to the attribution or projection by the patient of an authority figure to the analyst.

In *countertransference,* the analyst transfers elements from his or her past (or present) unconscious or unresolved emotional conflicts or needs to the analytic situation. It is avoided by the analyst refusing to become personally involved with the patient and by becoming aware of sources of countertransference by means of his or her own analysis.

Interpretation.   Interpretation attempts to provide the patient with the meaning of material revealed in free association, reports of dreams, slips of the tongue, symptoms, and transference. It is the means of relating present behavior to its origins in childhood; repressed and unconscious material enters the preconscious and consciousness. Interpretation helps the patient gain insight into the defense mechanisms and resistances that the ego uses to cope with repressed material and to thwart the therapy process. Part of the work of interpretation is to fill in memory gaps. The analyst reveals and interprets the impulses that have become subject to repression and the objects to which they have become attached, in order to help the patient replace the repression with judgments appropriate to the present situation rather than to the childhood situation. The analyst allies with the patient's ego, thus encouraging it to take control of the hitherto repressed libidinous energy. Unconscious impulses are exposed to criticism by being traced back to their origin.

The timing of interpretations is important. Premature interpretations meet with resistance. The material preferably should be in the preconscious, and the patient should be close to the moment of insight for interpretation to be effective. (Reflecting the importance of this topic, a recent special section of the *American Journal of Psychotherapy* was devoted entirely to transference interpretation [Piper, 1993].)

Resistance.   Resistance includes a number of behaviors on the part of the patient: omitting thoughts in free association because of shame or distress; claiming that the associations lack importance; having no thoughts to express; arriving late for appointments; forgetting appointments; losing interest in exploring problems and in the therapy; trying to win the love of the analyst; and engaging in a battle with the analyst. Acting out problems or difficulties in life rather than dealing with them in therapy also constitutes resistance, which may also involve withholding material because of distrust of the analyst, the desire to make a good impression on the analyst or to gain the analyst's approval, or fear of rejection by the analyst.

The threat of anxiety represented by the analysis and by the analyst's interpretations arouses the defense system of the ego, which attempts to maintain the repression through resistance. Resistance is a conservative force that seeks to maintain the status quo. Secondary gains, or the advantages of symptoms in the patient's life, are also a source of resistance. The unconscious sense of guilt or the need for punishment emanating from the superego is also a powerful source of resistance to recovery. The struggle to overcome resistance is a major part of analysis and requires time.

LENGTH AND LIMITATIONS OF TREATMENT

Length. Freudian psychoanalysis is generally recognized as being a long process; it takes much time and effort for an analytic cure to be effected. "Experience has taught us that psycho-analytic therapy—the freeing of someone from his neurotic symptoms, inhibitions and abnormalities of character—is a time-consuming business" (Freud, 1937, p. 373). As Arlow (1989) explains, "to maintain continuity of the analytic process, at least four sessions a week are indicated. Each session lasts at least 45 minutes. The course of treatment may run for several years" (p. 37).

Limitations. Freud's was a therapeutic approach focused on the treatment of the neuroses. He seemingly did not see his approach as viable with those more difficult, severe conditions, such as the psychoses. Again, to draw on the words of Arlow (1989), consider the following.

> Impulsive, willful, self-centered, and highly narcissistic individuals may not be able to accommodate themselves to [the analytic situation]. People who are basically dishonest, psychopathic, or pathological liars obviously will not be equal to the task of complete and unrelenting self-revelation. Furthermore, . . . psychoanalysis can rarely be used in the treatment of [the psychoses] except under very special circumstances. (pp. 40–41)

This passage is reflective of Freud's original thinking and also communicates some of the many demands imposed on the patient by psychoanalysis.

EXAMPLES

There are, of course, no typescripts of Freud's work. Thus, it is not clear just how he practiced therapy. He did publish a number of case histories, one of which, the Shreber case (Freud, 1911/1933) was not that of a patient of Freud. Another, Little Hans (Freud, 1909/1933a), was treated by the boy's father under Freud's guidance. Four of the cases were treated by Freud: "Dora" (Freud, 1905/1933), the "Rat Man" (Freud, 1909/1933b), the "Wolf Man" (Freud, 1918/1933), and the case of female homosexuality (Freud, 1920/1933). The notes in these cases were made after interviews, since Freud felt that note taking during the interview would interfere with therapy and that the therapist would remember important material and forget the trivial.

The following brief report of a patient suffering from obsessions gives the flavor of Freud's (1908/1924) case studies:

> A young woman who in five years of married life had only one child complained to me of an obsessive impulse to throw herself from the window or balcony, and also the fear of stabbing her child which seized her at the sight of a sharp knife. She confessed that marital relations seldom occurred, and only with precautions against conception; but she added that this was no privation to her as she was not of a sensual nature. I ventured to tell her that at the sight of a man she had erotic ideas and that she had therefore lost confidence in herself and regarded herself as a depraved person, capable of

anything. The re-translation of the obsession into the sexual was successful; in tears she confessed at once to her long-concealed misery in her marriage and later on related in addition some painful thoughts of an unchanged sexual nature, such as the often-recurring sensation of something forcing itself under her skirts. (p. 71)

An excerpt from the case of Dora involves the interpretation of a dream. Dora was an 18-year-old girl brought to Freud by her father. She was

in the first bloom of youth—a girl of intelligent and engaging looks. But she was a source of heavy trials for her parents. Low spirits and an alteration in her character had now become the main features of her illness. She was clearly satisfied neither with herself nor with her family; her attitude towards her father was unfriendly, and she was on very bad terms with her mother . . . [When] one day, after a short passage of words between [the father] and his daughter, she had her first attack of loss of consciousness—an event which was subsequently covered by amnesia—it was determined, in spite of her reluctance, that she should come to me for treatment. (Freud, 1953, p. 23)

Freud had met the father and daughter about two years earlier and had recommended treatment for the girl, but her father had declined the suggestion.

The analysis lasted from October 1900, on a six-day-week basis, to December 31, 1900, when Dora broke off the analysis, being unable, according to Freud, to accept the truth of his insights. The case is not a sequential account of the therapy, but a reconstruction of Dora's problems based on Freud's analysis and interpretations. The treatment appears to have been quite forceful, with Freud pressing insight and interpretations on her. About two years later, she returned to Freud for treatment, but he refused to accept her because he felt that she was not sincere in her desire to change.

The Herr K. referred to in the following was a friend of the family; his wife was the mistress of Dora's father, and on two occasions in the past, he had made sexual advances to Dora, the first time at L———. Here is the dream as related by Dora, with Freud's analysis (Freud, 1959b):

A house was on fire.[1] My father was standing beside my bed and woke me up. I dressed myself quickly. Mother wanted to stop and save her jewel-case; but father said "I refuse to let myself and my two children be burnt for the sake of your jewel-case." We hurried downstairs, and as soon as I was outside I woke up.

As the dream was a recurrent one, I naturally asked her when she had first dreamt it. She told me she did not know. But she remembered having had the dream three nights in succession at L——— (the place on the lake where the scene with Herr K. had taken place), and it had now come back again a few nights earlier, here in Vienna.[2] My expectations from the clearing up of the dream naturally heightened when I heard of its connection with the events at L———. But I wanted to discover first what had been the exciting cause of its recent occurrence, and I therefore asked Dora to take the dream bit by bit and tell me what occurred to her in connection with it. She had already had some training in dream interpretation from having previously analyzed a few minor specimens.

"Something occurs to me," she said, "but it cannot belong to the dream, for it is quite recent, whereas I have certainly had the dream before."

"That makes no difference," I replied. "Start away! It will simply turn out to be the most recent thing that fits in with the dream."

"Very well, then. Father has been having a dispute with mother in the last few days, because she locks the dining-room door at night. My brother's room, you see, has no separate entrance, but can only be reached through the dining-room. Father does not want my brother to be locked in like that at night. He says it will not do: something might happen in the night so that it might be necessary to leave the room."

"And that made you think of the risk of fire?"

"Yes."

"Now, I should like you to pay close attention to the exact words you used. We may have to make use of them. You said that *'something might happen in the night so that it might be necessary to leave the room.'*[3]

But Dora now discovered the connecting link between the recent exciting cause of the dream and the original one, for she continued:

"When we arrived at L——— that time, father and I, he openly said he was afraid of fire. We arrived in a violent thunderstorm, and saw the small wooden house without any lightning-conductor. So his anxiety was quite natural."

What I now had to do was to establish the relation between the events at L——— and the recurrent dreams she had had there. I therefore said: "Did you have the dream during your first nights at L——— or during your last ones? In other words, before or after the scene in the wood by the lake of which we have heard so much?" (I must explain that I knew the scene had not occurred the very first day, and that she had remained at L——— for a few days after it without giving any hint of the incident.)

Her first reply was that she did not know, but after a while she added: "Yes, I think it was after the scene."

So now I knew that the dream was a reaction to that experience. But why had it occurred there three times? I continued my questions: "How long did you stop on at L——— after the scene?"

"Four days more. On the fifth day I went away with father."

"Now I am certain that the dream was an immediate effect of your experience with Herr K. It was at L——— that you dreamed it the first time, and not before. You have only introduced this uncertainty in your memory so as to obliterate the connection in your mind. But the figures do not quite fit in to my satisfaction yet. If you stayed at L——— for four nights longer, the dream might have occurred four times over. Perhaps this was so?" She no longer disputed my contention; but instead of answering my question she proceeded:[4] "In the afternoon after our trip on the lake, from which we (Herr K. and I) returned at midday, I had gone to lie down as usual on the sofa in the bedroom to have a short sleep. I suddenly awoke and saw Herr K. standing beside me . . ."

"In fact, just as you saw your father standing beside your bed in the dream?"

"Yes. I asked him sharply what it was he wanted there. By way of reply he said he was not going to be prevented from coming into his own bedroom when he wanted; besides, there was something he wanted to fetch. This episode put me on my guard, and I asked Frau K. whether there was not a key to the bedroom door. The next morning (on the second day) I locked myself in while I was dressing. In the afternoon, when I wanted to lock myself in so as to lie down on the sofa, the key was gone. I am convinced that Herr K. had removed it."

"Then here we have the theme of locking or not locking a room which appeared in the first association to the dream and also happened to occur in the exciting cause of the recent recurrence of the dream.[5] I wonder whether the phrase *I dressed myself quickly* may not also belong in this context?"

"It was then that I made up my mind not to stay with Herr K. without father. On the subsequent mornings I could not help feeling afraid Herr K. would surprise me while I was dressing: so *I always dressed myself very quickly.* You see, Father lived at the hotel, and Frau K. used always to go out early so as to go on expeditions with him. But Herr K. did not annoy me again."

"I understand. On the afternoon of the second day after the scene in the woods you resolved to escape from his persecution, and during the second, third and fourth nights you had time to repeat that resolution in your sleep. (You already knew on the second afternoon—before the dream, therefore—that you would not have the key on the following—the third—morning to lock yourself in with while you were dressing; and you could then form the design of dressing as quickly as possible.) But your dream recurred each night, for the very reason that it corresponded to a resolution. A resolution remains in existence until it is carried out. You said to yourself, as it were: 'I shall have no rest and I can get no quiet sleep until I am out of this house.' In your account of the dream you turned it the other way and said: *'as soon as I was outside I woke up.'*"

---

[1] In answer to an inquiry Dora told me that there had never been a fire at their house.

[2] The content of the dream makes it possible to establish that in fact it occurred for the first time at L———.

[3] I laid stress on these words because they took me aback. They seemed to have an ambiguous ring about them. Are not certain physical exigencies referred to in the same words? Now, in the line of associations ambiguous words (or, as we may call them, "switch words") act like points at a junction. If the points are switched across from the position in which they appear to lie in the dream, then we find ourselves upon another set of rails; and along this second track run the thoughts which we are in search of and which still lie concealed behind the dream.

[4] This was because a fresh piece of material had to emerge from her memory before the question I had put could be answered.

[5] I suspected, though I did not as yet say so to Dora, that she had seized upon this element on account of a symbolic meaning it possessed. "Zimmer" [room] in dreams stands very frequently for "Frauenzimmer" [a slightly derogatory word for women; literally, women's apartments]. The question whether a woman is "open" or "shut" can naturally not be a matter of indifference. It is well known, too, what sort of "key" effects the opening in such a case.

SUMMARY AND EVALUATION

Summary.   Freud divided human instincts into two broad categories: Eros, the erotic or life instincts; and Thanatos, the death or destruction instincts. The energy of the life instincts is the libido. Mental life includes conscious, preconscious, and unconscious levels. The mental apparatus consists of three agencies: the id, which is constantly striving for instinctual satisfaction; the ego, which aims to meet the instinctual demands of the id in conformity with the reality principle; and the superego, which represents parental and moral influences. The ego has three taskmasters—the external world, the id, and the superego—each of which may cause it anxiety. Psychic energy is distributed among the three mental agencies, which may be in harmony or in conflict with one another.

Individuals are sexual from infancy, although they tend to be subject to amnesia about sexual feelings and experiences. There are four stages of sexual development: the oral, the anal, the phallic (grouped as pregenital)—followed by the latency period—and the genital. The normal development of personality may be seen as three interrelated strands. One involves the individual's libidinal development, which starts with a combination of constitutional and infantile predispositions that mature into genital sexuality in successive but overlapping stages. The second strand involves the development of both the ego, as it gains in ability to mediate between the demands of the instincts and the reality of the external world, and the superego, based on identification with parental influences. The third strand is the establishment by the ego of favored defense mechanisms to ward off the anxiety caused by the strength and persistence of the libidinal impulses of the id. Thus, normal development consists of passing through successive stages of sexual maturation without major fixations and regressions; developing an ego that can cope reasonably effectively with the external world; developing a superego based on identifications that are constructive and are not punitively moralistic; and evolving defense mechanisms that drain off some of the energies of the id without serious restriction of the ego's functioning. The failure to achieve this balance provides the basis for the neuroses.

Excessive repression results in an ego weakened by having to maintain the repression and in susceptibility to stress. The repressed impulses become transformed into neurotic symptoms. Psychoanalysis aims to strengthen the ego by lifting the childhood amnesia and repression, thus allowing the ego to act from strength rather than from weakness. Free association, dream analysis, interpretation, and analysis of transference are the major methods of psychoanalysis.

It must be remembered that this chapter presents Freud's theories and practice only. Freud's contributions were complete by the mid-1920s. But beginning about 1910, other theorists had begun to modify and add to his contributions. The early modifiers include Adler, Rank, Ferenczi, Abraham, Reich, Jung, Sullivan, Horney, and Fromm; more recent adapters include the ego-analysts, such as Hartmann and Erikson, and the object relations theorists, such as Klein, Kernberg, and Fairbairn.

Evaluation. The theorists mentioned above and many other writers have provided numerous critiques of Freud's views (Grunbaum, 1984, 1993; Torrey, 1993). An adequate evaluation would require much more space than is available here. It will have to suffice to list the major contributions and criticisms of Freud's psychoanalysis.

Freud's major contributions include the following (not necessarily in order of importance):

1. Probably the most important contribution of Freud is his discovery that early childhood experiences are significant for later personality development and that

the effects of these experiences continue to influence the adult without his or her awareness of their operation.

2. Related to this contribution is Freud's recognition of the sexual aspects of childhood.

3. Freud developed the first comprehensive theory of personality, including the origins of personality characteristics in childhood experiences.

4. The discovery of unconscious processes, the activities going on in mental life without the individual's awareness, is a significant contribution to psychology.

5. The recognition of unconscious determinants of or influences on behavior contributed to the theory of motivation.

6. Freud's development of the method of free association was a major contribution to the field of psychotherapy. Ernest Jones (1955), Freud's major biographer, rated this as one of the two great achievements of Freud. (The other was his self-analysis.)

7. The discovery of transference was also a major contribution to the psychotherapy process.

8. Freud provided a major example of the study of single cases in psychotherapy as a source of insights about psychological development.

The criticisms of Freud have been numerous and varied. A few of the major ones are as follows.

1. Freud overemphasized the biological factors—hereditary, constitutional, and maturational—in human development. The almost exclusive emphasis on sexual development is a basic part of this biological focus.

2. Freud's view of human behavior is deterministic and therefore pessimistic. All behavior, including even the simplest—such as slips of the tongue—are, he held, determined by past experiences, especially those of the earliest years, which are no longer conscious. These experiences, in turn, are determined by innate biological strivings, most of which are also unconscious. These internal forces are sexual and aggressive energies that are basically antisocial or destructive and must be controlled. This negativistic determinism would appear to pose a problem in explaining how psychotherapy can change behavior.

3. The focus on organic, constitutional, and sexual aspects of development is accompanied by an almost complete neglect of social aspects of development as positive rather than as purely restrictive. Interpersonal relationships—with the parents early in life and with others later (except for sexual aspects)—were ignored by Freud.

4. Freud failed to recognize that much of what he saw in his patients was related to a particular time and place in human history. As a result, he overgeneralized from nineteenth-century Vienna to all humanity, failing to recognize cultural differences in human development.

5. Critics among the psychoanalysts note that Freud failed to recognize adequately the autonomy of the ego as against the dominance of the id and to realize that the ego has its own sources of energy, interests, motives, and objectives independent of those of the id.

6. Freud recognized that his ideas and theories influenced his patients' "free" associations. His theories, biases, and predilections (expectations) also entered into his observations and interpretations of the data he observed. Thus, the reliability of his methods of investigation has been questioned, as has the representativeness of the sample of cases he studied.

7. Related to Freud's influence on his patients is his apparent use of interpretation as a method of indoctrination. This is particularly clear in his report of the case of Dora.

In spite of these and many other criticisms and of the many changes in and additions to Freud's theories by other psychoanalysts, Freud's niche in history remains secure. "Freud's genius has won him a permanent place in the history of psychology and in the intellectual history of the world" (Hilgard & Bower, 1975, p. 373).

Hall and Lindzey (1970) summarized Freud's contributions this way.

> But a fine literary style and an exciting subject matter are not the main reasons for the great esteem in which Freud is held. Rather it is because his ideas are challenging, because his conception of man is both broad and deep, and because his theory has relevance for our times. Freud may not have been a rigorous scientist nor a first-rate theoretician, but he was a patient, meticulous, penetrating observer and a tenacious, disciplined, courageous original thinker. . . . For many people [his] picture of man has an essential validity. (p. 72)

Such opinions are also reflected in Jacobs' (1992) recent book on Freud.

Psychoanalysis—the theory and treatment—continues to make its presence felt in contemporary psychotherapy. Such societies as the American Psychoanalytic Association, the American Academy of Psychoanalysis, and the International Psychoanalytical Association see to that. Furthermore, psychoanalysis appears to be well represented in current journal offerings, e.g., the *International Journal of Psychoanalysis,* the *Journal of the American Psychoanalytic Association,* and *The Psychoanalytic Quarterly* (see Arlow, 1989).

But with all that recognized, what has research had to say about psychoanalysis, particularly of the classical form? It is true that psychoanalytic forms of therapy have been the subject of increasing research in the past 10 to 20 years, but to our knowledge, research specifically examining classical or Freudian psychoanalysis has been very limited. Of those limited studies, "it is generally agreed that research in psychoanalysis has so far not produced impressive results" (Kernberg, 1993, p. 48).

Perhaps one of the most (if not the most) extensive efforts to study psychoanalysis proper can be found in the Psychotherapy Research Project (PRP) of the Menninger Foundation. This project began in the early 1950s and followed 42 patients—with some in psychoanalysis and some in psychoanalytic psychotherapy—through treatment and for two to three years after termination. The PRP has been described in numerous publications (e.g., Kernberg et al., 1972; Wallerstein, 1989). Yet when all was said and done, Wallerstein (1986) reported that the success of psychoanalysis was "less than expected," that psychoanalysis "was more limited in the outcomes achieved than had been predicted or anticipated—*with these patients*" (p. 727). There certainly were mitigating factors to consider with these results, as Wallerstein indicated (his "*with these patients*" emphasized). Still, the findings were less than hoped for and seemingly point to some of the limits that attend psychoanalysis (i.e., that it clearly is not a treatment for all conditions).

Going along with this limited experimental data on analysis, too often psychoanalysts seemingly have accepted anecdotal case reports or case descriptions as "evidence" of their treatment's efficacy. As Wallerstein and Weinshel (1989) made clear, the "clinical case study . . . is still the source of most of what we know in psychoanalysis" (p. 361). "These case studies, for example Freud's case reports of Dora and the Rat Man, have had a tremendous impact on clinical practice. Unfortunately, when only the therapist's report is available, the case study has to be viewed with caution because the lack of corroborating evidence can lead to subjective distortions" (Hill, 1989, pp. 17–18). Or to put it more bluntly, "psychoanalysts must begin to face the fact that their primary and typical form of research, the uncontrolled clinical case study, is devoid of scientific value *except* as a source of hypotheses" (Holt, 1985, p. 296). If the case study is to inform psychoanalytic treatment, a systematic, data-based approach must be adopted for research purposes. Such an approach, which holds interesting possibilities, has been described by Jones and Windholz (1990).

From our perspective, then, it still remains for Freudian psychoanalysis to prove itself by means of research (cf. Gray, 1993). A more empirical analysis, or at least a systematic, data-based case study approach, should be brought to bear on the efficacy of Freudian analysis. Until that is done, this form of treatment will remain without any solid experimental basis; that is unfortunate, because it still appears to have a fair number of followers even today.

And what of the future of psychoanalysis? That is a question that has been much on the minds of contemporary psychoanalysts. For instance, a series of papers entitled "The Future of Psychoanalysis" appeared in *The Psychoanalytic Quarterly* this past decade (see Arlow & Brenner, 1988; Cooper, 1990; Michels, 1988; Orgel, 1990; Rangell, 1988; Reiser, 1989; Richards, 1990; Spruiell, 1989; Wallerstein & Weinshel, 1989). Kernberg (1993) also considered current challenges that face psychoanalysis now and in its future.

Some of what lies ahead for psychoanalysis, however, may be more a function of geography than anything else at this time. For example, consider the following quote from Wallerstein (1991).

Worldwide, psychoanalytic ranks. . . , although stable only in the United States and also, interestingly, in Great Britain, are in most other places on a remarkable accelerating upward spiral. Psychoanalysis is in fact a major growth industry all over Latin America and Europe, with truly explosive growth in such major nations as Argentina, Brazil, France, West Germany, and Italy, to say nothing of the burgeoning interest and growth in Asia, with South Korea as the most recently emergent center of psychoanalytic ferment, and of course . . . with the collapse of the East European communist world and its pell-mell rush westward, an intense new surge of psychoanalytic activity in Czechoslovakia and Poland and East Germany and Lithuania and even in the Soviet Russian heartland, where after decades of being totally forbidden, Freud's major writings have been newly translated and published in Russian—less than a year ago—and sold out fully in its first week in Soviet bookstores. What all this adds up to . . . is that psychoanalysis per se is growing in strength and influence worldwide, even as the American component . . . is diminishing. . . . (p. 438)

From this we can see that any reports about the demise of psychoanalysis are clearly false and premature.

Yet, within the United States at least, psychoanalysis has a major problem: The era of managed cared is upon us. And Freudian analysis has two pressing issues—accountability and cost containment—that it cannot ignore:

> Finally, whether one likes it or not, psychotherapeutic practice of all kinds will be significantly influenced by developments in the area of *managed care*, with its emphasis on short-term treatments for specific disorders, limited goals, and cost containment. This trend is less concerned with the goal of achieving a better understanding of change processes than with issues of practical utility. Open-ended dynamic psychotherapy (*including psychoanalysis* [emphasis added]) will clearly remain a luxury that relatively few members of our society can afford. (Strupp, 1992, p. 26)

In that same vein, we could also ask "What impact will President Clinton's health care reforms have on analytic treatment?" In a recent *Time* article, entitled "The Assault on Freud," Gray (1993) offered the following: "Whatever [health-care reform] package finally winds its way through Congress, many experts concede that insurance will not be provided for Freud's talking cure" (p. 47). Thus, psychoanalysis—at least within the United States—appears to be entering an uncertain period, and it most likely will be negatively affected in the process. Only time will tell us, however, just how negative those effects will be.

We suspect, though, that Freudian analysis will endure—with a recognizable number of adherents supporting the approach worldwide but with no increase, most likely a decrease (see Norcross, Alford, & DeMichele, 1992), of adherents in the United States. More and more American practitioners seem to be adopting a modified Freudian stance now anyway—which reflects ego psychology and object relations contributions. That has been and we believe will continue to be the *Zeitgeist* for contemporary psychoanalytic treatment in the United States.

REFERENCES

Arlow, J. A. (1989). Psychoanalysis. In R. J. Corsini (Ed.), *Current psychotherapies* (pp. 19–62). Itasca, IL: F. E. Peacock.

Arlow, J. A., & Brenner, C. (1988). The future of psychoanalysis. *The Psychoanalytic Quarterly, 57,* 1–14.

Cooper, A. M. (1990). The future of psychoanalysis: Challenges and opportunities. *The Psychoanalytic Quarterly, 59,* 177–196.

Freud, S. (1900/1913). *The interpretation of dreams.* New York: Macmillan.

Freud, S. (1905/1933). Fragments of an analysis of a case of hysteria. In *Collected papers* (vol. VII). London: Hogarth Press.

Freud, S. (1905/1962). *Three contributions to the theory of sex.* New York: Dutton.

Freud, S. (1908/1924). "Civilized" sexual morality and modern nervousness. In *Collected papers* (vol. II). London: Hogarth Press, pp. 76–99.

Freud, S. (1909/1933a). Analysis of a phobia in a five-year-old boy. In *Collected papers* (vol. III). London: Hogarth Press, pp. 149–295.

Freud, S. (1909/1933b). Notes upon a case of obsessional neurosis. In *Collected papers* (vol. III). London: Hogarth Press, pp. 296–398.

Freud, S. (1911/1933). Psychoanalytic notes upon an autobiographical account of a case of paranoia (dementia paranoides). In *Collected papers* (vol. III). London: Hogarth Press, pp. 390–472.

Freud, S. (1915/1925). Repression. In *Collected papers* (vol. IV). London: Hogarth Press, pp. 84–97.

Freud, S. (1918/1933). From the history of an infantile neurosis. In *Collected papers* (vol. III). London: Hogarth Press, pp. 473–605.

Freud, S. (1920/1933). The psychogenesis of a case of homosexuality in a woman. In *Collected papers* (vol. II). London: Hogarth Press, pp. 202–231.

Freud, S. (1920/1950). *Beyond the pleasure principle.* New York: Liveright.

Freud, S. (1923/1962). *The ego and the id.* London: Hogarth Press.

Freud, S. (1930/1962). *Civilization and its discontents.* New York: Norton.

Freud, S. (1933). *New introductory lectures on psychoanalysis.* New York: Norton.

Freud, S. (1935). *An autobiographical study.* London: Hogarth Press.

Freud, S. (1937). Analysis terminable and interminable. *International Journal of Psychoanalysis, 18,* 373–405.

Freud, S. (1949). *An outline of psychoanalysis.* New York: Norton.

Freud, S. (1953). Fragments of an analysis of a case of hysteria. In *The standard edition of the complete psychological works of Sigmund Freud* (vol. VII). London: Hogarth Press.

Freud, S. (1959a). *Sigmund Freud: Collected papers* (vol. II). New York: Basic Books.

Freud, S. (1959b). *Sigmund Freud: Collected papers* (vol. III). New York: Basic Books.

Freud, S., & Breuer, J. (1895/1956). *Studies on hysteria.* London: Hogarth.

Gray, P. (1993, November 29). The assault on Freud. *Time,* 47, 49, 51.

Grunbaum, A. (1984). *The foundations of psychoanalysis: A philosophical critique.* Berkeley, CA: University of California Press.

Grunbaum, A. (1993). *Validation in the clinical theory of psychoanalysis: A study in the philosophy of psychoanalysis.* New York: International Universities Press.

Hall, C. S., & Lindzey, G. (1970). *Theories of personality* (2nd ed.). New York: Wiley.

Hilgard, E. R., & Bower, G. H. (1975). *Theories of learning* (4th ed.). Englewood Cliffs, NJ: Prentice-Hall.

Hill, C. E. (1989). *Therapist techniques and client outcomes.* Newbury Park, CA: Sage.

Holt, R. R. (1985). The current status of psychoanalytic theory. *Psychoanalytic Psychology, 2,* 289–315.

Jacobs, M. (1992). *Sigmund Freud.* London: Sage.

Jones, E. (1955). *The life and work of Sigmund Freud* (vol. II). New York: Basic Books.

Jones, E. E., & Windholz, M. (1990). The psychoanalytic case study: Toward a method for systematic inquiry. *Journal of the American Psychoanalytic Association, 38,* 985–1015.

Kernberg, O. F. (1993). The current status of psychoanalysis. *Journal of the American Psychoanalytic Association, 41,* 45–62.

Kernberg, O. F., Burstein, E. D., Coyne, L. Appelbaum, A., Horwitz, L., & Voth, H. (1972). Psychotherapy and psychoanalysis: Final report of the Menninger Foundation's Psychotherapy Research Project. *Bulletin of the Menninger Clinic, 36,* 1–275.

Norcross, J. C., Alford, B. A., & DeMichele, J. T. (1992). The future of psychotherapy: Delphi data and concluding observations. *Psychotherapy, 29,* 150–158.

Michels, R. (1988). The future of psychoanalysis. *The Psychoanalytic Quarterly, 57,* 167–185.

Orgel, S. (1990). The future of psychoanalysis. *The Psychoanalytic Quarterly, 59,* 1–20.

Piper, W. E. (Ed.). (1993). Transference interpretation: Special section. *American Journal of Psychotherapy, 47,* 477–557.

Rangell, L. (1988). The future of psychoanalysis: The scientific crossroads. *The Psychoanalytic Quarterly, 57,* 313–340.

Reiser, M. F. (1989). The future of psychoanalysis in academic psychiatry: Plain talk. *The Psychoanalytic Quarterly, 58,* 185–209.

Richards, A. D. (1990). The future of psychoanalysis: The past, present, and future of psychoanalytic theory. *The Psychoanalytic Quarterly, 59,* 347–369.

Rieff, P. (Ed.). (1965). *Freud: Therapy and techniques.* New York: Collier.

Spruiell, V. (1989). The future of psychoanalysis. *The Psychoanalytic Quarterly, 58,* 1–28.

Strupp, H. H. (1992). The future of psychodynamic psychotherapy. *Psychotherapy, 29,* 21–27.

Thompson, C. (1957). *Psychoanalysis: Evolution and development.* New York: Grove Press.

Torrey, E. F. (1993). *Freudian fraud: The malignant effect of Freud's theory on American thought and culture.* New York: Harper Perennial.

Wallerstein, R. S. (1986). *Forty-two lives in treatment: A study of psychoanalysis and psychotherapy.* New York: Guilford Press.

Wallerstein, R. S. (1989). The Psychotherapy Research Project of the Menninger Foundation: An overview. *Journal of Consulting and Clinical Psychology, 57,* 195–205.

Wallerstein, R. S. (1991). The future of psychotherapy. *Bulletin of the Menninger Clinic, 55,* 421–443.

Wallerstein, R. S., & Weinshel, E. M. (1989). The future of psychoanalysis. *Psychoanalytic Quarterly, 58,* 341–373.

chapter *2*

Analytical Psychotherapy: Jung

Carl G. Jung (1875–1961) was born in Kesswil, Switzerland, a small village on Lake Constance. His father was a pastor of the Swiss Reform Church, his mother a housewife. Jung's parents had two boys, both of whom died in infancy, prior to his birth. Some nine years after he was born, his parents had another child—this time a girl.

Shortly after Jung's birth, the family moved to Laufen, another small Swiss village. Jung's father was assigned to a parish there. Some three years later, the family again moved—to yet another parish in the village of Klein-Hüningen. It was there, in this village near Basel, that Jung spent the better part of his early childhood years. He attended the local school until he was eleven, when he transferred to a larger school, the Gymnasium, in Basel.

After high school, Jung went on to attend medical school at the University of Basel, receiving his M.D. degree in 1900. He first worked as an assistant physician to Eugen Bleuler at the Burgholzi mental hospital in Zurich. He later studied at the Saltpetrière in Paris with Pierre Janet. He also served as a lecturer at the University of Zurich. Jung married Emma Rauschenbach in 1903; they had five children—four daughters and one son. Emma died in 1955.

Among his many distinctions, Jung served as president of the International Psychoanalytic Society (1910–1913) and editor of the *Annual for Psychoanalytical and Psychopathological Research.* In 1909 he resigned his position at the Burgholzi mental hospital. In 1913 he resigned his position at the University of Zurich. This allowed him to devote more time to his private practice as well as to other pursuits (e.g., traveling). Some 20 years later, he took a position as professor of psychology at the Federal Polytechnical University at Zurich. In 1948 the C. G. Jung Institute was formed in Zurich.

Jung was the first president. He remained an active writer, scholar, and practitioner until his death in 1961.

BACKGROUND AND DEVELOPMENT

Jung's childhood and adolescence were by no means problem free. In his autobiography, *Memories, Dream, Reflections* (Jung, 1961), he speaks of his isolation and loneliness as a child, his parents' marital problems, his mother's emotional problems, and his coming close to death on a couple of occasions. He speaks of having vague fears and vivid dreams, fantasies, and images. Later, he speaks of having fainting spells, becoming bored with school, and having persistent troublesome religious conflicts. Over time, however, Jung seemed to get a better handle on the concerns that plagued him. He became more self-confident, he became deeply interested in philosophy, he read widely and voraciously, and he began to move down a path that would ultimately make him a major figure in psychiatry and psychotherapy.

On entering medical school, philosophy, dreams, fantasies, occult phenomena, and parapsychology remained of much interest to Jung. While attending medical school, he also attended seances on the side and read philosophy when he was able. He even did his M.D. dissertation, entitled "On the Psychology and Pathology of So-Called Occult Phenomena," on the behavior of his 15-year old cousin, a medium, who performed at the seances he attended (Jung, 1902/1970). All of this—what we might call Jung's interest in and desire to understand "the mysteries of life"—eventually led him to psychiatry, psychopathology, and psychotherapy.

During his study and practice of psychiatry, Jung became acquainted with the works of Freud; he even sent Freud copies of his published works (e.g., Jung, 1907/1960). Later, in 1907, on Freud's invitation, they met, became close friends, and maintained a close personal/professional relationship for several years. Throughout this time, Jung—always the independent thinker—continued to develop his own ideas about personality and psychopathology. In 1912 came Jung's (1912/1967) *Symbols of Transformation.* This book further reflected the development of Jung's thought, was critical of Freud's system, and ultimately led to the end of Jung and Freud's relationship. That *Symbols of Transformation* would cause this relationship's ending deeply troubled Jung. But that was not to be reversed.

In the years that followed, Jung continued his study of personality. He also pursued his other diverse, eclectic interests as well (e.g., religious symbolism, alchemy, flying saucers, clairvoyance, and seances). In 1921, what some regard as his finest or certainly one of his finest books appeared: *Psychological Types* (Jung, 1921/1966). He made travels to North Africa, New Mexico (to study the Pueblo Indians), Kenya, Uganda, India, and Rome. He of course continued to publish (e.g., *Modern Man in Search of a Soul* [1933] and *Psychology and Alchemy* [1944/1968]). In 1957 he began work on his autobiography, *Memories, Dreams, Reflections,* which was first published in 1961.

The development of Jung's psychology can be seen as a result of the following: Jung's interests were broad and far-ranging; Jung was forever a creative, intuitive, independent thinker; and he forever worked to pull together varied information, varied ideas, and varied experiences under the umbrella of analytical psychology. In what follows, we will consider what that means for Jung's approach to psychotherapy.

We would like first to say, however, that Jung's approach is by no means easy to get a firm handle on. There are some good reasons for that:

> Jung never presented a psychological theory in the straight sense of a theory: that is, a body of generalizations and principles developed in association with the practice of psychotherapy and forming its content as an intellectual discipline. . . . Jung does not offer a methodology, a technique for procedure, a series of "applications" that the Jungian analyst can use from the insights and formulations of the master. (Singer, 1973, p. 6)

Understandably, then, piecing together a Jungian approach to psychotherapy is in our opinion a difficult task. But, still, it is one worth the effort.

Since Jung is not always clear about his approach, particularly his methods and techniques, other sources are occasionally drawn on, as indicated by citations.

PHILOSOPHY AND CONCEPTS

To understand Jung one must first try to understand the concepts that he proposed. Some of the primary ones are as follows.

Concepts

Consciousness.   This refers to awareness, the thoughts, feelings, and experiences that are known and available to the individual.

Ego.   "The important fact about consciousness is that nothing can be conscious without an ego to which it refers" (Jung, 1968b, p. 10). But what then is the ego? "The ego is a complex datum which is constituted first of all by a general awareness of your body, of your existence, and secondly by your memory data; you have a certain idea of having been, a long series of memories. Those two are the main constituents of what we call the ego" (Jung, 1968b, p. 10). The ego is that which "gives life to consciousness" in a sense; it is the center of consciousness.

Personal Unconscious.   In the personal unconscious lie all the memories and experiences that have been forgotten or repressed (Jung, 1936/1968); they were conscious at one time, and may even become conscious again if the right circumstances prevail (e.g., by focusing attention or by seeing something that causes you to remember an earlier event). "The personal [unconscious] layer ends at the earliest memories of infancy. . . ." (Jung 1956, p. 87).

Within the personal unconscious, complexes of various sorts can be found. "A complex is an agglomeration of associations—a sort of picture of a more or less complicated psychological nature—sometimes of traumatic character, sometimes simply of a painful and highly toned character" (Jung, 1968b, p. 79). For example, an individual could have a "mother complex" or "father complex," be very sensitive to mother or father stimuli, with all this then reflecting some type of unresolved issues with one's parents. Just as we have our complexes, so too do our complexes have us. A major task in Jungian psychotherapy, then, is to help patients resolve their problematic, traumatic complexes.

Collective Unconscious.   "[T]he contents of the collective unconscious have never been in consciousness, and therefore have never been individually acquired, but owe their existence exclusively to heredity" (Jung, 1936/1968, p. 42). The contents of the collective unconscious are images, potentialities, and predispositions that we have inherited from our ancestors (e.g., fears, attractions, symbol meanings)—our racial, evolutionary, and ancestral inheritance. The collective unconscious is "universal," "preexistent," "identical in all individuals," "made up essentially of *archetypes*" (Jung, 1936/1968).

By understanding archetypes, a better understanding can be gained of the collective unconscious itself.

> An archetype means a *typos* [imprint], a definite grouping of archaic character continuing, in form as well as in meaning, *mythological motifs.* Mythological motifs appear in pure form in fairytales, myths, legends, and folklore. Some of the well-known motifs are: the figures of the Hero, the Redeemer, the Dragon (always connected with the Hero, who has to overcome him), the Whale or the Monster who swallows the Hero. (Jung, 1968b, p. 41)

> Archetypes refer to "primordial images;" they are not ideas "for they lack the language structure which ideas must embody. . . . They must be beckoned forth by circumstance" (Rychlak, 1973, p. 145).

> [A]rchetypes are not to be regarded as fully developed pictures in the mind like memory images of past experiences of one's life. The mother archetype, for example, is not a photograph of a mother or a woman. It is more like a negative that has to be developed by experience (Hall & Nordby, 1973, p. 42)

The archetypes are many, including the Hero, Mother, Father, Family, Soul, and Trickster, among others (see Jung's *Collected Works*, volume 9, parts 1 and 2 [1936/1968, 1968a], for an extensive treatment of the archetype and collective unconscious concepts). The archetypes that are accorded the most significance are the persona, anima and animus, shadow, and self.

Persona literally means "the mask worn by an actor, signifying a role he played" (Jung, 1956, p. 167); the persona is "designed on the one hand to make a definite impression upon others, and, on the other, to conceal the true nature of the individual" (Jung, 1956, p. 203). It can be thought of as one's "public personality" that is adopted to meet social demands; behind that public face lies one's "private personality" (Hall & Lindzey, 1970). The persona can be, ideally is, flexible—allowing the person to behave differently depending on what different circumstances warrant. But if the persona becomes rigid, adaptability tends to be impaired.

Jung defined the *anima* as follows:

> Every man carries within him the eternal image of woman, not the image of this or that particular woman, but a definitive feminine image. This image is fundamentally unconscious, an hereditary factor of primordial origin engraved in the living organic system of

the man, an imprint or archetype of all the ancestral experiences of the female, a deposit, as it were, of all the impressions ever made by woman. (Jung, 1925/1954, p. 198)

This eternal, unconscious image is a primary reason for intimacy, relatedness, attraction, or aversion. If the anima is not well integrated into one's personality, relatedness can be negatively affected. The anima, then, is the feminine side within male personality and can be seen reflected in certain dreams, visions, fantasies, and symbols, about females (e.g., the Mother, the Witch).

"Since the anima is an archetype that is found in men, it is reasonable to suppose that an equivalent archetype must be present in women; for just as the man is compensated by a feminine element, so woman is compensated by a masculine one" (Jung, 1968a, p. 14). The woman's masculine archetype is the *animus*. "[I]n the same way that the anima gives relationship and relatedness to a man's consciousness, the animus gives to woman's consciousness a capacity for reflection, deliberation, and self-knowledge" (Jung, 1968a, p. 16). If the animus is not well integrated into one's personality, this capacity can be negatively affected. The animus is reflected in certain dreams, visions, fantasies, and symbols about males (e.g., the Father, the Devil).

The *shadow* refers to the "dark side" of our personalities, the animal instincts. It contains our inferiorities, the aspects that we prefer to keep hidden, the aspects we are ashamed of (Singer, 1973). It is

that hidden, repressed, for the most part inferior and guilt-laden personality whose ultimate ramifications reach back into the realm of our animal ancestors and so comprise the whole historical aspect of the unconscious. . . . [It consists of] morally reprehensible tendencies, but also displays a number of good qualities, such as normal instincts, appropriate reactions, realistic insights, creative impulses, etc. (Jung, 1968a, p. 266)

Because the shadow is unconscious and contains the personal aspects we do not like and wish to keep hidden, its contents are often projected onto others (e.g., seeing someone as arrogant and vain).

The *self* is the central archetype, the center of personality. "The self is not only the centre but also the whole circumference which embraces both conscious and unconscious; it is the centre of this totality . . . " (Jung, 1944/1968, p. 41). The self provides unity, organization, and stability in personality functioning. It can be seen reflected in the mandala symbol, the circle, Christ (Jung, 1968a).

Individuation is "the process by which a person becomes a psychological 'in-dividual,' that is, a separate, indivisible unity or 'whole'" (Jung, 1939/1968, p. 275).

The Attitudes.   These are introversion and extroversion.

The first attitude is normally characterized by a hesitant, reflective, retiring nature that keeps itself to itself, shrinks from objects, is always slightly on the defensive and prefers to hide behind mistrustful scrutiny. The second attitude is normally characterized by an outgoing, candid, and accommodating nature that adapts easily to a given situation, quickly forms attachments, and . . . will often venture forth with careless confidence into unknown situations. (Jung, 1956, p. 54)

We each possess some degree of each of these attitudes, but one often will be dominant.

The Four Functions. These are thinking, feeling, sensation, and intuition.

> The essential function of sensation is to establish that something exists, thinking tells us what it means, feeling what its value is, and intuition surmises whence it comes and whither it goes. Sensation and intuition I call irrational functions, because they are both concerned simply with what happens and with actual or potential realities. Thinking and feeling, being discriminative functions, are rational. (Jung, 1921/1971, appendix)

The Types. Crossing the two attitudes and four functions produces a theory of psychological type—with there being eight types in all (e.g., the extroverted sensation type, the introverted feeing type, etc.). By means of a person's type, you can tell about how that individual characteristically approaches and operates in the world (Jung, 1921/1966). (It is this type approach that has been incorporated into what is now one of the more popular objective personality inventories, the Myers-Briggs Type Indicator.)

A Concluding Note. These are by no means all the concepts that Jung put forth, but these appear to be among the most important. For still further concepts and definitions, the glossary in Jung's *Memories, Dreams, Reflections* (1961) can be consulted. Other useful sources include the personality theory introductions of Hall and Lindzey (1970) and Hall and Nordby (1973), as well as Samuels, Shorter, and Plaut's (1986) dictionary of Jungian analysis. But having identified and defined some of Jung's primary concepts here, let us now consider how they might all fit together. To help us with that, we will move next to assumptions.

Assumptions

Fifteen assumptions underlie Jung's system of thought. [These assumptions (italics added) have been taken from Maduro and Wheelwright, 1977, pp. 89–105.]

1. *Personality is influenced by the existence and potential activation of a collective transpersonal unconscious.* This again speaks to the existence of a collective unconscious, which we all possess and which affects us all in our day-to-day functioning.

2. *Unconscious elements unacceptable to the ego are located in the personal unconscious.* Those acceptable but forgotten or suppressed elements can also be found in the personal unconscious, too. But it is the unacceptable elements that, of course, cause pain, misery, and suffering and which are of primary concern in psychotherapy.

3. *Complexes are structured and energized over time around an activated archetypal image.* Complexes, the "psychic fragments which have split off owing to traumatic influences or certain incompatible tendencies" (Jung, 1937/1968, p. 121), are found in the personal unconscious. But complexes are organized and given life by some archetypal image. It is a purpose of treatment to make conscious problematic complexes, so that they can ultimately be resolved and integrated into the personality.

4. *The ego mediates between the unconscious and the outside world.* The ego, then, is the go-between; it functions as the bridge between that which is unconscious and that

which is external. Being the "go-between," the ego plays a crucial role in mental health and healthy functioning (or lack thereof); it is important for purposes of continuity, boundary establishment, and "filtering" essential from nonessential stimuli.

5. *The self represents wholeness, and is an organizing archetype.* As stated earlier, the self is seen as the center of conscious and unconscious; it also is seen as the central archetype, reflected in the mandala circle or other such symbols of "wholeness."

6. *Archetypes function as organs of the collective unconscious psyche.* Archetypes reside in the collective unconscious and exert their influence from there; they are largely the "contents" of the collective unconscious, just as complexes are largely the contents of the personal unconscious.

7. *Psychic reality, the unconscious inner world, is as important as the external world.*

The unconscious is continually active, combining its material in ways which serve the future. It produces, no less than the conscious mind, subliminal combinations that are prospective; only, they are markedly superior to the conscious combinations both in refinement and scope. For these reasons the unconscious could serve man as a unique guide, provided that he can resist the lure of being misguided. (Jung, 1956, p. 126)

The unconscious is what analytical psychology is all about. "By 'analytical' I mean a procedure that takes account of the existence of the unconscious" (Jung, 1939/1968, p. 275).

8. *Jung's psychology concerns itself more with central preoedipal experiences, anxieties, and defenses than with oedipal conflicts.* Oedipal conflicts can exist; however, Freud's oedipal drama is recast archetypally. Jung's system focuses more on the pre-oedipal period as a point of interest.

9. *Personality growth occurs throughout the entire life cycle and can be accelerated by the "individuation" process in later life.* While growth can occur over the course of the entire life span, it is around midlife when the individuation process can be realized and growth thereby accelerated.

We could therefore translate individuation as 'coming to selfhood' or 'self-realization.' . . . Individuation . . . can only mean a process of psychological development that fulfills the individual qualities given; in other words, it is a process by which a man becomes the definite, unique being he in fact is. (Jung, 1956, pp. 182-183)

10. *The psyche, a self-regulating system, utilizes the principle of constructive unconscious compensation.*

[W]e can lay it down that the unconscious processes stand in a compensatory relation to the conscious mind. I expressly use the word "compensatory" . . . because conscious and unconscious are not necessarily in opposition to one another, but complement one another to form a totality. (Jung, 1956, p. 186)

For example, what we may not experience in consciousness (e.g., certain thoughts, images, affects) can be manifested (compensated, made up for) in our dreams.

11. *Normal and pathological ego defenses are basic oppositional forces to handle conflict in a self-regulating psyche.* Ego defenses should not be thought of as "all bad"; they serve useful protective, maintenance functions, enabling us to deal with stress and

conflict. But defenses also can go "too far," can become pathological, and can pose major problems for treatment efforts.

12. *The psyche spontaneously strives toward psychological wholeness, integration of conscious and unconscious materials, and self-healing.* Life is movement, striving toward completion, wholeness, integration. The same could be said for each individual—whether pathological or healthy. Unfortunately for the pathological individual, the striving—while still there—fails to bear fruit.

13. *Regression may have adaptive significance and take place "in the service of the ego," and "in the service of the self."* Regression, moving back into the deepest recesses of the unconscious, is critical to treatment. Such regression is adaptive, giving patients the opportunity to get in touch with and integrate powerful early experiences and images into the personality. *"[T]herapy must support the regression"* (Jung, 1912/1967, p. 329).

14. *Psychic energy (libido) is a general hypothetical energic force that invests mental processes and representations.* Psychic energy is that which makes personality happen; it infuses our being with life, energy, vitality. Without psychic energy, there is nothing.

15. *Individuation processes proceed throughout life in relation to one's "psychological type."* Again, this recognizes the importance of the two attitudes (introversion and extroversion), the four functions (sensing, intuiting, thinking, and feeling), and how they become manifested in a "psychological type." Life is experienced and unfolds through the lenses of one's type; this is true for the process of individuation as well.

Psychopathology

> A neurosis is a dissociation of personality due to the existence of complexes. To have complexes is in itself normal; but if the complexes are incompatible, that part of the personality which is too contrary to the conscious part becomes split off. If the split reaches the organic structure, the dissociation is a psychosis. . . . Each complex then lives an existence of its own, with no personality left to tie them together.
>
> As the split-off complexes are unconscious they find only an indirect means of expression, that is, through neurotic symptoms. Instead of suffering from a psychological conflict, one suffers from a neurosis. . . . The idea of psychic dissociation is the most general and cautious way I can define a neurosis. (Jung, 1968b, p. 188)

Psychosis is but "an extension of neurosis that occurs when repressed and unconscious forces overpower consciousness" (Ryckman, 1993, p. 87), or to put it another way, "an extension of the division of personality which begins with neurotic conditions" (Rychlak, 1973, p. 174). Complexes, then, are integral to health and psychopathology; for that reason, the analytical approach has even been referred to as "complex psychology" (Hochheimer, 1969).

But while complexes were at one time referred to as "*the* morbid cause" of disorder (Jung, 1972), Jung later backed off from specifying any uniform theory of disturbance.

> I myself have long discarded any uniform theory of neurosis, except for a few quite general points like dissociation, conflict, complex, regression, *abaissement du niveau mental,* which belong as it were to the stock-in-trade of neurosis. In other words, every neurosis is characterized by dissociation and conflict, contains complexes, and shows

traces of regression and *abaissement*. These principles are not, in my experience, reversible. (Jung, 1926/1954, p. 114)

Thus, for every neurosis, the therapist could at least expect to see these facets—dissociation, conflict, complexes, regression, and *abaissment*—to some degree.

Summary. Analytical psychology consists of or involves such concepts as "complex," "archetype," "the personal unconscious," "the collective unconscious," "psychological type," and "individuation." Complexes, those "agglomerations of associations," are the stuff of which the personal unconscious is made. Archetypes, our "primordial images," are the stuff of which the collective unconscious is made. The most important archetypes are the persona, anima, animus, shadow, and self. Understanding archetypal information and resolving complexes are integral to treatment.

Jung's psychology is more concerned with pre-oedipal as opposed to oedipal phenomena. The conscious and unconscious are complementary, not opposed to one another. Neurosis, earlier thought to be caused by "complexes," was later said to involve several elements—of which complexes is one. Psychosis is viewed as being but an extension of neurosis. Neurosis and psychosis inteferes with, or prevents individuation. Individuation is the ultimate goal—that of "coming to selfhood" or "self-realization."

ELEMENTS OF ANALYTICAL PSYCHOTHERAPY

Goals of Therapy

While there are some general goals of therapy, the uniqueness and individuality of each patient guides treatment objectives. "The fundamental rule for the psychotherapist should be to consider each case new and unique. That, probably, is the nearest we can get to the truth" (Jung, 1934/1970, p. 168).

The aim of therapy is as far as possible, to "let pure experience decide the therapeutic aims. This may perhaps seem strange, because it is commonly supposed that the therapist has an aim. But in psychotherapy it seems to me positively advisable for the doctor not to have too fixed an aim" (Jung, 1931/1966, p. 41).

Yet Jung states,

the immediate goal of the analysis of the unconscious . . . is to reach a state where the unconscious contents no longer remain unconscious and no longer express themselves indirectly as animus and anima phenomena; that is to say a state in which animus and anima become functions of relationship to the unconscious. So long as they are not this, they are autonomous complexes, disturbing factors that disrupt conscious control and act like true "disturbers of the peace." (Jung, 1956, p. 244)

Also, "my aim is to bring about a psychic state in which my patient begins to experiment with his own nature—a state of fluidity, change, and growth where nothing is eternally fixed and hopelessly petrified" (Jung, 1931/1966, p. 46). Thus, the unconscious is made conscious and the process of individuation is facilitated.

Aims do, however, differ according to age, and the therapist should take this into account when providing analysis:

> the age of the patient seems to me a most important *indicium*. It seems to me that the basic facts of the psyche undergo a very marked alteration in the course of life, so much so that we could almost speak of a psychology of life's morning [i.e., younger patients] and a psychology of its afternoon [i.e., older patients]. (Jung, 1931/1966, p. 39)

With older patients, there is a midlife crisis of sorts (perhaps archetypally determined) that brings a different slant to treatment:

> As a rule, the life of a young person is characterized by a general expansion and a striving towards concrete ends; and his neurosis seems mainly to rest on his hesitation or shrinking back from this necessity. But the life of an older person is characterized by a contraction of forces, by the affirmation of what has been achieved, and by the curtailment of further growth. His neurosis comes mainly from his clinging to a youthful attitude, which is now out of season. (Jung, 1931/1966, p. 39)

Process of Therapy

Diversity and the Dialectic. Patients are diverse and require a diverse, flexible treatment approach: "the method of treatment is determined primarily by the nature of the case. . . . The stubborn application of a particular theory or method must be characterized as basically wrong" (Jung, 1926/1954, p. 113). For example, "round common sense and good advice," "thorough confession or 'abreaction,'" and "a reductive analysis . . . along the lines of Freud or . . . Adler" are all fitting for some patients (Jung, 1935/1966a, p. 19).

> But when the thing becomes monotonous and you begin to get repetitions, and your unbiased judgment tells you that a standstill has been reached, or when mythological or archetypal contents appear, then is the time to give up the [Freudian or Adlerian] analytical-reductive method and to treat the symbols analogically or synthetically, which is equivalent to the [Jungian] dialectical procedure and the way to individuation. (Jung, 1935/1966a, p. 20)

It is in these particular situations that Jungian analysis seems indicated.

Therapy is a dialectical process—a dialogue or discussion between analyst and patient in which both parties affect and are affected by each other.

> [The dialectic] is not so much an elaboration of previous theories and practices as a complete abandonment of them in favor of the most unbiased attitude possible. In other words, the therapist is no longer the agent of treatment but a fellow participant in a process of individual development. (Jung, 1935/1966a, p. 8)

Therapist Characteristics. The therapist is a human, humane participant in the therapeutic process, respecting patients and their views: "[T]he doctor should, as a matter of principle, let nature rule and himself do his utmost to avoid influencing the patient in the direction of his own philosophical, social, and political bent" (Jung, 1935/1966b, p. 26). Furthermore, the concern and caring of the therapist are critical therapeutic elements.

> This influence on the part of the doctor. . . . I . . . call it his human interest and personal devotion. These are the property of no method, nor can they ever become one; they are moral qualities which are of the greatest importance in all methods of psychotherapy. (Jung, 1921/1966, p. 132)

Analytical therapy first and foremost emphasizes the value of the analyst's personal qualities for the analytic endeavor.

Stages.   Treatment can be divided into four phases, which are not necessarily consecutive or mutually exclusive (Adler, 1967): Confession (or catharsis), elucidation (gaining understanding or insight), education (or retraining), and transformation (on the way to wholeness and individuation). "The first beginnings of all analytical treatment . . . are to be found in its prototype, the confessional" (Jung, 1929/1966, p. 55).

The saying, "give up what thou hast, and then thou wilt receive [is] a motto for the first stage in psychotherapeutic treatment" (*ibid.*, p. 59). "Confession" is important since "there would appear to be a sort of conscience in mankind which severely punishes everyone who does not somehow and at some time . . . confess himself fallible and human. Until he can do this, an impenetrable wall shuts him off from the vital feeling that he is a man among other men" (*ibid.*, pp. 58–59).

But

> the intervention of the doctor is absolutely necessary. One can easily see what it means to the patient when he can confide his experience to an understanding and sympathetic doctor. His conscious mind finds in the doctor a moral support against the unmanageable affect of his traumatic complex. No longer does he stand alone in his battle with these elemental powers, but someone whom he trusts reaches out a hand, lending him moral strength to combat the tyranny of uncontrolled emotion. In this way the integrative powers of his conscious mind are reinforced until he is able once more to bring the rebellious affect under control. (Jung, 1921/1966, p. 132)

Abreaction, catharsis, *confessional,* then, serve the purpose of supporting the patient in his/her battle with intense affect.

Within stage two, *elucidation,* regression, and transference emerge and require attention. With regression, how far—ideally—should it be allowed to go in therapy?

> *Therapy must support the regression,* and continue to do this until the "prenatal" stage is reached. It must be remembered that the "mother" is really an imago, a psychic image merely, which has in it a number of different but very important unconscious contents. The "mother," as the first incarnation of the anima archetype, personifies in fact the whole unconscious. Hence the regression leads back only apparently to the mother; in reality she is the gateway into the unconscious, into the "realm of the Mothers." Whoever sets foot in this realm submits his *conscious ego personality to the controlling influence of the unconscious,* or if he feels that he has got caught by mistake, or that somebody has tricked him into it, he will defend himself desperately, though his resistance will not turn out to his advantage. For regression, if left undisturbed, does

> not stop short at the "mother" but goes back beyond her to the prenatal realm of the "Eternal Feminine," to the immemorial world of archetypal possibilities where, "thronged round with images of all creation," slumbers the "divine child," patiently awaiting his conscious realization. This son is the germ of wholeness, and he is characterized as such by his specific symbols. (Jung, 1912/1967, pp. 329–330)

By means of such regression in therapy, growth becomes possible.

Transference, transferring past unresolved experience (particularly in regard to one's parents) onto the therapist, can be an important part of treatment. "[A]lmost all cases requiring lengthy treatment gravitate round the phenomenon of transference, and . . . success or failure of the treatment appears to be bound up with it in a very fundamental way" (Jung, 1946/1966, p. 164). To dissolve the transference, four steps need to take place: (1) "make the patient realize the *subjective value* of the personal and impersonal contents of his transference;" (2) *"discrimination between personal and impersonal contents;"* (3) *"to differentiate the personal relationship to the analyst from impersonal factors;"* and (4) *"objectivation of impersonal images"* (Jung, 1968b, pp. 173–186). Another form of transference—the archetypal transference (i.e., transferring archetypal, ancestral elements onto the analyst)—can also come forth during treatment and require further analysis as well.

After elucidation, we next move on to *education,* stage three. This is a period of retraining, much like Adler's educational method.

> Nor should it be forgotten that the crooked paths of a neurosis lead to as many obstinate habits, and that for all our insight these do not disappear until replaced by other habits. But habits are won only by exercise, and appropriate education is the sole means to this end. (Jung, 1929/1966, p. 68)

[But, as Rychlak (1973) has pointed out, "Jung did not offer any set recipe of training aids at this point" (p. 177). Since Jung seemed to associate education with Alfred Adler, he appears to have drawn on Adler's techniques (see Chapter 3) as he saw fit during this stage of treatment.]

Last comes the stage of *transformation.* This refers to something much, much more than confession, elucidation, or education. It is a higher-level process—of self-realization, of moving toward individuation. This stage has been referred to as Jungian analysis proper—where Jung's unique ideas and thoughts about personality and treatment come forth (Adler, 1967). The work of this stage builds on and furthers previous therapeutic efforts. Therapists continue to draw on some if not all of the techniques used before (e.g., catharsis, dream work).

While there is a four-stage treatment process, again these stages are not necessarily consecutive or mutually exclusive.

> The three stages of analytical psychology [confessional, elucidation, education] so far dealt with are by no means of such a nature that the last can replace the first or the second. All three quite properly co-exist and are salient aspects of one and the same problem; they no more invalidate each other than do confession and absolution. And the same is true of the fourth—the stage of transformation: it must not claim to be the finally-achieved and only valid truth. Its part is to make up a deficit left by the previous stages; it comes to meet an additional and still unsatisfied need. (Jung, 1933, p. 47)

Techniques of Therapy

"The course of treatment is . . . rather like a running conversation with the unconscious" (Jung, 1956, p. 122). But, as Dehing (1992) put it, "unfortunately, C. G. Jung is rarely explicit with regard to his analytical practice; he always refused to lay down technical rules and little is known of his actual psychotherapeutic interventions" (p. 31).

Analysis of the Transference.   Some of this was described above, under stage two, elucidation, of the therapeutic process. Analysis of the transference can, among other possibilities, involve (1) becoming aware of and integrating complexes and (2) becoming aware of and assimilating one's shadow (Mattoon, 1986).

Dream Analysis.   The therapist analyzes dreams because "the dream is specifically the utterance of the unconscious" (Jung, 1934/1966, p. 147), "the dream describes the inner situation of the dreamer" (*ibid.,* p. 142), "dreams provide information about the hidden inner life and reveal to the patient those components of his personality which . . . appear merely as neurotic symptoms" (*ibid.,* p. 151). Indeed, dream analysis is "the most important method of getting at the pathogenic conflicts" (Jung, 1956, p. 30). "[S]ince . . . the unconscious possesses an etiological significance, and since dreams are the direct expression of unconscious psychic activity, the attempt to analyze and interpret dreams is theoretically justified" (Jung, 1934/1966, p. 140).

Yet, Jung states, "I have no theory about dreams. I do not know how dreams arise. And I am not at all sure that my way of handling dreams even deserves the name of a 'method'" (Jung, 1934/1966, p. 42). But Jungian therapists do seem to have a method or strategy that they apply to dream analysis. According to Henderson (1980), four ways of approaching dreams can be used: Free association (having patients associate freely to their own dreams); direct association (directing patients to associate to certain aspects of their dreams); amplification by the patient (elaborating and clarifying the dream contents); and amplification by the therapist. With amplification, patients are asked to give multiple associations to a particular aspect of their dreams. "Amplification enriches a dream image with the meanings of that image or motif in myths, religion, fairy tales, art and literature" (Whitmont, 1978, p. 55). Jung tended to engage in dream series analysis (i.e., analyzing a series of patient dreams) as opposed to focusing on a single dream. [Though free association is one dream analysis method that some Jungians use, Jung (1934/1966) himself spoke out against this; for those Jungians that do use free association, "the continuing use of [it] is not encouraged" (Henderson, 1980, p. 369), and general opinion is that direct association is preferable.]

As for the validity of a dream interpretation, "I allow myself only *one* criterion for the result of my labours: Does it [the interpretation] work?" (Jung, 1931/1966, p. 43). An interpretation works, according to Mattoon (1978), if there is an affirmative answer to one or more of the following questions (p. 178):

1. "Does the interpretation 'click' with the dreamer?"
2. "Does the interpretation 'act' for the dreamer?"
3. "Is the interpretation confirmed (or disconfirmed) by subsequent dreams?"
4. "Do the events anticipated by the interpretation occur in the dreamer's waking life?"

Interpretation. Interpretation thus plays a key role in dream analysis. It also is involved in dealing with transference and archetypal phenomena as well, for example, as with an archetypal interpretation.

> An interpretation is composed of that part of the patient's unconscious digested and thought about by the analyst. The result is then communicated to the patient in such a way as to give meaning to the patient's material. To do this it must have a clear structure and contain a verb. It can be short or long, clumsy, beautiful, poetic, and the tones of voice can make it musical. (Fordham, 1991, p. 169; see also, Fordham, 1978)

But whether musical or not, the important point to be remembered here is simply this: "interpretation is the main work of the [Jungian] analytic process" (Kaufman, 1989, p. 135).

Active Imagination. The active imagination technique can be applied to dreams and, more broadly, to fantasy experience in general.

> This process can . . . take place spontaneously or be artificially induced. In the latter case you choose a dream, or some other fantasy image, and concentrate on it by simply catching hold of it and looking at it. You can also use a bad mood as a starting point, and then try to find out what sort of fantasy-image it will produce, or what image expresses this mood. You then fix this image in the mind by concentrating your attention. (Jung, 1970, p. 495)

As the image is focused on, it often changes in some way. By tracking and reflecting on these changes, dialogue between the unconscious and ego can be stimulated (Singer, 1973).

Expressive Methods. There are yet other ways of accessing the unconscious.

> But why do I encourage patients, when they arrive at a certain stage in their development, to express themselves by means of brush, pencil, or pen at all? . . . To start off with, he puts down on paper what he has passively seen, thereby turning it into a deliberate act. He not only talks about it, he is actually doing something about it. (Jung, 1931/1966, p. 48)

These methods can also be used in conjunction with active imagination.

Other Techniques. Dehing (1992), in a paper that appeared in the *Journal of Analytical Psychology,* provided a critical inventory of interventions used by Jungian analysts. Some of these included silence, questioning, clarifying, confronting, supporting, and self-disclosing.

LENGTH AND LIMITATIONS

Length. Jung, 1935/1966b, p. 24, states that

> [M]odern psychotherapy . . . can no longer be mass produced but it is obliged to give undivided and generous attention to the individual. The procedure is necessarily detailed and lengthy. . . . The point is that most neuroses are misdevelopments that have

been built up over many years, and these cannot be remedied by a short and intensive process. Time is therefore an irreplaceable factor in healing.

Treatment, then, is to be long rather than short. (Interestingly, whereas Freud advocated the use of the couch for the analysand to lie on during analysis, Jung advocated a no-couch approach, with both parties sitting in chairs looking at each other for the duration of treatment).

As for the frequency of sessions, patients should "be seen as often as possible. I content myself with a maximum of four consultations a week. With the beginning of synthetic treatment . . . I then generally reduce them to one or two hours a week" (Jung, 1935/1966a, p. 20). But Kaufman (1989) has stated that a growing number of current Jungian therapists prefer to see their patients just once a week.

Limitations.   Jungian therapy proper—"transformation"—clearly is not for everyone. Not every patient is up to or even interested in studying the unconscious process, archetypes, and individuating. "[M]y contribution to psychotherapy confines itself to those cases where rational treatment does not yield satisfactory results" (Jung, 1931/1966, p. 41). Kaufman (1989) has stated that "analytical psychology originally was considered applicable primarily to persons who had adjusted to the outer world very well, had accomplished what was expected of them by society" (p. 142). Analytical psychotherapy today is still probably best suited for those who are relatively adequately adjusted, are intact, have relatively strong egos, are inclined to deep introspection and self-analysis, are self-aware, and have a good capacity for insight.

EXAMPLE

The following example, which further shows Jung's interest in dreams and symbolism, is taken from the appendix, entitled "The Realities of Practical Psychotherapy," of *Collected Works,* volume 16, pp. 330–338:

> I remember a case that caused me no end of trouble. It concerned a 25-year-old woman patient, who suffered from a high degree of emotivity, exaggerated sensitiveness, and hysterical fever. She was very musical; whenever she played the piano she got so emotional that her temperature rose and after ten minutes registered 100°F. or more. She also suffered from a compulsive argumentativeness and a fondness for philosophical hair-splitting that was quite intolerable despite her high intelligence. She was unmarried, but was having a love-affair which, except for her hypersensitivity, was perfectly normal. Before she came to me, she had been treated by an analyst for two months with no success. Then she went to a woman analyst, who broke off the treatment at the end of a week. I was the third. She felt she was one of those who were doomed to fail in analysis, and she came to me with pronounced feelings of inferiority. She didn't know why it hadn't worked with the other analysts. I got her to tell me her somewhat lengthy anamnesis, which took several consulting hours. I then asked her: "Did you notice that when you were treated by Dr. X [the first], you had at the very beginning a dream which struck you, and which you did not understand at the time?" She remembered at once that during the second week of the treatment she had an impressive dream which she had not understood then, but which seemed clear

enough to her in the light of later events. *She had dreamt that she had to cross a frontier. She had arrived at a frontier station; it was night, and she had to find where the frontier could be crossed, but she could not find the way and got lost in the darkness.* This darkness represented her unconsciousness, that is, her unconscious identity with the analyst, who was also in the dark about finding a way out of this unconscious state—which is what crossing the frontier meant. As a matter of fact, a few years later this analyst gave up psychotherapy altogether because of too many failures and personal involvements.

Early in the second treatment, the dream of the frontier was repeated in the following form: *She had arrived at the same frontier station. She had to find the crossing, and she saw, despite the darkness, a little light in the distance showing where the place was. In order to get there, she had to go through a wooded valley in pitch-blackness. She plucked up her courage and went ahead. But hardly had she entered the wood than she felt somebody clinging to her, and she knew it was her analyst.* She awoke in terror. This analyst, too, later gave up her profession for very much the same reasons.

I now asked the patient: "Have you had a dream like that since you have been with me?" She gave an embarrassed smile and told the following dream: *I was at the frontier station. A customs official was examining the passengers one by one. I had nothing but my handbag, and when it came to my turn I answered with a good conscience that I had nothing to declare. But he said, pointing to my handbag: "What have you got in there?" And to my boundless astonishment he pulled a large mattress, and then a second one, out of my bag.* She was so frightened that she woke up.

I then remarked: "So you wanted to hide your obviously bourgeois wish to get married, and felt you had been unpleasantly caught out." Though the patient could not deny the logical rightness of the interpretation, she produced the most violent resistances against any such possibility. Behind these resistances, it then turned out, there was hidden a most singular fantasy of a quite unimaginable erotic adventure that surpassed anything I had ever come across in my experience. I felt my head reeling, I thought of nymphomaniac possession, of weird perversions, of completely depraved erotic fantasies that rambled meaninglessly on and on, of latent schizophrenia, where at least the nearest comparative material could be found. I began to look askance at the patient and to find her unsympathetic, but was annoyed with myself for this, because I knew that no good results could be hoped for while we remained on such a footing. After about four weeks the undeniable symptoms of a standstill did in fact appear. Her dreams became sketchy, dull, dispiriting, and incomprehensible. I had no more ideas and neither had the patient. The work became tedious, exhausting, and barren. I felt that we were gradually getting stuck in a kind of soggy dough. The case began to weigh upon me even in my leisure hours; it seemed to me uninteresting, hardly worth the bother. Once I lost patience with her because I felt she wasn't making any effort. "So here are the personal reactions coming out," I thought. The following night *I dreamt that I was walking along a country road at the foot of a steep hill. On the hill was a castle with a high tower. Sitting on the parapet of the topmost pinnacle was a woman, golden in the light of the evening sun. In order to see her properly, I had to bend my head so far back that I woke up with a crick in the neck.* I realized to my amazement that the woman was my patient.

The dream was distinctly disturbing, for the first thing that came into my head while dozing was the verse from Schenkenbach's "Reiterlied":

She sits so high above us,
No prayer will she refuse.

This is an invocation to the Virgin Mary. The dream had put my patient on the highest peak, making her a goddess, while I, to say the least, had been looking down on her.

The next day I said to her: "Haven't you noticed that our work is stuck in the doldrums?" She burst into tears and said: "Of course I've noticed it. I know I always fail and never do anything right. You were my last hope and now this isn't going to work either." I interrupted her: "This time it is different. I've had a dream about you." And I told her the dream, with the result that the superficial symptomatology, her argumentativeness, her insistence on always being right, and her touchiness vanished. But now her real neurosis began, and it left me completely flabbergasted. It started with a series of highly impressive dreams, which I could not understand at all, and then she developed symptoms whose cause, structure, and significance were absolutely incomprehensible to me. They first took the form of an indefinable excitation in the perineal region, and she dreamt that a white elephant was coming out of her genitals. She was so impressed by this that she tried to carve the elephant out of ivory. I had no idea what it meant, and only had the uncomfortable feeling that something inexplicable was going on with a logic of its own, though I couldn't see at all where it would lead.

Soon afterwards symptoms of uterine ulcers appeared, and I had to send the patient to a gynecologist. There was an inflamed swelling of the mucous membrane of the uterus, about the size of a pea, which refused to heal after months of treatment and merely shifted from place to place.

Suddenly this symptom disappeared, and she developed an extreme hyperaesthesia of the bladder. She had to leave the room two or three times during the consulting hour. No local infection could be found. Psychologically, the symptom meant that something had to be "expressed." So I gave her the task of expressing by drawing whatever her hand suggested to her. She had never drawn before, and set about it with much doubt and hesitation. But now symmetrical flowers took shape under her hand, vividly coloured and arranged in symbolic patterns. She made these pictures with great care and with a concentration I can only call devout.

Meanwhile the hyperaesthesia of the bladder had ceased, but intestinal spasms developed higher up, causing gurgling noises and sounds of splashing that could be heard even outside the room. She also suffered from explosive evacuations of the bowels. At first the colon was affected, then the ileum, and finally the upper sections of the small intestine. These symptoms gradually abated after several weeks. Their place was then taken by a strange paraesthesia of the head. The patient had the feeling that the top of her skull was growing soft, that the fontanelle was opening up, and that a bird with a long sharp beak was coming down to pierce through the fontanelle as far as the diaphragm.

The whole case worried me so much that I told the patient there was no sense in her coming to me for treatment, I didn't understand two-thirds of her dreams, to say nothing of her symptoms, and besides this I had no notion how I could help her. She looked at me in astonishment and said: "But it's going splendidly! It doesn't matter that you don't understand my dreams. I always have the craziest symptoms, but something is happening all the time."

I could only conclude from this peculiar remark that for her the neurosis was a positive experience; indeed, "positive" is a mild expression for the way she felt about it. As I could not understand her neurosis, I was quite unable to explain how it was that all these extremely unpleasant symptoms and incomprehensible dreams could give her such a positive feeling. One can, with an effort, imagine that *something* is better than nothing, even though this something took the form of disagreeable physical symptoms. But so far as the dreams were concerned, I can only say that I have seldom come across a series of dreams that seemed to be so full of meaning. Only, their meaning escaped me.

In order to elucidate this extraordinary case, I must return to a point in the anamnesis which has not been mentioned so far. The patient was a full-blooded European, but had been born in Java. As a child she spoke Malay and had an *ayah,* a native nurse. When she was of school age, she went to Europe and never returned to the Indies. Her childhood world was irretrievably sunk in oblivion, so that she could not remember a single word of Malay. In her dreams there were frequent allusions to Indonesian motifs, but though I could sometimes understand them I was unable to weave them into a meaningful whole.

About the time when the fantasy of the fontanelle appeared, I came upon an English book which was the first to give a thorough and authentic account of the symbolism of Tantric Yoga. The book was *The Serpent Power,* by Sir John Woodroffe, who wrote under the pseudonym of Arthur Avalon. It was published about the time when the patient was being treated by me. To my astonishment I found in this book an explanation of all those things I had not understood in the patient's dreams and symptoms.

It is, as you see, quite impossible that the patient knew the book beforehand. But could she have picked up a thing or two from the *ayah?* I regard this as unlikely because Tantrism, and in particular Kundalini Yoga, is a cult restricted to southern India and has relatively few adherents. It is, moreover, an exceedingly complicated symbolical system which no one can understand unless he has been initiated into it or has at least made special studies in this field. Tantrism corresponds to our Western scholasticism, and if anyone supposes that a Javanese *ayah* could teach a five-year-old child about the *chakra* system, this would amount to saying that a French nanny could induct her charge into the *Summa* of St. Thomas or the conceptualism of Abelard. However the child may have picked up the rudiments of the *chakra* system, the fact remains that its symbolism does much to explain the patient's symptoms.

According to this system, there are seven centres, called *chakras* or *padmas* (lotuses), which have fairly definite localizations in the body. They are, as it were, psychic localizations, and the higher ones correspond to the historical localizations of consciousness. The nethermost *chakra,* called *mulādhāra,* is the perineal lotus and corresponds to the cloacal zone in Freud's sexual theory. This centre, like all the others, is represented in the shape of a flower, with a circle in the middle, and has attributes that express in symbols the psychic qualities of that particular localization. Thus, the perineal *chakra* contains as its main symbol the sacred *white elephant.* The next *chakra,* called *svadhisthāna,* is localized near the bladder and represents the sexual centre. Its main symbol is water or sea, and subsidiary symbols are the sickle moon as the feminine principle, and a devouring water-monster called *makara,* which corresponds to the biblical and cabalistic Leviathan. The mythological whale-dragon is, as you know, a symbol for the devouring and birthgiving womb, which in its turn symbolizes certain reciprocal actions between consciousness and the unconscious. The patient's bladder symptoms can be referred to the *svadhisthāna* symbolism, and so can the inflamed spots in the uterus. Soon afterwards she began her drawings of flowers, whose symbolic content relates them quite clearly to the *chakras.* The third centre, called *manipura,* corresponds to the solar plexus. As we have seen, the noises in the abdomen gradually moved up to the small intestine. This third *chakra* is the emotional centre, and is the earliest known localization of consciousness. There are primitives in existence who still think with their bellies. Every-day speech still shows traces of this: something lies heavy on the stomach, the bow-els turn to water, etc. The fourth *chakra,* called *anāhata,* is situated in the region of the heart and the diaphragm. In Homer the diaphragm (*phren, phrenes*) was the seat of feeling and thinking. The fifth and sixth, called *vishuddha* and *ajña,* are situated re-spectively in the throat and between the eyebrows. The seventh, *sahasrāra,* is at the top of the skull.

The fundamental idea of Tantrism is that a feminine creative force in the shape of a serpent, named *kundalinā,* rises up from the perineal centre, where she had been sleeping, and ascends through the *chakras,* thereby activating them and con-stellating their symbols. This "Serpent Power" is personified as the *mahādevishakti,* the goddess who brings everything into existence by means of *māyā,* the building ma-terial of reality.

When the *kundalini* serpent had reached the *manipura* centre in my patient, it was met by the bird of thought descending from above, which with its sharp beak pierced through the fontanelle (*sahasrāra chakra*) to the diaphragm (*anāhata*). Thereupon a wild storm of affect broke out, because the bird had implanted in her a thought which she would not and could not accept. She gave up the treatment and I saw her only occasionally, but noticed she was hiding something. A year later came the confession: she was beset by the thought that she wanted a child. This very ordinary thought did not fit in at all well with the nature of her psychic experi-ence and it had a devastating effect, as I could see for myself. For as soon as the *kundalini* serpent reached *manipura,* the most primitive centre of consciousness, the patient's brain told her what kind of thought the *shakti* was insinuating into her: that she wanted a real child and not just a psychic experience. This seemed a great let-down to the patient. But that is the disconcerting thing about the *shakti:* her building material is *māyā,* "real illusion." In other words, she spins fantasies with real things.

This little bit of Tantric philosophy helped the patient to make an ordinary human life for herself, as a wife and mother, out of the local demonology she had sucked in with her *ayah*'s milk, and to do so without losing touch with the inner, psychic figures which had been called awake by the long-forgotten influences of her childhood. What she experienced as a child, and what later estranged her from the European con-sciousness and entangled her in a neurosis, was, with the help of analysis, trans-formed not into nebulous fantasies but into a lasting spiritual possession in no way in-compatible with an ordinary human existence, a husband, children, and housewifely duties.

Although this case is an unusual one, it is not an exception. It has served its purpose if it has enabled me to give you some idea of my psychotherapeutic proce-dure. The case is not in the least a story of triumph; it is more like a sage of blunders, hesitations, doubts, gropings in the dark, and false clues which in the end took a favourable turn. But all this comes very much nearer the truth and reality of my proce-dure than a case that brilliantly confirms the preconceived opinions and intentions of the therapist. I am painfully aware, as you too must be, of the gaps and shortcomings of my exposition, and I must rely on your imagination to supply a large part of what has been left unsaid. If you now recall that mutual ignorance means mutual uncon-sciousness and hence unconscious identity, you will not be wrong in concluding that in this case the analyst's lack of knowledge of Oriental psychology drew him further and further into the analytical process and forced him to participate as actively as pos-sible. Far from being a technical blunder, this is a fate-sent necessity in such a situation. Only your own experience can tell you what this means in practice. No psychotherapist should lack that natural reserve which prevents people from riding roughshod over mysteries they do not understand and trampling them flat. This reserve will enable him to pull back in good time when he encounters the mystery of the patient's difference from himself, and to avoid the danger—unfortunately only too real—of committing psychic murder in the name of therapy. For the ultimate cause of a neurosis is something *positive* which needs to be safeguarded for the patient; otherwise he suffers a psychic loss, and the result of the treatment is at best a defective cure. The fact that our patient was born in the East and spent the most important years of her childhood under Oriental influences is something that cannot be eliminated from her life. The childhood experience of a neurotic is not, in itself, negative; far from it. It becomes negative only when it finds no suitable place in the life and outlook of the adult. The real task of analysis, it seems to me, is to bring about a synthesis between the two.

SUMMARY AND EVALUATION

Summary.   Jung, who as a boy was beset by fears, fainting spells, religious conflicts, and feeling the misfit, ultimately rose to become one of the major figures in the fields of psychiatry, psychology, and psychotherapy. He developed a broad, far-reaching system of thought—analytical psychology—which has had and continues to have broad applications. In psychotherapy, Jung emphasized the uniqueness and individuality of each case. He fought hard not to be hemmed in by any preconceptions about his patients, instead choosing to meet each one of them openly, being guided by a sense of discovery and an appreciation for their potential and possibility.

For Jung, therapy was conceived of as having four stages: catharsis, elucidation, education, and transformation. But it is in "transformation"—what has been referred to as Jungian therapy proper—where Jung's unique insights and concepts truly come to the forefront. Transference analysis was and is a part of treatment, but Jung saw this differently from Freud. For example, Jung spoke of the archetypal transference and the need to analyze it. Some of the primary techniques of the Jungian analyst include the following: dream analysis, using expressive methods, active imagination, and amplification. Therapy is a process of making the unconscious conscious, of resolving problematic complexes. The ultimate goal of treatment is individuation. Jung's primary writings about psychotherapy can be found in volumes 7 and 16 of his *Collected Works*.

Evaluation.   Jung presents us with some interesting views on the therapeutic experience. We especially like his emphasis on patient uniqueness and individuality. His belief in and valuing of those aspects is refreshing.

There is merit to be found in Jung's ideas about the aims of psychotherapy. While Jung (1931/1966) did specify some aims, he also said "let pure experience decide the therapeutic aims;" "in psychotherapy it seems to me positively advisable for the doctor not to have too fixed an aim" (p. 41). We have surely seen cases where therapists seem overly focused on quickly deciding what the goals of therapy are to be. But sometimes patients, on entering therapy, do not know their goals, they may not have any specific goal in mind—they just want to feel better. By letting "pure experience" run its course, however, goals can emerge and be defined. But for the therapist to want to do this hurriedly or for the therapist to push his/her own agenda about change is ill-advised. That seems to be the point Jung was making.

Jung emphasized a caring, concerned doctor–patient relationship for psychotherapy. He took the analysand "off the couch" so that they could see each other eye to eye. Jung of course knew the importance of maintaining an appropriate therapeutic distance, but he appeared to know equally well that the foundation of any psychotherapy lay in the therapist–patient relationship. We find that to be a positive aspect of his views.

Another strength of Jung's approach (which can also be a weakness, as we will explain subsequently) can be found in his introduction of such concepts as archetype, complex, and collective unconscious. By defining these and their personality implications, Jung brought a whole new perspective to bear on the treatment process—what can happen there, what can be explored, what can be uncovered. His ideas stretched psychotherapeutic thinking and led to the incorporation of some interesting, unique elements (e.g., archetypes) into therapy that we do not see reflected in any other approach.

With these positive features recognized, what might be some negative features we could mention about Jungian psychotherapy? To begin, let us again quote Singer (1973): "Jung never presented a psychological theory in the strict sense of a theory; that is, a body of generalizations and principles developed in association with the practice of psychotherapy and forming its content as an intellectual discipline" (p. 6). That Jung did not do this certainly makes it more difficult to connect his theory and his therapy, and piecing the two together can be a real struggle.

"Jung does not offer a methodology, a technique for procedure, a series of 'applications' that the Jungian analyst can use from the insights and formulations of the master" (Singer, 1973, p. 6). This too does not help to clarify the Jungian therapy process. Dieckmann (1991) has also picked up on this point: "Many Jungians experience an aversion and a deeply ingrained distrust of the idea of methodology and technique, especially the latter. Consequently, analytical psychologists have written precious little in this area" (p. 10). But this "aversion," "deeply ingrained distrust," and "precious little writing" all lead to continued murkiness about the Jungian analytic process and analytic procedure—What is it exactly? What exactly do you do as therapist? How do you do it? Why do you do it? Even after reading about Jungian therapy, these are still not uncommon questions for readers to ask.

In recent explications, Jung's personality theory has been referred to as "vague," "riddled with inconsistencies," "highly ambiguous," "imprecise," "untestable," "unparsimonious," "a fairly loose collection of theoretical ideas" (see Aiken, 1993, p. 128; Ryckman, 1993, pp. 93–94). Some of these same descriptors, in accordance with the "murkiness" mentioned above, could be applied to Jung's psychotherapy as well. Without question, if the personality theory is vague, inconsistent, ambiguous, and unparsimonious in some respects, how could the same not be said for analytical psychotherapy? The fact of the matter is that the same can be said. For example, just how parsimonious are the concepts of archetype or collective unconscious? Are such broad, mystical concepts really needed for therapy to occur? Are they really necessary for deep and meaningful change to happen?

And what of research? Is there any research to support Jungian psychotherapy? There certainly is much research that can be found on some of Jung's concepts, such as psychological type. There is, for instance, even a *Journal of Psychological Type* which publishes empirical work. But research into the process and outcome of Jungian psychotherapy is lacking. It appears that Jungians, much as with Freudian analysts, have relied largely on the anecdotal-type case study as their evidence. Actual experimental work evaluating the treatment process, or systematic case study analysis (e.g., Hill, 1989) have not been done as yet.

Is there a future for Jung's psychotherapy? Without question, there does appear to be. Books about Jung, his personality theory, and his psychotherapy continue to appear (e.g., Clarke, 1991; Daniels, 1991; Jacoby, 1994; Ryce-Menuhin, 1991; Spiegelman, 1988; Storr, 1991; Whitmont & Perera, 1992). The *Journal of Analytical Psychology,* which has been in existence for decades now, remains a primary outlet for articles on Jungian analysis. Kaufman (1989) pointed out that "Jungian training institutes have been established in the United States in New York, Los Angeles, Chicago, Seattle, Boston, and San Francisco" (p. 126). He further adds that "the number of Jungian analysts has been steadily growing all over the world," with there being "important centers in Switzerland, Britain, Germany, Israel, France, and Italy" (p. 126). Erica Goode, in a 1992 *U.S. News and World Report* article, said the following: "Thirty-one years after the Swiss psychiatrist's death, Jung's theories are surging in popularity, becoming a cultural touchstone, a lens for processing experience, in some cases almost a religion" (December 7, 1992, issue). A year later McCullough (1993) reiterated that point:

> Psychiatrist Carl Jung's ideas are spreading throughout the country. . . . Books influenced by the Swiss psychiatrist are selling widely, and interest in Jungian societies . . . is growing. Mental health professionals are applying Jung's ideas in their practices and encountering clients that are reading Jungian influenced books.

So there clearly is much current interest to be found in Jung and his analytical psychology.

About 20 years ago, Maduro and Wheelwright (1977) predicted that Jung's analytical school of thought would be increasingly integrated with other psychoanalytic and nonanalytic theories. Some efforts in that direction have been made, but perhaps more of that will be forthcoming. They further predicted: "in addition to the analysis of symbolic content and process, Jung's influence will continue to grow within the social and behavioral sciences in the following . . . domains: (1) art and culture, (2) human development and aging, (3) medical anthropology, (4) folklore studies, and (5) clinical psychology" (Maduro & Wheelwright, 1977, p. 118). The reports of Goode (1992) and McCullough (1993) seemingly lend some support to that prediction.

But as Maduro and Wheelwright (1977) also stated, "if analytical psychology is to survive and thrive it will have to consider interpersonal issues and make itself socially relevant to a changing world" (p. 118). For analytical psychology, and for analytical psychotherapy specifically, that statement—made almost two decades ago—seems as true now as it was then.

Yet, Hall and Lindzey's 1957 statement would still appear to hold, too:

> When all is said and done, Jung's theory of personality as developed in his prolific writings and as applied to a wide range of human phenomena stands as one of the most remarkable achievements in modern thought. The originality and audacity of

Jung's thinking have few parallels in recent scientific history, and no other man aside from Freud has opened up more conceptual windows into what Jung would choose to call "the soul of man." (p. 110)

REFERENCES

Adler, G. (1967). Methods of treatment in analytical psychology. In B. Wolman (Ed.), *Psychoanalytic techniques* (pp. 338–378). New York: Basic Books.

Aiken, L. R. (1993). *Personality: Theories, research, and applications.* Englewood Cliffs, NJ: Prentice Hall.

Clarke, J. J. (1991). *In search of Jung.* New York: Routledge.

Daniels, M. (1991). *Self-discovery the Jungian way: The watchword technique.* New York: Routledge.

Dehing, J. (1992). The therapist's interventions in Jungian analysis. *Journal of Analytical Psychology, 37,* 29–47.

Dieckmann, H. (1991). *Methods in analytical psychology: An introduction.* Wilmette, IL: Chiron.

Fordham, M. (1978). *Jungian psychotherapy.* London: Karnac Books.

Fordham, M. (1991). The supposed limits of interpretation. *Journal of Analytical Psychology, 36,* 165–175.

Goode, E. E. (1992, December 7). Spiritual questing. *U.S. News and World Report.*

Hall, C. S., & Lindzey, G. (1957). *Theories of personality.* New York: Wiley.

Hall, C. S., & Lindzey, G. (1970). *Theories of personality* (2nd ed.). New York: Wiley.

Hall, C. S., & Nordby, V. J. (1973). *A primer of Jungian psychology.* New York: New American Library.

Henderson, J. L. (1980). The dream in Jungian analysis. In J. M. Natterson (Ed.), *The dream in clinical practice* (pp. 369–387). New York: Jason Aronson.

Hill, C. E. (1989). *Therapist techniques and client outcomes.* Newbury Park, CA: Sage.

Hochheimer, W. (1969). *The psychotherapy of C. G. Jung.* Great Britain: Barrie & Rockliff.

Jacoby, M. (1994). *Shame and the origins of self-esteem: A Jungian approach.* New York: Routledge.

Jung, C. G. (1902/1970). On the psychology and pathology of so-called occult phenomena. In *Psychiatric studies, Collected works of C. G. Jung* (vol. 1, pp. 3–88). Princeton, NJ: Princeton University Press.

Jung, C. G. (1907/1960). The psychology of dementia praecox. In *The psychogenesis of mental disease, Collected works of C. G. Jung* (vol. 3, pp. 1–151). Princeton, NJ: Princeton University Press.

Jung, C. G. (1912/1967). *Symbols of transformation, Collected works of C. G. Jung* (vol. 5). Princeton, NJ: Princeton University Press.

Jung, C. G. (1921/1966). The therapeutic value of abreaction. In *Psychological types, Collected works of C. G. Jung* (vol. 16, pp. 129–138). Princeton, NJ: Princeton University Press.

Jung, C. G. (1925/1954). Marriage as a psychological relationship. In *The development of personality, Collected works of C. G. Jung* (vol. 17, pp. 189–201). Princeton, NJ: Princeton University Press.

Jung, C. G. (1926/1954). Analytical psychology and education. In *The development of personality, Collected works of C. G. Jung* (vol. 17, pp. 65–132). Princeton, NJ: Princeton University Press.

Jung, C. G. (1929/1966). Problems of modern psychotherapy. In *The practice of psychotherapy, Collected works of C. G. Jung* (vol. 16, pp. 53–75). Princeton, NJ: Princeton University Press.

Jung, C. G. (1931/1966). The aims of psychotherapy. In *The practice of psychotherapy, Collected works of C. G. Jung* (vol. 16, pp. 36–52). Princeton, NJ: Princeton University Press.

Jung, C. G. (1933). *Modern man in search of a soul.* New York: Harcourt, Brace, & World.

Jung, C. G. (1934/1966). The practical use of dream-analysis. In *The practice of psychotherapy, Collected works of C. G. Jung* (vol. 16, pp. 139–161). Princeton, NJ: Princeton University Press.

Jung, C. G. (1934/1970). The state of psychotherapy today. In *Civilization in transition, Collected works of C. G. Jung* (vol. 10, pp. 157–178). Princeton, NJ: Princeton University Press.

Jung, C. G. (1935/1966a). Principles of practical psychotherapy. In *The practice of psychotherapy, Collected works of C. G. Jung* (vol. 16, pp. 3–20). Princeton, NJ: Princeton University Press.

Jung, C. G. (1935/1966b). What is psychotherapy? In *The practice of psychotherapy, Collected works of C. G. Jung* (vol. 16, pp. 21–28). Princeton, NJ: Princeton University Press.

Jung, C. G. (1936/1968). The concept of the collective unconscious. In *The archetypes and the collective unconscious, Collected works of C. G. Jung* (vol. 9, part 1, pp. 3–41). Princeton, NJ: Princeton University Press.

Jung, C. G. (1937/1968). Psychological factors determining human behavior. In *The structure and dynamics of the psyche, Collected works of C. G. Jung* (vol. 8, pp. 114–125). Princeton, NJ: Princeton University Press.

Jung, C. G. (1939/1968). Conscious, unconscious, and individuation. In *The archetypes and the collective unconscious, Collected works of C. G. Jung* (vol. 9, part 1, pp. 275–289). Princeton, NJ: Princeton University Press.

Jung, C. G. (1944/1968). *Psychology and alchemy, Collected works of C. G. Jung* (vol. 12). Princeton, NJ: Princeton University Press.

Jung, C. G. (1946/1966). The psychology of the transference. In *The practice of psychotherapy, Collected works of C. G. Jung* (vol. 16, pp. 163–323). Princeton, NJ: Princeton University Press.

Jung, C. G. (1956). *Two essays on analytical psychology.* Cleveland: World Publishing (also vol. 7 in the *Collected works* series).

Jung, C. G. (1961). *Memories, dreams, reflections.* New York: Vintage Books.

Jung, C. G. (1968a). *Aion, Collected works* (vol. 9, part 2). Princeton, NJ: Princeton University Press.

Jung, C. G. (1968b). *Analytical psychology: Its theory and practice.* New York: Vintage Books.

Jung, C. G. (1970). *Mysterium coniunctionis, Collected works of C. G. Jung* (vol. 14). Princeton, NJ: Princeton University Press.

Jung, C. G. (1972). *Experimental researches, Collected works of C. G. Jung* (vol. 2). Princeton, NJ: Princeton University Press.

Kaufman, Y. (1989). Analytical psychotherapy. In R. J. Corsini & D. J. Wedding (Eds.), *Current psychotherapies* (4th ed., pp. 119–152). Itasca, IL: F. E. Peacock.

Maduro, R. J., & Wheelwright, J. B. (1977). Analytical psychology. In R. J. Corsini (Ed.), *Current personality theories* (pp. 83–123). Itasca, IL: F. E. Peacock.

Mattoon, M. A. (1978). *Applied dream analysis: A Jungian approach.* Washington, DC: Winston & Sons.

Mattoon, M. A. (1986). Jungian analysis. In I. L. Kutash & A. Wolf (Eds.), *Psychotherapist's casebook* (pp. 124–143). San Francisco: Jossey-Bass.

McCullough, L. (1993). Interest in Carl Jung's ideas is growing. *Guidepost, 36*(1), 1, 12–13.

Ryce-Menuhin, J. (1991). *Jungian sandplay: The wonderful therapy.* New York: Routledge.

Rychlak, J. F. (1973). *Introduction to personality and psychotherapy.* Boston: Houghton Mifflin.

Ryckman, R. M. (1993). *Theories of personality* (5th ed.). Pacific Grove, CA: Brooks/Cole.

Samuels, A., Shorter, B., & Plaut, F. (1986). *A critical dictionary of Jungian analysis.* New York: Routledge.

Singer, J. (1973). *Boundaries of the soul: The practice of Jung's psychology.* New York: Anchor Books.

Spiegelman, J. M. (Ed.). (1988). *Jungian analysts: Their visions and vulnerabilities.* Phoenix, AZ: Falcon Press.

Storr, A. (1991). *Jung.* New York: Routledge.

Whitmont, E. C. (1978). Jungian approach. In J. L. Fosshage & C. A. Loew (Eds.), *Dream interpretation: A comparative study* (pp. 53–77). New York: Spectrum Publications.

Whitmont, E. C., & Perera, S. B. (1992). *Dreams, a portal to the source: A guide to dream interpretation.* New York: Routledge.

chapter 3

Individual Psychology: Adler

Alfred Adler (1870–1937) was born in Penzing, Austria, a town on the outskirts of Vienna, to middle-class parents. His mother was a housewife, his father a Jewish grain merchant. He had an older brother and sister and two younger brothers (one of whom died when Adler was three) and two younger sisters as well.

During the period of Adler's birth, Jews had two choices about where they could live—in voluntary ghettoes or in predominantly gentile neighborhoods. The Adlers lived in the latter. While the 1870s, 1880s, and 1890s were a time of increasing antisemitism, reports say this had little effect on Adler and his upbringing. "Alfred grew up just a boy of the Vienna outskirts. . . . Adler's early experiences made him unable to feel the differences between Jews and gentiles as something personally important" (Furtmuller, in Ansbacher & Ansbacher, 1979, p. 331).

As a child, Adler was said to have been "sickly." He had rickets, a vocal cord spasm problem, and came close to death from pneumonia at the age of four. His early school years have been described as difficult, though not much is known about them. He experienced adjustment problems, had little confidence in himself physically, and did quite poorly in math.

Supposedly, Adler's brush with death by pneumonia at age four significantly affected his decision to become a medical doctor. He entered the Vienna medical school, graduating from there in 1895 with a specialty in ophthalmology. He then opened a general practice in internal medicine and soon thereafter began developing a line of thinking about organ inferiority and overcompensation, which culminated in the book *Study of Organ Inferiority and Its Psychical Compensation* (Adler, 1907/1917). And so began his journey into psychiatry and psychotherapy.

During this time, Adler met, fell in love with, and, in 1897, married Raissa Epstein. They had four children—Valentine born in 1898, Alexandra in 1901, Kurt in 1905, and Nelly in 1909. Alexandra and Kurt went on to become psychiatrists and continue their father's pioneering work.

In the late 1800s, Sigmund Freud was in the process of developing and presenting his dream theory. His ideas met with great opposition, and Adler came to Freud's defense—asking that people objectively evaluate Freud's ideas rather than dismissing them out of hand. In 1902, Adler (along with three other individuals) was invited by Freud to join a discussion group of sorts, where theory, philosophy, and psychopathology would be taken up and considered. Adler did so. This group came to be called the "Vienna Psychoanalytic Society." During this period, Adler learned from Freud, but he continued to develop his own ideas and refine his own thinking as well.

In 1910, the International Psychoanalytical Association was founded; its first president was C. G. Jung, it second, Adler. That same year a new journal—*Zentralblatt fur Psychoanalyse*—was founded through the cooperation of Freud and Adler. Adler was co-editor, Freud the editor-in-chief. But as Adler continued to develop his own ideas further, as he continued to publish these, and as he began to criticize Freud's thinking, tension developed between Adler and Freud. This became so problematic that Adler resigned as journal co-editor and as Association president. Adler, along with some of his followers, later founded and then became president of the Society for Free Psychoanalytic Research. In 1912 or 1913, the Society's name became the Society for Individual Psychology. The journal, *Zeitschrift fur Individual-psychologie,* began publication in 1914 with Adler as its co-editor.

Adler was drafted in 1915—into the Austro-Hungarian army—all the while continuing to develop his system of "Individual Psychology." With the war over, he became involved in the Austrian school reform movement and started the first child guidance clinic in Vienna in 1922; many other such clinics were established in Vienna and Germany.

Adler first came to the United States in the latter part of 1926. He lectured widely, was visiting professor at Columbia University in 1929, and became first chair of Medical Psychology at Long Island Medical College in 1932. During this period, he worked on improving his English (which has been described as "halting") and even learned at the age of 60 to drive a car.

In the mid-1930s, the Fascists came to power in Austria. Because of that, Adler and his wife came to live in New York City permanently in 1935. Three of his children came as well, with Valentine fleeing to Russia (where she soon died as part of a Stalinist purge). While in the United States, Adler maintained a very busy schedule—lecturing and writing as always. On May 28, 1937, shortly before he was to lecture to a group in Aberdeen, Scotland, he died of heart failure. (Biographical material on Adler was obtained from several sources: Bottome, 1957; Furtmuller, in Ansbacher & Ansbacher, 1979; Manaster, 1977; Manaster & Corsini, 1982; Manaster, Painter, Deutsch, & Overholt, 1977.)

BACKGROUND AND DEVELOPMENT

Some of the personal background that ultimately affected Adler's theorizing can be found in the above biographical description: his being "sickly," weak, and frail and his efforts to overcome those. Later having a general medical practice in which he saw a lot of "waiters, acrobats, and artists whose livelihood depended on bodily skills" (Manaster, 1977, p. 10) is also said to have influenced Adler's ideas about physical weakness, organic inferiority, and their effects on personality formation. All of this eventually led to the concepts of compensation and overcompensation (to make up for felt deficiencies), which had application to both biological as well as psychological processes.

H. L. Ansbacher (1978), perhaps the foremost Adlerian scholar in the world, has divided Adler's writings (1898–1937) into four periods of development. First was 1898–1907, the "prior to an explicit concept of man" period. Here the focus was primarily on the organic, physiological understanding of the individual—the organ inferiority years (see Chapter 1 in Ansbacher & Ansbacher, 1964). The second period was 1908–1917, the "prior to social interest" period. Here the aggression drive was first emphasized, then came the "masculine protest" and "will to power" (see Chapters 1 and 2 in Ansbacher & Ansbacher, 1964), and ultimately, a shift toward a more subjective, individualistic psychology began to take hold.

The third ran from 1918 to 1927, the "social interest as counterforce" period. Here social interest (feeling for and with others) emerged as an important force that placed limits on or countered one's aggression drive and will to power. At this point, then, there were two opposing motivational forces in Adler's theory: The aggressive, will to power force and the social interest force. But according to Ferguson (1989), "Adler placed social bonding as more fundamental for humans than the individualistic striving . . . " (p. 357).

Ansbacher classified 1928–1937 as the "social interest as cognitive function" period. Here social interest, what Ansbacher (1968) has referred to as Adler's most distinctive concept, came to be seen as a cognitive function that must be developed and that provides direction to individual strivings. Other important changes to occur during this period have been identified as follows (Ferguson, 1989, pp. 357–359):

(a) Adler "shifted from striving for individualistic supremacy to the fundamental motivation of human beings to belong. . . ."

(b) He "shifted his meaning regarding superiority, from an emphasis on social superiority to one of task superiority."

(c) He "recognized that the feeling of social inferiority reflects a lack of one's sense of worth and adequacy, and that this differs from more transient feelings of inferiority about a given task or situation."

(d) "The need to belong and bond with others as the fundamental human motivation became linked to the goal of contribution."

Adler's system of Individual Psychology shows some interesting evolution of thought; our subsequent treatment will most reflect the last period—"social interest as cognitive function." From this brief sketch of background and development, we see that by the 1930s, "Adler had come from an early emphasis on organ inferiority, and a later emphasis on striving for power and social superiority, to an evolutionary emphasis that focused on the need to belong and on striving to contribute to human welfare" (Ferguson, 1989, p. 361). With those changes recognized, Ansbacher's (1978) words seem a fitting conclusion to this section: "Adler's untimely death at the age of 67 leaves the question wide open how this development would have continued had he lived longer" (p. 145).

PHILOSOPHY AND CONCEPTS

Some of the words often used to describe Adler's Individual Psychology include the following: holistic (as opposed to reductionistic), phenomenological (focusing on the subjective, personal view of each individual), teleological (focusing on movement toward goals rather than being impelled by one's past), field-theoretical (focusing on the individual and the field within which he/she operates), and socially oriented (viewing the person as a social being who lives in a world of others) (Ansbacher, 1977; Manaster & Corsini, 1982; Mosak, 1989). "Adlerian psychology stresses consciousness and cognition, responsibility, meanings, and values. It is optimistic in that it considers man as creator and essentially captain of his soul and believes he can overcome obstacles" (Ansbacher, 1977, p. 45). But to better understand the philosophy of Adler's psychology, let us first consider some of the concepts that have long been and continue to be so integral to it.

Concepts

Inferiority Feeling.   For Adler the inferiority feeling was universal; we all experience it. In his view, this came about first through one's experiences as an infant—being weak, vulnerable, dependent. To feel inferior then was to feel "less than." This feeling served as motivation for the individual to overcome. "The individual is continuously filled by an inferiority feeling and motivated by it" (Adler, in Ansbacher & Ansbacher, 1964, p. 117). But as Adler was quick to say, "the degree of the feeling of insecurity and inferiority depends primarily on the interpretation of the child" (*ibid.,* p. 116).

Goal Striving.   "The psychic life of man is determined by his goals" (Adler, 1927/1954, p. 29). We all move toward goals, hence teleology. We are purposive beings. "In each mind there is the conception of a goal or ideal to get beyond the present state [of inferiority] and to overcome the present deficiencies and difficulties by postulating a concrete aim for the future. . . . Without the sense of a goal individual activity would cease to have any meaning" (Adler, 1929/1969, p. 2). The goals toward which persons strive are decided on in the first few years of life, become the organizers of one's personality functioning, and push us forward from there.

Striving for Superiority.   This too refers to goal striving but adds a little more concreteness to that concept; striving for superiority has also been called "striving for perfection" or "the great upward striving." It is a ceaseless force, "common to all men" (Adler, 1931/1958, p. 68). It is a striving to overcome, to move toward completion. "It is the striving for superiority which is behind every human creation and it is the source of all contributions which are made to our culture. The whole of human life proceeds along this great line of action—from below to above, from minus to plus, from defect to victory" (*ibid.,* p. 69). Human dynamics, then, are viewed dialectically—with there being a goal (the striving for superiority or completion) and a starting point (the feeling of inferiority) (Ansbacher, 1977). Thus, striving for superiority (or goal striving) and the feeling of inferiority are complementary forces in personality—one does not exist without the other (Adler, 1930, 1929/1969).

Style of Life.   The style of life, or "life style" as it is now often called, is the major organizing concept. Life style can be thought of as the "personality," the "ego," or the "self." It consists of the individual's orienting goal, views about self, views about others, views about the world at large, and one's ethical convictions (Mosak, 1989). It is our cognitive map—a map that provides a consistent framework for making sense of, understanding, reacting to, and acting in the world around us. The life style is a self-consistent unity, which if understood can provide insight into personality functioning. "In order to understand a person's future we must understand his style of life" (Adler, in Ansbacher & Ansbacher, 1964, p. 195). Understanding the life style is critical to the conduct of Adlerian psychotherapy.

Social Interest.   Ansbacher (1968) referred to social interest as Adler's most distinctive concept; he also referred to this as Adler's most difficult concept to grasp. In its simplest form, social interest means "to see with the eyes of another, to hear with the ears of another, to feel with the heart of another" (Adler, in Ansbacher & Ansbacher, 1964, p. 135). In a more complex definition, social interest "means particularly the interest in, or feeling with, the community *sub specie aeternitatis* (*Webster's* definition: Under the aspect of eternity; in its essential or universal form or nature.) It means the striving for a community that must be thought of as everlasting, as we could think of it if mankind had reached the goal of perfection" (p. 142). Social interest involves empathy, identification with others, a movement toward others. Social interest is the criterion of mental health. Those possessing social interest are more apt to be mentally healthy, happy, contributing members of society. Those lacking in social interest are the opposite: "All failures—neurotics, psychotics, criminals, drunkards, problem children, suicides, perverts, and prostitutes—are failures because they are lacking in fellow-feeling and social interest" (Adler, 1931/1958, p. 8).

Life Tasks.   We each have three tasks of life to confront: Love, work, friendship. These are each viewed as social tasks, requiring cooperation and social interest if they are to be met successfully.

Family Atmosphere and Constellation.   Family atmosphere refers to the type of home environment that the parent or parents create for the children. Such atmospheres, for example, may be primarily rejective, authoritarian, inconsistent, overprotective, or competitive in nature (Dewey, 1971); whatever its character, the family atmosphere provides the child with his/her first consistent view of the world and this can ultimately affect life style development.

Family constellation refers to the set-up of the family and the child's place in it. This includes, for instance, the position of the child within the sibling group. Was the child a firstborn, secondborn, middleborn, lastborn, or an only child? The position of the child in the sibling group can influence personality development, and we can sometimes find certain identifiable characteristics associated with a particular birth position (e.g., with firstborns tending to be more responsible, more rule-bound, and taking charge). But Adler (1937) also emphasized that "it is not, of course, the child's number in the order of successive births which influences his character, but the *situation* into which he is born and the way in which he *interprets* it" (p. 211).

Inferiority Complex.   The inferiority feeling was seen by Adler as universal and "a stimulant to healthy, normal striving and development" (Adler, in Ansbacher & Ansbacher, 1964, p. 258). When the feeling becomes too much or too burdensome the result is an inferiority complex—where the individual becomes overwhelmed with and overtaken by inferiority—which is crippling and causes hesitation as well as intense personal distress. The inferiority feeling escalates into "a pathological condition only when the sense of inadequacy overwhelms the individual and, far from stimulating him to useful activity, makes him depressed and incapable of development" (*ibid.,* p. 258). The neuroses are fueled by an inferiority complex (Adler, 1931/1958).

Superiority Complex.   Going hand in hand with this pathological inferiority complex is the superiority complex. "We should not be astonished if in the cases where we see an inferiority complex we find a superiority complex more or less hidden" (Adler, in Ansbacher & Ansbacher, 1964, p. 259). Out of this intense feeling of inferiority comes intensely superior type behaviors, affects, and thinking. Some such examples can be found in disdain, vanity, tyrannical behavior, nagging, depreciating others, anger, loudness, inattention to others, arrogance, and snobbishness (*ibid.,* p. 261). These too are part and parcel of the neuroses.

The Neurotic Disposition.   There is a fundamental dynamic unity behind all mental disorders, neurotic and otherwise:

> (1) An individual with a mistaken opinion of himself and the world, that is, with mistaken goals and a mistaken style of life, (2) will resort to various forms of abnormal behavior aimed at safeguarding his opinion of himself, (3) when confronted with situations which he feels he cannot successfully meet, due to his mistaken views and resulting inadequate preparation. (4) The mistake consists in being self-centered rather than taking the human interrelatedness into account. (5) The individual is not consciously aware of these processes. (Ansbacher & Ansbacher, 1964, p. 239)

Neurotic symptoms, part of the neurotic disposition, have a safeguarding function—protecting the self-esteem while also serving as an excuse of sorts (e.g., "I can't do that because of my anxiety"). Neurosis, then, is an "I can't . . . , because . . ." or "Yes, but . . ." type of disorder.

Propositions

Building on these concepts, there are twelve main propositions (Ansbacher & Ansbacher, 1964, pp. 1–2); these are as follows:

1. *There is one basic dynamic force behind all human activity, a striving from a felt minus situation towards a plus situation, from a feeling of inferiority towards superiority, perfection, totality.* This then is the striving—that one basic dynamic force that moves us to act.

2. *The striving receives its specific direction from an individually unique goal or self-ideal, which though influenced by biological and environmental factors is ultimately the creation of the individual. Because it is an ideal, the goal is a fiction.* Humans are a cre-

ative lot. We are ultimately the masters of our fate. Biology and environment certainly have their effects upon us, but they are not the determining, decisive factors in making us who we are. Rather, it is our own creativity—our setting a goal, our selecting means by which to move toward that goal—that is the ultimate determiner.

3. *The goal is only "dimly envisaged" by the individual, which means that it is largely unknown to him or her and not understood by him or her. This is the unconscious: the unknown part of the goal.* Though our creativity may be brought to bear on striving for a goal, the goal is not something of which we are consciously aware. For example, we do not go around thinking that "at age three, I decided my life style goal would be the 'pursuit of control'—to be in charge." Yet "to be in charge" can become an organizing life style theme or goal, even though we do not consciously recognize it. We are "unaware" or "unconscious" of it.

4. *The goal becomes the final cause, the ultimate independent variable. To the extent that the goal provides the key for understanding the individual, it is a working hypothesis on the part of the mental health professional.* Life style goals can take many forms, e.g., to please, to be fair, to be knowledgeable, to achieve (see Kopp, 1986). But whatever form it takes, it is the goal that brings organization to the life style.

5. *All psychological processes form a self-consistent organization from the point of view of the goal, like a drama constructed from the beginning with the finale in view. This self-consistent personality structure is the "style of life." It becomes firmly established at an early age, from which time forward behavior that is apparently contradictory is only the adaptation of different means to the same end.* The life style becomes established in the first few years of life and remains a stable, organizing framework from which the person operates. There are four life style types—the ruling type, the getting type, the avoiding type, and the socially useful type. (Several life style types have been put forth by Mosak [1971]. And Kopp's [1986] exposition—in which he breaks down life style types according to type, goal, role strategy, tactics, and presence or absence of social interest—we find particularly instructive [see also, Wheeler, 1989]).

6. *All apparent psychological categories, such as different drives or the contrast between conscious and unconscious, are only aspects of a unified relational system and do not represent discrete entities and quantities.* We are unities—not, for example, an id, an ego, and a superego—and we function in a unified, self-consistent manner. This is exemplified by the designation of the system as Individual Psychology. "Adler chose the term *individual* in its Latin meaning of indivisible, for he regarded the person as an indivisible organic unit" (Ansbacher, 1977, p. 46).

7. *All objective determiners, such as biological factors and personal history, become relative to the goal idea; they do not function as direct causes but provide probabilities only. The individual uses all objective factors in accordance with his or her style of life.* All is in service of the life goal, and everything is given meaning only in the presence of that goal. The life goal is the ultimate organizer.

8. *The individual's opinion of himself or herself and the world, his or her "apperceptive schema" and interpretations, all as aspects of the style of life, influence every psychological process.* What we think—our beliefs, ideas, attitudes—are the stuff of which we are made. "[A] person's behavior springs from his opinion" (Adler, in Ansbacher & Ansbacher, 1964, p. 182). And it is thoughts—how we think—that fuel happiness, unhappiness, and disorder.

9. *The individual cannot be considered apart from his or her social situation. "Individual Psychology regards and examines the individual as socially embedded. We refuse to recognize and examine an isolated human being. . . . "* Hence, Adler's psychology is a social psychology. We each are part of a social context, and to get an understanding of any one individual, social context must be taken into account.

10. *All important life problems, including certain drive satisfactions, become social problems. All values become social values.* The life problems—love, friendship, work—are social problems.

11. *The socialization of the individual is not achieved at the cost of repression, but is afforded through an innate human ability, which, however, needs to be developed. It is social feeling or social interest. Because the individual is embedded in a social situation, social interest becomes crucial for his or her adjustment.* Social interest can be seen as the glue that bonds us to one another; it makes social and cultural survival and advancement possible. To survive, to advance, we must cooperate. Such is the nature of social interest. But social interest does not spring forth in full bloom. Rather, it is an innate ability that must be nurtured and developed so that it may come to fruition.

12. *Maladjustment is characterized by increased inferiority feelings, underdeveloped social interest, and an exaggerated uncooperative goal of personal superiority. Accordingly, problems are solved in a self-centered "private sense" rather than a task-centered "common sense" fashion. In neurotic persons this leads to the experience of failure because they still accept the social validity of their actions as their ultimate criterion. Psychotic persons, on the other hand, while objectively also failures, that is, in the eyes of common sense, do not experience failure because they do not accept the ultimate criterion of social validity.* In psychopathology, then, a dynamic unity—exaggerated inferiority, low social interest, and self-centered striving for a goal—can be found. That unity or dynamic configuration applies to the neuroses, psychoses, and other behavioral/emotional disorders as well.

ADLERIAN THERAPY

Goals

The goals of therapy include the following: reducing exaggerated feelings of inferiority, heightening social interest, and correcting the basic mistakes (i.e., errors in thinking) or faulty logic that have been incorporated into the life style. Behavior change and symptom removal are fine but not enough. "We do not attempt primarily to change behavior patterns or remove symptoms. If a patient improves his behavior because he finds it profitable at the time, without changing his basic premises, then we do not consider that as a therapeutic success. We are trying to change goals, concepts, and notions" (Dreikurs, 1963, p. 1046). Again, it is these goals, concepts, and notions that give life to behaviors and symptoms.

Therapeutic Process

The therapeutic process is all about understanding the patient's life style, identifying the basic mistakes in that life style, and correcting them. Therapy can be seen as having four phases (Dreikurs, 1967):

1. relationship formation;
2. life style assessment and analysis;
3. insight; and
4. reorientation

Relationship Formation.   Relationship formation consists of getting to know the patient, "breaking the ice," and engaging him/her in treatment. Mutual respect and trust are critical ingredients of the therapeutic relationship (Dreikurs, 1967). Furthermore, "for successful treatment it is absolutely necessary that the physician have a great deal of tact, renounce superior authority, be equally friendly at all times, be alertly interested, and have the cool-head feeling" (Adler, in Ansbacher & Ansbacher, 1964, p. 338). Other words such as empathic, encouraging, attentive, understanding, and socially interested describe the therapist during this beginning phase of treatment (cf. Dinkmeyer, Dinkmeyer, & Sperry, 1987).

Life Style Assessment and Analysis.   The life style is crystallized in the first five years of life—when one's reasoning and powers of logic are not at their height. "Because judgment and logical processes are not highly developed in young children, many of their growing convictions contain errors or only partial 'truths'" (Mosak, 1989, p. 78). These errors and partial truths can become part of who and what we are, can become defining components of the life style, and become manifest as basic mistakes. Five such basic mistakes have been identified (*ibid.*, p. 87).

1. *Overgeneralization.* "People are hostile." "Life is dangerous."
2. *False or impossible goals of "security."* "One false step and you're dead." "I have to please everybody."
3. *Misperceptions of life and life's demands.* Typical convictions might be "Life never gives me any breaks" and "Life is so hard."
4. *Minimization or denial or one's worth.* "I'm stupid." "I'm undeserving." "I'm just a housewife."
5. *Faulty values.* "Be first even if you have to climb over others."

All of these reflect rigid, absolutistic, inflexible ideas, which affect one emotionally, behaviorally, and conatively as well.

A life style assessment includes five foci:

According to my experience, so far the most trustworthy approaches to the exploration of personality are given in a comprehensive understanding of (1) the earliest childhood recollections, (2) the position of the child in the birth order, (3) childhood disorders, (4) day and night dreams, and (5) the nature of the exogenous factor that causes the illness. (Adler, in Ansbacher & Ansbacher, 1964, pp. 327–328)

1. Earliest childhood recollections are just that—our earliest memories from childhood:

Among all psychological expressions, some of the most revealing are the individual's memories. His memories are the reminders he carries about with him of his own limits and of the meaning of circumstances. There are no "chance memories:" out of the incalculable number of impressions which meet an individual, he chooses to remember only those which he feels, however darkly, to have a bearing on his situation. Thus his memories represent his "Story of My Life;" a story he repeats to himself to warn him or comfort him, to keep him concentrated on his goal, and to prepare him by means of past experiences, so that he will meet the future with an already tested style of action. (Adler, in Ansbacher & Ansbacher, 1964, p. 351)

These early recollections, or ERs as they are often referred to, are seen as reflections of the present (Verger & Camp, 1970)—revealing current information about the life style. In a life style assessment, the best, simplest way to collect ERs is to just to ask for them: "What are your earliest childhood recollections?" (Adler, in Ansbacher & Ansbacher, 1964, p. 409). ER criteria have been stated by Mosak (1958). Early memories are defined as (a) occurring before the age of eight, (b) being a single, specific incident, and (c) being visualizable. Patients then can be first told what an early memory actually is and then asked to share several. By collecting ER data, the therapist looks for consistency and pattern in the memories. Do the ERs, for example, reflect isolation? hurt? persecution? cooperativeness? going with or against others? By arriving at consistencies or patterns, the therapist begins to arrive at life style understanding in the process.

2. With the position of the child in the birth order, the therapist is interested in knowing how the child fit and found a place in the family. "How many brothers and sisters have you? What is your position in the birth order? What is your siblings' attitude toward you? How do they get along in life? Do they also have any illness?" (Adler, in Ansbacher & Ansbacher, 1964, p. 409). Such information may yield insight into how one strived for significance and belonging within the family. Also critical to this understanding is finding out about the parents as well. "Describe your parents as to their character, and their health. If not alive, what illness caused their death? What was their relation to yourself? . . . Who was your father's or your mother's favorite? What kind of upbringing did you have?" (Adler, in Ansbacher & Ansbacher, 1964, p. 409). These questions tap into family constellation and family atmosphere issues.

3. Childhood disorders can also shed light on the life style. With the life style taking form in the first five or six years of life, knowing about childhood disorders can be quite important. Such disorders include habit disorders, fears, stuttering, overt aggression, daydreaming and isolation, laziness, and lying and stealing, among other possibilities (see Adler, in Ansbacher & Ansbacher, 1964, pp. 386–392).

4. Dreams, like ERs, are also projective material that can be useful in gaining insight into the life style. In finding out about patient dreams, the therapist is quite direct: "What dreams do you have?" (Adler, in Ansbacher & Ansbacher, 1964, p. 409). With dreams, as with ERs, the therapist looks for the "private logic" or personal views of the patient (see Gold, 1978). What do the dreams say? How do they reflect life style functioning? But dreams are but one source of information and must be understood as such:

> [W]e cannot explain a dream without knowing its relationship to the other parts of the personality. Neither can we lay down any fixed and rigid rules of dream interpretation. . . . The only valid dream interpretation is that which can be integrated within individual's general behavior, early memories, problem, etc. (Adler, in Ansbacher & Ansbacher, 1964, pp. 362–363)

5. The nature of the exogenous factor that causes the illness consists of a stressful event or task that demands social interest and cooperation from the individual. It is "the ex-

ogenous situation which sets the match to the fire [leads to disorder]" (Adler, in Ansbacher & Ansbacher, 1964, p. 296). That exogenous factor, whatever it might be, ultimately comes back to one of the three life problems—love, friendship, work.

The therapist may use an interview guide to investigate these five variables— ERs, family constellation, childhood disorders, dreams, and exogenous factors (see Ansbacher & Ansbacher, 1964, pp. 404–409). A life style interview, then, is a structured, question-directed means by which to gather critical personal, theory-relevant data—all of which are then used to gain life style understanding and comprehension of basic mistakes. But this format is not followed rigidly, without flexibility. [Indeed, some Adlerians use no life style guide at all, preferring to "simply interview their clients with the idea that over time meaningful (life style) knowledge of the patient or client will come" (Manaster & Corsini, 1982, p. 178). Other life style interviews, building on Adler's original work, have been presented by Dinkmeyer et al. (1987), Dreikurs (1954), Ekstein, Baruth, & Mahrer (1978), Powers & Griffith (1987), and Shulman & Mosak (1988).]

Insight.   Once the therapist has gained insight into the patient's life style, the next step is to help the patient to gain that insight as well. During this phase of therapy, the therapist attempts to help the patient understand his/her orienting goal; views of self, others, and the world at large; and basic mistakes. Helping the patient gain such insight, of course, takes time, effort, and patience. "The uncovering of the neurotic life-plan proceeds apace in friendly and free conversation, in which it is always indicated that the patient take the initiative" (Adler, in Ansbacher & Ansbacher, 1964, p. 334).

This uncovering and understanding of the life-plan unfolds over the course of therapy. This uncovering/understanding process can be approached in a rather unstructured manner, with the therapist inserting basic mistake data into therapy when the time seems right. In other cases, the therapist may choose to present the patient directly with life style summary information, with this serving as the basis for therapeutic discussion and dialogue (e.g., Powers & Griffith, 1987).

Reorientation.   Once the therapeutic relationship has been solidly established, once the life assessment and analysis have been completed, and once the patient has gained insight into his/her life style, it is then time for reorientation—time for a reorienting of the life style convictions. Reorientation is all about change; it involves modifying basic mistakes and changing dysfunctional thinking to functional thinking. So if a patient is found to be engaging in the basic mistake of overgeneralization, the therapist's job is to help him/her stop or reduce overgeneralizing and think more realistically. With reorientation, then, the goal is "to replace the great mistakes by small ones. . . . [For it is the] big mistakes [that] can produce neuroses, but little mistakes a nearly normal person" (Adler, in Ansbacher & Ansbacher, 1964, p. 62). In making big into little, it is important that the following be recognized as preeminent: "as an Adlerian, the battlefield is cognition" (Manaster & Corsini, 1982, p. 156).

A Final Word on the Therapy Process.   The way in which these four phases of the therapeutic process are approached varies, with some Adlerians being highly unstructured in following this framework and others following it very closely. Adler himself probably varied between these two possibilities or some combination of them in his work. As a final comment on this process aspect, though, we find the therapy outline developed by Rudolf Dreikurs, Adler's foremost pupil, to be instructive. His approach to therapy consisted of five parts:

1. A first interview of about one hour.
2. A social and family history from a questionnaire of about one hour.
3. A projective test, *Early Recollections,* which usually takes about one hour.
4. The development from the above of a Life Style, . . . , which also takes about one hour.
5. The therapy proper. . . . This can take several months, and even years, but ordinarily Adlerian therapy lasts about 20 to 30 hours." (Manaster & Corsini, 1982, p. 260)

Techniques of Therapy

The following quote about Adlerian therapists probably would have fit for Adler himself.

> We Adlerians are not limited in any way in our operations: everything depends on the therapist's judgment; while our theory is solid, our methods vary. In short there is no "Adlerian way" of doing psychotherapy and counseling which excludes techniques, as long as the technique "fits" the theory and the client or patient. (Manaster & Corsini, 1982, p. 148)

The following techniques are drawn either from Adler's original writings or from the works of other Adlerians.

Modeling. The therapist should first and foremost be a good model to the patient—modeling cooperation, concern, sensitivity, fellow feeling, and social interest. "The task of the physician or psychologist is to give the patient the experience with a fellow man, and then to enable him to transfer this awakened social interest to others" (Adler, in Ansbacher & Ansbacher, 1964, p. 341). Empathy, respect, and caring are all important characteristics to model.

Paradoxical Strategies. According to Mozdzierz, Macchitelli, and Lisiecki (1976), Adler was the first person in Western civilization to use and write about paradoxical strategies. Patients might be told "never do anything you don't like," "refrain from doing anything you dislike," or "don't stop worrying; but at the same time you can think now and then of others" (Adler, in Ansbacher & Ansbacher, 1964, pp. 346–347). Or a prediction might be made that the patient was going to backslide or regress in some way. Such a prediction would be designed to evoke reaction in the patient and prevent the prediction from coming true. In still other cases, patients might be instructed to increase the very symptoms they wish to be rid of (e.g., recommending that the compulsive hand washer wash his/her hands even more). By not fighting and instead exaggerating the symptom, the patient is in theory confronted with its foolishness and has the opportunity to gain a better perspective on it all.

Encouragement.   Since emotional disturbance ultimately reflects discouragement, then encouragement would be a crucial component of the treatment process. "Altogether, in every step of the treatment, we must not deviate from the path of encouragement" (Adler, in Ansbacher & Ansbacher, 1964, p. 342). But just what is encouragement anyway? According to Ansbacher and Ansbacher (1964), Adler's definition of this would be "activating social interest." But, from a more practical standpoint, the following is of help:

> Encouragement can take many forms, depending on the phase of the counseling process. At the beginning, you let your clients know you value them by really listening to their feelings and intentions, and stimulate their confidence by accepting them as full and equal participants in the process. In the assessment phase . . . , you recognize and encourage the counselees' growing awareness of their power to choose and their attempts to change. In the reorientation phase, you promote change by stimulating the individual's courage. Thus, encouragement is a vital element of every aspect of the counseling process. (Dinkmeyer et al., 1987, p. 124)

Interpretation.   As with Freudian and Jungian analysis, interpretation plays a role in Adlerian psychotherapy as well. The focus of interpretation, however, is different in Adler's system. Interpretation is directed toward the teleology or goal-directed aspect of the patient—toward that for which the individual is striving. Interpretations are phrased tentatively, for example, beginning with such phrases as "Could it be . . ." or "I wonder if. . . ." For instance, some examples of Adlerian interpretations would be as follows: "Could it be you are acting that way because you want to show her you are in charge?" or "I wonder if you are doing that because you want to get back at her?" In the former instance, the goal could be one of power; in the latter, the goal could be one of revenge. By means of interpretation, patient awareness can be enhanced.

Catching Oneself.   Patients can be instructed to catch themselves in the act, that is, while engaging in the behavior or symptom they dislike. This requires some awareness of the symptom and when it is happening (e.g., catching oneself being nonassertive). By continuing to catch oneself, the hope is that this "catching" can occur a little earlier each time. Eventually, the patient may be able to stop the symptom before it even starts and behave in a more constructive fashion at the outset.

Acting As If.   Patients often say "I can't do it" (e.g., "make friends," "speak in a crowd," "be relaxed"). Therapists urge their patients to act as if they can; they are asked to take on a role, albeit a very limited one. If a patient is afraid of approaching people and striking up a conversation he/she is asked to pretend he/she can do just that and, for example, in the next two days, to approach an individual sitting alone and talk to that person for one minute. By "acting" as if they can, patients can try on the role of doing that which they fear.

Avoiding the "Tar Baby."   Each patient has dysfunctional ideas, beliefs, or expectations that he/she brings to therapy; though these cause problems, they are what the patient knows, and they provide a measure of comfort; therefore, the patient can strive to maintain these dysfunctional expectations and fit the therapist into them. The therapist's task then becomes that of sidestepping those dysfunctional expectations or "avoiding the tar baby."

While this "avoiding" is typically listed as a technique, it really seems to be more of a goal that the therapist keeps in mind and attempts to realize as needed.

Spitting in the Soup.   Adler is said to have referred to this technique as "besmirching a clean conscience." It involves "an attempt to reduce a problem by undermining its utility in the eyes of the client" (Allen, 1971, p. 41), by changing its meaning. To do this, the therapist first "must determine the purpose and payoff of the behavior and [then] spoil the game by reducing the behavior's pleasure or usefulness" (Dinkmeyer et al., 1987, p. 125). Dinkmeyer et al. (1987) provide an example of this—in which the therapist tells the client, Alan, that (a) he can continue to try and be first (his goal) if he chooses (his choice), and (b) he can continue to restrict himself and miss possible enjoyments in the process (negative consequences of his choice and goal). Thus, Alan's soup is made less tasty as a result. There is no set way to go about this technique; it instead appears that the therapist must have the idea of "spitting" in mind and do it when "the soup" presents itself.

Other Techniques.   Many other techniques for use in therapy have been described—giving advice, humor, homework, and task setting (Adler, in Ansbacher & Ansbacher, 1964; Dinkmeyer et al., 1987; Manaster & Corsini, 1982). Some therapists even use confrontation and arguing if they seem needed (Manaster & Corsini, 1982).

A Final Word on Therapy Style and Technique Implementation.   As mentioned earlier, Adlerians vary widely in their actual conduct of therapy. But from reading Adler's work, it comes across very clearly that he was highly active, educative, and instructive in his therapy style. Such a style still permeates the Adlerian approach today, with psychotherapy seen as a "cooperative educational enterprise" (Mosak, 1989, p. 83), with the therapist largely seen as an educator, and with the patient largely seen as a student of sorts (Nikelly & O'Connell, 1971).

LENGTH AND LIMITATIONS

Length.   "The usual question about the duration of treatment is not easy to answer. This queston is quite justified. . . . An Individual Psychology treatment, if properly carried out, should show at least a perceptible partial success in three months, often even sooner" (Adler, in Ansbacher & Ansbacher, 1964, p. 344). Further, to repeat Manaster and Corsini (1982) on this issue: Treatment "can take several months, and even years, but ordinarily Adlerian therapy lasts about 20 to 30 hours" (p. 260).

Limitations.   Adler wrote about treating a wide range of disorders, ranging from neuroses to psychoses to sociopathy. Contemporary Adlerians have followed suit (e.g., Peven & Shulman, 1983; Slavik, Sperry, & Carlson, 1992). But if Adlerian therapy has been discussed in light of these varying conditions, for who then is it not appropriate? For whom is it ill-suited? Since Adlerian treatment is more about motivation modification (i.e., changing dysfunctional premises and beliefs) than behavior modification, it stands to reason that patients must have the requisite ability and willingness to examine and reflect on their life style convictions, to see and grasp the dysfunctional nature of those convictions, and to then implement and complete a program designed to change them. Where such ability or willingness is lacking, then it would seem that Adlerian therapy would be lacking there as well.

EXAMPLE

Adler's works primarily contain conceptual case material; to our knowledge, there are no verbatim therapy transcripts by him from which to draw. Therefore, to give you some idea of how an Adlerian-oriented therapy might proceed, we have chosen to use the therapy case reconstruction provided by Manaster and Corsini, (1982, pp. 261, 278–283). The first session provides a brief description of the patient. Session four presents the therapist's interpretation of the patient's life style—with the life style data having already been collected in the two previous sessions. Session ten shows a bit of the treatment process as it advances beyond the assessment/insight stages.

Session 1

Ronald was a 40-year-old self-referred male. Short and stocky, with a wild mane of undisciplined hair, he was an extremely intense person, a man in a hurry, with no time for nonsense. He came into the first session, sat on the edge of the chair, spoke rapidly, replied quickly and pertinently, and gave the impression of great eagerness to get things done. He explained that he had already had some psychotherapy with a Rogerian therapist and from that he had gained a good deal, but he felt that he needed some more directive psychotherapy since he had a great many problems, did not feel he was effective in his life, had few friends, was not getting along with his wife, and needed some direction. He was in the field of the social sciences, had read a considerable amount in the field of personality theory and psychotherapy, and believed that Adlerian psychology was the best system for him. "Less bullshit in it" is the way he put it.

Session 4

THERAPIST: Good morning. How do you feel?
PATIENT: Pretty good. I have been thinking about the early memories and your interpretations. They seem simplistic.
TH: Possibly. Adlerian psychotherapy operates on a commonsense basis. A lot of people want complications. People are paradoxical, simple and complex at the same time. But let us try to avoid any judgments about Adlerian theory now. Did you have any other thoughts?
PA: I cried again about my father. He has been dead now for over 35 years. I hardly knew him. I have had some more memories. Some violent and some not, but always emotional. Then I thought of how my mother always beat me in reality and yet I didn't recall any violent or punitive scenes with her. I am all mixed up. My whole life was one of violence. As a kid I was always being beaten up by my teachers, the kids in the street, and my mother.
TH: Well, let me complete my life style analysis of you, and then we can begin to try to straighten things out. I have gone over your materials, and this is my summary. But please keep in mind that everything is tentative. Ready?

* * * * *

Ronald is the older of two living children out of a total of six boys. He was expected to replace his parents' first two dead twins, Robert and Albert, since his name combined both their names. After him, two additional boys died, so that his parents had five children and only one—Ronald—lived. [A sixth child, Albert was later born and did live, being five years younger than Ronald.] Mother treated him like a prince. He could do no wrong. He became a monster and no one else could control him. Two relatives gave up on him. He wanted his own way at any cost and he became a terror. His father, who had a short fuse and a violent temper, reacted strongly against this child who possibly had competed successfully for the mother's attention. Mother in effect said that she was glad that father had died. Ronald became a tyrant against his brother [Albert] and kept him down. Later on, his mother possibly had enough of him, and possibly felt that he was somehow implicated in the father's death and became excessively punitive. However, Ronald fought everyone and was punished by mother, by the school authorities and by the children in the street. The world was against him. He had no friends.

He developed a strong and inconsistent attitude toward women: He respected and feared them. His attitude toward men was fearful but also disrespectful, every man was his enemy.

Overconcerned with power, he unnecessarily struggled, making enemies on all sides, and has sabotaged his good potentials.

Private Logic (from the Early Recollections)

I don't know where I belong, and I am not sure anyone wants me. I do what I want, but people are against me, catch me and punish me. I never get away with anything. I feel everyone is holding me back and I have to get things on my own. I respect women and see them as superior and I am afraid of men who are brutal. There is little use in struggling since everything ends in failure.

Basic Mistakes

1. He is essentially a pessimist, and does not believe in his success.
2. He is excessively fearful of men and shows them hostility unnecessarily.
3. He is excessively dependent on women and fearful of them.
4. He operates to generate hostility in others.
5. He has little insight into his behavior, sees others, but not himself.

Assets

1. He is very bright and creative.
2. He seems to be open to understanding.
3. He has a strong feeling for people.

TH: Well, Ronald, this is more or less the way I see you. This is your life style. Please remember it is a tentative diagnosis. What did you get out of it?

PA: It seems like the mountain labored and brought forth a mouse. Nothing seems new or wonderful. Also, I can't agree with much of it. And I can't see where you got all your conclusions.

TH: Which ones?

PA: Well, the first basic mistake, about my pessimism. I see myself as an optimist. I take chances. I do things, I don't hold back. I am always a gambler.

TH: Yes, I agree with that, but your credo is, "Don't worry; everything is absolutely certain to go wrong." As a matter of fact the one thing I am absolutely certain about you is that you are a pessimist, you are certain everyone is against you, that you cannot have friends, that people will take advantage of you, that professors will not like you. You are absolutely convinced of the hostility of the world against you.

PA: But it's true!

TH: Of course it's true. But can I make a very simple point? It is true because you have made it true, and you make it true. For example, take your relationship with me. How did you treat me?

PA: I gave you my honest opinions. I spoke frankly.

TH: Yes, but what did you say?

PA: Like I wasn't sure of you. I still am not!

TH: You insulted me. You told me I wasn't very bright. You expressed openly—honestly—your contempt. As your therapist, this didn't bother me, but as a human being, it hurt. You said in effect you were superior to me. As a therapist, I knew that it was a facade; you possibly feel inferior. You don't believe that I or anyone can really like you—or that we won't punish you—but you don't realize your pessimism about being accepted that makes you strike out at others. When they retaliate you start everything.

PA: Let me get what you are saying. You claim that I hit out first?

TH: You start hostilities with your so-called honesty and your teasing. Then, people react to your hostility with their hostility. But you don't realize what you do. You only see what others do to you. But your hostility comes out of your pessimism. You think they are going to get you so you want them to know first that they'd better be careful of you.

PA: Christ! You seem to be saying that I set people up. I expect them to attack me, so I get the first blow in. That's quite a bundle you are handing me. I am to blame about everything. I can't buy it. How do you explain my bad grades in school when I am so smart? Why was I only average in high school and yet when I took entrance tests in college I was in the top one tenth of 1 percent? Why did I get a master's degree with not a single grade of A—and yet when I took a civil service test on the subject I got the highest grade? How come everyone is against me?

TH: Any hypotheses?

PA: None.

TH: Could it be that you do something to antagonize people?

PA: Not on purpose.

TH: I repeat my question.

PA: I must. But I don't see how. After all, I took 15 courses for my master's. I studied hard. I knew my subject. The civil service tests proved it. How could I be at the very bottom of my class in terms of grades and at the very top in terms of tests? And this has happened many times in my life. Like I really know my stuff but no one believes it . . . or maybe something else.

TH: Like what?

PA: Maybe they know I know it and dislike me for knowing it.

TH: Like teachers are jealous of you because you are so smart.

PA: It could be.

TH: Fifteen of them, all insecure about you, all of them giving you poor grades, because of your superiority?

PA: It could be. Maybe I threaten them somehow. Maybe I am a genius, they know it, they resent it, they then give me poor grades. One teacher had to miss a class session. He asked me to teach that session. I took over for him. But do you know what grade he gave me?—B! Does that make sense? Or, in this course I took recently. The professor gave a midterm examination. I got the highest mark. I was sure of an A. But again, I got a B at the end.

TH: I think you have established solidly one point: you really are smart. You really know your stuff. And yet your professors almost uniformly give you poor grades. Good knowledge—poor grades. What you don't see is how it is that this discrepancy comes about. Your hypothesis is that it is jealousy. These professors see you as bright and knowledgeable so they then punish you by giving you poor grades. What other hypothesis can you establish?

PA: According to you I do something to antagonize them! I can't see that.

TH: But don't we both agree that you do something—whether it be making them feel inferior to you because of your brilliance or whether it is something else—to explain the discrepancy between your good knowledge and your poor grades?

PA: Yes, but I don't know what it could be.

TH: Neither do I, but in view of your life style, it seems to me very probably that you antagonize them, whether it be because of your brilliance or because of your attacks on them.

PA: Attacks? How do I attack them?

TH: I don't know. But they misjudge you, they give you poor grades, and even if objective tests show you know your stuff they still give you poor grades.

(We have gone into one session in quite some depth to give a feeling of what the verbal interaction between the therapist and the client might be. Essentially, the therapist now has gained some insight into his client. He "sees" the client as pessimistic, fearful, not sure of his place in society, wanting to be accepted, but hostile, contact shy, and so on. He attempts to get the client to begin to see himself objectively. The client, however, responds with excuses, explanations, defenses, and avoids "owning" the problem. This is resistance, found in all therapies. Below is reported part of a later session which "broke the case" as it were.)

Session 10

PA: Look, you keep telling me how I antagonize people, I upset people. I deny that. I really try to get along. I try to help people. I go out of my way. I want to give you a good example. Sunday night, my wife and I were invited to a party, given by two friends of ours, Stan and Evelyn. They had invited two other couples. Stan had to talk to someone on the telephone. Evelyn was in the kitchen, coming back and forth. My wife and I were talking to one another. The other two couples were talking to each other. It was an awkward situation. So, I tried to make the evening successful. I got everyone's attention by saying "Do you know the game called *Napoleon in the Icebox?*" The other two couples said they didn't. "It's a lot of fun," I told them, and I started to explain it. Well, they were interested, and just as I was about to finish the explanation how to play the game, Evelyn comes in and announces, "Coffee is ready." Then, she yells at Stan to get off the phone. He comes in, and starts to tell everyone about the phone call. Then, Evelyn goes after the coffee. So, I start to finish telling about the game, when the husband of one of the couples got up to go to the bathroom. So, I gave up. That's how *that* went. Screw them!

TH: Is this an example of how unfair people are to you? You try to help out, make a party lively, and it all turns out poorly.

PA: That's right. That's exactly how it went, and how it goes for me.

TH: That is not my interpretation of what went on.

PA: What possible alternative explanation would you have?

TH: First, you are a guest in these people's house. Second, you decide that things are not going the way you think they should. People are talking to their mates, but that is not the way you think it should be. So, you take the initiative. You decide you want to play and explain the game. When the hosts do whatever they want to do, like feed their guests, you feel they are unfair to you. As I see it, you were rude, bossy, and tried to run the show, and when you didn't succeed, you sulked.

(The client was speechless. For more than five minutes, therapist and client looked at each other, with not a word said. The therapist waited, excited, since the client, who was usually very voluble, now was thinking, reflecting.)

PA: If you are right, then everything is explained. My poor grades, why I don't have friends, why I have gotten fired.

TH: What do you think?

PA: I meant well, like to help the party get going.

TH: I am sure of that.

PA: I think those people I tried to help didn't like me. The couple that started talking avoided me. I suppose I showed my displeasure.

TH: Probably.

PA: My friends probably thought I was intruding on their prerogative. After all, it was their home.

TH: Well, what do you think?

PA: Maybe that is the way it is. Maybe I want to be the boss. Just like when I was a kid. I didn't sit on the seat between my parents, but decided to slide off and explore. Like I want my own way.

TH: Does this have anything to do with school?

PA: Well, I would never study the assigned textbook. I'd study a different textbook.

TH: What do you mean?

PA: Like in biology. We have one text, but I would study another.

TH: Did you think the other texts were better?

PA: I didn't want to study the same text everyone else did.

TH: Why?

PA: I don't know. But maybe it has to do with not wanting to be controlled, to do my own thing, like I wanted to learn but didn't want to submit to their discipline. Like I didn't trust them. I wanted to compete with them, or something. I guess I didn't trust them. Wanted to do things my own way.

TH: Can you put it together? All of it?

PA: It is starting to come together. I am afraid of people, especially men. They can harm me. I must not let them direct me. So, in an attempt to be free of them, I do stupid things, like when I slid off the seat on the train, and I get them mad the way I got my father mad when I didn't wind up the string the right way. It's all crazy.

SUMMARY AND EVALUATION

Summary. Adler's system emphasizes teleology, holism, cognition, consciousness, unity, social psychology, field theory, and values. It does not deny biology and environment but places ultimate responsibility on the individual for being the creator of his/her own destiny. It is a psychology of use, not possession—asserting that it is not so much what we have but what we do with what we have that matters the most in the end. For Adler, the inferiority feeling and the striving for superiority (or significance or completion) was the dialectic that fueled human behavior. And it was the degree of social interest that took that dialectic in a positive or negative direction.

Adlerian psychotherapy has been described as educative, cooperative, and teacher-student in nature. It has been viewed as having four phases: relationship, life style assessment and analysis, insight, and reorientation. Its goals have been described thus: reducing inferiority, heightening or awakening social interest, and modifying dysfunctional life style beliefs or convictions, among others. The techniques of Adlerian therapy are varied, and the approach seems more eclectic than otherwise in implementation.

Evaluation. Adler's focus on teleology, the social side, growth, and values we find we like. There is an optimism in Adler's system that seems to pervade the theory, therapy, and its implementation as well. Adler's is a psychology of possibility—as stated above, of use not possession. Adler's views provide an interesting alternative to the more deterministic model of Freud and have a nice nonreductionistic feel to them.

Adler's theory is also easy to grasp and understand. It is not burdened by complex, undecipherable concepts and jargon. His is a simple, straightforward, user-friendly theory. It has been termed a "common-sense view." In our opinion, that is one of its greatest strengths.

(Because of the user-friendly nature of Adler's theory, it has enjoyed and continues to enjoy popularity in educational circles, e.g., through the STEP, STEP/Teen, and STET programs [Dinkmeyer & McKay, 1976, 1983; Dinkmeyer, McKay, & Dinkmeyer, 1980]. It too has been found useful for marriage enrichment training [Dinkmeyer & Carlson, 1984] and has had an impact with regard to couples and family therapy as well [Dinkmeyer & Dinkmeyer, 1982, 1983]. Our focus in this chapter is on individual psychotherapy, but the impact of Adlerian concepts and principles for these other areas seemed at least to merit mention here.)

Adler's emphasis on therapy as cooperative, as involving respect for the patient, and as a process between equals is to our liking as well. Those variables seem critical for any fruitful treatment endeavor, and for Adler to accord them such importance is just as it should be.

Along with these positive criticisms, however, there are some negative criticisms or at least some critical-type questions to raise. First, is there really too much time spent on life style assessment and analysis in Adlerian therapy? Again, Adlerians do vary in the ways they do life style analysis, but some easily devote several hours at the outset of therapy to this task. Is all that really needed? We imagine that those particular Adlerians in question would answer "yes," but still it is a good question to consider. Ellis (1992), for example, expresses a debt to Adler but expresses reservations about his possible overemphasis on life style (and, by extension, life styling). It could well be that basic mistake and other important life style information emerge early on in the therapy process with many patients anyway, without extensive life style assessment and analysis even having to be conducted at all.

While we value Adler's espousal of a cooperative, egalitarian therapy relationship, much of his work as well as the work of some Adlerians who have succeeded him has a highly directive, didactic, intrusive quality to it. The work of therapy comes off with more of a "pushy," "confrontive," "therapist-dominating" sound to it than otherwise. Such therapy endeavors may espouse cooperation and equality on one level, yet, conversely, do just the opposite on another level—conveying that the therapist is the real authority, is the "one who really knows," and is the "one who will make everything right." Those at least are possibilities that merit consideration when thinking about the practice of Adlerian therapy.

As stated earlier, Adler's theory is distinctive and brings a useful view to the understanding of persons. In practice, however, Adlerian therapy seems more an eclectic brand of treatment than otherwise. If a technique fits the theory, if it works, then use it. This on the one hand can be seen as a strength—reflecting flexibility and openness on the part of the therapist. But on the other hand, it would seem that almost all if not all techniques could be seen as "fitting" Adler's theory. Conceptually, could it not be said that virtually any technique—be it called "encouragement," "systematic desensitization," "therapist silence," "rational-emotive imagery," even "scream therapy"—ultimately may facilitate a diminution of one's inferiority and enhance one's striving for completion in some form or fashion? If yes, then any technique is potentially an "Adlerian technique." What would make a technique "not Adlerian" is unclear. And if any and everything is potentially Adlerian, could it then be said that Adlerian therapy is basically a mishmash, hodgepodge form of eclecticism more than anything else? Those, too, are questions worth some consideration.

And to belabor this issue just a bit more, it seems worth adding that some of the more distinctive Adlerian practice ideas—such as "avoiding the tar baby"—come across more like basic operational therapy principles than techniques, per se. Do not all therapists want to "avoid the tar baby" anyway? With others, such as "spitting in the soup," how much of this do you need to do to affect basic mistakes, to affect a dysfunctional life style pattern, to bring about change, be it short-term or long-term? These are further important questions that could be asked and that need to be kept in mind when considering Adlerian techniques.

Having raised some issues or questions about Adlerian therapy, let us now move on to research. Does the research support Adlerian therapy? Over 30 years ago, Rotter (1962) called for a research orientation to be brought to bear on Adlerian psychology. In some respects, that has happened—with numerous studies of basic Adlerian concepts such as birth order, early recollections, and social interest being conducted (see Watkins, 1992a, 1992b, 1992c, 1994). But what about Adlerian therapy? There is not much research to speak of. As a group, Adlerians have done little research on Adlerian therapy. A growing body of research—by Adlerians and non-Adlerians alike—has been carried out on paradoxical strategies, and some support for some such strategies has been reported (e.g., Hill, 1987). Furthermore, if Adlerian therapy is viewed as a "cognitive treatment," then research supporting cognitive therapy and rational-emotive therapy might also be seen by some as supporting Adlerian therapy, too. But whether such treatment generalizations could be made is surely open to question.

Perhaps if there is one recommendation that might be made on this subject, it is this: That a research orientation, just as it has been brought to bear on the study of some Adlerian constructs, should also be brought to bear on the study of the Adlerian therapy endeavor as well. Rotter's (1962) call has indeed been answered in some respects, but when it comes to Adlerian therapy, it appears that no one has really "picked up the phone" as yet.

Who will carry on the torch of Adler's Individual Psychology and Adlerian therapy in the years to come? There is the primary Adlerian association within the United States—the North American Society of Adlerian Psychology, which is an active group composed of therapists, counselors, and educators. At the international level, there is the International Society for Individual Psychology. The primary Adlerian journal, *Individual Psychology: The Journal of Adlerian Theory, Research, and Practice,* is published four times a year; two issues are devoted to theory/research, the other two to practice/application. These associations and publications, among others, have kept and will no doubt continue to keep the essence of Adler's thinking alive. Further interest in Adler's thinking can also be seen in recent translations of his work (Brett, 1992; see also, Ansbacher's review, 1994).

But with that said, let us also point out that within the Adlerian ranks there has been a charge to go "beyond Adler." This charge was first issued by Carlson (1989), calling on Adlerians "to modify Adlerian ideas to today's tough issues, issues that did not exist in the 1920s" (p. 411). He continued, "If Adlerian psychology is to continue . . . we must become neo-Adlerians and integrate our ideas and techniques with those already proven effective methods of other approaches" (p. 413). Carlson's words did not fall on deaf ears; they led to an article by Hartshorne (1991), in which he said "much of what we do as Adlerians is to pick the bones of Adler and Dreikurs, trying to distill what they mean, rather than burying them and thereby becoming their descendants" (p. 322). Carlson's words also led to an entire special issue of *Individual Psychology,* which was entitled "On Beyond Adler" (Huber, 1991).

Exactly what particular changes lie in store for Adlerian psychotherapy in the future is difficult to say now. But it does appear that many contemporary Adlerians are striving to update Adler's thinking, extend it, and expand its applicability in the therapy arena. This effort to go "beyond Adler" seemingly poses myriad interesting possibilities for the Adlerian psychotherapy of tomorrow.

REFERENCES

Adler, A. (1907/1917). *Study of organ inferiority and its psychical compensation.* New York: Nervous & Mental Diseases Publishing.

Adler, A. (1927/1954). *Understanding human nature.* New York: Fawcett Premier.

Adler, A. (1929/1969). *The science of living.* New York: Anchor Books.

Adler, A. (1930). *The education of children*. South Bend, IN: Gateway Editions.

Adler, A. (1931/1958). *What life should mean to you*. New York: Capricorn Books.

Adler, A. (1937). Position in family constellation influences life style. *International Journal of Individual Psychology, 3,* 211–227.

Allen, T. W. (1971). Adlerian interview strategies for behavior change. *The Counseling Psychologist, 2*(1), 40–48.

Ansbacher, H. L. (1968). The concept of social interest. *Journal of Individual Psychology, 24,* 131–141.

Ansbacher, H. L. (1977). Individual Psychology. In R. J. Corsini (Ed.). *Current personality theories* (pp. 45–82). Itasca, IL: F. E. Peacock.

Ansbacher, H. L. (1978). The development of Adler's concept of social interest: A critical study. *Journal of Individual Psychology, 34,* 118–152.

Ansbacher, H. L. (1994). Review of *What life could mean to you: A new translation by Colin Brett. Individual Psychology, 50,* 125–126.

Ansbacher, H. L., & Ansbacher, R. R. (Eds.) (1964). *The Individual Psychology of Alfred Adler: A systematic presentation in selections from his writings*. New York: Harper & Row.

Ansbacher, H. L., & Ansbacher, R. R. (Eds.) (1979). *Superiority and social interest: A collection of later writings*. New York: W. W. Norton.

Bottome, P. (1957). *Alfred Adler: A portrait from life* (3rd ed.). New York: Vanguard.

Brett, C. (Ed.) (1992). *[Adler's] What life could mean to you: A new translation by Colin Brett*. Oxford, England: Oneworld Publications.

Carlson, J. (1989). On beyond Adler. *Individual Psychology, 45,* 411–413.

Dewey, E. A. (1971). Family atmosphere. In A. G. Nikelly (Ed.). *Techniques for behavior change* (pp. 41–47). Springfield, IL: Charles C Thomas.

Dinkmeyer, D., & Carlson, J. (1984). *Training in marriage enrichment*. Circle Pines, MN: American Guidance Service.

Dinkmeyer, D., & Dinkmeyer, J. (1982). Adlerian marriage therapy. *Individual Psychology, 38,* 115–122.

Dinkmeyer, D., & Dinkmeyer, J. (1983). Adlerian family therapy. *Individual Psychology, 39,* 116–124.

Dinkmeyer, D. C., Dinkmeyer, D. C., Jr., & Sperry, L. (1987). *Adlerian counseling and psychotherapy* (2nd ed.). Columbus, OH: Merrill Publishing Co.

Dinkmeyer, D., & McKay, G. D. (1976). *Systematic training for effective parenting*. Circle Pines, MN: American Guidance Service.

Dinkmeyer, D., & McKay, G. D. (1983). *Systematic training for effective parenting of teens*. Circle Pines, MN: American Guidance Service.

Dinkmeyer, D., McKay, G. D., & Dinkmeyer, D., Jr. (1980). *Systematic training for effective teaching*. Circle Pines, MN: American Guidance Service.

Dreikurs, R. (1954). The psychological interview in medicine. *American Journal of Individual Psychology, 10,* 99–122.

Dreikurs, R. (1963). Psychodynamic diagnosis in psychiatry. *American Journal of Psychiatry, 119,* 1045–1048.

Dreikurs, R. (1967). *Psychodynamics, psychotherapy, and counseling*. Chicago: Alfred Adler Institute.

Ekstein, D., Baruth, L., & Mahrer, D. (1978). *Life style: What it is and how to do it*. Dubuque, IA: Kendall/Hunt.

Ellis, A. E. (1992). Questions and answers. In J. K. Zeig (Ed.), *The evolution of psychotherapy: The second conference* (pp. 95–99). New York: Brunner/Mazel.

Ferguson, E. D. (1989). Adler's motivational theory: An historical perspective on belonging and the fundamental human striving. *Individual Psychology, 45,* 354–361.

Gold, L. (1978). Life style and dreams. In L. G. Baruth & D. G. Ekstein (Eds.). *Life style: Theory, practice, and research* (pp. 24–30). Dubuque, IA: Kendall/Hunt.

Hartshorne, T. S. (1991). The evolution of psychotherapy: Where are the Adlerians? *Individual Psychology, 47,* 321–325.

Hill, K. A. (1987). Meta-analysis of paradoxical interventions. *Psychotherapy, 24,* 266–270.

Huber, C. H. (Ed.). (1991). Special issue: On beyond Adler. *Individual Psychology, 47,* 431–553.

Kopp, R. R. (1986). Styles of striving for significance with and without social interest: An Adlerian typology. *Individual Psychology, 42,* 17–25.

Manaster, G. J., & Corsini, R. J. (1982). *Individual Psychology: Theory and practice.* Itasca, IL: F. E. Peacock.

Manaster, G. J., Painter, G., Deutsch, D., & Overholt, B. J. (Eds.). (1977). *Alfred Adler: As we remember him.* Chicago: North American Society of Adlerian Psychology.

Manaster, J. (1977). Alfred Adler: A short biography. In G. J. Manaster, G. Painter, D. Deutsch, & B. J. Overholt (Eds.). *Alfred Adler: As we remember him* (pp. 9–15). Chicago: North American Society of Adlerian Psychology.

Mosak, H. H. (1958). Early recollections as a projective technique. *Journal of Projective Techniques, 22,* 302–311.

Mosak, H. H. (1971). Lifestyle. In A. G. Nikelly (Ed.). *Techniques for behavior change* (pp. 77–81). Springfield, IL: Charles C Thomas.

Mosak, H. H. (1989). Adlerian psychotherapy. In R. J. Corsini & D. Wedding (Eds.). *Current psychotherapies* (4th ed. pp. 65–113). Itasca, IL: F. E. Peacock.

Mozdzierz, G. J., Macchitelli, F. J., & Lisiecki, J. (1976). The paradox in psychotherapy: An Adlerian perspective. *Journal of Individual Psychology, 32,* 169–184.

Nikelly, A. G., & O'Connell, W. E. (1971). Action-oriented methods. In A. G. Nikelly (Ed.). *Techniques for behavior change* (pp. 85–90). Springfield, IL: Charles C Thomas.

Peven, D., & Shulman, B. (1983). The psychodynamics of affective bipolar disorders: Some empirical findings and their implication for cognitive therapy. *Individual Psychology, 39,* 2–16.

Powers, R. L., & Griffith, J. (1987). *Understanding life-style: The psycho-clarity process.* Chicago: The American Institute of Adlerian Studies.

Rotter, J. B. (1962). An analysis of Adlerian psychology from a research orientation. *Journal of Individual Psychology, 18,* 3–11.

Shulman, B. H., & Mosak, H. H. (1988). *Manual for life style assessment.* Muncie, IN: Accelerated Development.

Slavik, S., Sperry, L., & Carlson, J. (1992). The schizoid personality disorder: A review and an Adlerian view and treatment. *Individual Psychology, 48,* 137–154.

Verger, D. M., & Camp, W. L. (1970). Early recollections: Reflections of the present. *Journal of Counseling Psychology, 17,* 510–515.

Watkins, C. E., Jr. (1992a). Adlerian-oriented early memory research: What does it tell us? *Journal of Personality Assessment, 59,* 248–263.

Watkins, C. E., Jr. (1992b). Birth order research and Adler's theory: A critical review. *Individual Psychology, 48,* 357–368.

Watkins, C. E., Jr. (1992c). Research activity with Adler's theory. *Individual Psychology, 48,* 107–108.

Watkins, C. E., Jr. (1994). Measuring social interest. *Individual Psychology, 50,* 69–96.

Wheeler, M. S. (1989). A theoretical and empirical comparison of typologies. *Individual Psychology, 45,* 335–353.

chapter *4*

Psychoanalytic Object Relations Theory and Therapy: Fairbairn, Winnicott, and Guntrip

The nature of this chapter will be different from that of the other chapters in this book. Whereas other chapters present an exposition of one primary theorist's contributions (e.g., Freud, Jung, and Adler), this chapter will focus on a form of analytic therapy to which several theorists have contributed. This focus seems justified because the object relations school has increasingly made itself felt in recent decades and has emerged as a major force within psychoanalytic thought. As Greenberg and Mitchell (1983) have put it, "the common 'landscape' of psychoanalysis today consists of an increasing focus on people's interactions with others, that is, on the problem of object relations" (p. 2).

Deciding on which particular object relations theorists to focus on in this chapter was not an easy decision to make. Those identified as making important contributions to this school of thought are many, including Margeret Mahler, Harry Stack Sullivan, Melanie Klein, and Michael Balint, among others. From our observations, however, some of the most positive attention and interest has been directed toward the works of W. R. D. Fairbairn, who has been identified with the English or British school of object relations. Fairbairn, it has been said, presented "the most systematic and comprehensive account of object relations theory" (Eagle & Wolitzky, 1992, p. 127); furthermore, Fairbairn has been termed a "system-builder" (Greenberg & Mitchell, 1983) because he developed a theory of his own. For those reasons, our primary focus in this chapter will be given to his theory.

But two other object relations thinkers associated with the British school—D. W. Winnicott and Harry Guntrip—deserve mention as well. Winnicott gave us such terms as "good enough mothering" and "facilitating environment"; some of his work has been referred to as "the most revolutionary . . . yet produced within psychoanalysis" (Guntrip, 1973, p. 122). Guntrip, who was analyzed by both Fairbairn and Winnicott (see Guntrip,

1975), gave a nice accounting of schizoid phenomena and supplemented Fairbairn's theory; he is said to have moved object relations theory "in a very specific direction, according to his own unique vision of human experience and suffering" (Greenberg & Mitchell, 1983, p. 210). But Guntrip and Winnicott, unlike Fairbairn, were not system builders; instead, they primarily extended the theories of others. For those reasons, our coverage of them will be more brief overall. This chapter, then, will focus on the theoretical contributions of these three. For a comprehensive, critical analysis of contributions made by these three individuals as well as other object relations theorists, we refer you to the excellent volume by Greenberg and Mitchell (1983).

Object relations theory has been defined as "psychoanalytical theory in which the subject's need to relate to objects occupies the central position; in contrast to INSTINCT THEORY, which centres round the subject's need to reduce instinctual TENSION" (Rycroft, 1973, p. 101). To further draw this distinction with Freudian theory, Guntrip (1973) wrote: "Object relations theory . . . is the emancipation of Freud's psychodynamic personal thinking from . . . bondage to . . . [its] natural science, impersonal, intellectual heritage" (p. 20). With object relations theory, then, there is a significant shift in emphasis—from that of pleasure seeking to that of object seeking (Butler & Strupp, 1991). Thus, "of foremost concern to object relations theorists is the role that human relationships play in personality development" (*ibid.*, 1991, p. 520). In what follows, we hope to give you some idea of how that is specifically so for Fairbairn, Winnicott, and Guntrip.

BACKGROUND AND DEVELOPMENT

Much like Thompson (1957) who was mentioned in Chapter 1, Rapaport (1959) has also considered the evolution that has taken place in psychoanalytic theory construction. He has identified four such periods, beginning in the latter part of the nineteenth century and ending in the late 1950s. First came Freud's pre-1900 work, when he was associated with Breuer and introduced the concept of defense. Then came the 1897–1923 period, during which primary focus was on instinctual drives and unconscious fantasy. During the 1923–1937 period, Freud's structural theory and revised anxiety theory came to be. And 1937–1959 saw the beginnings and advancement of ego psychology—ushered in by Heinz Hartmann's (1939/1958) classic book, *Ego Psychology and the Problem of Adaptation.*

Building on Rapaport's four periods, Blanck and Blanck (1986) have brought them up to date. They redefined 1923 to 1937 as early ego psychology and referred to 1937 to 1975 as late ego psychology (see Blanck & Blanck, 1974). From 1975 on, Blanck and Blanck saw a further burgeoning out of psychoanalytic theory—to become psychoanalytic developmental psychology (Blanck & Blanck, 1979) and developmental object relations theory (Blanck & Blanck, 1986). Corresponding with this burgeoning since 1975, Eagle and Wolitzky (1992) have noted that "it is mainly within the past 20 years that the contributions of the British object relations theorists . . . have heavily influenced American psychoanalysis" (p. 110). With this increasing emergence of object relations theory has come the following: Shifts (a) from a drive/structure model to a relational/structure model (Greenberg & Mitchell, 1983); (b) from a "drive discharge model to a person point of view"; and (c) from "emphasis on insight into unconscious conflicts (primarily oedipal ones) to an increasing stress on relationship factors in treatment and their efficacy in ameliorating the maladaptive impact of early defects, deficits, and developmental arrests" (Eagle & Wolitzky, 1992, p. 110).

While this increasing emergence of object relations theory in American psychoanalysis has been linked to the past 20 to 25 years, it seems important to recognize that our three principals—Fairbairn, Winnicott, and Guntrip—were writing about object relations long before that. Many of Fairbairn's and Winnicott's publications came during the 1940s and 1950s, many of Guntrip's in the 1950s and 1960s. While some of their volume of work was in existence up to half a century ago, it took some time for it to be picked up by and incorporated into American psychology.

SOME BASIC CONCEPTS

Before presenting the theoretical ideas of Fairbairn, Winnicott, and Guntrip, some definitions of concepts seem in order. For these definitions, Rycroft's (1973) *A Critical Dictionary of Psychoanalysis* and Hamilton's (1988) *Self and Others: Object Relations Theory in Practice* have been primarily relied upon (cf. Dorpat, 1981).

Object. "In psychoanalytical writings, objects are nearly always persons, parts of persons, or SYMBOLS of one or the other. This terminology confuses readers who are more familiar with 'object' in the sense of a 'thing,' i.e., that which is not a person" (Rycroft, 1973, p. 100). Objects can be *internal* or *external, good,* or *bad.* "An external object is [an actual] . . . person, place, or thing invested with emotional energy [e.g., something or someone we can actually see or touch]. An internal object is an idea, fantasy, or memory pertaining to a person, place, or thing" (Hamilton, 1988, p. 7).

Object-Representation.   "The mental *representation* of an object" (Rycroft, 1973, p. 101).

Self.   "[C]onscious and unconscious mental representations that pertain to one's own person. . . . [A]n internal image" (Hamilton, 1988, p. 12).

Self-Representation.   Since the "self" is defined as "mental representations," the definition of self-representation would seem to be the same, i.e., the mental representation of the self.

Self-Object   "When the distinction between self and object . . . is unclear, it is called a self-object" (Hamilton, 1988, p. 20). This refers to a loss of boundaries, where what is self and what is object get blurred. Fusion, merger experiences would be an example of this.

Part Object.   "An object which is part of a person, e.g., a PENIS or a BREAST. The distinction between whole [defined below] and part object is . . . [respectively] that between recognizing an object as a person whose feelings and needs are as important as one's own [versus] treating an object as existing solely to satisfy one's own needs" (Rycroft, 1973, p. 101).

Whole Object.   "An object whom the subject recognizes as being a person with similar rights, feelings, needs, etc., as himself" (Rycroft, 1973, p. 102). This means essentially being able to respond to others as feeling, breathing human beings, with hopes, insecurities, strengths, and weaknesses just like oneself. Part object recognition, however, is not anywhere near that level.

Object Relations.   This refers to "the structural and dynamic relationships between the self-representations and object-representations. . . " (Horner, 1984, p. 4). Horner (1991) indicates that these "representations" are "complex cognitive schemata, an enduring organization of psychic elements. . . " (p. 7). The following passage further clarifies the importance of this:

> The internal object relations function as a kind of template that determines one's feelings, beliefs, expectations, fears, wishes, and emotions with respect to important interpersonal relationships. It is important to keep in mind that those intrapsychic imagos are not exact replicas of early experience but that they are constructed by the very small child with its limited cognitive abilities and primitive mental mechanisms. The inner world is thus an amalgam of actual experience and perception, and these mental representations evolve over the early years in accordance with the child's maturing cognitive capacities and actual experience. (Horner, 1991, p. 8)

(Interestingly enough, this mention of schemata and statement that imagos "are constructed by the very small child with its limited cognitive abilities and primitive mental mechanisms" seems consistent with Adler's thinking; see Chapter 3; also notice of this has been made by Sperry, 1992, as well.)

Object Constancy.   "The ability to maintain a lasting relationship with a specific, single object; or, inversely, the tendency to reject substitutes for a familiar object, e.g., an infant who displays object-constancy rejects mothering from anyone other than his MOTHER and misses her specifically when she is absent" (Rycroft, 1973, p. 100). Margeret Mahler, who made enormous contributions to our understanding about the development of object relations, viewed object constancy in this way: the "capacity to recognize and tolerate loving and hostile feelings toward the same object; the capacity to keep feelings centered on a specific object; and the capacity to value an object for attributes other than its function of satisfying needs" (Mahler, Pine, & Bergman, 1975, p. 328). If the process of object relations development proceeds as would be hoped, object constancy is achieved; so too is identity consolidation.

Summary.   These are some of the basic concepts integral to object relations thinking in general and more specifically to the works of Fairbairn, Winnicott, and Guntrip. We can see, then, that with the term *object* a mental representation of a person or part of a person (e.g., the mother's breast) is being referred to, that objects can be represented in part or whole, that objects can be represented in "good" or "bad" fashion (with good meaning satisfying, bad meaning unsatisfying), and that object relations refer to what might be thought of as our self and object schemas and the interactions between them.

   Object relations theorists have an especial interest in the earliest years of life, because our "self and object images are built out of myriad daily affective experiences that begin on day one or before" (Blanck & Blanck, 1986, p. 50). Furthermore, much interest is placed in the relation of the infant to his/her primary caretaker, usually seen as the mother. "[W]hatever a baby's genetic endowment, the mother's ability or failure to 'relate' is the *sine qua non* of psychic health for the infant. To find a good parent at the start is the basis of psychic health" (Guntrip, 1975, p. 156). Some examples of well matched and poorly matched mother-child pairs, each of which would contribute to the types of object relations the infant would ultimately develop, have been identified in the literature (e.g., Blanck & Blanck, 1986, pp. 51–52).

Fairbairn

Biographical Sketch.   William Ronald Dodge Fairbairn was born in Edinburgh, Scotland, in 1889. He received his education at the Merchiston Castle School, then Edinburgh University, then did postgraduate work in divinity and Hellenistic Greek. He served in World War I, later got his medical degree, worked in a psychiatric hospital for a year, and then went into private practice (in which he continued until his death in 1964). He held the following positions: lecturer in psychology at Edinburgh University, psychiatrist at the University Psychological Clinic for Children, visiting psychiatrist to Carstairs Hospital, and consultant psychiatrist to the Ministry of Pensions.

Among his many distinctions, Fairbairn was a member of the British Psycho-Analytical Society and had a special issue of the *British Journal of Medical Psychology* published in his honor. His publications appeared in such journals as the *International Journal of Psycho-analysis* (e.g., Fairbairn, 1941, 1958, 1963) and the *British Journal of Medical Psychology* (Fairbairn, 1952b, 1954, 1955). Many of his papers were collected in *Psychoanalytic Studies of the Personality* (1952a), which was published in England. The book appeared in America under the title, *An Object-Relations Theory of the Personality,* in 1954.

Fairbairn was married, had two sons and one daughter. His wife died in 1952. He remarried seven years later. He died in 1964 at the age of 76. (Source for biographical information: Sutherland, 1965.)

Differences from Freud.   Fairbairn had much to say about Freud's libido theory and his problems with it. The basic, most important difference between their theories, however, seems largely to come down to one fundamental assumption: That libido, in Fairbairn's view, was object seeking (in search of others) as opposed to pleasure seeking.

> [W]hilst at every point there is a recognizable analogy between my present views and those of Freud, the development of my views follows a path which diverges gradually from that followed by the historical development of Freud's views. This divergence of paths itself admits of only one explanation—a difference in certain theoretic principles. The central points of difference are not difficult to localize. They are two in number. In the first place, although Freud's whole system of thought was concerned with object-relationships, he adhered theoretically to the principle that libido is primarily pleasure-seeking, i.e., that it is directionless. By contrast, I adhere to the principle that libido is primarily object-seeking, i.e., that it has direction. . . . In the second place, Freud regards impulse (i.e., psychical energy) as theoretically distinct from structure,

whereas I do not accept this distinction as valid and adhere to the principle of dynamic structure. (Fairbairn, 1954, p. 126)

Fairbairn, then, took a view fundamentally different from that of Freud—saying that not only is libido object seeking but that energy and structure are not separable entities. In Fairbairn's opinion, Freud's views on impulse and structure were affected by "the scientific atmosphere of the nineteenth century . . . [which] was dominated by the Helmholtzian conception that the physical universe consisted in a conglomeration of inert, immutable and indivisible particles to which motion was imparted by a fixed quantity of energy separate from the particles themselves" (*ibid.*, pp. 126–127). But, whatever the factors affecting Freud's views, Fairbairn disagreed with them.

Another difference between Freud and Fairbairn can be found in the following: "The pristine personality of the child consists of a unitary dynamic ego" (Fairbairn, 1954, p. 107). As Guntrip (1973, pp. 92–93), an explicator of Fairbairn's ideas (also see Guntrip, 1961), put it,

the baby starts life as a whole psychic self however primitive and undeveloped and undifferentiated. . . . Fairbairn believed that we must be primarily aware of the fundamental dynamic wholeness of the human being as a person, which is the most important natural characteristic. . . . [H]e saw the human being, not as built up of layers like a brick wall, but as a psychosomatic whole

Fairbairn also took issue with Freud's views about the erogenous or erotogenic zones (i.e., oral, anal, phallic). Erogenous zones were reconceptualized as a means to have object relationships; they were seen as being in the service of object seeking, not the other way around.

The conception of fundamental erotogenic zones constitutes an unsatisfactory basis for any theory of libidinal development because it is based on a failure to recognize that the function of libidinal pleasure is essentially to provide a signpost to the object. According to the [Freudian] conception of erotogenic zones the object is regarded as a signpost to libidinal pleasure; and the cart is placed before the horse. (Fairbairn, 1954, p. 33)

The Development of Personality.   Fairbairn (1954) presented a sequence of stages or scheme whereby object relations develop. In his view, the distinctive feature of his scheme was that it was "based upon the nature of the object-relationship, and that the libidinal attitude [was] relegated to a secondary place" (p. 39). His scheme consisted of three stages, which are as follows (Fairbairn, 1954, p. 39):

    I. Stage of Infantile Dependence, characterized predominantly by an Attitude of Taking.
        I. Early Oral—Incorporating—Sucking or Biting (Pre-Ambivalent)
        II. Late Oral—Incorporating—Sucking or Biting (Ambivalent)
    II. Stage of Transition between Infantile Dependence and Mature Dependence, or Stage of Quasi-Independence—Dichotomy and Exteriorization of the Incorporated Object.
    III. Stage of Mature Dependence, characterized predominantly by an Attitude of Giving—Accepted and Rejected Objects Exteriorized.

"the norm for the development of object-relationships conforms to the . . . scheme" (*ibid.,* p. 38).

With Stage I, the focus is on infancy, breast-feeding, and taking in by means of the mouth. This is also the time of one's first object relationship. "The infant is completely dependent upon his object not only for his existence and physical well-being, but also for the satisfaction of his psychological needs" (*ibid.,* p. 47).

Fairbairn indicated that certain objects were appropriate for one's attention at the different stages of development; he said the breast of the mother—a part-object—was appropriate for the Early Oral part of Stage I, whereas "Mother with the Breast—Whole Object treated characteristically as a Part-Object" (*ibid.,* p. 41) was appropriate for the Late Oral part of Stage I.

With Stage II, the focus moves still more toward higher-order whole object relations. "Between . . . infantile and mature dependence is a transition stage characterized by an increasing tendency to abandon the attitude of infantile dependence and an increasing tendency to adopt the attitude of mature dependence" (*ibid.,* p. 35). The objects appropriate to Stage II are thought to be "Whole Object treated characteristically as Contents" (*ibid.,* p. 41).

Two concepts—dichotomy of the object and defensive techniques—become important during this stage. The former is significant because "the transition stage only begins to dawn when the ambivalence of the later oral phase [Stage I] has already commenced to give way to an attitude based upon dichotomy of the object" (*ibid.,* p. 35). Dichotomy of the object can "be defined as a process whereby the original object, towards which both love and hate have come to be directed, is replaced by two objects—*an accepted object,* towards which love is directed, and *a rejected object,* toward which hate is directed" (*ibid.,* p. 35).

This dichotomization gives way to the use of four techniques—obsessional, paranoid, hysterical, and phobic—which "are four alternative methods for attempting to deal with the difficulties of the transition stage" (*ibid.,* p. 146). These defensive techniques have also been referred to as rejective techniques, though they are not necessarily all exclusively rejective in operation. With the four techniques, dichotomization is thought to proceed as follows (*ibid.,* p. 46):

Technique	Accepted Object	Rejected Object
Obsessional	Internalized	Internalized
Paranoid	Internalized	Externalized
Hysterical	Externalized	Internalized
Phobic	Externalized	Externalized

(Fairbairn later said that the Rejected Object should be changed to the plural, objects, because both "exciting" and "rejecting" elements or objects would be included here; see Addendum to Chapter 4 in 1954 book.) Each technique, then, can be viewed as a means of attempting to cope with the key, unresolved conflict of the transition stage, with that conflict being "one between (a) a developmental urge to advance to an attitude of mature dependence upon the object, and (b) a regressive reluctance to abandon the attitude of infantile dependence upon the object" (*ibid.,* p. 38). With all this, it comes down to "separation from the object—a situation which is both desired and feared" (*ibid.,* p. 46).

With Stage III, Mature Dependence, the focus is on the development of self-other differentiation and the capacity for giving as well as taking. The objects appropriate to this stage are defined as "Whole Object with Genital Organs" (*ibid.*, p. 41). But why is this stage still referred to as one of "dependence" rather than "independence"? "[T]he final stage appears best described as . . . 'mature dependence' rather than 'independence,' since a capacity for relationships necessarily implies dependence of some sort" (*ibid.*, p. 145).

Yet it must be understood that the object relations of the individual in Stage III are comparatively further developed and more qualitatively advanced. Stage III "is characterized by a capacity on the part of a differentiated individual for co-operative relationships with differentiated objects . . . [I]t is a relationship involving evenly matched giving and taking between two differentiated individuals . . . " (*ibid.*, p. 145). Thus, in getting to Stage III, "there is a gradual expansion and development of personal relationships with objects, beginning with an almost exclusive and very dependent relationship with the mother, and maturing into a very complex system of social relationships of all degrees of intimacy" (*ibid.*, p. 144).

The Structure of Personality.   In Fairbairn's theory of endopsychic structure, there are five structural factors, two dynamic factors, and three levels of consciousness. The three levels of consciousness are the unconscious, the preconscious, and the conscious. These seem basically to correspond with the levels identified and defined by Freud (see Chapter 1).

The five structural factors are as follows:

1. central ego
2. libidinal ego
3. internal saboteur
4. rejecting object
5. exciting object

The *central ego* is the original source of mental life and cuts across conscious, preconscious, and unconscious; it

> is not conceived as originating out of something else (the 'id'), or as constituting a passive structure dependent for its activity upon impulses proceeding from the matrix out of which it originated. . . . On the contrary, the 'central ego' is conceived as a primary and dynamic structure, from which . . . the other mental structures are subsequently derived. (Fairbairn, 1954, p. 106)

The *libidinal ego* is somewhat similar to Freud's id; "but, whereas according to Freud's view the 'ego' is a derivative of the 'id,' according to my view the 'libidinal ego' . . . is a derivative of the 'central ego' (which corresponds to the ego) . . . a dynamic structure" (*ibid.*, p. 106). Compared to the central ego, however, the libidinal ego is described as "more infantile," having "a lesser degree of organization," having "a smaller measure of adaptation to reality," and having "a greater devotion to internalized objects" (*ibid.*, p. 106).

The *internal saboteur* is described as an aggressive and persecutory ego. But Fairbairn (1954) points out that the internal saboteur, "which largely corresponds to Freud's superego in function" (p. 108), is not identical to it; the saboteur is "wholly an ego structure" (p. 106). The internal saboteur later came to be called the antilibidinal ego.

The internalized bad object, i.e., unsatisfying aspects of the mother object, is split into two objects: the rejecting object and the exciting object. This is done in an effort to control the unsatisfying object. The *rejecting object* is frustrating; the *exciting object* is alluring. "[T]he unsatisfying object has . . . two facets. On the one hand, it frustrates; and, on the other hand, it tempts and allures. Indeed its essential 'badness' consists precisely in the fact that it combines allurement with frustration" (*ibid.,* p. 111).

The two dynamic factors are libido and aggression. Libido refers to "orientation toward and need for relations with others—rather than a specific form of energy or sensuality" (Greenberg & Mitchell, 1983, p. 158). Aggression, though different from libido, was seen as subordinate to it. "[W]hilst I regard aggression as a primary dynamic factor in that it does not appear capable of being resolved into libido . . . at the same time I regard it as ultimately subordinate to libido, not only metaphysically, but also metapsychologically" (Fairbairn, 1954, p. 109).

In Fairbairn's view, as might be expected, his theory of mental structure had much to offer over and above Freud's.

> Thus, with five structural factors and two dynamic factors to conjure with, my theory permits of a much greater range of permutations and combinations than does Freud's theory. . . . [M]y theory possesses all the features of an explanatory system enabling psychopathological and characterological phenomena of all kinds to be described in terms of the patterns assumed by a complex of relationships between a variety of structures. It also possesses the advantage of enabling psychopathological symptoms to be explained directly in terms of structural conformations, and thus of doing, justice to the unquestionable fact that, so far from being independent phenomena, symptoms are but expressions of the personality as a whole. (Fairbairn, 1954, p. 129)

Psychopathology.   Psychopathology can be traced back to problems in either the infantile dependence or transition stages of development. Problems in the infantile dependence stage can give rise to schizophrenia and depression.

> Schizophrenia and depression are etiologically related to disturbances of development during the stage of infantile dependence—schizophrenia being related to difficulties arising in object-relationships over sucking (loving), and depression being related to difficulties arising in object-relationships over biting (hating). (Fairbairn, 1954, p. 163)

These disorders, then, reflect fixations in or regressions to infantile dependence (Guntrip, 1961).

Problems during the transition stage can give rise to more neurotic-type conditions.

> Obsessional, paranoid, hysterical, and phobic symptoms derive their etiological significance from the fact that they reflect the operation of four specific techniques employed by the ego in an attempt to deal with difficulties arising over object-relationships during the *transitional* stage. . . . The four transitional techniques operate functionally as defenses against the emergence of schizoid and depressive tendencies originating during the first stage of ego-development. (Fairbairn, 1954, p. 163)

The characteristic affect of the depressive state was of course depression, whereas the characteristic affect of the schizoid state of mind was futility.

Summary.   Fairbairn's theory departs radically from Freud's—asserting that libido is object seeking rather than pleasure seeking. Fairbairn (1963) conceptualized a mental structure in which there is no id because everything originates from the ego, which is present at birth. Early relationships, particularly with the mother, are seen as decisive and critical for the development of object relations. Psychopathology has its origins in those early years and largely in that early relationship with the primary caretaker. Fairbairn's contribution is significant, and his thinking continues to generate much interest (e.g., Grotstein & Rinsley, 1993). In this regard the words of Guntrip (1973), though penned over 20 years ago, still seem as relevant today as they were then: "[W]e must concede to Fairbairn recognition as the one psychoanalytic thinker, who . . . unequivocally stressed object-relations experience as the determining factor, the all-important desideratum, for ego development" (p. 101).

Winnicott

Biographical Sketch.   Donald Woods Winnicott was born in 1896 in Plymouth, England. His mother was a housewife, his father a corsetry merchant. He had two older sisters, Violet and Cathleen.

Winnicott attended the Leys School in Cambridge, the Jesus College in Cambridge, did a stint in the Navy, and later returned to London to complete his medical training (at Bartholomew's Hospital). He began to specialize in pediatrics in 1920. Some of the positions in which he served were as follows: consultant in children's medicine to Paddington Green Children's Hospital, consultant in children's medicine to Queen's Hospital, and psychiatric consultant to the Government Evacuation Scheme. He also maintained a private practice. Some of his honors and awards include being made Fellow in the Royal College of Physicians and British Psychological Society, being president of the British Psycho-Analytical Society on two occasions, and being awarded the James Spence Medal for Pediatrics. During this time he was analyzed by James Strachey and later by Joan Riviere.

Winnicott was a prolific writer. Some of his books are *Clinical Notes on Disorders of Childhood* (1931), *The Child and the Family: First Relationships* (1957), *Collected Papers: Through Paediatrics to Psycho-Analysis* (1958, 1975, 1992), *The Maturational Processes and the Facilitating Environment: Studies in the Theory of Emotional Development* (1965b), *Playing and Reality* (1971), *Home is Where We Start From: Essays by a Psychoanalyst* (1987), and *Human Nature* (1988). His book, *Holding and Interpretation: Fragment of an Analysis* (1986), provides a "fragment of an analysis" in which he served as the analyst. A book containing his selected letters has been edited by Rodman (1987). *Winnicott Studies: The Journal of the Squiggle Foundation* is published annually by the Squiggle Foundation in London; the journal's purpose is to further the study and application of Winnicott's ideas.

Winnicott first married in 1923. He divorced some 26 years later and remarried in 1951. He died in 1971. (Source for biographical information: Phillips, 1988; cf. Khan, 1971; Tizard, 1971; C. Winnicott, 1978.)

The Theoretical Substrate.   Winnicott viewed his work as being a continuation of efforts begun by Freud and Melanie Klein; theirs was the theoretical ground from which he began. Winnicott, however, took his thinking in directions quite different from those of either Freud or Klein. Some of that difference, for example, can be seen reflected in this statement: "There is no id before ego" (Winnicott, 1965b, p. 56). In contrast to Fairbairn, however, Winnicott believed that there could be oedipal as well as pre-oedipal pathology.

The Mother-Child Relationship.   Being a pediatrician, Winnicott had ample opportunities to observe mothers and their infants interact. And, for Winnicott, this interaction and how it played out over time is critical for infant growth and development (or lack thereof). The infant is seen as being born with inherited potential, which includes "a tendency towards growth and development" (Winnicott, 1965a, p. 43). But even with that being the case, the following must be kept uppermost in mind: "*the inherited potential of an infant cannot become an infant unless linked to maternal care*" (*ibid.*, p. 43).

Satisfactory parental care can be grouped into "three overlapping stages:

(a) Holding.
(b) Mother and infant living together. Here the father's function (of dealing with the environment for the mother) is not known to the infant.
(c) Father, mother, and infant, all three living together." (p. 43)

Holding, an important concept, refers to actual physical holding as well as "caring for" the infant over time. Such holding, then, is psychological as well as physical. During the holding stage, numerous developments occur (e.g., qualitative changes in one's capacity for object relations). But "without a good enough holding these . . . cannot be attained, or once attained cannot become established" (p. 45).

The infant moves from absolute dependence to relative dependence toward independence. Through "holding" and care provided by the mother, continuity of being takes form. In considering the infant's care, such terms as *good enough care, good enough environment, average expectable environment,* and *facilitating environment* are invoked. By these terms, it is not meant that the environment should be perfect, all-gratifying; that is impossible. Instead, with the "good enough environment," there is consistent, stable, reliable care—"good enough care." Guntrip (1973) put it this way: "Winnicott implies a continuously helping, fostering, nurturing environment, accepting the infant's immature dependence while supporting his tentative adventures into independence, individuality, and finding a life of his own in and through personal relationships" (*ibid.*, p. 113).

This holding/maternal care "leads up to, includes, and co-exists with the establishment of the infant's first object relationships and his first experiences of instinctual gratification" (Winnicott, 1965b, p. 49). It is this maternal care—the nature of it—that contributes to the infant's later development of mental health (or lack thereof).

> The mental health of the individual, in the sense of freedom from psychosis or liability to psychosis (schizophrenia), is laid down by this maternal care. . . . This environmental provision . . . provides . . . vitally important ego-support. In this way schizophrenia or infantile psychosis or a liability to psychosis at a later date is related to a failure of environmental provision. (Winnicott, 1965b, pp. 49–50)

Other pathologies that Winnicott links with "defective ego support by the mother" include false self-defense and schizoid personality (*ibid.*, pp. 58–59). All these pathologies, then, "can be related . . . to various kinds and degrees of failure of holding, handling, and object-presenting at the earliest stage" (*ibid.,* p. 59).

Other Important Terms.   Some other concepts integral to Winnicott's thinking include the true self, the false self, transitional objects, and transitional phenomena. The true self refers to the part of the infant that feels "creative," "spontaneous," and "real" (*ibid.,* p. 148). The false self refers to the part of the infant "built up on the basis of compliance . . . [having] a defensive function, which is the protection of the true self" (*ibid.,* p. 133). With "good enough" care the true self is enabled to emerge, but with lack of "good enough" care the false self emerges (*ibid.,* p. 145). Transitional objects, discussed in Winnicott's (1953) paper, "Transitional Objects and Transitional Phenomena," refers to the infant's first not-me possessions, e.g., a blanket or doll. These are tangible—something that can be held on to, grasped, hugged; they lessen the stress of separation and function to soothe the infant. "Transitional phenomena" refers to behaviors (e.g., repetitive actions such as rocking) or fantasies which, like a tangible object, lessen the stress of separation and function to soothe.

Summary.   Winnicott, because of his work as a pediatrician and psychoanalyst, provides useful insights into the mother-infant relationship and its facilitating and non-facilitating aspects. As Phillips (1988) has stated, "Winnicott's work was devoted to the recognition and description of the good mother, and the use of the mother-infant relationship as the model of psychoanalytic treatment" (p. 3). Through this focus on infant and child observation, object relations theory is said to have achieved "its greatest impetus" (Pine, 1985, p. 59).

Winnicott's terms *facilitating environment, holding, good enough mother, average expectable environment, transitional objects,* and *transitional phenomena,* have all come to have a prominent place in object relations thought today. In 1981, Tuttmann summed up Winnicott's place:

> Although he did not conceptualize along metapsychological lines and did not reconstruct theory [as did Fairbairn], important object relations concepts were elaborated and an invigorating thrust to psychoanalytic technique was stimulated by . . . [his] cryptic, paradoxical style, poignant observations, and inspiring creativity. (p. 36)

Guntrip

Biographical Sketch.   Henry James Samuel Guntrip (or Harry) was born May 29, 1901, in London, England. His father was a clerk, his mother a housewife. He was educated at the University of London, receiving his B.A. in 1926, his B.D. in 1928, and his Ph.D. in 1952 from there.

He was a minister in England from 1928 to 1946. In 1946 he began work as a psychotherapist and lecturer for the Department of Psychiatry at the University of Leeds. He maintained this position throughout his career. He was a Fellow of the British Psychological Society.

He published a number of works. Some of his books were as follows: *Psychology for Ministers and Social Workers* (1949), *Psychotherapy and Religion* (1957), *Personality*

Structure and Human Interaction: The Developing Synthesis of Psycho-dynamic Theory (1961), *Clinical Studies of the Schizoid Personality* (1966), *Schizoid Phenomena, Object-Relations, and the Self* (1969), and *Psychoanalytic Theory, Therapy, and the Self* (1973). His books have been translated into various languages, including Norwegian, Swedish, Japanese, Italian, and Spanish. Some of Guntrip's papers have recently been collected into a volume, entitled *Personal Relations Therapy* (Hazell, 1994).

He married Bertha Kind in 1928, They had one child, Gwenda. Harry Guntrip died February 18, 1975.

The Theoretical Substrate.   Guntrip was very much a follower of Fairbairn. He did, however, see the need for some changes or additions to Fairbairn's theory.

The Regressed Ego.   "Guntrip's own innovation in theory and practice centers on his development of the concept of the 'regressed ego'" (Greenberg & Mitchell, 1983, p. 211). This refers to "a part of the infantile libidinal ego in which the infant found his world so intolerable that the sensitive heart of him fled into himself" (Guntrip, 1973, p. 152). Or, to put this another way, it could be said that:

> The *regressed ego* denotes, not a freely available generalized "fear and flight" reaction but *the deepest structurally specific part of the complex personality, existing in a settled attitude of fear, weakness, withdrawal, and dissolute dependence not in the active post-natal infantile sense but in a passive ante-natal sense. It represents the most profoundly traumatized part of the personality and is the hidden cause of all regressive phenomena.* (Guntrip, 1969, p. 77)

Guntrip (1961) viewed his regressed ego concept as having ties not only to Fairbairn's theory but to some of Winnicott's concepts as well. Fairbairn said that Guntrip's concept was "an original contribution of considerable explanatory power" (see Guntrip, 1969, p. 77). As for Winnicott, Guntrip (1961) said "I have thus come to regard the phenomena of regression as implying and deriving from a specific, structurally persisting Regressed L.E. [libidinal ego]. This appears to me to be equally implied in Winnicott's view about the 'true self' and 'therapeutic regression'" (p. 433).

For Guntrip, the regressed ego is the ultimate base from which psychopathology derived. With that being the case, the primary focus of treatment is accordingly the regressed ego as well.

Guntrip (1969) gave much attention to the theory of and therapy for the schizoid personality. In this way, he continued on and extended some of Fairbairn's work. The schizoid's emotional dilemma is conceived thus:

> he feels a deep dread of entering into a real personal relationship, i.e., one into which genuine feeling enters, because, though his need for a love-object is so great, he can only sustain a relationship at a deep emotional level on the basis of infantile and absolute dependence. . . . You are always *impelled into* a relationship by your needs and at once *driven out* again by the fear either of exhausting your love-object by the demands you want to make or else losing your own individuality by over-dependence and identification. This "in and out" oscillation is the *typical schizoid behavior,* and to escape from it into detachment and loss of feeling is the *typical schizoid state.* (Guntrip, 1969, p. 48)

The schizoid problem is ultimately the result of poor relations at the outset—in one's first object relationship.

> *The schizoid core develops in the infant who is "left without adequate object relations," left alone in a psychic vacuum in which he can only develop an "out-of-touchness" which erupts in later life as an inability to relate because he was not related to in the beginning.* (See Guntrip's comments, in Mendez & Fine, 1976, p. 375)

The schizoid personality, because of its dread of personal relationship and "feeling," is particularly difficult to treat and various roadblocks and defenses against psychotherapy are to be expected (see Guntrip, 1961).

Summary.   Guntrip, in making his theoretical contributions, drew freely from the works of other analytic theorists. However, he most aligned himself with Fairbairn; he primarily extended Fairbairn's theory by introducing the concept of regressed ego. For Guntrip, the regressed ego was the ultimate source of psychopathology and, thereby, the focus of analytic treatment as well. He devoted much attention to schizoid personality. All patients were not schizoid; none, however, escaped some degree of "schizoidness." As Guntrip (1969) asked, "what patients are not schizoid at bottom to some extent?" (p. 290).

OBJECT RELATIONS THERAPY

Eagle & Wolitzky, 1992, p. 129, stated,

> Because most of the writing in this area [object relations] is highly theoretical, it is often difficult to determine what therapists . . . actually do. . . . Detailed clinical data (as would be available, for example, from tape recorded sessions) are simply not available. The result is that, although we know a great deal about Fairbairn's theory, we know very little about how and to what extent his theory was expressed and implemented in his treatment.

That last sentence would seem equally applicable to Winnicott and Guntrip, too.

Eagle (1984; cf. Eagle & Wolitzky, 1992) has identified six implications that object relations theory has for treatment:

1. A greater general flexibility with regard to hours, scheduling, and the therapeutic situation.
2. A greater stress on the therapeutic relationship beyond a concern with transference and transference interpretations. The therapeutic relationship is conceptualized as providing a "holding" environment (Winnicott, 1958, 1965b).
3. While interpretations continue to be an important aspect of therapy, the *contents* of many interpretations are likely to differ from those provided by traditional analysts. Generally, one would expect less emphasis on sexual and aggressive wishes and oedipal issues and much greater attention to pre-oedipal issues, relationships with internalized objects, and feelings of lack of an intact sense of self. . . .

4. Perhaps because they are more willing to work with more disturbed patients, object relations therapists seem more willing to adapt treatment to periods requiring primarily management and even periods of hospitalization.

5. Because the therapeutic relationship is so strongly emphasized and because of a departure from strict analytic neutrality, object relations therapists would need to be especially concerned with issues of countertransference. The intense interest in countertransference issues that is now rather widespread in psychoanalytic circles may be partly attributable to the influence of object relations theory.

6. Although regression is seen as a necessary and inevitable aspect of therapy by traditional analysts, it plays a more central role in descriptions of therapy given by object relations theorists. The latter believe that marked regression—to points of early trauma, early experience of ego weakness, and early pathological defensive formations (e.g., establishment of a "false self")—is necessary in order for basic personality changes to occur. (pp. 90–91)

With those six orienting points in mind, let us now consider what Fairbairn, Winnicott, and Guntrip had to say about therapeutic treatment. Also, to provide a more comprehensive view on the treatment process, we have drawn on some more recent object relational therapy books (e.g., Horner, 1991) to flesh out our presentation further.

Goals

The goals of object relations psychotherapy or analysis have sometimes been described in rather dramatic terms—to exorcise the patient's demons, to provide the patient with "salvation," to assist the patient in achieving a rebirth, being born again (e.g., Fairbairn, 1954, 1955; Guntrip, 1953, 1969, 1973). Such terms reflect the nature of object relations therapy as conceived by Fairbairn, Winnicott, and Guntrip—a long-term process in which the work of treatment was replacing bad objects with good objects.

Fairbairn, in his 1958 paper, "On the Nature and Aims of Psycho-Analytical Treatment," identified four goals of analytic treatment. These were:

> to promote a maximum "synthesis" of the structures into which the original ego has been split. . . ; a maximum reduction of persisting infantile dependence. . . ; a maximum reduction of that hatred of the libidinal object which . . . is ultimately responsible for the original splitting of the ego. . . ; and to effect breaches of the closed system which constitutes the patient's inner world, and thus to make this world accessible to the influence of outer reality. (p. 380)

Treatment, then, strives to promote integration, to foster movement toward mature dependence, and to open the patient up to the outer world, that is, the world of others.

Winnicott (1965b), in his paper, "The Aims of Psycho-Analytical Treatment," viewed ego independence and ego integration as goals of treatment. Increasing ego strength was also one of treatment's goals.

Guntrip (1961) said that "the purpose of psychotherapy may be simply stated as that of helping the patient to grow till he feels strong enough in himself to be capable of living without unrealistic fears of internal origin and their attendant hates, guilts, defenses and conflicts" (p. 418). Symptom removal, in and of itself, is not seen as sufficient for treatment success. "Similarly, the real meaning of a 'cure' for the patient is not removal of symptoms, or any degree of social and vocational rehabilitation, but the achievement of reasonable or optimum maturity as a person" (Guntrip, 1953, p. 116).

But what of recovering repressed memories? What of releasing repressed impulses? What of breaking up repressed complexes? These are all important, though not primary goals of treatment.

> *The technique of psycho-analysis becomes an endeavor, not to release repressed impulses and recover repressed memories, nor even to break up repressed complexes, all of which are intermediate matters which are incidental to the ultimate aim, namely, to help the patient to tolerate the conscious re-experiencing of his profoundly repressed and fundamentally weak infantile ego, which he has spent his life trying to disown in his struggle to feel adult.* (Guntrip, 1961, p. 419)

Other writers (e.g., Horner, 1991), building on the works of Fairbairn, Winnicott, Guntrip, and other object relational therapists, have identified the following goals: modification of pathological structures (such as Winnicott's false self) and repairing structural deficits. Since object relations theorists seem to converge on the point "that basic structural ego-weakness is the starting-point of all later psychopathological processes" (Guntrip, 1961, p. 419), then some "ego" repair or "self" repair are typically called for in therapy.

In summary, while each of our theorists may have brought his own particular wording to bear on treatment goals, some consistencies can be found: ego synthesis or ego integration, mature dependence or reasonable maturity, strengthening the ego or diminishing ego-weakness. Again, much of this seems to come down to replacing bad objects with good, making "peace" with one's past, and consolidating one's identity. Such goals do not seem to lend themselves to a short-term treatment process.

Process of Therapy

Guntrip (1969) has spoken of the treatment process as involving three stages: rapport, transference, and regrowing or maturing. With rapport, the patient is thought to need "a parent-figure as a protector against gross anxiety" (p. 336). Transference, the second stage, "involves the analysis of all the ways in which . . . [patient functioning] is interfered with by the legacy of old inadequate relationships with the actual parents and in the family group" (*ibid.*, p. 336). With stage three,

> the patient begins . . . to feel that what he really needs is the basically non-erotic love of a stable parent in and through which the child grows up to possess an individuality of his own, a maturing strength of selfhood through which he becomes separate without feeling "cut-off," and the original relationship to parents develops into adult friendship. (Guntrip, 1969, p. 336)

Let us now take these three stages—rapport, transference, and maturing —and discuss them in more detail.

Rapport.   With but one exception, Rogers' client-centered therapy (see Chapter 13), the object relations theorists give more attention and emphasis to the therapeutic relationship than any other approach covered in this book. This emphasis is heartily reflected in the works of Fairbairn, Winnicott, as well as Guntrip. While technique is seen as having its place, it is secondary and nothing has any meaning without the analyst-patient relationship. The relationship is *the* treatment. Only through the relationship is cure effected.

> [T]he difficulties from which the patient suffers represent the effects of unsatisfactory and unsatisfying object-relationships experienced in early life and perpetuated in an exaggerated form in inner reality; and, if this view is correct, the actual relationship existing between the patient and the analyst as persons must be regarded as in itself constituting a therapeutic factor of prime importance. The existence of such a personal relationship in outer reality not only serves the function of providing a means of correcting the distorted relationships which prevail in inner reality and influence the reactions of the patient to outer objects, but provides the patient with an opportunity, denied to him in childhood, to undergo a process of emotional development in the setting of an actual relationship with a reliable and beneficent parental figure. (Fairbairn, 1958, p. 377)

Again, the replacing of bad objects with good is allowed to take place by means of the analytic relationship.

Guntrip (1953), in his interesting paper, "The Therapeutic Factor in Psychotherapy," defines the relationship—the good-object relationship of the analyst and patient—as *the* "therapeutic or 'saving' factor in psychotherapy" (p. 125). The treatment relationship is viewed as a most powerful medium: "[I]t is only the kind of knowledge that is arrived at as a living insight, which is felt, experienced, in the medium of a good personal relationship, that has therapeutic value" (*ibid.,* p. 125). Guntrip continues: "[T]he important point is that . . . *therapeutic change can only come about in, and as a direct result of, a good-object relationship*" (p. 125).

These sentiments about the analyst-patient relationship are also echoed in the works of Fairbairn. "In my own opinion, the really decisive factor is the relationship of the patient to the analyst, and it is upon this relationship that the other factors mentioned by Gitelson [catharsis, insight, recall of infantile memories] depend not only for their effectiveness, but for their very existence" (Fairbairn, 1958, p. 379).

In still an earlier paper, "Observations in Defence of the Object-Relations Theory of Personality," Fairbairn (1955) had this to say:

> For I am convinced that it is the patient's relationship to the analyst that mediates the "curing" or "saving" effect of psychotherapy. Where long-term psychoanalytical treatment is concerned, what *mediates* the "curing" or "saving" process more specifically is the development of the patient's relationship to the analyst, through a phase in which earlier pathogenic relationships are repeated under the influence of transference, into a new kind of relationship which is at once satisfying and adapted to the circumstance of outer reality. (p. 156)

Thus, for Fairbairn as well as Guntrip, the "curing," the "saving," or *the* therapeutic factor was the treatment relationship itself.

The model for the analyst-patient relationship is derived from the mother-infant relationship. This comes through in the following passage from Winnicott (1965a).

> In our *therapeutic* work over and over again we become involved with a patient; we pass through a phase in which we are vulnerable (as the mother is) because of our involvement; we are identified with the child who is temporarily dependent on us to an alarming degree; we watch the shedding of the child's false self or false selves; we see the beginning of a true self, a true self with an ego that is strong because like the mother with her infant we have been able to give ego support. If all goes well we may find that a child has emerged, a child whose ego can organize its own defenses. . . . A "new" being is born, because of what we do, a real human being capable of having an independent life. My thesis is that what we do in therapy is to attempt to imitate the natural process that characterizes the behavior of any mother of her own infant. If I am right, it is the mother-infant couple that can teach us the basic principles on which we may base our therapeutic work. (p. 15)

This conceptualization of the treatment relationship, according to Guntrip (1969), has implications for working with those "most ill" as well as those "lesser ill" patients. Key to this mother-infant model of the psychotherapy relationship is this: Just as the mother-infant relationship evolves to reflect and adapt to the changing needs and growth of the infant, so too does the analyst-patient relationship evolve to reflect and adapt to the changing needs and growth of the patient.

Some of the characteristics of the analyst in the treatment relationship include compassion, helpfulness, openness, and flexibility (Gitelson, 1952). Genuineness and empathy also seem quite important:

> I . . . think of psychotherapy as . . . the provision . . . of a genuine, reliable, understanding, and respecting, caring personal relationship in which a human being whose true self has been crushed . . . can begin at last to feel his own true feelings, and think his own spontaneous thoughts, and find himself to be real. (Guntrip, 1973, p. 182)

Continuity would be yet another important characteristic of the relationship—that the analyst be there consistently for the patient over time. "*It is the continuing relationship of analyst and patient on an emotional level that enables the patient to deal with what is made conscious*" (Guntrip, 1953, p. 124).

Thus, treatment is not seen as a technique-oriented process (though technique has its place). Technique is secondary to and acquires meaning only in the context of the analyst-patient relationship. This attitude is clearly reflected in Guntrip's (1953) "therapeutic factor" paper: "*The analyst is not a good object merely by virtue of being a good technician. The technique of psycho-analysis as such does not cure*" (p. 124). "*The technique makes problems accessible to treatment. It is the relationship with the therapist that enables the problem to be solved*" (p. 127).

Twenty years later, in *Psychoanalytic Theory, Therapy, and the Self*, Guntrip (1973) reiterated his views about this. "I cannot think of psychotherapy as a technique" (p. 182). "Terms such as 'analysis' and 'technique' are too impersonal. They remind me more of engineering than of personal relations" (p. 183). "[O]ne cannot practice a stereotyped technique on patients: one can only be a real person for and with the patient" (p. 185). Fairbairn

(1958), like Guntrip, also spoke out against practicing analysis in a stereotyped way, making patients conform to the sanctity of method rather than making method conform to the sanctity of patients.

The analyst's relationship to the patient was conceived of in terms of mature adult, parental love—*agape* (Fairbairn, 1954; Guntrip, 1953). This is not love in the erotic or sexual sense. It is a deep, abiding caring for the patient—a nonerotic parental love that respects and fosters the patient's growth, separation, identity, and independence. "This kind of parental love . . . *agape* . . . is the kind of love the psycho-analyst and psychotherapist must give the patient because he did not get it from his parents in sufficient measure or in a satisfactory form" (Guntrip, 1953, p. 125). It is this *agape* or nonerotic parental love that is "*the real condition of the child's* [*and patient's*] *ability to grow up*" (p. 119). (Interestingly enough, Adler's [see Chapter 3] key therapeutic relationship construct—social interest—has also been compared to agape; Watts, 1992).

Transference.   Therapeutic regression and transference analysis are viewed as critical in the treatment process by Fairbairn, Winnicott, and Guntrip. "Transference analysis is the slow and painful experience of clearing the ground of left-overs from past experience, both in transference and countertransference, so that therapist and patient can at last meet 'mentally face to face' and know that they know each other as two human beings" (Guntrip, 1969, p. 353). By means of regression, i.e., going back to earlier modes of thinking, behaving, and relating, the maladaptations of the past can be dealt with now and resolved through the analyst-patient relationship. This entails a process of "working through" the transference.

> Fairbairn's "object-relations" view of psychotherapy was certainly that it is a process in which transference relationships, both positive and negative, are worked through until they lead on and give way to a good realistic relationship of whatever kind is possible and appropriate between therapist and patient. (Guntrip, 1969, p. 331)

By working through the transference, transformation (to borrow from Jung) occurs. But this process is by no means fast, is by no means easy, and instead, as noted above, is slow and painful.

In Fairbairn's view, much of what the patient does is to try to force the analyst into the inner, closed system he/she had built up about others and the outside world. Much of what the analyst has to do, then, is to make his/her way into that system and open it up to outer reality.

> Thus, in a sense, *psycho-analytical treatment resolves itself into a struggle on the part of the patient to press-gang his relationship with the analyst into the closed system of the inner world through the agency of transference, and a determination on the part of the analyst to effect a breach in this closed system and to provide conditions under which, in the setting of a therapeutic relationship, the patient may be induced to accept the open system of outer reality.* (Fairbairn, 1958, p. 385)

The critical point here is that transference is to take place only within a good, caring, concerned, nonstereotypic, flexible (i.e., not bound by the rigidity of Frued's "stultifying" treatment set-up) analyst-patient relationship (Fairbairn, 1958). It is this relationship in conjunction with transference that makes cure possible. To repeat Fairbairn (1955, p. 156):

> Where long-term psychoanalytical treatment is concerned, what *mediates* the "curing" or "saving" process more specifically is the development of the patient's relationship to the analyst, through a phase in which earlier pathogenic relationships are repeated under the influence of transference, into a new kind of relationship which is at once satisfying and adapted to the circumstances of outer reality.

Through transference, the patient's bad objects are released, "worked through," and replaced with good objects. "The bad objects can only be safely released, however, if the analyst has become established as a sufficiently good object for the patient" (Fairbairn, 1954, p. 70). So, for bad to be replaced with good, the analyst must have first come to be a "good-enough" object in the patient's mind—allowing the patient to feel secure enough, "held" enough, so that such release and replacement could be made. For "at the deepest level, psychotherapy is replacement therapy, providing for the patient what the mother failed to provide at the beginning of life" (Guntrip, 1973, p. 191).

Winnicott's views about transference show definite similarities to Fairbairn's and Guntrip's views. Through regression and transference, though, he would say that the true self could become "unfrozen" and be allowed to emerge and grow.

Maturing.   Much of what was said earlier about mature dependence—Fairbairn's Stage III of personality development—applies here. The person, as a result of analysis, becomes increasingly differentiated, is increasingly able to engage in "co-operative relationships with differentiated objects" (Fairbairn, 1954, p. 145). Ideally, a differentiated, consolidated self emerges; the capacity for mature relationships, adult love, *agape,* emerges as well. The person acquires a sense of wholeness and integration. With such changes, the character of treatment itself changes.

> As progress is made, it is certainly true that the patient can more and more "take analysis," and treatment becomes increasingly something more than a co-operation in terms of infantile dependence, something that grows into a partnership of two increasingly equal adults as the child-patient grows up to the parent-analyst's level. Analysis has by then long ceased to be felt in terms of a psychotic terror of being torn to pieces and can be accepted as the helpful and friendly insight of one with whom the patient is developing a steadily more realistic relationship. (Guntrip, 1961, p. 413)

This metaphor of the child-patient, parent-analyst is further extended to the termination of analysis, the ultimate in maturation—when the patient, much like late adolescents or young adults who leave home, is now ready to strike out on his/her own.

> [T]he relationship between the matured patient and the analyst, after the close of treatment, . . . become[s] something analogous to that of a child who has grown up, developed his own proper personality, left home to marry and run his own life and affairs, but whose affection for his parents, respect for their experience and good qualities, and pleasure in their interest and goodwill remains on an adult level. (Guntrip, 1953, p. 131)

Techniques

Inquiry.   "The purpose of inquiry is to elicit data, not only for our own information, but to deepen and widen the patient's self-awareness" (Horner, 1991, pp. 137–138). This can involve having patients clarify or make more specific what they have said; it can also involve having patients provide examples of something they have said. Inquiry, then, serves to clarify, to render patient verbalizations more concrete and specific.

Observation.   "The therapist makes observations of what he or she has noticed when it seems clinically useful, timely, appropriate, and in keeping with what is known about the patient's ability to make use of such observations" (Horner, 1991, p. 139). Therapist observations can take the form of juxtaposing different pieces of data from treatment and asking the patient if he/she sees a connection; in other cases, the therapist may "wonder aloud" about the possible relationship between the juxtaposed data (e.g., "I wonder if . . ."). Horner (1991) provides the following example: "I wonder if there could be a connection between your feelings of rejection and your detachment. Somehow they seem to go together" (p. 139).

Interpretation.   Again, interpretation—as with Freudian, Jungian, and Adlerian analysis—has its place in object relation analysis, too. But as with everything else in object relations therapy, interpretation acquires its meaning only in a caring, concerned therapeutic relationship. For example, Guntrip (1975) said the following of Fairbairn: "[H]e held that psychoanalytic interpretation is not therapeutic *per se,* but only as it expresses a personal relationship of genuine understanding" (p. 145). Consider this passage.

> The psychotherapeutic implication . . . is that the interpretation of transference phenomena in the setting of the analytical situation is not in itself enough to promote a satisfactory change in the patient. For such a change to occur, it is necessary for the patient's relationship with the analyst to undergo a process of development in terms of which a relationship based on transference becomes replaced by a realistic relationship between two persons in the outer world. (Fairbairn, 1958, p. 381)

Winnicott seemed no different in his views. Psychoanalysis "is not just a matter of interpreting the repressed unconscious [but] . . . the provision of a professional setting for trust" (Winnicott, 1987, pp. 114–115). For Winnicott, interpreting was not something done with abandon; rather, it was an intervention offered with circumspection and in small doses. "My interpretations are economical. . . . One interpretation per session satisfies me if it has referred to the material produced by the patient's unconscious co-operation. I say one thing, or say one thing in two or three parts. I never use long sentences" (Winnicott, 1965b, p. 167).

But how does an object relations interpretation differ from traditional analysts' interpretations? Again, to repeat Eagle (1984), "generally, one would expect less emphasis on sexual and aggressive wishes and oedipal issues and much greater attention to pre-oedipal issues, relationships with internalized objects, and feelings of lack of an intact sense of self" (p. 91).

Horner (1991) has said that, in object relations psychotherapy, "interpretations are best made in the form of a question, which allows the patient the opportunity to consider the interpretation and to decide if it feels right or not." She offers the following as an example: "You've been telling me how seductive your mother was. I wonder if this doesn't have something to do with your avoidance of sexual relationships now" (p. 140). (Interestingly, this question-type format for interpretations—using phrases such as "I wonder if . . ."—follows the format that Adlerians would use for interpretations as well; see Chapter 3.)

Dream Analysis.   The analysis and interpretation of dreams are important in object relations psychotherapy. As is true of Freudian psychoanalysis, the object relational viewpoint also considers the dream to be "the royal road to the unconscious" (Padel, 1978, p. 134). But how does dream work in object relations treatment differ from dream work in classical analysis? "Perhaps we now recognize more readily in the dream and also interpret more readily the features of the current transference relationship. We look less for the wish underlying the trains of association than for the attempts to deal with bad or threatening object relationships and to put what once went wrong right" (Padel, 1978, p. 134).

Integration.   This type of intervention pulls together or "integrates" various awarenesses the patient has come to in treatment; it brings perspective to the patient's troubles, struggles toward growth, and how they fit into his/her overall experience. Consider the following example.

> You have had to deny your aggression in order to protect an image of yourself as always good. If you were to acknowledge your aggressive impulses, you would have had to give up the moral superiority you claimed over your father. At the same time, if you were able to own your aggression, you would not be caught in the helpless position of victim whose anger takes the form of justifiable and righteous indignation but is not useful for extricating yourself from the passive and helpless position. As you have been able to own those feelings and impulses you were afraid made you bad and deserving of your father's harshness, you find yourself much more effective and unafraid in the world. (Horner, 1991, p. 142)

Confrontation.   This involves bringing to the patient's attention something he/she "may or may not want to see or know" (Horner, 1991, p. 143). It can involve setting limits on dangerous acting-out behavior. It can even involve demanding that the patient change in some way (e.g., stop using drugs so that treatment can proceed; what Horner refers to as a "heroic confrontation").

LENGTH AND LIMITATIONS

Length.   If the goal of treatment is "replacement," that is, to replace bad with good, then it stands to reason that therapy can be a long-term process. For example, Guntrip (1975), in writing about his own analysis, indicated that he was seen by Winnicott for over 150 sessions; he noted that, in his analysis by Fairbairn, he was seen for over 1000 sessions. However long the therapy may last, we can confidently say that object relations work (at least as conceived by Fairbairn, Winnicott, and Guntrip) cannot be rushed, takes considerable time, patience, and empathy, and requires "being with" the patient in continuous fashion across space and time.

The couch—the staple of Freudian analysis—may or may not be used in object relations therapy; this appears to be at the discretion of the therapist. For instance, Guntrip (1973) made his position on this clear: "I do not instruct a patient to lie on the couch. I wait to see what he will do, and when and why he wants to do something different" (p. 184).

Limitations.   Schizoid, borderline, neurotic, and psychotic conditions have all been considered from an object relations treatment perspective. It is seen as being a viable treatment for pre-oedipal and even oedipal disorders. (After all, oedipal pathology—at least in the view of Fairbairn and Guntrip—can be traced back to pre-oedipal origins anyway.) But just as Jung's "transformation" process (Chapter 2) is not for everyone, the transformation to be wrought by object relations therapy is not for everyone either. We are talking here about a process that is lengthy, in which insight is vital, in which willingness to endure the pain of regression and transference is required, in which patients are "reborn," and in which some measure of personality reconstruction occurs. Patients who have neither the time, money, motivation, capacity for insight, nor capacity to endure "the slow and painful experience" of transference analysis would not fit the object relations model of treatment (again, at least as conceptualized by Fairbairn, Winnicott, and Guntrip).

EXAMPLE

Since regression plays such an important role in object relations therapy, we have chosen as our example Winnicott's case description entitled "Withdrawal and Regression." This was first read at the XVII Conference des Psychanalystes de Langues Romanes, Paris, November 1954, was read to the British Psycho-Analytical Society on June 29, 1955, and appears in Winnicott's *Through Paediatrics to Psycho-Analysis: Collected Papers* (1975, pp. 255–261); it also appears as an Appendix in Winnicott's *Holding and Interpretation* (1986, pp. 187–192).

> In the course of the last decade I have had forced on me the experience of several adult patients who made a regression in the transference in the course of analysis.
>
> I wish to communicate an incident in the analysis of a patient who did not actually become clinically regressed but whose regressions were localized in momentary withdrawal states which occurred in the analytic sessions. My management of these withdrawal states was greatly influenced by my experience with regressed patients.
>
> (By withdrawal in this paper I mean momentary detachment from a waking relationship with external reality, this detachment being sometimes of the nature of brief sleep. By regression I mean regression to dependence and not specifically regression in terms of erotogenic zones.)
>
> I am choosing to give a series of six significant episodes chosen out of all the material belonging to the analysis of a schizoid-depressive patient. The patient is a married man with a family. At the onset of the present illness he had a breakdown, in which he felt unreal and lost what little capacity he had had for spontaneity. He was unable to work until some months after the analysis started, and at first he came to me as a patient from a mental hospital. (This patient had had a short period of analysis with me during the war, as a result of which he had made a clinical recovery from an acute disturbance of adolescence, but without gaining insight.)

The main thing that keeps this patient consciously seeking analysis is his inability to be impulsive and to make original remarks, although he can join very intelligently in serious conversation originated by other people. He is almost friendless because his friendships are spoiled by his lack of ability to originate anything, which makes him a boring companion. (He reported having laughed once at the cinema, and this small evidence of improvement made him feel hopeful about the outcome of the analysis.)

Over a long period his free associations were in the form of a rhetorical report of a conversation that was going on all the time inside, his free associations being carefully arranged and presented in a way that he felt would make the material interesting to the analyst.

Like many other patients in analysis, this patient at times sinks deep into the analytic situation; on important but rare occasions he becomes withdrawn; during these moments of withdrawal unexpected things happen which he is sometimes able to report. I shall pick out these rare happenings for the purpose of this paper from the vast mass of ordinary psychoanalytic material which I must ask my reader to take for granted.

Episodes 1 and 2

The first of these happenings (the fantasy of which he was only just able to capture and to report) was that, in a momentary withdrawn state on the couch, he had *curled up and rolled over the back of the couch.* This was the first direct evidence in the analysis of a spontaneous self. The next withdrawn moment occurred a few weeks later. He had just made an attempt to use me as a substitute for his father (who had died when the patient was 18) and had asked me my advice about a detail in his work. I had first of all discussed this detail with him, pointing out, however, that he needed me as an analyst and not as a father-substitute. He had said it would be a waste of time to go on talking in his ordinary way, and then said that he had become withdrawn and felt this as a flight from something. He could not remember any dream belonging to this moment of sleep. I pointed out to him that his withdrawal was at that time a flight from the painful experience of being exactly between waking and sleeping, or between talking to me rationally and being withdrawn. It was at this point that he just managed to tell me that he had again had the idea of being *curled up,* although in actual fact he was lying on his back as usual, with his hands together across his chest.

It is here that I made the first of the interpretations which I know I would not have made twenty years ago. This interpretation turned out to be highly significant. When he spoke of being curled up, he made movements with his hands to show that his curled-up position was somewhere in front of his face and that he was moving around in the curled-up position. I immediately said to him: "In speaking of yourself as curled up and moving round, you are at the same time implying something which naturally you are not describing since you are not aware of it; you imply the *existence of a medium.*" After a while I asked him if he understood what I meant and I found that he had immediately understood; he said, "Like the oil in which wheels move." Having now received the idea of the medium holding him, he went on to describe in words what he had shown with his hands, which was that he had been twirling round forwards, and he contrasted this with the twirling round backwards over the couch which he had reported a few weeks previously.

From this interpretation of the medium I was able to go on to develop the theme of the analytic situation and together we worked out a rather clear statement of the specialized conditions provided by the analyst, and of the limits of the analyst's capacity for adaptation to the patient's needs. Following this the patient had a very important dream, and the analysis of this showed that he had been able to discard a shield which was now no longer necessary since I had proved myself capable of supplying a suitable medium at the moment of his withdrawal. It appears that *through my immediately putting a medium around his withdrawn self I had converted his withdrawal into a regression,* and so had enabled him to use this experience constructively. I would have missed this opportunity in the early days of my analytic career. The patient described this analytic session as "momentous."

There was a very big result from this detail of analysis: a clearer understanding of the part I could play as analyst; a recognition of the dependence which must at times be very great even although painful to bear; and also a coming to grips with his reality situation both at work and at home in a completely new way. Incidentally he was able to tell me that his wife had become pregnant and this made it very easy for him to link his curled-up state in the medium with the idea of a foetus in the womb. He had in fact identified with his own child and at the same time had made an acknowledgement of his own original dependence on his mother.

The next time he met his mother after this session he was able for the first time to ask her how much the analysis was costing her, and to allow himself to feel concerned about this. In the next sessions he was able to get at his criticisms of me and to express his suspicion that I was a swindler.

Episode 3

The next detail came some months later, after a very rich period of analysis. It came at a time when the material was of an anal quality and the homosexual aspect of the transference situation, an aspect of analysis which especially frightened him, had been reintroduced. He reported that in childhood he had had a constant fear of being chased by a man. I made certain interpretations and he reported that while I had been talking he had been *far away, at a factory.* In ordinary language his "thought had wandered." This wandering off was very real to him, and he had felt as if he was actually working at the factory to which he had gone when he ended the earlier phase of his analysis with me (which had had to be terminated because of the war). Immediately I made the interpretation that he had gone away *from my lap.* The word lap was appropriate because in his withdrawn state and in terms of emotional development he had been at a stage of infancy, so that the couch had automatically become the analyst's lap. It will readily be seen that there is a relationship between my supplying the lap for him to come back to, and my supplying the medium on which depended his capacity to move round in a curled-up position in space.

Episode 4

The fourth episode that I wish to pick out is not so clear. It came in a session in which he said that he was unable to make love. The general material enabled me to interpret the dissociation in his relation to the world; on the one hand spontaneity from the *true* self which has no hope of finding an object except in imagination; and, on the other hand, response to stimulus from a self that is somewhat *false* or unreal. In the interpretation I pointed out that he was hoping to be able to join up this split in himself in his relation to me. At this point he sank into a withdrawn state for a brief period, and then was able to tell me what had happened when he was withdrawn; *it had become dark, clouds had gathered and it had started to rain; the rain had beaten down on his naked body.* On this occasion I was able to put into this cruel, ruthless environment himself, a newborn baby, and to point out to him what kind of environment he might expect should he become integrated and independent. Here was the "medium" interpretation in reversed form.

Episode 5

The fifth detail comes from the material presented after a break of nine weeks which included my summer holiday.

The patient came back after the long break saying that he was not sure why he had come back; and that he found it difficult to start again. The main thing he reported was a continued difficulty in making a spontaneous remark of any kind either at home or among friends. He could only join in a conversation, and this was easiest when there were two others present who were taking the responsibility by talking to each other. If he made a remark he felt he was usurping the function of one of the parents (that is to say in the primal scene) whereas what he needed was to be recognized by the parents as an infant. He told me enough about himself to keep me in touch with current affairs.

The fifth episode was reached through consideration of an ordinary dream.

The night after this first session he had a dream which he reported the following day. It was unusually vivid. He went on a weekend trip abroad, *going on the Saturday and returning on the Monday.* The main thing about the trip was that he would meet a patient who had gone abroad from a hospital for treatment. (This turned out to be a patient who has had a limb amputated. There were other important details that do not specifically concern the subject of this communication.)

My first interpretation was the comment that in the dream *he goes and comes back.* It is this comment that I wish to report, since it joins up with my comments on the first two episodes in which I had provided a medium and a lap, and with that on the fourth episode in which I put an individual in the bad environment that had been hallucinated. I followed with a fuller interpretation, namely that the dream expresses the two aspects of his relationship to analysis; in one he goes away and comes back, and in the other he goes abroad, the patient from hospital standing for this part of himself; he goes and keeps in touch with the patient, which means that he is trying to break down the dissociation between these two aspects of himself. My patient followed this up by saying that in the dream he was particularly keen to make contact with the patient, implying that he was becoming aware of dissociation or splitting in himself, and wishing to become integrated.

This episode could begin in the form of a dream dreamed away from analysis because it contained both elements together, the withdrawn self and the environmental provision. The medium aspect of the analyst had become introjected.

I further interpreted: the dream showed how the patient dealt with the holiday; he had been able to enjoy the experience of escaping from the treatment while at the same time he knew that although he had gone away he would come back. In this way the particularly long break which might have been serious in this type of patient was not a great disturbance. The patient made a particular point that this matter of going off and away was closely associated in his mind with the idea of making an original remark or doing anything spontaneous. He then told me that he had had, on the very day of the dream, a return of a special fear of his, that he would find that he had sud-denly kissed a person; it would be anyone who happened to be next him; this might turn out to be a man. He would not make such a fool of himself if he found he had un-expectedly kissed a woman.

He now began to sink more deeply into the analytic situation. He felt he was a little child at home, and if he spoke it would be wrong; because he would then be in the parents' place. There was a feeling of hopelessness about having a spontaneous gesture met (and this fits in with what is known of the home situation). Much deeper material now emerged and he felt that there were people going in and out of the doors; my interpretation that this was associated with breathing was supported by fur-ther associations on his part. Ideas are like breath; also they are like children, and if I do nothing to them he feels they are abandoned. His great fear is of the abandoned child or the abandoned idea or remark, or the wasted gesture of a child.

Episode 6

A week later the patient (unexpectedly from his point of view), came up against the fact that he had never accepted his father's death. This followed a dream in which his father had been present and had been able to discuss current sexual problems with him in a sensible and free way. Two days later he came and reported that he had been seriously disturbed because he had had a *headache,* quite different from any that he had ever had before. It dated more or less from the time of the previous session two days earlier. This headache was temporal and sometimes frontal and *it was as if it were situated just outside the head.* It was constant and made him feel ill and if he could have got sympathy from his wife he would not have come to analysis but would have gone to bed. He was bothered because as a doctor he could see that this was certainly a functional disorder and yet it could not be explained in terms of physiology. (It was therefore like a madness.)

In the course of the hour I was able to see what interpretation was applicable and I said: "The pain being just *outside* the head represents your *need to have your head held* as you would naturally have it held if you were in a state of deep emotional distress as a child." At first this did not mean very much to him but gradually it became clear that the person who was more likely to have held his head at the right moment and in the right way when he was a child was not his mother but his father. In other words, after his father's death there was no one to hold his head should he break down into experiencing grief.

I linked up my interpretation with the key interpretation of the medium, and grad-ually he felt that my idea about the hands was right. He reported a momentary with-drawal with a feeling that I had a machine which I could activate and which would sup-ply the trappings of sympathetic management. This meant to him that it was important that I did not hold his head actually and in fact, as this would have been a mechanical application of technical principles. *The important thing was that I understood immedi-ately what he needed.*

At the end of the hour he surprised himself by remembering that he had spent the afternoon holding a child's head. The child had been having a minor operation un-der local anaesthetic and this had taken more than an hour. He had done all he could to help the child but without much success. What he had felt the child must need was that his head should be held.

He now felt in rather a deep way that my interpretation had been the thing for which he had come to analysis on that day, and he was therefore almost grateful to his wife that she had offered no sympathy whatever and had not held his head as she might have done.

Summary

The idea behind this communication is that if we know about regression in the analytic hour, we can meet it immediately and in this way enable certain patients who are not too ill to make the necessary regressions in short phases, perhaps even almost momentarily. I would say that *in the withdrawn state a patient is holding the self* and that if immediately the withdrawn state appears *the analyst can hold the patient,* then what would otherwise have been a withdrawal state becomes a regression. The advantage of a *regression* is that it carries with it the opportunity for correction of inadequate adaptation-to-need in the past history of the patient, that is to say, in the patient's infancy management. By contrast the *withdrawn* state is not profitable and when the patient recovers from a withdrawn state he or she is not changed.

Whenever we understand a patient in a deep way and show that we do so by a correct and well-timed interpretation we are in fact holding the patient, and taking part in a relationship in which the patient is in some degree regressed and dependent.

It is commonly thought that there is some danger in the regression of a patient during psycho-analysis. The danger does not lie in the regression but in the analyst's unreadiness to meet the regression and the dependence which belongs to it. When an analyst has had the experience that makes him confident in his management of regression, then it is probably true to say that the more quickly the analyst accepts the regression and meets it fully the less likely is it that the patient will need to enter into an illness with regressive qualities.

SUMMARY AND EVALUATION

Summary.   With object relations theory, the shift—from instinct to relation—is what emerges most substantially. All of this is perhaps best captured by Fairbairn's (1954) phrase "libido is primarily object-seeking . . . rather than pleasure-seeking" (p. 82). To understand individuals, then, requires understanding their self-representations, object representations, and object relationships. This ultimately means understanding individuals' earliest relationships with the primary caretaker, typically the mother. From this earliest experience, "templates" or "schemas" are laid down—which influence and affect later ways of perceiving, thinking, feeling, and relating. Thus, instinct is not that which is decisive or determining; instead, it is now relationships—how they affected self-development, how they got taken in, how they got incorporated into our being.

Psychopathology can all be traced back to these early relationships and their failure. "[I]t is to disturbances in the object-relationships of the developing ego that we must look for the ultimate origin of all psychopathological conditions" (Fairbairn, 1954, p. 82). For Winnicott, "environmental deficiency" or lack of "good-enough" mothering was *the* problem. But Winnicott, in contrast to Fairbairn and Guntrip, accepted the view of there being oedipal as well as pre-oedipal pathology. Fairbairn and Guntrip saw everything ultimately going back to the pre-oedipal period.

Psychotherapy is, to use Guntrip's words, "replacement therapy." It involves replacing bad objects with good objects. It essentially involves providing the patient with a relationship in which "frozen parts" of the self can be unfrozen, in which derailed development can be put back on track, in which "rebirth" of the self can occur. The treatment requires first and foremost a good analyst-patient relationship; this is *the* curative factor. "[P]sychotherapy is simply the application of the fundamental importance of personal relationships, in the sense of using good relationships to undo the harm done by bad ones" (Guntrip, 1973, p. 194). Regression and analysis of the transference are important parts of treatment. The "good-enough" mother-infant relationship can be seen as the model for the analyst-patient relationship. The analyst corrects, belatedly, what the "not-good-enough" mother failed to do originally.

Evaluation.   Object relations theory has some definite positive, attractive features. Much of what we like best about it can be summed up thus: "The emergence of object relations . . . graced psychoanalytic theory with a more positive view of human nature . . . increased attention to subjective experience and a greater inclination to believe that people can control their own destiny . . ." (Weiner, 1991, p. 33; cf. Blatt & Lerner, 1991). Object relations moved the primary focus from instincts to relationships. By doing so, it opened up a whole new realm of experience that had not been given its due in traditional analytic theory and that is critical for understanding personality development, psychopathology, and cure.

Object relations theory also gives us reason to see that pathology can be pre-oedipal as well as oedipal in origin. The object relational emphasis on pre-oedipal phenomena has enabled us to get a far better handle on early development, how it unfolds, how it is stunted, and how it contributes to overall growth (e.g., Mahler, Pine, & Bergman, 1975). This emphasis has further enabled us to extend our theoretical lines toward an explication of pre-oedipal pathology (see Horner, 1984, p. 37).

We also like the object relational emphasis on the "good-enough" therapeutic relationship, in which the analyst is empathic, attuned to the patient's needs, sensitive, and compassionate. Going along with this is the recognition that the patient comes first and should not be subordinated to any "analytic technique," that analytic neutrality can actually be more mistake than anything. "If the analyst persists in being, in reality, a merely objective scientific intelligence with no personal feeling for the patient, he will repeat on the patient the original trauma which laid the foundations of the illness" (Guntrip, 1953, p. 119). Such thinking has merit in our view.

However, it is not clear that practice follows or adheres to the principle that therapy *is* the relationship. Techniques appear to occupy a prominent place. There are certainly many criticisms that can be brought to bear on object relations theory. For example, Holt (1985), in his highly critical, stinging examination of psychoanalytic theory, referred to object relations work as a current fad. He said that

> Fairbairn (1952a), Guntrip (1969), and Winnicott (1958) . . . all incorporate far too many of the defective parts of psychoanalytic theory to make their corrections much more than cosmetic. . . . Moreover . . . they show the same familiar obliviousness to the need for cogent evidence, the same willingness to accept unspecified "clinical ex-

perience" as a sufficient factual basis for confident assertions of fact as the traditional Freudians whom they claim to have transcended, but on scientifically unacceptable grounds (pp. 304–305)

Again, this latter statement relates back to something we addressed earlier about what seems to be the case for many Freudian (Chapter 1) as well as Jungian (Chapter 2) analysts, that being the tendency to rely all too heavily on anecdotal-type case descriptions as confirmations of their theory and treatment reality. And, again, the problem of such "therapist evidence" is that "the lack of corroborating evidence [from the patient] can lead to subjective distortions" (Hill, 1989, p. 18).

In much of the object relations thinking reviewed here, there appears to be a tendency to place the locus of responsibility for any and all pathology on the mother. Without question, mothers can have a substantial, decisive influence on growth and development. But what about the role of the father—who Fairbairn (1954) referred to as that "parent without breasts"? Does he have a role at all? Isn't he more than just a "breastless being"? Can he not have a substantial, decisive influence—be it for the good or for the bad—as well? Greenberg and Mitchell (1983) have made note of the tendency for some object relations theorists, particularly Fairbairn, Winnicott, and Guntrip, to cast the infant and developing child as the "innocent victim" in the hands of the "victimizing, bad mother." They facetiously make the point that, since all pathology goes back to the mother, the ultimate source of all psychopathology must be Eve—who in the Garden of Eden failed us all. This view about pathology has been referred to as "unpersuasive and overly simplistic" (Greenberg & Mitchell, 1983, p. 181).

Going back to the preceding chapter on Adler, a couple of ideas from there seem relevant to our discussion here. Adler spoke of the creative self—that, though we were subject to influence by our environment, there is a creative part to us that has a say too. Where is such a creative self in object relations thinking? Adler also gave attention to siblings and their potential influence on personality development. With object relations thought, it seems to focus all too exclusively on the mother-infant dyad and to exclude or greatly restrict any mention of other family members. Again, do they not matter?

Next, how accurate is it to compare the analyst-patient relationship with that of the mother-infant relationship? Eagle and Wolitzky (1982) have stated that "the fact is . . . that an adult patient, however disturbed and regressed, is not a chronological infant. Hence, the parallel between the therapeutic relationship and the mother-child relationship cannot be complete" (p. 371). To that, they add the following useful statement:

A more meaningful comparison between the parent-child relationship and the therapeutic one is, as Strupp (1976) points out, likely to center on the fact that the patient is in a dependent relationship, is subject to the influences that such a relationship entails, and is encouraged to substitute inner control and autonomy for such external influences—a process not unlike socialization. (Eagle & Wolitzky, 1982, p. 372)

Furthermore, it could certainly be maintained that there is a certain arrogance that attends the parent-child/analyst-patient analogy. After all, the mother has "done it all wrong." She was a failure. But the analyst can "do it all right." Or, to paraphrase some of Fairbairn's and Guntrip's therapy/religion comparisons, the mother is the Devil, the analyst is God—the savior sent to "save" patients from their inner devils, which are but a product of the ultimate source of evil: the Mother-Devil. There is, as Greenberg and Mitchell (1983) have noted, something "overly simplistic" about all this.

Some other criticisms of object relations theory and therapy are that its concepts are imprecise and that there is a lack of clarity about the "how" and "why" of certain key treatment foci. Again, Morris Eagle has raised these concerns. "Although ideas such as replacing bad objects with good objects are evocative and one has a general sense of what they mean, they are far from precise. And Fairbairn does not attempt to make them more precise" (Eagle & Wolitzky, 1992, p. 130). With regard to the second point above, Eagle (1984) has stated that "just how and why presumed regression by a chronological adult to certain early development points should lead to a resumption of psychological development and rebirth is not made entirely clear by object relations theorists" (p. 92). Imprecision and lack of clarity seem to be basic criticisms often leveled against psychoanalytic theory in general (see Holt, 1985).

In developing a relational structure model and in repudiating the drive structure model, might some object relations theorists actually have gone too far? There are certainly those who think so, with Otto Kernberg being one of them. Kernberg (1976) has attempted to blend the drive, ego, and object relations psychologies in his theorizing; he does not see those frames of reference as incompatible.

> Guntrip . . . has recently extended Fairbairn's thinking into a total opposition to psychoanalytic instinct theory, denying in the process the importance of instincts in determining personality in general. I disagree with this view and certainly do not consider object-relations theory to be opposed in any way to the modern conception of instincts or to psychoanalytic instinct theory. (p. 119)

Whether the object relations theorists might have gone too far is a good question, which is still open to debate.

What of research and the object relations approach? As mentioned before, one problem has been the tendency to rely too much on anecdotal case descriptions—which are unilateral in perspective and subject to possible bias and distortion. But some interesting, novel research work incorporating object relations thought can be found in the literature—in the efforts of Weiss and Sampson (1986) and their San Francisco Psychotherapy Research Group.

> Weiss and Sampson's . . . unconscious control theory can be seen as an extension and elaboration of ego psychology, in the sense that a major emphasis is placed on unconscious ego processes of belief, judgment, testing, and so on. However, unconscious-control theory is also interactional and object relational, in the sense that unconscious pathogenic beliefs are acquired through interactions with and communications from parental figures and are tested in treatment through interaction with the therapist. (Eagle & Wolitzky, 1992, pp. 142–143)

The theory of the Weiss/Sampson group, while not designed to focus so much so on the techniques of therapy, is designed to explain how therapy works (Silberschatz, Curtis, Sampson, & Weiss, 1991, p. 56). There is concern about the patient's plan, that is, an often unconscious strategy that patient's use in therapy to disconfirm their pathogenic beliefs, the testing of those pathogenic beliefs in treatment, and the therapist's passing the tests put forth by the patient. Thus far, research has supported Weiss and Sampson's ideas about patient plans, patient tests, what happens when the therapist passes or fails those tests. For a description of their research program, its accomplishments, and its future directions, see Sampson and Weiss (1992), Silberschatz et al. (1991), Weiss (1988, 1993), and Weiss and Sampson (1986).

But with the promise of the work of the Weiss/Sampson/San Francisco group recognized, still what about the effectiveness of object relations therapy? Perhaps the best we can say here is again to quote Eagle and Wolitzky (1992), who had the following to say about object relations as well as other analytic models of therapy: "[T]o what extent the use of one or another or some combination of these models is in fact associated with variations in the effectiveness of treatment outcome . . . [is] among the [most] important questions we need to answer in the future" (p. 151).

And what may we say about the future of object relations theory and therapy? Object relations, at least at this point in time, appears to be highly popular and well received in many analytic circles. Going back to two of our principals, many recent books on Fairbairn and Winnicott and their thinking have been published (Docker-Drysdale, 1989; Giovachinni, 1990; Goldman, 1993; Grotstein & Rinsley, 1993; Hughes, 1989; Little, 1990; Sutherland, 1989; Winnicott & Shepherd, 1989). Books on object relations family therapy, couple therapy, group and individual therapy can easily be found (e.g., Cashdan, 1988; Horner, 1991; Scharff & Scharff, 1987, 1991, 1992). Workshops and seminars on this subject abound. Indeed, we do not currently lack for interest in and availability of materials about object relations.

But is object relations, as Holt (1985) has said, only a fad? In our opinion, no. Object relations presents us with an alternative, viable vision about development, change, and cure. There is much meat to be found in the object relational work of Fairbairn, Winnicott, and Guntrip. As for others we have not covered here, for example, Melanie Klein, Harry Stack Sullivan, and Michael Balint, there is much meat to be found in their work as well. The influence of these people's efforts on theory and therapy will continue to be felt, analyzed, explored, and extended. Continued efforts, we believe, will be made to apply object relations therapy further to varied therapeutic problems and varied treatment modalities, to consider how its concepts apply to and can be integrated with other theories, and to adapt its concepts and vision to more brief treatment models. We believe object relational work is here to stay, that it will not pass away from the psychoanalytic scene as might be the case for some passing fad.

But with that said, let us conclude this chapter and this entire first section by drawing once more from the fine book by Greenberg and Mitchell (1983). Here is what they have to say about the future of psychoanalysis—the relational/structure (or object relations) model and drive structure (or Freudian) model.

> It is difficult to predict the future direction of a discipline as complex as psychoanalysis. It may be that the drive/structure model will prove compelling and resilient enough to incorporate within its boundaries all the data and concepts generated by the study of object relations. In that case the relational structure models will wither away, having served a useful purpose in prodding and provoking an expansion of the earlier approach. On the other hand, relational models may prove to be more and more compelling, expanding and combining to provide a more encompassing and enticing

framework for theory and practice. If so, the drive model will slowly lose adherents, becoming an important, elegant, but no longer functional technique.

We suspect that neither of these two scenarios will come to pass. The paradox of man's dual nature as a highly individual yet social being runs too deep and is too entrenched within our civilization to be capable of simple resolution in one direction or the other. It seems more likely that both the drive model and the relational model will persist, undergoing continual revision and transformation, and that the rich interplay between these two visions of human experience will generate creative dialogue. (pp. 407–408)

Thus far, both models have persisted, both continue to be subject to revision, and the rich interplay between them has certainly generated creative dialogue. We do not see any of that changing in the near future.

REFERENCES

Blanck, G., & Blanck, R. (1974). *Ego psychology: Theory and practice.* New York: Columbia University Press.

Blanck, G., & Blanck, R. (1979). *Ego psychology II: Psychoanalytic developmental psychology.* New York: Columbia University Press.

Blanck, R., & Blanck, G. (1986). *Beyond ego psychology: Developmental object relations theory.* New York: Columbia University Press.

Blatt, S. J., & Lerner, H. (1991). Psychodynamic perspectives on personality theory. In M. Hersen, A. E. Kazdin, & A. S. Bellack (Eds.). *The clinical psychology handbook* (2nd ed., pp. 147–169). New York: Pergamon.

Butler, S. F., & Strupp, H. H. (1991). Psychodynamic psychotherapy. In M. Hersen, A. E. Kazdin, & A. S. Bellack (Eds.). *The clinical psychology handbook* (2nd ed., pp. 519–533). New York: Pergamon.

Cashdan, S. (1988). *Object relations therapy: Using the relationship.* New York: W. W. Norton.

Docker-Drysdale, B. (1989). *Provision of primary experience: Winnicottian work with children.* New York: Columbia University Press.

Dorpat, T. L. (1981). Basic concepts and terms in object relations theories. In S. Tuttman, C. Kay, & M. Zimmerman (Eds.). *Object and self: A developmental approach* (pp. 149–178). New York: International Universities Press.

Eagle, M. N. (1984). Psychoanalysis and modern psychodynamic theories. In N. Endler & J. Hunt (Eds.). *Personality and the behavioral disorders* (pp. 73–112). New York: Wiley.

Eagle, M. N., & Wolitzky, D. L. (1982). Therapeutic influences in dynamic psychotherapy: A review and synthesis. In S. Slipp (Ed.). *Curative factors in dynamic psychotherapy* (pp. 349–378). New York: McGraw-Hill.

Eagle, M. N., & Wolitzky, D. L. (1992). Psychoanalytic theories of psychotherapy. In D. K. Freedheim (Ed.). *History of psychotherapy: A century of change* (pp. 109–158). Washington, DC: American Psychological Association.

Fairbairn, W. R. D. (1941). A revised psychopathology of the psychoses and neuroses. *International Journal of Psycho-analysis, 22,* 250–279.

Fairbairn, W. R. D. (1952a). *Psychoanalytic studies of the personality.* London: Tavistock Publications, Ltd.

Fairbairn, W. R. D. (1952b). Theoretical and experimental aspects of psychoanalysis. *British Journal of Medical Psychology, 25,* 122–127.

Fairbairn, W. R. D. (1954). *An object-relations theory of the personality.* New York: Basic Books.

Fairbairn, W. R. D. (1955). Observations in defence of the object-relations theory of the personality. *British Journal of Medical Psychology, 28,* 144–156.

Fairbairn, W. R. D. (1958). On the nature and aims of psycho-analytical treatment. *International Journal of Psycho-analysis, 39,* 374–385.

Fairbairn, W. R. D. (1963). Synopsis of an object-relations theory of the personality. *International Journal of Psycho-analysis, 44,* 224–225.

Giovachinni, P. (Ed.). (1990). *Tactics and techniques in psychoanalytic therapy: The implications of Winnicott's contributions* (vol. 3). New York: Jason Aronson.

Gitelson, M. (1952). The emotional position of the analyst in the psychoanalytical situation. *International Journal of Psycho-analysis, 33,* 1–10.

Goldman, D. (Ed.). (1993). *In one's bones: The clinical genius of Winnicott.* Northvale, NJ: Jason Aronson.

Greenberg, J. R., & Mitchell, S. A. (1983). *Object relations in psychoanalytic theory.* Cambridge, MA: Harvard University Press.

Grotstein, J. S., & Rinsley, D. B. (Eds.). (1993). *Fairbairn and the origins of object relations.* New York: Plenum.

Guntrip, H. (1949). *Psychology for ministers and social workers.* London: Independent Press.

Guntrip, H. (1953). The therapeutic factor in psychotherapy. *British Journal of Medical Psychology, 26,* 115–132.

Guntrip, H. (1957). *Psychotherapy and religion.* New York: Harper.

Guntrip, H. (1961). *Personality structure and human interaction: The developing synthesis of psycho-dynamic theory.* New York: International Universities Press.

Guntrip, H. (1966). *Clinical studies of the schizoid personality.* London: Hogarth Press.

Guntrip, H. (1969). *Schizoid phenomena, object-relations and the self.* New York: International Universities Press.

Guntrip, H. (1973). *Psychoanalytic theory, therapy, and the self.* New York: Basic Books.

Guntrip, H. (1975). My experience of analysis with Fairbairn and Winnicott. *International Review of Psycho-analysis, 2,* 145–156.

Hamilton, N. G. (1988). *Self and others: Object relations theory in practice.* Northvale, NJ: Jason Aronson.

Hartmann, H. (1939/1958). *Ego psychology and the problem of adaptation.* New York: International Universities Press.

Hazell, J. (Ed.). (1994). *Personal relations therapy: The collected papers of H.J.S. Guntrip.* Northvale, NJ: Jason Aronson.

Hill, C. E. (1989). *Therapist techniques and client outcomes.* Newbury Park, CA: Sage.

Holt, R. R. (1985). The current status of psychoanalytic theory. *Psychoanalytic Psychology, 2,* 289–315.

Horner, A. J. (1984). *Object relations and the developing ego in therapy* (2nd ed.). New York: Jason Aronson.

Horner, A. J. (1991). *Psychoanalytic object relations therapy.* Northvale, NJ: Jason Aronson.

Hughes, J. M. (1989). *Reshaping the psychoanalytic domain: The work of Melanie Klein, W.R.D. Fairbairn, & D. W. Winnicott.* Berkeley, CA: University of California Press.

Kernberg, O. F. (1976). *Object relations theory and clinical psychoanalysis.* New York: Jason Aronson.

Khan, M. M. R. (1971). Obituary: Donald W. Winnicott. *International Journal of Psycho-analysis, 52,* 225–226.

Little, M. (1990). *Psychotic anxieties and containment: A personal record of an analysis with Winnicott.* Northvale, NJ: Jason Aronson.

Mahler, M., Pine, F., & Bergman, A. (1975). *The psychological birth of the human infant.* New York: Basic Books.

Mendez, A. M., & Fine, H. J. (1976). A short history of the British School of object relations and ego psychology. *Bulletin of the Menninger Clinic, 40,* 357–382.

Padel, J. H. (1978). Object relational approach. In J. L. Fosshage & C. A. Loew (Eds.). *Dream interpretation: A comparative study* (pp. 125–148). New York: Spectrum Publications.

Phillips, A. (1988). *Winnicott.* Cambridge, MA: Harvard University Press.

Pine, F. (1985). *Developmental theory and clinical process.* New Haven, CT: Yale University Press.

Rapaport, D. (1959). An historical survey of psychoanalysis. *Psychological Issues, 1,* 5–17.

Rodman, F. R. (Ed.). (1987). *The spontaneous gesture: Selected letters of D. W. Winnicott.* Cambridge, MA: Harvard University Press.

Rycroft, C. (1973). *A critical dictionary of psychoanalysis.* Totowa, NJ: Littlefield, Adams & Co.

Sampson, H., & Weiss, J. (1992). The Mt. Zion psychotherapy research group. In D. K. Freedheim (Ed.). *History of psychotherapy: A century of change* (pp. 432–436). Washington, DC: American Psychological Association.

Scharff, D., & Scharff, J. S. (1987). *Object relations family therapy.* Northvale, NJ: Jason Aronson.

Scharff, D., & Scharff, J. S. (1991). *Object relations couple therapy.* Northvale, NJ: Jason Aronson.

Scharff, J. S., & Scharff, D. (1992). *Scharff notes: A primer of object relations therapy.* Northvale, NJ: Jason Aronson.

Silberschatz, G., Curtis, J. T., Sampson, H., & Weiss, J. (1991). Mount Zion Hospital and Medical Center: Research on the process of change in psychotherapy. In L. E. Beutler & M. Crago (Eds.). *Psychotherapy research: An international review of programmatic studies* (pp. 56–64). Washington, DC: American Psychological Association.

Sperry, L. (1992). The centrality of life style convictions across psychotherapy systems. *The NASAP Newsletter, 25* (7), 3–4.

Strupp, H. (1976). The nature of the therapeutic influence and its basic ingredient. In A. Burton (Ed.). *What makes behavior change possible?* (pp. 96–112). New York: Brunner/Mazel.

Sutherland, J. D. (1965). Obituary: W.R.D. Fairbairn. *International Journal of Psycho-analysis, 46,* 245–247.

Sutherland, J. D. (1989). *Fairbairn's journey into the interior.* London: Free Association Press.

Thompson, C. (1957). *Psychoanalysis: Evolution and development.* New York: Grove Press.

Tizard, J. P. M. (1971). Obituary: Donald W. Winnicott. *International Journal of Psycho-analysis, 52,* 226–227.

Tuttmann, S. (1981). A historical survey of the development of object relations concepts in psychoanalytic theory. In S. Tuttman, C. Kay, & M. Zimmerman (Eds.), *Object and self: A developmental approach* (pp. 3–51). New York: International Universities Press.

Watts, R. E. (1992). Biblical agape as a model of social interest. *Individual Psychology, 48,* 35–40.

Weiner, I. B. (1991). Theoretical foundations of clinical psychology. In M. Hersen, A. E. Kazdin, & A. S. Bellack (Eds.). *The clinical psychology handbook* (2nd ed., pp. 26–44). New York: Pergamon.

Weiss, J. (1988). Testing hypotheses about unconscious mental functioning. *International Journal of Psycho-analysis, 69,* 87–95.

Weiss, J. (1993). *How psychotherapy works: Process and technique.* New York: Guilford Press.

Weiss, J., & Sampson, H. (1986). *The psychoanalytic process: Theory, clinical observations, and empirical research.* New York: Guilford Press.

Winnicott, C. (1978). D.W.W.: A reflection. In S.A. Grolnick, L. Barkin, & W. Muensterberger (Eds.). *Between reality and fantasy: Transitional objects and phenomena* (pp. 17–33). New York: Jason Aronson.

Winnicott, C., & Shephard, R. (Eds.). (1989). *Psycho-analytic explorations, D. W. Winnicott.* Cambridge, MA: Harvard University Press.

Winnicott, D. W. (1931). *Clinical notes on disorders of childhood.* London: Heinemann.

Winnicott, D. W. (1953). Transitional objects and transitional phenomena. *International Journal of Psycho-analysis, 34,* 89–97.

Winnicott, D. W. (1957). *The child and the family: First relationships.* London: Tavistock.

Winnicott, D. W. (1958). *Collected papers: Through paediatrics to psycho-analysis.* New York: Basic Books.

Winnicott, D. W. (1965a). *The family and individual development.* London: Tavistock.

Winnicott, D. W. (1965b). *The maturational processes and the facilitating environment: Studies in the theory of emotional development.* New York: International Universities Press.

Winnicott, D. W. (1971). *Playing and reality.* London: Tavistock.

Winnicott, D. W. (1975). *Through paediatrics to psycho-analysis.* New York: Basic Books.

Winnicott, D. W. (1986). *Holding and interpretation: Fragment of an analysis.* New York: Grove Press.

Winnicott, D. W. (1987). *Home is where we start from: Essays by a psychoanalyst.* London: Pelican Books.

Winnicott, D. W. (1988). *Human nature.* London: Free Association Books.

Winnicott, D. W. (1992). *Through paediatrics to psycho-analysis: Collected papers.* New York: Brunner/Mazel.

part two

LEARNING THEORY APPROACHES

Learning may be defined as changes in behavior that are not due to native response tendencies, maturation, or temporary states of the organism, for example, fatigue or drugs (Hilgard & Bower, 1975). Psychotherapy is concerned with behavior change and must, therefore, involve learning and learning theory. Psychotherapy would thus be an application of principles of learning or learning theory.

This reasoning may be essentially acceptable to many therapists, but the actual situation is not as simple as such reasoning may suggest. Most approaches to psychotherapy have not developed from learning theory. Although it would appear that any approach must be consistent with or explainable by learning theory, most approaches have not been systematically evaluated from this point of view.

Two reasons apparently account for this lack of rapprochement. First, learning theory is still in a stage where it cannot be automatically applied widely to practical situations, particularly to situations involving abnormalities of behavior or deviation from normal behavior. While experimentation and research have burgeoned beyond the laboratory, they are limited for the most part to relatively simple behaviors in controlled situations.

Kimble (1967), summarizing the situation regarding conditioning, wrote:

It may, some day, be known whether the laws of conditioning do or do not explain (say) psychopathological behavior. But that day is still far in the future. For the time being all that is possible is to attempt the explanation of complex phenomena in simpler terms. It is to be expected that the resulting explanations will be incomplete and imperfect. Complex behavior, if it is explainable at all in these terms, certainly involves the simultaneous operation of many principles of conditioning. Unfortunately, these principles are not exactly known, and we know even less about the way in which they combine and function together. (p. 436)

This statement should be kept in mind when reading accounts of therapy based on learning theory and principles. These accounts usually state or imply that the methods are based on known and experimentally demonstrated principles of learning.

Second, it is not possible to speak of *a* learning theory or *a* theory of learning. There is no single theory, but many theories usually related, in the case of human beings, to limited areas of behavior, such as paired-associates learning of nonsense syllables or learning a simple psychomotor performance. Thus, when the claim is made that a particular approach or method of psychotherapy is an application of, or is based on, learning theory or learning principles, one must ask, "What theory?" or "What principles?"

The two major sources in learning for the various methods and techniques of learning based approaches to psychotherapy are classical (or respondent) conditioning and operant (or instrumental) conditioning. Classical conditioning derives from the work of Pavlov. Although others before him had recognized and studied conditioning, he was the first to study it systematically and intensively. The paradigm for classical conditioning is the presence of an unconditioned stimulus that automatically evokes an unconditioned response and a conditioned stimulus that evokes a conditioned response—which is similar to, or a part of, the unconditioned response—when paired with (presented shortly before) the unconditioned stimulus.

Three aspects of classical conditioning are overlooked or ignored by many of those who apply this model to complex behavior in counseling or psychotherapy. The first is that the conditioned response is not identical with the unconditioned response, sometimes being quite different and constituting an anticipatory response. The second is that (as Pavlov noted in his work with dogs) the specific response is not the only behavior evoked by the unconditioned or the conditioned stimulus; the total organism responds, so that there are what might be termed "side effects" in conditioning. The third is that in laboratory work on conditioning, the subject is in a situation from which it cannot escape by developing avoidance (or instrumental) responses.

In operant conditioning, voluntarily or spontaneously emitted (operant) behavior is strengthened by positive reinforcement (reward) or is discouraged by negative reinforcement, which is a stimulus whose removal increases the probability of the behavior it follows, by lack of reinforcement (failure to reward either positively or negatively), or by punishment. The terms *operant* and *instrumental* derive from the concept that the conditioned behavior operates on the environment or is instrumental in obtaining the reinforcement or the reward. In this sense, the behavior appears to be beyond the control of the experimenter. Behavior, it is emphasized, is controlled by its consequences. Yet, since the experimenter controls the consequences or the application of reinforcers or punishment, he or she does control the behavior of the subject. There is an implication of cognitive awareness and choice, yet awareness is not necessary for conditioning to occur; in fact, strict behaviorists reject the existence of choice.

Classical and operant conditioning are not distinctly separable. In classical conditioning, the unconditioned stimulus follows the conditioned stimulus. Thus, the unconditioned stimulus may be seen, in operant conditioning terms, as reinforcing the association between the conditioned stimulus and the response. In operant conditioning, the reinforcement follows the responses that it is desired to strengthen, and this response may be said to become associated with the action (or stimulus) that preceded it. In operant conditioning, the voluntary, spontaneously emitted behavior that is said to "produce" the reinforcement may be seen as the unconditioned stimulus. In classical conditioning, the unconditioned stimulus is independent of the subject's behavior. As Yates (1970) pointed out, if a classical conditioning experiment, in which a conditioned stimulus is associated with a shock leading to a dog's involuntarily lifting its paw when the conditioned stimulus is presented alone, is changed so that the animal is allowed to escape or avoid the shock by lifting its paw before the unconditioned stimulus has occurred, then classical aversive conditioning becomes instrumental, or operant, aversive conditioning.

Attempts have been made to combine or integrate the two types of conditioning into one model. Pavlov tried to reduce instrumental conditioning to classical conditioning. Hull's system sought to reduce classical conditioning to instrumental conditioning. Mowrer (1947), who earlier had proposed a two-factor theory of learning based on distinction between classical and instrumental conditioning, later attempted to bring them together under the classical position (Mowrer, 1960).

Concern about the relationship between learning and psychotherapy dates back many years (Bandura, 1961; Kanfer, 1961; Magaret, 1950; Shaffer, 1947; Shaw, 1946; Shoben, 1948, 1949, 1953). The early discussions were mainly concerned with reinforcement theory and were mainly limited to interpretation or translation of methods of psychotherapy, such as psychoanalysis, into learning theory terms. The work of Dollard and Miller (1950) is classic and is, therefore, included in this section. Two other systematic attempts are those of the Pepinskys (1954) and of Pascal (1959). Phillips's (1956) interference theory approach is also a variant of reinforcement theory.

In contrast to these essentially reinforcement theory approaches is Salter's (1949) application of classical conditioning. Wolpe's (1958) method, included here, is also based essentially on classical conditioning. The classical conditioning approach to modifying human behavior dates back to the work of Jones (1924) with Peter and the rabbit, under the influence of Watson (Watson & Rayner, 1920).

Learning approaches to psychotherapy are not restricted to either the classical or the instrumental paradigm, however. Salter is probably closest to the classical approach. Wolpe is less restricted to classical conditioning, although his theoretical base derives essentially from this paradigm. Dollard and Miller, developing their work from Hull's theory, emphasize reinforcement and are thus closer to the operant paradigm.

The recent work in operant conditioning derives from Skinner (1938, 1953). Operant conditioning was first considered in relation to psychotherapy in terms of verbal conditioning in interviews (Greenspoon, 1950, 1955; Hildum & Brown, 1956; Kanfer, 1966; Krasner, 1958, 1962, 1963, 1965; Salzinger, 1959, 1969). This work has not been developed into an integrated systematic approach to psychotherapy, which is no doubt because of the atheoretical and operationalistic influence of Skinner.

The use of operant conditioning in modifying the behavior of hospitalized psychiatric patients was apparently first explored by Peters (1952, 1955; Peters & Jenkins, 1954) and by Lindsley (1956; Lindsley & Skinner, 1954). Its application in institutional settings, including the classroom, has burgeoned tremendously since then.

The term *behavior therapy* probably was first used by Lindsley (Lindsley, Skinner, & Solomon, 1953). (Lazarus [1958] and Eysenck [1959] later used the term independently of Lindsley and of each other.) It has come into common use and refers to the application of a wide variety of techniques derived from or related to learning principles or theory in order to modify more or less specific abnormal behaviors, both in the therapy interview and outside. The term *behavior modification* is also widely used, often interchangeably with *behavior therapy,* particularly in this country, to refer to operant conditioning methods as distinguished from the behavior therapy of Wolpe or, more generally, to cover the application of learning principles in a wide variety of situations outside the therapy interview. Here we are limiting our concern to interview-mediated behavior change; programs or systems for changing behavior in institutions, such as token economies, are not considered.

Research and writing in this area proliferated rapidly in the 1960s, with new journals being established to accommodate reports of research and case studies (for example, *Journal of the Experimental Analysis of Behavior, Behavior Research and Therapy, Journal of Applied Behavior Analysis*), edited books being published to provide surveys and reviews (Eysenck, 1960, 1964; Franks, 1964, 1970; Krasner & Ullmann, 1965; Krumboltz & Thoreson, 1969; Levis, 1970; Osipow & Walsh, 1970; Rubin & Franks, 1969; Ullmann & Krasner, 1965), and case studies and books being written to include more extensive treatments of the field (Bandura, 1969; Eysenck & Rachman, 1965; Kanfer & Phillips, 1970; Yates, 1970). The extent of the activity and the implications for psychotherapy and behavior change have led to the application of the word *revolution* to the movement (Krasner, 1966; Krumboltz, 1966). Levis (1970) suggested that behavior therapy constitutes the fourth revolution (following Pinel, Freud, and community mental health).

Unlike earlier approaches to psychotherapy, and although the term *learning theory* is frequently used, behavior therapy or behavior modification is essentially empirical, experimental-analytic, and inductive rather than deductive. Ullmann and Krasner (1969) noted that "while there are many techniques, there are few concepts or general principles involved in behavior therapy" (p. 252). Books on behavior therapy thus are essentially compendiums of techniques and methods. They are not systematic in the sense that an author has adopted a theoretical point of view, developed its philosophy and assumptions, and presented techniques derived from, or consistent with, the assumptions and theory. Behavior therapy, Yates (1970) claimed, is inductive rather than deductive, is based on experiments, and applies the experimental method to the treatment of the individual client. Thus, Yates stated that Dollard and Miller were not behavior therapists and that even Wolpe is not considered a behavior therapist in the British usage of the term. Yates defined behavior therapy as

the attempt to utilize systematically that body of empirical and theoretical knowledge which has resulted from the application of the experimental method in psychology and its closely related disciplines (physiology and neurophysiology) in order to explain the genesis and maintenance of abnormal patterns of behavior; and to apply that knowledge to the treatment or prevention of those abnormalities by means of controlled experimental studies of the single case, both descriptive and remedial. (p. 18)

Not all those who call themselves behavior therapists function in this manner or only in this manner, however. Nor is the atheoretical, empirical limitation accepted by all behavior therapists. Franks (1969), for example, wrote:

In the best of all possible worlds, it would seem highly desirable for the therapist to aspire to be a scientist even if this goal were difficult to realize. To function as a scientist, it is necessary to espouse some theoretical framework. . . . How the behavior therapist practices (including his choice of technique, his approach to the problems or general strategy, and his specific relationships with his patient) thus depends both upon his explicit theoretical orientation and upon his implicit philosophical and cultural milieu. (p. 21)

There is evidence that behavior therapists are becoming more diverse and are moving toward so-called traditional psychotherapy, particularly in recognizing the importance of the therapist-client relationship (see Glass & Arnkoff, 1992). (The importance of the experimenter-subject relationship in verbal conditioning has been demonstrated by the research referred to earlier.) Many behavior therapists are acknowledging the importance of cognitive and affective variables, including awareness or consciousness (Glass & Arnkoff, 1992). There appears to be a movement away from the application of techniques taken from laboratory research to the recognition of the complexities of human *in situ* behavior, as compared with the behavior of animals in the laboratory. Franks (1969), for example, asked:

Can it be assumed, on the basis of a concomitance that is sometimes observed between certain measures of acquisition and extinction in the laboratory, that there must inevitably be a high positive relationship between the rapidity and strength with which new responses are acquired during behavior therapy and the resistance to the therapeutic extinction of possibly quite different responses which are already in existence? Similar issues arise with respect to the generalization of conditional responses during therapy. If the basic parameters of laboratory conditioning are still in dispute, it is hardly surprising that the relationships between conditioning in the laboratory and conditioning in the clinical situation remain unclear. Unfortunately, many clinical investigators proceed as if the relationships were clear. (p. 22)

With such diversity among those who call themselves behavior therapists, it may be questioned whether there is a behavior therapy or behavior *therapies*. Nevertheless, Franks (1969) argued for the term *behavior therapy*, even though he admitted that "there is a bewildering conglomeration of techniques," on the basis that "all forms of behavior therapy are predicated upon the common, explicit, systematic, and a priori usage of learning principles to achieve well-defined and pre-determined goals" (p. 2). He stated that the term *behavior therapies* "implies little more than a grab bag of behaviorally oriented therapeutic techniques." Yates (1970) took the same position. The Association for the Advancement of the Behavioral Therapies changed its name to the singular in 1968, and the singular is used by most writers, even though they include or refer to a variety of methods or approaches that are not integrated into any system.

Yet the observer may obtain the strong impression that behavior therapy is essentially little more than a grab bag of techniques, applied to specific problems with little theoretical justification or support. Certainly, no systematic, integrated, theoretically oriented presentation of behavior therapy has appeared. Perhaps this represents the state of the field at the present time, and it is too early to expect an integration of the proliferating techniques and methods into a systematic approach. Certainly, any such attempt would be exceedingly difficult. It is not the function of this book, nor is it within the capabilities of these authors, to present a systematic position when none exists or has been attempted by proponents of the position.

Krasner (1971) noted that "as one plods through the vast literature on behavior therapy, one is reminded of the parable of the blind men who described the elephant solely on the basis of their feeling the animal." Each described a different part of the elephant. Krasner wrote that "the elephant of behavior therapy does indeed exist and can be discriminated from other creatures of the jungle." He proposed to do so in his review and listed 15 streams of development of behavior therapy, including social psychology and social learning, and reviewed the literature of the latter 1960s to give a broad overview of behavior therapy, but he does not articulate the parts of the elephant into a whole. Kanfer and Phillips (1969) also called for "establishing a well integrated framework from which a practitioner can derive new techniques with clearly stated rationales with predictable effects and with well defined criteria and methods for examining their efficacy" (p. 448). So far, no well-integrated framework seems to exist.

Wolpe's work, including his 1958 book and its supplementation in 1969, 1973, 1982, and 1990, offers a relatively systematic view of behavior therapy based mainly on classical conditioning theory and research. There appears to be no comparable presentation of therapy based on operant conditioning theory and research, nor is there a systematic attempt to integrate both these approaches under a broader, more comprehensive learning theory. However, there is a broadly based compendium of behavior therapy that includes both of these approaches, presenting them as separate models, and therapeutic procedures that partake of both models, presenting them as mixed models. This is the work of Kanfer and Phillips (1970), which probably presents the best statement of a comprehensive behavior therapy to date. The previous edition of this book included a summary of that work.

Space does not permit an adequate evaluation of behavior therapy here. A number of critiques (and rejoinders) have been published (Breger & McGaugh, 1964, 1968; Grossberg, 1964; Patterson, 1969; Rachman & Eysenck, 1966; Weitzman, 1967; Wiest, 1967), as have research reviews and evaluations (Emmelkamp, 1986, 1994; Ollendick, 1986). As experience and research accumulate, behavior therapists show increasing recognition of the complexities of human behavior and behavior problems and a realization that behavior therapy is not a panacea. The book by Kanfer and Phillips (1970) is a case in point.

Lazarus (1971), who has been identified as a behavior therapist and who was associated with Wolpe for several years, has presented a critical review of behavior therapy. He wrote that

the methods of behavior therapy are extremely effective when applied to carefully selected cases by informed practitioners. But when procedures overstep the boundaries of their legitimate terrain, ridicule and disparagement are most likely to ensue. Far from being a panacea, the methods are then held to have no merit whatsoever, and the proverbial baby gets thrown out with the bath water. (p. 1)

He continued:

The danger lies in a premature elevation of learning principles into unwarranted scientific truths and the ascription of the general term of "modern learning theory" to what in reality are best described as "modern learning theories." . . . Thus, Eysenck's insistence that behavior therapy denotes "methods of treatment which are derived from modern learning theory" amounts to little more than a beguiling slogan. (pp. 5–6)

He regarded Wolpe's 20 or so behavioral techniques as "a useful *starting point* for increased clinical effectiveness rather than a complete system which can put an end to 90 percent of the world's neurotic suffering" (pp. 6–7). He regarded behavior therapy as an objective psychotherapeutic adjunct. He stated that "several behavior therapists now acknowledge the fact that more varied and complex interactional processes other than reciprocal inhibition and operant conditioning permeate their interviews and contaminate or facilitate the application of their specific techniques" (p. 9).

The more complex and varied processes, to use Lazarus's term, include not only processes associated with the relationship between the therapist and the client, but also cognitive processes. Cognitive elements have always been present in learning theory approaches to psychotherapy. Dollard and Miller explicitly considered higher mental processes in the development and treatment of emotional problems. Kanfer and Phillips also acknowledged cognitive aspects. Many behaviorists now acknowledge cognitive elements and openly espouse purely cognitive methods and techniques (Goldfried & Davison, 1976; Mahoney, 1974; Martin & Pear, 1978; O'Leary & Wilson, 1975; cf. Glass & Arnkoff, 1992).

Behavior therapists have not, however, systematically integrated cognitive methods or techniques with standard behavioristic techniques (which also include cognitive elements) on any theoretical basis, nor have they attempted to use any particular cognitive theory. Probably because behavior therapy has been essentially atheoretical or empirically oriented, cognitive methods have been included with its other techniques. This incorporation of cognitive techniques has been questioned by Wickramasekera (1976):

It appears to me that it is highly unlikely that this approach by itself will advance our ability to reliably and powerfully control private events. This simplistic approach to forcing a marriage between operant conditioning and cognitive learning ignores the richness of investigative effort, which has collected around the construct, cognition. (p. 2)

The question is whether the marriage between behaviorism and cognition is compatible or whether it is simply a pragmatic association to keep behaviorism respectable. There appear to be basic inconsistencies between a strict or orthodox behaviorism, which rejects mental events as causally important or significant, and cognitive psychology.

In what follows, we offer summaries of Dollard's and Miller's as well as Wolpe's approaches to psychotherapy. Dollard and Miller represent the first meaningful attempt to integrate learning theory and psychoanalytic thought. Though it may seem somewhat arbitrary to place their work in the learning theory section, we thought a focus on them here might serve as a nice bridge from the previous (psychoanalytic) section to this one. Wolpe's view of behavior therapy can be seen as reflecting a neobehavioristic mediational stimulus-response model (see Wilson, 1984). There are no doubt other behavior therapy models to draw upon, but our emphasis in this section will be on these two.

REFERENCES

Bandura, A. (1961). Psychotherapy as a learning process. *Psychological Bulletin, 58,* 143–159.

Bandura, A. (1969). *Principles of behavior modification.* New York: Holt, Rinehart and Winston.

Breger, L., & McGaugh, J. L. (1964). Critique and reformulation of "learning theory" approach to psychotherapy and neuroses. *Psychological Bulletin, 63,* 338–358.

Breger, L., & McGaugh, J. L. (1968). Learning theory and behavior therapy: A reply to Rachman and Eysenck. *Psychological Bulletin, 65,* 170–173.

Dollard, J., & Miller, N. E. (1950). *Personality and psychotherapy: An analysis in terms of learning, thinking, and culture.* New York: McGraw-Hill.

Emmelkamp, P. M. G. (1986). Behavior therapy with adults. In S. L. Garfield & A. E. Bergin (Eds.). *Handbook of psychotherapy and behavior change* (3rd. ed., pp. 385–442). New York: Wiley.

Emmelkamp, P. M. G. (1994). Behavior therapy with adults. In A. E. Bergin & S. L. Garfield (Eds.). *Handbook of psychotherapy and behavior change* (4th ed., pp. 379–427). New York: Wiley.

Eysenck, H. J. (1959). Learning theory and behavior therapy. *Journal of Mental Science, 195,* 61–75.

Eysenck, H. J. (Ed.). (1960). *Behavior therapy and the neuroses.* New York: Pergamon Press.

Eysenck, H. J. (Ed.). (1964). *Experiments in behavior therapy.* New York: Pergamon Press.

Eysenck, H. J., & Rachman, S. (1965). *The causes and cures of neurosis: An introduction to modern behavior therapy based on learning theory and principles of conditioning.* San Diego: Knapp.

Franks, C. M. (Ed.). (1964). *Conditioning techniques in clinical practice and research.* New York: Springer.

Franks, C. M. (Ed.). (1969). *Behavior therapy: Appraisal and status.* New York: McGraw-Hill.

Franks, C. M. (Ed.). (1970). *Assessment and status of the behavioral therapies.* New York: McGraw-Hill.

Glass, C. R., & Arnkoff, D. B. (1992). Behavior therapy. In D. K. Freedheim (Ed.). *History of psychotherapy* (pp. 587–628). Washington, DC: American Psychological Association.

Goldfried, M. R., & Davison, G. C. (1976). *Clinical behavior therapy.* New York: Holt, Rinehart and Winston.

Greenspoon, J. S. (1950). The effect of a verbal stimulus as a reinforcement. *Proceedings of the Iowa Academy of Science, 59,* 287.

Greenspoon, J. S. (1955). The reinforcing effect of two spoken sounds on the frequency of two responses. *American Journal of Psychology, 68,* 409–416.

Grossberg, J. M. (1964). Behavior therapy: A review. *Psychological Bulletin, 62,* 73–88.

Hildum, D. C., & Brown, R. W. (1956). Verbal reinforcement and interviewer bias. *Journal of Abnormal & Social Psychology, 53,* 108–111.

Hilgard, E. R., & Bower, G. H. (1975). *Theories of learning* (4th ed.). Englewood Cliffs, NJ: Prentice-Hall.

Jones, M. C. A. (1924). A laboratory study of fear: The case of Peter. *Journal of Genetic Psychology, 31,* 308–315.

Kanfer, F. H. (1961). Comments on learning in psychotherapy. *Psychological Reports, 9,* 681–699.

Kanfer, F. H. (1966). Implications of conditioning techniques for interview therapy. *Journal of Counseling Psychology, 13,* 171–177.

Kanfer, F. H., & Phillips, J. S. (1969). A survey of current behavior therapies and a proposal for classification. In C. M. Franks (Ed.). *Behavior therapy: Appraisal and status.* New York: Pergamon Press.

Kanfer, F. H., & Phillips, J. S. (1970). *Learning foundations of behavior therapy.* New York: Wiley.

Kimble, G. A. (Ed.). (1967). *Foundations of conditioning and learning.* Englewood Cliffs, NJ: Prentice-Hall.

Krasner, L. (1958). Studies of the conditioning of verbal behavior. *Psychological Bulletin, 55,* 148–170.

Krasner, L. (1962). The therapist as a social reinforcement machine. In H. H. Strupp & L. Luborsky (Eds.). *Research in psychotherapy* (vol. 2). Washington, DC: American Psychological Association.

Krasner, L. (1963). Reinforcement, verbal behavior and psychotherapy. *American Journal of Orthopsychiatry, 33,* 601–613.

Krasner, L. (1965). Verbal conditioning and psychotherapy. In L. Krasner & L. P. Ullmann (Eds.). *Research in behavior modification.* New York: Holt, Rinehart and Winston.

Krasner, L. (1966). Review of *The causes and cures of neurosis* by H. J. Eysenck and S. Rachman. *Contemporary Psychology, 11,* 341–344.

Krasner, L. (1971). Behavior therapy. *Annual Review of Psychology, 22,* 483–532.

Krasner, L., & Ullmann, L. P. (Eds.). (1965). *Research in behavior modification.* New York: Holt, Rinehart & Winston.

Krumboltz, J. D. (Ed.). (1966). *Revolution in counseling.* Boston: Houghton Mifflin.

Krumboltz, J. D., & Thoresen, C. E. (Eds.). (1969). *Behavioral counseling: Cases and techniques.* New York: Holt, Rinehart and Winston.

Lazarus, A. A. (1958). New methods in psychotherapy: A case study. *South African Medical Journal, 33,* 660–664.

Lazarus, A. A. (1971). *Behavior therapy and beyond.* New York: McGraw-Hill.

Levis, D. J. (1970). Behavioral therapy: The fourth therapeutic revolution? In D. J. Levis (Ed.). *Learning approaches to therapeutic behavior change.* Chicago: Aldine.

Levis, D. J. (Ed.). (1970). *Learning approaches to therapeutic behavior change.* Chicago: Aldine.

Lindsley, O. R. (1956). Operant conditioning methods applied to research in chronic schizophrenia. *Psychiatric Research Reports, 5,* 118–139.

Lindsley, O. R., & Skinner, B. F. (1954). A method for experimental analysis of the behavior of psychotic patients. *American Psychologist, 9,* 419–420.

Lindsley, O. R., Skinner, B. F., & Solomon, H. C. (1953). *Studies in behavior therapy. Status Report I.* Waltham, MA: Metropolitan State Hospital.

Magaret, A. (1950). Generalization in psychotherapy. *Journal of Consulting Psychology, 14,* 64–70.

Mahoney, M. J. (1974). *Cognition and behavior modification.* Cambridge, MA: Ballinger.

Martin, G., & Pear, J. (1978). *Behavior modification: What it is and how to do it.* Englewood Cliffs, NJ: Prentice-Hall.

Mowrer, O. H. (1947). On the dual nature of learning: A reinterpretation of "conditioning" and "problem solving." *Harvard Educational Review, 17,* 102–148.

Mowrer, O. H. (1960). *Learning theory and behavior.* New York: Wiley.

O'Leary, K. D., & Wilson, G. T. (1975). *Behavior therapy: Application and outcome.* Englewood Cliffs, NJ: Prentice-Hall.

Ollendick, T. H. (1986). Behavior therapy with children and adolescents. In S. L. Garfield & A. E. Bergin (Eds.). *Handbook of psychotherapy and behavior change* (pp. 525–564). New York: Wiley.

Osipow, S. H., & Walsh, W. B. (Eds.). (1970). *Behavior change in counseling: Readings and cases.* Englewood Cliffs, NJ: Prentice-Hall.

Pascal, G. R. (1959). *Behavioral change in the clinic—A systematic approach.* New York: Grune & Stratton.

Patterson, C. H. (1969). Some notes on behavior theory, behavior therapy and behavioral counseling. *Counseling Psychologist, 1,* 44–56.

Pepinsky, H. B., & Pepinsky, P. (1954). *Counseling: Theory and practice.* New York: Ronald Press.

Peters, H. N. (1952). An experimental evaluation of learning as therapy in schizophrenia. *American Psychologist, 7,* 354.

Peters, H. N. (1955). Learning as a treatment method in chronic schizophrenia. *American Journal of Occupational Therapy, 9,* 185–189.

Peters, H. N., & Jenkins, R. L. (1954). Improvement of chronic schizophrenics with guided problem-solving, motivated by hunger. *Psychiatric Quarterly Supplement, 28,* 84–101.

Phillips, E. L. (1956). *Psychotherapy: A modern theory and practice.* Englewood Cliffs, NJ: Prentice-Hall.

Rachman, S., & Eysenck, H. J. (1966). Reply to a "critique and reformulation" of behavior therapy. *Psychological Bulletin, 65,* 165–169.

Rubin, R. D., & Franks, C. M. (Eds.). (1969). *Advances in behavior therapy: 1968.* New York: Academic Press.

Salter, A. (1949). *Conditioned reflex therapy.* New York: Creative Age Press. (Capricorn Books, 1961)

Salzinger, K. (1959). Experimental manipulation of verbal behavior: A review. *Journal of General Psychology, 61,* 65–94.

Salzinger, K. (1969). The place of operant conditioning of verbal behavior in psychotherapy. In C. M. Franks (Ed.). *Behavior therapy: Appraisal and status* (pp. 375–395). New York: McGraw-Hill.

Shaffer, L. F. (1947). The problem of psychotherapy. *American Psychologist, 2,* 459–467.

Shaw, F. J. (1946). A stimulus response analysis of repression and insight in psychotherapy. *Psychological Review, 53,* 36–42.

Shoben, E. J., Jr. (1948). A learning theory interpretation of psychotherapy. *Harvard Educational Review, 18,* 129–145.

Shoben, E. J., Jr. (1949). Psychotherapy as a problem in learning theory. *Psychological Bulletin, 46,* 366–392.

Shoben, E. J., Jr. (1953). Some observations on psychotherapy and the learning process. In O. H. Mowrer (Ed.). *Psychotherapy: Theory and research.* New York: Ronald Press.

Skinner, B. F. (1938). *The behavior of organisms.* Englewood Cliffs, NJ: Prentice-Hall.

Skinner, B. F. (1953). *Science and human behavior.* New York: Macmillan.

Ullmann, L. P., & Krasner, L. (Eds.). (1965). *Case studies in behavior modification.* New York: Holt, Rinehart and Winston.

Ullmann, L. P., & Krasner, L. (Eds.). (1969). *A psychological approach to abnormal behavior.* Englewood Cliffs, NJ: Prentice-Hall.

Watson, J. B., & Rayner, R. (1920). Conditioned emotional reactions. *Journal of Experimental Psychology, 3,* 1–14.

Weitzman, B. (1967). Behavior therapy and psychotherapy. *Psychological Review, 74,* 300–317.

Wickramasekera, I. (Ed.). (1976). *Biofeedback, behavior therapy and hypnosis.* Chicago: Nelson-Hall.

Wiest, W. M. (1967). Some recent criticisms of behaviorism and learning theory with special reference to Breger and McGaugh and Chomsky. *Psychological Bulletin, 67,* 214–225.

Wilson, G. T. (1984). Behavior therapy. In R. J. Corsini (Ed.). *Current psychotherapies* (pp. 239–278). Itasca, IL: Peacock.

Wolpe, J. (1958). *Psychotherapy by reciprocal inhibition.* Stanford, CA: Stanford University Press.

Yates, A. J. (1970). *Behavior therapy.* New York: Wiley.

chapter 5

Reinforcement Theory and Psychoanalytic Therapy: Dollard and Miller

The learning theory developed by Hull and his students and associates, including Neal Miller, has been applied to psychotherapy by John Dollard and Neal Miller (1950) in their book, *Personality and Psychotherapy: An Analysis in Terms of Learning, Thinking, and Culture.* John Dollard (1900–1980), after taking his Ph.D. at the University of Chicago in 1931, went to the Institute of Human Relations at Yale University, where he became professor of psychology in 1952. He was the author of *Caste and Class in a Southern Town* (1937), among other books.

Neal E. Miller was born in 1909, earned his Ph.D. in 1935 at Yale, and remained there until 1966, except for a postdoctoral year of training at the Psychoanalytic Institute in Vienna and during the Second World War, when he was associated with the Air Force selection and classification program. He was James Rowland Angell Professor of Psychology at Yale from 1952 to 1966, when he went to Rockefeller University as professor of psychology. In addition to being the author of numerous articles in the field of learning and learning theory, he is coauthor with Dollard of *Social Learning and Imitation* (1941) and with Dollard, Doob, Miller, and Sears of *Frustration and Aggression* (1939).

In 1964 Miller received the National Medal of Science. In 1959 he received an Award for Distinguished Scientific Contributions from the American Psychological Association (APA). In 1983 he received an Award for Distinguished Professional Contributions (also from the APA). The announcement of the award included a biography and a bibliography of his publications to 1983 (*American Psychologist,* 1984, *39,* 291–298). In 1991, he received a Citation for Outstanding Lifetime Contribution to Psychology from the APA.

BACKGROUND AND DEVELOPMENT

Unlike the approaches that attempt to apply principles of conditioning to psychotherapy, the approach of Dollard and Miller attempts to integrate learning theory—essentially Hullian behaviorism—with the insights of psychoanalysis about human behavior and personality and with the contributions of social science to the social conditions of learning. The result, Dollard and Miller hoped, would be a general science of human behavior. The nature and treatment of neurosis would be included as part of this science. Psychotherapy, particularly psychoanalysis, is seen as providing a window that allows one to look into the mental life in a way that cannot usually be done in the study and observation of the normal individual. The laws and theory of learning applied to psychotherapy should provide a rational foundation for psychotherapy.

PHILOSOPHY AND CONCEPTS

Neurosis is a product of experience rather than primarily of instinct or organic damage. Therefore, it must be learned, and learning is governed by laws, some of which are known and some of which, now unknown, may be discovered through the study of neuroses by means of psychotherapy. Thus, learning theory and psychotherapy supplement each other. In their book, however, Dollard and Miller (1950) attempt "to give a systematic analysis of neurosis and psychotherapy in terms of the psychological principles and social conditions of learning," (p. 9).

What is a Neurosis?   The neurotic person is miserable, is stupid in handling emotional problems, and suffers from a variety of symptoms. Neurotic persons are capable of normal activity but are unable to function normally or to enjoy life. The more common symptoms are sleeplessness, restlessness, irritability, sexual inhibitions, phobias, headaches, irrational fears, distaste for life, and lack of clear personal goals. This condition is the result of conflict produced by two or more strong drives leading to incompatible responses. The neurotic person is unable to solve these conflicts because he or she is not clearly aware of them. The neurotic person's conflicts are repressed—that is, unlabeled—and "he has no language to describe the conflicting forces within him," (*ibid.*, p. 15). Neurotic persons appear to be stupid because of an inability to use higher mental processes to deal with problems, since they do not know what the problems are.

Although neurotic symptoms cause suffering, they actually reduce the neurotic's conflict. "When a successful symptom occurs it is reinforced because it reduces neurotic misery. The symptom is thus learned as a habit" (Dollard & Miller, 1950, p. 15).

Basic Principles of Learning.   The behavior of all human beings, which ranges from the child's very simple avoidance of a hot radiator to the scientist's construction of a theory, is learned. Four basic factors are important for all learning.

The first factor is *drive,* or motivation. Drives are strong stimuli that impel action. Certain classes of stimuli are primary, or innate, drives: pain, thirst, hunger, and so on. There are also secondary, or learned, drives, which "are acquired on the basis of primary drives, represent elaborations of them, and serve as a facade behind which the functions of the underlying innate drives are hidden" (*ibid.*, pp. 31–32). (In subsequent publications [1959,1964], Miller has modified his views to include the channeling by learning of certain presumably innate drives such as curiosity.) Many of the most important drives are learned. Fear (or anxiety) is a major learned drive.

The second factor in learning is the *cue,* or stimulus. When a person is impelled by a drive, "cues determine when he will respond, where he will respond, and which response he will make" (*ibid.,* p. 32). Both external and internal stimuli may function as cues (as well as being drives) for specific responses. Changes in, differences among, and patterns of stimuli serve as cues. Fear has the properties of a strong external cue. "When fear is learned as a response to a new situation, it serves as a cue to elicit responses that have previously been learned in other frightening situations" (*ibid.,* p. 77), such as verbal responses expressing fear, meek muteness, or withdrawal. Fear may also become a cue to avoid an act or a response that leads to punishment when it has become attached to cues produced by the thought of performing the prescribed act. After effective punishment for an act, the individual feels afraid when he or she thinks about or begins to perform the punished act and is thus led to stop or withdraw. The fear is reduced, and thus the stopping or withdrawing becomes reinforced.

Fear produces or is associated with certain innate responses, such as increase in stomach acidity, increase in and irregularity of heartbeat, muscular tension, trembling, being startled, freezing (with fear), perspiration, dryness of mouth and throat, feelings of unreality, mutism, and amnesia. Many of these reactions are the symptoms of neurosis or psychosis.

The third factor in learning is *response.* Cues lead to responses, which may be arranged in a hierarchy in terms of their probability of occurrence. A dominant response (one high in the hierarchy) has a strong connection with the stimulus. The nature of this causal connection is unknown. The changing of the strength of connections between stimuli and responses (or the changing of the position of responses in the hierarchy) is learning, but a response must occur before it can be connected with a stimulus. Such new responses may occur as the result of trial and error, of imitation, or of verbal direction. All these methods are ways of producing responses that can be rewarded. In conditioning, the response to the unconditioned stimulus is the dominant response. Fear is an innate response to certain stimuli.

The fourth factor is *reinforcement,* or reward. "Any specified event . . . that strengthens the tendency for a response to be repeated is called reinforcement" (*ibid.,* p. 39). The reduction or cessation of a painful or noxious stimulus acts as a reinforcement, as does the reduction in the strength of a strong drive or stimulus. There are learned, or secondary, reinforcements, for example, money, as well as innate reinforcements. Learned rewards function in the same way as unlearned rewards. While reinforcement may operate in a situation of awareness on the part of the subject, reinforcement may also operate directly, occurring without awareness.

In addition to these four factors or conditions of learning, there are several other aspects of the learning process that require definition. One of these is *extinction.* When a learned response is repeated without continued reinforcement, it tends to occur less and less often; that is, it is extinguished. If responses were not subject to extinction, they would persist indefinitely, even responses that were rewarded by chance. Responses are extinguished at different rates, with strong responses persisting longer than weak ones. The strength of the drive during learning, the magnitude of the previous reward, and the strength of the drive during extinction influence the rate of extinction. Although the extinction process may be prolonged, all learned habits that have been studied have been found to be extinguished eventually when they are no longer reinforced. "This statement is no longer accurate. At present it is not known whether all learned responses would extinguish if given enough unreinforced trials" [N. E. Miller (personal communication, July 8, 1964).]

When a response has been extinguished, it may recur after a time without having been rewarded in the meantime. This is known as *spontaneous recovery* and indicates that the response or habit has only been inhibited, not destroyed. After repeated extinctions, however, the response does disappear. (Same comment as above applies to this statement.)

The reinforcement accompanying a particular stimulus not only increases the tendency of that stimulus to elicit the response, but also spreads to similar stimuli, so that they tend to elicit the same response. The less similar the stimuli or cues, the less the tendency for the response to occur. This spread or transfer to other stimuli is termed *generalization,* and the variation in tendency for responses to occur is known as the *gradient of generalization.* No two stimuli or stimulus situations are exactly the same, and if there were no generalization, learning could not occur.

If the response occurred with any stimulus, though, learning would not occur either. Dissimilar stimuli are differentiated and not responded to. Or *discrimination* between responses may be established by not rewarding or by punishing responses to stimuli that differ in some way or degree from the rewarded stimulus.

Reinforcement is more effective the closer the response is to the reinforcement, so that delayed reinforcement is less effective than immediate reinforcement. There is thus a *gradient of reinforcement:* responses occurring before the final reinforced response are also reinforced but less so than is the final response.

The gradients of generalization and of reinforcement lead to the principle that "responses near the point of reinforcement tend, whenever physically possible, to occur before their original time in the response series, that is, to become anticipatory" (*ibid.,* p. 57). *Anticipatory responses* thus crowd out useless acts. Withdrawal from a painful stimulus will occur prior to touching the object that causes pain. The anticipatory tendency is involuntary and may lead to errors or nonadaptive responses as well as to adaptive elimination of useless acts. Use of reinforcement, such as punishing or not rewarding responses that are not preceded by desirable anticipatory responses, may prevent the elimination of these desirable responses.

The importance of fear in behavior becomes apparent when it is realized that fear is one of the most significant of the learned drives. Fear is easily learned and transferred to new stimuli and can develop into a powerful drive, thus becoming involved in the production of conflicts leading to neurotic behavior. When fear becomes attached to a new situation, it is accompanied by many of the reactions that are a part of the innate pattern of fear. It serves as a cue to elicit responses that have been learned in other fearful situations. When drive-reducing responses are punished, fear is learned and will then motivate responses that prevent reduction of those drives, leading to inhibitions that result in disturbance and neurotic symptoms. Fear seems to be a part of many socially learned drives, such as guilt, shame, pride, the need for social conformity, and the desire for money or power. Fear of the loss of love or status, of failure, and of poverty seem to be socially learned. The reduction of fear is reinforcing for the learning and performance of new responses such as avoidance responses. Fears are often highly resistant to extinction, and sometimes they appear not to be extinguished completely. Like other responses, fear can be inhibited by incompatible responses such as eating.

There are many other learned social motives, but some that are especially important for personality development and psychotherapy are gregariousness, sociability, dependence and independence, conformity and nonconformity, the need to receive and show affection, the desire for approval from others, pride, fairness, and honesty. Learned drives and their reinforcements vary among cultures and among social classes within a culture. Therapists must be aware of this variability.

Normal Use of Higher Mental Processes in Solving Emotional Problems.   Little is known today about the solution of social and emotional problems, compared with the solution of problems posed by the physical environment. Psychotherapy itself, which is concerned with social and emotional problems, offers an opportunity to learn more about this area.

Behavior may be divided into two "levels": the first consists of immediate, automatic responses; the second includes behavior that follows or is mediated by a series of internal responses, images, or thoughts called *higher mental processes.* It is this latter kind of behavior with which we are concerned. In the former kind of behavior, responses are instrumental acts in that they influence the individual's relationship to the environment directly and immediately: they are instrumental in changing the environment. In the second kind of behavior, the intervening responses are called "cue-producing responses." They may or may not be verbalized. Their main purpose is to produce a cue that functions as a part of the stimulus pattern for another response. Such cues, when verbalized, may serve as substitutes for instrumental responses, stimulating another person to perform the response—as, for example, in asking another person to do something for you. The important function here is that of serving as cues to the person making the responses. These cue-producing responses are usually in the form of words and sentences. It is assumed that language and other cue-producing responses, rather than thoughts that have not been articulated, are central to the higher mental processes. The laws that apply to responses to external cues are assumed to apply to such internal response-produced cues.

Attaching the same label (cue-producing response) to different objects gives them a certain "learned equivalence" resulting from verbally mediated generalization. Giving different labels to similar objects increases their distinctiveness and facilitates their discrimination. Labeling is important "because language contains those discriminations and equivalences that have been found useful by generations of trial and error in a given society" (*ibid.,* p. 103).

Labels or words can arouse drives; that is, learnable drives can be attached to words. Drives elicited by words are called *mediated learned drives.* Words, spoken or unspoken, can also provide reassurance, thus mediating rewards. Verbal and other cue-producing responses are important in helping people respond to future possibilities and thus in producing foresight. The association of motivational and instrumental responses with verbal cues makes possible great economy in verbal learning, so that much of human learning is in terms of verbal responses or hypotheses that may lead to sudden changes in many other responses (a process often called "insight"). Verbal learning is often described as logical learning, in contrast to rote learning; in this light, it is apparent why logical learning is superior to rote learning.

Verbal cue-producing responses make possible reasoning and planning. Reasoning involves, but is not restricted to, verbal or symbolic trial and error. Verbal cue-producing responses are not limited to a single sequence, as are instrumental responses, but "it is possible for certain cue-producing responses that have been associated with the goal to move forward in the sequence and provide cues that have a selective effect on subsequent responses" (*ibid.,* p. 111). These are called *anticipatory goal responses.* It is also possible for a chain of cue-producing responses to begin at the goal and work backward to the correct response in the problem situation. Reasoning and planning require the inhibition of immediate instrumental responses, the occurrence of appropriate cue-producing responses, and the execution of appropriate instrumental responses in place of the direct responses that have been inhibited.

Society has developed solutions to many problems and passes these solutions on to its new members through education and training. Social training in language is important in leading to problem solving. Words and sentences copied from others can be used in reasoning and planning. Verbal responses are learned in social interaction, but the process is not clearly understood. Imitation plays a central role in the process of learning to talk (Dollard & Miller, 1941). Training that involves listening, following the suggestions of others, stopping to think, matching words correctly to the environment, making oneself understood, being logical, being oriented, and responding to verbal cues with appropriate action and emotion helps to make a person's behavior appropriate to the social situation. When such training is not too effective, the individual may appear to have a poor sense of reality or a weak ego. Cue-producing responses that are not socially evident, such as images of various kinds, are not subject to direct social training; they may be less inhibited but also less orderly and less useful in problem solving.

How Neuroses Are Learned.   Neurotic behavior is based on an unconscious emotional conflict, usually originating in childhood. "Neurotic conflicts are taught by parents and learned by children" (Dollard & Miller, 1950, p. 127). The patterns of child training contain inconsistencies and, thus, inherent conflicts, and parents vary in their consistency, effectiveness, and ability in conducting child training. The task is complex and difficult, and the appropriate rules and conditions are only partly known. There is also the problem of determining what kind of child it is desirable to produce. Although our knowledge is inadequate, we know that the period of childhood is important, and we must attempt to reconstruct childhood in order to understand adult life.

Children are helpless and thus are at the mercy of confusing patterns of training. "The young child is necessarily disoriented, confused, deluded, and hallucinated—in short, has just those symptoms that we recognize as psychosis in the adult. Infancy, indeed may be viewed as a period of transitory psychosis" (*ibid.,* p. 130). Rather than being indulged, supported, and gradually trained during infancy, the child is pushed by incompatible and impossible demands and is expected to control impelling drives and to learn rapidly.

The child is faced with training demands in four critical situations. The ways in which this training is handled lead to the development of learned responses that persist throughout life. The *feeding situation* may be handled so as to lead to optimism or apathy, to security or apprehension, to sociability or lack of social feeling, to fear of being alone or later compulsive sociability. Premature or rigid *cleanliness training,* which must proceed without verbal aids, arouses strong emotions—anger, defiance, stubbornness, and fear. Anxiety, conforming behavior, feelings of unworthiness, and guilt may result. *Sex training* may lead to conflicts generated by taboos, sexual anxieties, and heterosexual fears and conflicts deriving from the Oedipus situation. Finally, the *treatment of anger responses* in the child may give rise to anger-anxiety conflicts as fear is attached to anger cues. Anger is inevitable because of the many frustrations produced in the child during training, of sibling rivalry, and of the helplessness and mental limitations of the child. Repression of anger may go beyond inhibition of aggression to inhibition of feelings of anger and thus lead to an overinhibited personality.

These early conflicts of the child occur before he or she can verbalize or at least do so adequately. They are therefore unlabeled and unconscious. They cannot be reported later in life. We cannot learn from the individual (except to some extent in psychotherapy) the nature of these conflicts. Much of what we know about these conditions has come from neurotic persons in psychotherapy. Normal people may not have as severe conflicts; some individuals may be less able to handle conflicts through higher mental processes or may be more predisposed than others to neurotic reactions.

How Symptoms Are Learned. *Phobias* are learned fears whose basic origins currently are not understood. The avoidance response reduces the fear and thus is strongly reinforced. Phobias tend to persist because the avoidance of the phobia situation reinforces them through reduction of fear and so prevents extinction. Like phobias, *compulsions* are acts that reduce anxiety of unknown origin. They persist because they reduce the anxiety temporarily. *Hysterical symptoms* are likewise learned responses that avoid or reduce fear. The factors that determine the specific hysterical response, such as an arm paralysis, are unclear, although the origin of the fear, such as active combat in war, may be clear. *Regression* is the occurrence of the next strongest response (usually one learned as a strong habit during childhood) when the dominant (adult) habit is blocked by conflict or extinguished through lack of reward. When the dominant response is replaced by another response that is strong because of generalization, rather than by an earlier response, the process is called *displacement*. *Rationalizations* occur when, as a result of social training, the individual feels the necessity for logical explanations for his or her behavior but cannot accept the true explanation because it would provoke anxiety or guilt. *Delusions* are different from rationalizations only quantitatively; socially acceptable explanations are more difficult to find, and delusions are resorted to—and persist—to reduce the strong anxiety or guilt. *Hallucinations* are a result of wide generalization of strongly motivated perceptual responses. When external cues become highly disturbing, the shifting of attention to internal images (hallucinations) may reduce the fear. *Projection* results from the many factors that lead people to think that others are motivated as they are. When individuals erroneously impute motivation in others, it is called "projection." The individual often is incorrect in labeling his or her own motives as well as those of others. Projection is reinforced by the reduction of anxiety when blame is shifted to someone else. *Reaction formations* are thoughts, statements, or behaviors opposite to those that the individual is motivated toward but of which the individual fears or disapproves. *Alcoholism* results from the reinforcement of the use of alcohol to reduce fear.

Although in the long run, many symptoms are maladaptive, they delay the increase in misery, and the immediate results are favorable, thus reinforcing the symptoms. The strengthening effect of an immediate reinforcement may be much greater than the deterring effect of a much stronger but delayed punishment. When there appears to be an immediate increase in misery, the explanation of the persistence of the symptoms presents a problem, but the situation can be accounted for theoretically in various ways consistent with a drive-reduction interpretation of reinforcement theory.

While any strong drive can motivate symptoms and its reduction can reinforce them, certain drives appear to be more likely to do so in our society than others. Fear is perhaps the most common motivating drive. Sex, aggression, and the striving for social mobility are others. The repression of verbal responses to these drives increases the likelihood of the appearance of maladaptive behavior or symptoms. When it is physically possible to perform direct drive-reducing responses, such responses may be prevented by conflict, so that the drive must be reduced by symptomatic behavior. Two strong drives may have incompatible dominant responses, but some of the less dominant responses may be compatible and will tend to occur. Symptoms are often such compromise responses, which are strongly reinforced because they reduce both drives.

Symptoms are resistant to elimination, or extinction, apparently because they have been strengthened by long reinforcement, they continue to be reinforced, and their interruption makes the individual feel worse.

> If the symptom is reinforced by drive reduction so that interrupting it causes the drive to mount, we would expect this increased drive to motivate the learning and performance of new symptoms. Thus treatment that is aimed only at eliminating specific symptoms by such means as hypnosis or physical punishment should tend to be followed by the appearance of new symptoms. As is well known, this is indeed the case. (Dollard & Miller, 1950, p. 196)

Elimination or reduction of the drive that motivates a symptom leads to the disappearance of the symptom. If the drive reappears, the symptom reappears, particularly if the elimination of the drive did not involve the pitting of incompatible responses against it, as in interpretation.

How Repression Is Learned.   In the individual's psyche, the repressed or the unconscious, as Freud pointed out, is the unverbalized. Drives, cues, and responses that never have been labeled are unconscious. Most of what is repressed originates in childhood before the acquisition of language, but even later in life, some aspects of life remain unverbalized or poorly labeled. Suppression is the conscious avoidance of unpleasant thoughts, but repression is automatic; since it is not under the control of verbal cues, repression cannot be revoked by the individual. Repression is reinforced by the reduction of the unpleasant drive. The removal of repression results in an increase of the drive. An innate response to the drive of fear may be to stop thinking. For example, children learn to fear saying certain words, and the fear generalizes to the thoughts represented by those words. Thoughts themselves may become attached directly to fears, as when the thoughts precede acts that are immediately punished. Even delayed punishment may result in attachment of fear to thoughts when the punishment is accompanied by an explanation of the reason for the punishment. Sometimes parents can tell what a child is going to do and warn or reprimand the child while he or she is only thinking about the act, thus attaching fear to the thought.

Repression may intervene in a drive sequence in three ways.

1. The drive may not be labeled, or it may not be recognized for what it is and be mislabeled.
2. The drive may be inhibited by stronger competing responses. For example, fear may lead to the inhibiting of the sexual drive. Hunger may even inhibit fear if

the hunger is strong and the fear is weak to begin with, as in the experiment of Jones with Peter and the rabbit (referred to in the introduction to Part Two of this book).

3. In the case of mediated learned drives, the inhibition of the mediating responses, which produce the cues that elicit the drive-producing responses, will eliminate the drive. Thus, for example, if one stops thinking about another's comments as insults, this can reduce anger.

It is the first type of repression, in which the drive is present at full strength but unlabeled, that leads to symptomatic behavior.

Repression may be viewed as the result of an approach-avoidance conflict, that is, a conflict between trying to remember or think about something and trying to avoid the topic because of its fear-producing quality.

The superego, or conscience, is in part unconscious. This may be because the emotional components of the moral sanctions were learned before language developed or because the responses were so strongly learned that they have become direct responses to nonverbal cues, like strong habits that may function without thought.

The presence of repression generates deficits in the higher mental processes, which involve verbal cue-producing responses. The inability to use labels leads to primary stimulus generalization or inadequate discrimination and thus to displacement. Inability to attach the same label to similar situations results in a decrease in learned (secondary) generalization. Absence of verbal responses removes the capacity for responding to remote goals or stimuli or for dealing with the future with foresight. Reasoning and planning will be affected, as well as the ability to communicate with others and to obtain their help. Behavior is more childish and thus abnormal as compared with that of other adults. Since repression usually is limited to certain areas or topics, not all behavior is affected, of course, or else the individual would not be able to function at all. These expectations drawn from behavior theory are all supported by clinical data and fit Freud's description of the results of repression.

To summarize, the neurotic person is one in whom there is a conflict between drives such as sex and aggression, and a strong fear. The satisfaction of these drives is prevented, resulting in a state of chronic high drive described as misery. The strong drives tend to evoke behavior that elicits fear. The neurotic person responds by avoiding such behavior and thus not approaching the goal, which reduces the fear and thus reinforces these responses. The state of conflict also results in tension, and the fear, too, is accompanied by unpleasant physiological reactions. In addition, the fear leads to repression of verbal and other cue-producing responses, so that thinking and reasoning are prevented and stupidity results. Symptoms are produced by the strong drives and/or fear and are reinforced by reduction of these drives or fear.

THE THERAPY PROCESS

The neurotic person who comes for psychotherapy has suffered long, and relatives, friends, and even a personal physician have given up attempts to help the individual. Neurotic persons become hopeless and do not know what to do. They cannot explain themselves, are afraid to express themselves or attempt to satisfy their drives, and are confused and cannot think adequately. They have failed in many areas of life, sense that others know that they are failures, and thus lack self-esteem. Neurotic persons cannot solve their own problems and require new conditions of therapeutic learning to achieve a better adjustment. Psychotherapy offers these new conditions of learning. The therapy process is essentially a situation in which neurotic responses are extinguished and better, normal responses are learned.

Selection of Clients.   Since psychotherapy is a learning process, it is desirable for the therapist to exercise selection of those who can learn under the conditions of psychotherapy. If these conditions and the principles of learning are known, such selection should be possible. The rules of selection based on these principles seem to agree quite well with those developed from clinical experience and psychoanalytic theory.

First, the disorder must be learned, not organic. To be unlearned, the condition must first be a product of learning. Second, there must be motivation for therapy, since motivation is important in learning. A person who is miserable and suffering is more motivated than one who is self-satisfied. A person who seeks therapy on his or her own is better motivated than one who is compelled or forced into therapy. The more disadvantageous the symptoms, the stronger the motivation for therapy. Third, the more strongly the symptoms are reinforced, the poorer the prognosis. Secondary gains, such as pensions or compensation, may reinforce symptoms and reduce motivation for therapy. Fourth, the greater the potential rewards for improvement, the better the prognosis. Good physical health, youth, beauty, intelligence, education, special skills, a satisfactory position, a good social-class status, wealth, and a supportive marital partner or prospects of one increase the possibility of reward. Fifth, a certain minimum achievement in social learning is necessary, since psychotherapy does not provide the basic training that should be received in the family. A minimum ability to use and respond to language is required; this is related to intelligence, of course. The potential for higher mental functioning, evidenced by previous high-level functioning or by the presence of such functioning in some areas, increases the favorability of the prognosis. If age-graded achievements, such as aspects of the conscience or superego, are lacking, psychotherapy will be difficult. Sixth, a history of neurosis going back into childhood is unfavorable. Finally, habits that interfere with psychotherapy—such as inability to listen or to talk reasonably, extreme suspiciousness, excessive passivity and dependence, or great independence and pride—are unfavorable signs.

Elements of Therapeutic Learning.   The therapeutic process consists of a number of aspects. The first is the *lifting of repression* through extinguishing or counterconditioning the fear or anxiety associated with repressed material. "In therapy a new type of social situation is created, the opposite of that responsible for learning repression," (Dollard & Miller, 1950, p. 240). That is, the client says the words that have been attached to fear, shame, and guilt in a permissive, warm, and accepting atmosphere, and this verbalization leads to the extinction of the fear and guilt. The extinction generalizes from words to thoughts and from painful but not repressed topics to more repressed topics. The drives that motivate repression become weakened, and cycles of extinction and generalization occur until "the repression is gradually unlearned under permissive social conditions that are the opposite to the punitive ones under which it was learned" (*ibid.*, p. 240). Thus, the therapeutic situation is characterized by permissiveness, which leads to the lifting of repression.

The process is slow and difficult because fear and anxiety accompany the discussion of repressed ideas. Even though the therapist is permissive and neutral, the therapist is also seen as a specialist in whom the client can have trust and confidence and who thus provides reassurance. The client experiences fear and anxiety while talking, which is a necessary condition for extinction. At the same time, the client experiences the benign attention of the therapist. Punishment does not occur, and the fear attached to the forbidden sentences is not reinforced. In terms of the approach-avoidance conflict that characterizes repression, the avoidance gradient is reduced by the attitudes and activity of the therapist, so that the client, as a result of the approach drive, can begin to move toward the goal that will satisfy his or her drive.

In addition to the client's verbalizations about himself or herself and the past, the *transference relationship* is the second necessary part of therapy. It provides information that the client is not able to give directly. The client reacts to the therapist emotionally—with fear, hate, and love—without being aware of it. These emotional reactions are called "transference," since they are not elicited by the therapist as the therapist actually is but are transferred to her or him as a representative of other figures, to whom they were originally directed.

Transference occurs in all areas of normal life, for emotional reactions are evoked by many situations that would not be considered adequate stimuli for them. In therapy, these transferred reactions are utilized to obtain information that is useful in helping the client. The therapist stimulates transference reactions by attempting to remain ambiguous, which allows the client to generalize more easily. The weakening of repression through permissiveness also facilitates transference—avoidance reactions to the therapist thus are not as strong as they are to others.

The generalization, or transfer, of many previously learned adaptive habits to the therapy situation makes therapy possible to begin with. These habits include being sensible, logical, and reasonable; being self-critical; speaking in an orderly, intelligent way; listening; being influenced by experts; expressing appropriate emotions; having hope, trust, and confidence in the therapist and in science; and wishing to please the therapist.

These generalizations, or transference reactions, facilitate therapy. Others interfere with therapy. Fear and dependence or helplessness may be immediately transferred to therapy. False hopes of quick or easy cure may transfer from experience with doctors. The client also brings more specific responses to therapy that obstruct the process. These reactions are the client's habitual ways of escaping from anxiety situations; they include stopping talking or being silent, obscuring or confusing issues by quibbling, focusing on minor or irrelevant matters, talking in circles, and being repetitious. Fear may be reacted to with anger directed toward the therapist, or anger may evoke fear responses. A common well-learned response to an anxiety-producing situation is to leave it, and the client may thus break off therapy. These reactions are considered transference reactions because they are not appropriate to the therapy situation. It is, of course, possible that at times the emotional reactions directed toward the therapist are appropriate, as when the therapist is hasty, stupid, or cruel (which are indications of incompetence) or when the therapist makes a mistake (in which case it is best for her or him to admit it).

While transferred reactions in the client may be considered as resistance on the part of the client, it must be recognized that they are generalized automatically to the therapy situation and are not purposely produced by the client. The transference situation is not a duel, but a real battle. Therapy is not simply a verbal intellectual discussion. The emotions involved in the neurosis must be brought out in therapy, at least to some extent.

The appearance of emotional responses in therapy entails responses that the client cannot talk about because they have never been labeled. They are, therefore, brought out where they can be discussed and labeled. Thus, the third aspect of the therapy process is *learning to label,* or to think about new topics. The feelings that arise with the lifting of repression and those that are manifested in transference must be dealt with verbally.

> The neurotic is a person who is in need of a stock of sentences that will match the events going on within and without him. The new sentences make possible an immense facilitation of higher mental processes. . . . By labeling a formerly unlabeled response he can represent this response in reasoning. (Dollard & Miller, 1950, p. 281)

Labeling must not be misunderstood as mere intellectualization. Therapy involves a new emotional experience with the therapist, which leads to learning that may occur unconsciously, but "the learning is more transferable, and therefore more efficient, when adequate labeling occurs" (*ibid.,* p. 303). The client must have his or her own emotional experience and must correctly label it. It is not sufficient for the client to acquire a collection of sentences that are not related to emotional or instrumental responses.

The fourth aspect of therapy is the *learning of discriminations.* The neurotic person

> must clearly see that the conflicts and repressions from which he suffers are not justified by the current conditions of reward and punishment. He must further learn that the conditions in the past which produced these conflicts are sharply dissimilar from those of the present. (Dollard & Miller, 1950, p. 305)

Only then can the neurotic person have the courage to try new responses, which, when rewarded, can break the neurotic impasse.

Discrimination, by enabling the client to recognize that the situation is different now, is useful in reducing the anxiety that prevents the client from making a formerly punished and now inhibited response. Simply using the labels *past* to refer to the dangerous situation and *present* to denote the harmless situation may provide a discrimination that can quickly reduce anxiety. Labeling thus facilitates discrimination, and discrimination tends to generalize to similar situations.

The importance of recovering past conditions is in contrasting them with present conditions so that differentiation or discrimination can occur. Describing the past constitutes a kind of reliving of it, with some of the emotions it generates. The past can thus be brought to some extent into the present and compared with it, thereby facilitating discrimination. The realization of the contrast between the client's present habit of repression and inhibition and the positive opportunities for gratification that exist in the environment helps the client mobilize his or her drives to be sensible and realistic; with the therapist's help, such realization may inhibit anxiety and stimulate action.

Verbal responses are important in discrimination, making possible the recognition of dissimilar stimuli to which similar responses are made and of similar stimuli to which dissimilar responses are made. Verbal cues can prevent generalization of anxiety from the past to the present. When anxiety is reduced by discrimination, new responses become possible; and as these responses reduce neurotic drives, they can become the basis for new habits that permanently resolve the neurotic conflict.

Result: Restoration of the Higher Mental Processes. Therapeutic gains can occur without improved labeling or insight. The permissive attitude of the therapist probably reduces the client's fear, and this lessening of fear should generalize from the therapeutic situation, leading to general improvement. This is usually not sufficient for complete cure, however; the removal of repression, new labeling, and improvement in discrimination and in the higher mental processes must also occur. The higher mental processes require verbal and other cue-producing responses and thus depend on the removal of repression and on labeling. A number of changes in thinking result.

One of the changes is the ability to make *adaptive discriminations,* which leads to the reduction of primary stimulus generalization and of irrational fears. The second is the ability to make *adaptive generalizations,* which improves secondary stimulus generalization and leads to adaptive responses to culturally defined similarities. The third change or improvement is anticipating danger and *motivating foresightful behavior.* Verbal and other cue-producing responses can mediate hope, as well as enable the individual to reward himself or herself for subgoal achievement and to wait for delayed rewards. The fourth is improvement in *reasoning and planning* through becoming aware of the real problem and defining it accurately. The fifth is the better *utilization of the cultural storehouse of tested problem solutions* that are available. The sixth is the *avoidance of the waste of contradictory behavior* through logical thinking. Finally, the verbalization of previously repressed material does not result in uninhibited behavior but in *behavior that is under better social control.* Such verbal control of behavior requires that the words be attached to proper emotional and instrumental responses and not merely to other words.

Considerable practice or "working through" is needed before appropriate labeling, and thus discrimination and generalization, becomes a habit. Also, thoughts and plans must be translated into action, which is then rewarded, if behavior is to improve. All this takes time, so that therapy is a long process, and improvement may continue after therapy sessions have ended.

Real-World Aspects of Therapy. The therapy sessions are the "talking" phase of therapy. The second phase is the outside, or real-world, aspect. Real-life problems must be solved with new behavior outside of therapy. An aspect of this is the generalization of responses to the therapist to other persons. This is an important part of cure. These responses will be strengthened or extinguished depending on whether they are rewarded or punished.

The performing in the real world of responses learned in therapy is not sufficient, however. Responses never performed in therapy will be necessary. Therapy can prepare for these responses by reducing the anxiety associated with them, but the responses must be made to persons in the client's real world. The extinction of fear of talking about such actions must generalize to fear of performing them. Once this fear is reduced, the drives leading to these actions increase and overcome inhibitory drives or stimuli. As the goal becomes nearer, strong anxiety reactions may arise, but they are overcome by the drive to respond. The approach-avoidance conflict must be resolved. Therapy contributes to this by reducing the avoidance gradient. In the neurotic, the attempt to increase the approach gradient leads only to increase in conflict and misery, with possible breaking off of the therapy. Therapy may be a slow process of trying and failing or of trying and succeeding in part, until success is achieved. Risks must be taken, and failures sometimes result. Therapy is not complete until actions follow verbalization.

Freudian theory seemed to assume that responses outside of therapy would occur automatically, although some analysts do encourage or direct real-life trials. While there is a tendency for such responses to occur without direction, it is not innate. However, if therapy is to be successful, verbal cues must be connected to overt responses; the client must act. Some clients are apathetic about acting, in which case the therapist must "get some 'action' responses following upon the cues of plans, and this connection must be slowly rewarded and strengthened" (*ibid.*, p. 338). In the later stages of therapy, when fear (avoidance) has been reduced, increasing motivation (approach) may have a good effect.

Since the major sources of drive reduction are not in the therapeutic situation, the therapist cannot provide the rewards that the client needs. They must come in real life. The nature of the life conditions or environment of the client are thus important for the success of therapy, and the therapist has no control over these conditions. Therapists do attempt to select clients whose life conditions are favorable.

Therapy is limited in what it can do. It cannot give all that the client may wish—better speech, social advancement, an advantageous marriage, and so forth. It cannot remake the person, particularly the older person, nor can it remedy all the deficiencies of early development and training. Solutions must also be within the moral codes of society, otherwise the client exchanges an unconscious mental conflict for an open social conflict, which is likely to be still more maladaptive.

IMPLEMENTATION: TECHNIQUES OF THERAPY

The techniques of psychotherapy are not completely separate, or discrete, but are blended or combined in infinite variety. Nevertheless, they can be identified and discussed separately.

Permissiveness

From the patient's standpoint, the novelty of the therapeutic situation lies in its permissiveness. He is allowed a good turn to talk. His statements are received by the therapist with an even, warm attention. The therapist is understanding and friendly. He is willing, so far as he can, to look at matters from the patient's side and make the best case for the patient's view of things. The therapist is not shocked by what he hears and does not criticize. The frightened patient learns that here is a person he can really talk to—perhaps the first such person in his life. (Dollard & Miller, 1950, pp. 243–244)

In the accepting, permissive situation, fears attached to repressed topics are gradually extinguished. Without this, therapy could not occur. Through permissiveness, lack of judgmental behavior, and lack of criticism, therapists set themselves apart from those who are not accepting and permissive. The permissiveness applies to thoughts but not to actions. Therapy attempts to remove repression of thoughts but not restraint of antisocial acts. There are also definite restrictions of actions during therapy: the client is asked not to take important steps, such as making changes in his or her marital status, job, or other significant areas. Such actions are to be suppressed until the client is in a position to take action that is free from neurotic influences. The client may also be asked to limit therapeutic conversation to the therapy hours.

Free Association

While permissiveness allows the client to speak, the rule of free association requires the client to speak without the inhibitions and censorship that influence ordinary conversation and without the consistencies and logic of such conversation. The client must report everything that comes to mind, immediately and without reservations. "The rule is a force which is applied against the force of neurotic fear. Without it, and unless he follows it, the patient will remain fixed in his neurotic habits and cannot recover the free use of his mind" (Dollard & Miller, 1950, pp. 241–242). Clients must talk; that is their responsibility. The therapist cannot obtain the relevant information by questioning, since he or she does not know the relevant questions. Furthermore, clients must volunteer information in the presence of fear, or extinction cannot occur. Thus, free association is not free and easy.

The client begins with material that is less important and less anxiety producing; then, as the anxiety is extinguished by the therapist's responses and attitudes and as the effects generalize, the client proceeds to more important, significant, and relevant material. This cycle of fear, extinction, generalization, and fear again is repeated in a process that appears to be a testing of the therapist. The result of this process is a gradual lifting of repression—the remembering of forgotten experiences, events, repressed sentences, and emotions. The therapist listens to it all with no a priori hypotheses in order to obtain a complete and rational verbal account of the client's life. As the therapist attempts to make sense of it all, he or she will see gaps and inconsistencies and will develop hypotheses about them. The therapist's own thoughts may describe what remains repressed in the client's mental life. Blockings in the client's association serve as aids to the therapist, since they point to areas where repression exists. Failure to deal with common important areas, as well as dreams and slips of the tongue, also points to repressed material. The therapist deals with these gaps and indications of repression essentially by following to the letter the rule of free association, urging and encouraging the client to further exploration and pointing out certain omissions, attitudes, and so on ("permissive interpretation").

Rewards for Talking

The client must be rewarded for talking while fearful and anxious in order to reinforce the talking and to enable the client to continue and to progress in uncovering repression. The therapist may reward such talking in various ways. One is by listening—giving full, free, and exclusive attention to what the client is saying. Another reward is the therapist's acceptance of what the client says and avoidance of judging and condemning. The client's talking without acceptance and forgiveness, or catharsis, is not effective. A third reward is the therapist's understanding and remembering what the client has said in the past. The therapist's calmness in the face of important revelations that the client is ashamed of or anxious about is a fourth reward. The therapist may even reward the client by expressions of sympathy or approval, but this is used sparingly. Finally, the therapist does not cross-question or make definite pronouncements but speaks tentatively and suggests possible implications or relationships. The therapist is patient and adapts to the pace of the client.

These rewards, instead of punishment for forbidden sentences spoken with fear, lead to the extinction of the fear. However, the fear of real dangers, of punishment for antisocial behavior, is not extinguished. "This discrimination must be made quite clearly by the therapist. The therapist can, so to say, promise nonpunishment for certain activities—those which were once punished but are now no longer forbidden—but the therapist cannot tamper with life's realities" (Dollard & Miller, 1950, p. 250).

Handling the Transference

The transference provides the therapist with indirect information about the client, in addition to what is obtained during free association. The therapist can label such data, while the client cannot.

The therapist is in many ways similar to teachers, parents, and age-graded superiors, which facilitates transference of responses learned in interaction with authoritative figures. The therapist encourages or produces such transference by remaining as ambiguous as possible. In addition, the extinction of anxiety related to speaking about forbidden matters under the permissiveness of the therapist generalizes to the fears that lead to avoidance and inhibition of emotional responses, so that these responses appear and are directed toward the therapist.

When the client impedes therapy because of transference-induced reactions, the therapist attempts to overcome the obstruction. If the client falls silent, the therapist may interpret this silence, assure the client that he or she cannot have a blank mind, or give a clue as to what thoughts the client might have. When obfuscation occurs, the therapist points out that it is an escape and urges the client to resume work.

> The therapist is under stress in accepting, identifying, and using transferred reactions for the ends of therapy. Though informative, transference emotions are often obstinate and difficult to deal with. . . . It is particularly important that the therapist should not imply that the patient is purposely producing these reactions, else he will confuse his patient and possibly give real cause for a feeling of injustice. The therapist's task is to identify these responses as transferred and find out how they arose. (Dollard & Miller, 1950, p. 274)

While the client feels that his or her reactions must be real, the therapist must prove to the client that they are not. The angry client may criticize obvious defects of the therapist (for example, a foreign accent), but the therapist must not respond with anger or irritation.

The therapist may have to identify the existence of the transferred response, show that it is not objectively justified as directed toward the therapist, and raise questions about its origin and the person from whom it is transferred. Since transferred responses are learned responses, they are a source of inference about early conditions in the client's life. When the inappropriateness of the transference response and its obstruction of therapy are pointed out, the acquired drives to be logical and to progress in therapy lead the client to resume work and free association.

If the therapist does not know how to recall the patient to his proper task, such responses may persist and may end therapeutic progress. Failure to understand transference manifestations is one of the commonest sources of failure for the amateur in psychotherapy. The therapist lost many patients in this way, and inexperienced therapists still do. (Dollard & Miller, 1950, p. 278)

Labeling

Free association and transference produce emotional responses that have never been labeled. The therapist must help the client label these responses. In order to do this, the therapist, on the basis of the material provided by free association and the transference, must develop an understanding of the client, so that he or she not only can empathize with the client (feel the client's feelings), but also can label the client's feelings. Labeling consists of producing new verbal responses by connecting words to the correct emotional or environmental cues. The client may acquire these new verbal responses in at least three ways.

1. The client may discover or create the new verbal units under the compulsion of free association. Anxiety associated with the responses is extinguished by the therapist's permissiveness. The production of the responses increases during therapy, both because anxiety is reduced and because there is increasingly more to build on. "The more of the essential work the patient can perform by himself during therapy, the more certain he is to be able to do what he needs afterward. The therapist should be careful not to deprive the patient of the pleasure of making his own discoveries" (Dollard & Miller, 1950, p. 287).

2. Therapists may selectively strengthen client responses that they think are important without contributing their own ideas. The therapist may reward the client in various ways, such as by saying "uh-huh," including the client's ideas in summaries, and repeating what the client has said. Questions that are asked for clarification of material already introduced by the client may also serve this purpose by focusing attention on the client's responses.

3. The client may rehearse responses provided by the therapist as interpretations. Strong anxiety or the failure of the label and the cues produced by the emotion to occur at the same time may prevent the client from being able to label his or her own responses. The therapist may provide the labels at the appropriate time. The client's rehearsal may be in paraphrase, using the client's own words, or may take place in the client's thoughts rather than verbalizations. The client is rewarded by the reduction of anxiety, the increase of hope, and the feeling of progress. Sometimes anxiety is increased, however, and the client resists the interpretation. Resistance may be related to the client's strong desire to be independent and do it all alone, or it may occur when the therapist makes a stupid or an awkward interpretation.

An incorrect label may give some temporary relief by reducing anxiety, but because it is not correct, it will not continue to be rewarded and will not persist. Verbal responses may be attached to emotional cues, to environmental cues, to instrumental acts, and to other verbal cues. The last relationship may be termed clarification and often involves ordering responses, linking events in a temporal and causal order.

Interpretation, or "prompting," by the therapist is necessary if therapy is to be efficient and maximally successful, since the client usually cannot do it all alone, although this is to be preferred. The client who can do this makes rapid progress and is ready for dismissal when he or she can do it well alone. The second of the methods described above is necessary when the client makes a number of different and confusing or contradictory hypotheses or statements.

The third method, although sometimes necessary, has some disadvantages. The therapist cannot be certain that the client uses interpretation when the client rehearses the responses silently rather than saying them aloud. Silent responses are probably weaker and less effective than verbalizations. Weakening also occurs through generalization from the therapist's voice to the client. Finally, there is the resistance, or "interpretation shock."

The therapist should not intervene with interpretations until clients cease to make progress on their own, and then only to the extent that the therapist feels clients can bear. Moreover, "the skillful therapist . . . does not make interpretations on mere hunches. He waits until he has strong evidence for his hypothesis before he supplies a label, points out a transferred response, or teaches a discrimination. If the patient is to be convinced, the evidence must be convincing. The fewer ill-founded notions the therapist utters, the greater his authority when he does speak" (Dollard & Miller, 1950, p. 284).

Teaching Discrimination

Discrimination involves attaching different verbal cues to stimulus patterns that are actually different. The therapist uses various methods to teach the patient to discriminate. One technique is to call attention to a problem area in order to evoke new discriminations by failing to understand the client, which stimulates the client to reexamine the area. This is similar to the Socratic method of teaching. Applying a word or a label to which an elaborate series of responses is already attached transfers these responses to the new situation. The therapist may discourage certain responses by labeling them as false or doubtful. The therapist is thus "an operator in the field of language, exciting learned drives and administering learned rewards, eliciting adequate sentence chains to guide instrumental responses" (Dollard & Miller, 1950, p. 312). Generalizations to similar sets of stimuli can be facilitated if the therapist points out their similarity. The therapist may also foster discrimination by pointing out the difference between the past and the present and assuring the client that the present environment is benign.

LENGTH AND LIMITATIONS OF TREATMENT

Length.   There are no set time limits for therapy. The length of treatment can be expected to vary—all depending on the patient and his/her particular problems and issues.

Some patients will need only minor encouragement to make effective use of their higher mental skills. Others may require many months of laborious work to revoke repression and restore higher mental activity. Some patients may need only a nudge to take the vital step into drive-reducing action. Others will require a long period of slow testing in the therapeutic situation before inhibition of action is reduced. The goal is the same in every case, i.e., an active mental life and effective behavior in the real world. The demands on the therapist, however, will vary according to the severity of repression and the strength of the conflict. (Dollard & Miller, 1950, p. 423)

Limitations.   This approach is oriented toward the treatment of neuroses. However, a number of circumstances that can lead to the failure of therapy are as follows (Dollard & Miller, 1950, pp. 424–427):

1. if the patient is too proud to come to the therapist (for help);
2. if the patient cannot meet the therapist's conditions of treatment (e.g., being able to pay a certain fee);
3. if the patient is unable to learn;
4. if the patient is not strongly motivated;
5. if the patient does not try new responses outside the therapeutic situation;
6. if real life does not reward new responses of the patient;
7. if reality circumstances do not remain favorable.

EXAMPLE

Dollard, Auld, and White (1953) have presented an analysis of a case of brief psychotherapy using techniques based on the theories of Dollard and Miller. The student would benefit from reading the complete presentation and analysis of this case, but only a portion of the verbatim transcript of the eleventh interview, which is given under the heading "Tactics: Examples of Therapeutic Techniques in This Case," is included here without comment. It is perhaps well to note that the authors felt that the therapist was too active and, thus, that this interview does not illustrate free association well, or not as well as other interviews in the case.

The Eleventh Hour of Therapy

PATIENT: We've had a hectic day today. We've been working like slaves, my mother and I, all morning, since seven-thirty. For a big family dinner tonight. And I'm tired. But she's doing all the cooking. . . . I haven't that to worry about, but the little things, you know. Do you know I've been thinking about the conversation that we had last week . . . and . . . my life is very boring and dull . . . but it really is my own fault. I really should go out and get a job and work, I think, so that during the day my mind is occupied—my time is taken up at night—I'll be very contented to sit home and do nothing. And . . . and I guess I shouldn't complain about it . . . being so dull. Because it really is my fault.

THERAPIST: How do you mean, it's your fault?

PA: Well, I mean I shouldn't . . . I should be so busy during the day that at night I won't mind staying in and being bored or leading a quiet life. But . . . I don't know what I . . . I'm not qualified to do anything really—I mean to get a job. I used to take those parts in our theater group plays but I could never go into show business professionally. I could only work in a gift shop or as a reception-ist or a telephone-answering service, or something like that. But I suppose I could do it. Now I could take up bookkeeping or typing and shorthand.

TH: Yes, un huh.

PA: I could get . . . you know, take that course and six easy lessons, is that what they. . . . (laugh) You see it advertised. It's a short course. I was thinking about doing that. But, it's funny, I don't know what's the matter with me, I . . . have two lovely children, I have a wonderful husband, I have a lovely home . . . but I'm not happy. That doesn't make sense.

TH: I don't understand, you say is life too easy. . . .

PA: Well, I mean is it because I . . . I have things too easy that I'm . . . discon-tented. . . . [I]f I had it harder would I feel that I shouldn't complain about any-thing?

TH: How does that sound to you?

PA: It seems logical. It seems that my life is too easy for me. That . . . I have no complaints to make at all for. . . . I mean as far as . . . having a wonderful hus-band and a wonderful daughter and son and a lovely home, and I entertain when I want to . . . and it seems as though I'm discontented. I'm not happy and I complain all the time.

TH: Well, there must be some reason, don't you think?

PA: Well, I don't know, that's what I can't understand; why should I feel this way? Why should I feel that I'm discontented, that I'm looking for something all the time? Why shouldn't I be contented to stay home and . . . and have the things I have? I can . . . I don't know. I still can't understand it. Why should I complain about my boring life or monotonous life? I have no right to, really.

TH: How's that?

PA: Well, people . . . many people are worse off than I am, that haven't got the things that I have. Why should I complain? Why should I be unhappy? Does it all have to do with what I went through as a child?

TH: Well, I don't see . . . of course other people have it more difficult and other peo-ple have greater problems. . . .

PA: Yes.

TH: . . . but I don't think we should judge your problem on the basis of what other people's problems are but should try to understand your problems and see why you should have. . . .

PA: What am I looking for? I don't know what I want in life. What am I . . . what's . . . what . . . I don't know what is my aim in life. Shouldn't I be contented—the way it is? But I'm not. I'm unhappy.

TH: Well, isn't that then our problem?

PA: Yes, but. . . .

TH: Not the question whether you should or should not be contented, but the fact that you are not and that we want to find out why.

PA: But I'm ashamed to complain about it. Because I have so much. I mean I have a . . . a good husband and a nice house and a wonderful daughter and son. It really makes me ashamed. Am I making a mountain out of a molehill?

TH: Well, there's something in this picture which seems to be missing; I mean you mention all these things that are seemingly satisfying and yet you are not satis-fied. . . .

PA: But I'm not.

TH: . . . and there must be something that is wrong.

PA: I don't know why—I can't put my finger on it, really. Well, I don't know what I'm striving for. What do I want? What do I expect from life? Why should I get bored all the time? Why should life be so monotonous? Is it because I don't have enough to do? Is it because I have time on my hands? If I went out and worked I probably wouldn't feel this way. I kept asking myself that for the past two days. I don't know what I want out of life, what I'm striving for, but I expect what I want . . . my husband is good to me, my daughter is wonderful, and I have a fine boy. I entertain nicely. People have said that they feel very welcome in . . . and I'm a cordial hostess, and they were comfortable in my home. Doesn't everybody do that? Isn't that everybody's life?

TH: Well, if this were all so, then it would be very amazing that you shouldn't be satisfied. And I wonder whether these things really are so.

PA: But, they are all so, but still I'm unhappy, still I'm unhappy, still I want to run away . . . and . . . get away from my house. But I think it's lack of something to do, lack of interest, lack of . . . working maybe, that's what I need. Paul has gone away to school. Doris is growing up now, she doesn't need me for anything, really . . . except to get her meals and things like that, but that's nothing. And Paul is away at school all winter and at camp in the summer. My husband only needs me for the meals and things like that.

TH: What kind of things?

PA: Dinner, and washing, and cleaning, but outside of that I . . . my time is my own.

TH: Is that really the only thing that your husband needs you for?

PA: Well . . . he's very . . . he seems to be very contented with the life that he lives . . . leads. I don't interfere with his life. He seems to . . . like to come home, and stay home and relax, after putting in a tough day with those law cases of his. I certainly can't . . . interfere with that. It wouldn't do me any good if I tried. We are . . . . a . . . two very different personalities completely. He's very placid and reserved and I'm the opposite. I'm happy-go-lu- . . . I mean I used to be . . . happy-go-lucky and nothing bothered me too much. I like to have a good time. I like to have fun. I don't feel as though I'm old . . . too old to enjoy life. But he . . . he likes quiet things . . . the quiet life.

TH: But this difference in personality hasn't been bothering you—at least you haven't said so—all through the last sixteen years or so.

PA: Oh, I thought about it . . . yes, I have. I've thought about it a long time . . . how we can be visiting and I'll have a good time and all of a sudden he'll say, "Come on, let's go home." So, quick like that I have to leave and go home. . . . I mean it's been going on for years. It isn't anything new. And as I told you before, if we're invited out and he's tired, we don't go. I mean things like that. But I guess I can't be a playgirl all the time. But I don't feel old . . . really, I mean, where I have to stay home all the time. I feel as though I want to have fun and enjoy myself. Is that wrong?

TH: No. Of course, you are young; you are quite young enough to have an enjoyable life, and I think that you have a right to that kind of thing, but I'm just wondering. . . .

PA: You mean it isn't wrong to still feel young in your heart and to want to get fun out of life.

TH: If one considers such a thing as "right" or "wrong," I'm quite sure that it is not wrong.

PA: Do I sound immature, do I sound like a child when I say things like that? Childish?

TH: Do you think you do?

PA: I'm afraid to say I do. I think it is childish just to want to have a good time and enjoy myself. I think now that my children are growing up and I'm getting older I should want to settle down and not do anything—and just lead a very quiet, simple life.

TH: Why do you think you should?

PA: We . . . I don't know, I just feel as though I . . . I can't go out and do the things I used to do, although I still feel as though I could . . . I mean, inside. But it doesn't look right; it isn't right to do it.

TH: With Doris getting older and more independent, do you feel that you are, well let us say, getting old, being an old woman now?

PA: No. It doesn't bother me. I never think of it that way. Is that wrong?

TH: No, what you say, that you feel that you should. . . .

PA: Well, I do . . . I mean, I feel I should on account of the people around me, convention's sake, you know what I mean, having people talk about me. I still feel that I can . . . I ought to have fun . . . and . . . and enjoy myself, even though the children are growing up and don't need me as much now. I think I really could have a better time . . . but I'm afraid of what people will say. My friends, my husband.

TH: What do you think they might say?

PA: They'll say that she ought to grow up, she's not . . . she's got growing children, she should act like a mother. (embarrassed laugh) But Bob is very restrained . . . not restrained but placid; he's very quiet. We have been away—as a matter of fact I don't even enjoy going away with Bob, because he likes to go to a place where you can just eat, and sleep, and you know, relax, go to bed early. I do that every night. All the time. I don't even like to go away on vacations with him, or anyplace . . . but I go. He wants to relax all the time; I'm not tired, I don't feel that kind of tired that . . . I want fun, I want life, I want people around. Is that wrong?

TH: Just . . . how do you feel about this? You seem to feel. . . .

PA: Well, I don't know. . . . I can't understand . . . I mean, this . . . feeling that I've had about Bob being . . . placid . . . I've always . . . held it in, I mean I've never said anything about it. I've never said, "Oh, I'd like to go someplace where it's fun." I've always kept my mouth shut and not said anything about it . . . because I knew it wouldn't do any good to say it. I mean it's always been in the back of my mind. We went on a vacation once for four days, and all I did was sit on the porch and read. I can do that at home. I . . . and people said, "Oh, you must have had a wonderful time on your vacation." I was bored to death! I hated every minute of it. Of course, I didn't say anything to him. I said it was very nice . . . but I hated it. And I won't go away with him anymore. And I can't go alone, so I'm stuck. (half-laugh) So I . . . so I guess for me the only way I can go . . . I mean get away . . . is to go with him and do what he wants to do. So you see how different we are? Exact—just like night and day. Maybe it's better. Maybe he holds me down. Maybe I need that sort of thing. But I feel that I've missed so much in my younger days. I wasn't allowed to do anything. But I thought being married, and . . . it would be different. But it hasn't changed a bit. I mean as far as . . . pleasure . . . and enjoyment. It sounds crazy, doesn't it? (pause) But he's so good that I can't . . . . I guess I can't be any different with him, I mean I can't . . . I can't go . . . a . . . I can't disagree with him, as far as things like that go. I can't say, "I'm going out to a nightclub tonight and you can stay home." I've never done it.

TH: At the time you were telling me about, when you used to be active in that amateur dramatic group and so on. . . .

PA: The rehearsals were sometimes in the afternoon.

TH: Yes, but you were then also going out and having . . . fun. Did that have any relationship to this feeling?

PA: Sure. It made me feel that I could have fun one or two afternoons or evenings a week, and I could sit home the other evenings. At least I had some fun; I got that in. But he . . . I . . . listen . . . I . . . I feel he's entitled to living the kind of life he wants to live. I don't object to it, I mean, as far as he's concerned. He puts in a hard day; he's tired. He really—I'd never deprive him of going to bed at nine o'clock or ten o'clock; I would never say anything to make him feel that . . . that I was unhappy about it, I just don't say anything. Course I feel terrible, but I don't say anything about it. We . . . we refuse a million invitations on account of him. Is it wrong to feel that you still want to have fun in life?

TH: Well, there might be other compensations. . . .

PA: Well. . . .

TH: . . . for this, and I wonder whether you feel that there are or there are not . . . and, I mean, other compensations in your relationship.

PA: Well, he's . . . he's a . . . he's good.

TH: How do you mean?

PA: He's . . . reliable, he's honest, he's a hard worker . . . he's a homebody. (apologetic laugh) He likes to stay home. Maybe I haven't . . . maybe I'm not mature; maybe I'm still a child—I haven't matured enough, maybe I'm not grown-up enough, I don't know.

TH: Well now, the things you mentioned as . . . the good points of your husband. Are those really the only things you would expect from a husband?

PA: No, I think a husband should be . . . as excited to do something as the wife should. I feel that . . . Bob should feel like I feel, about having a good time, about going out and being with people. That he should be as congenial as I am. (pause) Even when we were younger—I mean even before we were married and . . . we were engaged, it was the same way, although I always figured, well, he has a hard day the next day and I wouldn't interfere. I would let him . . . he would . . . we . . . when we used to have dates he left me at ten-thirty or eleven o'clock, early. We never stayed up past midnight, ever. I never remember staying out till twelve or one o'clock. I sound silly, though, to make an issue of it, don't I?

TH: Well, this is a problem which is bothering you, and I don't see why you consider that silly.

PA: Yes, but how . . . I . . . I can't straighten it out. How can I do anything about it? There's no way of . . . of changing it. I certainly couldn't say to Bob, "I'm going out on a date tonight, good-by." (throaty laugh) Or, "I'm going out to have fun." I couldn't do that; I'm not built that way. As much as I would probably love to do it, I wouldn't do it. Is it . . . is it because I feel that I missed so much when I was younger that I feel that now I want to . . . do the things I didn't do before?

TH: Is that what you think it is?

PA: Yes, I do. I think I never really had a chance to . . . really go out and . . . well, I don't know, it sounds silly to even talk about. It's ridiculous. Can't do anything about it anyway. I sound like a child. Once the pattern is made you have to stick to it, I guess. Once you start your life the way you do you can't change. Especially your married life. I've never told Bob how I felt about this . . . because I knew it wouldn't do any good. I'm sure it wouldn't. Because he wouldn't understand, he wouldn't . . . he . . . he'd think I was acting like a baby. So, if I get myself something to do during the day, where I'd get busy and not think about it, maybe it'll be better to a . . . at night I'd be contented to stay home. It's like knocking your head against a stone wall, isn't it? Can you straighten out a problem like that? Is it possible?

TH: Well, I'm not sure whether we really have the whole problem in front of us.

PA: Well, what do you mean? I don't understand; I've told you how I felt about it.

TH: But you say yourself, again and again, it sounds childish and it doesn't make sense.

PA: But it's because there's no way of solving it. There's no way of solving that problem. How can I go to Bob and say, "I want to go out tonight. I want to have fun. I'm tired of staying home." If I did, he'd say, "I'm sorry, I'm tired." So what am I going to do? Go out by myself? Can I do that?

TH: Well, that's a question you'd have to ask yourself.

PA: Well, I can't, I've never done it, I wouldn't know where to—how to start. So I keep asking myself, well am I str—what do I want out of life? What am I striving for, what am I working for? Where am I getting? I have a nice home, a nice daughter and son, a nice husband, but that's all. It sounds stupid, doesn't it?

TH: No, it doesn't sound stupid; it sounds like an incomplete picture to me.

PA: Well, it isn't incomplete. That's exactly how I feel. I feel that I . . . do what I have to do, but I still want to get some pleasure out of life too. But why am I different from most people? Most people, I guess, don't feel the way I do. They don't complain about not going out. Well, what's wrong with me? Why should I feel like I want to enjoy myself and have fun?

TH: Well, of course, again we can't say what happens to most people, because we are dealing with—appraising—your problem rather than other people. . . .

PA: Well, that's what I mean, there's no comparison, I mean I don't understand it. There are . . . there's a friend of mine who . . . who's in worse circumstances than I am, but she never complains. Maybe because she has three kids to take care of during the day and she's probably tickled to death when they go to bed so she can relax at night. Maybe it's because I don't have enough to do during the day. (pause) I don't know. But I've felt like this for a long time. I feel that I'm not getting everything out of life that I would like to.

TH: What would you like to get out of life? That you're not. . . .

PA: I don't know. That's what I'd like to know. That's what I wonder. What do I want? What do I? That's where I can't put my finger on it. There's something that I . . . that I . . . I'm hoping for, but I don't know what.

TH: When you were engaged to your husband and this pattern had already been . . . you know, you say this pattern had already been established back then—was there something that you were hoping for that might compensate you for some of the socially unexciting times?

PA: There was nothing. Nothing. I was young, I didn't know, I was madly in love. I thought he was wonderful and I adored him. I thought he was a wonderful guy. I didn't look for anything else. He was sweet, he was . . . oh, I didn't need . . . I didn't want anything else. He was thoughtful and he was considerate. I used to work in a gift shop; I was substituting there one summer. He used to pick me up in the morning and drive me to work, pick me up at five-thirty in the afternoon. I thought he was just marvelous. And Bob is very secure. As far as I can see, he . . . he . . . nothing seems to bother him too much. And he's had a very tough life, too, because he worked his way through college . . . as a salesman . . . in the summertime. And his family were poor. He was really, he's really a terrific guy. Self-made. (pause) And I always felt that Bob was the "old reliable," I mean somebody you could depend on all the time. That was the feeling I had, he was always there when you wanted him, when you needed him. He still is, I mean that's the w . . . you know. That's what he is today.

TH: And yet, somehow you sound as if you were disappointed. . . . I can't quite put my finger on it.

PA: Disappointed? (pause) No, I don't know. Maybe it's because I . . . that he's older that I'm disappointed. I mean, maybe if I had married somebody younger that . . . that wasn't so . . . set in their ways. Bob is a lot like I remember my father to be. He had a wonderful disposition, easygoing, reliable, I mean, those are the traits.

TH: Well, isn't there something that one expects from a husband that one doesn't expect from one's father?

PA: Love and companionship? Romance? (pause) That's when you're young. When you're older it doesn't mean anything anymore. Or when you're married a long time it changes completely, doesn't it?

TH: How do you mean, it changes completely?

PA: Well, I don't know, when you're young it's kid stuff I guess, but when you get older you don't . . . think about it, or . . . it doesn't mean anything. It's like . . . being married when you're older . . . it's like a habit. I mean it's like brushing your teeth. It's . . . it's . . . your husband is there and you're . . . and that's the way it is.

TH: I wonder whether that is the way it really has to be.

PA: Well, I don't know. I mean I can't answer that question. I don't know.

TH: Well, let me put it this way, could it be that you would rather that it were not that way?

SUMMARY AND EVALUATION

Summary.   Neurosis is learned in early childhood. Although a single drive can be raised to traumatic heights and cause pain and suffering, neurosis is usually the product of the conflict of drives originating in the feeding situation, cleanliness training, sex training, and anger-anxiety situations. These conflicts are repressed; that is, they are unconscious. The unconscious is that which cannot be verbalized, that which is unlabeled. Fear is the most basic and the strongest drive involved in conflict; it inhibits the expression of other drives, thus preventing their satisfaction. Both fear and the conflicting drive produce symptoms that consist of responses—often compromise responses—that lead to some drive reduction. Thus, they are rewarded or reinforced and persist. Neurotic persons are miserable because of their conflicts, which prevent the satisfaction of drives and appear to be stupid because repression prevents neurotic persons from knowing the nature of their problem.

The therapeutic situation provides the conditions for new learning. Free association leads to the uncovering of repression. The transference further reveals the nature of the conflicting drives. The client and the therapist engage in the process of labeling these drives, experiences, feelings, and conflicts. Such labeling makes possible both the discrimination of experiences and situations that are apparently similar but actually different and the appropriate generalization to situations that are actually similar. Labeling and the resultant insight enable the client to engage in the higher mental activities that are necessary for adaptive behavior.

Neurosis is essentially an approach-avoidance conflict, that is, a situation in which the individual has strong tendencies to both approach and to avoid the same goal. The gradient of avoidance (the increase of the tendency for avoidance, or fear, with increasing proximity to the goal) is stronger than the gradient of approach (the increase of the tendency for approach with increasing proximity to the goal). The neurotic person has strong avoidance tendencies. An attempt to increase the neurotic person's motivation to approach the goal will increase only his or her fear and conflict. This is often what well-meaning relatives and friends try to do. If the therapist does the same, the client will tend to leave therapy. Therefore, rather than attempt to raise the approach gradient, the therapist attempts to reduce the avoidance gradient and, thus, the client's fears through acceptance, permissiveness, and understanding.

In one publication, Miller (1964) referred to the situation in which the client's fears are realistic and the achievement of the goal results in punishment. The client is then punished if the goal is reached or suffers strong fear or conflict if the punishment keeps the client just barely away from the goal.

> In such cases, attempting to decrease fear and avoidance will indeed produce a negative therapeutic effect, while conversely, a positive therapeutic effect may be produced by increasing the strength of fear and avoidance to the point where the subject remains far enough away from the forbidden goal that he is no longer strongly punished or even tempted enough to be in conflict. (p. 154)

When punishment occurs some time after achieving the goal, strong fear (or guilt) is felt after the goal has been reached but only moderate fear, before it has been reached. Again, increasing the height of the avoidance gradient might produce therapeutic changes.

Evaluation.   Dollard and Miller present a meticulous, systematic, and reasoned approach based on reinforcement learning theory. They have integrated learning theory with the clinical system of psychotherapy developed by psychoanalysis. They have shown essentially that psychoanalysis is consistent with, or can be rationalized to appear consistent with, reinforcement learning theory. The concept of reinforcement is substituted for Freud's pleasure principle. The concept of ego strength is translated into that of the higher mental processes and of culturally-valued learned drives and skills. Repression becomes the inhibition of the cue-producing responses that mediate thinking and reasoning. Transference is a special case of generalization. Conflict is seen in terms of learning theory. Additional concepts and principles, such as inhibition and restraint, are added to extend some of those of psychoanalysis. The concept of reality is extended, or concretized, in terms of the physical and social conditions of learning. The need for responses to be made and reinforced outside of therapy, in real life, is emphasized.

Compared with the approaches of Wolpe (1990; see Chapter 6) and of Salter (1949), that of Dollard and Miller is broad, comprehensive, and authoritative. Rather than rejecting psychological and social factors, such as the nature of the client-therapist relationship, this approach incorporates them and indicates their consistency with learning theory. There is a major point of disagreement with the techniques of Salter and Wolpe. On the assumption, supported by empirical evidence, that the avoidance gradient is stronger than the approach gradient in an approach-avoidance conflict, Dollard and Miller base their techniques on the reduction of the avoidance gradient. (However, they do recognize the need to motivate some clients to go beyond talking and take action, although they do not specify how this is to be done.) In direct contrast to this, the techniques of Salter and Wolpe appear to be directed toward the raising of the approach gradient. Since Dollard and Miller present empirical evidence and suggest clinical evidence for their position, how, then, can Wolpe and Salter achieve success with their techniques? Two possible explanations present themselves. First, many of Wolpe's clients may not be clinically neurotic but possess isolated symptoms or limited disturbances that can be helped by these approaches; that is, they are individuals in whom the approach gradient, although somewhat weak, can easily be made stronger by techniques such as those used by Salter and Wolpe. Second, it is possible that their success is the result, not of the techniques to which they ascribe it, but of other aspects of the treatment, such as their earnest, sincere interest in, concern for, and efforts to help their clients.

The contrasting views of treatment in terms of the approach-avoidance gradient appear to be related to contrasting views of whether behavior changes first and feelings and attitudes change later or vice versa. Wolpe and Salter appear to accept the former position. Dollard and Miller appear to adhere to the latter. For them, fear is an attitude or a feeling, and their approach is to reduce fear through the therapeutic relationship before they expect behavior to change.

There is another related and somewhat contradictory aspect of this basic difference. Wolpe emphasizes that the client must be relaxed when engaging in desirable new behavior, such as sexual activity, so that behavior is reconditioned by being associated with a pleasant or nonanxious feeling. (Wolpe also describes it as the inhibition of fear by another incompatible response.) Dollard and Miller (1950), on the contrary, advocate that the client make a sexual response while feeling afraid, so that when the behavior is not followed by punishment, extinction will occur. It is, of course, likely that in the case of Wolpe's method, some anxiety or fear does exist, even though the client is somewhat relaxed, and that in the case of Dollard and Miller's technique, fear or anxiety has been reduced sufficiently to permit the client to act when he or she could not before. Wolpe emphasizes reconditioning, while Dollard and Miller emphasize extinction.

Dollard and Miller also disagree with Salter and Wolpe and other behavior therapists in the latter's belief that symptoms are the neurosis and that removal of the symptoms is equivalent to a cure of the neurosis. Dollard and Miller (1950) stated that since

> a learned symptom produces a certain amount of reduction of the state of high drive motivating it . . . interfering with the symptom . . . will be expected to throw the patient back into a state of high drive and conflict. This will tend to motivate the learning of new responses. These new responses may be either more adaptive ones or new, and possibly worse, symptoms. (p. 385)

Dollard and Miller conceded that "after the inhibitions blocking the more adaptive goal responses have been sufficiently reduced, however, we might expect different results" (*ibid.,*

p. 386). Then the therapist might interfere with a symptom by means of an unfavorable interpretation, which might cause the goal response to become stronger than the weakened inhibition. This may be a factor in the apparent success of Wolpe's and Salter's methods. Dollard and Miller also rely more on discrimination than on automatic conditioning. Their approach is thus more verbal and more rational than are conditioning approaches. Although they recognize the affective and emotional aspects as essential, their emphasis on verbal labeling, discrimination, and generalization gives a more verbal-rational cast to their approach than traditional psychoanalysis has. It is interesting that at the close of the chapter on labeling, Dollard and Miller (1950) feel it necessary to note that they "are not advocating any mere intellectualization of the therapeutic process" (p. 303). Yet, while there is concern with affective elements, there is emphasis on rational analysis. The therapist is seen as performing a teaching function to a great extent.

There are some gaps and inconsistencies in Dollard and Miller's approach. For example, what repression *is* receives attention, but the *process* of repression itself is given inadequate treatment. In discussing free association, they claim that speaking is easier or less anxiety producing than thinking, so that "the extinction effects which are first attached to talking out loud generalize swiftly to 'talking without voice' (thinking)" (*ibid.,* p. 250). Later, however, discussing client obstructiveness, they suggest that "even though the patient goes on thinking the sentences which produce anxiety, it may be that this anxiety is considerably less than when he makes the same response out loud" (*ibid.,* pp. 270–271). These are minor things, however. A more general criticism is that Dollard and Miller's approach is derived from a learning theory that has been developed mainly from experiments with animals and then extended to human behavior, often by analogy (Miller & Butler, 1952). It suffers also from the limitations of reinforcement theory (Raimy, 1952), which does not appear to account adequately for all learning and behavior change, particularly the complex behavior of human beings. Dollard and Miller's approach is thus oversimplified and restricted to a view of the human being as a reaction system responding to situational stimuli that reduce its drives. Secondary, or learned, drives, which derive from the primary drives, are recognized, but their nature and their development, or derivation from the primary drives, remain rather vague.

Dollard and Miller present their ideas as hypotheses, not proven principles. They stress that their book is not complete or adequate for the practice of psychotherapy. They contemplated further books to fill in the gaps and deal with unsolved problems. It is a pity that this plan was not realized, and it is also a pity that *Personality and Psychotherapy* (Dollard & Miller, 1950) has not been given the attention it deserves by others interested in psychotherapy or in the education of psychotherapists.

Dollard and Miller's is one of the few really systematic approaches to therapy. Their integration of so-called insight psychotherapy with learning theory anticipated current efforts by almost 30 years. As Arkowitz (1992) has stated,

> Dollard and Miller's book . . . went far beyond its usual description as a simple attempt to translate psychoanalytic concepts into behavioral language. In fact, it was far more than that. It was an attempt to synthesize and integrate ideas about neurosis and psychotherapy from two perspectives in order to provide a unifying theory for the field. (p. 264)

He continues, "the work of Dollard and Miller still stands as one of the most comprehensive and ambitious attempts to integrate these two seemingly diverse approaches" (*ibid.,* p. 265). "Now that psychotherapy integration is more established as a field, perhaps their work will be rediscovered as it deserves to be" (*ibid.,* p. 265).

REFERENCES

Arkowitz, H. (1992). Integrative theories of therapy. In D. K. Freedheim (Ed.). *History of psychotherapy* (pp. 261–303). Washington, DC: American Psychological Association.

Dollard J. (1937). *Caste and class in a southern town.* New Haven: Yale University Press.

Dollard, J., Auld, F., Jr., & White, A. M. (1953). *Steps in psychotherapy.* New York: The Macmillan Company.

Dollard J., Doob, L. W., Miller, N. E., & Sears, R. R. (1939). *Frustration and aggression.* New Haven: Yale University Press.

Dollard, J., & Miller, N. E. (1941). *Social learning and imitation.* New Haven: Yale University Press.

Dollard, J., & Miller, N. E. (1950). *Personality and psychotherapy: An analysis in terms of learning, thinking, and culture.* New York: McGraw-Hill.

Miller, J. G., & Butler, J. M. (1952). Review of *Personality and psychotherapy* by J. Dollard and N. E. Miller. *Psychological Bulletin, 49,* 183–185.

Miller, N. E. (1959). Liberalization of basic S-R concepts: Extensions to conflict behavior, motivation, and social learning. In S. Koch (Ed.). *Psychology: A study of science. Study I: Conceptual and systematic.* Vol. 2. *General systematic formulations, learning, and special processes* (pp. 196–292). New York: McGraw-Hill.

Miller, N. E. (1964). Some implications of modern behavior theory for personality change and psychotherapy. In D. Byrne & P. Worchel (Eds.). *Personality change* (pp. 149–179). New York: Wiley.

Raimy, V. C. (1952). Clinical methods: Psychotherapy. *Annual Review of Psychology, 3,* 321–350.

Salter, A. (1949). *Conditioned reflex therapy.* New York: Farrar, Straus.

Wolpe, J. (1990). *The practice of behavior therapy* (4th ed.). New York: Pergamon.

chapter *6*

Behavior Therapy: Wolpe

Joseph Wolpe (b. 1915) was educated in South Africa and received his M.B. and B.Ch. in 1939 and his M.D. in 1948 from the University of Witwatersrand, Johannesburg. While engaged in the private practice of psychiatry, he was lecturer in psychiatry at Witwatersrand from 1949 to 1959, except for the year 1956–1957, when he was a fellow at the Center for Advanced Study in the Behavioral Sciences at Stanford University. From 1960 to 1965, Wolpe was research and clinical professor of psychiatry at the University of Virginia Medical School in Charlottesville, Virginia. In 1965, he became professor of psychiatry in the Department of Behavioral Sciences of the School of Medicine at Temple University and the Eastern Pennsylvania Psychiatric Institute in Philadelphia, where he remained for approximately 20 years. He currently is affiliated with Pepperdine University and the University of California, Los Angeles.

In 1979, Wolpe received a Distinguished Scientific Award for the Applications of Psychology from the American Psychological Association. The announcement of the award in the *American Psychologist* (1980, *35*, 44–51) includes a bibliography of his publications through 1979. Wolpe received the Lifetime Achievement Award from the Phobia Society. In 1993, he also received the James McKeen Cattell Fellow Award from the American Psychological Association.

Wolpe's M.D. thesis was entitled "An Approach to the Problem of Neurosis Based on the Conditioned Response." Publication of journal articles in 1952, 1954, and 1956 preceded publication of his book *Psychotherapy by Reciprocal Inhibition* (1958). With Lazarus, he wrote *Behavior Therapy Techniques: A Guide to the Treatment of Neuroses* (1966). Wolpe also is the author of *The Practice of Behavior Therapy* (1969; 2nd ed., 1973; 3rd ed., 1982; 4th ed., 1990) and *Theme and Variations: A Behavior Therapy Casebook*

(1976). He cofounded the *Journal of Behavior Therapy and Experimental Psychiatry* and since 1970 has served as its editor.

BACKGROUND AND DEVELOPMENT

Wolpe dates the beginning of his method of psychotherapy to 1944, when his reading led him to a questioning of psychoanalysis. He learned that psychoanalysis was not accepted in the Soviet Union, and when he looked into the reason for this, he was led to Pavlov, Hull, and studies of experimental neuroses in animals. This resulted in his conducting experiments in which neurotic reactions were induced in cats by administering electric shock; these reactions then were removed by getting the animal to eat in the presence of small, and then increasingly larger, doses of anxiety-evoking stimuli. Thus, there occurred a conditional inhibition of the anxiety responses (Wolpe, 1958). These results led to the idea that human neurotic anxieties might be dealt with—as in Jones's experiments with Peter—by counterconditioning them with eating. Wolpe never actually attempted this and instead used other anxiety-inhibiting responses.

All behavior conforms to causal laws. There are three classes of processes that lead to lasting changes in an organism's behavior: growth, lesions, and learning.

> Learning may be said to have occurred if a response has been evoked in temporal contiguity with a given sensory stimulus and it is subsequently found that the stimulus can evoke the response although it could not have done so before. If the stimulus could have evoked the response before but subsequently evokes it more strongly, then, too, learning may be said to have occurred. (Wolpe, 1958, p. 19)

The strengthening of the connection between the new stimulus and the response is called "reinforcement," and the events that lead to strengthening are reinforcements.

A number of factors are related to reinforcement. The new, or conditioned, stimulus must precede the unconditioned stimulus at an optimal interval. The shorter the interval between the response and the reduction of a strong drive (by reward), the greater the reinforcement. The greater the number of reinforcements, the greater the strength of the connection; spaced reinforcements are more effective than massed reinforcements. In general, the greater the reinforcement, the greater the reduction in drive, although there appear to be instances when increase in drive is reinforcing.

When a conditioned stimulus occurs repeatedly without the unconditioned stimulus or without reinforcement, the response ceases to occur or is extinguished, although there is partial recovery if the stimulus is not applied for some time and then is reapplied. The disappearance of the response is the result of negative conditioning and of reactive inhibition due to fatigue, which dissipates with time, allowing for recovery.

Reciprocal inhibition is the inhibition, elimination, or weakening of old responses by new ones. "When a response is inhibited by an incompatible response and if a major drive reduction follows, a significant amount of conditioned inhibition of the response will be developed" (Wolpe, 1958, p. 30).

Wolpe performed a series of experiments in which neurotic reactions (anxiety and fear, with their behavioral and physiological concomitants) were induced in cats by electric shock. These symptoms were generalized, occurring outside the experimental cage. They were intensified by an auditory stimulus that had been presented with the shock. The magnitude of the symptoms varied directly with the similarity of the environment to the room in which the neuroses had been induced.

The neurotic reactions were produced in a feeding situation, which provided the possibility of removing them by reciprocal inhibition. Two methods were used. The first was the addition to the stimulus situation in the experimental cage of a factor to favor or strengthen or induce the feeding response. Since in their living cages, the cats were fed by hand, it was expected that the hand had become a conditioned stimulus that evoked approach responses to food. Food was therefore presented on a spatula held in the experimenter's hand. Four of the nine cats so treated were induced to eat in this manner and gradually were led to eat from the food box. Three cats were forcibly led to eat from the food box. Over several days, the neurotic reactions decreased and finally were eliminated.

A second method consisted of feeding the animals under conditions in which the anxiety-reducing stimuli were less potent. The five (out of nine) cats who did not respond to the hand-feeding method were offered food outside the experimental cage in surroundings that aroused decreasing symptoms of anxiety, until they were able to eat the food. When all were able to eat in some situation, they were then offered food in situations that had evoked increasing symptoms of anxiety. Eventually, all apparently were brought to the point where they could eat from the food box inside the experimental cage, and their symptoms of anxiety disappeared.

When the conditioned auditory stimulus was presented, however, anxiety recurred. Two cats were induced to eat at gradually decreasing distances from the auditory stimulus, until they were able to eat in the cage with no anxiety. The remaining seven cats were given food in the experimental cage, followed by a brief presentation of the auditory stimulus, followed by more food, and so forth, with the result that the cats' delay in eating the food decreased. Then the duration of the stimulus was increased until the cats were able to eat with no anxiety in the presence of the auditory stimulus. Eventually, the stimulus became a conditioned stimulus for food-seeking movements. To determine whether the neurotic reactions were still present but dormant, the food-seeking response to the auditory stimulus was extinguished by not following the response with food. Then food was offered, and when the cat approached it, the auditory signal was presented continuously, with no effect either in anxiety or in inhibition of eating.

Prior to the removal of the anxiety-evoking effects of the auditory stimulus, two cats were offered food, and then the stimulus was presented as they moved toward it. Neurotic anxiety developed, and eating was inhibited in the situations in which the stimulus was presented.

Are the experimental neuroses in animals and the clinical neuroses in humans the same? The criteria of a clinical neurosis are anxiety, nonadaptive behavior, persistence, and acquisition through learning. These criteria appear to have been met by the cats in these experiments. The responses of the cats in the experimental environment without the shock were the same responses made in the presence of shock, thus conforming with the definition of learning given above. Learning under shock occurs very rapidly because of the great reduction in drive on cessation of the shock and because of the secondary reinforcement of stimuli from the experimental environment that become anxiety inducing; so removal from the experimental environment reduces anxiety and at the same time reinforces the anxiety responses to the environment's stimuli.

The question arises as to the persistence of neurotic habits that are not reinforced, that is, their resistance to extinction. Since neurotic responses are nonadaptive, they are unrewarded. However, they have an antecedent drive that is reduced when the neurotic is removed from the action of the anxiety-producing stimulus. Thus, responses associated with such removal are reinforced. Responses such as autonomic reactions, which are continuously evoked and inevitably present at the time of such drive reductions, are therefore highly persistent, whereas more variable or intermittent motor responses may be extinguished.

The removal or cure of the experimental neurosis is the result of making possible the feeding response in the presence of stimuli conditioned to anxiety responses that otherwise inhibit feeding.

> When stimuli to incompatible responses are present simultaneously, the occurrence of the response that is dominant in the circumstances involves the reciprocal inhibition of the other. As the number of feedings increased, the anxiety responses gradually became weaker, so that to stimuli to which there was initially a response of the anxiety pattern there was finally a feeding response with inhibition of anxiety. (Wolpe, 1958, p. 67)

It seems that there are a number of aspects to this process:

1. Neurotic (anxiety) responses are inhibited.
2. There is a positive conditioning of the feeding response by reduction of the hunger drive.
3. There is a reduction of the drive antecedent to the anxiety responses by the reciprocal inhibition.

"With repetition more and more conditioned inhibition was built up, so that the anxiety-evoking potential of the stimuli progressively diminished—eventually to zero" (Wolpe, 1958, p. 71). The general principle formulated on the basis of the experiments is as follows: "If a response antagonistic to anxiety can be made to occur in the presence of anxiety-evoking stimuli so that it is accompanied by a complete or partial suppression of the anxiety responses, the bond between these stimuli and the anxiety responses will be weakened" (Wolpe, 1958, p. 71).

PHILOSOPHY AND CONCEPTS

Learned versus Physiopathological Psychiatric Syndromes

There are two kinds of maladaptive habitual behavior: organically based and learned. The latter includes neuroses, other maladaptive habits (e.g., nail biting, tardiness), psychopathic personality (antisocial personality disorder), drug addictions, and nonadaptive behavior of schizophrenics. Psychotherapy, including behavior therapy, is feasible only with psychiatric syndromes that involve learning. Only the neuroses are dealt with by Wolpe.

Manifestation of Neuroses

Neuroses are "persistent maladaptive habits that have been acquired in anxiety-generating situations and in which anxiety responses are almost invariably central" (Wolpe, 1990, p. 8). Fears, particularly social fears, are most common; phobias can also be seen. Free-floating anxiety may be present. Anxiety often has secondary effects that cause suffering—shyness, stuttering, sexual inadequacy, kleptomania, exhibitionism, fetishism, obsessions, compulsions, and neurotic depression.

Cause of Neuroses

Definition of Anxiety.   Anxiety is *"the individual organism's characteristic pattern of autonomic responses to noxious stimulation"* (Wolpe, 1990, p. 23). Fear is synonymous with anxiety.

How Fear is Learned.   This definition of anxiety refers to an unconditioned response. "Neutral stimuli making impact on the person when fear is evoked are liable to be conditioned to fear" (Wolpe, 1990, p. 25). Further fear responses may develop not only through second-order classical conditioning of conditioned fear responses, but also on the basis of information by which fears are associated with ideas of "danger" through language.

Etiology of Neurotic Fears.   Neurotic fears develop just as do normal fears—on the basis of classical conditioning or of information or misinformation (cognitive learning). Neurotic fears, though, are a reaction to a stimulus situation that is not objectively a source or a sign of danger. Some predisposing factors include emotional sensitivity, preconditioning, lack of information or misinformation, and physiological factors (e.g., fatigue, infections).

Experimental and Clinical Neuroses.   Experimentally induced neuroses in animals and neuroses in humans are similar.

1. The neurotic behavior resembles that evoked in the precipitating situation.
2. The neurotic responses are under the control of the same or similar (generalized) stimuli as were present in the precipitating situation.
3. The neurotic responses are most intense when the stimuli are most like those to which the behavior was originally conditioned.
4. The neurotic responses are resistant to extinction.
5. The neurotic responses are subject to second-order conditioning.

"The main *difference* between experimental and clinical neuroses is that, whereas in the former the original fear aroused is by an unconditioned stimulus such as electric shocks, in clinical neuroses it is a conditioned stimulus such as the comprehension of a grave danger. Clinical neuroses originate in second-order conditioning" (Wolpe, 1982, p. 41).

THE THERAPY PROCESS

Behavior therapy is "the use of experimentally established principles and paradigms of learning to overcome maladaptive habits" (Wolpe, 1990, p. 3). The therapist views the patient as the product of his or her genetic endowment and the learning that has taken place through exposure to stimuli in the environment, resulting in maladaptive attitudes, thoughts, verbal behavior, and emotional behavior. Thus, the therapist never blames or disparages the patient, but offers sympathy, empathy, sensitivity, and objectivity.

Behavior Analysis

Therapy is preceded by behavior analysis. "Behavior analysis is the process of gathering and sifting information for use in the conduct of behavior therapy" (Wolpe, 1990, p. 59). Psychotic illness and organically based conditions must be ruled out.

Establishing Stimulus Antecedents of Reactions.   The therapist explores the patient's fears and other complaints to obtain information about their determinants and their later extensions through second-order conditioning. Current stimulus-response relationships are scrutinized, since they usually will be the focus of therapy. Complaints other than anxiety—stuttering, compulsions, "psychosomatic" illnesses—complicate a stimulus-response analysis. The therapist must determine whether a fear is based on classical conditioning or on misinformation.

Gathering Background History.   Following the exploration of the presenting reactions, the patient's life history is obtained, focusing on family relationships, education, employment, sexual development, and social relationships. The patient is then given the Willoughby Personality Schedule, the Fear Survey Schedule developed by Wolpe and Lang (1964, 1969), and the Bernreuter Self-Sufficiency Scale. A medical examination is obtained if there is any suggestion of organic disease. Anxiety attacks with no constant stimulus antecedents may be caused by hypoglycemia, hyperthyroidism, or, less commonly, other neurological or physiological disturbances.

Therapeutic goals and strategies are discussed with the patient, although the therapist decides (on the basis of the degree to which a neurotic habit is handicapping the patient) which areas should be given priority. Therapy is an individual matter, but there are some general rules.

1. The emotional climate is a blend of objectivity and permissiveness with regard to acts and attitudes that the patient may deplore.
2. The patient must be assured that reactions, having been learned, can be unlearned.
3. Misconceptions about symptoms must be corrected as soon as possible.
4. Unless there are extreme phobia reactions against it, assertive behavior should be instigated early in the treatment.

5. For many maladaptive anxiety response habits, systematic desensitization is the treatment of choice.

Preparing for Behavior Therapy.   Although most patients are aware that fear (anxiety) is involved in their neurosis, the central role of fear must be emphasized, in statements such as the following:

> You know that your trouble is having too much fear. It is an emotion that is normal in everybody's life whenever a real threat arises—for example, walking alone and unarmed at night in an unsafe neighborhood, learning that one's firm is about to retrench its staff, or being confronted by a poisonous snake. It is a different matter when fear is aroused by situations that contain no real threat—such as seeing somebody receive an injection, entering a crowded room, or riding in a car—to take examples other than your own. To be fearful in such situations is obviously inappropriate, and this is what we call neurotic fear. It is the task of therapy to detach this from the stimuli or situations that provoke it.
>
> Let us consider how neurotic fears originate. The process is really what common sense would lead you to expect. A severe fear reaction that is aroused in the presence of a particular sight or sound becomes "attached" to it. As a result, the later occurrence of the sight or sound under any circumstances automatically triggers the fear reaction. For example, an American lieutenant "went through hell" in the bursting of high explosive in a pass in Vietnam. A few weeks after he returned to the United States, when he and his wife were walking to a wedding in New York City, a truck backfired near them. He reacted with instant panic, "rolled up next to a parked car, cringing in the gutter."
>
> Your own fears were likewise acquired in the course of unpleasant experiences, which we touched upon in your history. The unpleasant emotions you then had became conditioned, or connected, to aspects of the situation that made an imprint on you at the time. This means that subsequent similar experiences led to the arousal of these same unpleasant feelings. Now, just because this happened as a result of a process of learning it is possible to eliminate the reactions by the application of principles of learning. If, as in the case of the Vietnam lieutenant, your fears are automatic emotional habits, we will have to use other emotions to break down those habits. If any of your fears are due to misinformation, we will provide corrective information. (Wolpe, 1982, p. 87)

In addition to such preparatory statements, the therapist provides patients with an outline that explains what behavior therapy tries to do. The therapist also attempts to gauge patients' anxiety by means of the SUD (subjective units of distress) scale. For example, consider the way that Wolpe introduces the SUD scale.

> Think of the worst anxiety you can imagine and assign to it the number 100. Then think of being absolutely calm—that is, no anxiety at all—and call this zero. Now you have a scale of anxiety. At every moment of your waking life you must be somewhere between 0 and 100. How do you rate yourself at this moment? (Wolpe, 1990, p. 91)

The SUD scale can be used to identify patients' level of anxiety at various times, for example, during sessions, outside sessions, and across situations.

IMPLEMENTATION: TECHNIQUES OF THERAPY

Cognitive Procedures

Cognitive elements are present in all psychotherapies. Besides the cognitive activity that is part of all human interaction, and contrary to allegations of some cognitive therapists, "cognitive *procedures* have always been part of the stock-in-trade of behavior therapy as a matter of common sense" (Wolpe, 1982, p. 86). In addition to the gathering of information for behavioral analysis and the preparing of the patient for therapy, there are a number of other cognitive procedures.

Combating Cognitively Based Fears.   Cognitively based fears can be the result of mis-information about the dangerousness of a situation rather than a conditioned reaction to a situation. Corrective information similar to the following is provided and sometimes is am-plified with detailed instructions, demonstrations, and arguments:

> Your fears are based on faulty thinking. In the instances where this is a matter of in-correct information, I will point this out and provide correct information, in as much de-tail as necessary. To the extent that, even with correct information, you are in the habit of making self-defeating, fear-arousing statements to yourself, I will attempt to reveal this, and will help you break the habit. (Wolpe, 1982, p. 89)

Thought Stopping.   Thought stopping is used to eliminate unrealistic, unproductive, anx-iety-arousing persistent, or obsessive thoughts. The patient is asked to close his or her eyes and recite the thought sequence; the therapist shouts "Stop!" and points out to the patient that the thoughts did stop. This procedure is repeated a number of times, and the patient is told to practice stopping thoughts by saying "Stop" to himself or herself. The method may be modified by accompanying the stop signal with an uncomfortable shock or by having the patient press a buzzer when a useless thought occurs, at which the therapist shouts "Stop!"

Contrary to the assertions of cognitive therapists, cognitive errors, distortions, or misconceptions are not the only cause of neuroses.

> For the cognitivists, emotional conditioning, and specifically, learned automatic trig-gering of fear responses do not exist. I reject the view that the psychotherapeutic task is a matter of nothing but cognitive correction, both because it is contrary to estab-lished facts about autonomic responses, and because it is substantially contradicted by clinical data. (Wolpe, 1982, pp. 114–115; cf. Wolpe, 1990, pp. 131–134)

Assertiveness Training

"*Assertive behavior* is the socially appropriate verbal and motor expression of any emotion other than anxiety " (Wolpe, 1990, p. 135). While this includes affectionate and positive behaviors, it more often involves negative or oppositional statements or behaviors. Normal

assertive behavior is inhibited because of fear. Suppression of feeling resulting from inhibitory actions about which one feels strongly causes inner turmoil and psychosomatic reactions. Therapy is directed toward eliciting the inhibited responses, which leads to reciprocal inhibition of anxiety and weakening of the anxiety response. Thus, counterconditioning and operant conditioning both occur, facilitating each other.

Patients may question the morality of assertive behavior. Three possible approaches
to interpersonal relations may be pointed out to them. The first is to consider yourself only,
attempting to get what you want regardless of the effects on others. The second is submis-
sion, unselfishly putting others before yourself. Both of these approaches lead to difficulty.
The third is the golden mean, in which you come first but others are considered.

The patient's need for assertiveness training may emerge naturally from his or her
complaints, from the Willoughby Personality Schedule, or from questions by the therapist,
such as "What do you do if somebody pushes in front of you in a line?" Patients must recognize and accept the need for assertiveness as reasonable and desirable and not in conflict
with their religious or ethical beliefs.

Simple instruction often is sufficient to get patients to try assertive behavior. If the
patient finds assertive behavior very difficult, more vigorous efforts are necessary; the therapist may even refuse to see a patient until some actions are taken. When assertive actions
are taken, the patient reports his or her experiences and is commended for successes, and
mistakes are corrected. It usually is desirable to give the patient graded-task assignments,
as in systematic desensitization, particularly when there are "phobic" reactions to assertiveness or fear of aggression from others. A basic rule is "*never instigate an assertive act that
is likely to have punishing consequences*" (Wolpe, 1990, p. 145).

Behavior rehearsal, in which the therapist takes the role of a person toward whom the
patient is maladaptively anxious and inhibited, may be used when the patient seems to be
unable to become assertive in real life. It gives the patient the opportunity to practice assertive statements and to be coached in improving them. For situations in which direct assertion may be inappropriate (as in dealing with one's boss), indirect ways of controlling
the situation, such as those in Potter's "lifemanship" (or one-upmanship) approach, may be
encouraged. The case of Mrs. Schmidt, presented later in this chapter, illustrates assertiveness training. Although used less than the method of systematic desensitization, it is frequently used early in therapy, since it is simple and effective and involves the patient in the
therapy.

Systematic Desensitization

Systematic desensitization is the step-by-step breaking down of habits of neurotic anxiety
response. A state that is physiologically inhibitory to anxiety, usually relaxation, is induced, after which the patient is exposed to a weak anxiety-arousing stimulus. Progressively stronger stimuli are introduced as the weaker ones are tolerated, until the strongest
stimulus is reacted to with the degree of anxiety that the mildest stimulus evoked, which is
then reduced to zero. The method parallels closely the technique of feeding cats in the presence of increasing amounts of anxiety-evoking stimuli. Systematic desensitization is useful
in the treatment of noninterpersonal neuroses for which training in assertive behavior is not

useful, such as phobias, or of patients in whom the mere presence of another person evokes fear.

Desensitization requires the training of the patient in relaxation, following Jacobson (1938), for about six or seven lessons, interspersed with the patient's practicing at home for two quarter-hour periods a day. Relaxation of the arm muscles is first, followed by those of the head and face (second and third session), the neck and shoulders (fourth session), the back, the abdomen and thorax (fifth session), and finally, the lower limbs (sixth session).

Concurrent with training in relaxation, anxiety hierarchies are constructed. "An anxiety hierarchy is a thematically related list of anxiety-evoking stimuli, ranked according to the amount of anxiety they evoke" (Wolpe, 1990, p. 160). Hierarchies are constsructed from the patient's history, from responses to the Willoughby Personality Schedule and to the Fear Survey Schedule, and from probings, including having the patient list (as homework) all situations, thoughts, or feelings that are fearful or disturbing in any way. The various fears are grouped into themes. Stimuli or situations need not have been experienced to be included but can be imaginary. Basically objective fears are not included and are not, of course, treated by desensitization.

These items are general and must be developed into specific situations that can be placed in a hierarchy. There may be multiple dimensions, such as room size and duration of confinement in claustrophobia. The hierarchy may be constructed by having the patient rate the items according to the amount of anxiety they would evoke, using a scale of 0 to 100. An example of a hierarchy (with SUD scale ratings) constructed for a highly test anxious patient follows (Wolpe, 1990, p. 167):

1. On the way to the university on the day of an examination (95)
2. In the process of answering an examination paper (90)
3. Standing before the unopened doors of the examination room (80)
4. Awaiting the distribution of examination papers (70)
5. The examination paper lies face down before her (60)
6. The night before an examination (50)
7. One day before an examination (40)
8. Two days before an examination (30)
9. Three days before an examination (20)
10. Four days before an examination (15)
11. A week before an examination (10)
12. Two weeks before an examination (5)

If the patient cannot achieve adequate relaxation, drugs (diazepam or codeine), carbon dioxide–oxygen mixtures, hypnotism (in about 10 percent of cases), or the imaging of relaxing scenes may be used. When the patient is adequately relaxed, the therapist presents a neutral scene and asks the patient to imagine it. Then the procedure itself begins: the patient is asked to imagine the least anxiety-arousing stimulus in the hierarchy (e.g., no. 12 in the examination hierarchy above) and to raise a finger when he or she sees it clearly; the therapist allows the scene to remain for a few seconds (5 to 7), terminating it by saying "Stop the scene" and then asking the patient to rate the degree of induced anxiety felt (using the scale of 0 to 100). Relaxation is then induced again for 10 to 30 seconds, with the number of scenes presented varying with the patient. Sessions are usually 15 to 30 minutes in length, once or twice a week.

Systematic desensitization involves the imagining of anxiety-evoking scenes, not the actual experiencing of them. Yet progress is reflected in improvement in reaction to real situations. Difficulties or failures usually reflect difficulties in relaxing, misleading or irrelevant hierarchies, or inadequate imagery.

In the cases of 39 patients randomly selected from Wolpe's (1961) files, systematic desensitization was judged effective in 35 patients (or 90 percent) with the median number of sessions per patient being 10. Wolpe (1990, pp. 186–190) also cites other studies supportive of systematic desensitization; all of these studies, however, were conducted prior to 1970, and he mentions none of the more recent work that has been done in this area.

Technical Variations of Standard Desensitization Procedure

Two ways have been used to reduce the amount of time the therapist has to spend with patients, as discussed below.

Mechanical Aids to Systematic Desensitization.   A specially modified tape recorder has been used to enable patients to desensitize themselves. Relaxation instructions are taped, and a pause switch enables patients to stop the tape while relaxing according to the specific instructions. Before the presentation of the first scene, brief general relaxation directions are given, followed by the direction to pause until visualization is clear and then to continue. After 10 seconds of silence comes the instruction to stop visualizing and, if anxiety is felt, to press the repeat button, which winds the tape to the beginning of the general relaxation instructions, where a metal foil stops it. The process of visualization can then be repeated. If the repeat button is not pressed, the tape continues to the next relaxation instructions (also preceded by a metal foil), followed by the second scene and so on. The tape is recorded by patients themselves, following instructions. A simpler tape recording has also been developed.

Group Desensitization.   Patients with the same phobia have been treated successfully in groups, not only by Wolpe, but also by others.

Alternative Counteranxiety Responses for Use with Imaginal Stimuli

Responses Evoked by Therapy.   The therapy situation itself evokes positive emotions—hopeful expectation, confidence in the expert, and so forth—that inhibit weak anxiety responses. Patients who are unable to learn to relax may be presented with hierarchical scenes in the hope that the therapist-evoked positive emotions will inhibit the anxiety associated with the scenes.

Relaxation Substitutes.   A number of procedures result in the calmness and autonomic effects produced by relaxation. *Autogenic training* uses suggestions of heaviness and warmth to produce muscle relaxation. *Transcendental meditation* encourages the physiological changes that accompany muscle relaxation. *Yoga* exercises also lead to control of autonomic responses. *Electromyographic biofeedback* can reduce tension levels, leading to muscle relaxation.

Responses Triggered by Electrical Stimulation. In the first technique, *desensitization based on inhibition of anxiety by a conditioned motor response,* the patient is asked to imagine a mildly anxiety-arousing scene in the usual way. When the patient signals that the scene is clear, he or she receives a mild electric shock in the forearm, at which time the patient flexes the arm, as the therapist has instructed. The muscle activity and the weak electrical stimulation itself weaken anxiety. In the second technique, *external inhibition,* two mild to moderate electric half-second shocks are administered when the patient imagines a scene; the shocks are repeated 5 to 20 times until the scene no longer arouses anxiety, the anxiety having been inhibited by the shocks.

Responses Evoked by Verbally Induced Imagery. Three methods are included in this category. In the *emotive-imagery technique,* the hierarchical stimuli are presented to the patient while he or she is in a suggested imaginary situation that includes emotional states counteractive to anxiety. The anxiety-arousing scenes are then introduced into this setting. The induced situation, with its emotional state, is a substitute for relaxation. In the second technique of *induced anger,* anger-arousing imagery is paired with fear-arousing imagined scenes, suppressing the fear or anxiety. Hostility or aggression does not replace the fear. In the third technique, *direct suggestion,* various responses, including relaxation, are induced, which act as counteranxiety responses.

Responses Encouraged by Physical Activity. Numerous physical activities may be a source of reciprocal inhibition of anxiety when engaged in during the imagining of fear or anxiety-arousing scenes. These include oriental defense exercises—such as karate, kung fu, and aikido—yoga, and transcendental meditation.

Responses Produced by Relief from Distress. In the *aversion-relief* technique, the patient is presented with a phobic or an anxiety-arousing stimulus on the termination of a period of unpleasant electrical stimulation. In the *anxiety-relief* technique, the word *calm* is paired with "the cessation of a moderately unpleasant continuous electrical stimulus applied to the patient's forearm" (Wolpe, 1990, p. 204). Another technique, *respiratory-relief,* is to present the phobic or anxiety-arousing stimulus at the moment of respiratory relief after the patient holds in his or her breath for as long as possible.

Desensitization to Exteroceptive Stimuli to Anxiety

Either the actual feared objects or pictorial representations of them are used in these procedures.

Desensitization in Vivo. Having patients expose themselves to the actual stimulus situation up to the level in the hierarchy to which they have been desensitized in imagination has been used to consolidate progress and to get feedback. It also can be the prime method in the 10 to 15 percent of patients who cannot imagine hierarchical scenes or do not respond to them emotionally. Natural stimuli can be used, with graded exposure and the therapist present, as a guide and anxiety inhibitor.

Modeling. Bandura (1969) and his associates have demonstrated that observation of filmed or live models engaging in fear-provoking interactions is effective in eliminating or reducing fears or phobias.

Use of Chemical Agents in Deconditioning of Anxiety

Conventional Drugs.   To reduce anxiety, many people resort to alcohol and other nonprescription sedatives, as well as to numerous prescription drugs such as diazepam (Valium), chlordiazepoxide (Librium), trifluoperazine (Stelazine), thioridazine (Mellaril), and tranylcypramine (Parnate). Conditions that presumably are secondary to anxiety (enuresis, encopresis, premature ejaculation) can be controlled by drugs. Amelioration of premenstrual reactions may be obtained by the administration of female-sex hormone preparations.

Carbon Dioxide–Oxygen to Reduce Pervasive Anxiety.   Drugs can be used to facilitate relaxation in systematic desensitization. In cases of pervasive free-floating anxiety, the most satisfactory measure is one to four single, full-capacity inhalations of a mixture of 65 percent carbon dioxide and 35 percent oxygen. The mechanism of anxiety reduction is not known. It is not simply pharmacological, and may be based on reciprocal inhibition of anxiety by the responses produced by the gas, the postinhalation state of relaxation, or both. The effect may last from hours to weeks or months.

Drugs for Specific Deconditioning.   Chlorpromazine meprobamate, codeine, and alcohol have been prescribed for patients to take before exposure to disturbing situations. It has been found that after use of several weeks, or months, the drug is no longer necessary. Classroom anxiety and phobias have responded to such treatment. Chlordiazepoxide and related drugs [diazepam and oxazepam (Serax)] have been used effectively.

"It is reasonable to think that reciprocal inhibition [is] the mechanism of the observed relearning" (Wolpe, 1982, p. 230) associated with the use of drugs. Avoidance responses apparently are inhibited by other responses to other stimuli in the environment. The effectiveness of programs of in vivo systematic desensitization that use tranquilizing drugs "almost certainly depends upon insuring that *high-anxiety evocation never occurs,* for whenever it does it may recondition a substantial degree of anxiety and lose hardwon ground. . . . [T]he hazard of addiction is small when the administration of drugs is limited to assignments" (Wolpe, 1990, p. 208).

Intravenous Anxiety Inhibitors.   Methahexitone sodium (Brietal or Brevital) acts as a primary anxiety-inhibiting agent and can be used with or instead of relaxation instructions in systematic desensitization.

Procedures Involving Strong Anxiety Evocation

Abreaction. Abreaction is not strictly a behavioral technique; its occurrence and outcome are not controllable or predictable by the therapist. It is not always therapeutic, but its dramatic success in some cases warrants attempts to elucidate its mechanisms; it may work through the same processes as flooding.

Abreaction is "the reevocation with strong emotional accompaniment of a fearful past experience" (Wolpe, 1990, p. 217). It is most useful with patients whose maladaptive emotional responses were conditioned to intricate stimulus compounds that are not present in current or contrived stimulus situations; recalled images can thus be introduced into therapy. The effectiveness of abreaction is related to the protective psychotherapeutic relationship and may be "a special case of nonspecific effects" (Wolpe, 1982, p. 237). Abreaction may occur during the application of other methods: history taking, desensitization, and so on.

Flooding. The first successful case of flooding appears to have been reported by Crafts and colleagues (1938). The therapist ordered the patient, a young woman who was afraid to ride in an automobile on strange roads, especially over bridges and through tunnels, to be driven the 50 miles from her home to his office, over bridges and through the Holland Tunnel. During the ride, the patient was panicked, but her terror diminished as she neared the physician's house. On the return trip and later trips, there were no problems.

Flooding thus presents the patient with maximum stimulation, or the highest anxiety-provoking scene in a hierarchy. Stampfl's implosive therapy (Stampfl & Levis, 1967) is an example of flooding, using the patient's imagination.

Flooding techniques apparently are based on the paradigm of experimental extinction, but "so far, nobody has cured an experimental neurosis simply by exposing the animal for long periods (hours or days) to the stimuli to which anxiety has been maximally conditioned. . . . [I]t seems most unlikely that [flooding] leads to change on the same basis as extinction" (Wolpe, 1982, p. 241, p. 245). There are two other possibilities: (1) that "the anxiety is inhibited by the patient's response to the therapist" or (2) "that if the stimulation is not so strong as to cause the subject to withdraw or to 'switch off' entirely, the continuing strong stimulation may lead, after a varying time, to transmarginal inhibition of the response" (Wolpe, 1982, p. 246; cf. Wolpe, 1990, pp. 224–225).

Flooding is an important addition to behavior therapy, but because of its unpleasant nature, it should not be the first choice for use except when it can be shown to be more effective than desensitization. One such case is the obsessive-compulsive neurotic person with fear and avoidance of contamination.

Paradoxical Intention. Paradoxical intention, developed by Frankl (1960), resembles flooding in that it brings about high response levels by having patients expose themselves to feared situations and deliberately try to precipitate feared symptoms. With this technique, patients are instructed to bring on or exaggerate their symptoms—actually do that which they fear. For example, a patient who feared having a heart attack could be encouraged to try to have one. By helping patients see that that which they fear does not occur, they are then helped to overcome their fears.

Operant Conditioning Methods

> There is only one *kind* of learning process. The distinction between respondent
> and operant conditioning is not in the nature of the conditioning, but in the fact that
> in the former nonvoluntary, especially autonomic, behavior is predominantly in-
> volved, whereas in the latter the behavior is predominantly motor. (Wolpe, 1982,
> p. 249)

Operant procedures, thus, are not prominent in the treatment of neuroses, which are primarily autonomic habits. Nevertheless, autonomic responses can be brought under the control of reward contingencies.

Operant conditioning is involved in assertiveness training and is central in the treatment of many other maladaptive habits that have no particular relation to conditioned anxiety—for example, nail biting, enuresis, encopresis, and chronic tardiness. Some important
operant techniques are as follows.

Positive Reinforcement.   Establishing a habit by arranging for a reward or reinforcement
to follow each or many of its performances is a powerful means of changing behavior. Its
therapeutic potentials have been demonstrated mainly with schizophrenics, in whom it effects changes in behavior but does not "cure" the psychosis, which probably is an organic
illness. Anorexia nervosa is one of the few neurotic conditions for which positive reinforcement has been used successfully as the main method of treatment. Operant procedures also
may be used in treating the phobias in whose maintenance physical avoidance is a major
factor, such as school phobias. They are also increasingly being used with problem behaviors in children and delinquent behavior.

Negative Reinforcement.   Negative reinforcement, which increases the rate or strength
of a response by removing an unpleasant stimulus, often requires the therapist to introduce
the aversive stimulus in the first place.

Extinction.   When a response is made repeatedly without reinforcement, it is extinguished. Extinction may be slow in clinical cases because the responses have been sus-
tained by long periods of intermittent reinforcement. Dunlap's (1932) method of "negative
practice," which is now mainly used in the treatment of tics, depends on extinction through
massed responses without reinforcement. The undesirable response must be performed to
the point of exhaustion in order to produce strong reactive inhibition.

Aversion Therapy

Aversion therapy is a special application of the principle of reciprocal inhibition in which
an aversive stimulus is administered simultaneously with an unwanted response (thus differing from punishment, which follows the response), inhibiting the response. Although
not usually the treatment of first choice, it is useful in the treatment of obsessions, compulsions, fetishes, and attraction to inappropriate objects. If the maladaptive habit has a basis
in neurotic anxiety, the anxiety should be deconditioned first, in which case the undesirable

behavior may disappear. Even after successful aversion therapy, anxiety may remain and need to be deconditioned.

When a strong aversion stimulus (such as an electric shock) is administered in the presence of the stimulus for the undesired response, it will elicit an avoidance response and inhibit the undesired emotional response, thereby establishing a conditioned inhibition of the response. Electric stimulation is advantageous because the strength and timing of administration can be precisely controlled and can be tailored to the individual patient. It can be used in relation to actual objects or situations or with imagery. Drugs have been used extensively in the aversion treatment of alcoholism. The procedure is difficult and not highly successful: if successful, it does not allow social drinking. Other unpleasant stimuli have been used in aversive treatment of smoking, obesity, and other conditons.

LENGTH AND LIMITATIONS OF TREATMENT

Length.   The length of behavior therapy can be expected to vary, depending on the type of problems that patients present and the severity of those problems. Yet "Across the spectrum of the neuroses well-trained behavior therapists achieve lasting recovery or marked improvement in more than 80 percent of neurotic cases in an average of about 25 sessions, with relapse and symptom substitution rarely occurring" (Wolpe, 1987, p. 137).

Limitations.   "Behavior therapy, in general, is relevant only in those syndromes that owe their existence to learning" (Wolpe, 1990, p. 8). There are five such categories into which these syndromes fall: the neuroses, maladaptive learned habits not associated with anxiety (e.g., nail-biting, enuresis), psychopathic personality, drug addictions, and learned behavior of schizophrenics. These categories, by identifying that for which behavior therapy is considered appropriate, also identify the limits of the approach—that which falls outside these categories would not be appropriate for treatment by means of behavior therapy.

EXAMPLE

The following material consists of excerpts from two interviews held with a client before a seminar audience, to demonstrate the behavioristic approach. The comments between the two interviews are Wolpe's (1965).

First Interview

THERAPIST: Good morning, Mrs. Schmidt. What's your trouble?
CLIENT: I get very upset sometimes.
TH: What upsets you?
CL: Lately the children.
TH: What, what is there about the children that upsets you?
CL: Uh, before I moved where I am now, I used to . . . they used to listen to me and all that. It disturbs me also that my husband is to—not enough home with them. He is, doesn't spend enough time with the children and I feel like I am raising them by myself.

TH: What does your husband do?

CL: He works as a barber now.

TH: What prevents him from being home enough?

CL: He has long hours.

TH: What are his hours?

CL: He leaves at seven, and he comes home half past eight.

TH: Certainly very long. Well, that's a practical problem. Is there anything else that upsets you?

CL: Yes, many things.

TH: Well, for example?

CL: The things that I read in the paper.

TH: Like what?

CL: Oh, like, uh, I have seen plenty killings in the war and now I feel the same like over here. When I first came here I . . . I just thought there is no place like this, I . . . I thought that you could live in peace and there would never be any trouble. You, you couldn't, you wouldn't hear of anything and now, I . . . I hear more and more things and I get very upset about it.

TH: What year did you come here?

CL: In '47.

TH: In '47. How old were you then?

CL: 21.

TH: Now let me get one thing clear. If you had gone on feeling the way you felt during those few years, then you would not be here?

CL: I would not have to come here.

TH: Right. Can you say what happened to make you unhappy again after that?

CL: I don't know. It might be . . . you see, uhm, when I was born my mother died in childbirth and she never wanted to even look at me, my grandmother used to tell me . . . she didn't even want to hold me once and as she was dying she was sorry that she was leaving the house behind. She had a feeling for home but she never said that she was leaving the child behind and my grandmother used to always talk about that, which she shouldn't have. And so hard things, I have so many things to talk about and uh. . . .

TH: Was your grandmother with you here?

CL: No, my grandmother got killed.

TH: Oh, well. . . . But, can you say more or less what year you began to feel that you were not so happy anymore?

CL: You see, I was disappointed in the family life. I was always looking for somebody like a mother, you know. A somebody. And they would tell me that they would be like a mother to me. And then I found out different—many things and ever since then and—like if I would find somebody and I would get, I can't get too close to them. When I get too close I am afraid that I get hurt and then I run.

TH: Does that mean that at first when you came here you were trusting people and you . . . you felt you could easily form close relationships with them and then . . . and then at some stage you found that these people were disappointing you?

CL: Uh, uh, I had a few but one I remember is my aunt. She told me that she wanted to be like a mother to me when I came here and I thought that she would and—well, many things happened but if I remember very closely I was expecting my first one. When I was in the hospital waiting, uh, to give birth, I had the baby at 11:55 and my hus . . . 10:55 and my husband called her to say . . . to tell her the news so she said, "You woke us up and we couldn't go back to sleep." She said, "Couldn't it wait till the morning?" And he shouldn't have even told me that—I was very sad. But there were many, many things I knew happened but this I remember.

TH: Are the other things that happened of this kind? Were they always things that somebody who should have been friendly to you was in some way uh. . . .

CL: I don't get that close. I don't wait to find out.

TH: Yes, well, but in that case you did get close.

CL: Yes.

TH: You mentioned that your children don't obey you properly and you mentioned that your husband works too much; therefore, he doesn't help you with the children. Now, both of these things are things that any person could be expected to be upset by and, well, maybe solutions could be worked out. But, if you come for psychiatric treatment it means that you feel that there is some kind of situation where you're not reacting as you should . . . where you are perhaps more upset than you ought to be.

CL: There were many times, days that I just didn't feel like going on living. If I had the courage I would have just killed myself many times and I still feel like that. I used to feel like that when I was a child. If I, uh, where I lived with my grandparents, my uncle and my aunt lived there and they just didn't want me. They used to call me all kinds of names and my grandmother used to tell me it would be good if I run away because they didn't want me and that's the time I started feeling that, I just felt like I didn't want to go on living.

TH: Uh-huh. I want to ask you how you react in certain rather common situations. Suppose that you're standing in a line and somebody gets in front of you. What do you do?

CL: Sometimes I let—if I, if I feel that there is a reason for it I let them go. But if I, if I have to make time, I just don't like it.

TH: What do you do?

CL: I don't do nothing. I get upset. (laughs)

TH: If you go into a shop and you buy, say, a woolen pullover like that and when you come home you inspect it and you see there is a little moth hole in the sleeve, what do you do?

CL: I take it back. I show it to them.

TH: You don't mind taking it back?

CL: I don't know.

TH: I mean, can you do it quite easily or is it difficult to take it back?

CL: I, I don't like to bother people too much. I don't like to—for that reason I don't like to take it back. I—if something goes wrong in the house—they don't fix things right or they don't make them right, my husband has to force me to talk and he, he tells it often that I can't do it. He says that's why people take advantage of me, because I don't have the courage to speak up.

TH: Well, that is very much a matter of habit. Now, it's a thing that one can learn to change.

CL: So far, I haven't succeeded.

TH: Well, but, I . . . I want to tell you how you can succeed. Look, let's, let's take this, uh, little example that we used first where somebody gets in front of you in the line. Suppose you're in a hurry and somebody does that. You get cross. You are annoyed. But when you, when you have any thought of doing anything about it, you're kept back at the same time by feeling you don't want to hurt his feelings, you don't want to distress him, maybe it will make a scene, things like that.

Now, what I want you to do in the future in this little situation is express these feelings. Now, of course it's difficult, but if you will express this feeling that you have and say, "Will you kindly get to the back of the line?" then, in the act of doing it, you will sort of push back the fear feelings. You will push them down to some extent. And if you do that, the next time it will be a little easier.

CL: I will try.

TH: Well, the more you try, the easier it will become, and of course there are many situations like this. But it requires action.

CL: But if somebody asks me for a favor and I know I can't do it, I just can't tell them *no.* I go out of my way and I do it. There has to be a *no* which I am trying to learn.

TH: That's right. You can only learn to make the *no* a part of action if you say the *no* and it's usually easier if you start saying *no* in a small situation.

CL: Maybe at home to the children?

TH: Yes, that kind of thing. Now, oddly enough, last month I had a patient who has exactly this problem but probably much worse than you—this is a man who works in a university and the situation has been that if his secretary says to him, "Will you go to the post . . . to the post office and register this letter?" he can't say *no.* He has to do it for his secretary. And you see how ridiculous this is. The first—I, I said to him, "Will you please crawl across the room for me?" (patient laughs) And it was very hard for him to say *no,* but he said *no* and after a little while it became easy. So, anyway, there are many many things of this kind where it is reasonable and right for you to express your feelings, to do according to your feelings and you must learn to be able to—of course that does not mean that you are becoming rude or nasty. There is one general thing I want to tell you that if you get into the habit of saying *no* correctly at the right time, then you don't have to become violent about it. But if you, if you don't exert your authority immediately, and the other person goes on doing what you don't want, then you become more and more annoyed and eventually you can't control yourself and it comes out in violence. I would like to consider for a moment some of these situations where you feel that, that people are rejecting you.

CL: I don't try to get that close to them to find out. I don't want to find it out.

TH: Yes, but there are other kinds of rejection and, which are a smaller kind, and I would also like to know about those. For example, suppose you walk in the street and there is an acquaintance, a person you don't know well, and you expect that person to greet you and she just walks past. Does that worry you?

CL: Yeah, I don't like it. Because I say hello to everybody that I know.

TH: Now, what about this kind of sitution. Suppose you are having afternoon coffee with two friends and you notice that one of the friends is speaking more to the other one than to you. Does that bother you at all?

CL: I don't know.

TH: Can you think of any other situations that happen nowadays between you and other people that upset you?

CL: My aunt came up last time and, uh, she, she was complaining that I don't invite the family for dinner and I just, I just thought that I wasn't up to invite them because I always get upset with them.

TH: What upsets you?

CL: They always, you know, uh, they always think you don't, you don't do enough for them. And every time I have them over, there's always something, she likes to boss me around—set the table this way—feed this one like that—she always tries to tell me what to do and I, I think I'm capable of taking care of the people myself and if she, I don't do what she wants me, she gets very angry.

TH: What do you do or say when she tries to boss you around?

CL: Sometimes I take it and sometimes I just tell her that—"Don't worry about it, I'll do it, I'll take care of it myself." Things like that. Sometimes I just don't answer but then I get upset inside.

TH: Yes, Well this is another example of what we were talking about a few minutes ago. That here, also, where she is, where she is taking unreasonable advantage of you and it's your home and your right to control the matter, you should say to her, "Please keep out of this. I will organize it my way."

CL: I don't want to hurt her feelings, to say that.

TH: Well, it won't hurt her feelings and if you don't do it, you're hurting yourself. In a way that is much more important than anything you can be doing to your aunt. Well, these are the things you have to learn. You have to learn to express your personality because in doing that you will gradually weaken these fears.

CL: But when I think of telling her that or something then I think of myself, I mean, I don't have to expect really anything of her, why should I expect those things of her?

TH: But all you're expecting is justice. Is justice too much to expect? Well, Mrs. Schmidt, that's about all I want to do with you today.

Comments

From the contents of the first interview it was clear that the patient acceded too readily to the wishes of others and required training in assertive behavior to overcome this and related anxieties. Systematic desensitization was indicated for her gross fear of rejection. In the second interview details are found of her training in muscle relaxation, which was done in a much more skimpy way than is usual in clinical practice.

The later part of the second interview demonstrates systematic desensitization. In this technique, progressively more disturbing scenes on a particular theme are presented to the imagination of the deeply relaxed patient. Each scene is presented until it ceases to evoke any anxiety. The particular scenes used here came from a list set up with the patient's help between the interviews on the basis of information that had been obtained during the first interview. The list consisted of people known to her, ranked according to the degree to which rejection by them would disturb her. Of the two individuals named, Mrs. Benning and Selma, Mrs. Benning aroused very little anxiety as a rejecting figure, Selma substantially more. The image of Selma was introduced only after it had been ascertained that Mrs. Benning did not arouse anxiety when imagined as ignoring the patient. Imagining of rejection by Selma did disturb her, and when presentations of this were repeated, disturbance decreased progressively. The presentations were repeated until the patient ceased to have any disturbance at all. In later sessions, increasingly anxiety-arousing items from this and other relevant lists of stimulus situations would have been subjected to desensitization.

A didactically fortunate coincidence occurred that afternoon. When the patient was on her way home, she encountered Selma outside the subway station, and Selma was preoccupied and did not respond to her. The patient telephoned her clinical psychologist in gleeful excitement that evening to tell him that she had been quite unconcerned at not being greeted by Selma.

Second Interview

TH: We are now going to go on to the demonstration of the technique of relaxation training and also a small demonstration of desensitization which we've worked out rather hastily; and it will be tentative. If there are therapeutic effects, we will regard ourselves as fortunate. Altogether, this is going to be a very condensed session because the training in relaxation ordinarily takes anything between five and seven sessions to accomplish. I will of course show you my own standard way of doing this. There is nothing absolute about this; other people use a different order of training in relaxation and there are all sorts of little details of technique which can be varied.

Well, now Mrs. Schmidt, I'm going to show you how to relax your muscles. . . . As you know, when you relax you become more comfortable, and if you're anxious you feel less anxious. Now, I'm going to show you how to bring about a deep relaxation so that you can fight the anxiety more effectively than you have been able to in the past. Now, what I want you to do is, with your left hand, hold the arm of your chair quite tight. I want you to observe certain things that are a result of your holding this chair tight. First of all, there are certain sensations. To begin with, you have sensations in you . . . in your hand and you may have other sensations. With your right hand, point out to me all the places where you get any kind of feeling which seems to be a result of holding the chair tightly.

CL: (Points to left hand and top of forearm. Points to left biceps.)

TH: Now, I want to show you the main idea of the action that you take if you want to relax deeply. When you relax ordinarily, you let go. Now, I want to show you how to let go more than the usual way, and what I'm going to do is this—I'm going to hold your wrist again and ask you to pull against it. When you pull, you will notice that the muscle becomes tight again. Then I will say to you, "Let go gradually." Now, when you let go, I want you to notice two things. The tight feeling will become less, and I want you also to notice that the letting go is something that you do—something active that you put in the muscle. Well, your forearm will eventually come down to rest on the arm of the chair and ordinarily that would seem to you as though that's the end of the matter. You have let go. But it will not really be quite the end, because some of the muscle fibers will still be contracted, so that when your forearm has come down to the chair I will say to you, "Keep on letting go. Go on doing that in the muscle, that activity which you were doing while it was coming down." Now, pull against me. Now, do you get the feeling up there in the muscle? Tight feeling? OK now, let go gradually. Come on, let go. And notice how the feeling changes. Try and make it go further and further. Now, you see, this is difficult. It takes quite a lot of practice, really, to do it properly. You just have to keep on trying to let your muscle go in a negative direction. At this time, when you have never done it before, it could easily take you twenty or thirty minutes to make any important change in the muscle, but you'll find later on, when you've been practicing, that you can relax the whole body quite well in a few seconds. Meanwhile, you just have to keep on trying and you have to practice. You should try and practice for fifteen minutes twice a day. Now, do you get the idea of what I'm trying to do?

CL: Yes, I feel much more relaxed already. (she laughs)

TH: Good. Keep on relaxing. Let's try and make it go further and further. We're going to rush ahead today. So we are going now to do the muscles of the face. So here are these very tense muscles and now I'm going to start relaxing, so I relax a little ... more ... more ... more. Now, from about this point onwards there is very little that you can see, but relaxation continues; and this part that you can't see is the important part because this is what takes us beyond the normal point of relaxation, and this is the part that brings about the calm feeling that we are trying to get. You can contract them to be sure where they are and then just spend a few minutes relaxing. If you find it's easier to close your eyes, then close your eyes.

Next we do the muscles of the neck. The muscles of the neck that we are mainly concerned with are those at the back of the neck, the muscles that hold the head up. Well, if you let them go, then of course your head will fall forward. Now, let that happen. Do you feel anything in the back of your neck when you do this?

CL: It's the pressure over here.

TH: You'll find that if you do this as I suggested twice a day, that in about a week or two your chin will come right down onto your chest and you won't feel this pulling in the back of your neck at all. Well, we'll go on to the muscles of the back. Try and arch your back backwards. You would feel two columns of muscles on either side of the spine. OK. Now, we do the muscles of the abdomen; now, that means, make your stomach tight, as though you were expecting somebody to punch you in the stomach. Can you feel it? All right, so we've now done all of the usual muscles, certainly rather skimpily toward the end.

Well, let's go on now to the next step. I want you to close your eyes. Now, with your eyes closed I want you to try and make use of all the information I have just given you and get as relaxed as possible. So, let's go through these muscles in a systematic order. OK, now, you are quite nice and relaxed. Now, keep your eyes closed and I'm going to ask you to imagine some scenes. Now, you will imagine these scenes very clearly, and generally speaking they will not affect your state of relaxation. But if by any chance anything does affect your state of calm, you'll be able to signal that to me by raising your right forefinger about an inch. So now, I want you to imagine just that you're standing on a street corner and you're watching the traffic. Just a nice, pleasant, peaceful day, and you're watching the cars, and the taxis and trucks, and people all passing at this corner. OK, now stop imagining this scene. Now, if the scene didn't worry you at all, do nothing. If that scene disturbed you, raise your finger now. (no finger movement) OK, that's fine, now just keep on relaxing.

Now, I want you to imagine that you're walking along the sidewalk and you see, walking toward you from the other side, Mrs. Benning. Now, as you pass Mrs. Benning, you see she is looking toward you and you get ready to greet her, and she just walks past as though she didn't recognize you. Now, stop imagining that. Now, if that, if imagining that disturbed you even a very small bit, I want you to raise your right index finger now. If it didn't worry you, don't do anything. (no finger movement)

Now, I want you to imagine again that you're walking on the sidewalk and you see, moving toward you, Selma and you get ready to greet her, and she seems to see you but she walks right on—she doesn't greet you. Now, stop imagining this. If you felt any disturbance at that. ... (right forefinger rises)

OK. Thank you. Now, just keep relaxed. Now, don't think of anything except muscles. Let yourself sink more and more deeply into this calm, relaxed state. Now, again imagine that you're walking along the sidewalk and you see

Selma approaching and she seems to see you, and you expect her to make some response but she just walks right on. Stop imagining this scene—just relax. Again, think only of your muscles. Just be calm and comfortable.

Again imagine that you're walking along the sidewalk and you see Selma coming toward you, but there are also other people on the sidewalk, and you think she sees you but she walks right past without greeting you. Now, stop imagining. Now, if you felt any disturbance when you imagined it this last time, raise your finger now. (finger rises) OK. Now, if the amount of the disturbance that you have been feeling, if the amount is getting less, do nothing. If it is not getting less, raise your finger again. (finger does not rise) OK, now, just keep relaxing as well as you can.

Again imagine that you are walking along the sidewalk and Selma approaches and passes you without recognition or greeting. Stop the scene. Only relax.

Now, again imagine that you're walking along the sidewalk and you see Selma coming and she seems to see you, and then you pass each other without her greeting you. Stop imagining. If there was any disturbance this last time, raise your finger. (finger rises) OK. If the amount of disturbance is still getting less, do nothing. If it is not getting less, raise your finger. (finger does not rise) All right. Keep on relaxing. Think only of relaxing.

You're walking along the sidewalk and you see Selma approaching. You expect her to recognize and greet you but she just walks straight past. Stop the scene. Just relax.

Again imagine that you are walking on that sidewalk and you see Selma approaching and she seems to see you, and you are ready to greet her but she just walks past without any recognition. Stop the scene. If there was any disturbance, raise your finger. (finger does not rise) OK, now. Just relax. Now, I'm going to count up to 5 and then you will open your eyes and feel calm and refreshed. 1-2-3-4-5. How do you feel?

CL: I feel like, I wouldn't feel like doing any work today anymore. The last time when I seen her I just didn't care whether she said hello or not.

TH: How did you feel the first time?

CL: I was very mad. At least, the least she could do is say hello when I live just across the way from her. The last time it was, if she didn't think enough of me to say hello, then let her just go.

TH: Very good. Thank you very much. You've been a great help to us.

SUMMARY AND EVALUATION

Summary.   Emotional disturbance, or neurosis, is characterized by nonadaptive behavior, usually accompanied by anxiety, which has been learned through conditioning. Emotional disturbance originates when an individual is punished for behavior motivated by a bodily need or drive, with the result that the person experiences anxiety and becomes inhibited when the need again arises. Fear or anxiety has been aroused by some noxious stimulus or an idea conditioned to such a stimulus or as the result of a conflict situation; it has become associated, through conditioning and generalization, with other neutral stimuli.

Treatment consists of eliminating the association, thus removing the inhibition, mainly by the technique of reciprocal inhibition, which is essentially counterconditioning or experimental extinction. This is accomplished by means of the performance and practice in the anxiety-evoking situation of responses that are antagonistic to anxiety, which results in the suppression of the anxiety responses. Therapy involves motivating and enabling the client to perform responses antagonistic to anxiety. Techniques of motivating the client include explanation and instruction concerning the nature and origin of his or her condition, the prescription of specific activities, reasoning and assurance that the prescribed activities will remedy the situation, and encouragement, support, and pressure to engage in the activities.

Evaluation.   Wolpe's behavior therapy has several positive features that merit mention. First, it has long been and continues to be closely tied with science and experimental psychology; it is a therapy that draws from and is informed by learning principles, the experimental method, and scientific research. Second, assessment and therapy are closely tied as well; behaviorists typically want to get a base-line evaluation (e.g., How much is a problematic behavior being performed?) that they then use to examine treatment effects and treatment outcome. Third, as an approach, behavior therapy is based on certain assumptions and has a definite structure that patients often will find easy to understand. The ideas that "maladaptive behaviors can be eliminated" and that "new, adaptive behaviors can be learned in their place" can be easily grasped by patients and give them hope. Furthermore, by explicitly describing how treatment will proceed and why, behaviorists help demystify and actively engage patients in the therapeutic process.

But having mentioned these positive features, what questions or concerns could be raised about Wolpe and behavior therapy? Our discussion will focus on three questions: Is behavior therapy really a superficial treatment? Is the therapeutic relationship adequately recognized in behavior therapy? and At what point does behavior therapy get stretched too far?

The idea that behavior therapy is "superficial" is a well-worn criticism. Because this criticism has been leveled at behavior therapy for quite some time, let us give some attention to it. What does it actually mean? Typically, whenever this criticism has been made, it has referred to the following: that behavior therapy is superficial because it does not provide patients with insight into their behavior and that behavior therapy is superficial because it only removes symptoms, not the true underlying problem. Whether these concerns have any validity depends on one's point of view. Wolpe's position seems to correspond to that of Eysenck (1960): "There is no neurosis underlying the symptom, but merely the symptom itself. Get rid of the symptom and you have eliminated the neurosis" (p. 9).

Since symptoms (as viewed in behavior therapy) are not necessarily part of a deeper personality disturbance, their removal should not be followed by the development of other symptoms; their removal should be sufficient and constitute "cure." The value of symptom removal as a goal of therapy, however, can be questioned. It may not be sufficient or adequate in comparison with other goals, and it may have some undesirable accompaniments or consequences. As London (1964) said, "the relief from symptomatic pain in . . . therapy may encourage its parties to disregard the cost or consequences of that relief" (p. 119). Mowrer (1964) suggests that the method may remove symptoms at the expense of character.

In considering the "behavior therapy as superficial" idea, other related issues also come to mind. The first has to do with the nature and origin of neuroses, or nonadaptive behavior. The analogy between experimental neuroses in animals and clinical neuroses in humans is only an analogy and, indeed, one whose validity has been questioned. Wolpe agrees that noxious stimuli usually do not operate in the production of human neuroses.

Nor are the conflicts that give rise to anxieties in humans the same kinds of ambivalent stimuli that result in animal neuroses. Conflicts of needs, desires, and so on are equated with discriminatory ambivalence, although they do not appear to be the same. Wolpe (1958) seemed to recognize a weakness in the analogy when he wrote: "*Apparently,* simultaneous, strong, conflicting action tendencies *somehow* generate high degrees of anxiety within the nervous system" (p. 79, emphasis added). This kind of reasoning and evidence is characteristic of the application of the animal analogy to human neuroses.

Lazarus, who was associated with Wolpe for several years, has voiced several criticisms of Wolpe's approach. Responding to Wolpe's (1969) definition of behavior therapy as "the use of experimentally established principles and paradigms of learning to overcome unadaptive behavior" (Lazarus, 1971), he asked,

> Just what are these so-called "experimentally established principles of learning?" Do they apply to human beings as well as to animals? . . . Some established principles of learning may exist in animal laboratories, but insofar as their relevance for human behavior is concerned, there are, to say the least, many debatable points of issue. (pp. 3–4)

Again, Lazarus pointed out that although there is considerable evidence that neurotic behavior is learned, it is still a hypothesis, while Wolpe treats it as an established fact. Finally, he criticized the narrowness of Wolpe's approach, which treats human beings as animals without a cerebral cortex, a "hypothalamic, subcortical creature dominated by a primitive autonomic nervous system" whose neuroses are in essential respects like those experimentally induced in animals. But, Lazarus continued,

> when confronted by people intent on self-destruction, torn asunder by conflicting loyalties, crippled by too high a level of aspiration, unhappily married because of false romantic ideals, or beset by feelings of guilt and inferiority on the basis of complex theological beliefs, I fail to appreciate the clinical significance of Wolpe's neurotic cats and sometimes wish that life were really as simple as he would have us believe. (p. 6)

Wolpe (1958) also seemed to imply that second-order conditioning is involved in human neuroses. Since second-order conditioning is not as stable or as persistent as first-order conditioning, the problems of the persistence of nonadaptive neurotic anxiety and other behavior must be faced. As Mowrer (1964) pointed out, in ordinary life (as in the laboratory), fears that are not reinforced spontaneously are extinguished, contrary to the assumptions of behavior theory and of psychoanalysis.

As for the concept of reciprocal inhibition, it may be questioned whether what Wolpe includes under this term is anything more than what already is covered by the concepts of extinction or counterconditioning. Extinction consists of the disappearance of anxiety and nonadaptive behavior and is made possible by the inhibition of the neurotic (or anxiety) responses by any means. Essentially, the stimulus for anxiety is allowed to occur in a situation in which it is not reinforced. If the neurotic responses are inhibited, the activity causing them to be inhibited becomes (positively) conditioned to the former anxiety-arousing stimulus. Thus, in addition to experimental extinction, Wolpe instigates other behavior in the presence of the anxiety-evoking stimulus. It would appear that an aspect of his approach and a reason for his success is the inducement of such behavior. He does this by encouragement, support, suggestion, command, and, in the interview, suggestion and hypnosis. His method can thus be viewed as reconditioning.

In the therapy situation, the client faces anxiety-evoking situations in his or her imagination and learns that they are not to be feared. Outside the therapy session, the client is led or forced to face such situations and finds that they are not to be feared. In effect, the client is put into the anxiety-producing situation and learns that there is no reason to fear it; that is, the unconditioned stimulus receives no reinforcement. The methods and techniques for inducing or forcing the client to enter and stay in the anxiety-producing situation are devices to create a situation in which extinction can take place. The client cannot do it alone because of this fear. In effect, Wolpe's approach consists of changing attitudes or feelings by first changing behavior. As London (1964) said, "In effect, by his own admission then, a large part of reciprocal inhibition therapy consists simply of getting people to do the very things they fear" (p. 91).

Having considered the "behavior therapy as superficial" idea, let us next ask, "at what point does behavior therapy get stretched too far?" In other words, for what problems is behavior therapy not appropriate? It does not seem to be applicable to problems of meanings or goals and the fears and aspirations related to them. This is a definite limitation of which to make note. Not all the problems for which people seek help are due to excesses or deficiences of function; many involve systems of meaning. But behavior therapy does not pick up on such issues; they are not addressed in treatment.

The behavior therapist must, as London (1964) noted, "drastically curtail the range of persons and problems he attacks. Courting specificity, the Actionist [or behaviorist] risks wedding triviality" (p. 122). If the therapist widens the concept of symptoms, as many do, until it includes meaning, his or her position becomes scientifically tenuous, according to London. One might ask the behavior therapist how he or she would decondition the pain or suffering of the client who realizes that he or she is not functioning up to full potential or up to his or her aspiration level, who has a concept of himself or herself as a failure, or who experiences a lack of meaning in life. As London (1964) suggested,

> there must be men who, freed of all their symptomatic woes, discover then a truer misery, until now buried underneath a lot of petty ills. Preoccupied no more with pedantries, with headaches, phobias, or vile thoughts, a nauseating emptiness appears to them ahead, a nameless terror of a nameless end. Can this still be a symptom, and if so, still violable by some concrete act, by formulation of a habit or association with some pleasantness-arousing stimulus pulled from a bag of therapeutic tricks? (p. 38)

Exactly how Wolpe would respond to such a charge is unclear. As mentionied earlier, Wolpe (1990) has said that behavior therapy "is relevant only in those syndromes that owe their existence to learning" (p. 8)—including the neuroses, maladaptive learned habits not associated with anxiety, psychopathic personality, drug addictions, and learned behavior of schizophrenics. But what of value conflicts, concerns about meaning, and confusion over one's life goals? In Wolpe's system, none of these would appear to be relevant.

And now our third question: Is the therapeutic relationship adequately recognized in behavior therapy? Let us note that Wolpe himself agrees that the relationship between therapist and patient is probably the most important factor in conventional therapy, but he claims that behavior therapy has effects other than the relational effects common to all forms of psychotherapy. A reading of transcripts of Wolpe's interviews demonstrates clearly that a great deal besides the behavior therapy techniques enter into his therapy. Included are acceptance, expressions of concern and of interest, reassurance, and a desire to help. Marmor (1987) has also described Wolpe as a warm, caring, genuine therapist who strives to understand his patients (and uses psychoanalytic interpretations in the process!). Wolpe (1969) says that "no basis exists for the idea that others have more compassion than the behavioristic psychotherapists." Thus, there appear to be strong relationship variables in his work, including those contributing to a powerful placebo effect.

Klein, Dittman, Parloff, and Gill (1969), after closely observing Wolpe and Lazarus, wrote: "Perhaps the most striking impression we came away with was of how much use behavior therapists make of suggestion and of how much the patient's expectations and attitudes are manipulated" (p. 263). Lazarus, who was at that time associated with Wolpe, commented on this statement: "Both Wolpe and I have explicitly stated that relationship variables are often extremely important in behavior therapy. Factors such as warmth, empathy, and authenticity are considered necessary but often insufficient." Later he wrote: "If suggestion enables the person to attempt new responses, these may have positive effects. One thus endeavors quite deliberately to maximize the 'placebo' effect." He agreed that "even the results of a specific technique like systematic desensitization cannot be accounted for solely in terms of graded hierarchies and muscle relaxation." Wolpe probably would not go as far as Lazarus, but it would appear that in the absence of any evidence to the contrary, Wolpe's success could be the outcome of relationship variables, including the placebo effect, which would result in desensitization, counterconditioning, and extinction. Indeed, the argument could be made that Wolpe has reversed the true situation: What he regards as the placebo effect is the psychotherapy, and what he labels the specific effect is the placebo.

Brown (1967) analyzed Wolpe's therapy and concluded that Wolpe's personality as well as cognitive factors were important elements; his therapy is far from being a pure behavior therapy but is an amalgam of his personality, verbal and cognitive activities, and specific behavior techniques. Marmor (1987) has even said that Wolpe "works in a combined behavioral and psychodynamic way" (p. 145). Whatever the case, the cognitive elements are clear and pervasive from a reading of Wolpe's presentation of his methods and cases, with such elements as cognitive restructuring, correction of misconceptions, teaching, suggestions, and persuasion being used.

That Wolpe's procedures are not behavioristic has been argued by Locke (1971), who pointed out that they require the patient to be introspective about the content and intensity of his or her negative emotional states and to think, reason, remember, judge, discriminate, and imagine, none of which are behavioristic. Wilkins (1971) questioned the theoretical formulations that Wolpe puts forward for the effectiveness of systematic desensitization. He pointed out that "neither hierarchy construction or training in muscle relaxation, but only instructed imagination of fear-relevant scenes, is a necessary element of Wolpe's procedure." He suggested that its effectiveness is due to cognitive and social factors involved in the patient-therapist relationship, including the therapist's social-reinforcing qualities, information feedback of success, training in the control of attention, and the client's expectation of improvement (p. 313). Wilkins (1972) supported his evaluation against criticism by Davison and Wilson (1972). His position was also supported by an extensive review by Kazdin and Wilcoxon (1976), who concluded that the apparent greater effectiveness of desensitization over other methods was due to the presence of expectation of improvement in the experimental groups but not in the control groups.

> A review of the research that has controlled for expectancies for improvement does not support the proposition that desensitization has a specific therapeutic ingredient ... nonspecific treatment effects, at least at present, cannot be ruled out in accounting for the effects of desensitization.

Wolpe has attempted to answer some of these criticisms. While admitting that nonspecific factors contribute to the results of behavior therapy, he insisted that desensitization involves more than expectation and includes specific factors. To the charge that relaxation does not contribute to the efficacy of systematic desensitization, he argued that many of the studies cited by Yates (1975) and by Kazdin and Wilcoxon (1976) were analogue studies that included subjects who had weak fears and that sometimes used inadequate relaxation. Wolpe (1990) also denied that relaxation is indispensable to desensitization, a position that he said has been attributed erroneously to him (p. 190), noting that "*numerous* responses can compete with anxiety, including the emotional response that the patient makes to the therapist" (1982, p. 178).

Wolpe's therapy, as well as behavior therapy in general, may well be effective, not for the reasons claimed, but for the same reasons that other methods may be effective: The relationship provided by the therapist and the patient's expectations. This relationship engenders, among other things, an environment in which the patient can experience anxieties without their being reinforced, which allows them to be extinguished. Rotter (1959), in reviewing Wolpe's (1958) *Psychotherapy by Reciprocal Inhibition*, makes the following point about patient expectations:

> One could say, after a careful reading of the wide variety of methods and the great variety of behaviors which [Wolpe] attempts to substitute for the patient, that he has one basic principle: when the patient presents certain unadaptive behavior or symptoms, then other behavior, which the therapist considers to be more adaptive and possible to substitute in specific situations, should be taught directly to the patient by whatever method is possible. Apparently, what has frequently been referred to in the past as prestige-suggestion is the method he relies on most heavily. The patient is led to expect that his problems will be solved if he will do as the therapist suggests, and at least in many cases the patient is willing to try out these behaviors, finds them successful and so maintains them. (p. 178)

Thus, patient expectations and the therapeutic relationship are two variables that may account for a fair amount if not many of the positive effects that result from behavior therapy. This still remains a viable hypothesis worth entertaining. [See Emmelkamp (1986, 1994) for some discussion about research, the therapeutic relationship, and behavior therapy.]

Let us now move on to consider research and behavior therapy. This has surely been a heated topic for Wolpe and other ardently committed behaviorists over the past 10 to 15 years. Wolpe (1987) has said that the work of Smith, Glass, and Miller (1977, 1980) and related psychotherapy outcome reviews and studies (e.g., Luborsky, Singer, & Luborsky, 1975)—which have supported the idea that the various psychotherapies are more alike than different in their ultimate effects—are flawed, have set behavior therapy back significantly, and merit a close reexamination. More to the point, Wolpe has said that such "equivalence" reviews and studies have unfairly led to the devaluation of behavior therapy.

To refute the idea of equivalence, Wolpe (1986a, 1987, 1990) himself cited several studies and reviews (e.g., Andrews & Harvey, 1981; Giles, 1983a, 1983b; cf. Latimer & Sweet, 1984) that support the superiority of behavior therapy over other therapeutic approaches. For example, he gave much weight to Andrews and Harvey (1981), who drew neurotic patient studies from the original data of Smith et al. (1980) and reanalyzed them. Andrews and Harvey found that the behavioral psychotherapies produced better outcomes when compared with some other forms of psychotherapy. Giles (1983a) criticized three often-cited comparative psychotherapy studies (Sloane, Staples, Cristol, Yorkston, & Whipple, 1975; Smith & Glass, 1977; Luborsky et al., 1975), saying that, while these are frequently taken to support "equivalence," they actually support behavior therapy if closely examined. Giles cried foul, asserting that "this apparent bias against behavioral interventions is ubiquitous in the literature" (p. 31; cf. Giles, 1993). This is an opinion with which Wolpe (1986a, 1987, 1990) appeared to agree heartily.

In a related review focusing on psychotherapy outcome, Giles (1983b) concluded that "other psychotherapies, compared with behavior therapy, are neither as effective nor as efficient" (p. 192). He went on to add, however, that "against the weight of this evidence, the non-behavioral psychotherapies are the choice of the great majority of clinicians. . . . [M]ost patients are presently being treated by inferior means" (p. 192; cf. Giles, 1990; 1993). In still another related paper, Latimer and Sweet (1984) reviewed the effectiveness of behavioral versus cognitive procedures in therapy. They concluded that "the efficacy of cognitive therapy (excluding behavioral components) has not been demonstrated in clinical populations and what evidence there is suggests that the 'cognitive' procedural component of the cognitive therapies is less potent than established behavioral methods such as exposure *in vivo*" (p. 14). This too is a conclusion echoed by Wolpe (1990) in his work.

Much of the foregoing reviews have been done in an effort to correct what some perceive, to use Wolpe's words, as the devaluation and misrepresentation of behavior therapy. The critiques of Wolpe (1986a, 1986b, 1987, 1989) and Giles (1983a, 1983b), among others, on this matter are certainly worth reading and reflecting on. With that said, however, we must also add that some of this writing smacks of evangelical fervor and a lack of objectivity. It is an aggressive compaign or counterattack (see Franks, 1984) that is so aggressive it almost seems more defensive than otherwise. Exactly why such a strong, vociferous counterattack is needed is unclear to us. Whatever the reasons, we still highly recommend that you read these papers that claim bias against and misrepresentation of behavior therapy and draw your own conclusions.

In completing our discussion of research and behavior therapy, let us mention two last items: recent or relatively recent psychotherapy outcome reviews and more on behavior therapy research. While Wolpe (1987, 1990) has continued to decry the so-called equivalence studies and reviews, it seems only fair to say that the effects of behavior therapy have actually been recognized in some of this literature. For example, Lambert and Bergin (1994), based on their comprehensive review, stated the following:

> Although there is little evidence of clinically meaningful superiority of one form of psychotherapy over another with respect to moderate outpatient disorders, behavioral and cognitive methods appear to add a significant increment of efficacy with respect

to a number of difficult problems (e.g., panic, phobias, and compulsion) and to provide useful methods with a number of nonneurotic problems with which traditional therapies have shown little effectiveness (e.g., childhood aggression, psychotic behavior, and health-related behaviors). (p. 181; cf. Lambert, 1991; Lambert, Shapiro, & Bergin, 1986)

The cognitivists, Hollon and Beck (1986), said that "it is not clear that either cognitive or cognitive-behavioral approaches necessarily add anything over and above the purely behavioral approaches" (p. 476). While such statements may not be strong enough for Wolpe, that the positive effects of behavior therapy have been recognized in recent reviews—even in what could be called "equivalence" reviews (e.g., Lambert & Bergin, 1994)—seems clear.

Other research reviews specifically on behavior therapy (beyond those of Giles and Latimer & Sweet) can easily be found, and to get a more complete picture about the effectiveness of behavior therapy, the reader may wish to read these (see Emmelkamp, 1986, 1994; Ollendick, 1986). For example, Emmelkamp nicely discussed some of the successes and promise of behavior therapy (e.g., in treating some phobic disorders and sexual dysfunctions) as well as some of its disappointments (e.g., in treating chronic alcoholics) and also considers directions for future research. Such a review is helpful in providing a good, overall perspective on what has happened and needs to happen in behavior therapy and, in our view, brings a bit of balance to the words of Giles (1983a, 1983b, 1990) and Wolpe (1986a, 1987, 1990).

To conclude, what of the future of behavior therapy? This is really an interesting question to consider. On the one hand, there is Wolpe (1986b, 1989, 1990), who sees the need for fighting against what he refers to as the "new wave"—with the "new wave" referring to the emergence and acceptance of the "cognitive" in behavior therapy. Wolpe views the blending of cognitive and behavioral as undesirable, something that "dilutes and weakens the field" (Glass & Arnkoff, 1992, p. 618). As he puts it,

by bringing out in the open the rationality and depth of traditional behavior therapy, and contrasting it with the superficiality of the "new wave," we may look forward to a restoration of traditional behavior therapy to its rightful place as the spearhead of modern psychotherapy. (Wolpe, 1990, p. 352)

In contrast to Wolpe are those behaviorists (e.g., Wilson & Agras, 1992) who believe that the broadening of behavior therapy to include the cognitive is good (Glass & Arnkoff, 1992). Whatever the differences of opinion, we at least seem safe in saying that this is an issue that will occupy the attention of some behavior therapists in the future and that some will continue to debate it.

In addition to this area of contention, several directions—what is expected to happen or what should happen—have been charted for behavior therapy's future. According to Wilson and Agras (1992), some of these are as follows: the refinement and improvement of existing treatment methods, improvement in the way in which treatment methods can be disseminated more broadly and implemented more efficiently, the continued application of behavior therapy to an expanded range of psychiatric disorders and health problems, and the development of operationally explicit treatment manuals for different clinical disorders (pp. 40–41). According to Glass and Arnkoff (1992), some future directions are as follows:

greater integration of behavioral self-help, relaxation, and self-management programs into medical practice; increasing emphasis on changing behavior in the real world (i.e., patient's natural environment); and a focus on risk factors and prevention of childhood emotional disorders (pp. 616–617). That many if not all of these directions will be realized to some degree in the years ahead, we suspect, will occur.

Through it all, we also suspect that close ties with experimental psychology will be maintained, that close ties to science and empiricism will be maintained, and that close ties to measuring change and documenting change will be maintained. But none of this should be really surprising. These "close ties" have long been and are now basic hallmarks of the theory and practice of behavior therapy. That this would also be so for the future is only to be expected.

REFERENCES

Andrews, G., & Harvey, R. (1981). Does psychotherapy benefit neurotic patients? *Archives of General Psychiatry, 38,* 1203–1208.

Bandura, A. (1969). *Principles of behavior modification.* New York: Holt, Rinehart, & Winston.

Brown, B. M. (1967). Cognitive aspects of Wolpe's behavior therapy. *American Journal of Psychiatry, 124,* 162–167.

Crafts, L. W., Schneirla, T. C., Robinson, E. E. and Associates (1938). *Recent experiments in psychology.* New York: McGraw-Hill.

Davison, G. C., & Wilson, G. T. (1972). Critique of "Desensitization: Social and cognitive factors underlying the effectiveness of Wolpe's procedure." *Psychological Bulletin, 78,* 28–31.

Dunlap, K. (1932). *Habits: Their making and unmaking.* New York: Liveright.

Emmelkamp, P. M. G. (1986). Behavior therapy with adults. In S. L. Garfield & A. E. Bergin (Eds.). *Handbook of psychotherapy and behavior change* (3rd ed., pp. 385–442). New York: Wiley.

Emmelkamp, P. M. G. (1994). Behavior therapy with adults. In A. E. Bergin & S. L. Garfield (Eds.). *Handbook of psychotherapy and behavior change* (4th ed., pp. 379–427). New York: Wiley.

Eysenck, H. J. (1960). Learning theory and behavior therapy. In H. J. Eysenck (Ed.). *Behavior therapy and the neuroses.* New York: Pergamon.

Franks, C. M. (1984). Behavior therapy: An overview. In C. M. Franks, G. T. Wilson, P. C. Kendall, & K. P. Brownell (Eds.). *Annual review of behavior therapy* (vol. 10). New York: Guilford.

Frankl, V. E. (1960). Paradoxical intention: A logotherapeutic technique. *American Journal of Psychotherapy, 14,* 520–535.

Giles, T. R. (1983a). Probable superiority of behavioral interventions—I. Traditional comparative outcome. *Journal of Behavior Therapy and Experimental Psychiatry, 14,* 29–32.

Giles, T. R. (1983b). Probable superiority of behavioral interventions—II: Empirical status of the equivalence of therapies hypothesis. *Journal of Behavior Therapy and Experimental Psychiatry, 14,* 189–196.

Giles, T. R. (1990). Bias against behavior therapy in outcome reviews: Who speaks for the patient? *The Behavior Therapist, 13,* 86–87.

Giles, T. R. (Ed.). (1993). *Handbook of effective psychotherapy.* New York: Plenum.

Glass, C. R., & Arnkoff, D. B. (1992). Behavior therapy. In D. K. Freedheim (Ed.). *History of psychotherapy* (pp. 587–628). Washington, DC: American Psychological Association.

Hollon, S., & Beck, A. T. (1986). Research on cognitive therapies. In S. L. Garfield & A. E. Bergin (Eds.). *Handbook of psychotherapy and behavior change* (pp. 443–482). New York: Wiley.

Jacobson, E. (1938). *Progressive relaxation.* Chicago: University of Chicago Press.

Kazdin, A., & Wilcoxon, L. (1976). Systematic desensitization and non-specific treatment effects: A methodological evaluation. *Psychological Bulletin, 83,* 729–758.

Klein, M., Dittman, A. J., Parloff, M. B., & Gill, M. M. (1969). Behavior therapy: Observations and reflections. *Journal of Consulting & Clinical Psychology, 33,* 259–266.

Lambert, M. J. (1991). Introduction to psychotherapy research. In L. E. Beutler & M. Crago (Eds.). *Psychotherapy research: An international review of programmatic studies* (pp. 1–11). Washington, DC: American Psychological Association.

Lambert, M. J., & Bergin, A. E. (1994). The effectiveness of psychotherapy. In A. E. Bergin & S. L. Garfield (Eds.). *Handbook of psychotherapy and behavior change* (4th ed., pp. 143–189). New York: Wiley.

Lambert, M. J., Shapiro, D. A., & Bergin, A. E. (1986). The effectiveness of psychotherapy. In S. L. Garfield & A. E. Bergin (Eds.). *Handbook of psychotherapy and behavior change* (pp. 157–212). New York: Wiley.

Latimer, P. R., & Sweet, A. A. (1984). Cognitive versus behavioral procedures in cognitive-behavior therapy: A critical review of the evidence. *Journal of Behavior Therapy and Experimental Psychiatry, 15,* 9–22.

Lazarus, A. A. (1971). *Behavior therapy and beyond.* New York: McGraw-Hill.

Locke, E. A. (1971). Is "behavior therapy" behavioristic? (An analysis of Wolpe's psychotherapeutic methods.) *Psychological Bulletin, 76,* 318–327.

London, P. (1964). *The modes and morals of psychotherapy.* New York: Holt, Rinehart and Winston.

Luborsky, L., Singer, B., & Luborsky, L. (1975). Comparative studies of psychotherapy: Is it true that "Everyone has won and all must have prizes"? *Archives of General Psychiatry, 32,* 995–1008.

Marmor, J. (1987). Discussion. In J. K. Zeig (Ed.). *The evolution of psychotherapy* (pp. 142–146). New York: Brunner/Mazel.

Mowrer, O. H. (1964). Freudianism, behavior therapy and "self-disclosure." In O. H. Mowrer (Ed.). *The new group psychotherapy.* New York: Van Nostrand Reinhold.

Ollendick, T. H. (1986). Behavior therapy with children and adolescents. In S. L. Garfield & A. E. Bergin (Eds.). *Handbook of psychotherapy and behavior change* (3rd ed., pp. 525–564). New York: Wiley.

Rotter, J. B. (1959). Substituting good behavior for bad. (Review of *Psychotherapy by reciprocal inhibition* by J. Wolpe.) *Contemporary Psychology, 4,* 176–178.

Sloane, R. B., Staples, F. R., Cristol, A. H., Yorkston, N. J., & Whipple, K. (1975). *Psychotherapy versus behavior therapy.* Cambridge, MA: Harvard University Press.

Smith, M. L., & Glass, G. V. (1977). Meta-analysis of psychotherapy outcome studies. *American Psychologist, 37,* 752–760.

Smith, M. L., Glass, G. V., & Miller, T. I. (1980). *The benefits of psychotherapy.* Baltimore: Johns Hopkins University Press.

Stampfl, T. G., & Levis, D. J. (1967). Essentials of implosive therapy: A learning based psychodynamic behavioral therapy. *Journal of Abnormal Psychology, 72,* 496.

Wilkins, W. (1971). Desensitization: Social and cognitive factors underlying the effectiveness of Wolpe's procedure. *Psychological Bulletin, 76,* 311–316.

Wilkins, W. (1972). Desensitization: Getting it together with Davison and Wilson. *Psychological Bulletin, 78,* 32–36.

Wilson, G. T., & Agras, W. S. (1992). The future of behavior therapy. *Psychotherapy, 29,* 39–43.

Wilson, G. T., & Davidson, G. C. (1971). Processes of fear reduction in systematic desensitization: Animal studies. *Psychological Bulletin, 76,* 1–14.

Wolpe, J. (1958). *Psychotherapy by reciprocal inhibition.* Stanford, CA: Stanford University Press.

Wolpe, J. (1961). The systematic desensitization treatment of neuroses. *Journal of Nervous and Mental Disease, 112,* 189–193.

Wolpe, J. (1965). *The case of Mrs. Schmidt.* Typescript and record published by Counselor Recordings and Tests, Box 6184, Acklen Station, Nashville, TN. Typescript reproduced by permission.

Wolpe, J. (1969). *The practice of behavior therapy.* New York: Pergamon.

Wolpe, J. (1973). *The practice of behavior therapy* (2nd ed.). New York: Pergamon.

Wolpe, J. (1976). *Theme and variations: A behavior therapy casebook.* New York: Pergamon.

Wolpe, J. (1982). *The practice of behavior therapy* (3rd ed.). New York: Pergamon Press.

Wolpe, J. (1986a). Misrepresentation and underemployment of behavior therapy. *Comprehensive Psychiatry, 27,* 192–200.

Wolpe, J. (1986b). Retreat from principles. *Journal of Behavior Therapy and Experimental Psychiatry, 17,* 215–218.

Wolpe, J. (1987). The promotion of scientific psychotherapy: A long voyage. In J. K. Zeig (Ed.). *The evolution of psychotherapy* (pp. 133–142). New York: Brunner/Mazel.

Wolpe, J. (1989). The derailment of behavior therapy: A tale of conceptual misdirection. *Journal of Behavior Therapy and Experimental Psychiatry, 20,* 3–15.

Wolpe, J. (1990). *The practice of behavior therapy* (4th ed.). New York: Pergamon.

Wolpe, J., & Lang, P. J. (1964). A fear survey schedule for use in behavior therapy. *Behavior Research and Therapy, 2,* 27–30.

Wolpe, J., & Lang, P. J. (1969). *Fear survey schedule.* San Diego, CA: Educational and Industrial Testing Service.

Wolpe, J., & Lazarus, A. A. (1966). *Behavior therapy techniques: A guide to the treatment of neuroses.* New York: Pergamon.

Yates, A. J. (1975). *Theory and practice in behavior therapy.* New York: Wiley.

part three

COGNITIVE APPROACHES

Cognitive approaches to psychotherapy are those that tend to emphasize more of *a logical, intellectual approach* to the process and/or the solution of the client's problems or difficulties. These approaches can be relatively eclectic; that is, a variety of techniques can be accepted or adopted. This may be predicated on the belief that different problems and different clients require different methods or techniques; the choice of techniques usually is made on the basis of empiricism or one's experience.

Some earlier editions of this book included the so-called Minnesota point of view of Williamson as a cognitive approach. The previous edition also included a chapter on Raimy and his cognitive misconception hypothesis. Individuals interested in those theories should consult previous editions.

Ellis was the first to develop a rational psychotherapy. More than a decade passed before others, such as Beck and Meichenbaum, developed their cognitive therapies. The approaches of Ellis, Beck, and Meichenbaum are each described in the chapters of this section. These approaches share a number of similarities, as the reader will recognize. They present the therapist largely as a teacher who attempts to get the client to apply information, logic, or reasoning to correct the faulty interpretations and inferences and the irrational thinking that are assumed to be the bases of emotional disorders.

The nature of American culture would appear to be conducive to a cognitive approach to psychotherapy because of its emphasis on science. Frank (1961) pointed this out and in doing so also indicates a possible weakness of this approach to psychotherapy. The scientific ideal, he said, values objectivity and intellectual comprehension, and these features may not be entirely advantageous for psychotherapy. They tend to result in an overevaluation of the cognitive aspects. From the patient's standpoint "insight" in the sense of ability to verbalize self-understanding may be mistaken for genuine attitude change. From the therapist's standpoint, the scientific attitude may lead to undue stress on the niceties of interpretation and avoidance of frankly emotion-arousing techniques . . . even though there is universal agreement that in order to succeed, psychotherapy must involve the patient's emotions. (pp. 219–220)

REFERENCE

Frank, J. D. (1961). *Persuasion and healing.* Baltimore: Johns Hopkins University Press.

chapter 7

Rational-Emotive Psychotherapy: Ellis

Perhaps one of the best known and earliest attempts to introduce logic and reason into psychotherapy is the approach of Albert Ellis, first presented in several journal articles. Originally called *rational psychotherapy,* it became *rational-emotive psychotherapy* in 1962 and is now often referred to as RET.

Albert Ellis (b. 1913) earned a B.B.A. at the City College of New York in 1934; he obtained his M.A. in 1943 and Ph.D. in 1947, both at Columbia University. He began private practice in the field of marriage, family, and sex counseling in 1943. Ellis became interested in psychoanalysis, so he obtained analytic training and underwent a three-year personal analysis. He held positions briefly as a clinical psychologist in a mental-hygiene clinic and in a state diagnostic center, as a chief psychologist for the New Jersey Department of Institutions and Agencies, and as an instructor at Rutgers University and New York University. The major part of his professional life, however, has been spent in private practice. Even with that being the case, he has lectured extensively and conducted workshops in RET around the world and continues to do so. In 1958, he established the Institute for Rational Living, and in 1968, the Institute for Advanced Study in Rational Psychotherapy, of which he is the executive director. In addition to offering training in RET, the institute operates the Living School—where normal children are taught the principles of rational-emotive psychology.

Ellis has been the recipient of numerous awards. He has received the Distinguished Professional Contribution to Knowledge Award from the American Psychological Association (see *American Psychologist,* 1986, *41,* pp. 381–397), the Humanist of the Year Award from the American Humanist Association, and the Personal Development Award from the American Counseling Association, among others.

Ellis, a Diplomate in Clinical Psychology of the American Board of Professional Psychology, has been a prolific writer throughout his career. He is the author of numerous popular books dealing with sex, as well as more scientific discussions about sex and sexuality. He appeared as one of the three therapists in the film series, *Three Approaches to Psychotherapy: I,* produced by Everett L. Shostrom. He has extended the rational-emotive approach to group psychotherapy and encounter groups. He has published summaries of his approach in a number of edited books as well as other publications. An Ellis biography has been prepared by Wiener (1988).

BACKGROUND AND DEVELOPMENT

In his early practice of marital counseling, Ellis was concerned essentially with giving authoritative information. However, he became aware that the problems brought to him involved more than the lack of valid information or knowledge; his clients also were psychologically or emotionally disturbed. He then turned to psychoanalysis for help and, after his training and personal analysis, began practicing orthodox psychoanalysis. Although he feels that he was as successful as other analysts (he claims that 50 percent of all his patients and 70 percent of the neurotic patients were significantly helped), he was dissatisfied with the results and, more importantly, with the theory and techniques of psychoanalysis. He felt that there was a lack of correspondence between the passivity and inactivity of orthodox analysis and his own personality and temperament.

> Why when I seemed to know perfectly well what was troubling a patient, did I have to wait passively, perhaps for a few weeks, perhaps for months, until he, by his own interpretive initiative, showed that he was fully "ready" to accept my own insight? Why, when patients bitterly struggled to continue to associate freely, and ended up by saying only a few words in an entire session, was it improper for me to help them with several pointed questions or remarks? (Ellis, 1962, p. 7)

As a result of his dissatisfaction, Ellis changed to a neo-Freudian approach and then to psychoanalytically oriented psychotherapy, becoming more active in the process. Although he feels that his effectiveness increased (with 63 percent of all patients and 70 percent of neurotic patients showing significant improvement) and that results were achieved in less time and with fewer interviews, he was still dissatisfied. Even though his patients achieved insight into their behavior and its origins, they did not necessarily change or improve their behavior.

Ellis then became interested in learning theory (that is, conditioning) and attempted to apply it in deconditioning his patients by directing them to engage in pertinent therapeutic activities. Again, he felt that his activity-directed eclectic therapy was more effective, but he still remained unsatisfied. His rational approach began to develop at this point (in 1954). He became convinced that irrational, neurotic early learnings persisted, because individuals persisted in reindoctrinating themselves in these learnings and in resisting therapy and its insights. Ellis then turned to teaching his patients to change their thinking and adopt a rational approach to problems. He felt that about 90 percent of those treated by this method for ten or more sessions showed distinct or considerable improvement.

RET was developed in a series of articles, beginning in 1955 (Ellis, 1955a, 1955b, 1956, 1957a, 1957b, 1958, 1959) and culminating in the book *Reason and Emotion in Psychotherapy* (Ellis, 1962). The more recent writings of Ellis (1987a, 1988b, 1989; Ellis & Dryden, 1987; Ellis & Grieger, 1977a; Ellis & Whiteley, 1979) have continued to build on, complement, and extend this early body of work.

PHILOSOPHY AND CONCEPTS

While early on calling his approach a "rational therapy," Ellis abandoned this designation because it led to confusion with other "rational" therapies and with the classical rationalist philosophy, which he does not accept. He is, however, sympathetic to modern rationalism or neorationalism, which applies reason and logic to science and to the search for truth and which is opposed to supernaturalism, mysticism, and dogmatism. He is also in sympathy with most of the modern existentialists' goals for living and accepts the following themes from Braaten (1961):

> (1) Man, you are free, define yourself; (2) Cultivate your own individuality; (3) Live in dialogue with your fellow man; (4) Your own experiencing is the highest authority; (5) Be fully present in the immediacy of the moment; (6) There is no truth except in action; (7) You can transcend yourself in spurts; (8) Live your potentialities creatively; (9) In choosing yourself, you choose man; and (10) You must learn to accept certain limits in life.

Ellis claims no originality for the concepts that make up his system. While he discovered many of them through his own experience, he recognizes that they were already formulated by many ancient and modern philosophers, psychologists, psychotherapists, and social thinkers (Ellis, 1979c, 1987a).

Assumptions

Rational-emotive therapy (RET) makes certain assumptions about the nature of human beings and about the nature and genesis of their unhappiness or emotional disturbances (Ellis, 1988b, 1989, 1993). Some of these assumptions are as follows:

1. Human beings are uniquely rational, as well as irrational. When they are thinking and behaving rationally, they are more apt to be effective, happy, and competent.
2. Emotional or psychological disturbance—neurotic behavior—is a result of irrational and illogical thinking. Thought and emotion are not separate or different functions. Emotion accompanies thinking, and thinking is, in effect, usually biased, prejudiced, highly personalized, and irrational.
3. Human beings are biologically predisposed toward irrational thinking, and environmental conditions and experiences build on this predisposition. Seriously disturbed (psychotic) individuals have stronger predispositions toward disturbed thinking.

4. Human beings are verbal animals, and thinking usually occurs through the use of symbols or language. Since thinking necessarily persists if the emotional disturbances persist, irrational thinking necessarily persists if the emotional disturbances persist. This is just what characterizes disturbed individuals: They perpetuate their disturbance and maintain illogical behavior by internal verbalization of their irrational ideas and thoughts. "For all practical purposes the phrases and sentences that we keep telling ourselves frequently *are* or *become* our thoughts and emotions" (Ellis, 1962, p. 50). This perpetual stimulation is the reason that disordered behavior and emotions are not extinguished and that simple understanding of the origins of the disturbance, obtained through psychoanalysis, is not sufficient to eliminate the disturbance.

5. Continuing states of emotional disturbance, which are a result of self-verbalizations, are thus determined, not by external circumstances or events, but by the perceptions and attitudes toward these events that are incorporated in the internalized sentences about them. Ellis finds the origin of this concept in Epictetus, who wrote: "Men are disturbed not by things, but by the views which they take of them." He also quotes a similar phrase from Hamlet: "There's nothing either good or bad but thinking makes it so" (Ellis, 1962, p. 54).

6. Negative and self-defeating thoughts and emotions thus must be attacked by a reorganization of perceptions and thinking so that thinking becomes logical and rational rather than illogical and irrational. The goals of the therapist in the psychotherapy process are to demonstrate to clients that their self-verbalizations have been the source of their emotional disturbance, to show that these self-verbalizations are illogical and irrational, and to straighten out their thinking so that their self-verbalizations can become more logical and efficient and be dissociated from negative emotions and self-defeating behavior (also see Dryden, 1989; Ellis & Dryden, 1987).

Irrational Ideas

Ellis identified eleven ideas or values that are irrational, superstitious, or "senseless" and that are universally inculcated in Western society and "would seem inevitably to lead to widespread neurosis" (Ellis, 1962, p. 61).

1. *It is essential that a person be loved or approved of by virtually everyone in the community.* This is irrational because it is an unobtainable goal, and if strived for, the person becomes less self-directing, more insecure, and more self-defeating as a result. It is desirable to be loved; however, the rational person does not sacrifice his or her own interests and desires for this goal.

2. *A person must be perfectly competent, adequate, and achieving to be considered worthwhile.* This, again, is an impossibility, and to strive compulsively for it can result in psychosomatic illness, a sense of inferiority, an inability to live one's own life, and a constant sense of fear of failure. The rational individual strives to do well for his or her own sake rather than to be better than others, to enjoy an

activity rather than to engage in it solely for the results, and to learn rather than to try to be perfect.

3. *Some people are bad, wicked, or villainous and therefore should be blamed and punished.* This idea is irrational because there is no absolute standard of right or wrong and very little free will. "Wrong" or "immoral" acts are the result of stupidity, ignorance, or emotional disturbance. All people are fallible and make mistakes. Blame and punishment do not usually lead to improved behavior, because they do not then result in less stupidity, more intelligence, or a better emotional state; in fact, they often lead to worse behavior and greater emotional disturbance. Rational individuals do not blame others or themselves. If other people blame them, they try to improve or correct their own behavior if they have been wrong; if they have not been wrong, they realize that such blame is an indication of disturbance in others. When others make mistakes, they try to understand them and, if possible, to stop them from continuing their misdeeds; if this is not possible, they try not to let others' behavior seriously upset them. When they make mistakes, they admit and accept their own behavior but do not let it become a catastrophe or lead them to feel worthless.

4. *It is a terrible catastrophe when things are not as a person wants them to be.* This is irrational thinking because to be frustrated is normal, but to be severely and prolongedly upset is illogical, since there is no reason that things should be different from what they are in reality, getting upset only rarely changes the situation and usually makes it worse, if it is impossible to do anything about the situation, the only rational thing to do is to accept it, and frustration need not result in emotional disturbance if we do not define the situation in such a way as to make obtaining our desires a necessity for satisfaction or happiness. The rational person avoids exaggerating unpleasant situations and works at improving them or at accepting them if they cannot be improved. Unpleasant situations may be disturbing, but they are not terrible or catastrophic unless we define them as such.

5. *Unhappiness is caused by outside circumstances, and a person has no control over it.* Actually, outside forces and events, while they can be physically assaulting, usually are psychological in nature and cannot be harmful unless we allow ourselves to be affected (by means of our attitudes and reactions). People disturb themselves by mentally going over how horrible it is when someone is unkind, rejecting, annoying, and so on. If we realize that our own perceptions, evaluations, and internalized verbalizations cause disturbances, then the disturbances can be controlled or changed. People who are intelligent realize that unhappiness comes largely from within, and while they may be irritated or annoyed by external events, they will recognize that their reactions can be changed by their definitions and verbalizations of these events.

6. *Dangerous or fearsome things are cause for great concern, and their possibility must be continually dwelt on.* This is irrational because worry or anxiety prevents an objective evaluation of the possibility of a dangerous event, often interferes with dealing with a dangerous event effectively if it should occur, may contribute to bringing about a dangerous event, leads to exaggerating the possibility of a dangerous event's occurrence, cannot possibly prevent inevitable

events, and makes many dreaded events appear worse than they actually are. People who are rational recognize that potential dangers are not as catastrophic as they fear; they also recognize that anxiety does not prevent feared events from happening, may increase the likelihood of their occurrence, and may be more harmful in and of itself. The rational person also realizes that he or she should do the things that are feared in order to prove that they are not actually frightful.

7. *It is easier to avoid certain difficulties and self-responsibilities than to face them.* This is irrational because avoiding a task is more difficult and more painful than performing it and leads to later problems and dissatisfactions, including loss of self-confidence. Also, an easy life is not necessarily a happy one. People who are rational do what has to be done, although they intelligently avoid unnecessary painful tasks. When they find themselves avoiding necessary responsibilities, they analyze the reasons, engage in self-discipline, and then realize that a challenging, responsible, problem-solving life is an enjoyable life.

8. *A person should be dependent on others and should have someone stronger on whom to rely.* While we all are dependent on others to some extent, there is no reason to maximize dependency; it leads to loss of independence, individualism, and self-expression. Dependency causes greater dependency, failure to learn, and insecurity, because we are then at the mercy of those on whom we depend. The person who is rational strives for independence and responsibility but does not refuse to seek or accept help when necessary. The person recognizes that risks, while possibly resulting in failures, are worth taking and that failing itself is not a catastrophe.

9. *Past experiences and events are the determinants of present behavior; the influence of the past cannot be eradicated.* On the contrary, what was once necessary behavior in certain circumstances may not be necessary at present; past solutions to problems may not be relevant in the present. The presumed influence of the past may be used as an excuse for avoiding changing behavior. Although it may be difficult to overcome past learning, it is not impossible. People who are rational, while recognizing that the past is important, also realize that the present can be changed by analyzing past influences, questioning the acquired beliefs that are harmful, and forcing themselves to act differently.

10. *A person should be quite upset over other people's problems and disturbances.* This is erroneous because other people's problems often are just that: Other people's problems. Such problems may have nothing to do with us. Even when others' behavior does affect us, it is our definition of it that is upsetting. The person who is rational determines whether the behavior of others warrants becoming disturbed and, if so, attempts to do something that will help them to change. If nothing can be done, the person accepts and makes the best of it.

11. *There is always a right or perfect solution to every problem, and it must be found or the results will be catastrophic.* This is irrational because there is no perfect solution, the imagined results of failure to find a perfect solution are unreal and can lead to anxiety or panic, and such perfectionism results in poorer solutions than are actually possible. The person who is rational attempts to find various possible solutions to a problem and accepts the best or most feasible one, recognizing that there is no perfect answer.

These fallacious ideas are almost universal in our society; when accepted and reinforced by continual self-indoctrination, they can lead to emotional disturbance or neurosis because they cannot be lived up to.

> For once a human being believes the kind of nonsense included in these notions, he will inevitably tend to become inhibited, hostile, defensive, guilty, ineffective, inert, uncontrolled, unhappy. If, on the other hand, he could become thoroughly released from all these fundamental kinds of illogical thinking, it would be exceptionally difficult for him to become intensely emotionally upset, or at least to sustain his disturbance for any extended period. (Ellis, 1962, p. 89)

While the Freudians are right in pointing out the influences of early childhood experience on emotional disturbance, these influences are only secondary causes; they continue to be influential only because the individual has adopted some of the basic illogical ideals listed above. It is not early experiences alone that cause disturbance but the individual's attitudes and thoughts about them (Ellis, 1989).

While these eleven ideas show some of the varied ways in which our thinking can be irrational, Ellis has also attempted to pare down this list further—to identify a few core irrational beliefs that capture the essence of the eleven. Ellis (1979b) has identified three such ideas:

> I MUST be competent, adequate, and achieving, and I MUST win approval of virtually all the significant people in my life. It is *awful* when I don't. I *can't stand* failing in these all-important respects. I am a *rotten person* (R.P.) when I don't do what I must do to act competently and to win others' approval. . . . Others MUST treat me kindly, fairly, and properly when I want them to do so. It is *terrible* when they don't. I *can't bear* their acting obnoxiously toward me. They are damnable, worthless people when they don't do what they MUST do to treat me satisfactorily. . . . I need and MUST have the things I really want. The conditions under which I live and the world around me MUST be well ordered, positive, certain—just the way I want them to be. I MUST gratify my desires easily and immediately, without having to deal with too many difficulties or hassles. It is *horrible* when conditions are not this way. I *can't tolerate* their being uncomfortable, frustrating, or merely not ideal. The world is a rotten place and life is hardly worth living when things are not as they *should be* in this respect. (pp. 3–4)

These core irrational beliefs, which really seem to be various combinations of the eleven ideas compacted into three, reflect yet another key RET concern: The use of "shoulds," "oughts," and "musts" in our thinking. According to Ellis (1988b, 1993), it is the use of such absolute thinking ("I MUST...," "I SHOULD...," "I OUGHT...") that gets people into trouble. Absolutes of this type reflect irrationality, can cause or significantly contribute to emotional disturbance, and are best dealt with by means of rational disputation (i.e., combatting one's absolutistic thinking with rational analysis). Indeed, it is this "must," "should," and "ought" element that appears to actually define a belief as irrational or illogical in the RET system.

The A-B-Cs of RET

While rational-emotive therapy recognizes that human events can include external causal factors, people are not viewed as being completely determined by such factors. Instead, people are seen as having the potential to transcend their biological and social limitations, difficult though it may be, and act in ways to change and control their future (Ellis, 1976, 1979d). This recognition of individuals' ability to determine, in good part, their own behavior and emotional experience is expressed in the A-B-C theory of behavior and personality disturbance (Ellis, 1989).

In this A-B-C model, A refers to the activating event or experience; B to the individual's belief system; and C to the consequences. For example, let us say you were traveling down the highway and had a flat tire; this would be an A (activating event). In response to this event, you might think, "This SHOULD not have happened. It is AWFUL. I *can't stand* it. I *can't* handle it." These thoughts would reflect the B (belief system) part of the model. Then, assuming you had these thoughts, you may well feel highly anxious, exasperated, disgusted, and angry; such feelings would be the C (consequences) of your problematic thinking. So the A would not be the direct cause of the C that you experience. Instead, the consequences would be caused by your belief system—that mediating component of the A-B-C model.

Belief systems can be rational or irrational. If the belief system is rational, reasonable, or realistic (rB), then the consequences will be rational or reasonable (rC). If the belief system is irrational, unreasonable, or unrealistic (iB), then the consequences will be irrational or unreasonable (iC). The recognition of this A-B-C relationship leads to the possibility of changing and controlling one's attitudes and behaviors in reaction to circumstances.

THE THERAPY PROCESS

Goals of Therapy

One goal of therapy is to help clients eliminate or reduce irrational consequences (iCs) or emotional disturbances. Another goal is to minimize anxiety (self-blame), hostility, and anger (blaming others or circumstances). Still another goal is to provide clients with a method—through rational analysis of their disturbances—by which they can maintain a state of minimum anxiety and hostility (Ellis & Harper, 1975).

Other positive goals of mental health are implicit, if not explicit, in rational-emotive psychotherapy. These include but are not limited to an enlightened self-interest (that recognizes the rights of others); social interest, self-direction, independence, and responsibility; tolerance of human fallibility; acceptance of uncertainty; flexibility and openness to change; scientific thinking; commitment to something outside of oneself; risk taking or willingness to try new things; self-acceptance; and non-utopianism (recognizing that utopias are not possible) (Ellis, 1979c). These goals are shared with many philosophers and other psychotherapists (Ellis, 1967, 1979c).

Steps of RET

In view of the above philosophy and concepts regarding the nature of emotional disturbance, it follows that psychotherapy, according to Ellis, is the curing of unreason by reason. While there are other ways of controlling emotions—by electrical or chemical means, by sensorimotor techniques, or by doing something out of love or respect for someone else—psychotherapy does so by using the cerebral processes. Humans, as rational beings, are able to avoid or eliminate most emotional disturbance or unhappiness by learning to think rationally.

The task of the therapist is to help clients get rid of illogical, irrational ideas and attitudes and substitute logical, rational ideas and attitudes for them (Ellis, 1989). The first step in this process is to show clients that these ideas and attitudes are illogical, to help them understand how and why they are so, and to demonstrate (by means of the A-B-C model) the relationship between their irrational ideas and unhappiness and emotional disturbance. Ellis recognizes that most therapeutic approaches do this; but they do it passively, indirectly, and stop there.

In the second step, rational-emotive therapy shows clients that they maintain their disturbance by continuing to think illogically; that is, their present irrational thinking, not the continuing influence of early events, is responsible for their condition.

The third step in the therapeutic process is to get clients to change their thinking and to abandon irrational ideas. While some approaches depend on clients to do this themselves, rational-emotive therapy recognizes that illogical thinking can be so ingrained that clients cannot change it without help. Therapy, then, essentially consists of attacking irrational beliefs by disputing (D) them. By means of this disputation, it is hoped that desirable cognitive effects (cE), emotional effects (eE), and behavioral effects (bE) will result.

The fourth and final step goes beyond dealing with the specific illogical ideas of clients; it gives consideration to irrational ideas in general (such as the eleven mentioned earlier), along with a more rational philosophy of living. The result of this process is that clients acquire a rational philosophy of life; they substitute rational attitudes and beliefs for irrational ones. Once this is accomplished, the negative, disturbing emotions can be eliminated, along with self-defeating behavior (Ellis, 1962).

Rational-emotive therapy also deals with the problem of self-depreciation, or low self-esteem and feelings of worthlessness. The problem of personal worth arises when persons evaluate themselves on the basis of their acts, behavior, or performance, which reveal their inadequacies, mistakes, and failures. One approach to this problem—the usual one—is to help clients believe that they are worthwhile simply because they exist as persons, whatever their behaviors or opinions of others might be. While this is effective if clients can accept this belief, it is more effective if they can be shown that they do not have to evaluate themselves at all (Ellis, 1988a). Without engaging in any self-evaluation, they can recognize that they are alive and that they can choose to remain alive and to enjoy life. Clients then do not ask such questions as "Who am I?" "What is my identity?" or "What is my worth?" Rather, they ask, "What are my traits?" "What sort of things do I enjoy and not enjoy doing?" "How can I improve some of my traits and find more things to experience, so that I will continue to live and to have a maximally satisfying existence?" They can rate their traits, but this does not require them to rate themselves as either good or bad (Ellis, 1973, 1993).

IMPLEMENTATION: TECHNIQUES OF THERAPY

Ellis has stated that "all effective psychotherapists, whether or not they realize what they are doing, teach or induce their patients to reperceive or rethink their life events and philosophies and thereby change their unrealistic and illogical thought, emotion, and behavior" (Ellis, 1962, pp. 36–37). But he further believes that the techniques other therapists use to accomplish this are relatively indirect and inefficient. Techniques such as abreaction, catharsis, dream analysis, free association, interpretation of resistance, and transference analysis can be successful, at least in bringing clients to recognize their illogical thinking. However, Ellis (1979a) believes that even when most successful these methods are wasteful. The relationship itself and expressive-emotive, supportive, and insight-interpretive methods, although used in rational-emotive therapy, are preliminary techniques to establish rapport, to enable clients to express themselves, and to show them that they are respected. The therapist provides either nonjudgmental acceptance or unconditional positive regard of the client as a person, demonstrating the worth of the individual regardless of his or her behavior.

> If, because the patient is exceptionally upset when he comes to therapy, he must first be approached in a cautious, supportive, permissive, and warm manner, and must sometimes be allowed to ventilate his feeling in free-association, abreaction, role playing, and other expressive techniques, that may be a necessary part of effective therapy. But the rational therapist does not delude himself that these relationship-building and expressive-emotive methods are likely to really get to the core of the patient's illogical thinking and induce him to cogitate more rationally. (Ellis, 1962, p. 95)

While occasionally this is sufficient, more often it is not.

The essential technique of rational-emotive therapy is teaching. After the initial stage, the therapist assumes an active teaching role to reeducate the client. The therapist demonstrates the illogical origin of the client's disturbance and the role of illogical self-verbalizations in continuing it.

> Patients should be shown that their internalized sentences are quite illogical and unrealistic in certain respects. . . . The effective therapist should continually keep unmasking his patient's past, and, especially, his present illogical thinking or self-defeating verbalizations by (a) bringing them forcefully to his attention or consciousness; (b) showing him how they are causing and maintaining his disturbance and unhappiness; (c) demonstrating exactly what the illogical links in his internalized sentences are; and (d) teaching him how to re-think, challenge, contradict, and reverbalize these (and other similar) sentences so that his internalized thoughts become more logical and efficient. (Ellis, 1962, pp. 58–59)
>
> Rational-emotive psychotherapy makes a concerted attack on the disturbed person's illogical positions in two main ways: (1) The therapist serves as a frank counter-propagandist who directly contradicts and denies the self-defeating propaganda and superstitions which the patient has originally learned and which he is now self-instilling. (2) The therapist encourages, persuades, cajoles, and occasionally even insists that the patient engage in some activity (such as doing something he is afraid of doing) which itself will serve as a forceful counterpropaganda agency against the nonsense he believes. (Ellis, 1962, pp. 94–95)

The rational-emotive therapist thus uses logic and reason, instruction, suggestion, persuasion, confrontation, deindoctrination, indoctrination, and prescription of behavior to show the client what his or her irrational philosophies are, to demonstrate how these lead to emotionally disturbed behavior, and to change the client's thinking—and thus emotions—by replacing these irrational philosophies with rational, logical ones (Ellis, 1989). In addition, as was indicated earlier, the therapist goes further to instruct the client, as a protective measure, in the major irrational ideas of our culture and to provide the client with more effective rational ones (Ellis & Dryden, 1987).

In effect, any method or technique that will induce clients to look at, question, and change their irrational assumptions or beliefs can be used. Clients may be literally forced "to look at the simple exclamatory sentences that they are telling themselves to create their emotions of anger and hostility."

> Whenever a client tells me, for example, "My wife accused me of being unfaithful to her, and that got me terribly angry, because it was so untrue and so unfair of her to accuse me of it," I stopped him immediately and ask: "What do you mean *that* got you angry? How could her false accusations do anything whatever to you? You mean, don't you, that your wife accused you unjustly and then *you* got yourself angry by idiotically telling yourself: (1) "I don't like her false accusation," and (2) "Because I don't like it, she shouldn't make it." Isn't *that* what got you upset, your own irrational premise, rather than her accusation? (Ellis, 1973, pp. 153–154)

The rational-emotive therapist is also verbally active. As Ellis stated:

> I do a great deal of talking rather than passively listening to what the client has to say. I do not hesitate, even during the first session, directly to confront the client with evidences of his irrational thinking and behaving. I most actively interpret many of the things the client says and does, without being too concerned about possible resistance and defenses on his part. I consistently try to persuade and argue the person out of his firmly held irrational and inconsistent beliefs, and unhesitatingly *attack* his neurosis-creating ideas and attitudes after first demonstrating how and why they exist. (Ellis 1973, p. 154)

The therapist not only deals with the specific irrational beliefs of the client, but also teaches the client the rational-emotive theory of emotional disturbances by assigning reading materials. The relationship is thus one of teacher and student.

> I am deliberately not very warm or personal with most of my clients, even those who crave and ask for such warmth, since, as I quickly explain to them, their main problem is usually that they think they need to be loved, when they actually do not; and I am there to teach them that they can get along very well in this world *without* necessarily being approved or loved by others. I therefore refuse to cater to their sick love demands. (Ellis, 1973, p. 155)

Rational-emotive therapy is an insight-producing form of therapy. The insights are not of the usual kind—explaining the origins or historical causes of the client's behavior. There are three kinds of insight (Ellis, 1979c). The first consists of the recognition that present dysfunctional behavior has antecedent causes, which includes past experiences. More important is the second: Understanding that these original causes are disturbing because of the irrational beliefs the client continues to harbor and recall about them. The third insight is the acknowledgment that

> there is no other way for him to overcome his emotional disturbance but by *his* continually observing, questioning, and challenging his own belief systems, and his working

and practicing to change his own irrational philosophic assumptions by verbal and by motor counterpropagandizing activity. (Ellis, 1973, p. 158)

The first two insights are of little value without the third.

Rational-emotive therapists, in addition to the direct disputing of beliefs, draw on a number of varied cognitive as well as emotive and behavioral techniques to help their clients (see Walen, DiGiuseppe, & Dryden, 1992). Ellis (1979a) has provided a list of such techniques. In the cognitive area, therapists make use of bibliotherapy (having clients read RET books), imaging methods, and cognitive homework (e.g., using an RET self-help form that is structured according to the A-B-C model; see Sichel & Ellis, 1984). In the emotive area, therapists make use of unconditional acceptance (i.e., accepting their clients without conditions; see Ellis, 1991), role playing, modeling, rational-emotive imagery (which gives clients the opportunity to practice their RET learnings via imagination), and shame-attacking exercises (to help people not feel shameful). In the behavioral area, therapists make use of operant conditioning and self-management, relaxation methods, and skill training. This listing of techniques is by no means exhaustive.

All told, RET therapists tend to use perhaps 40 or 50 regular techniques, . . . But they may also employ any number of "irregular" methods—including somewhat idiosyncratic ones like body massage or psychodynamic abreaction—as long as these methods are used in a general RET philosophical framework and are not employed in a hit-or-miss manner because the therapist has some vague idea that they might work with certain clients. (Ellis, 1979a, p. 66)

By using such varied techniques, all within the context of a cognitive restructuring framework, Ellis considers RET to be a comprehensive treatment approach—one that addresses the cognitive, emotive, and behavioral domains.

LENGTH AND LIMITATIONS OF TREATMENT

Length.   Rational-emotive therapy may be either short-term or long-term. The usual range is from five to fifty individual sessions (Ellis, 1989). Individual and group therapy can be combined and often nicely complement each other.

Limitations.   Ellis cautions about overexpectations from any method of psychotherapy. He feels that many biological tendencies (which he enumerates) lead to the development and persistence of emotional disturbance and neurotic behavior (see Ellis, 1976). In addition, socioenvironmental factors have a strong influence on the impressionable child. Therefore, if clients are to benefit from and maintain gains made in psychotherapy, they have to work hard during therapy and continue working hard when therapy is ended.

Although most clients have strong self-actualizing and regenerating capacities, some, such as the severely psychotic and the seriously mentally deficient, may not have the capacity to help themselves much. Nevertheless, "all kinds of clients can be helped with the rational-emotive method, including disturbed individuals whose traits include fixed homosexuality, psychopathy, schizophrenic reactions, mental deficiency and other syndromes that are usually unresponsive to most therapeutic methods" (Ellis, 1973, p. 35; cf. Ellis,

1987b). It is less effective with "those who will not face their problems or who refuse to work at therapy, such as individuals with character disorders and overt psychotic reactions." It is "more effective with younger and brighter clients" (Ellis, 1973, p. 51).

Results largely depend on the characteristics of the therapist. "Usually, RET gets best results when employed by a vigorous, active-directive, outgoing therapist who is willing to take risks and to be little concerned about winning his clients' approval." However, it can be successfully used

> by less outgoing therapists, as long as they are sufficiently active to keep challenging and questioning their clients' irrational ideas and as long as they persist at teaching these clients a more scientific method of looking at themselves and the world and of working against their own self-indoctrination. (Ellis, 1973, p. 51)

EXAMPLE

The following case example is taken from Yankura and Dryden's (1990) book, *Doing RET: Albert Ellis in Action* (pp. 102–111).

> In the following transcript, Ellis works with an unemployed middle-aged female client who is assiduously avoiding the task of job-hunting. It is apparent that this session is not the client's first exposure to RET, as she makes statements which indicate some degree of familiarity with Ellis's writings and approach. Nevertheless, it appears that she is a novice at applying rational-emotive concepts and techniques to the resolution of her problem areas. The session begins with the client making a specific request for some assistance in overcoming her task-avoidance:

CLIENT: I was reading *A New Guide to Rational Living* again, and two chapters in it were very helpful to me—the chapters on self-discipline and getting rid of inertia. I'm looking for a job, and I want to see if I can get some extra help in getting off of my ass.

ELLIS: All right—what's blocking you from getting off your ass?

CL: I'm scared!

EL: Avoid using a word like "scared"—it's too vague. Now, see if you can answer this question: "If I got off my ass and went out into the world. . . ," what might happen?

CL: (Pause) Well, I think it's just habit. I've never done it before.

EL: It's not just habit! You're probably inert because of low frustration tolerance. But let's keep on the "scared" part for a moment—what are you afraid of? Forget about "habit" for the time being—we'll get back to that later.

CL: I don't really know if I'm scared. I'm just guessing that I am.

EL: Then why'd you say that? You must have some indication that you're scared. . . .

CL: I'm either scared, or else I think the world owes me a living.

EL: Let's start with the "scared." Those two things are not the same.

CL: Well, I once heard someone tell a story about a little animal that was peeking out of its hole because it was hungry. It was hungry, but it was too scared to come out—so it finally starved to death, peeking out of its hole. I sort of identify with that animal, so that's what makes me think I'm scared.

EL: I think that you *are* scared. I don't doubt that you have the other thing—the low frustration tolerance—which we'll get back to, but let's just stick to the anxiety, the scariness. *What* is scary?

CL: I think I'm scared about job-hunting because I've never done it before.

EL: That's not true—there are millions of things you've never done before. If I gave you a million dollars and told you to go to the Kentucky Derby—which presumably you've never done—would you be scared of going?

CL: Well, not really. Not like this.

EL: Right. There are a lot of things you wouldn't be scared of—which are much more frightening than looking for a job. If you've never skied, for example, and again you had plenty of money—and I said, "Go skiing," you probably would go skiing—even though there really *is* danger involved. So, you're not scared just because you've never done it before—you're scared of something more concrete. Now, think about it—don't give up! If you don't get beyond merely recognizing that you're scared, you'll never solve the problem. What would you really be afraid of if you went out day after day and pushed to find a job?

Less than ten minutes into this session, Ellis has already accomplished several important therapeutic tasks. He has begun to make a distinction between ego anxiety and discomfort anxiety . . . (without explicitly employing these terms), and has rather forcefully directed the client to examine her "anxiety" before jumping to consideration of her low frustration tolerance. In addition, he has encouraged the client to become specific with regard to the nature of her anxiety ("Avoid using a word like 'scared'—it's too vague."), and has presented a logical argument to counter her view that it stems merely from a lack of experience with the behaviors involved in seeking employment. This intervention can be viewed as operating in the service of a depth-centered approach, as Ellis uses it to help the client get at the beliefs behind her anxiety.

CL: Oh, Dr. Ellis! (Pause) Well, what are most people afraid of?

EL: I know the answer to that question—but first let's see if *you* can figure out what *you're* afraid of.

CL: Do you think it's because I'm afraid I can't do it, that I won't get hired? I'm afraid that someone won't grab me on my first try, and then I'll think I'm. . . .

EL: You'll think you're what?

CL: I'll think maybe . . . that someone out there isn't all excited about having the Queen of the May come to work for them. That I'll then think I'm worthless. . . .

EL: Right—but think that through—don't just say it because you think that it might apply to other people. Think about what would really occur in your *gut* if you went out for twenty or thirty job interviews and they all didn't want you. How would you tend to feel?

CL: I think I'd just be completely passive like many women; that it's just something new. But you don't agree. . . .

EL: No—that's a falsehood! Unless you face things, you're not going to solve them! That's an easy way to cover up! And as I said before, we'll get back to that other thing later—that's a different feeling. Let's stick to the anxiety.

CL: (Musing to self) Why am I scared? Why am I scared to go out and get a job? (To Ellis) I'm scared I'll be turned down—but why should I be scared about that?

EL: Because . . . how would you feel if twenty or thirty times in a row. . . .

CL: . . . And I'll think, "Here I am, a middle-aged woman turned down," . . . and then I'd just get to feeling worse and worse.

EL: Because you'd be concluding what? What would be your conclusion?

CL: That nobody wants me.

EL: And that would be. . . ?

CL: That would be terrible.

EL: All right—now, did you just *say* that, or do you believe that that would probably occur?

CL: I just don't know!

EL: Well, think about it! You're avoiding thinking about it. I would know perfectly well, for example, how I would feel if I got turned down for thirty jobs.

CL: Of course I'd feel very upset!

EL: Well, what would the upsetness be?

CL: The upsetness would be that there's something wrong with *me!*

EL: And that that's *awful.*

CL: Right.

Through confrontation/insistence, Ellis encourages the client to make an effort at examining her own thoughts and feelings, rather than adopting a helpless stance or merely responding to his questions with what she believes to be the "right" answers. He again refocuses her to the issue at hand, and helps her to begin gaining some insight as to the negative self-rating issues which underlie her anxiety.

EL: But why would those be two nutty conclusions?

CL: Because working would be better than sitting home—that's awful, too!

EL: No, that's not the reason. You see, you're not zeroing in—you're not using your head.

CL: The obvious answer is that I would probably be getting turned down for economic reasons.

EL: That's right—it *doesn't* prove that there's something *wrong* with you! These are lousy times, and there are relatively few jobs available.

CL: Yeah—but you know, I remember now . . . all of my life, I've never gone out and gotten a job—I've never gone out and done one thing! I just waited 'till something happened.

EL: Because, "If I stuck my neck out. . . ."

CL: I might find out that. . . .

EL: What?

CL: I wasn't any good!

EL: Right—"I would *conclude* that I wasn't any good." You see, you *wouldn't* find out that you weren't any good—that's practically impossible.

CL: It has nothing to do with being middle-aged now, because I was that same way when I was nineteen.

EL: Yeah—but you remind me that at seventeen or eighteen I would never go out and look for a job—because I would be so afraid of rejection!

CL: (Surprised) *You?*

EL: That's right! But at nineteen I started getting over it—today, I have infinitely *less* anxiety.

CL: You have less today?

EL: Yes—because I've worked against my anxiety, and you never have!

CL: Mm-hm.

EL: So I think you're quite right—it has very little to do with your age. The chances of your getting rejections may have increased—but that's not necessarily true! Lots of women your age are considered highly desirable as employees, while many times the younger ones aren't. (A discussion as to the reasons that an older woman may be preferred by some employers occurs here. It is omitted for the sake of brevity.)

CL: Well now, I get mixed up when I read your book—because I see so many things to be working on.

EL: But you're moving from one thing to another! Now, stick to the anxiety—you're going to get mixed up if you keep jumping around and using one as an excuse for another. You'd better face the fact—which we've just barely gotten into—that you've always been scared shitless of rejection.

CL: So, the same thing would apply to making new friends, new boyfriends, everything! I still *wait*—wait for it to come to me!

EL: That's right. Your passivity is not *merely* laziness—although I'm not saying that that's not an element that's involved. . . .

CL: No . . . but it is laziness, too . . . and being spoiled as a child.

EL: It's not "being spoiled"! That has practically nothing to do with it! That's just a cop out.

CL: Really?

EL: Well, Nelson Rockefeller was spoiled!

CL: Right, right.

EL: He never had to do one day's work in his life—but as far as I know, Rocky always worked his ass off!

CL: Well, I don't mean spoiled—I mean . . . well, you know . . . no discipline, or anything—not trained. . . .

EL: But we don't know that Rockefeller got any discipline. It's a little unlikely that he got *much*, because he was probably raised by nurses—and they're not going to discipline a child who has ten million dollars!

Ellis begins this portion of the transcript by asking a question which is intended to prompt the client into seeing the erroneous nature of the meanings she attaches to rejection experiences. When she responds in an irrelevant fashion, he quickly intervenes and again insists that she "use her head."

When the client makes reference to childhood experiences ("being spoiled") as being responsible for her current passivity, Ellis moves in with a strong dispute by citing the example of Nelson Rockefeller. The response he makes here is quite important, as it serves to illustrate that "A" doesn't cause "C" and encourages the client to take responsibility for her problems. It is possible that this intervention serves its purpose, as the client moves into new territory:

CL: Well, then—what do I say to myself about rejection and all of these different things? Not just jobs, but. . . .

EL: Well, what *are* you saying to yourself? Because as I said, you'd better vividly picture yourself trying for twenty or thirty jobs, and getting rejected for various reasons.

CL: You mean you want me to definitely picture that.

EL: That's right.

CL: And then picture my reaction?

EL: That's right—what your feeling would be and what you would be saying to yourself to create that feeling.

CL: You want me to do that now? Picture that?

EL: Yeah—picture it and see what you're feeling in your gut, as you get rejected for the twentieth time.

CL: Well, I know that I must be planning to go out and look for a job, because for the last few weeks I've had a feeling in my gut of such anxiety and nervousness. . . .

EL: So there's your answer. Now, what do you think you'd be telling yourself—and don't just give me an answer from my book—what do you think *you* would be telling yourself?

CL: I'm telling myself that I'm going to do it.

EL: "And if I do it. . . ."

CL: It's going to be hell, it's going to be like jumping into a pot of boiling water or something. . . .

EL: Because. . . ?

CL: Because I guess I think I'm going to be rejected.

EL: And that would mean. . . ?

CL: Or else I think I'm going to be . . . you know, it's a mixture of grandiose thoughts. . . .

EL: Well, wait a minute—first stick with this one: "If I got rejected, that would mean. . . ."

CL: That would mean that I'm right about myself.

EL: "That I'm really no good." Is that what you're saying?

CL: Yeah.

The client begins this section by displaying her awareness of the desirability of generating an alternative philosophy to deal with rejection experiences, but again evinces helplessness by asking, "[W]hat do I say to myself. . . ?" Ellis responds by turning her question back at her, thus creating an opportunity to uncover her current dysfunctional beliefs. His directive to "vividly picture yourself . . . getting rejected for various reasons" can be considered an example of thoroughgoingness in therapy (i.e., increasing efficiency by employing a variety of techniques), as he is attempting to prompt the client to use imagery as a vehicle for gaining insights into her irrational beliefs. The non-verbal cognitive content of an imagery experience can be seen to deviate considerably from the verbally-loaded interventions which Ellis mainly employs, and adds a multi-modal tone to the session.

Following the imagery directive, Ellis utilizes a series of "incomplete sentences" (e.g., "And that would mean. . . ?") to direct the client to her irrational conclusions regarding her worth in the face of rejections. This technique appears to be favored by Ellis, as he can be heard using it in a majority of his sessions.

EL: All right—now let's look at the other side for a moment. Let's suppose you picture getting *accepted*.

CL: Then I'd manage to say it must be a lousy job or something.

EL: What else would you say? Let's suppose you got interviewed a few times, and your fifth or sixth time out they say to you, "Well, you seem to be the one we want—we want a woman around your age, because we'd like her to stay, and it looks like you can handle this job." So they've accepted you. Now, you're about to go into work on Monday. . . .

CL: Yeah—well, I wouldn't mind that as much, because I'd be over the main hurdle. I'd be quite nervous about it, but. . . .

EL: Because. . . ? Wait a minute, you'd better not run over that quickly. You see, you run over things quickly—you sweep them under the rug. "I'd be quite nervous about Monday because. . . ."

CL: Because I'd think, "Oh, I'm going to make mistakes"—that kind of thing.

EL: And that would mean. . . .?

CL: And that would mean that I was right all along—that I'm a jerk!

EL: Now you see, you've just boxed yourself in completely!

CL: Even if I get hired, even if it's a lousy job, they wouldn't have hired a jerk.

EL: Or—"It's a good job, but I'm not going to be able to make it, and I'm a shit."

CL: Yeah. . . .

EL: So you see, you've closed just about all of the exits in your head. If you get interviewed and aren't accepted you'll think you're a jerk, and that will prove what you've always believed since the age of nineteen: That you'd better not try to do things, because you're no good. And if you actually get the job, it'll either prove that the job. . . .

CL: They'll find out I'm no good.

EL: That's right—they'll find out you're incompetent and no good, and that'll be a terrible thing. Now, unless you go over and over those two ideas. . . .

CL: The second one is that they'll find out I'm no good. What was the first?

EL: The first one is related to their refusing you—that they'll find out you're no good while interviewing you.

CL: Or else when I get hired they'll find out I'm no good.

EL: That's right. Now, is there any exit with your views?

CL: No!

In this portion of the transcript, Ellis shows the client how her self-rating issues will plague her whether she is rejected or hired with respect to a given job. This can be considered an example of his criterion for pervasiveness in psychotherapy, as he is helping the client to see the many manifestations of a particular form of irrational thinking to which she subscribes.

EL: There'll be no exit from anxiety—that's the issue. Now, let's jump to the other thing for a moment—let's just suppose that you get a job, and you're doing okay at it.

CL: Yeah—I always do very well on jobs, strangely enough.

EL: Well—where do you get the jobs, if you do okay?

CL: Well, somebody offers them to me. But I've never gone out and gotten one.

EL: Right—but suppose you now have a job, and you're doing alright on it. It's not the greatest job in the world, but it's okay, and you're doing all right on it. Now, would you feel—after a while—the inertia, the not wanting to get up in the morning and go to work, and things like that?

CL: Well, that happened to me two years ago! I worked for a year and a half.

EL: Doing what?

CL: Selling, in a boutique. And then I became the manager, sort of. And I did pretty well.

EL: And why did you quit?

CL: I just got bored with it. It was interesting to learn the business, but then it just got to be . . . there was nothing to do, and I had just gotten as far as I could go.

EL: Yeah—so it really was a boring job. . . .

CL: Well, it was all right while I was learning it, but after a year and a half there wasn't much to do.

EL: But you see, there were two avenues you could have taken there—one would've been to go look for another job—because the best time to look for a job is when you have one—and the second would have been to go open your own boutique or something.

CL: That's what a friend of mine was trying to get me to do, and I got panic-stricken.

EL: Because. . . ?

CL: "Oh, couldn't do it, couldn't do it; it would fail, it would fail. . . ." I got utterly panic-stricken.

EL: Yeah, but where'd you get *that* nutty idea—"It would fail, it would fail"—when you knew exactly how to run a boutique. How would it fail?

CL: Well—actually, I didn't have any knowledge of the business end of it, at all. I was just in charge of the sales girls and some of the stock—things like that. I didn't have anything to do with the business end of it.

EL: But wait a minute—there's an obvious thing you could do. Do you know what that is?

CL: Well . . . get a job someplace where I could learn the business end of it.

EL: Right—why didn't you do the obvious?

CL: Because I was a neurotic slob!

EL: But that's vague, you see. Now you're going back to the vagueries.

CL: Because I had no confidence that I'd be able to do it.

EL: Well, you began as a saleswoman there, and then they let you run the place, and it got boring because it was easy for you. Now what's the evidence that you couldn't also learn to do buying, and pay bills, et cetera? What's the evidence for that?

CL: None.

EL: But you concluded that.

CL: I concluded that—right.

EL: And with every job you've ever had, somehow or other you did okay. . . .

CL: But I've always concluded that—I told you that before—that I was there under false pretenses, and they were going to find it out eventually.

EL: But take that boutique job—what were the false pretenses? You were managing the thing and it became too boring, easy. So what were the false pretenses?

CL: Well, I couldn't possibly learn to do the business end of it—I don't know anything about business.

EL: (Unintelligible) . . . we're back now to the anxiety! You see, it doesn't look like real passivity and inertia in the sense that, "I just don't wanna work"—although there may be some of that in there too.

CL: Not so much—because I like *doing,* you know.

EL: You like activity. But there's *extreme* anxiety. . . .

CL: I feel like I'm tearing in two directions! You know—wanting to do something and being terrified to do it.

EL: The terror seems to be, one, "I'm going to be refused if I try for a job," two, "Even if I get it, I can't make it," and three, "Even if I make it, then it's a crummy job or there are aspects of it I never could do well at."

CL: I'm just *determined* to be boxed in!

EL: Well, you're determined not to explore the hypotheses that you are *able* to do more in life than you let yourself do, and that even when you fail at something, you're not a shit.

Here, Ellis again applies his criterion for pervasiveness by exploring the possibility that low frustration tolerance might be contributing to this client's job-related difficulties. This route, however, seems to lead back to the client's ego anxiety and self-rating issues. In relation to this, Ellis utilizes repetition in order to reinforce the message that failure is not evidence of one's worthlessness.

CL: Well—how can I counteract it?

EL: By asking, "How could I possibly be a shit?" There are four disputing questions that we give to everybody. . . .

CL: Yeah—"What am I saying to sustain it; is it true?"

EL: Right. "Where is the evidence, and what's the worst thing that could happen if I fail at this, whatever it is." If, for example, you went out and looked for a job and fell on your face—or if you got a job and failed at it—what's the worst thing that could happen? Now, you don't seem to be *doing* that about this area—asking yourself these questions and thinking them through to the right answer. You've indulged yourself all your life in the nutty conclusion that failure proves you're a shit.

CL: So what you want me to work on . . . is that I can go ahead and fail, be turned down and fail, and I'm still not a shit!

EL: That's right! Whether it's with regard to a job, or socially, or anything—you can't legitimately devalue *you* just because you've failed at something—and just because you may have failed many times.

CL: Even though I *haven't* really failed at these things—you still think that's the thing I should work on?

EL: Well, you haven't failed mainly because you haven't gotten yourself into anything complicated. In your whole life, what was the most complicated work you ever did?

CL: Oh, I've had a lot of jobs. . . .

EL: What was the most *complicated*—where you really had responsibility and did a variety of things?

CL: Um, never.

EL: Well, you see—and yet on the. . . .

CL: Well, I ran a bar in Chicago.

EL: Who owned the bar?

CL: My husband and me—but I used to run it plenty of times when he was away.

EL: So you did practically everything—buying, bartending, managing the employees, et cetera. Now, did you only do that because you were married?

CL: Probably.

EL: Because let's suppose you weren't married. . . .

CL: I never would have had the courage to go to Chicago and open a bar! (Laughs) You know that! I had somebody with me to do it—somebody to take care of me.

EL: And did he have prior experience at that?

CL: Oh, not much. But he was the kind who did all sorts of things like that.

EL: So that time you had a fairly complicated job. You got into it through him, but then you made the wrong conclusions, again: "Unless some man is around and leading me by the hand, I can't make it at a thing like that."

CL: I know it.

EL: That's a nutty conclusion—because you could go right back to Chicago—assuming that you had the money—and do exactly the same thing without him. Why would you need him, now that you know that kind of business?

CL: Well, I don't understand what I'm supposed to work on—am I supposed to work on the idea that I *won't* fail?

EL: No . . .

CL: I'm going to work on the idea that I can fail, and can get refused, and that I'm still not a shit.

EL: That's right! But while you're working on that, you could also realize that somebody with your intelligence and experience could practically never fail completely. As I said before, if you tried enough interviews, you'd get a job. If you tried enough jobs, you'd succeed at some of them. But if you do fail, you're never a shit—you're never devalued as a human being. Now *that's* what you'd better work on, and I really mean work on it! Okay. . . .

CL: Thank you—see you Monday.

SUMMARY AND EVALUATION

Summary.   Rational-emotive therapy assumes that, although there are powerful biological and social forces leading to irrationality, human beings have the potential for being rational. Emotional disturbance and neurosis *are,* in fact, irrational thinking and can be remedied by changing one's thinking and, in consequence, one's emotions and behavior to reflect logic and rationality. The process of psychotherapy is thus to teach the client to think rationally. While other commonly practiced techniques of therapy—such as reflection of feeling, abreaction, and reassurance—may be used at the beginning of the process, the rational-emotive therapist quickly moves into an active-directive, didactic, teaching process, wherein the irrational ideas and beliefs of the client are pointed out, their relationship to the client's emotional disturbance or unhappiness is explicated, and the client's thinking is changed by logic and reasoning, suggestions, argument and persuasion, and prescription of activities.

The aims or goals of therapy as stated by Ellis are similar to those of many other psychotherapies. Ellis speaks not only of the elimination or minimization of anxiety, hostility, depression, feelings of inferiority and inadequacy, unhappiness, and other related symptoms, but also the development or enhancement of happiness, effective living, rational behavior, independence, responsibility, and even self-actualization. Chief among the goals of RET is the modification of clients' thinking—changing it from irrational to rational.

Other therapists, as Ellis recognizes, often place most if not all of the responsibility for correction of irrational and illogical ideas and beliefs on the client. Ellis does not do so. He recognizes that clients have the potential for growth and health, but he believes that this potential is so overgrown with longstanding irrational attitudes, beliefs, and emotions that only an active, direct attack on the part of the therapist can uncover it. "Unless these current residuals of his old cognitive errors are vigorously and persistently attacked, there is little chance of his modifying them significantly" (Ellis, 1973, p. 35).

Evaluation.   But how well does such an approach help clients learn to think for themselves? By taking such an active, directive, didactic stance throughout treatment, is it possible that the rational-emotive therapist may actually deprive clients of the opportunity to think and act for themselves? That the RET approach may foster dependency on the therapist and may prevent clients from becoming self-initiating and autonomous are concerns worth bearing in mind. Less active, directive, didactically oriented therapists might argue that it takes time for clients to mobilize their growth potential, that it is better for them to do this themselves, that it is better for them to reach their own solutions than for the therapist to present them with ready solutions for their problems. It could also be argued that the obsession of many therapists with efficiency, their emphasis on speeding up the therapeutic process, and their desire to achieve results quickly may have some significant disadvantages, even undesirable results for clients (e.g., depriving them of the satisfaction of achieving their own solutions).

We could also ask the following of Ellis and RET: How many patients hold beliefs in the extreme form that he states them? Could the irrational beliefs that Ellis (1962, 1979b) has identified be absolutist or extremist forms of what patients actually think? These are reasonable questions worth entertaining. In his own way, Ellis may impose, project, or assume an extreme form of beliefs in his clients in order to attack and argue against them. Wolpe (1978) has made this point: "In practice, . . . he often seems to project onto the patient the irrational beliefs he supposes the patient ought to have" (p. 441; cf. Wolpe, 1990). While we imagine Ellis would disagree with this assertion, Wolpe's point still merits consideration. Could it be that the rational-emotive approach, in its own way, is an extremist vision about people, their problems, and problem remediation?

Ellis agrees that the essence of effective psychotherapy is the changing of attitudes. But there are other therapists who believe that, since attitudes are emotion laden, a direct attack on them is ineffective. Goldfried and Davison (1976) commented on Ellis's reliance on argument and persuasion:

> Rather than arguing with the client and trying to convince him how foolish he is for accepting any of these beliefs, it would be far more effective for the client *himself* to offer arguments to refute these expectations. The social-psychological literature suggests that this method is more effective in creating attitude change. (p. 176)

Young, in his comments in the Ellis-Young-Lockwood (1987, p. 247) dialogue, put it this way.

> I think the more you dispute and debate in an aggressive manner, the more you put a certain percentage of clients on the defensive. They feel threatened by it, and as a result you often get people agreeing when they don't really agree. They nod and say, "Yes, I see your point of view," but they are actually too threatened to say that they don't agree and to explain their reasons why. As a result, I would predict that the client dropout rate would be higher in RET.

Ellis surely does not appear to be all that concerned that direct attacks on a client's resistance may constitute a threat, may serve to increase resistance, and may make change more difficult if not impossible. Yet there seems to be sufficient evidence that threat results in impairment of learning and reasoning. With this in mind, we think it best that therapists exercise much caution when using such direct, active methods which might be quite threatening to some if not many clients.

This leads to a comment on the imparting of values in psychotherapy. There is, of course, no question that values are involved in therapy; that the values of the therapist must be considered; and that all therapists, since they determine the goals of therapy, are, to that extent at least, directive. Still, there are degrees of indoctrination of, or imposition of values or philosophies on clients. It would appear that rational-emotive psychotherapy is rather extreme in the extent and detail of the values it imposes on its clients. Ellis (1962) noted the danger that the therapist "may use his authority to induce his patient to acquire *his,* the therapist's, particular brand of beliefs" (p. 367), yet he does not seem to recognize that this is essentially what he does, although, to be sure, he uses reason and logic, together with authority.

Other concerns that could be raised about RET include its seeming overemphasis on cognition and its overlooking, or at least giving minimal attention to, the clients' past, their ego defenses, and the unconscious. That RET would emphasize cognition is understandable; after all, it is a cognitively oriented approach. But does RET overemphasize cognition and give clients' emotions short shrift in the process? Again Ellis would probably strongly respond "no," yet this is another question worth thinking about. It would seem possible that RET, with its primary and intense focus on ideas, thoughts, and beliefs, may diminish, downplay, even ignore clients' affective experience some if not much of the time. This inattention or ignoring of such a significant part of clients' lives may well lead to problems (e.g., clients feeling that they are not being listened to and heard fully) of which therapists need to be aware.

That RET places little to no emphasis on the past, ego defenses, and the unconscious seems clear. This could definitely be seen as a limitation of the approach. As Corey (1992) states, "I find it hard to believe clients can make lasting and significant changes until they first recognize and accept their history and then come to terms with past unfinished conflicts so that these feelings do not interfere with their present functioning" (p. 360). Thus, for those who share Corey's view, RET would seem largely to omit still another significant component of clients' being and experience, and this omission could have negative implications for helping clients improve in treatment.

These then are some (but by no means all) of the issues that can be seen as attending the RET approach. We have no doubts that RET has its merits. Furthermore, we realize that therapists do not have to adopt Ellis' hard-hitting approach to do RET. However, for anyone thinking of doing RET, and for anyone thinking of trying to ape Ellis in some shape or form, reflection on and consideration of the above issues would seem important.

Let us next consider research. Based on the research evidence, how effective is RET? Ellis has said that

> the rational-emotive approach to psychotherapy is not only unusually effective clinically but is now backed by a considerable amount of experimental evidence which almost consistently supports phenomenological tenets and indicates that human emotions are enormously influenced by cognition. . . . There is clinical, experimental, and other support for rational-emotive therapy. (Ellis, 1973, p. 27; cf. Ellis, 1977a)

Since Ellis wrote those words, we have not lacked for RET research (e.g., see the reviews of DiGiuseppe, Miller, & Trexler, 1977; Haaga & Davison, 1989a; Hollon & Beck, 1986, 1994; Lyons & Woods, 1991; McGovern & Silverman, 1986; Zettle & Hayes, 1980). If we consider the conclusions drawn in some of the most recent research reviews, opinion about the efficacy of RET appears to be mixed. For example, McGovern and Silverman (1986), in their review of 47 outcome studies, found RET to be quite effective, as did Silverman, McCarthy, and McGovern (1992) in their later review of 89 such studies. In still another review of 70 outcome studies, Lyons and Woods (1991) came to the same conclusion; they stated that "RET is an effective form of treatment. Compared to baseline assessments and control groups, those individuals receiving RET demonstrated significant improvement" (p. 368). Interestingly enough, Lyons and Woods (1991) went on to add the following:

> Perhaps it is time to stop the needless and inefficient discussion of the efficacy of this therapy. Rather a better focus of investigations and reviews would be to determine

which factors, or combinations thereof, contribute most to the effectiveness of RET. (p. 368)

Other reviewers, however, have not been as positive about the efficacy of RET. For example, Haaga and Davison (1989b), in commenting on their review (Haaga & Davison, 1989a) of rational-emotive therapy studies, said that

RET either (a) is supported only by preliminary, unreplicated findings. . . , (b) has not added anything to simpler treatments that do not strive for the profound philosophical change RET seeks. . . , or (c) works as well as other plausible treatments, but with little information on mechanisms of action or predictors of differential response. (p. 494)

More recently, Haaga and Davison (1991, 1993) have updated their review, basically reiterating the above conclusions.

These reviews have all been well-done, recent (or relatively recent) examinations of the RET literature, but what then can we conclude from them? Perhaps the best we can say from all this is that RET clearly shows promise, has been shown to be superior to no treatment or placebo controls (e.g., Engels, Garnefski, & Diekstra, 1993), is clearly continuing to garner a more solid empirical base, but still is in need of more adequate empirical testing and operationalization (cf. Haaga & Davison, 1991; Hollon & Beck, 1986, 1994). Even in the most favorable of reviews, it was well recognized that the research suffered from various methodological flaws (e.g., lack of follow-up data, small sample sizes, inadequate statistical power), and that those flaws tempered the positive conclusions that could be drawn about RET. It could be, as Lyons and Woods (1991) asserted, that research would be best served by considering what factors make RET most effective. Or further still, it could be as Haaga and Davison (1993) have asserted that

it is time to consider the possibility that RET is not susceptible to traditional scientific outcome evaluation. . . . [P]erhaps studies of RET will be replaced by studies of specific tactics in particular circumstances. . . . Such studies could begin to address the theoretically and clinically interesting issue of when and for whom RET's distinctive methods are helpful. (p. 218)

Whatever the case, there still appears to be some controversy here about RET. For that to change, it seems that RET research will need to address better some of the methodological problems identified previously by Haaga and Davison (1989a, 1989b, 1991, 1993).

To conclude, what about the future of RET? This is a question that Ellis has dealt with at various points. Some future directions and needs that he has noted include the following: using research to further refine RET theory and practice, working to integrate rational-emotive theory with cognitive psychology better, and giving RET to the masses (by means of various media; Ellis, 1987b, 1993; Ellis & Grieger, 1977b). Other events, such as proposals to reformulate rational-emotive theory (Rorer, 1989a, 1989b), proposals to reformulate the A-B-C model (Muran, 1991), and insightful critiques of how RET research could be improved (Haaga & Davison, 1989b, 1993), may also ultimately affect the future of RET (see Ellis, 1992, for some indications of this).

But all this remains to be seen. For now, we can surely say that there appears to be much ferment, vigor, and activity within the RET camp. The Institute for Rational-Emotive Therapy continues to be a prime force in offering RET training, workshops, and making available all manner of RET materials. There are affiliated RET training centers throughout the United States; there, too, are several international affiliated training centers—in such countries as Australia, Germany, Italy, and the Netherlands, among others. The *Journal of Rational-Emotive and Cognitive-Behavior Therapy* continues to provide a useful forum for the presentation of RET theory, research, and practice articles. In addition, there are numerous practitioners (such as the Wesslers, DiGiuseppe, and Dryden) who appear commited to furthering the rational-emotive approach. It may well be that this evident ferment, vigor, and commitment will be RET's greatest strength as it attempts to realize those future directions and meet those needs mentioned above.

REFERENCES

Braaten, L. J. (1961). The main theories of existentialism from the viewpoint of the psychotherapist. *Mental Hygiene, 45,* 10–17.

Corey, G. (1992). *Theory and practice of counseling and psychotherapy* (4th ed.). Pacific Grove, CA: Brooks/Cole.

DiGiuseppe, R. A., Miller, N. J., & Trexler, L. D. (1977). A review of rational-emotive psychotherapy outcome studies. *The Counseling Psychologist, 7*(1), 64–72.

Dryden, W. (Ed.). (1989). *The essential Albert Ellis.* New York: Springer.

Ellis, A. (1955a). New approaches to psychotherapy techniques. *Journal of Clinical Psychology Monograph Supplement, 1.*

Ellis, A. (1955b). Psychotherapy techniques for use with psychotics. *American Journal of Psychotherapy, 9,* 452–476.

Ellis, A. (1956). An operational reformulation of some of the basic principles of psychoanalysis. *Psychoanalytic Review, 43,* 163–180.

Ellis, A. (1957a). Outcome of employing three techniques of psychotherapy. *Journal of Clinical Psychology, 13,* 344–350.

Ellis, A. (1957b). Rational psychotherapy and individual psychotherapy. *Journal of Individual Psychology, 13,* 38–44.

Ellis, A. (1958). Rational psychotherapy. *Journal of General Psychology, 59,* 35–49.

Ellis, A. (1959). Rationalism and its therapeutic applications. In A. Ellis (Ed.). *The place of values in the practice of psychotherapy.* New York: American Academy of Psychotherapists.

Ellis, A. (1962). *Reason and emotion in psychotherapy.* Secaucus, NJ: Citadel Press.

Ellis, A. (1967). Goals of psychotherapy. In A. R. Mahrer (Ed.). *The goals of psychotherapy.* Englewood Cliffs, NJ: Prentice-Hall.

Ellis, A. (1971). *Growth through reason: Verbatim cases in rational-emotive therapy.* Palo Alto, CA: Science and Behavior Books. (Paperback published by Wilshire Books, North Hollywood, CA.)

Ellis, A. (1973). *Humanistic psychotherapy: The rational-emotive approach.* New York: Julian Press. (Paperback published by McGraw-Hill, New York.)

Ellis, A. (1976). The biological basis of human irrationality. *Journal of Individual Psychology, 32,* 145–168.

Ellis, A. (1977a). Rational-emotive therapy: Research data that support the clinical and personality hypotheses of RET and other modes of cognitive-behavior therapy. *The Counseling Psychologist, 7* (1), 2–44.

Ellis, A. (1979a). The practice of rational-emotive therapy. In A. Ellis & J. M. Whiteley (Eds.). *Theoretical and empirical foundations of rational-emotive therapy* (pp. 61–100). Monterey, CA: Brooks/Cole.

Ellis, A. (1979b). Rational-emotive therapy. In A. Ellis & J. M. Whiteley (Eds.). *Theoretical and empirical foundations of rational-emotive therapy* (pp. 1–6). Monterey, CA: Brooks, Cole.

Ellis, A. (1979c). The theory of rational-emotive therapy. In A. Ellis & J. M. Whiteley (Eds.). *Theoretical and empirical foundations of rational-emotive therapy* (pp. 43–60). Monterey, CA: Brooks/Cole.

Ellis, A. (1979d). Toward a new theory of personality. In A. Ellis & J. M. Whiteley (Eds.). *Theoretical and empirical foundations of rational-emotive therapy* (pp. 7–32). Monterey, CA: Brooks/Cole.

Ellis, A. (1987a). The evolution of rational-emotive therapy (RET) and cognitive-behavior therapy (CBT). In J. K. Zeig (Ed.). *The evolution of psychotherapy* (pp. 107–124). New York: Brunner/Mazel.

Ellis, A. (1987b). Rational-emotive therapy: Current appraisal and future directions. *Journal of Cognitive Psychotherapy: An International Quarterly, 1,* 73–86.

Ellis, A. (1988a). Can we legitimately evaluate our selves? A reply to Robert C. Roberts. *Psychotherapy, 25,* 314–316.

Ellis, A. (1988b). *How to stubbornly refuse to make yourself miserable about anything—yes anything!* Seacaucus, NJ: Lyle Stuart.

Ellis, A. (1989). Rational-emotive therapy. In R. J. Corsini & D. Wedding (Eds.). *Current psychotherapies* (4th ed., pp. 197–238). Itasca, IL: Peacock.

Ellis, A. (1991). Rational-emotive treatment of simple phobias. *Psychotherapy, 28,* 452–456.

Ellis, A. (1992). The revised ABC's of rational-emotive therapy. In J. K. Zeig (Ed.). *The evolution of psychotherapy: The second conference* (pp. 79–92). New York: Brunner/Mazel.

Ellis, A. E. (1993). Reflections on rational-emotive therapy. *Journal of Consulting and Clinical Psychology, 61,* 199–201.

Ellis, A., & Dryden, W. (1987). *The practice of rational-emotive therapy.* New York: Springer.

Ellis, A., & Grieger, R. (Eds.). (1977a). *Handbook of rational-emotive therapy* (vol. 1). New York: Springer.

Ellis, A., & Grieger, R. (1977b). The present and future of RET. In A. Ellis & R. Grieger (Eds.). *Handbook of rational-emotive therapy* (pp. 421–433). New York: Springer.

Ellis, A., & Harper, R. A. (1975). *A new guide to rational living.* North Hollywood, CA: Wilshire Books.

Ellis, A., & Whiteley, J. M. (Eds.). (1979). *Theoretical and empirical foundations of rational-emotive therapy.* Monterey, CA: Brooks/Cole.

Ellis, A., Young, J., & Lockwood, G. (1987). Cognitive therapy and rational-emotive therapy: A dialogue. *Journal of Cognitive Psychotherapy: An International Quarterly, 1,* 205–255.

Engels, G. I., Garnefski, N., & Diekstra, R. F. W. (1993). Efficacy of rational-emotive therapy: A quantitative analysis. *Journal of Consulting and Clinical Psychology, 61,* 1083–1090.

Goldfried, M. R., & Davison, G. C. (1976). *Clinical behavior therapy.* New York: Holt, Rinehart & Winston.

Haaga, D. A. F., & Davison, G. C. (1989a). Outcome studies of rational-emotive therapy. In M. E. Bernard & R. DiGiuseppe (Eds.), *Inside rational-emotive therapy: A critical appraisal of the theory and therapy of Albert Ellis* (pp. 155–197). San Diego, CA: Academic Press.

Haaga, D. A. F., & Davison, G. C. (1989b). Slow progress in rational-emotive therapy outcome research: Etiology and treatment. *Cognitive Therapy and Research, 13,* 493–508.

Haaga, D. A. F., & Davison, G. C. (1991). Cognitive change methods. In F. H. Kanfer & A. P. Goldstein (Eds.). *Helping people change: A textbook of methods* (4th ed., pp. 248–304). New York: Pergamon.

Haaga, D. A. F., & Davison, G. C. (1993). An appraisal of rational-emotive therapy. *Journal of Consulting and Clinical Psychology, 61,* 215–220.

Hollon, S. D., & Beck, A. T. (1986). Cognitive and cognitive-behavioral therapies. In S. L. Garfield & A. E. Bergin (Eds.). *Handbook of psychotherapy and behavior change* (3rd ed., pp. 443–482). New York: Wiley.

Hollon, S. D., & Beck, A. T. (1994). Cognitive and cognitive-behavioral therapies. In A. E. Bergin & S. L. Garfield (Eds.). *Handbook of psychotherapy and behavior change* (4th ed., pp. 428–466). New York: Wiley.

Lyons, L. C., & Woods, P. J. (1991). The efficacy of rational-emotive therapy: A quantitative review of the outcome research. *Clinical Psychology Review, 11,* 357–369.

McGovern, T. E., & Silverman, M. (1986). A review of outcome studies of rational-emotive therapy from 1977 to 1982. In A. Ellis & R. Grieger (Eds.). *Handbook of rational-emotive therapy* (vol. 2, pp. 81–102). New York: Springer.

Muran, J. C. (1991). A reformulation of the ABC model in cognitive psychotherapies: Implications for assessment and treatment. *Clinical Psychology Review, 11,* 399–418.

Rorer, L. G. (1989a). Rational-emotive theory: I. An integrated psychological and philosophical basis. *Cognitive Therapy and Research, 13,* 475–492.

Rorer, L. G. (1989b). Rational-emotive theory: II. Explication and evaluation. *Cognitive Therapy and Research, 13,* 531–548.

Sichel, J., & Ellis, A. (1984). *RET self-help form.* New York: Institute for Rational-Emotive Therapy.

Silverman, M. S., McCarthy, M., & McGovern, T. (1992). A review of outcome studies of rational-emotive therapy from 1982–1989. *Journal of Rational-Emotive and Cognitive-Behavior Therapy, 10,* 111–186.

Walen, S., DiGiuseppe, R., & Dryden, W. (1992). *A practitioner's guide to rational-emotive therapy.* New York: Oxford University Press.

Wiener, D. N. (1988). *Albert Ellis: Passionate skeptic.* New York: Praeger.

Wolpe, J. (1978). Cognition and causation in human behavior and its therapy. *American Psychologist, 33,* 437–446.

Wolpe, J. (1990). *The practice of behavior therapy* (4th ed.). New York: Pergamon.

Yankura, J., & Dryden, W. (1990). *Doing RET: Albert Ellis in action.* New York: Springer Publishing Co.

Zettle, R. D., & Hayes, S. C. (1980). Conceptual and empirical status of rational-emotive therapy. *Progress in Behavior Modification, 9,* 125–166.

chapter 8

Cognitive Therapy: Beck

Aaron T. Beck (b. 1921) received his M.D. from Yale University School of Medicine in 1946. From 1946 to 1948, he served an internship and residency in pathology at the Rhode Island Hospital; following that, he did a residency in neurology and psychiatry at the Cushing Veterans Administration Hospital in Framingham, Massachusetts. Beck has been on the faculty of the University of Pennsylvania Medical School since 1954 and is now professor of psychiatry and the director of the Center for Cognitive Therapy. He also has been a fellow in psychiatry at the Austen Riggs Center in Stockbridge, Massachusetts; a consultant to the Philadelphia Veterans Administration Hospital; a member of the board of directors of the West Philadelphia Mental Health Consortium; a trustee of the American Academy of Psychoanalysis; and the president of the Society of Psychotherapy Research.

Beck was certified in psychiatry by the American Board of Psychiatry and Neurology in 1953, and he graduated from the Philadelphia Psychoanalytic Institute in 1958. He is a recipient of the Foundations' Fund Award for Research in Psychiatry from the American Psychiatric Association; he is also a recipient of the James McKeen Cattell Fellow Award from the American Psychological Association. In 1989, he received an Award for Distinguished Scientific Contribution to Psychology from the American Psychological Association (see *American Psychologist*, 1989, *44*, pp. 458–460).

Beck is on the Advisory Board of the journal *Cognitive Therapy and Research;* he is on the Board of Consulting Advisors for the *Journal of Cognitive Psychotherapy*. Beck is the author of numerous journal articles and the author or coauthor of *Depression: Causes and Treatment* (1972); *Cognitive Therapy and the Emotional Disorders* (1976); *Cognitive Therapy of Depression* (1979; with Rush, Shaw, & Emery); *Anxiety Disorders and Phobias: A Cognitive Perspective* (1985; with Emery & Greenberg); *Love Is Never Enough*

(1988); and *Cognitive Therapy of Personality Disorders* (1990; with Freeman and Associates), among other publications. He also appeared as one of the three therapists in the film series, *Three Approaches to Psychotherapy III.* A recent book, part of the Key Figures in Counselling and Psychotherapy book series, has focused on Beck's life, his contributions, and overall influence (Weishaar, 1992).

BACKGROUND AND DEVELOPMENT

Beck, like Ellis, was trained in and engaged in the practice of orthodox psychoanalysis. But he became dissatisfied with its complexity and abstractness, and his studies that attempted to validate psychoanalytic concepts were not supportive of the theory. Beck's encouragement of his patients to focus their attention on their "automatic thoughts" (a term that we will explain later) ultimately led him to reformulate concepts of depression, anxiety, phobias, and obsessive-compulsive neuroses in terms of cognitive distortions. He developed various maneuvers to correct patients' faulty thinking and thus relieve neurosis.

Beck also was attracted to the newly developing field of behavior therapy, which he studied and practiced. He felt that behavioral techniques were effective, but not for the reasons given by behavior therapists. Rather, these techniques were effective because they brought about attitudinal or cognitive changes in patients. Thus, Beck viewed behavior therapy as limited; it ignored patients' thinking about themselves, about the therapist, and about the therapy itself. Still, behavior therapy's emphases on obtaining objective data from patients, on systematic planning of the treatment process, and on quantifying behavioral change were of some value to Beck in developing his treatment approach.

In addition to these influences, there are yet others to mention. Beck has acknowledged that the writings of such neo-Freudians as Karen Horney, Alfred Adler, and Harry Stack Sullivan contributed to his initial theoretical formulations and gave him support in his break from classical psychoanalysis. As cognitive therapy has evolved, the work of such individuals as George Kelly, Richard Lazarus, Albert Bandura, and Walter Mischel has had influence as well. In most recent years, work in cognitive psychology, social psychology, and evolutionary biology has been increasingly drawn on and incorporated into Beck's views on cognitive theory and therapy (see Beck, 1985, 1991b).

PHILOSOPHY AND CONCEPTS

A Common-Sensical Approach

Cognitive therapy rejects the views of the three major therapeutic schools: psychoanalysis, which posits the unconscious as the source of emotional disturbance; behavior therapy, which regards only overt behavior as significant; and traditional neuropsychiatry, which considers physiological or chemical disorders to be the cause of emotional disturbances. Cognitive therapy is based on the common-sensical idea that what people think and say about themselves—their attitudes, ideas, and ideals—are relevant and important.

In the course of development, people acquire a vast store of information, concepts, and formulas for dealing with the psychological problems of living. This knowledge is applied through observing, developing and testing hypotheses, and making judgments—essentially acting as a practical scientist. From their cultural heritage and through education and experience, people learn to use the tools of common sense—forming and testing hunches, making discriminations, and reasoning—to resolve conflicts and judge whether they are reacting realistically to situations.

Common sense, however, fails to provide explanations for emotional disorders. The thoughts and behaviors of depressed patients, for example, contradict the basic principle of human nature—that is, the survival instinct. The thinking of depressed patients is controlled by erroneous ideas about themselves and their world. Beck (1976) points out that his "formulation of psychological problems in terms of incorrect premises and a proneness to distorted imaginal experiences represents a sharp deviation from generally accepted formulations of the psychological disorders" (p. 19). Cognitive therapy does not require a concept of the unconscious. Psychological problems

> may result from commonplace processes such as faulty learning, making incorrect inferences on the basis of inadequate or incorrect information, and not distinguishing adequately between imagination and reality. Moreover, thinking can be unrealistic because it is derived from erroneous premises; behavior can be self-defeating because it is based on unreasonable attitudes. (Beck, 1976, pp. 19–20)

Principles

There are eight principles on which the cognitive model is based. These principles are listed (Beck, 1987b, pp. 150–151), and subsequently elaborated on.

1. *The way that individuals structure situations determines how they behave or feel.* Our *interpretation* of events is a key, highly critical variable in cognitive therapy. Based on our interpretations, we feel and act; people react to events via the meanings that they assign to them (Beck, 1991a). Personal interpretations of an event can lead to varied emotional responses to the same situation by different people or by any one person at different times. "The thesis that the special meaning of an event determines the emotional response forms the core of the cognitive model of emotions and emotional disorders" (Beck, 1976, p. 52).

Emotional and behavioral reactions, then, are not direct or automatic responses to external stimuli. Rather, stimuli are processed and interpreted by an internal cognitive system. A major discordance between the internal system and external stimuli can lead to psychological disorders. Specific thoughts take place between an external event and a certain emotional response. Patients' thoughts often reflect negative themes or a negative view about the past, present, and future (Beck, 1983). Although patients ordinarily are not aware of or ignore these thoughts and therefore do not report them, they can be taught to observe them introspectively before experiencing an emotion.

These thoughts are "automatic." Automatic thoughts are specific and discrete, occur in an abbreviated style, do not arise from deliberation or reasoning, are relatively autonomous and involuntary, and are regarded as reasonable by the patient, even when they appear to be implausible to others or are contradicted by objective evidence (Beck & Weishaar, 1989).

> Internal signals in a linguistic or visual form [e.g., automatic thoughts] play a significant role in behavior. The way a person instructs himself, praises and criticizes him-

self, interprets events, and makes predictions not only illuminates normal behavior, but sheds light on the inner workings of emotional disorders. (Beck, 1976, p. 37)

2. *Interpretation is an active, ongoing process comprised of appraisals of the external situation, coping capacities, and the potential benefits, risks, and costs of different strategies.* Interpretation is a complex, continuous process. In the process of interpretation, multiple factors are taken into account. We consider the demands of the external situation, what capacities we have available to us to cope with that situation, and what strategies we can bring to bear on that situation.

A critical variable in this interpretation process is our "personal domain," at the center of which is the self or self-concept. "The nature of a person's emotional response—or emotional disturbance—depends on whether he perceives events as adding to, subtracting from, endangering, or impinging upon his domain" (Beck, 1976, p. 56). *Sadness* results from the perception that something of value has been lost, thus subtracting from the personal domain. The perception or expectation of a gain leads to *euphoria* or *excitation.* Threats to the physical or psychological self or of the loss of something important causes *anxiety. Anger* arises from a perceived direct attack, intentional or unintentional, or from the violation of laws, morals, or standards held by the person. The person takes the attack seriously and focuses on the wrongfulness of the offense rather than on any injury suffered. The kind of ideation leading to sadness, euphoria, anxiety, or anger, if it involves a distortion of reality, can result in depression, mania, anxiety reactions, or paranoid states.

3. *Each individual has idosyncratic sensitivities and vulnerabilities that result in psychological distress.* Each of us is different; what proves stressful for one individual may not be stressful for another. We each have our own particular vulnerabilities to stress. Vulnerabilities, which tend to be triggered by certain stressors, lead to distress.

4. *Some of the wide variations in individual sensitivities or vulnerabilities are attributable to basic differences in personality organization.* The concepts of autonomous personality and sociotropic personality account for these variations (see Beck, 1983; Beck, Epstein, & Harrison, 1983). These two concepts reflect a new addition (Haaga, Dyck, & Ernst, 1991) to Beck's thinking about depressed patients. As Beck (1991a, p. 370) noted,

Patients who were heavily invested in autonomy (independent achievement, mobility, solitary pleasures) were prone to become depressed after an "autonomous stressor" such as failure, immobilization or enforced conformity. Patients who deeply valued closeness, dependency, and sharing [the sociotropics] were hypersensitive to and prone to become depressed after "sociotropic traumas" such as social deprivation or rejection. (Beck, 1983)

Thus, the primary idea is that one's personality can be vulnerable to and is most apt to respond to particular stressors—with the autonomous personality responding to autonomous stressors and the sociotropic personality responding to sociotropic stressors.

5. *The normal activity of the cognitive organization is adversely affected by stress.* "The primitive, egocentric cognitive system is activated when one determines that his [or her] vital interests are threatened" (Beck, 1987b, p. 150). When this happens, various negative sequelae—the making of extreme, absolutist judgments, emergence of problematic thinking, and impairments in reason and concentration—can occur.

6. *Psychological syndromes, such as depression and anxiety disorders, consist of hyperactive schemas with idiosyncratic content that characterizes the particular syndrome.* Hyperactive schemas refer to hyperactive beliefs, which are negative in tone and content. Each psychological syndrome, be it depressive or anxiety or personality disturbance, has its own unique set of beliefs that characterize it; each syndrome has its own cognitive profile (Beck, 1976; Beck et al., 1979; Beck et al., 1990). For example, the depressive person's thought centers on loss, the patient with anxiety has thoughts centered on threat and danger, and the thoughts of a patient with a personality disorder can center on rejection, neediness, or responsibility (depending on the type of personality disorder manifested), among other possibilities.

7. *Stressful interactions with other people create a mutually reinforcing cycle of maladaptive cognitions.* Since stress adversely affects the normal activity of one's cognitive organization and can impair reasoning and judgment (see principle 5), it does not seem surprising that stressful interactions would then create such a mutually reinforcing cycle. The following example, (Beck, 1991a, p. 372), illustrates this principle.

> Obviously, the depressed individual's psychological systems continue to interact with those of other people even after depression has occurred. A depressed wife, for example, may interpret her husband's frustration at not being able to help her as a sign of rejection (husband's cognitions: "I can't do anything to help her"; wife's cognitions: "He has given up on me because he doesn't care"). The wife reacts with further withdrawal, which triggers further withdrawal of support by the husband. (Beck, 1988)

Thus, this depressed wife misreads her husband's frustration, attributes a negative meaning to his frustration, further thinks negatively about herself and about herself in relation to her husband, withdraws, and thereby her maladaptive cognitions are further perpetuated and reinforced.

8. *The individual will exhibit the same somatic response to threat whether the threat itself is physical or symbolic.* Threat can be physical (e.g., physical assault) or symbolic (e.g., verbal assault). The individual will respond somatically to threat—be it physical or symbolic—in the same way. For example, we most likely will respond to both physical and verbal assault with anxiety, fear, or anger, or some combination of the three.

Summary. Following these eight principles several factors are important in explaining dysfunction from a cognitive perspective. These factors include (but are not necessarily limited to) distorted, unrealistic beliefs, individual sensitivities or vulnerabilities, one's personality type, and the occurrence of an apt stressor (one that can interact with one's personality and thereby activate problematic schemas). There are, then, various factors to consider when asking, "In the cognitivist's view, what gives rise to psychological disturbance?"

Beck (1991a) has noted that some if not many have mistakenly viewed his theory as assuming that cognitions cause psychological disturbances. But in speaking about depression, Beck (1987a) makes the following statement: "It seems unwarranted to assert that 'cognitions cause depression.' Such statements would be akin to saying that 'delusions cause psychosis'" (p. 10). Thus, "deviant cognitive processes [are] as intrinsic to the depressive disorder, [but] not a cause or consequence" (p. 10). Further: "I believe that it is counterproductive to speak of *The Cause* of the affective disorders" (Beck, 1983, p. 267). There can be a whole host of predisposing *and* precipitating factors that contribute to affective disorder, these factors can combine in varied ways in causing the disorder, and they can vary in how much they each contribute to the development of the disorder. Some of these predisposing factors can include developmental traumas, physical diseases, inadequate personal experiences, and counterproductive cognitive patterns. Some of these precipitating factors can include severe external stresses, chronic insidious external stresses, specific external stresses, and physical diseases.

Key Concepts

The causation of disturbance in the cognitive model and the role of cognition are involved in the key concepts of cognitive therapy.

Schema.   Schemas can be defined as "cognitive structures that organize experience and behavior . . ." (Beck et al., 1990, p. 4). They are involved in classifying, labeling, and interpreting (Beck et al., 1985; Kovacs & Beck, 1978). They allow us to make meaning of our world.

Such terms as *beliefs, schemas,* and *rules* are used interchangably at times (e.g., Beck et al., 1990). It appears that schema refers to a "belief system" or "network of beliefs." That system or network is made up of a host of beliefs about people, events, situations, or stimuli. These schematic beliefs are maintained in a conditional form, e.g., "If I don't win, I am a failure." A depressive schema, for instance, would be composed of depressive-type beliefs. To assist us in navigating through our world, we make use of cognitive, affective, and motivational schemas, among others (Beck et al., 1990).

Law of Rules.   People's reactions to many situations are consistent, which suggests that their responses are guided by a "set of rules." These rules form the basis for the individual's interpretations, expectations, and self-instructions and thus provide a framework for understanding life's experiences. Such guidelines include the formulas and premises by which people operate and make sense out of the world; these guidelines also include standards to guide actions and to evaluate the behaviors of oneself and others. Rules are a part of the social heritage and thus are absorbed through personal experience and observation of others.

The following example (Beck, 1976) illustrates this concept.

> An instructor, in a casual way, told two students (Miss A and Miss B), who were carrying on a side conversation in his seminar, "If you have anything to say, share it with the rest of us or else be quiet." Miss A responded angrily that she had simply been trying to clarify a point. During the open discussion that followed, she challenged the instructor repeatedly regarding the content of his presentation and expressed sharp criticisms of his point of view. Miss B, who was usually an active participant in the seminar discussions, appeared sad and withdrawn following the instructor's comment and remained silent for the rest of the class period.
>
> The contrasting responses of these two girls can be understood in terms of different rules they applied in interpreting the situation and then in guiding their overt responses. Miss A interpreted the teacher's remarks as "He is trying to control me. He is treating me like a child." Her emotional response was anger. The general rule leading to this interpretation was: "Correction by authority figures = domination and belittling."

Her self-instruction was: "Tell him off." The rule behind her retaliation was: "I must get even with people who treat me badly."

Miss B's interpretation: "He has caught me doing something wrong. He will dislike me from now on." Emotion: shame and sadness. Rule: "Correction by authority = exposure and weakness, fault, inferiority. Being corrected = disapproval." Self-instruction: "I should keep my mouth shut." Rule: "If I am quiet, I am less offensive." Also, "Being quiet will show I am sorry for my offensive behavior." (pp. 43–44)

As this example shows, "rules" affect the interpretations that we make and provide us with ideas about how we should and should not behave. By knowing the rules under which a patient operates, the therapist can better understand his/her illogical behavior and abnormal emotional responses. Patients' rules can be out of sync with reality, can reflect distortions, or can be applied arbitrarily; when any of these is the case, problems can result.

Cognitive Errors.   Disorders of thinking are a characteristic of all the common psychiatric disorders. All patients show distortions of reality to varying degrees. There are several different types of cognitive errors (or distortions) in which patients often engage (Beck, 1976; Beck & Weishaar, 1989). These are as follows.

1. *Selective abstraction:* Focusing one's attention on a single set of details, ignoring other relevant details of a situation, and drawing conclusions accordingly. The depressed patient, for example, may focus on the negative aspects of a situation, screen out the positive aspects, and thereby draw negatively oriented conclusions.

2. *Arbitrary inference:* Arriving at a conclusion when you have no evidence to support it or arriving at a conclusion when you actually have evidence to the contrary. For example, this can be seen where patients "assume the worst" when they do not need to do so at all (i.e., there may be no evidence whatsoever to support a worst-case scenario taking place).

3. *Overgeneralization:* Drawing conclusons, which are based on a single incident, and then generalizing them way beyond reason. For instance, a depressive patient might have failed in performing a certain task and then assume that he/she is a failure in performing all tasks.

4. *Magnification and minimization:* Making polarized assessments about oneself, situations, and events. We can see this error manifested when patients magnify the demands of a situation they must confront while also minimizing their ability to confront it.

5. *Personalization:* Viewing external events or happenings as being related to oneself when that is not the case at all. We can see this most clearly exemplified in paranoid patients, who often assume that others are talking about them when that is not so.

6. *Dichotomous thinking:* Refers to patients' tendencies to think in a dichotomous manner—either/or, black/white, yes/no—in which there are no in-between or gray areas. Depressed patients, for instance, can see others as "good" and themselves as "bad."

Again, these cognitive errors (or faulty ways of processing information) can lead to and help maintain emotional disturbance. Regardless of the type of disorder, the cognitive therapist can expect to see one or more of these errors in evidence.

7. *Cognitive shift:* This refers to a basic change that occurs in patients' thinking. As patients become emotionally disturbed and as they continue to experience that disturbance, a shift takes place in how they take in or allow admittance to certain information. For example, the negative cognitive shift that occurs in depression is defined as follows: "[T]here

is a change in the cognitive organization so that much positive information relevant to the individual is filtered out (cognitive blockade), whereas negative self-relevant information is readily admitted" (Beck, 1991a, p. 369). A cognitive shift often takes place in other disorders as well as in depression (Beck et al., 1985). For example, with anxiety disorder, the focus becomes "danger," and there is a shift in which the patient attends to and readily admits danger stimuli.

8. *Cognitive profile:* "Each disorder has its own specific cognitive conceptualization and relevant strategies that are embraced under the general principles of cognitive therapy" (Beck, 1991a, p. 368). In other words, patients with each disorder—whether depressive, anxiety-based, or personality-based—have certain beliefs, views of themselves, views of others, and action strategies that characterize it. This idea is nicely conveyed in Beck et al.'s (1990) book on the cognitive therapy of personality disorders, in which the cognitive profiles of nine different personality disorders are identified (see Beck et al., 1990, pp. 54–55). Since each disorder has its own characteristic set of beliefs, self-views, other-views, and action strategies, this has direct treatment implications. The cognitive profile becomes a primary target of attention in psychotherapy: "The understanding of the typical beliefs and strategies of each . . . disorder provides a road map for therapists" (Beck et al., 1990, p. 57). But with this noted (Beck et al., 1990), there is one caution worth keeping in mind: "[M]ost individuals with a specific . . . disorder will manifest attitudes and behaviors that overlap other disorders. Consequently, it is important for therapists to expose these variations in order to make a complete evaluation" (p. 57).

Summary.   What causes disturbance in the cognitive model? What role does cognition actually play? Haaga et al. (1991) have addressed these issues with regard to depression: "Dysfunctional beliefs are thus hypothesized to be diatheses for depression (see Riskind & Rholes, 1984). Before activation by specific experiences [i.e., stressors to which we are vulnerable], they are thought to be latent, not directly influencing mood or cognition and not necessarily readily available to awareness" (p. 216). Thus, the key concepts consist of the existence of a problematic schema (made up of dysfunctional beliefs) lying latent, the existence of a personality style (sociotropic versus autonomous), vulnerability to certain stressors, experiencing one or more of those stressors, which then interact with one's personality style, the activation of that problematic schema, the development of disorder, the occurrence of a negative cognitive shift, and the maintenance of disorder. While this sequence applies specifically to depression, a similar sequence could be expected to come into play in some other disorders as well (e.g., those that are anxiety-based).

The Emotional Disorders

"The nature of a person's emotional response—or emotional disturbance—depends on whether he perceives events as adding to, subtracting from, endangering, or impinging upon his domain" (Beck, 1976, p. 56). Thus, in considering each emotional disorder, it is important to ask, "How is the patient's personal domain affected?"

Depression.   The development of depression begins with an experience connoting loss to the patient. The loss may be real or it may be a hypothetical pseudo-loss; in either case, it is exaggerated, perceived as permanent and irreversible, and is viewed as a reflection on one-self, one's attributes, or one's competence. This can lead to a negative self-concept—the view of oneself as a "loser" or unworthy. Patients come to think that some self-defect is the cause of their adversities and, thereby, appraise every subsequent experience in terms of self-deficiency. Comparisons with others further lower self-esteem, and total self-rejection can result.

Negative views of the self lead to negative views of the future. Pessimism pervades the patient's outlook on life. Hopelessness results in loss of motivation. Since outcomes are expected to be negative, there is no point in making an effort. Such pessimism can lead to suicidal thoughts and suicide attempts. Another reason for patients' suicidal preoccupations is the belief that others would be better off if they (the patients) were dead. A negative view of self, a negative interpretation of events and experiences, and a negative view of the future constitute the *cognitive triad of depression* (Beck et al., 1979). Manifestations of depression, such as inertia, fatigue, and agitation, are outcomes of negative cognitions. Other manifestations, such as eating and sleep disturbances, reflect the physiological symptoms that can accompany depression.

Mania.   The thinking of manic patients is considered to be just the opposite of the thinking of depressive patients. They perceive "gain" rather than "loss" in their personal domain. They view most if not all happenings, events, people, whatever, as adding to their world in some way. This overinflation of one's personal domain is accompanied by exaggerated views about oneself, overly positive interpretations of one's experiences, and overly positive views of the future. In a sense, we have the cognitive triad of depression in reverse, and with it comes various emotional (euphoric, lability), behavioral (much heightened motor activity), and physiological (sleep, eating) disturbances.

Anxiety Neurosis.   Anxiety is abnormal and constitutes a neurosis when its degree exceeds that evoked by an actual threat or when no threat is present. Anxiety is the emotion that arises with the activation of fear.

> Common among patients with anxiety neurosis is fear of loss of control leading to feelings of humiliation, embarrassment, sadness. Among these fears are: losing control of one's faculties as in fear of becoming insane; not being able to function; not attaining crucial objectives; harming others. (Beck, 1976, pp. 141–142)

These fears seem plausible to the patient, whose thinking is dominated by themes of danger manifested in repetitive thoughts about danger; reduced ability to "reason" with the fearful thoughts (to evaluate them objectively); and generalization of anxiety-evoking stimuli to the point that almost any stimulus or situation may be perceived as a threat. The patient's attention is stuck on or bound to the concept of danger and its accompanying stimuli (Beck, 1987b; Beck et al., 1985). Danger is exaggerated, with a tendency to perceive events as catastrophic, and hypothetical dangers are equated with actual dangers.

Phobias.   A phobia is a "fear of a situation that, by social consensus and the person's own intellectual appraisal when away from the situation, is disproportionate to the probability and degree of harm inherent in that situation" (Beck, 1976, p. 159). Persons with phobias are not afraid of the situation itself but of the *consequences* of being in the situation, which they avoid in order to prevent the excessive anxiety. Each phobia is characterized by a specific central fear, which often is a composite of fears that varies with individuals (see Beck et al., 1985). The agoraphobic fears befalling a calamity when away from home. The acrophobic fears falling from a high place and being injured or killed. The person afraid of elevators fears getting stuck and suffering some harm. The person afraid of tunnels fears being suffocated. The person with a social phobia fears the reactions of other people toward him or her. The fear of consequences is the cognitive element behind phobias and makes them understandable.

Paranoid State. Persons who are paranoid are highly suspicious, mistrustful, and question the motives of others; they are forever on guard and believe others are out to get or hurt them in some way; they see enemies everywhere. Such patients are preoccupied with injustice, believing that they have been done some wrong—that their personal domain has been (or will be) attacked. The main theme in their thinking is as follows: "I am right, he is wrong." With that being the case, they believe that they have suffered at the hands of someone else, that they have suffered unfairly, and that they have been in the right all along.

Obsessions and Compulsions. Obsessions are repetitive thoughts about actions that patients believe they *should* have taken or actions that patients believe they *should not* have taken. Obsessive doubt leads to compulsions or repetitive actions to allay doubts. "Should" appears to be an important word here, pointing to some absolutistic thinking that the patient cannot rise above and that seems to largely fuel and maintain this disturbance.

Psychoses. With psychotic reactions, we typically see patients who manifest hallucinations, delusions, incoherence, bizarre behavior, and a loss of touch with reality. Diagnoses such as catatonic schizophrenia or undifferentiated schizophrenia would be examples of this. The psychotic patient's thought processes are characterized by the following descriptors: "ideation . . . bizarre, grotesque, extreme. . . , pronounced cognitive impairment. . . , perseverative ideation . . . more intense and less subject to modification. . . , capacity to view . . . erroneous ideas objectively is much more limited, . . . degree of illogical and unrealistic thinking . . . more pronounced" (Beck, 1976, p. 89). Even with this rather bleak picture, still some attention has been given to using cognitive therapy in the treatment of schizophrenia (Perris, 1988).

Hysterical Reactions. Hysteria consists of physical dysfunctions with no demonstrable organic disease or physical abnormality.

> As a result of an injury to himself or identification with a constellation of symptoms in others, the hysteric comes to believe that he has a physical disorder. As he thinks about having this disorder, he experiences physical sensations—somatic imaging. A circular mechanism is set up. The person "reads" his physical sensations as evidence that he has the disorder. His belief becomes consolidated, and the physical manifestations are proportionately intensified. (Beck, 1976, p. 211)

Psychosomatic Disorders.   Psychosomatic disorders include

(1) physiological disturbances or structural abnormalities in which psychological and constitutional factors combine to produce the disorder . . . (2) Primary physical disorders that are exacerbated by psychological processes . . . (3) Aberration of sensation or movement, but with no demonstrable tissue pathology or disturbed physiology. This category includes a broad spectrum of conditions ranging from "somatic imaging" and the hysterias to somatic delusions. (Beck, 1976, pp. 189–190)

Whether a psychosomatic disorder results instead of or in addition to anxiety is determined by genetic factors.

Under stress, all people tend to overreact, and their overreaction is most apt to manifest itself in a particular vulnerable physiological system. Thus, patients who overreact to the extent of developing continuing or severe psychosomatic disorders are similar to anxiety-prone or anger-prone patients in general: They conceptualize innocuous life experiences as threatening and exaggerate minor threats into major calamities. Actual stressful situations are less important than is the way they are perceived by the patient.

Most patients with psychosomatic disorders may not be under specific external stresses. But there are internal stresses; a major one is the demands these patients place on themselves. Hard-driving individuals manifest faulty cognitive appraisals concerning the importance and difficulty of the tasks they face, underestimate their capacity to deal with them, and exaggerate the consequences and probability of failure.

Summary.   With each disorder, we do indeed see that the patient's personal domain is impinged on in some way; it can be added to, subtracted from, or endangered, among other possibilities. Once that has happened and a disorder emerges, treatment is called for. Treating disturbance by means of the cognitive model is the subject of the next section.

PRINCIPLES OF COGNITIVE THERAPY

Cognitive therapy is most appropriate for those who have the capacity for introspection and reflection and who are able to think adequately in areas of their lives outside the problem area. It focuses on helping the patient overcome blind spots, blurred perceptions, self-deceptions, and incorrect judgments. Since the emotional reactions that bring the patient to therapy are the results of incorrect thinking, they are alleviated when that thinking is corrected. Cognitive therapy helps patients to use the problem-solving methods that they employ during normal periods of their lives. "The formula for treatment may be stated in simple terms: The therapist helps the patient to identify his warped thinking and to learn more realistic ways to formulate his experiences" (Beck, 1976, p. 20). This approach makes sense to patients because of their earlier application of their knowledge about correcting misconceptions and misinterpretations.

Some Targets of Cognitive Therapy

Automatic Thoughts.   Since automatic thoughts influence how we feel and act, and since they can prove so problematic, it is important that therapists teach their clients to identify automatic thoughts. This can be done by informing patients that between an event and their reaction to it exists a thought. Once patients get this concept down, they can then be taught to identify those intervening thoughts, e.g., "What happened between your losing your car keys and your feeling of anger? What thoughts did you have in between?" Thus, by learning to identify their problematic automatic thoughts, patients come to identify their illogical thinking (e.g., perceiving catastrophes; "should" statements) and distortions of reality.

Cognitive Errors.   Since patients often process information incorrectly, it can be helpful for them to know how they do that. Furthermore, when incorrect information processing can occur in consistent ways across time and across situations, this becomes all the more important to know about. So by learning to identify cognitive errors—selective abstraction, arbitrary inference, overgeneralization, magnification and minimization, personalization, and dichotomous thinking—patients can come to see how they get themselves into trouble.

Rules.   As indicated previously, rules include the formulas and premises by which we make sense of others' behavior and the world about us; for example, "Correction by authority figures = domination and belittling;" and those by which we act, for example, counterattack to offset the belittling and domination. As these examples illustrate, rules can prove to be problematic; yet they can continue to galvanize our behavior. In therapy, the cognitive therapist wants to help patients identify and change their maladaptive rules.

The Therapeutic Collaboration

The patient and the therapist must agree on the problem to be dealt with, the goals of therapy, the methods of achieving those goals, and the duration of therapy. Emphasis is on solving problems rather than on changing the patient's personal characteristics or defects. The therapist must be sensitive to the patient's need or desire to discuss certain topics at each session; the therapist should be accepting, warm, and empathic.

The cognitive therapist can be described as a "guide," a "catalyst," as active, flexible, and supportive (Beck, 1987b; Beck & Weishaar, 1989). Therapists must avoid authoritative methods that might lead some patients, on the one hand, to accept interpretations and suggestions blindly or, on the other hand, to be resistant. A cautious, trial-and-error approach, that attempts to involve patients actively in the therapeutic process, is followed.

Collaborative empiricism seems best to characterize the therapeutic relationship. This means that therapist and patient collaborate in *testing out* the faulty thinking and conclusions that seem to so negatively affect the patient's current functioning. Conclusions become hypotheses—to be examined, studied, put to the acid test of reality. For example, assume a patient thought, "When I walk down the street, everyone turns to look at me." This could be tested out by having the patient actually monitor how many people turn to look at him/her as she/he walks down the street. Thus, the faulty conclusion is first identified, gets framed as a hypothesis, and then gets tested.

Other important concepts that define the therapeutic relationship are Socratic dialogue and guided discovery. *Socratic dialogue* refers to a carefully designed series of questions used "to (1) clarify or define problems, (2) assist in the identification of thoughts, images, and assumptions, (3) examine the meaning of events for the patient, and (4) assess the consequences of maintaining maladaptive thoughts and behaviors" (Beck & Weishaar,

1989, p. 302). Such dialogue appears to be yet another way to assist patients in putting their thinking to the test (i.e., does their thinking follow the rules of logic?). *Guided discovery* refers to the therapist as "guide," who encourages patients in their use of facts, considering probabilities, gathering information, and putting all this to the test; it also refers to the therapist as designer of experiments and experiences, one who creates means by which patients can gain new skills and perspectives and question dysfunctional behaviors and thinking.

Whatever the therapist may do in cognitive therapy, it seems clear that questions are integral to and at the forefront of the therapeutic process (Beck & Young, 1985).

> Most of the therapist's verbal statements are in the form of questions. This reflects the empirical orientation of cognitive therapy and the immediate goal of changing the patient's closed belief system into a more open one. Questioning also provides the patient with a model for introspection which he can use on his own when the therapist is not present and after termination of formal treatment. Through questions, the therapist helps the patient uncover and modify cognitive distortions and dysfunctional assumptions. (Beck, 1987b, p. 157)

So whether you are engaged in collaborative empiricism, Socratic dialogue, or guided discovery, questioning is essential and usually the primary verbal response mode on which the therapist relies.

TECHNIQUES OF COGNITIVE THERAPY

The therapist attempts to clarify the patient's distortions of reality, the self-injunctions and self-reproaches that lead to distress, and the rules that underlie the faulty self-signals. The therapist draws on the problem-solving methods that patients have previously used successfully. Patients are encouraged to use their own problem-solving abilities to change their ways of interpreting experiences and controlling actions. When patients become aware that their self-signals are maladaptive, they can work at correcting them.

Recognizing Maladaptive Ideation. "The term 'maladaptive thoughts' is applied to ideation that interferes with the ability to cope with life experiences, unnecessarily disrupts internal harmony, and produces inappropriate or excessive emotional reactions that are painful" (Beck, 1976, p. 235). Patients may not be fully aware of these thoughts, but with instruction and training, they can become aware of and then focus on them.

Filling in the Blank. When patients report events and their emotional reactions to them, there is usually a gap between the stimulus and the response. It is the task of therapy to fill in this blank. Again, this is accomplished by instructing the patient to focus on the thoughts that occur while experiencing the stimulus and the response.

Distancing and Decentering. *Distancing* refers to the process of coming to view one's thoughts objectively. It involves recognizing that automatic thoughts may not reflect reality, may not be reliable, and may be maladaptive.

Authenticating Conclusions. Although patients may be able to distinguish between internal mental processes and external stimuli, they still have to learn the procedures for obtaining accurate knowledge. This includes recognizing that a hypothesis is not fact and that an inference is not reality. By applying the rules of evidence, the therapist helps patients to explore their conclusions and to test them against reality.

Changing the Rules. Therapy attempts to replace unrealistic, maladaptive rules with more realistic, adaptive ones. Rules seem to focus on *danger versus safety* and on *pain versus pleasure.* Patients overestimate dangers and the risk involved in common situations. Psychosocial dangers are the source of most problems. Fears of humiliation, criticism, and rejection are challenged, and the serious consequences of their occurrence are questioned. Exaggerated estimates of the probabilities of physical harm or death are examined, leading to their reduction.

Beliefs and attitudes can act as rules. Some rules that predispose people to excessive sadness or depression include:

1. "In order to be happy, I must be successful, accepted, popular, famous, wealthy, ..."
2. "If I make a mistake, I am incompetent."
3. "I cannot live without love."
4. "When people disagree with me, they do not like me."

These rules are framed as absolutes or extremes and cannot be satisfied. In cognitive therapy, the therapist wants to identify the patient's rules clearly, examine how these rules might be problematic, and suggest alternative rules the patient might wish to adopt.

Rules, then, often are related to "shoulds" in some way or other. Some common shoulds are as follows:

1. "I should be generous, considerate, courageous, unselfish, ..."
2. "I should be able to endure hardship."
3. "I should be able to solve any problem."
4. "I should know and understand everything."
5. "I should never tire or become sick."
6. "I should always be at top efficiency."

Other Cognitive Techniques. In addition to the preceding cognitive techniques, which Beck (1976) described some 20 years ago, there are others that have since been identified. Some of these include:

(a) scaling—having patients translate their extreme thinking into scale values, which can work against dichotomous, either/or thought;
(b) reattribution—assigning responsibility for events or happenings based on an analysis of the available facts or data;
(c) deliberate exaggeration—taking an idea or conclusion and deliberately exaggerating it so that a more realistic perspective might ultimately be brought to bear on the patient's dysfunctional thinking; and
(d) decatastrophizing—helping patients to counter thinking in "worst possible" terms (Beck et al., 1990).

Behavioral Techniques.   Some of the behavioral techniques that the cognitive therapist uses include homework—assigning tasks for patients to perform outside therapy; relaxation training—training patients in how to relax; behavioral rehearsal and role playing—giving patients opportunities to practice new behaviors and skills; assertiveness training—providing training that helps patients become more assertive; activity monitoring and scheduling—using a *Daily Schedule of Activities* to help determine what patients are doing and when and formulating treatment strategies and plans accordingly; graded task assignment—working on assignments in a graded (from easy to more difficult) manner, so that success will most likely be accomplished; and in vivo exposure—going with the patient to a problematic setting or situation, observing how the patient thinks and responds there, and striving to help him/her better deal with this real-life exposure (Beck, 1987b; Beck et al., 1990).

COGNITIVE THERAPY OF DEPRESSION

Because Beck's attention to depression is longstanding (e.g., Beck, 1972, 1976, 1987a), and because a considerable amount of effort has gone into explicating and researching the cognitive model of depression (e.g., Beck et al., 1979; Haaga et al., 1991), a more specific look at this disorder and how the cognitive therapist would go about treating it follows (also see Hollon & Garber, 1990).

Rationale of the Cognitive Approach

Depression includes

> (a) the observable abnormal behavior or symptom, for example, easy fatigability, crying spells, suicidal threats; (b) the underlying motivational disturbances (if any), such as the wish to avoid activities or to escape from life; (c) underlying the motivation, a cluster of cognitions, such as the belief that striving toward a goal is futile, that there are no satisfactions ahead, and that he is defeated, deprived, and defective. (Beck, 1976, p. 265)

Intervention could be directed at any of these three areas, which constitute a cycle. Cognitive therapy attacks the underlying attitudes, although with the severely depressed patient intervention may be directed first at a behavioral target (Beck et al., 1979).

Symptom, Technique, and Maladaptive Attitude.   Although the therapeutic approach may begin at the behavioral level, the underlying attitude component must be changed. The ultimate goal, then, is *cognitive modification*. Engaging in activities leading to concrete successes (behavioral method) may help to counteract the attitude. But a multiple approach, focusing on a variety of targets, must be used.

Mechanics of Cognitive Reorganization.   The therapist helps the patient to identify the assumptions that underlie his or her depression. These assumptions are challenged and subjected to argument by means of questioning and debate. Experiments may be set up to test the assumptions.

Specialized techniques are used in the treatment of problem areas or "targets." Some of these (described previously) are as follows:

1. *Scheduled Activity.* Scheduling activities with patients actively structures time and enables them to observe their own potential effectiveness.
2. *Graded-Task Assignment.* Success in graded tasks can change patients' self-concepts.
3. *Mastery and Pleasure Therapy.* Patients keep records of all activities and designate each mastery experience with an *M* and each pleasure experience with a *P*, thus increasing their awareness of positive experiences.
4. *Cognitive Reappraisal.* Cognitive reappraisal involves the identification of maladaptive cognitions and attitudes.
5. *Alternative Therapy.* By considering alternative explanations for negative experiences, patients are helped to recognize their biases. By considering alternative ways of handling psychological and situational problems, patients find solutions to problems previously considered insoluble.
6. *Cognitive Rehearsal.* By imagining that they are carrying out an activity, patients report obstacles and conflicts, which can then be discussed.
7. *Homework Assignments.* Assignments are made at each session to counteract depressive symptoms. Patients keep records of negative cognitions in one column and of rational responses in another.

Targets of Cognitive Modification

Inertia, Avoidance, and Fatigue.   In cognitive therapy, an activity tailored to the patient may be proposed. Reasons against the proposal are elicited from the patient, who is then asked to weigh their validity. The therapist points out why these reasons are self-defeating and invalid and stimulates the patient's interest in attempting the activity. The activity is designed to test the validity of the patient's ideas; successful completion will refute the patient's assumption that he or she is incapable of doing it.

Hopelessness and Suicidal Wishes.   Skillful questioning can reveal the assumptions behind hopelessness and suicidal tendencies. Alternative therapy then shows the patient that there are other interpretations of his or her present and future and other choices than the current behavior.

Self-Criticisms and Self-Blame.   Depressed patients tend to blame themselves for all their difficulties. Cognitive therapy aims at making patients aware of their extreme self-criticisms and increasing patients' objectivity about the dysfunctionality and self-destructiveness of their self-criticisms. By means of questioning and role playing, the therapist can demonstrate the patient's distortions and false inferences. Training in recognizing and challenging the validity of automatic self-deprecatory thoughts also can be effective.

Painful Affect.   Encouraging emotional release may reduce the intensity of unpleasant emotions. Patients may feel sympathy for themselves or may direct anger at others. By eliciting amusement through irony or by stimulating patients to engage in an interesting activity, the therapist can raise the threshold for sadness. Encouraging the ignoring of unpleasant feelings may also raise the threshold for psychic pain.

Mastery and pleasure therapy helps patients to recognize that they have more positive and pleasant experiences than they might realize. By having patients record events and asking significant others to assist them in recalling pleasant events, the therapist stimulates patients to increase their sense of satisfaction and sense of competence. This leads to their attempting and succeeding at problem-solving activities, resulting in a more positive self-image. A program of graded-task assignments can be especially useful here. Imagery techniques can also be helpful in having patients recollect and recapture earlier pleasant events and successful experiences.

Exaggeration of External Demands.   Depressed patients often feel overwhelmed by everyday problems to the point of contemplating suicide.

> When the problems are discussed, however, it becomes apparent that the patient has greatly exaggerated their magnitude and importance. Through rational exploration, the patient may regain his perspective and then set about defining what has to be done and how to go about doing it. The therapist generally has to take the lead in helping the patient to list his responsibilities, set priorities, and formulate the appropriate course of action. (Beck, 1976, p. 300)

But the implementation of this new course of action can be blocked by self-defeating thoughts. Cognitive rehearsal can be used to prevent any such blocks from occurring.

LENGTH AND LIMITATIONS OF TREATMENT

Length.   Cognitive therapy is time limited (with treatment of the personality disorders excepted), and, as a result, often avoids termination problems (e.g., patients becoming unduly attached to the therapist at treatment's end). As Beck and Weishaar (1989) pointed out, however,

> Length of treatment depends primarily on the severity of the client's problems. The usual length for unipolar depression is 15 to 25 sessions at weekly intervals (Beck, Rush et al., 1979). Moderately to severely depressed patients usually require sessions twice a week for 4 to 5 weeks and then require weekly sessions for 10 to 15 weeks. Most cases of anxiety are treated within a comparable period of time. (p. 304)

Limitations.   Cognitive therapy is not for everyone (e.g., Beck, 1987a). But for whom is cognitive therapy best suited and for whom it is not well suited?

> Cognitive therapy is not recommended as the exclusive treatment in cases of bipolar affective disorder or psychotic depression. It is also not used alone for the treatment of other psychoses, such as schizophrenia. . . . Cognitive therapy produces the best

results with patients who have adequate reality testing (i.e., no hallucinations), good concentration, and sufficient memory functions. It is ideally suited to patients who can focus on their automatic thoughts, accept the therapist-patient roles, are willing to tolerate anxiety in order to do experiments, can alter assumptions permanently, will take responsibility for their problems, and are willing to postpone gratification in order to complete therapy. . . . Cognitive therapy works best with psychologically sophisticated patients. Lower-social-class and psychologically naive patients can also benefit after appropriate preparation for therapy. (Beck & Weishaar, 1989, pp. 306–307)

EXAMPLE

This example, which illustrates some of the process of cognitive therapy, shows how treatment would proceed with a panic-disordered patient. This case is taken from Beck and Greenberg, 1988, pp. 578–581.

Status at Intake

A 31-year-old elementary school teacher entered treatment with panic attacks two or three times a day. She frequently experienced anxiety and a rapid heart rate, which she feared were symptomatic of a life-threatening heart condition. Other symptoms— blurred vision, palpitations, dizziness, sweating, paresthesias, shaking—also occurred during the attacks. Because of the attacks she stopped working, driving her car, or staying at home alone. She became increasingly dependent on her husband, frequently checked her pulse, and was preoccupied with worries about her physical condition. Panic symptoms typically came "out of the blue" and disappeared within 30 minutes.

During a previous period of frequent panic attacks, Ann (not her real name) had consulted several cardiologists and was prescribed a variety of cardiac medications, which had produced little improvement. In fact, Ann attributed some of her more troubling symptoms to the medications. She had mitral valve prolapse and frequent migraine headaches.

Family Background and Precipitating Stresses

Circumstances that involved her family of origin were clear precipitants of the patient's problems. The obedient oldest child of fanatically religious parents, Ann had carried much of the responsibility for managing the household and her six siblings, including a disruptive, delinquent brother. While her mother worked a night shift, Ann would often be beaten by her authoritarian father.

Over time, tension had developed between Ann and her brother, who as an adult was troubled by joblessness and drug abuse. Despite the disturbing facts of his life, the patient felt her mother was partial to the brother and acted coldly and capriciously toward Ann. Eventually, the brother was arrested on burglary charges. In an emotional scene that followed the incident, Ann expressed anger at her brother's behavior, and her mother responded by defending him and angrily withdrawing from Ann. Almost immediately, Ann experienced panic symptoms, and a generalized anxiety state also began to develop.

Sessions 1–7

In her first sessions, Ann complained of a variety of symptoms that frightened her and reported automatic thoughts such as, "What if my heart beats faster while I'm driving the car?" When driving into the city that week, she had had severe anxiety accompanied by the thought, "What if I have to get home and have to wait to get my car out of a parking lot?" In both cases she pictured an incapacitating medical emergency.

She also identified fears of performing inadequately at work. She was able quickly to discern a pattern of expecting the worst of her own performance and of others' reactions, and she could see that these expectations had generally not been confirmed by subsequent events. Ann also realized that she constantly felt compelled to hurry.

In the third session, Ann agreed to try to overbreathe for two minutes. She had a strong physical and emotional reaction to the procedure—indeed, tearfulness interrupted the overbreathing. She described her experience as follows: "My heart is pounding. I feel very dizzy, lightheaded, spaced out, unreal. I don't feel particularly anxious. I'm a little afraid. It's a little scary. My palms are sweaty. My mouth feels dry. I'm a little shaky. I feel like I can't catch my breath . . . I did have a thought about my heart. I hope it doesn't beat very fast. I did feel that I feel safe here."

Thus, the procedure did evoke Ann's fear of having a potentially dangerous heart condition; the automatic thoughts also suggest an implicit appraisal of how perilous the symptoms might be, given particular circumstances. Ann concluded that it was plausible that overbreathing might be contributing to her symptoms and that regulating her breathing might help her.

At the following session, Ann had observed that when anxious she had been holding her breath. Breathing slowly and regularly had helped. Further, she had applied the idea of conscious pacing to other activities, and noted with satisfaction that the tactic had worked very well. Pacing herself had made it obvious that she would need to stand up to her principal, who had been extracting hours of uncompensated service from her each week.

Here some basic assumptions were elicited: "I'm not such a hot person because I don't want to do what's expected of me. You are supposed to do without getting back." For homework, Ann recorded her activities for a week to see whether it was *possible* comfortably to add responsibilities to her current schedule. By her next session, the "evidence" had convinced Ann that no time was available for additional work—and that turning down the principal had nothing to do with whether she was a "hot person," but merely with assessment of priorities.

In the fourth session, guided imagery was used to reduce Ann's fear of public places from which escape would be difficult. Ann pictured herself shopping in a large department store, her car blocks away in a huge garage. In her initial image, she saw herself gasping for breath, desperate to reach her car, finally collapsing for lack of medical attention. Asked to form an alternate image, she pictured herself managing symptoms on her own until they passed, aware that a rescue team would likely be summoned in the event of a true emergency.

Simultaneously, Ann was trained in testing danger-laden automatic thoughts regarding her health ("What if my blood pressure is high?" "If the anxiety keeps up, my heart won't be able to take it.") and her work performance ("I can't do it!" "What if something went wrong?"). By the sixth session, she was able to respond on her own to such thoughts. Ann was feeling better during the day, "churning" at night.

During the following week, Ann became frightened by symptoms that started when she drank wine. At the root of this may have been a church prohibition against drinking. Ann appeared to have interpreted signs of anxiety about breaking the prohibition as manifestations of a dangerous reaction to the alcohol itself. However, she had coped with a rapid heartbeat that awakened her that night by breathing slowly and reminding herself that such symptoms always passed. She was pleased to have achieved some control over her symptoms and her fears.

Sessions 8–12

Concerns about Ann's family began to move into the foreground at about session seven. She expressed fear that her helpless, troubled brother would become her responsibility as her parents aged, if the parents failed to correct his behavior. The assumption, "If others aren't doing the job, I am responsible," seemed to be at work. In retrospect, it had also been operating at school. The assumption accounted in part for her anger at her mother—"I have to assume this burden because you refuse to." Ann recalled that she had long been angry at her mother for abandoning her responsibilities: "Why didn't you protect me from Dad?"

Two related assumptions could soon be articulated: "If I don't take care of things, and do it properly, a catastrophe will happen," but at the same time, "There's more to taking care of things than I can handle." Visiting her family, which she had been avoiding since the beginning of her illness, Ann caught automatic thoughts such as, "Something bad will happen. I have to fix it." The assumptions could be traced readily to childhood, when she had been expected to manage potentially dangerous situations that were beyond her level of competence. A memory surfaced of having aborted a sister's suicide attempt while her mother sewed.

During this period of therapy, Ann was helped to reassess the probability that she or her parents *could* set her brother straight. She began to see that she was quite able to succeed at any *reasonable* goal she set for herself, although she would likely have to give up trying to change her brother: "I see I can't control some things."

Fear and anger about the mother were also addressed: "I might deserve her mistreatment." An alternative hypothesis was proposed to account for the mother's behavior. Far from disapproving of Ann, the mother might feel she must apologize to the successful sibling for the unsuccessful one.

Ann was encouraged to "gather data" related to this hypothesis by speaking assertively to her mother, assisted by in-session role plays and "cognitive rehearsals," and found the mother more accepting than she had imagined. Later, Ann said she had learned to "be more bold," and to try to express feelings and solve problems in a timely manner.

In later sessions, earlier lessons were reinforced. A short episode of "spaceyness" made Ann recall the period of florid symptoms and fear it would recur. She also was distraught that anger at her parents meant she was not fulfilling the commandment to "honor" them. In both cases, she learned that "all or nothing thinking" was at fault: Some anxiety did not inevitably foretell severe anxiety, and angry behavior was not a sign of total disrespect.

SUMMARY AND EVALUATION

Summary.   Cognitive therapy is based on the common-sensical idea that what people think and say is significant. Concurrent with thoughts at the level of awareness, however, is a stream of thoughts that usually is outside of awareness. Termed automatic thoughts, these consist of ideas that may be unreasonable to others but are plausible to the person having them and of rules and regulations used in self-monitoring and self-instruction. These rules can lead to maladaptive actions.

People respond to events on the basis of the meaning that they attribute to events, which are interpreted according to their relevance to the self or the personal domain. Different emotions are evoked by different interpretations. Interpretations that involve distortions of reality give rise to emotional disorders, which are actually disorders in thinking; disordered thinking tends to include the personalization of events, the polarization of thought, and the application of rules in an unconditional, absolute manner. Cognitive therapy attempts to alleviate emotional disorders by correcting faulty interpretations of reality and faulty reasoning. Therapist and patient establish a collaborative relationship, which emphasizes solving problems rather than changing personal defects.

Over time, cognitive therapy and its application to various psychopathological conditions has been increasingly fleshed out. Beck and his colleagues have expanded their work well beyond depression, showing the substantive relevance of cognitive therapy for anxiety and phobic disorders and personality disorders, among others (Beck et al., 1985; 1990). With the cognitive model, we have been introduced to such concepts as "the negative triad," "cognitive shift," "automatic thoughts," and "collaborative empiricism." Such concepts reflect the truly cognitive emphasis of Beck's therapy and its focus on hypothesis testing, setting up experiments, and designing experiences through which patients' dysfunctional thinking can be evaluated.

Evaluation.   The cognitive model has several positive features that, in our opinion, merit mention. We can see the value of helping patients test out their thinking, helping patients become better "personal scientists," and helping patients change in graded fashion. We can see value in the concepts of cognitive profile (which recognizes differences across disorders) and collaborative empiricism. We also think there is much to be said for cognitive therapists' efforts to increasingly put their theory and therapy to the test (through scientific experiments); in the past decade alone, the research on the cognitive model has been extensive (e.g., Haaga et al., 1991; Hollon & Beck, 1994).

There is no question that there is much to commend the cognitive model. But just as there are positive features, so too are there some issues of concern that surround the model. In what follows, we would like to mention a few of these: the neglect of affect, the neglect of history, the neglect of response modes other than questioning, and the limitations of reasoning in behavior change. After that, we conclude by briefly considering research on and the future of cognitive therapy.

What role does affect play in cognitive therapy? Beck's work mentions time and time again cognitive and behavioral techniques, but very little is said about affective techniques. It appears that Beck has departed, or progressed from a pure cognitive approach as originally developed, to include a number of behavioral or other techniques, but perhaps has not incorporated methods of dealing with affective elements. It appears that the role of the therapist is to change affect by means of cognitive and behavioral techniques, not to use affect itself to effect change. Yet patients' affect, being a primary domain of experience, would seem to offer much toward rounding out and enriching the treatment process (see Greenberg & Safran, 1987). Patients' affect, even when dysfunctional, still can provide a dimension of experience that expands understanding of psychopathology and brings fuller meaning about how treatment might best proceed. This limited role assigned to affect in cognitive therapy, then, could be seen as one matter of concern.

Much like affect, the patient's history seems to be given short shrift in cognitive therapy. Is the patient's past unimportant? Does it have no bearing on the present? We guess the cognitive therapist might respond to those questions as follows: "Yes, the past has a bearing on the present, but we do not need to explore the past intensively to effect therapeutic change now." That may be so, but some attention to the past (e.g., patient explanation of significant attachments and their effects) can be important for some patients. Considering past relationships, hurts, and wounds, not ignoring them, can provide patients with the opportunity to deal with unresolved issues, come to grips with them, and move ahead. It seems to be the case with a few exceptions (i.e., marital problems, abuse, and personality disorders; Beck et al., 1990; "Controversies in cognitive therapy," 1993), that cognitive therapy would not provide such an opportunity.

What about the primary reliance on questioning in cognitive therapy? It has been illustrated in the work of Hill (1986) that there are many response modes (e.g., reflection, interpretation, restatement) on which therapists can draw. But the cognitive therapist seems to draw primarily on only one: Questioning. This heavy reliance on questioning would no doubt restrict the nature and character of the therapeutic interaction. While such questioning would allow the therapist to test patients' thinking, whether it would do anything else beyond that is unclear. This is a concern worth keeping in mind. The hope of course is that patients would themselves incorporate the questioning process that takes place in cognitive therapy. But does this happen? Do patients actually incorporate this question-answer exchange to assist them in dealing with future problems? To what extent does this reliance on questioning in therapy actually limit the scope of therapy and, thereby, limit progress in therapy? To what extent might this heavy reliance on teaching patients a self-questioning process ill prepare them to deal with problems that fall outside of this question-answer strategy? These are questons that, in our opinion, merit consideration in thinking about the cognitive model and its treatment utility. Questioning has its place in therapy (e.g., to gather information), but it is by no means the "be all and end all" of techniques.

The focus on cognition and reason, to the neglect of emotion and affect, would appear to be a serious limitation. It is doubtful that reason alone could account for the claimed impairment of patients. Actually, it appears that other elements are present in Beck's therapy. Certainly Beck establishes a relationship with his patients that goes beyond reasoning, persuading, and instructing them. He certainly is concerned and caring. Relationship elements must be considered in looking at and evaluating cognitive therapy. In addition, common sense fails to provide explanations for the emotional disorders. The thoughts and behaviors of depressed patients, for example, contradict the basic principles of human nature—that is, the survival instinct.

Let us next consider research. What does resesarch have to say about cognitive therapy? Without question, Beck and the cognitive therapy camp have been and are very active researchers of their approach (Alford & Norcross, 1991). Research on cognitive theory and therapy has been summarized or critiqued in numerous publications (e.g., Beck, 1976, 1983, 1991; Beck et al., 1985, 1990; Dobson, 1989; Haaga et al., 1991; Hollon & Beck, 1986, 1994; Hollon & Najavits, 1988).

Beck's therapy approach seems to have its best showing with regard to depression. There are many studies that have shown cognitive therapy to be effective in treating this disorder (Dobson, 1989). In their review, Hollon and Najavits (1988) summarized the situation as follows:

> Beck's cognitive therapy for depression appears to be as effective as any other alternative intervention in the treatment of acute episodes, and more effective than other alternatives in terms of preventing post treatment relapse. Little is yet known about inpatient, psychotic, or bipolar populations. Indicators of differential response are few. Work is underway to identify the active components leading to change and the mechanisms mediating that change but, to date, that work is not sufficiently well developed to be conclusive. (p. 658)

That assessment, though made several years ago, still largely holds true now (Hollon & Beck, 1994; Hollon, Shelton, & Davis, 1993).

Studies of the cognitive model or theory of depression have fared well in some cases and not so well in others. For example, Haaga et al. (1991), in their excellent, comprehensive review, found support for the following hypotheses of Beck's theory: negativity, the depressive triad, universality, and specificity, among others. However, they found only mixed or no support for such hypotheses as automaticity, exclusivity, and necessity; furthermore, they found "little convincing support for [the] causal hypotheses of cognitive theory . . ." (p. 231; i.e., the causal sequence specified by Beck of how depression comes about). What all this may mean for the cognitive therapy of depression is unclear. But it would appear accurate to say that the cognitive model of depression, which seemingly would have implications for cognitive treatment, is well supported in some respects, is not supported at all in other respects, and could benefit from some theoretical revision and refinement at this time.

Aside from depression, how has cognitive therapy fared in the research? Cognitive therapy research on other disorders has been done, and promising results have emerged in some cases. This appears to be especially so in regard to some anxiety disorders (Chambless & Gillis, 1993) and eating disorders (Wilson & Fairburn, 1993). But still, as Robins and Hayes (1993) have noted, "much work remains to be done to subject the recent applications of CT [cognitive therapy] to empirical scrutiny" (p. 212).

Determining the mechanisms of change in cognitive therapy seems highly important. Could it be possible that the effects of cognitive treatment are really due to the so-called nonspecific factors (e.g., attention, therapist interest and concern)? Or is change due to the questioning, hypothesis-testing component of cognitive therapy? These are questions that require research. Other questions that also merit attention have been raised by Dobson (1989; e.g., to what extent does cognitive therapy achieve change in patients' cognitive distortions or depressogenic assumptions?), Chambless and Gillis (1993), Hollon et al. (1993), and Wilson and Fairburn (1993). If our understanding of cognitive therapy is to become more complete, their research questions and concerns must be taken up and answered (cf. Whisman, 1993).

In closing, what of cognitive therapy's future? In more recent papers, Beck (1991a, 1991b, 1993; Beck & Haaga, 1992) has made mention of the following: (1) that the cognitive model will tie itself more to emerging concepts in social and cognitive psychology; (2) that elements of other approaches (e.g., emotional restructuring) and theories (e.g., interpersonal) will be incorporated into cognitive therapy; (3) that cognitive therapy will draw more from and be informed more by developments in basic psychology and related sciences; and (4) that continued research work will be done to further test the efficacy of cognitive therapy across a variety of disorders. If those developments do occur, then they would bode well for the continued viability of cognitive therapy; they could lead to a more meaningful integration of affect into cognitive therapy, a more informed, expanded theory base for cognitive therapy, and a more solid, established research base upon which to ground one's practice. Let us see what the future brings. As Beck (1991a) has stated, "cognitive therapy . . . has demonstrated its capacity to fly under its own power. How far it will fly remains to be seen" (p. 374).

REFERENCES

Alford, B. A., & Norcross, J. C. (1991). Cognitive therapy as integrative therapy. *Journal of Psychotherapy Integration, 1,* 175–190.

Beck, A. T. (1972). *Depression: Causes and treatment.* Philadelphia: University of Pennsylvania Press.

Beck, A. T. (1976). *Cognitive therapy and the emotional disorders.* New York: International Universities Press.

Beck, A. T. (1983). Cognitive therapy of depression: New perspectives. In P. J. Clayton & J. E. Barnett (Eds.). *Treatment of depression: Old controversies and new approaches* (pp. 265–284). New York: Raven Press.

Beck, A. T. (1985). Cognitive therapy. In H. I. Kaplan & B. J. Sadock (Eds.). *Comprehensive textbook of psychiatry* (4th ed., pp. 1432–1438). Baltimore: Williams & Wilkins.

Beck, A. T. (1987a). Cognitive models of depression. *Journal of Cognitive Psychotherapy: An International Quarterly, 1,* 5–37.

Beck, A. T. (1987b). Cognitive therapy. In J. K. Zeig (Ed.). *The evolution of psychotherapy* (pp. 149–163). New York: Brunner/Mazel.

Beck, A. T. (1988). *Love is never enough.* New York: Harper & Row.

Beck, A. T. (1991a). Cognitive therapy: A 30-year retrospective. *American Psychologist, 46,* 368–375.

Beck, A. T. (1991b). Cognitive therapy as *the* integrative therapy. *Journal of Psychotherapy Integration, 1,* 191–198.

Beck, A. T. (1993). Cognitive therapy: Past, present, and future. *Journal of Consulting and Clinical Psychology, 61,* 194–198.

Beck, A. T., & Emery, G., with Greenberg, R. L. (1985). *Anxiety disorders and phobias: A cognitive perspective.* New York: Basic Books.

Beck, A. T., Epstein, N., & Harrison, R. (1983). Cognitions, attitudes and personality dimensions in depression. *British Journal of Cognitive Psychotherapy, 1,* 1–16.

Beck, A. T., Freeman, A., & Associates (1990). *Cognitive therapy of personality disorders.* New York: Guilford.

Beck, A. T., & Greenberg, R. L. (1988). Cognitive therapy of panic disorder. In A. J. Frances & R. E. Hales (Eds.). *American Psychiatric Press review of psychiatry* (vol. 7, pp. 571–583). Washington, DC: American Psychiatric Press.

Beck, A. T., & Haaga, D. A. F. (1992). The future of cognitive therapy. *Psychotherapy, 29,* 34–38.

Beck, A. T., Rush, A. J., Shaw, B. F., & Emery, G. (1979). *Cognitive therapy of depression.* New York: Guilford.

Beck, A. T., & Young, J. E. (1985). Cognitive therapy of depression. In D. Barlow (Ed.). *Clinical handbook of psychological disorders: A step-by-step treatment manual* (pp. 206–244). New York: Guilford.

Beck, A. T., & Weishaar, M. E. (1989). Cognitive therapy. In R. J. Corsini & D. Wedding (Eds.). *Current psychotherapies* (4th ed., pp. 285–320). Itasca, IL: F. E. Peacock.

Chambless, D. L., & Gillis, M. M. (1993). Cognitive therapy for anxiety disorders. *Journal of Consulting and Clinical Psychology, 61,* 248–260.

Controversies in cognitive therapy: A dialogue with Aaron T. Beck and Steve Hollon. *Journal of Cognitive Psychotherapy: An International Quarterly,* (1993)*7,* 79–94. (Transcript of dialogue that took place at 1992 World Congress of Cognitive Therapy.)

Dobson, K. S. (1989). A meta-analysis of the efficacy of cognitive therapy for depression. *Journal of Consulting and Clinical Psychology, 57,* 414–419.

Greenberg, L. S., & Safran, J. D. (1987). *Emotion in psychotherapy: Affect, cognition, and the process of change.* New York: Guilford.

Haaga, D. A. F., Dyck, M. J., & Ernst, D. (1991). Empirical status of cognitive theory of depression. *Psychological Bulletin, 110,* 215–236.

Hill, C. E. (1986). An overview of the Hill counselor and client verbal response modes category systems. In L. S. Greenberg & W. M. Pinsof (Eds.). *The psychotherapeutic process: A research handbook* (pp. 131–160). New York: Guilford.

Hollon, S. D., & Beck, A. T. (1986). Cognitive and cognitive-behavioral therapies. In S. L. Garfield & A. E. Bergin (Eds.). *Handbook of psychotherapy and behavior change* (3rd ed., pp. 443–482). New York: Wiley.

Hollon, S. D., & Beck, A. T. (1994). Cognitive and cognitive-behavioral therapies. In A. E. Bergin & S. L. Garfield (Eds.). *Handbook of psychotherapy and behavior change* (4th ed., pp. 428–466). New York: Wiley.

Hollon, S. D., & Garber, J. (1990). Cognitive therapy for depression: A social cognitive perspective. *Personality and Social Psychology Bulletin, 16,* 58–73.

Hollon, S. D., & Najavits, L. (1988). Review of empirical studies of cognitive therapy. In A. J. Frances & R. E. Hales (Eds.). *American Psychiatric Press review of psychiatry* (vol. 7, pp. 643–666). Washington, DC: American Psychiatric Press.

Hollon, S. D., Shelton, R. C., & Davis, D. D. (1993). Cognitive therapy of depression: Conceptual issues and clinical efficacy. *Journal of Consulting and Clinical Psychology, 61,* 270–275.

Kovacs, M., & Beck, A. T. (1978). Maladaptive cognitive structures in depression. *American Journal of Psychiatry, 135,* 525–533.

Perris, C. (1988). *Cognitive therapy with schizophrenics.* New York: Guilford.

Riskind, J. H., & Rholes, W. S. (1984). Cognitive accessibility and the capacity of cognitions to predict future depression: A theoretical note. *Cognitive Therapy and Research, 8,* 1–12.

Robins, C. J., & Hayes, A. M. (1993). An appraisal of cognitive therapy. *Journal of Consulting and Clinical Psychology, 61,* 205–214.

Weishaar, M. (1992). *Aaron Beck.* London: Sage.

Whisman, M. A. (1993). Mediators and moderators of change in cognitive therapy of depression. *Psychological Bulletin, 114,* 248–265.

Wilson, G. T., & Fairburn, C. G. (1993). Cognitive treatments for eating disorders. *Journal of Consulting and Clinical Psychology, 61,* 261–269.

chapter 9

Cognitive-Behavior Modification: Meichenbaum

Donald Herbert Meichenbaum (b. 1940) was born and obtained his early education in New York City. He received his B.A. from City College in 1962. He entered the University of Illinois at Urbana–Champaign in 1963 and received his M.A. in 1965 and Ph.D. in clinical psychology in 1966. During 1965 to 1966, he was a U.S. Public Health Service fellow. In 1966, he was appointed assistant professor of psychology at the University of Waterloo in Ontario, Canada, where he became associate professor in 1970 and is now professor.

Meichenbaum is a member of the American Psychological Association, the Canadian Psychological Association, and the Society for Research in Child Development. He is an author of *Facilitating Treatment Adherence: A Practitioner's Guide* (1987; with D. Turk), *Stress Reduction and Prevention* (1983; with M. Jaremko), *Pain and Behavioral Medicine* (1983; with D. Turk & M. Genest), *Cognitive-Behavior Modification* (1974), *Stress Inoculation Training* (1985), and *Cognitive-Behavior Modification: An Integrative Approach* (1977), on which this summary is based. He is the co-editor of *The Unconscious Reconsidered* (1984; with K. Bowers). He serves on the Advisory Board of the journal *Cognitive Therapy and Research,* and is on the Board of Consulting Advisors to the *Journal of Cognitive Psychotherapy.* He appeared as one of the three therapists in the film series, *Three Approaches to Psychotherapy III,* and has been awarded the Izaak Killam Fellowship Award from the Canada Council.

BACKGROUND AND DEVELOPMENT

Meichenbaum relates an experience during his doctoral studies at the University of Illinois that was the beginning of the research and theory development leading to his cognitive-behavioral approach to behavior modification and psychotherapy (or cognitive-behavior modification). His research involved training hospitalized schizophrenic patients to emit "healthy talk" by operant conditioning procedures. He observed that some of the patients, while they were being given a follow-up interview as part of the evaluation of the effectiveness of the treatment, repeated aloud to themselves the experimental instruction "Give healthy talk; be coherent and relevant," thus engaging in spontaneous self-instruction.

It might be noted that the use of such experimental instructions constituted a departure from strict operant conditioning, thereby introducing a cognitive element into the treatment. An incident reported by William Gilbert, director of the Counseling Center at the University of Illinois, occurred at about the same time that Meichenbaum was engaged in his research. A psychology student working in a mental hospital decided to attempt to eliminate an antagonizing behavior in a patient (sticking his tongue out at members of the hospital staff) by the method of aversive conditioning. After several interviews, the patient caught on to the psychology student's objective and said, "Say, Doc, if you're trying to get me to stop sticking my tongue out, just tell me and I'll be glad to" (Gilbert, 1968). Whether Meichenbaum was aware of and influenced by this incident is not known, but it points to the influence of cognitive factors in behavior change.

Meichenbaum's experience led him to wonder if schizophrenic patients and other patients or clients could be explicitly trained to talk to themselves in a way that would lead to changes in their behavior. He started on a program of research to study the role of cognitive factors in behavior modification. He focused on inner speech, or inner dialogue, seeking to alter it, and on images, hoping to learn if such changes would lead to changes in thinking, feeling, and behavior. He also began to develop a theoretical explanation for the operation of such factors in behavior change. His results are presented as a progress report, not as a finished or proven theory and practice.

Building on the research that shows that overt and covert private speech influence the behavior of children, Meichenbaum explored the use of self-instructional training with hyperactive, impulsive children. He found in laboratory studies that impulsive children manifested less verbal control of nonverbal behavior than did reflective children and that impulsive children used private speech differently in natural play situations. In the latter situation, impulsive children were deficient in outer-directed and self-regulatory speech. Impulsive children "do not habitually and spontaneously analyze their experience in cognitively mediated terms (i.e., both verbal and imaginal) and . . . they do not formulate and internalize rules that might guide them in new learning situations" (Meichenbaum, 1974, p. 30). Meichenbaum then developed a program to train hyperactive, impulsive children to talk to themselves differently so that they could better comprehend problem tasks, spontaneously produce verbal mediators and strategies, and use these mediators to guide, monitor, and control their behavior.

Meichenbaum and others have succeeded in changing the behaviors of impulsive, hyperactive, and aggressive children through a training program in which the experimenter models the self-instructions as well as the behaviors and in which the child rehearses the self-instructions. Conversely, the addition of self-instructional training to operant procedures enhanced the results over those obtained from operant procedures alone. However, extrinsic reinforcements were not effective with children who attributed results to luck or chance rather than to their own efforts. Self-instructional training was effective in helping children change their attributions from luck or lack of ability to effort. Meichenbaum concluded that self-instructional training can be effective in altering children's attributional and cognitive styles but cautioned that its effectiveness has not yet been fully demonstrated.

Meichenbaum also developed a program of training in self-instruction for patients diagnosed as schizophrenic. He began with structured sensorimotor tasks, rather than with social interactions, since there is evidence that interpersonal-relationship pressures increase symptoms such as bizarre verbalizations. The initial tasks included a digit-symbol test and the Porteus Maze Test. The patients were trained to develop and use self-controlling self-statements. As the patients developed proficiency, tasks such as a proverbs test and an interview were added. When a patient used symptoms to control the situation, he or she was made aware of this as a cue to use self-instructional controls learned earlier in the simpler tasks.

> Each subject was individually trained to first monitor and evaluate his own performance by means of self-questioning. Then, if he judged his performance to be inferior, he learned to self-instruct in a task-relevant fashion in order to produce a more desirable response. (Meichenbaum, 1974, p. 71)

The experimenter modeled verbalizations as he or she performed the task, and subjects overtly and then covertly used the same verbalizations as they in turn performed the task. Verbalization included a restatement of the task requirements, instructions to perform the task slowly and to think before acting, a cognitive strategy using imagery in seeking a solution, self-rewarding statements, an example of a poor or an erroneous response, followed by the reason it was inappropriate, and a statement describing how to cope with failure and come up with an adequate response. Early training sessions were simple, and later sessions gradually added more elements. In final sessions, the patient was asked to observe and report the reactions—verbal and nonverbal—of staff and other patients to inappropriate behavior. Discussion then led to suggesting self-statements the patient could use in such situations, such as "Be relevant, be coherent, make myself understood." Other self-statements, such as "I'm not making myself understood, let me try again," were used to maintain task relevance. Compared with control subjects who were trained by operant social reinforcement, the experimental subjects showed significantly greater improvement on all criterion tests except one (digit recall without distraction).

Self-instructional training is not effective unless the necessary concepts and skills are present. For example, self-instructional training will not improve performance in arithmetic if the basic skills are lacking. "Teaching children to respond to such self-directed verbal commands as 'stop and think' will not result in incremental improvement of performance in specific tasks unless the prerequisite performance skills are already in the repertoire" (Meichenbaum, 1974, p. 80). Also, actions may not follow self-verbalization if there is no incentive to perform the actions. Reinforcement of the sequence of verbal and nonverbal behavior increases the frequency of action following verbalization. Language alone may not change behavior; thought is also necessary. Thinking can occur without language, but language can significantly increase thinking and thus change behavior. "That is the promise of the self-instructional cognitive-behavior treatment approach" (Meichenbaum, 1974, p. 82).

ASSUMPTIONS AND CONCEPTS

Self-instructional training is based on the assumption that "the things people say to themselves determine the rest of the things they do" (Farber, 1963). Behavior is affected or influenced by various aspects of a person's activities, which are designated by various constructs: physiological responses, affective reactions, cognitions, and interpersonal interactions. Inner speech, or internal dialogue, is one of these activities or constructs.

> The goal of a cognitive-functional assessment is to describe, in probabilistic terms, the functional significance of engaging in self-statements of a particular sort [being] followed by an individual's particular behavior or emotional state (e.g., mood), or his physiological reactions or his attentional processes, etc. How does the internal dialogue influence, and, in turn, is it influenced by other events or behavioral processes? (Meichenbaum, 1977, p. 202)

There is little research on conscious thought or internal dialogue, as a variable affecting other behaviors. However, studies in three areas—interpersonal instructions, cognitive factors in stress, and the effects of instructional sets of physiological reactions—have dealt with the consequences of self-statements and are a source for suggestions regarding the functional value of inner speech.

Functions of Internal Dialogue

Interpersonal Instructions. Descriptions of the function of interpersonal instructions (by Gagne, 1964, for example) are very similar to the descriptions of self-instructions (by McKinney, 1973, for example). Both provide procedures and a rule or a principle for mediating behavior. Thus, it can be hypothesized that self-instructions operate in a similar fashion to interpersonal instructions. Self-instructions are derived from adults' instructions that children internalize or incorporate and use to control their behavior, as the Russian psychologists Vygotsky (1962) and Luria (1961) theorized.

Cognitive Factors in Stress. Although the psychosocial literature on coping with stress does not deal with self-statements, it does suggest that "how one responds to stress in large part is influenced by how one appraises the stressor, or to what he attributes the arousal he feels, and how he assesses his ability to cope" (Meichenbaum, 1977, p. 202). A person's self-statements about the stress situation and ability to handle it influence that person's behavior in the situation. Anxiety level is related to such self-appraisals in relation to the situation. High anxiety is associated with a person's focusing on the self and his or her inadequacy and self-deprecating thoughts. Low anxiety is associated with a person's focusing on the external situation, with a resulting higher level of coping. "[O]ne function of internal dialogue in changing affect, thought, and behavior is to *influence the client's attentional and appraisal processes*" (Meichenbaum, 1977, pp. 206–207).

Instructional Sets and Physiological Effects. There is considerable evidence that cognition influences physiology and emotions. Studies have shown that there is a relationship between self-statements and mood. Clients' thoughts and cognitive sets are related to psychosomatic disorders; hypnotized subjects who have been instructed to feel the attitudes reported by psychosomatic patients have suffered the symptoms of the patients. Cognitive activity has been postulated as a mediational factor in operant autonomic conditioning. Meichenbaum found that following cognitive-behavior-modification treatment, subjects labeled their physiological reactions as facilitative rather than inhibitive.

> Sweaty palms, increased heart and respiratory rates, muscular tension, now became "allies," cues to use the coping techniques for which they had been trained. . . . This shift in cognitions in itself may mediate a shift in autonomic functioning. The present theory postulates that it is not the physiological arousal *per se* that is debilitating but rather what the client says to himself about that arousal that determines his eventual reaction. (Meichenbaum, 1977, pp. 207–208)

Thus, there is considerable evidence that thought influences behavior. Yet it must be recognized that much of our behavior is automatic or the result of habit. We do not always think before we act (habits are useful for quick, efficient actions), but "*if we are going to change behavior then we must think before we act.* Such thinking (i.e., the production of inner speech) 'deautomatizes' the maladaptive behavior act and provides the basis for providing the new adaptive behavior" (Meichenbaum, 1977, pp. 210–211).

Structure of Internal Dialogue.   A second important function of inner speech is to influence and change cognitive structures. A construct such as cognitive structure is necessary to account for the nature of self-statements. Cognitive structure provides the system of meanings or concepts that gives rise to a particular set of self-statements.

> By *cognitive structure* I mean to point to that organizing aspect of thinking that seems to monitor and direct the strategy, route and choice of thoughts. I mean to imply a kind of "executive processor" which "holds the blueprints of thinking" and which determines when to interrupt, change, or continue thought. (Meichenbaum, 1977, pp. 212–213)

Learning or change occurs without a change in cognitive structure, but learning a new skill requires a change in cognitive structure. Structural changes occur by *absorption,* in which new structures incorporate old structures; by *displacement,* in which old structures continue to exist in a more comprehensive new structure (from Neisser, 1962, following Piaget's (1954) concepts of assimilation and accommodation). Cognitive structures determine the nature of inner speech, but inner dialogue changes cognitive structures, in what Meichenbaum calls a "virtuous cycle."

THE CHANGE/THERAPY PROCESS

There are certain underlying mechanisms of change common to all procedures (therapy systems) and contexts (in therapy and in nonprofessional contacts) in which change occurs. These mechanisms involve the individual's cognitive processes. First, the client must recognize or become aware of his or her inadequate behaviors. Second, this awareness is a cue that produces a certain internal dialogue. The nature of this dialogue is guided by the theoretical orientation of the therapist, to which the client adapts. Third, there is a change in the nature of the internal dialogue from that which the client engaged in prior to therapy. There is a "translation" process fostered by the therapist's reflections, explanations, interpretations, information giving, and cognitive modeling. In addition, outside of therapy the client engages in coping behaviors that are discussed and rehearsed in therapy, resulting in an internal dialogue that influences the client's cognitive structures as well as behaviors. "Some clients require explicit teaching of such coping responses, and this is where the technology of behavior therapy is of particular value" (Meichenbaum, 1977, pp. 218–219). The three phases are elaborated as follows.

Self-Observation.   Prior to therapy, the client's internal dialogue consists of negative self-statements and images. In therapy, clients, through heightened awareness and attention, focus on their thoughts, feelings, physiological reactions, and interpersonal behaviors. The translation process leads to new cognitive structures that allow clients to view their symptoms or problems differently and to produce thought and behaviors that are incompatible with the maladaptive ones. This reconceptualization process leads to a redefinition of problems in ways that give clients both a sense of understanding and a feeling of control and hope that are required for acts of change. Reconceptualization gives new or different meanings to thoughts, feelings, and behaviors. These meanings vary with different schools of therapy, and different conceptualizations may be effective in facilitating change. However, "one of the more essential variables that determines therapy outcome is the degree to which a given conceptualization leads to specific behavioral changes that can be transferred to the real-life situation" (Meichenbaum, 1977, p. 222).

Therapists vary in the directiveness and force with which they attempt to change their clients' conceptualizations. The therapist must be concerned with clients' self-statements, descriptions, definitions, and attributions of their problems and their conceptions of the therapy process and dependence on the therapist, but therapists do not simply uncritically accept clients' views. The reconceptualization is a joint process, and clients' acceptance of it is an implicit result of the interaction between therapist and client.

Incompatible Thoughts and Behavior.   In the second phase, the client's self-observation triggers an internal dialogue. "[I]f the client's behavior is to change, then what he says to himself and/or imagines, must initiate a new behavioral chain, one that is incompatible with his maladaptive behaviors" (Meichenbaum, 1977, p. 224). This new internal dialogue involves all the functional properties of inner speech indicated above (affecting attentional and appraisal systems and physiological responses, and instigating new behaviors). This inner speech, guided by the translation involved in the therapy, influences the client's cognitive structures, enabling the client to organize his or her experiences around the new conceptualization in a way that leads to more effective coping.

Cognitions Concerning Change.   The third phase has to do with the client's performing coping behaviors on a day-to-day basis and self-talk about the outcomes of these "personal experiments." It is not enough for the client to focus only on skills training.

> For what the client says to himself about his *newly* acquired behaviors and their resultant consequences will influence whether the behavioral change process will be maintained and will generalize. . . . To the extent that the client changes both his behavior

and his internal dialogues, to that extent therapy becomes a success. In other words, a person is how he behaves, as well as what he says to himself (including his attributions), which says much more than that a person is only how he behaves. (Meichenbaum, 1977, p. 225)

Thus, the effective change process involves new behavioral skills, new internal dialogues, and new cognitive structures. Different therapies emphasize one or another of these. The cognitive-behavior approach involves all three. There is the question of where to begin, which requires research to answer. Different types of clients may require the focus or emphasis on one or another of the three basic processes, but the others are also involved.

IMPLEMENTATION: METHODS AND TECHNIQUES

Cognitive-Behavioral Assessment

Since psychiatric patients suffer from disorders of affect, cognition, and volition, assessment should deal with these areas of functioning. Traditional assessment strategies in the study of psychological deficits have been inadequate for such assessment. Two research approaches have been used. The first is the *comparative-groups approach.* Clinical groups are given a series of tests, and the results are compared with those of matched normal control groups. Such results are of little assistance in revealing the nature of the deficit, what underlies or causes it, or what can change it. Deficient performance can arise from different reasons.

The second approach is the *specific-deficits approach,* in which tests are used to detect the client's deficient performance, the nature of which has been hypothesized. A normative control group is used, but the focus is on specific tests rather than on a global "shotgun" comparison. This approach may result in a new label for the deficiency, but it does not explain or define the problem. Speculation may result in hypothetical explanations derived from either of these approaches, but there is no basis for choosing among the various explanations or conceptualizations. A cognitive-functional approach to deficit analysis appears more promising.

Cognitive-Functional Approach. A *functional analysis of behavior* involves a detailed examination of environmental antecedents and consequences in relation to a response repertoire. It requires a careful definition of the response class, a knowledge of the responses' frequency in various situations, and the manipulation of environmental events to demonstrate causal relationships. A *functional-cognitive analysis* includes and focuses on the role of cognitions in the behavioral repertoire,

in order to determine which cognitions (or failure to produce which key cognitions), under which circumstances, are contributing to or interfering with adequate performance. . . . The cognitive-functional approach analyzes *sequential psychological processes* . . . required for adequate performance. . . . [A] failure in the internal dialogue of the client, what he says or fails to say to himself prior to, accompanying, and following his performance on a task, becomes the concern of the analysis. (Meichenbaum, 1977, pp. 236–237)

The clinician may engage in the task in order to speculate about the factors that lead to the client's poor performance.

Task analysis involves breaking down the task into its components or into the cognitive strategies required for its performance, beginning with comprehension of the nature of the task or the instructions. Then various manipulations are performed, and the changes that result are noted. There are three types of manipulation. The first is the *modification of the task* in a variety of ways, permitting assessment of the client's capabilities and deficits under different conditions. The second type of manipulation is the *alteration of nontask environmental variables,* such as presence or absence of distortions and interpersonal factors. This permits observation of aspects of the situation that facilitate or disrupt performance. The client is also a source of such information.

> Soliciting from the client his perception of the task, his description of his strategy, his appraisal of his performance, and his assessment of his own situation are key elements of a cognitive-functional analysis. . . . [O]ur clients have something to tell us if we would only ask and then listen. (Meichenbaum, 1977, p. 242)

The third type of manipulation consists of *providing the client with supports* in the form of various aids and suggestions and observing changes in performance. Thus, cognitive-functional assessment involves the client as the subject of an experimental investigation.

Such an experimental analysis leads directly into treatment suggestions. Assessment and treatment merge or overlap. "Assessment of deficiencies and capabilities go [sic] hand-in-hand with remediation" (Meichenbaum, 1977, p. 246).

Clinical Application of the Approach

In the individual assessment process two questions are asked: "First, what is the client failing to say to himself, which, if present, would help lead to adequate performance and adaptive behavior? Second, what is the content of the cognitions that interfere with adaptive behavior?" (Meichenbaum, 1977, p. 249). A number of procedures are used to answer these questions.

The Clinical Interview.   The initial interview begins with an exploration of the extent and the duration of the client's problem as the client presents it and of the client's expectations of therapy, following the outline provided by Peterson (1968), which involves a situational analysis of the client's behavior. Beyond this, the cognitive-behavior therapist asks the client to imagine incidents involving personal problem(s) and to report his or her thoughts, images,and behaviors before, during, and after these incidents. Then the therapist explores the presence of similar thoughts and feelings in other situations and/or at earlier periods in the client's life and may ask the client to look for them during the next week.

The cognitive-functional assessment leads clients to recognize that part of the problem derives from self-statements—that we can control and change our thoughts if we choose to do so. Clients may be unaware of what they have been saying to themselves, since because of "the habitual nature of one's expectations and beliefs, it is likely that such thinking processes and images become automatic and seemingly involuntary, like most overlearned acts" (Meichenbaum, 1977, p. 252).

Behavioral Tests.   In a behavioral test, the client engages in the behaviors involving his or her problem, either in a laboratory situation or in real life. This is followed by an exploration of thoughts and feelings during the experience. In the laboratory, the client can be videotaped, and the videotape can be viewed and discussed with the therapist, or the client can be asked to think aloud during the behavior test. Although such reconstruction and verbalization while engaging in the task are subject to inaccuracy or distortion, they can reveal the client's thinking style.

A TAT-Like Approach.   Pictures similar to those in the Thematic Apperception Test (TAT) but related to the client's problem behavior may be used to elicit thoughts and feelings related to the behaviors.

Other Psychometric Tests.   Tests of cognitive processes, such as creativity and problem-solving tests, may be administered, followed by the client reporting on his or her thinking while the test was taken.

Assessment may be conducted on a group basis, particularly if clients have the same problem. Exploration of thoughts and feelings in a group can help clients appreciate the role of cognitive factors in behavior and lead to self-disclosure and self-examination.

Cognitive Factors in Behavior Therapy Techniques

Behavior therapy techniques have overemphasized the importance of environmental events (antecedents and consequences) at the same time that they have overlooked or underemphasized the cognitive factors in these techniques. "Our research on cognitive factors in behavior therapy techniques has highlighted the fact that environmental events *per se,* although important, are not of *primary* importance; rather what the client says to himself about those events influences his behavior" (Meichenbaum, 1977, p. 108). However, behavior modification techniques can be used to modify the client's internal dialogue as well as behaviors, but when standard behavior therapy procedures are supplemented by self-instructional techniques, they are more effective, generalization is greater, and effects are more persistent. This raises questions about the learning theory basis of the standard techniques, which is a simple contiguity model. Research on cognitive factors in behavior therapy—testing the effectiveness of changing cognitions through behavior therapy techniques—suggests a new and different conceptualization.

Anxiety-Relief Conditioning.   In the behavioristic anxiety-relief procedure, the cessation of an aversive stimulus is paired with the emitting of a word such as *calm.* Anxiety can then be reduced by clients instructing themselves to be "calm." Meichenbaum, on the basis of an experiment in which subjects reported using coping verbalizations other than the words *calm* or *relax,* conducted a study incorporating such self-instructions. He also made the onset of shock punishing for some subjects. Thus, subjects said the name of the phobic object (for example, "snake"), followed by fear-engendering thoughts (for example, "It's ugly; I won't look at it.") that elicited the shock. Then the subjects said the coping self-statements (for example, "Relax, I can touch it."), which led to cessation of the shock, and the clients then relaxed. A control group of subjects were *shocked contingent on the coping self-statements,* and the shock was terminated by the *emission of fear-engendering* self-statements. The expanded anxiety-relief treatment was, as expected, effective in reducing fears, but, surprisingly, the inverted or reversed treatment was also effective. Both treatments were more effective than the standard procedure. The results of the inverted treatment are inconsistent with the "learning theory" model; these subjects should have done poorly.

Other studies have confirmed these results, both with aversive conditioning and with other behavior therapy techniques. Flooding techniques, for example, are difficult to explain by learning theory. Similar studies using covert conditioning have yielded similar results. The conditioning paradigm is inadequate for explaining such behavioral changes, questioning the so-called basic laws of learning.

In questioning the subjects in this study, Meichenbaum found that they emitted coping statements to prepare for the forthcoming shock and perceived the fear-engendering self-statements as signals to the experimenter to turn off the shock. "What seemed to be happening was that the subjects were learning a set of coping skills that could be employed *across* situations, including confronting the phobic object" (Meichenbaum, 1977, p. 117). The results also might be explained by psychosocial theories, such as social learning theory, dissonance theory, attribution theory, and self-perception theory. Essentially, what a client learns in behavior therapy are cognitive and behavioral skills, including changes in maladaptive beliefs as a result of nonconfirming experiences in therapy; changes in the self-concept and beliefs about others through information learning; and the development of new problem-solving and interpersonal skills (as in Murray & Jacobson, 1971).

Systematic Desensitization.   Systematic desensitization, according to Wolpe (1990), eliminates fear because fear is incompatible with relaxation. This counterconditioning explanation has been questioned by a number of writers. Observation of Wolpe's therapy sessions have shown the presence of cognitive factors, which were confirmed by reports of his clients.

Systematic desensitization can be modified to utilize the clients' cognitions explicitly. The relaxation component of desensitization can be simplified and shortened by having clients adopt a mental set of relaxation through self-instruction. The imaginal component can be improved by having clients see themselves as coping with the anxiety induced by visualizing the scene, breathing slowly and deeply, relaxing, and engaging in self-instructions. The anxiety-producing experience then becomes a cue to cope and to function in spite of the anxiety. Anxiety is thus seen by the client as facilitating rather than debilitating—it is a signal for coping behavior, as shown in experiments by Meichenbaum and others.

The proposed changes in the desensitization procedures are consistent with (a) observations that desensitization should be viewed as an active means of learning coping and self-control skills and (b) notions of the therapeutic value of the "work of worrying" (anticipatory problem-solving and cognitive rehearsal). (Meichenbaum, 1977, p. 124)

Modeling.   Bandura (1969) has emphasized that, in the modeling technique, the observer converts the information obtained from the model to covert perceptual-cognitive images and covert verbal, mediatory rehearsal responses that are used later as cues to overt behavior. Such responses are essentially self-instructions. Explicit modeling of such responses should facilitate behavior change. Models can think aloud as they perform, including the demonstration not only of the mastery behavior, but also of coping behavior, such as facing and dealing with self-doubts and frustrations, and ending with self-reinforcing statements following success. Research by Meichenbaum and others has shown this method to be more effective than the usual modeling technique.

Aversive Conditioning.   In aversive conditioning, an undesirable response is paired with an aversive condition such as shock, which is terminated by cessation of the response. In the cognitive-behavioral approach, the undesirable response is expanded to include cognitions in the form of self-statements and images. In treating smoking, for example, shock is terminated by having the client put out the cigarette *and* emit personally selected self-statements about smoking behavior, such as not wanting a "cancer weed." This approach was more effective than the usual approach in a study by Meichenbaum. The explanation of the facilitating effect of mental rehearsal is not yet clear, but it may be related to "a better representation of the implicit stimuli that contributed to the maladaptive behavior," to the involvement of "many more different situational cues in the training," and to "greater emotional involvement" (Meichenbaum, 1977, pp. 137–138). The acquisition of motor skills can be enhanced by mental practice involving similar processes, as well as imagery.

A number of behavior therapists have recognized the cognitive factors in behavior therapy and have made "comments that converge to suggest that the alteration of the client's self-statements may represent a common mediation of the behavioral change brought about by many of these behavior therapy techniques. . . . If the hypothesis that the client's self-instructions mediate behavior change is valid, one would expect that explicit self-instructional training would enhance treatment effectiveness" (Meichenbaum, 1977, p. 141). Research has confirmed this hypothesis.

Cognitive-behavior modification includes two other major methods, in addition to behavior therapy techniques—stress-inoculation training and cognitive-restructuring techniques.

Stress-Inoculation Training

Stress-inoculation training follows the biological model of immunization. It builds up resistance to stress through a program of teaching the client how to cope with graded stress situations. It incorporates suggestions from research on coping with stress. The training procedure is multifaceted in order to provide flexibility because of the complexity of coping devices, the variability of stress situations, and the differences among individuals and cultural factors. Stress-inoculation training consists of three phases (see Meichenbaum, 1985).

Educational Phase.   In the educational phase, the client is provided with a conceptual framework for understanding the nature of his or her reactions to stress. This should be in lay terms and be plausible to the client and lead naturally to the practice of specific cognitive and behavioral techniques. Thus, "the scientific validity of a particular conceptualization is less crucial than its face validity or air of plausibility for the client" (Meichenbaum, 1977, p. 151). The purpose of the framework is to help the client view a problem rationally and accept and collaborate in the appropriate therapy.

In a study of multiphobic clients, following an assessment interview, the client's anxiety was presented as involving two major elements: (1) heightened physiological arousal (increased heart rate, rapid breathing, sweaty palms, or other symptoms stated by the client) and (2) a set of anxiety-evoking avoidance thoughts indicated by the client (disgust, sense of helplessness, thoughts of panic, desire to flee, embarrassment, and so on). The client was then told that the self-statements during arousal led to emotional avoidance behavior and that treatment would be directed toward (1) helping the client control his or her physiological arousal and (2) changing the self-statements that were made under stress conditions. The client was then encouraged to view the phobic or stress reactions as consisting of four stages rather than being one undifferentiated reaction: (1) preparing for the stressor, (2) confronting or handling the stressor, (3) possibly being overwhelmed by the stressor, and (4) reinforcing himself or herself for having coped (cf. Meichenbaum, 1986).

Rehearsal Phase. In the rehearsal phase, the client was provided with coping techniques, including both direct actions and cognitive coping modes, to use in each of the four stages of the phobic reaction. Direct action included obtaining information about the phobic objects, arranging for escape routes, and learning physical relaxation exercises. Cognitive coping consisted of helping the client become aware of negative, self-defeating statements and using these as cues or signals for producing incompatible, coping self-statements. Examples for each of the four stages are

1. "You can develop a plan to deal with it."
2. "Relax, you're in control. Take a slow, deep breath."
3. "When fear comes, just pause."
4. "It worked; you did it."

Application Training. When the client became proficient in the coping techniques, he or she was exposed in the laboratory to a series of graded ego-threatening and pain-threatening stressors, including unpredictable electric shocks. The therapist modeled the use of the coping skills.

The training was thus multifaceted because it involved a variety of therapeutic techniques, including didactic training, discussion, modeling, self-instructional and behavioral rehearsal, and reinforcement. Research is necessary to determine which are the necessary and sufficient conditions for achieving change. The total procedure was more effective than systematic desensitization, more effective than the use of phase 1 and 2 techniques without phase 3, and more effective than no treatments (as shown by an untreated control group). Self-instructional rehearsal is thus a necessary but not a sufficient condition for the elimination of fears; application or practice training also is necessary. Both the total procedure and the treatment involving the first two phases only were more effective than desensitization in terms of generalization. Stress-inoculation training provided a way of altering the client's cognitive self from one of "learned helplessness" to one of "learned resourcefulness."

> It was quite common for clients in the stress-inoculation group to report spontaneously that they had successfully applied their new coping skills in other stressful situations, including final exams and dental visits. . . . The change in attitude seemed to encourage clients to initiate confrontations with real-life problems. (Meichenbaum, 1977, p. 159)

Stress-inoculation training has been successfully used to teach personal competence in managing provocations and regulating anger in individuals who have problems in controlling anger and in experiments on pain tolerance. There are reports of success in other clinical situations. Meichenbaum, however, is cautious in his claims for its effectiveness: "[T]he evidence for the efficacy of stress-inoculation is encouraging but not proven. The data on the full usefulness of the procedure have yet to be obtained. The stress-inoculation procedure is not offered as a panacea nor a replacement for other treatment approaches" (Meichenbaum, 1977, p. 181). It offers promise as a preventive measure with high-risk populations.

> An explicit training program that would teach coping skills and then provide application training in handling a variety of stressors is in marked contrast to the haphazard and chance manner in which people now learn to cope with stress. The research on stress seems to indicate the necessary skills required to cope, and the method of cognitive-behavior modification seems to provide a promising means for teaching such skills. (Meichenbaum, 1977, p. 182)

Cognitive-Restructuring Techniques

There are a variety of therapeutic methods subsumed under the names *cognitive-restructuring therapy* or *semantic therapy*. They focus on modifying the client's thinking and reasoning—the premises, assumptions (beliefs), and attitudes underlying his or her cognitions. Mental illness is viewed as a disorder of thinking that involves distorted thought processes leading to distorted views of the world, unpleasant emotions, and behavioral difficulties. These methods constitute what is often called "insight-oriented therapy." Actually, the diversity of methods is so great that they do not constitute a single therapy but, rather, differing therapies. Although they are concerned with clients' cognitions, different therapists conceptualize their clients' cognitions differently, leading to different treatment techniques.

Cognitions as Instances of Irrational Belief Systems. Ellis's rational-emotive therapy falls under the category of restructuring therapy. The basic irrational belief is that a person's self-worth is determined by others. The semantic therapist attempts to get clients to realize that their maladaptive behaviors and emotional disturbances are possibly related to or determined by what they say to themselves, although they may not be aware of what they are saying. Once clients accept this conceptualization (of the therapist), they are ready for any of a number of therapeutic approaches of a cognitive-restructuring nature. Ellis forcefully attempts to change the clients' beliefs.

Although leading clients to view their behavior from Ellis's conceptualization may result in change, the existence of self-negating beliefs is not necessarily the difference between clients and nonclients. Many, if not most, normal people may hold the same beliefs.

Rather, it may be that they differ in what they say to themselves about the irrational beliefs or in what mechanisms they employ in order to cope. Normal people "may be more capable of 'compartmentalizing' such events and be more able to use coping techniques such as humor, rationality, or what I have come to call 'creative repression'" (Meichenbaum, 1977, p. 191). Thus, other treatment techniques, such as self-instructional methods, may be useful.

Cognitions as Instances of Faulty Thinking Styles.   A second cognitive-restructuring approach is that of Beck (1976), whose focus is on clients' distorted thought patterns. Distortions include faulty inferences not supported by evidence; exaggeration of the significance of an event; cognitive deficiency, or disregard for an important element in a situation; dichotomous reasoning, or seeing things as either black or white (good or bad, right or wrong, with no in-betweens); and overgeneralization from a single incident. Clients are taught to identify these distortions through semantic and behavioral techniques. The therapist then challenges the "silent assumptions" underlying clients' attitudes and conceptions by demonstrating the clients' unrealistic interpretations of their experiences. The client then collaborates with the therapist in observing and analyzing his or her own experiences.

Cognitions as Instances of Problem-Solving Ability and Coping Skills.   An alternative cognitive-structuring approach is that of D'Zurilla and Goldfried (1971), among others (e.g., Goldfried & Davison, 1976). The focus is on identifying the *absence* of specific adaptive, cognitive skills and responses and on teaching clients problem-solving skills—how to identify problems, generate possible solutions, tentatively select one solution, and then test and verify its efficacy. Other therapists, including Meichenbaum, focus on coping skills. In problem solving, clients are taught how to face and solve future problem situations. Coping skills are taught in the actual crisis or problem situations.

These cognitive-restructuring methods differ in a number of ways, including the emphasis on formal logical analysis, the prescriptiveness of the treatment, and the relative use of adjunctive behavior therapy procedures. The cognitive-behavior therapist faces a dilemma in choosing among them and numerous other cognitive techniques. The result could be a technical eclecticism or a trial-and-error clinical approach and a preoccupation with "engineering" questions, such as which treatment, by whom, is most effective with what clients, with what specific problems, in what situations. More important are the questions of how and why change comes about. The answers to these questions require a theory of behavior change. Meichenbaum's theory attempts to provide a beginning toward such a theory.

SUMMARY AND EVALUATION

Summary.   Meichenbaum's cognitive-behavior modification is not simply behavior therapy with the addition of some cognitive techniques, as are the methods of a number of behavior therapists who have recognized the usefulness of cognitive techniques (for example, Goldfried & Davison, 1976, and O'Leary & Wilson, 1975). It is much more cognitive than behavioristic. Behavior therapy techniques include many cognitive elements. The "learning theory" on which behavior therapy is based is not adequate to account for the cognitive aspect of behavior therapy.

Meichenbaum has attempted to develop a theory- and research-based cognitive therapy. It recognizes the importance of what people say to themselves in determining their behavior. Thus, the focus of therapy is on changing the things clients say to themselves, implicitly if not explicitly, which lead to ineffective behavior and emotional disturbance. Therapy becomes training in modifying clients' self-instructions so that clients can cope with the problem situations they face. In addition to their independent use, these training methods can be incorporated into the standard behavior therapy techniques to increase the effectiveness of these techniques. They can also be incorporated into cognitive-restructuring techniques.

Evaluation.   Both the theory and practice are incomplete, as Meichenbaum recognizes. However, they continue to evolve, now incorporating information-processing and constructivist perspectives (Meichenbaum, 1992, 1993). His claim that the theory applies to all behavior change in any therapeutic procedure (Meichenbaum, 1977) may be true, in the sense that self-instruction is *part* of what goes on in all successful therapy. Other theories emphasize the importance of the client's self-exploration, which includes or involves an internal dialogue. Questions arise about the best way to facilitate this process in the client. Is it necessary or more efficient to teach the client directly? Is didactic instruction necessary for or the most effective way to achieve client learning? Is the client's failure to think logically or rationally always because of a lack of understanding of the nature of reasoning, logic, or problem solving? Is the most effective way to change the client's self-statements through teaching?

Teaching does not always lead to learning, and learning can occur without teaching. Learning by means of self-exploration and self-discovery may be more effective and more persistent than learning as a result of being taught, although it may not always be as rapid. If the client lacks necessary information or skills, certainly the client should acquire them; if this is all that is lacking, perhaps the client does not need therapy, and if this is not all that is lacking, perhaps the client can acquire them from persons other than the therapist. The issue is, then, is therapy teaching, even though it involves learning? Even if cognitive therapy is defined as teaching, is teaching a purely cognitive process?

Meichenbaum does not explore the nature and conditions of learning. He does appear to recognize that not all clients require explicit teaching of coping responses (Meichenbaum, 1977, p. 219), but his theory and practice appear to assume that all clients do. Affective factors are not dealt with adequately; his only explicit reference to affect is when he notes that in the process of giving oneself new self-instructions, the client must engage in meaningful and not simply mechanical self-instructions; nor does he consider the relationship between client and therapist in other than its cognitive, teaching aspect. However, in more recent publications, Meichenbaum (1992, 1993) does assign much importance to both affect and the therapeutic relationship for the treatment process. Indeed, it appears that these elements are now being increasingly accorded a far more significant place in cognitive-behavior therapy (e.g., Safran & Segal, 1990), and Meichenbaum's thinking seems to reflect that shift as well.

Ellis (1978), in his review of Meichenbaum's book, takes him to task for not having adequately indicated "how cognitive, emotive, and behavioral approaches to psychotherapy significantly interact and have profound reciprocal effects on each other." It might be noted, however, that it was not Meichenbaum's purpose to attempt this kind of integration.

Nevertheless, Meichenbaum has made a contribution. He has given theoretical support for the importance of internal dialogue in behavior and behavior change. He has gone beyond behavior therapy, not simply by adding a few cognitive techniques to behavior therapy but by providing a broader theory that can encompass behavior therapy and make it possible for those who have clung to a narrow behavior therapy because of its "learning theory" and research base to abandon it for a broader theory.

But is this theory base in turn supported by a research base? While Meichenbaum's 1977 book mentions supportive research of cognitive behavior modification up through the mid-1970s, how well has research on his approach fared since then? From our observations, research on Meichenbaum's approach has focused on two areas: (a) self-instructional training (SIT); and (b) stress-inoculation training (STI). With regard to SIT, Salovey and Singer (1991) stated that, "the efficacy of this approach is well documented, especially for dealing with conduct disordered children (Kendall & Wilcox, 1980), learning disabled children (Harris, 1986; Harris & Graham, 1985), mentally retarded children (Whitman, Burgio, & Johnston, 1984)" (p. 374). Some support for their assertion can be found in other reviews but some qualifying statements have been offered as well (e.g., Hollon & Beck, 1986, 1994; Meyers & Craighead, 1984). For example, Hollon and Najavits (1988) pointed out that while "Meichenbaum's self-instructional training appears to be effective in modifying impulsive behavior patterns in children, . . . the generalizability and full clinical significance of these findings remain unclear" (p. 658). Meichenbaum (1986) himself even said that while "the results of [cognitive-behavior modification] interventions are most encouraging, . . . demonstrations of long-term improvements that generalize across settings have *not* yet been forthcoming: (p. 355) (cf. Ollendick, 1986). With those qualifying points acknowledged, it also seems worth saying that research on SIT, comparatively speaking, "is far less conclusive" with adult disorders (Hollon & Najavits, 1988).

With regard to STI, Salovey and Singer (1991) said that its efficacy "has been reported in recent studies concerning the treatment of social anxiety (Emmelkamp, Mersch, Vissia, & van der Helm, 1985; Jerremalm, Jansonn, & Ost, 1986), chronic pain (Turk et al., 1983), and writer's block. . . , to name just a few" (p. 373). Research reviews have supported the efficacy or promise of STI with helping patients deal with anger and aggression and in helping patients with some behavioral medicine concerns (e.g., pain) (Hollon & Beck, 1986, 1994; Hollon & Najavits, 1988). But as with SIT, "the results [of STI] are far less conclusive with other disorders in adults" (Hollon & Najavits, 1988, p. 658). It remains, then, for STI to prove itself as an effective treatment across disorders and patient populations.

To conclude, what could be said about the future of Meichenbaum's approach? Meichenbaum has said that he sees the need "for cognitive principles to be incorporated into education, to teach children to self-regulate and treat themselves humanely" (Arnkoff & Glass, 1992, p. 670). Perhaps that is one direction in which his cognitive-behavior modification will move. We also suspect, with the empirical interest that continues to be shown in both STI and SIT, that more sophisticated, rigorous research into those interventions will be forthcoming, that more clear answers about the efficacy of those interventions will be forthcoming, and that more efforts to apply those interventions to more problems and patient populations will be forthcoming as well. Should these directions be realized, we should be able to get a much better picture on the applicability, generalizability, and efficacy of the cognitive-behavior modification approach to psychotherapy.

REFERENCES

Arnkoff, D. B., & Glass, C. R. (1992). Cognitive therapy and psychotherapy integration. In D. K. Freedheim (Ed.). *History of psychotherapy* (pp. 657–694). Washington, DC: American Psychological Association.

Bandura, A. (1969). *Principles of behavior modification.* New York: Holt, Rinehart and Winston.

Beck, A. T. (1976). *Cognitive therapy and the emotional disorders.* New York: International Universities Press.

Bowers, K., & Meichenbaum, D. (1984). *The unconscious reconsidered.* New York: Wiley.

D'Zurilla, T., & Goldfried, M. R. (1971). Problem solving and behavior modification. *Journal of Abnormal Psychology, 78,* 107–126.

Ellis, A. (1978). Review of *Cognitive-behavior modification: An integrative approach* by D. Meichenbaum. *Contemporary Psychology, 23,* 736–737.

Emmelkamp, P. M. G., Mersch, P. P., Vissia, E., & van der Helm, M. (1985). Social phobia: A comparative evaluation of cognitive and behavioral interventions. *Behaviour Research and Therapy, 23,* 365–369.

Farber, I. E. (1963). The things people say to themselves. *American Psychologist, 18,* 185–197.

Gagne, R. (1964). Problem solving. In A. Melton (Ed.). *Categories of human learning.* New York: Academic Press.

Gilbert, W. M. (1968). Discussion. In J. M. Whiteley (Ed.). *Research in counseling,* (pp. 30–35). Columbus, OH: Merrill.

Goldfried, M. R., & Davison, G. C. (1976). *Clinical behavior therapy.* New York: Holt, Rinehart and Winston.

Harris, K. R. (1986). The effects of cognitive-behavior modification on private speech and task performance during problem-solving among learning disabled and normally-achieving children. *Journal of Abnormal Child Psychology, 14,* 63–67.

Harris, K. R., & Graham, S. (1985). Improving learning disabled students' composition skills: Self-control strategy training. *Learning Disabilities Quarterly, 8,* 27–36.

Hollon, S. D., & Beck, A. T. (1986). Cognitive and cognitive-behavioral therapies. In S. L. Garfield & A. E. Bergin (Eds.). *Handbook of psychotherapy and behavior change* (3rd ed., pp. 443–482). New York: Wiley.

Hollon, S. D., & Beck, A. T. (1994). Cognitive and cognitive-behavioral therapies. In A. E. Bergin & S. L. Garfield (Eds.). *Handbook of psychotherapy and behavior change* (4th ed., pp. 428–466). New York: Wiley.

Hollon, S. D., & Najavits, L. (1988). Review of empirical studies of cognitive therapy. In A. J. Frances & R. E. Hales (Eds.). *American Psychiatric Press review of psychiatry* (vol. 7, pp. 643–666). Washington, DC: American Psychiatric Press.

Jerremalm, A., Jansson, L., & Ost, L. G. (1986). Cognitive and physiological reactivity and the effects of different behavioral methods in the treatment of social phobia. *Behaviour Research and Therapy, 24,* 171–180.

Kendall, P. C., & Wilcox, L. E. (1980). A cognitive-behavioral treatment for impulsivity: Concrete vs. conceptual training in non-self-controlled problem children. *Journal of Consulting and Clincial Psychology, 48,* 80–91.

Luria, A. (1961). *The role of speech in the regulation of normal and abnormal behavior.* New York: Pergamon Press.

McKinney, J. A. (1973). *A developmental study of the effects of hypothesis verbalizations and memory load on concept attainment.* Unpublished manuscript, University of North Carolina, Chapel Hill.

Meichenbaum, D. (1974). *Cognitive-behavior modification.* Morristown, NJ: General Learning Press. (A unit in University Programs Modular Studies series.)

Meichenbaum, D. (1977). *Cognitive-behavior modification: An integrative approach.* New York: Plenum.

Meichenbaum. D. (1985). *Stress inoculation training.* Elmsford, NY: Pergamon.

Meichenbaum, D. (1986). Cognitive-behavior modification. In F. H. Kanfer & A. P. Goldstein (Eds.). *Helping people change: A textbook of methods* (pp. 346–380). Elmsford, NY: Pergamon Press.

Meichenbaum, D. (1992). Evolution of cognitive behavior therapy: Origins, tenets, and clinical examples. In J. K. Zeig (Ed.). *The evolution of psychotherapy: The second conference* (pp. 114–127). New York: Brunner/Mazel.

Meichenbaum, D. (1993). Changing conceptions of cognitive behavior modification: Retrospect and prospect. *Journal of Consulting and Clinical Psychology, 61,* 202–204.

Meichenbaum, D., & Jaremko, M. (1983). *Stress reduction and prevention.* New York: Plenum.

Meichenbaum, D., & Turk, D. C. (1987). *Facilitating treatment adherence:* A practitioner's guide. New York: Plenum.

Meyers, A. W., & Craighead, W. E. (1984). *Cognitive behavior therapy with children.* New York: Plenum.

Murray, E. J., & Jacobson, L. I. (1971). The nature of learning in traditional and behavioral psychotherapy. In A. E. Bergin & S. L. Garfield (Eds.). *Handbook of psychotherapy and behavior change: An empirical analysis* (pp. 709–747). New York: Wiley.

Neisser, U. (1962). Cultural and cognitive discontinuity. In J. E. Gladwin & W. Sturtevant (Eds.). *Anthropology and human behavior.* Washington, DC: Anthropological Society of Washington.

O'Leary, K. D., & Wilson, G. T. (1975). *Behavior therapy: Application and outcome.* Englewood Cliffs, NJ: Prentice-Hall.

Ollendick, T. H. (1986). Child and adolescent behavior therapy. In S. L. Garfield & A. E. Bergin (Eds.). *Handbook of psychotherapy and behavior change* (3rd ed., pp. 525–564). New York: Wiley.

Peterson, D. (1968). *The clinical study of social behavior.* Englewood Cliffs, NJ: Prentice-Hall.

Paiget, J. (1954). *The construction of reality.* New York: Basic Books.

Safran, J., & Segal, Z. (1990). *Interpersonal processes in cognitive therapy.* New York: Basic Books.

Salovey, P., & Singer, J. A. (1991). Cognitive-behavior modification. In F. H. Kanfer & A. P. Goldstein (Eds.). *Helping people change: A textbook of methods* (4th ed., pp. 360–395). New York: Pergamon.

Turk, D. C., Meichenbaum, D., & Genest, M. (1983). *Pain and behavioral medicine.* New York: Guilford.

Vygotsky, L. S. (1962). *Thought and language.* Cambridge, MA: M.I.T. Press.

Whitman, T., Burgio, L., & Johnston, M. B. (1984). Cognitive-behavioral intervention with mentally retarded children. In A. W. Meyers & W. E. Craighead (Eds.). *Cognitive behavior therapy with children* (pp. 193–227). New York: Plenum Press.

Wolpe, J. (1990). *The practice of behavior therapy* (4th ed). New York: Pergamon.

part four

PERCEPTUAL-PHENOMENOLOGICAL APPROACHES

A number of approaches to psychotherapy, although differing in many significant respects, have in common a major concern with the perceptions or perceptual field of the individual client. These approaches assume, explicitly or implicitly, that since behavior is determined by the individual's perceptual field, a change in the perceptual field is necessary before behavior will change. Differences occur in the methods employed to achieve such change.

George Kelly's (1955; see also 1991 reissue) psychology of personal constructs is a perceptual-phenomenological theory. Personal constructs are perceptions, and changing personal constructs thus involves changing perceptions. Kelly's methods are rational or cognitive, which is probably the reason why he did not identify himself as a phenomenologist.

Another perceptual approach in psychology is labeled "transactional" by those associated with its evolution (Cantril, Ames, Hastorf, & Ittelson, 1949; Ittelson, 1952; Kilpatrick, 1952, 1961). It applies to the treatment of events as processes in time and environment. A segment of time in this process is labeled a "transaction" and includes, in the case of human beings, the individual organism and his/her environment. Activities of human beings cannot be treated as theirs alone or even as primarily theirs, but must be seen as processes of the interaction of the organism and its environment; that is, neither one exists or can be understood without the other.

Transaction is defined by English and English (1958) as "a psychological event in which all the parts or aspects of the concrete event derive their existence and nature from active participation in the event" (p. 561). In this respect, the transactional view differs from the concept of interaction, with which it is sometimes confused (see Kanfer, 1962). The concept of interaction implies two separate or independently existing objects that interact with each other without being changed by the interaction. In a transaction, both are changed by the process.

It appears that the transactional point of view has been adapted and used, at least to some extent, by many who did not use the term itself. These include George H. Mead, Kurt Goldstein, Gordon and Floyd Allport, Gardner Murphy, Prescott Lecky, and C. R. Rogers. Thus, there is perhaps some point to Levitt's (1962) comment that "transactionalism is a somewhat fancy label applied to a viewpoint which is far from new" (pp. 255–256). It is a point of view that is implicit in much of the research and writing on perception as well as on phenomenological psychology.

Two approaches in psychotherapy have adopted the term *transactional.* One was presented in *Psychiatric Social Work: A Transactional Case Book,* by Grinker, MacGregor, Selan, Klein, and Korman (1961). Their approach was included in the first two editions of this book. It did not seem to be generally or widely accepted or applied and has been omitted from this book.

In the same year that *Psychiatric Social Work* was published, Berne's (1961) first book-length publication on transactional analysis appeared. It was followed by other publications, including two that were published after his death in 1970, and an edited book of selections from his writings. Berne's work was independent of that of Grinker and his associates, and both were apparently independent of the development of transactional psychology. In the foreword to his book on group treatment, Berne (1964) notes the differing origins and nature of the approaches. Berne's transactional analysis developed out of and has been applied mainly in group situations, which was the main reason his approach was not included in the earlier editions of this book. It has relevance for individual psychotherapy, however, and has gained a wide popularity. A summary of Berne's work, then, is included here in order to supplement—or even counteract—the popularized versions.

Another popular perceptual or phenomenological approach to psychotherapy is Gestalt therapy. Its development is associated with Frederick (Fritz) Perls, whose 1947 book (republished in 1969) was followed by a book in collaboration with Ralph Hefferline and Paul Goodman in 1951 (republished in 1965) and by other books, including two published after his death in 1970. As has been the case with transactional analysis, numerous publications dealing with Gestalt therapy have appeared since Perls's death. However, the presentation here is based primarily on Perls's original writings.

Client-centered therapy is perhaps the first major approach to psychotherapy that is explicitly based on phenomenological psychology and explicitly concerned with the most effective or appropriate methods for changing the perceptions of clients. One of the sources for misconceptions of client-centered therapy is the lack of an adequate understanding of its phenomenological foundations. While Rogers (1951) does deal with this, he does not elaborate on it. The student should be familiar with phenomenological psychology as a basis for understanding client-centered therapy. A systematic treatment will be found in Combs, Richards, and Richards (1975). Although a number of writers have presented the client-centered approach, Rogers was its originator and, until his death, its chief exponent. Some of the newer developments of the approach have been included in Chapter 13 in this edition.

It might be noted that Ellis's rational-emotive approach (Chapter 7) is basically phenomenological. However, its rational elements dominate, even in the phenomenological view of behavior as determined by (irrational) beliefs.

Finally, all the perceptual approaches have existential elements, as their proponents recognize. However, these elements are subordinate and not systematically developed, so the perceptual approaches cannot be classified as existential therapies.

REFERENCES

Berne, E. (1961). *Transactional analysis in psychotherapy.* New York: Grove Press.

Berne, E. (1964). *Principles of group treatment.* New York: Oxford University Press.

Cantril, H., Ames, A., Jr., Hastorf, A. H., & Ittelson, W. H. (1949). Psychology and scientific research. *Science 110,* 461–464.

Combs, A. W., Richards, A. C., & Richards, F. (1975). *Perceptual psychology: A humanistic approach to the study of persons.* New York: Harper & Row.

English, H. B., & English, A. C. (1958). *A comprehensive dictionary of psychological and psychoanalytic terms.* New York: McKay.

Grinker, R. R., Sr., MacGregor, H., Selan, K., Klein, A., & Korman, J. (1961). *Psychiatric social work: A transactional casebook.* New York: Basic Books.

Ittelson, W. H. (1952). *The Ames demonstrations in perception.* Princeton, NJ: Princeton University Press.

Kanfer, F. H. (1962). Review of *Psychiatric social work: A transactional casebook* by R. R. Grinker, Sr., H. MacGregor, K. Selan, A. Klein, & J. Korman. *Contemporary Psychology, 7,* 295–296.

Kilpatrick, F. P. (Ed.). (1952). *Human behavior from the transactional point of view.* Hanover, NH: Institute for Associated Research.

Kilpatrick, F. P. (1961). *Explorations in transactional psychology.* New York: New York University Press.

Levitt, E. L. (1962). Review of *Perceptual changes in psychopathology* edited by W. H. Ittelson & S. B. Kutash. *Contemporary Psychology, 7,* 255–256.

Kelly, G. A. (1955). *The psychology of personal constructs.* Vol. 1: *A theory of personality.* Vol. 2: *Clinical diagnosis and psychotherapy.* New York: Norton. (Reissued 1991 by Routledge).

Perls, F. S. (1947). *Ego, hunger and aggression.* New York: Random House. (Republished in 1969).

Perls, F. S., Hefferline, R. F., & Goodman, P. (1951). *Gestalt therapy.* New York: Julian Press. (Paperback published 1965 by Dell).

Rogers, C. R. (1951). *Client-centered therapy.* Boston: Houghton Mifflin.

chapter 10

Psychology of Personal Constructs and Psychotherapy: Kelly

One of the most systematic approaches to psychotherapy is that developed by George A. Kelly on the basis of his psychology of personal constructs. Kelly (1905–1967) received his B.A. in 1926 at Park College, his M.A. at the University of Kansas in 1928, his B.Ed. in 1930 from the University of Edinburgh, and his Ph.D. from the State University of Iowa in 1931. Although his Ph.D. was in psychology, his earlier work included study in education, sociology, economics, labor relations, speech pathology, biometrics, and cultural anthropology. In 1931, he became an instructor at Fort Hays State College in Kansas and was an associate professor when he entered the navy for two years in 1943. He was an associate professor at the University of Maryland during 1945 and 1946. In 1946, he became professor of psychology at Ohio State University and served as director of the psychological clinic from 1946 to 1951 and in 1963, while continuing as professor of psychology until 1965. He then became professor of psychology at Brandeis University, where he remained until his death in 1967.

Kelly was a Diplomate in Clinical Psychology of the American Board of Professional Psychology. He served as president of the American Psychological Association's Division of Clinical Psychology and Division of Consulting Psychology. In 1969, Maher published a collection of Kelly's papers under the title *Clinical Psychology and Personality*. One of the papers in this book, "The Autobiography of a Theory," is a personal account of the development of the theory of personal constructs, beginning with Kelly's repudiation of stimulus-response determinism, through a Freudian period, to the present- and future-oriented view of constructive alternativism. A memoriam article about Kelly appeared in a 1990 issue of *History of Psychology* (Niemeyer, 1990).

BACKGROUND AND DEVELOPMENT

The Psychology of Personal Constructs (Kelly, 1955) began, Kelly reports, as a handbook of clinical procedures compiled 20 years before its publication as a two-volume work. The "how-to" approach was not satisfying, however, and he began to explore the "why." Kelly then discovered that the result he obtained was far different from traditional psychology. Many implicit assumptions were recognized, and this led to a third approach, that of system building, which required the development of explicit assumptions and the expression of convictions that had been taken for granted in clinical practice. The first task, then, was the construction of a theory of personality, followed by the development of its implications for psychological practice.

The resulting system differs from the familiar psychological systems. Far from occupying the central place, as it does in most contemporary systems, the term *learning* hardly appears. Concepts such as ego, emotion, motivation, reinforcement, drive, need, and unconscious do not appear. Instead, such concepts as foci of convenience, preemption, propositionality, fixed-role therapy, creativity cycle, transitive diagnosis, and the credulous approach are encountered. Other common concepts, such as anxiety, guilt, and hostility, carry new definitions. The result is an unorthodox theory of personality and of therapy.

PHILOSOPHY AND CONCEPTS

Philosophy of Constructive Alternativism

Points of Departure.   Two simple notions underlie Kelly's theory of personality. One is that human beings are better understood when they are viewed in the perspective of centuries; the other is "that each man contemplates in his own personal way the stream of events upon which he finds himself so swiftly borne" (Kelly, 1955, vol. 1, p. 3). Within these notions, there is the possibility of discovering ways in which individuals can restructure their lives. The long-range view focuses attention on humanity's progress and on *scientists,* seeking to predict and control the causes of events in which they are involved. Thus, human motivation is seen in a new light, instead of in terms of appetites, needs, and impulses.

Humanity exists in a real universe, which it is gradually coming to understand. Thoughts also really exist, but the correspondence between what people think exists and what really exists is imperfect, although it is in a constant state of change. The universe is integral, with all its parts having exact relationships to one another, but it is constantly changing, so that there is a dimension of time that must be considered. While some aspects of the universe make sense without the time dimension, life makes sense only when it is viewed in the perspective of time.

Life has the capacity to represent other forms of reality or to represent its environment, and can place alternative constructions on the environment; thus, it does more than respond to its environment. The individual may misrepresent the real phenomenon, but the misrepresentation will itself be real; "what he perceives may not exist, but his perception does" (Kelly, 1955, p. 8). Human beings look at the world through patterns, which are ways of construing the world, or *constructs.* Although people seek to improve their constructs by increasing their repertory, in order to provide a better fit between perceptions and the real environment, the larger system of which their constructs are a part may resist change because of their personal investment in or dependence on it.

Construction systems that can be communicated can be shared, and progress in such communication has been great. Systems may be designed to fit special fields or realms—for example, those of psychology and physiology—but realms may overlap or may give rise to alternative systems or ways of representing or viewing the same facts, as is the case with psychology and physiology. There is no universal system of constructs. All our systems are miniature systems with limited ranges. The system of personal constructs is limited to human personality and problems of interpersonal relationships. Systems have centers or points at which they work best. The theory of personal constructs tends to focus on the area of human readjustment to stress and thus proves to be most useful to the psychotherapist.

Constructs are used to predict events. They are thus tested in terms of their predictive efficiency. A construct may appear to be validated by events that are misrepresented because of the need to validate it. Constructs are more susceptible to revision when they are immediately tested on an experimental basis. The continuing course of events reveals constructs either as usefully valid or as misleading, and thus provides the basis for revision of constructs and construction systems. Some people are afraid to express and test their constructs; this is a problem in psychotherapy.

Philosophical Position.   The world may be construed in various ways. Interpretations constitute successive approximations of an absolute construction. *Constructive alternativism* assumes

> that all of our present interpretations of the universe are subject to revision or replacement. . . . We take the stand that there are always some alternative constructions available to choose among in dealing with the world. No one needs to paint himself into a corner; no one needs to be completely hemmed in by circumstances, no one needs to be the victim of his biography. (Kelly, 1955, p. 15)

Some alternatives are better than others; some lead to difficulty. The criterion is the specific predictive efficiency of each and of the system of which it could become a part.

Constructs are not necessarily symbolized by words, nor are they always capable of being verbalized; the concept as such may seem to be psychological rather than philosophical. Constructive alternativism is a philosophical point of view rather than a philosophical system. It bears some relation to various philosophical systems, however, falling within the area of epistemology called *gnoseology* (i.e., the nature of knowledge). It also relies on *empiricism* and *pragmatic* logic, although it is in a measure *rationalistic* and stands apart from traditional realism, which makes human beings victims of circumstances.

The notion of an integral universe implies determinism. However, since there is no repetition and each sequence of events is unique, "there is not much point in singling it out and saying that it was determined. It was a consequence—but only once!" (*ibid.*, p. 21). The sort of determinism that is important here is the control exercised by a superordinate construct over its elements. The elements do not determine the construct, which is thus free from or independent of them.

Determinism and freedom are then inseparable, for that which determines another is, by the same token, free of the other. Determinism and freedom are opposite sides of the same coin—two aspects of the same relationship. [Thus the individual,] to the extent that he is able to construe his circumstances, can find for himself freedom from their domination.... Theories are the thinking of men who seek freedom amid swirling events. The theories comprise prior assumptions about certain realms of these events. To the extent that the events may, from these prior assumptions, be construed, predicted, and their relative courses charted, men may exercise control, and gain freedom for themselves in the process. (Kelly, 1955, pp. 21–22)

For individuals whose constructs limit and restrict them, the theory of personal constructs is concerned with finding ways to help them reconstrue their lives in order to keep themselves from being victims of their past.

Basic Theory

Fundamental Postulate. A person's processes are psychologically channeled by the ways in which the person anticipates events. As a postulate, this assumption is not subject to question. It is accepted as a presupposition. The term *processes* indicates that the person is a behaving organism, so that it is not necessary to account for or establish the existence of some sort of mental energy. *Channeled* refers to a network of pathways, flexible but structured, that both facilitates and restricts a person's range of action. *Anticipates* indicates the predictive and motivational features, which point toward the future. "Anticipation is both the push and pull of personal constructs" (*ibid.,* p. 49). The psychology of personal constructs develops from this postulate through corollaries that in part follow from and in part elaborate it.

Construction Corollary. A person anticipates events by construing their replications. This means that events are predicted by placing an interpretation on or structuring the recurring aspects of events. Construing is not identical with verbal formulation; it may not necessarily be symbolized.

Individuality Corollary. Persons differ from one another in their construction of events. This is because no two persons participate in the same event in the same way.

Organization Corollary. Each person characteristically evolves, for convenience in anticipating events, a construction system that embraces ordinal relationships among constructs. A system of constructs minimizes incompatibilities and inconsistencies and involves a hierarchy of constructs, with some being superordinal and others, subordinal. An individual's system sometimes needs revision, but the individual may choose to conserve its integrity. While this appears to be similar to Lecky's (1945) concept of the need for self-consistency, it is not for consistency itself that the individual is seeking to preserve the system, but because the system is essential for an anticipation of events.

Dichotomy Corollary. A person's construction system is composed of a finite number of dichotomous constructs. Similarities and contrasts, which constitute replication, are in terms of the same aspect; that is, if we select an aspect in which A and B are similar but are different from C, this same aspect is the basis of the construct. "In its minimum context a construct is a way in which at least two elements are similar and contrast with a third" (Kelly, 1955, p. 61). Concepts are meaningless except in relation to or in comparison with their contrasts, opposites, or complements; for example, *good* has no meaning except in comparison with *bad.*

Choice Corollary.   A person chooses the alternative in a dichotomized construct through which he or she anticipates the greater possibility for extension and definition of a system. Choice consists of placing relative values on the alternatives of the dichotomies. Extension and definition include both elaboration, or comprehensiveness, and explicitness, or clarity. While the choices might be said to constitute "a seeking of self-protection" or "acting in defense of the self" or "the preservation of one's integrity . . . from our point of view a person's construction system is for the anticipation of events. If it were for something else, it would probably shape up into something quite different" (*ibid.,* p. 67). The individual does not seek pleasure, satisfactions, or rewards to satisfy needs or reduce tensions but seeks to anticipate events; "there is a continuing movement toward the anticipation of events, rather than a series of barters for temporal satisfactions, and this movement is the essence of human life itself" (*ibid.,* p. 69).

Range Corollary.   A construct is convenient for the anticipation of a finite range of events only. Constructs are limited and are applicable only with a restricted range of the perceptual field. Some persons use a construct more comprehensively than do others.

Experience Corollary.   A person's construction system varies as he or she successively construes the replication of events. Events subject a person's construct system to a validation process, which leads to revision of the system or to a reconstruing of events and a reconstruction of life through experience. Learning is inherent in this corollary and is thus a part of the assumptive structure of the theory; it is not a special class of psychological processes but is synonymous with any and all processes.

Modulation Corollary.   The variation in a person's construction system is limited by the permeability of the constructs within whose range of convenience the variants lie. *Permeability* is the admitting of new, as yet unconstrued, elements. Variants are the old and the new constructs. Change thus occurs within a system in which superordinate constructs admit new constructs to its context.

Fragmentation Corollary.   A person may successively employ a variety of construction subsystems that are inferentially incompatible with one another. Successive inconsistency between subsystems may be tolerated within a larger system. Successive formulations may not be derivable from each other; new constructs are not necessarily direct derivatives of old constructs but are derivatives of the larger system.

Commonality Corollary.   To the extent that one person employs a construction of experience that is similar to that employed by another, his or her psychological processes are similar to those of the other person. It is not the experiencing of the same events or stimuli but the placing of the same construction on events (which may be phenomenally dissimilar) that results in similar psychological processes. Identity of construction or processes is impossible, phenomenologically speaking.

Sociality Corollary.   To the extent that one person construes the construction process of another, the person may play a role in a social process involving the other person. This is more than seeing things as another does; it is also seeing the other's way of seeing, or outlook, for some measure of acceptance of that person, and his or her way of seeing things. This is a basis for playing a constructive role in relation to her or him. Construing what others are thinking enables us to predict what they will do. While commonality may make the understanding of another's construction system more likely, it is not essential.

Nature of Personal Constructs

Personal Usage of Constructs.   "A construct is a way in which some things are construed as being alike and yet different from others" (*ibid.,* p. 105). The contrast is included in the construct rather than considered irrelevant or as another concept, as it is in conventional logic. It differs in this respect from a concept. It includes not only the abstraction element of a concept, but also percepts. The dichotomy represents an aspect of all human thinking.

The individual is unable to express the whole of his or her construction system and may misconstrue what the construction of a situation will be in the future. The individual may not be able to express certain constructs in a way in which others can understand them or subsume them under their own systems without predicting the individual's behavior incorrectly. The individual may express constructs incompletely, omitting the contrast, by saying, for example, "Mary is gentle." To say that Mary is gentle implies that at least one other person is gentle and one other is not gentle or that at least two other persons are not gentle, since the minimum context for a construct is three things. Any other statement is illogical and unpsychological. To say that everyone is gentle, for example, has no meaning. Since constructs are primarily personal, they may not be easily understood by others. Thus, there are a number of conditions that may make it appear that a person does not mean what he or she says.

Constructs abstract repeated properties of events and imply that the replicated properties may reappear in another event. Prediction is therefore implicit in construing. It is not a specific event that is predicted but its properties intersecting in a prescribed way. The prediction is validated only when an event occurs that can be construed in the same way as the intersection.

Constructs provide the means of binding or grouping events so that they become predictable, manageable, and controllable. A person controls his own destiny "to the extent that he can develop a construction system with which he identifies himself and which is sufficiently comprehensive to subsume the world around him. . . . According to this view, mankind is slowly learning to control his destiny, although it is a long and tedious process" (*ibid.,* p. 127).

The individual has a choice between the two ends or dichotomies of the constructs but is controlled by the network of the construction system. However, new constructs can be developed to expand his or her system. A construct, in effect, represents rival hypotheses, on either of which the person can act.

The self is a construct. The use of the self as a datum in forming constructs leads to constructs that operate as rigorous controls on behavior, particularly behavior in relation to or in comparison with other people. These comparisons as the individual construes them control his or her social life. "As one construes other people, he formulates the construction system which governs his own behavior" (*ibid.*, p. 133)—that is, we each define our own roles. A person's construct system is revealed when the person talks about others.

Formal Aspects of Constructs.   Symbolism allows one of the elements of a construct to represent the construct itself. Communication is, then, the reproduction of the symbolic element to elicit a parallel construct in another person. Words are useful as symbols but are not always effective. Figures, such as the mother or father, may symbolize constructs. This sort of symbolization is characteristic of children. Such figures give clarity and stability or rigidity to the construct.

Dimensions against which the constructs of others can be evaluated may be set up. A commonly used dimension is abstract versus concrete, but this does not seem to be particularly useful; permeability versus impermeability, already referred to, is a more useful dimension. A *preemptive construct* is one that preempts its elements exclusively for its own realm—a ball can be nothing but a ball. It is a pigeon-holing, or nothing-but, approach. A *constellatory construct* permits its elements to belong to other specified realms concurrently (e.g., a ball shares bouncing with other objects). A *propositional construct* leaves its elements open to construction and does not specify all the other realms to which it may belong (e.g., "any roundish mass may be considered, among other things, as a ball," p. 155). It is at the other end of the continuum for preemptive and constellatory constructs. There are also other dimensions, such as *anxiety, hostility, transference,* and *dependence,* which will be mentioned later.

Changing Construction.   Validation is the payoff of an anticipation or prediction. Validation is not reinforcement; it is much broader, for it may include such things as the breaking of one's leg after it has been anticipated. Failure of validation leads not only to changes of prediction, but also to a turning to another construct on which to base a prediction or to a revising of the construct system. The formation of new constructs is favored by certain conditions, which include approaching the constructs in contexts that do not involve the self or family members and providing a fresh set of elements as a context. This is what therapy does. Other conditions are an atmosphere of experimentation, in which propositional constructs are "tried on for size," and the availability of validating data—knowledge of the results. Results must be seen from the subject's, not the experimenter's, point of view, however.

The most important condition unfavorable for the formation of new constructs is *threat.* "A construct is threatening when it is itself an element in a next-higher-order construct which is, in turn, incompatible with other higher-order constructs upon which the person is dependent for his living" (*ibid.*, p. 166); for example, "the construct of danger is a *threat* when it becomes an element in the context of death or injury" (*ibid.*, p. 166). Such elements have been excluded from the person's construct system because they are incompatible and are seen as threats when they are presented as elements of a new construct and thus cannot be easily used.

> The effect of threat is to compel the client to claw frantically for his basic construct. Threat arouses the necessity for mobilizing one's resources. It should be borne in mind that the resources which are mobilized may not always be mature and effective. Therefore a threatened person may often behave in childish ways. Another effect of introducing threatening elements, and frequently an undesirablae one, is the tendency for the traumatic experience to act as further subjective documentation or proof of the client's own maladaptive conceptual framework. (Kelly, 1955, pp. 167–168)

A second unfavorable condition for the formation of new constructs is preoccupation with old material or old impermeablae constructs or old habits. A third condition is the lack of a laboratory in which to try out new constructs in a relatively controlled or protected situation.

Meaning of Experience.   Our experience is the portion of the world's happenings that happens to us. However, things happen to us personally only when we behave in relaton to them, when we construe them—not when we just react to them. People do not learn *from* experience; learning constitutes experience. Successive construing or reconstruing of happenings increases experience.

The psychology of personal constructs accepts the individual's experience as phenomenological but attempts

> to lift our data from the individual at a relatively high level of abstraction. This is a little like saying that we deal concretely with a person's abstractions rather than abstractly with his concretisms. Behaviorism, for example, did it the other way; it created elaborate public abstractions out of minute personal concretisms. (Kelly, 1955, p. 173)

The personal-construct therapist observes the client's constructs or abstractions of behavior and takes what is seen and heard at face value, including what is seen and heard about the subject's constructs. This is commonly called *acceptance;* it is the *credulous attitude.* The abstractions in the subject's system are the concrete elements awaiting construction in the therapist's system. "All of this means that we cannot consider the psychology of personal constructs a phenomenological theory, if that means ignoring the personal construction of the psychologist who does the observing" (*ibid.,* p. 174).

Personal-construct theory, like perceptual theories, takes an ahistorical approach, which is the view that since a person's activity at a given moment is determined by that person's outlook at that moment, the past influences behavior only through current perceptions. The basis of perception includes "nonconscious" as well as conscious processes. The historical method of study may be used to help reveal the successive patterning of the elements entering into a person's personal constructs.

Other people are important in the validation of a person's constructs. Their opinions may be validators of constructs about nonhuman events. In the case of constructs involving other people as elements, when another person fails to perform according to expectations, that person becomes threatening. The individual is affected in turn, and even though the individual may reject the expectancies of others, he or she construes oneself in relation to those expectancies.

Another aspect of validation by group expectancies involves the construction of a role. The term *role* applies to a course of activity played out in the light of a person's construction of one or more other persons' construct systems. Thus, in playing a role, the individual acts according to what he or she believes others think, so that the construction of a role must be validated in terms of the expectancies of these others. This last situation illustrates the characteristic approach of the personal-construct therapist, who seeks to establish a role in relation to other people. Personal-construct theory is essentially "role theory."

The culture influences the personal constructs of the individual, resulting in similarities among its members. The therapist must understand these cultural influences and must see the group constructs as elements on which the individual builds personal constructs. Thus, both the similarities and the differences among persons in a culture must be recognized.

Diagnostic Constructs.   The purpose of diagnostic constructs is to give clinicians a set of professional constructs under which personal constructs of their clients can be subsumed; this allows the clinician to assume a professionally useful role in relation to clients. These constructs are not disease entities, types of people, or traits; rather, they consist of a set of universal coordinate axes with respect to which it is possible to plot any person's behavior and the changes occurring in the person's psychological processes. They are not used to pigeonhole clients but to represent different lines of movement open to them. The tentative structuring of the client's experience record by the clinician is termed *structuralization*. *Construction* refers to the better organized formulation that arranges the client's behavior under his or her inferred personal constructs and then arranges them or subsumes them under the clinician's own systems. The phenomenologist's approach is used to arrive at the individual's personal constructs, and then the normative approach is used to put these together with what is known about other persons, thus bringing each client's systems into the public domain.

A good diagnostic construct should have the characteristics of other good constructs, which include propositionality (relative independence), dichotomy, permeability, definability (operational), temporality, futurity (prognostic), sociality, and the ability to generate hypotheses, particularly treatment hypotheses.

General Diagnostic Constructs

Preverbal Constructs.   A preverbal construct is one that the client continues to use even though it has no consistent word symbol. Words facilitate the utilization and modification of constructs, while other symbols are more cumbersome, since they impede communication and discussion. Preverbal constructs usually originate in infancy and often relate to the client's dependence. They may represent a kind of core of the construction system and may be overlaid by misleading verbalized constructs. Signs of preverbal constructs are confusion in verbalization, greater ability to illustrate the construct than to verbalize it, the appearance of the construct in dreams that are not remembered clearly, and the remembering of events that the client is not sure actually happened. Preverbal constructs cover in part the concept of the unconscious. (Other aspects of this concept are included in the constructs described below.) The failure of the client to construe things in the same way as the clinician should not be interpreted to mean that the client really does construe things in this way but is unaware of it. The client's later ability to construe things as the clinician does constitutes a new construction for her or him, not a revelation of the unconscious.

Submergence.   Submergence refers to the omission or avoidance of one of the ends of the dichotomous construct, usually the contrast end. Constructs that have one end submerged cannot be tested.

Suspension.   As constructs are revised, some elements drop out and others become more prominent. "When a structure is rejected, because at the moment it is incompatible with the over-all system which the person is using, we may say that it has undergone *suspension*" (p. 472). This is similar to forgetting, dissociation, and repression. What is unstructured is "forgotten" or "repressed."

Level of Cognitive Awareness.   The preceding three constructs involve low levels of cognitive awareness. A high-level construct is one that is readily expressible in socially effective symbols, has alternatives that are both readily accessible, falls well within the range of convenience of the client's major constructions, and is not suspended by its superordinating constructs.

Dilation and Constriction.   Dilation is the broadening of the perceptual field to organize it more comprehensively, following a series of alternating uses of incompatible systems. Constriction occurs when the individual narrows the perceptual field to minimize apparent incompatibilities in the system.

Comprehensive Constructs and Incidental Constructs.   Comprehensive constructs subsume a wide variety of events; they are not necessarily superordinate constructs, however. Incidental constructs subsume a small variety of events.

Superordinate Constructs and Subordinate Constructs.   A superordinate construct utilizes another construct as its contextual element; the construct so utilized is a subordinate construct.

Regnancy.   A superordinate construct that assigns each of its elements to a category on an all-or-none basis is a regnant construct. For example, if we were to say that all spades are implements, then *implement* would be a regnant superordinate construct. This is an example of classical logic and simplifies one's personal-construct system.

Core Constructs and Peripheral Constructs.   Core constructs are those that the individual uses to maintain identity and existence. In the healthy person, they are comprehensive and permeable. Peripheral constructs may be altered without serious modification of the core structure. Their reformulation is a much less complicated affair than is the reformulation of a core construct.

Tight Constructs and Loose Constructs.   Tight constructs lead to unvarying predictions, while loose constructs lead to varying predictions. Loose constructs are like preliminary sketches of a design.

Transitional Constructs

Constructs provide a stable element in experience. Yet constructs change, and the transitions present problems. Transitional constructs concern this process of change and include the following.

Threat.   "Threat is the awareness of imminent comprehensive change in one's core structures" (*ibid.,* p. 489). The therapist, who expects the client to change, is thus threatening, especially when the client is on the verge of a major change.

Fear.   Fear is the awareness of an imminent change in an incidental core construct rather than in a comprehensive construct.

Anxiety.   Anxiety is the recognition on the part of the individual that the events confronting him or her lie outside the range of convenience of his or her construct system. Since the individual's constructs do not apply, an inability to construe the events meaningfully (an ambiguity) results. Loosening the superordinate constructs may increase tolerance for ambiguity and may be sufficient to reduce anxiety; if loosening proceeds too far, however, it may lead to schizophrenia. Redefinition and increase in the permeability of the superordinate system is also effective against anxiety. Tightening is another defense against anxiety.

Guilt.   Within the individual's core structure is the core role, which involves that part of the role structure by which the self as an integral being is maintained. Guilt is the experience resulting from the perception of an apparent loss of one's core role structure. The core role is not a superficial role but "a part one plays as if his life depended upon it. Indeed, his life actually does depend upon it" (*ibid.,* p. 503). When individuals discover that they have not been acting in accordance with this role, they feel guilt. Punishment is not the result of guilt, but vice versa. We punish those who threaten us in order to protect ourselves from the threat of being like them and to make them feel guilty.

Aggressiveness.   Aggressiveness is the active elaboration of one's perceptual field. The aggressive individual has a greater than average tendency to set up choice points, precipitating situations that require decision and action. Areas of anxiety tend to be areas of aggressiveness. The aggressive person is seen as threatening.

Hostility.   Hostility is the effort to force another person to validate a prediction that is invalid. "The other person is the victim, not so much of the hostile person's fiendishly destructive impulses, as of his frantic and unrealistic efforts to collect on a wager he has already lost" (*ibid.,* p. 511). Recurring evidence that he or she is wrong leads the hostile person to feel guilty.

Sequential Changes in Constructs

There are typical sequences of changes in constructs that people employ in order to function in everyday situations. Two of them are the C-P-C cycle and the creativity cycle.

C-P-C Cycle.   The C-P-C cycle is a sequence of construction from circumspection to preemption to control, resulting in a choice involving the self. *Circumspect construction* employs a series of propositional constructs. Thus, there is a process that goes from looking at elements in a multidimensional manner to focusing on one element and that results in a choice, or the control of the construct through superordination. To understand choice, we must understand the alternatives facing a person, from his or her point of view. *Impulsivity* is a form of control in which the period of circumspection preceding the choice or decision is shortened. It is an attempt at a quick solution.

In the C-P-C cycle, the actor—or person—begins by looking at a situation circumspectly, or in a multidimensional manner, considering various elements or alternatives. Then he/she establishes the regnancy or exclusiveness of a particular superordinate construct as if this were the crux of the situation, preempting the relevance of all other issues. This sets up a choice point for action or control.

Creativity Cycle.   The creativity cycle begins with loosened construction, involving exploration and experiment, followed by tightened and validated construction. The diagnostic constructs are chosen as consistent with personal-construct theory and as useful to the therapist. They represent, primarily, lines along which persons may change in reconstruing their lives and, secondarily, ways in which individuals vary within themselves, as well as from one another, at different times. They are not categories for classifying people.

Types of Psychological Disorders

To illustrate the use of the dimensions of diagnosis or the diagnostic constructs, the constructs are included in a multidimensional system that illustrates representative types of psychological disorders. The diagnostic constructs themselves do not necessarily refer to disorders, but they are designed to be relevant to various personal-construct systems. A disorder usually involves more than one dimension. Disorders are not nosologic categories or disease entities.

A disorder is any personal construction that is used repeatedly in spite of consistent invalidation. There may be other bases of explanation for psychological disorders, such as past events; but the past cannot be changed, and treatment on this basis is a tedious cancelling out of each old experience with a new one or a turning back of the clock. One can do something, however, about a person's personal-construct system. Repentance is substituted for atonement; reconstruction for compensation; and the future for the past.

There are two major groupings of disorders: disorders of construction and disorders of transition.

Disorders of Construction.   There are three disorders of construction. The first of these, *disorders of dilation,* occur when individuals have no superordinate constructs to order their dilated field. The individual may have lost or abandoned governing constructs and then reverted to inappropriate preverbal constructs of dependence, which are comprehensive and permeable. Dilation may occur with loose construction, which is an effort to span or embrace the dilated field. The so-called *manic client* is usually dilated. In the *depressive phase,* the client makes an effort to constrict the field. Dilation is also seen in cases diagnosed as paranoid.

The second of the disorder of construction is *disorders involving tightening and loosening of constructs.* The individual with tight constructions makes precise, exact predictions, but his or her other superordinate structure lacks permeability. The individual's anticipations fail to materialize, and constructs must be discarded. The individual becomes anxious and must resort to constriction or preverbal comprehensive structures. Suicide or psychosis may be the result. The person with loose constructs is variable, adapts to experiences by stretching constructions, and seldom misses in his or her other predictions because they are so broad. Extreme looseness of construing is difficult to follow and may lead to avoidance on the part of others and thus to social withdrawal. Such persons are often labeled *schizophrenic.* With the loss of a social role, guilt may develop if the individual is aware of the loss and does not deny it by constriction.

The third of the disorder of construction is *disorders involving core constructs.* Physical complaints often involve core constructs and also imply that dependence is involved. *Psychosomatic symptoms* are required, just as sustenance and safety are required. In *conversion reactions,* the client is thinking dualistically and translates a psychological into a physiological problem. In this preemptive construction, the problem is wholly physical.

Disorders of Transition.   *Aggression* and *hostility* are disorders of transition. Aggression is often a solution for hostility, giving rise to activities that relieve the hostility. Hostility requires solution by reconstruing, not draining by catharsis. Aggression may lead to ignoring one's role or failing to elaborate one's role, dealing with others as objects to be manipulated rather than as people to be understood. Coping with others as people rather than as objects requires time, which the impatient, aggressive person often is not willing to spend. The aggressive person has "authority problems" for this reason. Aggression may lead to guilt in various ways when the individual feels that his or her other role is jeopardized. Hostility is unrealistic, yet it may achieve results if it obliges others—in order to placate the hostile person or to indulge his or her whims—to provide the outcomes that the hostile person wants.

Disorders of Anxiety, Constriction, and Guilt.   The anxious person has a construction system that fails and has no better or new system available. In a sense, all disorders of construction involve anxiety. Anxiety cannot be observed, but it can be inferred from the measures undertaken to control or avoid it, such as weeping, impulsiveness, dilation, or constriction. All behavior may be seen as directed toward the avoidance of anxiety or of the perception of anxiety, but this would lead to nirvana. People usually seek to master rather than avoid anxiety.

Constriction may be viewed as an avoidance of anxiety. It is a way of shrinking one's world until it becomes manageable. Constriction and preemption often go together. The individual becomes narrow, limited, and restricted. Issues accumulate, which leads to insurmountable anxiety. *Involutional melancholia* is an example of what results.

Life is difficult in the face of extreme guilt, which involves the person's core role. Guilt may lead to hostility or to physical illness, if not to death. *Paranoid homosexuality* represents a disorder of guilt.

Disorders Involving Undispersed Dependence.   Dependence is not considered a principal axis of the diagnostic construct system, but it does constitute the basis for disorders. Everyone is dependent on others. The normal person dispenses his or her dependencies widely and in a discriminative fashion; the disordered person is indiscriminate in dependencies and seeks someone on whom all dependence can be unloaded at once. Hostility frequently results when the person's search does not turn out well.

"Psychosomatic" and "Organic" Problems.   Somatic symptoms in a person with a psychological conflict are difficult to reach because they are perceived as physical in the client's dualistic way of thinking. Many psychological disorders involve "psychosomatic" symptoms, but the term has no precise meaning in the system of personal constructs.

The characteristics of the organically deteriorated person stem from an attempt to reconstrue the self in a constricted world. Deteriorated constructs or constructs that have become relatively impermeable may be used. The "organic" picture may also be found in persons with a deep-seated feeling of inadequacy who find themselves "in over their heads."

Disorders Involving Control.   Disorders of control reflect faulty superordinate construction systems. The superordinate construct may be such that it subsumes or controls all new experiences, with no change in itself. Disorders involving impulsiveness represent difficulties with the phase of the circumspection-preemption-control cycle, resulting in foreshortening of the cycle.

Not all disorders are disorders of the *form* of personal constructs, although these forms constitute the elements of the diagnostic dimensions. Some difficulties arise from the *content* of the constructs. In addition, some therapy can take place without concern for diagnostic constructs. Not all the important learning takes place on the couch.

THE THERAPY PROCESS

Psychotherapy is a psychological process that changes a person's outlook on some aspect of life. It involves reconstruing, usually of the client's life role or the role that clients envision for themselves. Psychological disorders can be traced to the characteristics of a person's construction system. They manifest themselves in complaints—client complaints about oneself and others and complaints of others about the client. At the phenomenal level, then, the goal of psychotherapy is to alleviate complaints.

Client's Conceptions and Expectations.   The client's widely varying conceptions of psychotherapy must be accepted by the therapist at the outset. The therapist must be able to subsume the client's construction of psychotherapy in order to use it within a more comprehensive perspective. As therapy progresses, the client's concept changes and his/her view becomes more comprehensive. The client discovers that the outcome of psychotherapy is not a fixed state of affairs but a vantage point for viewing a life plan and the opening phase of a continuing process.

The client also conceptualizes the therapist and the therapist's role in relation to his or her (the client's) conceptualization of psychotherapy. Clients' perceptions may be stretched to construe the therapist as one who will meet their expectations. Clients may construe the therapist in various ways—as a parent, a protector, an absolver of guilt, an authority figure, a prestige figure, a possession, a stabilizer against change, a temporary respite from stress, a threat, an ideal person or companion, a stooge or foil, or a representative of reality. The last is best suited to achieve therapeutic goals, since it leads to a relationship in which clients can test constructs in an experimental, or laboratory, situation. The therapist is expected to play the parts of many figures, to be articulate, and to serve as a validator. Any but the most inept therapist can help clients in such a way. Yet some therapists fail, usually because they insist on an authoritarian rather than a cooperative relationship or because they are afraid of the outcome of such an experimental relationship.

Therapist's Conceptualization of His/Her Role.   Clinicians assist in the reconstruction or continual shifting of the client's construct system—a process that should continue throughout the client's lifetime. All change or movement, great or small, takes place as a function of change in constructs.

The role of the clinician is broad. It includes producing superficial change by creating an atmosphere of threat or anxiety, by consistently invalidating clients' devices, by precipitating clients into a situation in which they perceive a contrasting role that is expected of them, and by exhorting clients. Less superficial approaches include *controlled elaboration* or helping clients "work through" a construct system to bring certain minor constructs in line with the system.

The major or most fundamental role of the therapist is to help clients revise constructs. The therapist begins, however, by accepting the client's construction system as it is. Such acceptance does not mean approval, but readiness to use the client's system and to attempt to anticipate events the way the client would. Acceptance alone is not sufficient for therapeutic progress, except in simple cases. Therapists, while putting themselves in their client's place, maintain a professional overview of client problems. The therapist subsumes the client's construction system under a comprehensive frame (which the therapist provides).

Basic Approaches to the Revision of Constructs

The therapist helps the client develop new constructs or make major revisions of constructs in several ways.

   1. *The therapist selectively adds new conceptual elements.* These experiential elements must not fit too neatly into the client's present system, or they will not challenge it and will lead only to superficial movement. But if the new element leads the client to attempt a sweeping revision of constructs, there is a danger

that the client will become deeply disturbed. The therapist must be keenly aware of how the client is handling the new elements. The role of the therapist "includes the skillful introduction of new conceptual elements which challenge the client's construction system but which are carefully chosen so as not to precipitate a catastrophic revolution in it" (Kelly, 1955, vol. 2, p. 590).

2. *The therapist accelerates the tempo of the client's experience.* Life experience accelerates during therapy, both within and outside the interviews, with the therapist confronting the client with problems intended to pull the client through the normal succession of life experiences at an accelerated pace.

3. *The therapist imposes recent structures on old elements.* Although the emphasis of the approach is on the present, the way in which the adult sees the past influences the way that he/she sees the present. Thus, if the past is seen through the eyes of childhood, new events that are similar to those of the past may be dealt with in a childish way. The therapist helps the client apply his/her adult constructs in dealing with childhood recollections. The client then is better prepared to handle present and future events that may appear to be repetitions of the past.

4. *The therapist helps the client reduce certain obsolete constructs to a state of impermeability.* When it is not possible to get the client to reconstrue certain events or figures of the past, the therapist "may get the client to define the limits of the construct, to tie it firmly to past events and figures which are so unusual that there is little likelihood that their counterparts need be perceived in the future, and finally to wrap the construct up tightly with a word symbol by means of which it can be kept under control" (Kelly, 1955, p. 592).

5. *The therapist helps design and implement experiments.* Therapy is a laboratory for testing ideas, and the therapist helps the client survey new data and develop hypotheses for testing that do not involve too much risk at one time. The therapist may also participate in the experiment by enacting required parts.

6. *The therapist serves as validator.* By reacting to client constructs, the therapist should be a sample of the social world and a reasonably faithful example of the natural human reactions that the client will meet outside therapy.

The therapist does not try to pass on personal constructs to the client. If the therapist should do so, the client will try to translate them into his/her own construct system. Thus, a client who is told to be self-confident may respond with behavior that the therapist feels is conceited. Nevertheless, therapists do shape the client's system by the elements they introduce, by the constructs they validate or invalidate, and by the hypotheses of the client that they select for experimentation. "[The therapist's] very choice of points at which to clear his throat, nod his head, or murmur acceptance reflects his bias as to what is inconsequential, what is transitional, or what is understandable" (*ibid.*, p. 594).

Psychotherapy according to the psychology of personal constructs is an experimental process, since the system is built on the model of science. Constructs are hypotheses, with prediction the goal. The therapist helps the client to define hypotheses and to design and implement experiments, using the psychotherapy room as a laboratory. The therapist participates in the experiment, serving as a part of the validating evidence. "Psychotherapeutic movement may mean (1) that the client has reconstrued himself and certain other features of the world within his original system, (2) that he has organized his old system more precisely, or (3) that he has replaced some of the constructs in his old system with new ones" (*ibid.,* p. 941). The last is the most significant type of movement.

IMPLEMENTATION: PROCEDURES AND TECHNIQUES

Appraisal of Experiences

The case history is elicited by the use of schedules and outlines. The material is structured in the light of the client's deep-seated personal outlook. The case history is important, not in terms of what happened in the past, nor even just in terms of what the client thinks now, but in terms of what it reveals about the client's outlook. The chronicle of events is also important in providing validational evidence and checkpoints against which the client's constructs may be understood.

Culture and Experience.   The clinician must be aware of cultural variations, since the culture provides the client with evidence of what is "true" and with much of the data used in a personal-construct system. Culture controls in that it limits the data and evidence at the client's disposal, but there is a tremendous variety in the ways in which clients handle the data within their construct systems.

Clients' culture must be seen critically through their eyes. Cultural-group memberships throw light on clients' constructs. These include or are expressed in socioeconomic class, racial and national extraction, family migration history, retirement plans, complaints, and church membership. Although clients cannot describe their own culture as a culture, the clinician can assess cultural-experiential determinants by inquiring along appropriate lines.

Personal Experience.   The assessment of cultural influence can be made indirectly through the study of the client's community experiences. Information is first sought at a popular level of abstraction, with the psychological and sociological levels attempted after the data have been obtained. The inquiry regarding the community, and the neighborhood as well, covers descriptions of the population, community economics, transitions through which the community is going, religious organizations and mores, schools and educational patterns, and recreational resources.

An appraisal of the school will help in dealing with children from the school. Such an appraisal would include observation of the building, the playground, the classrooms, and classroom behavior, as well as interviews with teachers and the principal. In the interviews, the constructs of the teachers and principal indicate the directions along which the children can move. The teachers' attitudes toward tests and records are revealing of constructs.

The individual's community interrelationships should be studied through the eyes of the person. Groups, organizations, and individuals in the person's life reveal the influences on him/her. Educational experiences are analyzed. In the case of a child, the teachers are interviewed to determine what they consider to be the problem or how they construe the situation. The person's home relationships constitute important social expectancies and should therefore be explored. Although people are not slaves of their biographies, the family history is important as seen through the client's eyes.

Appraisal of Activities

Spontaneous Activity. All activity is spontaneous yet controlled in the sense that it is lawful and predictable. Interests direct activities along particular lines. Areas of spontaneous activity indicate areas of permeable constructs and thus areas in which optimal conditions for evolution exist. Inactivity, or "laziness," is the result of impermeable thinking. The analysis of the client's spontaneous activities is thus a basic task of the clinician. The discovery of permeable constructs provides leads to the client's capacity for psychotherapeutic change.

Spontaneous activities may be studied through verbal inquiry or by time-sampling observation. The way in which the individual interprets experiences is important, however. Activities include not only physical movements, but also conversation and reading. The observation of a child in a group is difficult but profitable. Observation of the child in the family is also revealing.

Vocational choice exercises a selective effect on experience. The vocation is usually an area of permeable constructs and thus gives an indication of the kinds of changes the individual may be prepared to make. A vocation or a course of study often represents the seeking of a compromise between what is challenging and what is safe. The vocation provides the system of validating evidence to which the individual's daily expectations are subject. It is also one of the principal means by which the individual's life role is given clarity and meaning.

Structural Interpretation of Experience. The biographical record is appraised by viewing it in five ways. The client must make sense from this. It reveals something of the person's past construction system and thus suggests behavior to which the client may have recourse if present constructs fail and become invalidated. It indicates the kinds of validators against which the client has to check his/her construct system. It throws light on the present construct system. Finally, it will have to be rationalized by the client in any therapeutic reformulation of a role. It is in these ways that birth, maturation, and physical care are evaluated, as well as behavior problems, interpersonal relations, education, and occupation.

The health of the client is a concern of the therapist, since it has a bearing on psychological evaluation. The individual's physical being constitutes both part of the facts against which constructs must be validated and the implements with which his/her world must be explored. Illness and disability limit activity and interests and require psychological adjustment. Old dependence patterns are reactivated; there may be regression to earlier modes of conceptualization.

The clinician must interpret the client's structuralizations. In this way, the clinician subsumes the client's structure and establishes a role relationship with the client. The clinician is then in a position to anticipate the client's perceptions and behavior. The clinician's construction of a case develops by successive approximations. Structuralization, then, refers to the preliminary formulations, while construction is the final organization of the record into a well-subsumed system. The former is descriptive, limited to the past and present; the latter is dynamic, related to the future.

The structuralization of a case, utilizing the client's experience record, may make use of the terms that follow. These are not constructs but *collecting terms.* They represent section headings that may be used in case presentations and case records. Since they refer to the kinds of events the client has had to anticipate, they are validators.

1. *Figure matrix.* This includes information regarding the kinds of people the client has known intimately. The individuals are *figure constructs,* which are assembled into the figure matrix.

2. *Cooperative relationships.* This section would consist of information regarding the client's participation in socially constructive processes.

3. *Characterizations of the client.* This heading includes the ways in which the client is described by people with whom he/she must live.

4. *Externally imposed group identifications.* This topic refers to how the client is seen by others in terms of the client's group memberships.

5. *Areas in which the client is incorporated or alienated. Incorporation* refers to the willingness to see others as like oneself; *alienation* is unwillingness to do this. This heading includes the groups who see the client as like themselves, and the ways in which they see the client like this.

6. *External patterns of conflict and solution.* This area is concerned with the social issues and conflicts in the client's milieu that he/she must experience and construe.

7. *Thematic repertory.* Thema are the themes and patterns of the social world surrounding the client, against which the client plays a part.

8. *Symbolic system.* The symbolic system includes the language, religious, nationalistic, institutional, proverbial, epigrammatic, and so on, background of the client.

9. *Climate of opinion out of which complaints arise.* What are the conventionalized complaints in the client's social setting?

10. *Versatility.* This includes the range or breadth of the client's activities or thinking, which indicate a freedom to experiment.

11. *Biographical turning points.* Are there points of change in the experience record? The presence and nature of such changes suggest the client's capacity for change and the manner in which future changes may be expected to take place.

12. *Physical resources.* These include not only personal resources of property, but also the resources of the community.

13. *Dependences.* Are there resources on which the client has become so dependent that their loss would interrupt his/her whole pattern of life?

14. *Supportive Status.* This section consists of items indicating how and in what manner the client is seen as necessary to other people.

The clinical constructs used to bring together or structuralize the client's experience are of intermediate rather than salient significance from the point of view of the psychology of personal constructs.

Steps in Diagnosis

Diagnosis is the planning stage of client treatment. Client treatment is broader than therapy or treatment: it includes all actions directed toward the client's welfare.

There are many ways in which the same facts may be construed. Since the therapist is interested in helping clients, clinical diagnosis construes the facts in terms of their relevance to a solution of the client's problem, or client reconstruction. The phrase *transitive diagnosis* is used to indicate the concern with transitions in the client's life, or bridges between the client's present and future. "Moreover, we expect to take an active part in helping the client select or build the bridges to be used and in helping him cross them safely. . . . If the psychologist expects to help him he must get up off his chair and start moving along with him" (*ibid.,* p. 775).

The diagnostic constructs or dimensions presented earlier represent avenues of movement as seen by the therapist, and they are the bases of transitive diagnosis. The psychology of personal constructs is directed against the tendency to impose preemptive constructs on human behavior, a tendency in which "diagnosis is all too frequently an attempt to cram a whole live struggling client into a nosological category" (*ibid.,* p. 775). The question in transitive diagnosis is not, "In what category should this client be classified?" but, "What is to become of this client?" A temporary preemptive construction is necessary for deciding the immediate disposition of the client, including whether to accept the client for treatment.

There are six practical issues that arise in the making of a transitive diagnosis. In outline form they are as follows:

I. Normative formulations of the client's problem
   (1) Description of the manifest deviant behavior patterns (symptoms)
   (2) Description of the correlates of the manifest deviant behavior patterns
   (3) Descriptions of the gains and losses accruing to the client through symptoms (description of validational experience)

II. Psychological description of the client's personal constructions
   (1) The client's construction of what he/she believes to be the problem area
   (2) The client's construction of life roles

III. Psychological evaluation of the client's construction system
   (1) Location of the client's areas of anxiety, aggressiveness (or spontaneous elaboration), and constriction
   (2) Sampling the types of construction the client uses in different areas
   (3) Sampling the modes of approach
   (4) Determination of the client's accessibility and levels of communication

IV. Analyses of the milieu in which adjustment is to be sought
   (1) Analyses of the expectancy system within which the client must make the life role function
   (2) Assessment of the socioeconomic assets in the case
   (3) Preparation of information to be used as contextual material in helping the client reconstrue life

V. Determination of immediate procedural steps
   (1) Physiological construction of the available data
   (2) Other professional constructions of the available data
   (3) Evaluation of the urgency of the case

VI.   Planning management and treatment
    (1) Selection of the central psychotherapeutic approach
    (2) Designation of the principally responsible clinician
    (3) Selection of adjunctive resources to be used
    (4) Designation of the responsible clinician's advisory staff
    (5) Determination of the *ad interim* status of the client
    (6) Setting of dates or conditions under which progress will be reviewed by the advisory staff.

The issues at the beginning of the outline are essentially descriptive; those in the middle require more scientific sophistication; and those at the end require therapeutic training for their resolution. "Effective diagnosis is a matter of making some reasonable predictions as to what a client will do under different circumstances and then proposing to create a set of circumstances which will lead to the client's doing what we think he generally ought to do" (*ibid.,* p. 829).

Psychological Testing in Diagnosis and Psychotherapy

One direct approach to the client's personal constructs is by means of psychological tests, which involve a formal assigned task. So-called objective tests are considered *dimensional measures* of personal constructs, for example, cultural commonality, rather than direct revelations of the constructs themselves. Other tests elicit the constructs themselves; these are the tests under consideration here. There are five functions of a test in a clinical setting:

1. Define the client's problem in usable terms.
2. Reveal the pathways or channels along which the client is free to move.
3. Provide clinical hypotheses that may subsequently be checked and put to use.
4. Reveal resources of the client that might otherwise be overlooked by the therapist.
5. Reveal problems of the client that might otherwise be overlooked by the therapist.

A diagnostic instrument that attempts to fulfill these functions and meets the above requirements has been developed to elicit personal constructs. It is the Role Construct Repertory Test (Rep Test), which is aimed at eliciting role constructs and is thus concerned with those persons with whom the subject has had to deal in daily life. The subject is given a Role Title List and asked to designate persons in his/her own realm of experience who fit the role titles. Then groups of three of the persons named are selected, and the subject is asked to tell in what important way two of them are alike but different from the third. There are various forms of the test, including tests for both group and individual administration.

The test has been developed on the basis of personal-construct theory. There are six assumptions in interpreting the results:

1. The constructs elicited are permeable.
2. Preexisting constructs are elicited by the test.

3. The figures are representative of the people to whom the subject must relate his/her self-construed role.
4. Constructs will be elicited that subsume, in part, the construction systems of the element figures.
5. The constructs elicited are regnant over the subject's own role.
6. The constructs elicited are adequate to communicate to the examiner some understanding of how the client organizes the elements in the test.

The test can be subjected to both formal and clinical analyses. Clinical analysis considers the number and overlap and the permeability or impermeability of the constructs elicited, fields of permeability, contrasting constructs, unique figures, linkage of constructs through contrasts and figures, preemptive constructs, superficial constructs, dependency constructs, and so forth. The test contributes to diagnosis in the area of the client's construction of a life role.

During therapy, tests may contribute to the understanding of the client's personal-construct system, thus broadening the therapist's perspective. They may also dispel some of the bias of the therapist or point to content related to one of the therapist's "blind spots."

Tests also affect the outlook of the client, bringing him/her face to face with issues that might otherwise be ignored or rejected as being the therapist's incorrect perceptions. Test material may be used as "entry material" or as a point of departure for beginning a therapy hour, although such material is probably not as useful as other entries devised by the therapist.

Tests may pose a threat to the psychotherapeutic relationship, more so later on in the relationship than at the start. Threat may be reduced by reassuring the client that there is no passing or failing involved and by structuring the use of the test as a help to the therapist in understanding the client better. Projective tests, particularly sentence-completion tests, are likely to be less damaging than objective tests. The word-association test seems to be most damaging.

Psychotherapeutic Approach: Basic Techniques

Setting Up the Relationship. The therapist does not allow himself or herself to become an intimately known and sharply delineated personality for the client; instead, the therapist maintains a personal ambiguity. This makes it more likely that the client will develop a secondary rather than a primary transference and allows the therapist to play the versatile roles required. This ambiguity enables the client to cast the therapist in the parts necessary in reconstructive experiments. The therapist, therefore, avoids social relationships with the client, as well as contacts with members of the client's family. Nor should the therapist treat two members of the same family.

Controlling Interviews. Because of the different ways clients may have of construing the world, the therapist must maintain a flexible relationship with clients. Each interview, nevertheless, requires some planning, although the plan can be altered as necessary within prescribed limits. As therapy proceeds, the therapist becomes aware of danger areas to be avoided and develops the ability to predict what the client will say. Special activities of the client may call for special interviewing plans. Interviews may be spaced to meet the client's needs for contact. For most purposes, a 45-minute interview is adequate. Notes or summaries of interviews should be kept to assist the therapist's memory from interview to interview. They should include predictions of what the client will do before the next interview. This is an important point because "if the therapist is able to 'call the shots' on his client, he can be reassured that he is developing a fairly adequate construction of the case" (Kelly, 1955, vol. 2, p. 635).

Since having prepared a plan, the therapist initiates the interview with that plan in mind. Interviews should be terminated on time and not continue out the door in "threshold therapy." The tempo of the interview is controlled by the therapist as necessary to broaden or narrow the scope of the client's immediate perceptual field and for other purposes. The therapist should avoid a guilt-laden dependence on the part of the client by not listening to outpourings of wrongdoings, unless the therapist is prepared to assume continuing responsibility for the client's welfare.

Psychotherapist's Manner. Communication is not limited to words. The therapist should appear to be physically relaxed and mentally receptive during interviews. Gestures should be of the accepting type. The therapist's voice should be responsive, and speech should be clear yet colorful and adapted to the client's vocabulary. While the therapist should appear to be "shockproof," he/she should not be so impassive that the client cannot observe the results of experiments.

Teaching the Client How to Be a "Patient." The client should be taught how to respond in the therapeutic relationship. In long-term relationships, this may take months. Such structuring may include formal verbal structuring as well as intermittent instructions and orientation.

Palliative Techniques

Reassurance. Reassurance is never more than a temporary expedient to give the client the impression that his/her behavior and ideas are consistent, acceptable, and organized. It helps to hold together the client's construction system until it can be rebuilt. Reassurance can backfire if things turn out badly after the therapist has assured the client they would not. It tends to support existing maladjustive mechanisms. Too much reassurance leads to dependence.

Some ways of providing reassurance are less likely to produce unfavorable results than are others. Predictions made as reassurance should not be sweeping. Acceptance of anxiety-laden material as not unexpected is reassuring. Both the process of structuring and the therapist's manner can be reassuring. But value labels used as reassurance can be hazardous because they prevent the client from changing any evaluations. Comfort as reassurance may create "resistance" in a client who is ambivalent about complaints. It may lead the client to feel that there is no solution, that the therapist feels this way also, and that all he or she can do is "grin and bear it."

Since reassurance slows therapeutic movement, it should be used only when retardation is desired. For example, it may be used as a temporary preventive of fragmentation of constructs. It may be used to encourage loosening of conceptualization, with less danger of fragmentation. Reassurance controls anxiety. It may also be used to keep an important chain of associations temporarily from being broken. It should always be used in minimal and calculated amounts.

Support.   Support is provided by acceptance without agreement or by understanding the client's communication without telling the client he/she is right before the client has had a chance to experiment. It is a response that allows the client to experiment widely and successfully. Support recognizes and accepts the client's dependence patterns of behavior; it thus may be threatening to the client and may arouse guilt feelings.

The therapist shows support by being on time for appointments, by remembering what the client has said in the past, and by construing things as the client does. This last is one of the therapist's main functions and is sometimes enough. Support includes adapting to changes in the client's thinking, helping the client to verbalize a new rationale, and doing things for the client outside the interview situation.

Support may be used in certain anxiety cases, as an approach to help a client understand his/her striving for dependence, or to stabilize a situation temporarily. Support, like reassurance, should be used sparingly and should be limited to situations in which the client cannot take everything in stride.

Transference.   Transference is a construct. In its broad sense, transference is the lifting of a construct from one's repertory and transferring it, or applying it, to a particular situation. When facing a therapist, the client takes a construct from his/her repertory and uses it in looking at and dealing with the therapist. In psychotherapy, transference is concerned with role constructs and refers to the way in which a person attempts to subsume the constructs of others. In reference to the client, it represents the effort of the client to construe the therapist by transferring role constructs onto the therapist. The therapist is constantly extricating himself/herself from the client's constructions, both those that are useful and those that are not useful. The client tends to cast the therapist into the form of a highly elaborated prejudicial stereotype, such as the father or father figure, which becomes fixed.

Transference Dependency.   Transference sometimes involves dependency constructs, which may be immature and may not lend themselves to verbalization. The client responds to the therapist as if life depended on the therapist. Therapists sometimes invite dependency transferences by the attitude that they know what is best for the client.

Counterdependency Transference.   If the therapist cannot adequately construe the client within a set of professional constructs, the therapist runs the risk of transferring his/her dependencies to the client. Prevention of such counterdependency transference requires an organized and meaningful set of diagnostic constructs acquired through thorough professional training and the use of the client's own personal constructs within the subsuming system. The therapist who is overly concerned with and preoccupied by the client's relationships to himself/herself and others, in almost a jealous manner, should be alert to the possibility that he/she has developed counterdependency transference.

Primary and Secondary Transference.   The application of a varying sequence of constructs from a variety of figures of the past is secondary transference. The therapist can use this transference to reorient the client's constructions of other persons by playing various parts. When the client construes the therapist preemptively, as a unique person (a type) and develops a personal identification with the therapist, a primary transference exists. This kind of relationship limits the experiments that the client can perform with the therapist. The client focuses on the therapist as a unique figure and is unable to generalize the lessons learned in the therapy situation to persons outside therapy.

Control of Transference.   Transference should be allowed only to the extent that it appears to be safe and useful; it seems to go in cycles. The therapist must determine at the end of each cycle whether to begin another or to terminate therapy. A transference cycle can be shortened by abandoning concept-loosening techniques, shifting to current material, dealing with lower levels of abstraction, and, in general, engaging in a more structured, superficial form of therapy. Primary transference, once it occurs, should be resolved immediately. Two methods may be used. In one, the therapist assumes a rigid, persevering, repetitive, and stereotyped role. In the other, less drastic, the therapist uses free roles, forcing the client to play opposite various other persons, whose parts the therapist enacts.

Elaborating the Complaint

Uncontrolled Elaboration.   Most therapeutic elaboration starts with an elaboration of the complaint. The elaboration may be uncontrolled, with the therapist being "nondirective." There are contraindications for this undirected elaboration. One is if the therapist is going to make a referral. Another is if there are excessive guilt feelings. A third is excessive repetition by the client. A fourth is in cases of loose construction.

Controlled Elaboration.   Controlled elaboration avoids the hazards of undirected elaboration; however, it does not avoid the serious hazard that the therapist may not be able to know precisely how the client managed to be incapacitated and, thus, may not be able to make contact with the client's personal-construct system (in order to establish a meaningful role in relation to the client). Questions should be used to get the client to place problems, if possible, on a time line; to see them as fluid and transient; and to interpret them as being responsive to treatment, the passage of time, and varying conditions. These procedures lead to construing the problems in ways in which they can be solved. Pressuring the client to explain why he/she has certain difficulties may be profitable but may lead to verbal rationalization. Questions about other people who have or have had the same problems put the complaint into a social framework. Sometimes it is advisable to confront the client with complaints or aspects of problems that have not been mentioned. This may clarify the diagnostic picture as well as the therapeutic realtionship. Most frequently, such confrontation is used to broaden the client's field as new constructs are being formulated.

Reflection of key terms or ideas may lead to elaboration by the client. Selected elements may be reflected to force the client to elaborate a theme. Review of previous sesions is a form of reflection and may be used to assure the client that the therapist was listening and to integrate or organize details on a higher level of superordination. It can also be used to draw contrasts between the past and the present. Review may threaten the client, however; it may block development by going back to the old material, or it may betray the therapist's prejudices. "The more the therapist talks or tries to place verbal structure on what the client has produced, the greater is the likelihood that the sensitive ear of the client will detect harsh notes of criticism and inflexibility" (*ibid.*, p. 975).

Elaborating the Personal System

The basic task of the therapist is to elaborate the construct system in which the client's difficulties are anchored.

Approach to the Construct System.   The turning from the complaint as a reference point to the client's system as a system broadens the picture, raises the issues to a higher level of abstraction, and places the emphasis on seeing alternatives. Tests, as already mentioned, are one approach to an elaboration of the client's construct system. Another is self-description through the self-characterization sketch used in fixed-role therapy, which will be mentioned later. Broad, general questions rather than an outline should be used to help the client produce a self-characterization. The client may be asked to elaborate life-role structure, including earlier plans and goals, as well as a projection into the future—what the client wants to be like after therapy.

Progressive confrontation with alternatives through use of the C-P-C cycle is another way to maintain the process of elaboration. Elaboration may take place in activities outside the therapy room, such as prescribed occupational, recreational, and social activities. The sorts of play and creative production in which the therapist can participate may also be used to encourage elaboration. Elaboration of the construct system must be done systematically and cautiously. Limits are ordinarily set on the areas to be elaborated in any one phase of the therapy. Elaboration may lead to loosening of the system and thus must be controlled to prevent too much or too general loosening.

Elaboration of Material Arising during the Course of Therapy.   The concern here is with the elaboration of bits of material to see where they fit into the total construct system and to determine their relationship to the sequence of developments in therapy. Since not all clues can be followed up, material must be selected for elaboration. What is selected is determined only partly by its suspected significance; the readiness of the client to deal with it must also be considered. Some of the kinds of material that should be chosen for elaboration are the following: Strange or unexpected material, material possibly indicative of an expected therapeutic movement or revision of the construct system, material apparently related to an area under intensive study, material lending itself to psychotherapeutic experimentation, material useful in validation of new constructs, material related to a construct taking shape, and material representing an extended range of convenience of an existing construct.

Recapitulation by the therapist or the client may point up the need for, and lead to, elaboration. Procedures used in recapitulation include the client's diaries and written summaries, playback of recordings, and discussions by the client in a therapy group of experiences in individual therapy.

Probing is a method of controlling the client's participation in the interview. It can be misused if it becomes an inquisition. Probing is used to get the client to explore an area. It may be immediate and done as soon as a cue has been given; but it is preferable to delay probing, so that it may represent a well-thought-out procedure for helping the client elaborate meaningful constructs. Probing can be used to elicit details about an important incident that may tie in with other incidents. Asking for the antecedents or consequences of an incident is also a means of elaboration. The therapist may ask the client to think of similar or contrasting incidents or experiences, which may lead to elaboration of the construct, or the therapist may try to relate client experiences, which also may lead to elaboration of the construct. In addition, the therapist may relate client experiences by asking the client how two are alike and how they are different from a third.

Enactment, in which the therapist plays a role in an incident described by the client, may be an effective way of helping the client to elaborate. Four principles are important in the use of enactment. First, there should be no long preliminary discussions or preparation. Second, the enactment should be brief. Third, there should be an exchange of parts, with the therapist taking various parts, including that of the client. Thus, the client may be led to think, "This therapist is both sympathetic and versatile; with him/her, the therapy room can become a well-equipped laboratory for experimenting with life's perplexing social relations, provided, of course, that I dare to experiment." The client, in taking the part of another, begins to know a little of how another person might be construing the situation and can begin to adapt to what the construction is. Fourth, portrayal of a caricature of the client must be avoided. Enactment should be introduced with a relatively innocuous incident.

Loosening and Tightening

Loosening.   The axis of loosened versus tightened construction is an important one and one with which the therapist deals early in therapy. Loosening is characteristic of constructs that lead to varying predictions—those whose elements may vary in their classification from one pole to the other. Dreaming is an illustration of loose thinking. It allows for resilience, inconsistencies, and a shifty defense. It is a necessary phase of creative thinking. It frees facts so that they can be seen in new aspects. Loosening prepares the ground for the changing development of constructs and the developing of new constructs. It is produced in psychotherapy in four principal ways:

1. *Relaxation.* The couch or chair, the surroundings, the relaxed manner of the therapist, and the therapist's systematic methods of eliciting physical relaxation induce relaxation in the client.
2. *Chain association.* Chain association is the free association of psychoanalysis. The client sometimes has to be helped by being given a starting point, being allowed to think without speaking, and being instructed to let his/her mind wander without being concerned about the importance of the content.
3. *Reporting dreams.* Dreams are so loose that it is difficult to report them. It is not the content of the dream, however, but the use of loosened construction in reporting it that is useful, even if the client can remember and verbalize little about the dream itself. In loosening, verbalization is slow. The manic flight of ideas is not loosening; the schizoid's thinking is. Interpretation of dreams tightens construction; therefore, the interpretation should not follow immediately on

the reporting of dreams but should take place when the therapist wants to move in the direction of tightening. Dreams are often preverbal and thus throw light on preverbal constructs. They often also involve submerged contrasting poles of constructs. This accounts for the fact that dream elements often appear to represent their opposites.

4. *Uncritical acceptance.* Acceptance is the attempt by the therapist to employ the client's construct system. It is uncritical when the client's thinking is not questioned by the therapist. "Essentially the technique of uncritical acceptance provides the client with a passive validation for his loosened construing which is elastic and nonexperimental" (*ibid.,* p. 1049).

There are difficulties involved in producing loosened constructions. The client has a tendency to move toward tightening of constructs; he/she has difficulty finding symbols or words to deal with ideas. Premature interpretation tightens up the client's construing. Distractions and interference from similar but tightly construed elements interfere with loosening.

Resistance to loosening may be dealt with not only by continuing to use the techniques to produce loosening, which have been mentioned, but also by using other special techniques. Enactment, or role playing, is one. The use of a context in which loosening is possible, followed by a gradual shifting to the desired area or context, is another. Reducing threat or increasing acceptance is a third technique.

Loosening has some hazards. Since it reduces anxiety, it may become like an addiction or an escape. Tight constructions may be a defense, and the loss of this defense may precipitate a severe anxiety state. The skillful use of loosening requires comprehensiveness and flexibility in the therapist's viewpoint.

Tightening.   The functions of tightening are to define what is predicted, to stabilize construction, to facilitate organization of the construct system, to reduce certain constructs to a state of impermeability, and to facilitate experimentation. Tightening is a form of elaboration, and techniques of elaboration apply to it also. Other techniques include the following:

1. *Judging or superordinating.* In judging or superordinating, the client is urged to cease free-associating, to judge rather than to experience, and to put a superordinate construction on a group of constructs that have been expressed unsystematically.
2. *Summarization.* In summarization, the client is asked to summarize what he or she has been saying. This leads to systematization, which involves the tightening of subordinated constructs. Written summaries between interviews may be assigned to the client.
3. *Historical explanation* of thoughts by the client.
4. *Relating the client's thinking* to that of others.
5. *Direct approach.* In the direct approach, the client is asked to be explicit—to explain or to clarify.
6. *Challenging the construction.* The therapist may ask the client to repeat what he/she has said, express confusion, misinterpret, question, or even label what the client is saying as nonsense.

7. *Enactment.* The demands of extemporaneous role playing may at times lead to the tightening up of certain minor constructions.
8. *Concept formation.* In concept formation, the client is asked to tell how two things are alike but different from a third.
9. *Asking for validating evidence.*
10. *Word binding.* The client is asked to name each construct and to stick with the name.
11. *Time binding.* The client is asked to date constructs, restricting them in time.

Difficulties occur in getting the client to tighten up certain constructions. The client may use a symbol consistently, but the construct itself may be vague and inconsistently applied. Tightness may be achieved at the expense of permeability, comprehensiveness, or superordination. Impulsive clients, who can hold themselves together only with a loose construction of themselves, may cause difficulty. Clients who want to limit their world to the therapy room and the therapy relationship and clients who are unwilling to test constructs can also cause difficulty. Loose constructs that are preverbal are difficult to tighten.

There are hazards involved in tightening, too. One is the danger of premature tightening, which may bring clients face to face with the implications of their construing and force them to test hypotheses before they have any appropriate alternative constructions. Hostility may result if constructs are invalidated, and since the therapist is also involved in the experiment, the therapist also may become hostile at the failure. A second principal hazard in tightening is the possible loss of comprehensiveness, permeability, and propositionality.

Therapy involves the weaving back and forth between tightening and loosening, essentially in the repetition of the creativity cycle. Therapy proceeds by successive approximations. In the process, clients learn a way of developing better modes of adjustment.

Producing Psychotherapeutic Movement

The techniques considered below are those employed in the stages of therapy in which the therapist urges clients to experiment with new ideas and behaviors.

Interpretation, Movement, and Rapport.   The client's constructs are personal, and the therapist must deal with them on an individual basis rather than in terms of general meanings. There is one basic principle in interpretation: *"All interpretations understood by the client are perceived in terms of his own system.* Another way of expressing the same thing is to say that it is always the client who interprets, not the therapist" (*ibid.,* p. 1090). Again, the therapist's job "is to help the client make discoveries of his own; it is not to shower him with blessed insights" (*ibid.,* p. 1053). The basic interpretive formats are those that invite the client to conceptualize in some new or generalized way what he/she has been discussing. In addition to interpretation, extending the range of convenience of the client's constructs and the use of elaboration are methods of increasing the permeability of the client's constructs.

Movement in psychotherapy is indicated by the client in various ways. One is the surprise of the client when things seem to fall into place; this is the "Aha!" experience. Another is the client's spontaneous documentation of the usefulness of a new construct. A third is the evidence of permeability when the client incorporates current experiences into a construct. A fourth is a positive change in mood or feeling. The perception of contrast between present and past behavior is a fifth indication. A sixth is the dropping of certain complaints or even the substitution of new ones for old ones. The client's summaries of previous interviews also indicate changes. Finally, the change in content, with the introduction of new content into the therapy, indicates movement.

There are also cues that indicate inadequate new construction. These include loose construction or erratic verbalization of a new construct, bizarre documentation, oversimplification, contrast behavor or "flight into health," and legalistic application of the new "insight."

How does the therapist know when the client's role relationship to him/her will support a certain type of inquiry into forbidden areas? There are several useful criteria, including relaxation, spontaneity, the ability to control loosening, and the dropping of guards. A fifth criterion is the contrasting of the client's present outlook with his/her outlook in the immediate past, and a sixth is the contrasting of the present with the future outlook. Optimism, flexibility, and the dropping of defensiveness constitute additional criteria. The ability to enact an aggressive role with the therapist is also a criterion. Another is the ability to construe the task of the therapist. Related to this is the individual's ability to relate attitudes and constructs to his/her role as a patient. Finally, lack of impulsiveness and of obliqueness in approaching a topic are useful criteria of readiness for new ventures.

Control of Anxiety and Guilt.   Anxiety and guilt are not necessarily all bad. "The task of the therapist is to assess them, take account of their functioning in his client, and deal with them in the light of the welfare of the particular personality" (*ibid.,* p. 1111). Anxiety is detected in various ways. The criteria for the client's readiness for movement listed above are related to anxiety. Knowledge of common anxieties and of the experiences of the client and observation of the client's behavior and communications are other sources for detecting client anxiety. Restriction of discussion, use of self-reassuring devices, and weeping may indicate anxiety.

One of the outcomes of therapy is to diminish or increase anxiety, as necessary. There are, however, temporary devices to keep anxiety under control. Support and reassurance techniques may be used to reduce anxiety as well as guilt. Acceptance, leading the interview into structured areas, allowing sufficient time for reconstruction before proceeding into another problem area, the use of binding, differentiating, introspection, anticipating hurdles, encouraging dependence, structuring the interview, and controlling the tempo of the interview are additional methods of controlling anxiety.

Guilt may be controlled by similar techniques. In addition, reconstruction of the core role—the awareness of the loss of this role being the cause of guilt—is an important method. Alternative roles may be sought with the client. Interpretation of the persons whom the client uses to delineate his/her role is useful. Broadening the base of the role relation to the therapist also temporarily replaces the lost role.

Psychotherapeutic Experimentation.   Psychotherapy and scientific research are similar. The client uses the scientific method in working out problems. The client first elaborates problems and then, in loosening, becomes creative in developing new ideas. Third, by tightening, the client formulates testable hypotheses. Finally, the client engages in experiments to test, or validate, his/her hypotheses.

Psychotherapeutic experimentation serves several functions. First, it provides a framework in which the client can anticipate alternative outcomes. Second, it places the client in touch with reality and tests the client's construct system. It also serves as a check on the therapist's construction of the case. In addition, experimentation opens up new vistas of experience. Finally, it puts the client in touch with other people and enables the client to see how others view their worlds, so that he/she may play a role in relation to them.

The therapist encourages experimentation, both inside and outside the interviewing room, by various techniques. Enactment, discussed earlier, is one of the most useful of these. Permissiveness, responsiveness, projecting the client into a novel situation, and seeing that the client has the necessary tools are methods that encourage and set the stage for actual experimentation. The therapist also gets the client to develop hypotheses or make specific predictions. The therapist asks the client to make interpretations of others' outlooks, to portray how another person views himself/herself, and to portray how another person views the client. Negative predictions may be encouraged. Or the client thinks his/her behavior would be different; this often leads to behaving differently. The therapist may directly encourage the client to take certain actions. Finally, the client may be placed in a social situation in which others are enthusiastically attempting what the client could do well if he/she wanted to.

Obstacles to experimentation include the client's hostility, anxiety, guilt, or dependence; the threat of outcomes; and the nonelaborative choice, that is, the client's belief that no matter what the outcome, he or she is trapped. Some of these difficulties also constitute hazards in experimentation. Other hazards are present: the client may constrict as a result of being "burned"; excessive loosening may result; or the therapist may urge the client to experiment in an inappropriate setting, with disastrous results.

Fixed-Role Therapy

Fixed-role therapy is a type of psychotherapy that is specifically derived from the psychology of personal constructs and is based on observations of the effects of dramatic experience. Fixed-role therapy begins with the therapist requesting the client to write a character sketch of himself/herself. The client does so in the third person with no detailed outline but with only the following instructions:

> I want you to write a character sketch of Harry Brown, just as if he were the principal character in a play. Write it as it might be written by a friend who knows him very *intimately* and very *sympathetically,* perhaps better than anyone even really could know him. Be sure to write it in the third person. For example, start out by saying, Harry Brown is. . . . (Kelly, 1995, vol. 1, p. 323)

The self-characterization is the basis for writing the fixed-role sketch. The sketch is designed to invite the client to explore certain sharply contrasting behaviors. It develops a major theme rather than correcting minor faults. It is intended to set the stage for the resumption of growth and movement rather than to attempt a major psychotherapeutic relocation. It sets up hypotheses that can be tested quickly. There is emphasis on role percep-tions and role relationships with other people. It is desirable that the sketch be developed by a group of experienced clinicians if possible.

The procedure involved in fixed-role therapy is introduced to the client following the diagnostic phase of therapy, in preparation for going into the client's problems. The charac-ter sketch is presented with a name other than the client's. Following the reading of the sketch, the *acceptance check* determines whether the client understands and accepts the sketch as representing someone he/she would like to know, not someone he/she would like to be. If the sketch is accepted as plausible and not threatening, the rehearsal sequence be-gins. This is initiated with the request that the client for the next two weeks act as if he/she were the person in the sketch with the therapist's help in interviews scheduled every other day. The client keeps the copy of the sketch, reads it at least three times a day, and tries to act, think, talk, and be like the person in the sketch.

Clients are skeptical and report failure during the greater part of the two weeks; if the process were easy, it would be ineffective. The client is given help in enacting the role in work situations, social relationships, family situations, and situations involving life orienta-tion and plan. Rehearsal takes place through role playing. The therapist treats the client as though the client were the person in the sketch. As interviews continue, the client con-tributes more and begins to feel like the person whose role he/she is playing. In the final in-terview, the role is withdrawn. The client is more active, while the therapist listens. The therapist does not resort to urging the client to adopt the new role. If the client has found it effective, the client will accept it. The therapist decides whether therapy should be contin-ued by another method, or the therapist may, if the client requests it, continue the rehearsals for another predetermined period.

The experience is kept realistic by creating a role that has many day-to-day implica-tions and by keeping the interviews geared to practical situations. Although it is not gener-ally helpful to schizoid individuals, it has helped put some in contact with reality. The haz-ard of unreality is thus not a great one. A greater hazard is that by pressuring the client to act, the therapist will force the client to act within his or her present construct system and push the client to the opposite extreme of his/her dichotomous constructs.

The client's insistence that although the role is working out, he/she is only acting is not undesirable. It indicates that the client has not been threatened. If this attitude persists to the end, however, and the role is too easily accepted, the sketch may not be adequate to lead the client to face crucial issues. The development of spontaneous behavior in which the client forgets that he/she is acting is a good sign as long as the client does not look back on it with embarrassment. The reactions of other people to the client as being different in-dicate progress in fixed-role therapy and lead to further progress by reducing threat. The best evidence of progress is when the client says, "I feel as if this were the *real* me." This is always accompanied by a marked shift in the client's formulation of problems.

While difficulty with the role and criticism of it are not bad signs, the failure of the client to accept the method or to see the role and its implications in contrast to old con-structs indicates that the method cannot be used as a vehicle for readjustment. Indications for fixed-role therapy include limited time for treatment, desirability of avoiding strong de-pendent transference, unavoidable client-therapist relationships outside therapy, inexperi-enced clinicians, the presence of obvious social and situational components in the case, need for termination of another type of therapy sequence, need for establishment of contact with everyday reality, uncertainty of the client's readiness for change, and defensiveness on the part of the client with respect to therapy. The method is relatively safe, even though it substitutes a new, prefabricated construction system rather than reworking parts of the old one, because the new system is enacted or play-acted with an artificial identity alongside the old structure, and there are no implications at the outset that the new structure may eventually replace the old one.

EXAMPLE

This example is taken from Neimeyer's (1980) chapter, "George Kelly as Therapist," which provides verbatim excerpts of Kelly working with a 28-year-old university student named Cal. Cal's presenting concerns focused on career choice and academic issues. The example that follows comes from the twenty-first session of their work together. We chose such an advanced session because it seemed to communicate so nicely the translation of Kelly's theory into practice. The explanatory comments that follow were made by Neimeyer.

By the 21st session Kelly has carried his investigation of Cal's interpersonal construing to deeper levels, and has begun to grapple with his *preverbal* constructions as they bear on the therapist and other important figures in his life. In Kellian terms, a preverbal construct "is one which continues to be used even though it has no consistent word symbol" (1955, p. 459) and is apt to deal with those sorts of elements of which the young child could be aware (1955, p. 461). In attending closely to the threat that Cal verbalizes at the prospect of becoming close to him, Kelly has begun to suspect the operation of an unspoken but very fundamental construction that governs Cal's relationships to others. Early in the session Cal contended that the psychotherapy client can be taken "strictly as a collection of various facts and fictions, worthy of critical inquiry," and has added, "I don't think it's necessary to go beyond that." Hearing a theme similar to that expressed during their earlier enactment [an earlier session], Kelly seeks an elaborated understanding of Cal's remark:

KELLY: So any kind of *tenderness* I might express toward you, anything of that order. . . .
CAL: No, because. . . .
K: Because this is not necessary?
C: Well, it may or may not be.
K: I see.
C: Uh, if the tenderness is . . . shown because of an emotional feeling toward the individual that is trying to prevent, what, an unpleasant occurrence for him . . . just out of kindness on your part, then no. . . .
K: So if it's merely tenderness in the sense of being, uh, being kind of butter-fingered, in the sense of being unwilling to get in there and go to work on the job, if it's an evasive kind of tactic. . . .
C: Yeah.
K: It has no place there. Now this makes sense with other things you've said, I think. You don't want tender-mindedness in the sense of being so tender that you can't come to grips with reality, come to grips with your problem.

C: Yeah. What I was thinking, though, uh, was being tender or kind, or nice simply because you don't want to be nasty.

K: Yeah, yeah. And that is just a kind of a, kind of a superficial social mannerism, huh?

C: Yeah.

K: Hardly worth the time and effort it takes to carry on the interview. 'Cause other people have been kind to you in this sense.

C: Oh sure, sure.

K: Uh, kind of *politeness,* just politeness.

C: As we refer to it here, yeah.

K: Yeah. I'm looking for a word to describe this kind of. . . .

C: Well, I think that's as good as any. Overpoliteness maybe would be more correct.

K: Let's call it *overpoliteness* then, you and I.

What Kelly is attempting to do is to assist Cal in *articulating* his preverbal construction, in finding an appropriate verbal symbol to represent the otherwise tacit dimension of meaning. Once articulated in a more communicable verbal medium, the preverbal construct may be more amenable to therapeutic reconstruction and experimentation (Kelly, 1955, p. 465). Having assigned the provisional label of "overpoliteness" to Cal's construct, Kelly goes on to investigate the interpersonal incidents that it was originally designed to construe.

K: Yeah, I see, overpoliteness. Yeah. Now this brings us to the next part that I wish you'd do some exploring on. And I'll help you as much as I can with the experience, but we've got to work on it together, you know. Have people been overpolite to you, in certain crucial ways?

C: I think the answer is yes. I don't think I can pinpoint any particular, isolated incident.

K: Let's work on it. Let's elaborate and see what we can get out of this, this kind of question.

In citing situations that exemplified his construction (e.g., his father's willingness to continue supporting him financially), Cal began to question the earlier designation of such behavior in terms of "overpoliteness." Kelly, sensitive to the difficulty of finding an appropriate verbal symbol, observes:

K: Well . . . we've got to the level of indulgence now, haven't we? We're talking about a kind of indulgence of you. Is this what you're talking about now?

C: Mmmm . . . would you express it again?

K: A while ago we talked about overpoliteness.

C: Ummm-hmm.

K: Then we moved in, asking about if you may get this sense of something like overpoliteness—maybe that's not the term—in your relations with your past. And you say, "yes and no"; you don't see this as anything that your father intends or that it is essentially inherent in his intent or his behavior. But you say it is a *sense* of overpoliteness. . . .

C: Well, I really define overpoliteness as sweet, syrupy politeness. I don't think that's exactly what you can say.

K: Yeah. There's another term we ought to have now, for what we're thinking of. I tried "indulgence," in the sense of being indulged? Being patted on the head as a child? Being treated too tenderly?

C: I don't think any of those terms define the situation.

K: Yeah. Let's find something, so we can deal with it.

C: "Indulged" may be the closest.

Having formulated a second, perhaps more adequate designation of Cal's pre-verbal discrimination, Kelly is prepared to change tacks. He moves Cal into the investigation of his problematic role relationships to others—both in the microcosm of therapy and the macrocosm of his familial and social world—with an eye to the operation of the client's tacit construction in these areas.

Kelly begins this exploration by focusing upon the character of the therapeutic relationship.

K: [Y]ou've said, both by implication and explicitly, you've said so often in here, "I don't want to get too close." There's something in the relationship that turns soft or something that does not enable us to get on with our job.

C: Now, may I throw something in there? When you meet an individual—and I think this goes for anybody—you mentally develop a picture of them. . . .

K: Yes.

C: And then you build upon this picture, embroider it, put sweet roses and lilacs and so on around it. (Laughs) In getting close to that person, you might tear this down. You might find out that your mental picture of beauty and so on is not entirely correct. The roses have thorns.

K: Yeah, you know before, you put it another way. You didn't want to get close because you didn't want that person to lose his objectivity. You wanted to always be prepared to, . . . for the surgeon's knife. That you might become. . . .

C: Yeah.

K: . . . protective of yourself. Now let's turn this a little bit differently. You're saying essentially you start with a rosy picture, but behind these roses you have a sense there may be thorns. And so by keeping at a distance, you can see him as a rosy person.

This line of inquiry is clearly an important one for Cal, and he spontaneously documents "a situation in which an individual doesn't seem to fit the pattern" in which he put him. He refers to an incident that occurred when he was quite young.

C: The time [was] up at Centerville where I was pushed into the goldfish pond.

K: Yes.

C: Now I'd say I'd pictured Tom, the fellow that pushed me in, in a certain way.

K: Mm-hm.

C: Well, he pushed me in . . . it's a perfectly natural reaction. I mean, there are times when you do it just for the heck of it. But this might not have fitted into that picture.

K: So there almost. . . .

C: So there goes my picture.

K: So there almost, in a literal and perfectly physical sense, you got close enough to him to get pushed into a pond (both laugh), and suddenly your picture of Tom had to be revised.

C: And I think the anger which exploded in me was not an anger directed at Tom alone.

K: But at the loss of your picture.

C: But at the loss of my picture. And it was a, what, radiating anger just booming out in all directions at anything and everything that comes in its path . . . it's not an anger that. . . .

K: It was barely that, being pushed in the fishpond, but the destruction of this beautiful picture you have drawn of Tom.

C: That follows.

Both Cal and Kelly recognize that this incident from the remote past remains significant, not because Tom had mischievously pushed Cal in the pond, but because, in so doing, he *invalidated* the "rosy" constructions Cal had used to anticipate the behavior of a friend. The client's experience of intense *anger* is particularly noteworthy here, since anger, in construct theory terms, can be conceptualized as "the awareness of invalidation of constructs leading to hostility" (McCoy, 1977, p. 121). Indeed, Cal shows remarkable perspicacity in recognizing that his rage is a reaction to the "loss of his picture" and not merely a response to Tom's literal behavior. To grasp the full implications of this scenario, however, one also must appreciate Kelly's unique definition of *hostility:* "The continued effort to extort validational evidence in favor of a type of social prediction which has already proved itself a failure" ([Kelly] 1955, p. 510). By defining hostility in terms of the phenomenology of the hostile person rather than in terms of his or her impact upon others, Kelly draws attention to its psychological function: it forces the social "facts" to fit a failing hypothesis, to buttress a shaky construction which might otherwise crumble under the weight of the evidence. Examining the scenario in this light, it is Cal, rather than Tom, who may be the hostile party. Rather than revising his "embroidered" conception of interpersonal relations in the face of invalidation, he continues to interpose sufficient distance between himself and other persons that the accuracy of his procrustean framework need not be called into question. The ramifications of this childhood incident continue to unfold in the therapeutic dialogue.

K: This spreading anger, spurting anger, was not so much directed at Tom but at something about having the whole situation fall apart on you . . .

C: Yeah. I would say yes. I would say that since he was the instigator of the collapse of the house of cards, the anger fell on his shoulders first.

K: Yeah.

C: But now, I'm trying to find something here. As I remember, I think my mother came to cajole me out of my anger. And I reacted in the same anger, that is, the same feeling of anger, against her.

Kelly suspects the reemergence of Cal's earlier preverbal construction relating to overpoliteness or indulgence at this point, and so remarks:

K: So you didn't want comfort then. The kind of comfort, or cajoling, or manipulation. . . .

C: Evidently not.

K: Was she being "overly polite" at the time or something? Soft-soaping?

C: Soft-soaping? A word people like not to fit.

K: Okay. "Soft-soaping" now comes; maybe it's a better expression for the moment. We may find better ones later.

C: Um-hm, um-hm.

K: In other words, here you were in an emergency, your house of cards having collapsed. . . .

C: Um-hm.

K: . . . and she came out with soft soap. We've got a double problem here, haven't we? Not only in relation to Tom. . . .

C: I'm trying to figure it out, trying to see it here. Would it be that she approached it—now "adult" is the word I see, but it isn't, doesn't quite fit—from the adult point of view. I mean, she was witnessing it all the time, and, I don't know. . . .

K: Superficial and alien, and *other*. . . .

C: But that isn't the way I saw it at that particular time.

K: That wasn't your problem. . . .

C: No. My problem was that I was soaking wet! (Both laugh)

Cal's remark that these new and very apropos interpretations of the childhood incident weren't the way he saw them at that particular time is worthy of mention. It reflects his growing appreciation of the "constructive alternativism" that Kelly is trying to inculcate in him, the sense that even the most "obvious" meanings attributed to past events are subject to liberating reinterpretations in the present. Such a philosophy implies, as Kelly states, that "man can enslave himself with his own ideas and then win his freedom by reconstruing his life" (1955, p. 21). This is, in large part, the goal of personal construct therapy.

Kelly first tests his understanding of Cal's experience before elaborating it further.

K: Now let me see if I've got it. You said not only was the house of cards fallen that involved a pictured relationship between you and your friend, between you and Tom . . . but when someone came to deal with it, it was kind of an outsider who did not understand; it was dealt with superficially by soft-soaping, without any appreciation for what the real issue was based on. . . .

C: Yeah—and yet looking at it, you can hardly say it was any other way; I mean you could hardly see it any other way if you were the other person.

K: Okay, of course. But we're talking about how it seemed to *you* at that moment.

C: Yeah.

K: And to come up to you and pat you on the head or try to hug you or something like this (made) you even more angry.

C: Um-hm.

K: You didn't want to be close to your mother at that time. It wasn't closeness, in that sort of soft-soaping, comforting way. You had yourself a problem.

C: Yeah.

K: And you're saying the same to me. "Don't cajole me out of my problems. Let's stand off here at arm's length. . . ."

C: Yeah.

K: . . . and make sure we understand this thing, something other than just . . . soft-soaping.

Cal then spontaneously begins to take Tom's perspective on the incident.

C: Tom, of course, had no intention of causing this to happen. Now, I don't mean pushing me in the pool (laughs), I mean my house of cards coming down . . . Tom . . . has always had a group to play in whereas I have not. So he understands, understood, a different relationship between boys.

K: Yeah.

C: Whereas I understood the essentially . . . *adult* relationship between myself and my parents.

K: So it was unthinkable to have . . . as unthinkable to have that other human being push you into the pond as it was to have your father push your mother into a pond, or push you into a pond.

C: Yeah—at that particular time it would have been unthinkable.

K: At that particular time.

C: Yeah.

K: So you perceived Tom in terms of a . . . a set of images of people in the world which were adult images.

C: Yeah.

K: Tom had behaved like . . . like children behave. He . . . it did not mean for him what it would have meant for you, or what it did mean for you. And, thus, this was *completely incoherent* behavior.

C: Um-hm.

K: Thus the structure of your social world was invalidated right at that moment. This was the falling of the house of cards.

Kelly then begins to draw together the separate but related themes woven through the dialogue.

K: You see, what I'm wondering is, you lost your framework within which you could perceive people.

C: Yeah.

K: I'm wondering if you lost an important friend at the same time.

C: In that, perhaps, at that particular time *any* friend was an important friend.

K: That makes sense.

C: Yes, That makes sense.

K: My goodness, we've got this thing falling down now in three ways. You lost the validity of a framework within which you see social relations. . . .

C: Yeah.

K: . . . completely irrational behavior on his part. Two, you lost *him,* since you didn't have too many "Toms" in your life.

C: Yeah.

K: And finally, you got treated by the soft-soap method. . . .

C: Yeah.

K: Which pulls together quite a number of things here.

Cal clarifies Kelly's second point, maintaining that he "did not lose Tom as a physical being, as a person, but as a house of cards." Kelly acknowledges this and continues.

K: Well, that's the part that you've made pretty clear, I think. That's a point that would be easy to overlook, 'cause you could look at it merely in terms of losing

Tom. But as you point out, that was not the key. It was perhaps a more important loss than the loss of any one person.

C: Yeah.

K: The loss of Tom you could stand. You might have regretted it for a few days, but
this was a specific loss. The loss of your framework within which to see interpersonal relationships is a devastating loss. Throws you right back at the beginning again, got to start all over, learning about people.

C: Um-hm, um-hm.

K: And you ain't never quite felt that you caught up, huh?

C: (Sighs) I'd say you're correct.

Cal takes the next step, relating this original incident to his present interpersonal aloofness.

C: Uh, in rebuilding, having once had—I don't think this comes entirely from one
event—but having once had this beautiful, false-fronted building knocked into
kindling wood, in rebuilding, there's a (sigh), what, sense of fear? That someone's going to come along and kick it down again. And perhaps each time
someone—well, I guess I'm getting fantastic in the description —someone
hauls off to swing his foot at it, you pull it down yourself, or duck, or dodge,
something like that. That follows anyway.

K: Here's my framework for looking at people, but don't you folks come too close
to it because I don't want you to kick it over.

By this point Cal seems to have established a revised, more communicable construction of the character of his role relationships which appears *permeable,* applicable to new as well as old experiences. Kelly tests the range of convenience of the new
structure by assessing its ability to subsume a specific problematic situation from the
recent past: Cal's intense, seemingly inexplicable anger at pledging a college fraternity and then being told he would have to go through an initiation period.

K: Now when the fraternity situation came up this fall and it looked as if. . . . They
decided you should go through an initiation. . . . This was like being pushed into
the fishpond? Adult relationships you would expect, and suddenly it turns out to
be kid stuff?

C: That might have been. . . .

K: You had a house of cards for your fraternity?

C: I wouldn't limit it to that.

K: Even broader than that, huh?

C: I would say—now this is supposition, I don't know—but following this on
through, my statement would be that it was not my house of cards for the fraternity, but the house of cards for my entire life.

K: I suppose the moral of this is to stay away from fishponds and fraternities. (Both
laugh) I think it's a very pointed issue.

Having recognized Cal's past and present hostility in forcing persons into his inflexible, if insubstantial, perceptual categories, and having dealt with the anxiety into
which he was precipitated whenever his "house of cards" fell apart, Kelly and his client
conclude by reflecting upon the therapeutic partnership which they seem to have
formed.

K: Well, we've been hitting it pretty hard and heavy here for an hour. You've . . . come to grips with this thing, I think, as well as I've ever seen you, if not better. I have a feeling of your . . . your helping me more, I mean working together as a team.

C: Uh, the feeling that I've come to grips with it better, thinking over the past session, would the way to describe it be that it's like facing, uh, let's say, going swimming? Until you get into it, that water's awfully cold. But once you're in there for a minute or two, it's okay. You get along fine.

K: Uh-hm. You have a feeling yet that you're in over your ears? Or at least up to your neck?

C: I don't know.

K: Yeah, that's a little hard to answer.

C: But very definitely there for a while I was having trouble keeping the thoughts together. And yet, what, the past minute or so I've been doing pretty good. I've been clicking right along.

K: We've been wrapping up a little bit, too.

C: Um-hm.

K: We had so many things kind of coming in at us there for a while, it was hard to keep together. It is for me, too. But if we work at it as a kind of team combination, I think between the two of us we can probably make a lot of sense that neither of us could make alone.

C: Um-hm.

K: Provided, of course, you help me.

C: Vice versa.

K: Yes.

SUMMARY AND EVALUATION

Summary.   The psychology of personal constructs is based on the philosophical position of constructive alternativism, which is the position that there are many workable ways for a person to construe the world. The system is developed on the basis of one postulate and its elaboration by means of eleven corollaries. The basic assumption is that "a person's processes are psychologically channelized by the ways in which he anticipates events" (p. 46). The individual's system of personal constructs determines the way the world is construed. Constructs are dichotomous, and the individual chooses the alternative through which he/she anticipates the greater possibility for extension and definition of the system. Constructs have certain formal characteristics and are organized into a hierarchy of subsystems. The characteristics of constructs form the basis for setting up a system of diagnostic constructs, which are used by the clinician to analyze, understand, and subsume the client's construct system. Changes in behavior involve changes in the personal-construct system.

Therapy is thus directed toward the reconstruction of the client's system of personal constructs. In therapy based on the psychology of personal constructs, the therapist is active, responding to the client in a great variety of ways. Enactment, or role playing, plays a large part in therapy, and in one specific approach to therapy—fixed-role therapy—the playing of an assigned role by the client constitutes the major aspect of the therapy.

The process of therapy is conceived as being similar to the process of scientific experimentation. The task of the therapist is to help the client develop hypotheses and test them experimentally, both within and outside the interview situation. Science is thus the model that clients use in reconstructing their lives. The therapist participates in the process as a helper and collaborator, using a wide variety of methods and techniques.

Evaluation.   Kelly's approach to psychotherapy is one of the most systematic, if not the most systematic, that has appeared. It is developed elaborately and in considerable detail, which makes it perhaps the most difficult approach to summarize of any of those included in this volume. Its detail makes it both fascinating and frustrating to read. Although the basic postulate and its corollaries are amazingly simple, their elaboration is amazingly complex. There are probably almost as many concepts as there are in psychoanalysis. Many common concepts or terms are used in somewhat different ways than is common in psychology or psychoanalysis. These include *anxiety, guilt, threat, hostility, aggressiveness,* and *fear.* There are also many new terms, such as *preemptive constructs, constellatory constructs, propositional constructs, submergence, suspension,* and *permeability.* It becomes difficult to keep all these in mind when reading about the development and application of the theory in therapy. The reader needs to have a system of constructs that is comprehensive, propositional, and permeable to be able to absorb the material.

The attraction of this approach could be limited by the formidability of the new concepts and the detail. Apparently, few have become attracted to it since its publication. To master it to the point of being able to practice it would require extensive study, training, and experience. In spite of its detail, the published material is not sufficient, as Kelly notes, for the application of the approach in therapy. While there is considerable discussion of method and technique, there are no actual therapy protocols to illustrate application.

Nevertheless, for the therapist who may not want to master this particular approach, there are an amazing number of details relating to problems and techniques in therapy—discussions of what the therapist should do when. For example, ten kinds of weeping are distinguished. There is a detailed discussion of what to look for in a classroom in appraising the school environment. The reader will also benefit from many other discussions, apart from the particular theoretical approach. There is a fresh, new way of looking at things, divorced from the usual clinical terminology or jargon. The approach is not diagnostically or externally oriented.

This lack of diagnostic orientation leads to a consideration of the phenomenological nature of the approach. One of its basic concepts is that "each man contemplates in his own personal way the stream of events upon which he finds himself so swiftly borne" (Kelly, 1955, vol. 1, p. 3). Kelly feels, however, that the phenomenological approach leaves the individual's personal constructs locked up in privacy, whereas they must be brought out for public view. At least the psychotherapist must be able to construe the personal constructs of the client, and this, according to Kelly, goes beyond phenomenology. It is difficult not to see this as an expression of the basic impossibility of avoiding a phenomenological approach, since the constructions of the therapist, while external, public, or objective from the client's viewpoint, are nonetheless phenomenological from the therapist's viewpoint. Here is one place where Kelly apparently is inconsistent in applying the basic concept noted above.

The same difficulty appears later when he says, "We attempt to use the phenomenologist's approach to arrive at personalized constructs which have a wide range of meaning for the given individual; then we attempt to piece together this high-level type of data with what we know about other persons" (*ibid.*, p. 455). How do we obtain this knowledge of other people, except phenomenologically? In most instances, however, Kelly is consistently phenomenological in his approach, although he does not feel that his system is neophenomenological. His basic conception of a role relationship is that the therapist, for example, subsumes the construct system of the client by an acceptance (defined as willingness to see the world through the client's eyes) and thus is able to construe things as the client does, which enables the therapist to predict or anticipate the client's behavior. This is exactly the approach taken by Combs and Snygg (1959) in their phenomenological system.

It is interesting to consider Kelly's approach as an alternative to client-centered therapy, since both have a common phenomenological base. Nothing in phenomenology leads only to the client-centered approach to psychotherapy. Perceptions or the personal constructs related to perceptions may be changed in various ways. Whereas in the client-centered approach, the therapist operates in one way to facilitate change, in therapy based on the psychology of personal constructs, the therapist functions in another way. In the latter approach, the therapist appears to be highly active, prodding, pushing, and stimulating the client.

It is this continually active nature of therapy that creates the need for the therapist to be constantly engaged in evaluation and judgment of the client and of his/her needs in order to make decisions about what to do next. This places a tremendous responsibility on the therapist. After reading Kelly's books, one may be left with the feeling that there are few therapists who would want to accept this responsibility. One is led again to the conclusion that it is not so much what is done as the way in which it is done that is important in therapy; the danger of damage is apparently minimized when the therapist is obviously interested and concerned. The client responds to the relationship rather than to the methods. The personal-construct therapist—or at least in Kelly's writings—gives the client the impression that he/she is in complete control. While it appears to be close to the "doctor-knows-best" approach, Kelly recognizes the dangers of this method and disavows it. He mentions several cases in which suicide attempts were precipitated and points out the errors of the therapists in terms of this theory. However, it may be that the errors were not so much due to a failure to apply the theory as to a failure to understand the client, together with excessive activity and manipulation, apparently in an effort to play the active, pushing role demanded by the approach. Kelly warns against the therapist playing God, but a therapist using this approach almost has to be God.

The fixed-role therapy is a method of instigating client activity that has some similarities to the prescriptions of client activity in other approaches, such as those of Salter (1949) and of Wolpe (1990). It is a much more systematic and individually adapted approach, however, than those of Salter and of Wolpe; the prescription is not a blanket one but varies with the client. It also appears to differ in that through the fixed-role sketch, the client's attitudes and perceptions are changed prior to the change in activity, rather than the client's being forced into actions that, it is presumed, will generate changes in attitudes and feelings following reinforcement.

In addition to its active, manipulative aspects, Kelly's approach is also apparently highly rational and intellectual. "Psychotherapy is the intelligent manipulation of various psychological processes" (Kelly, 1955, vol. 2, p. 1071). Psychotherapy is likened to a scientific experiment. Rogers (1956), in his review of Kelly, emphasized this aspect, noting, "He is continually thinking about the client, and about his own procedures, in ways so complex that there seems no room for entering into an emotional relationship with the client" (pp. 357–358). Nevertheless, it may be that Kelly's description of the way he practiced psychotherapy is not quite the way he actually practiced it. While he no doubt was highly active, and cognitively oriented, there is evidence that he was sensitive to the various possible meanings that a client's behavior (such as weeping) or statements may have had.

The approach is highly provocative and stimulating. The theory of behavior and personality is probably more significant than is the application of the approach in psychotherapy; the theory can be useful in connection with other methods, since there seems to be nothing inherent in it that would lead to these particular methods of therapy. Many of the methods are those commonly used in other approaches to psychotherapy, including psychoanalysis. The unique approach developed in fixed-role therapy is limited, since, as Rogers (1956) pointed out, it is useful only with clients who are not familiar with the method. Many of the concepts or constructs are similar to those of other theorists, but there are unique aspects that are more than the coining of new words for old concepts. The forward-looking aspect manifested in the basic postulate involving anticipation is unique; it is similar to the concepts of Rotter and of Phillips (see previous editions of this book), although Kelly develops it much more extensively. There is also some similarity between the concept of self-actualization and the concept of elaborative choice (that persons choose for themselves the alternative in a dichotomized construct through which they anticipate the greater possibility for extension and definition of their systems).

Perhaps one of the major unique concepts is the notion of the dichotomous nature of constructs. The notion of contrast is, of course, nothing new, but it is one that has never been given the place it appears to deserve in psychological theory. It is easily recognized that satisfaction exists only in contrast to or in relation to lack of satisfaction or dissatisfaction. This relativity relationship has been elevated by Garan (1963) into the basic psychological causal law. While perhaps it does not warrant such elevation, it does deserve more attention than it has received, and Kelly has made a real contribution here, which does not seem to have been recognized as yet. The relativity relationship contributes, for example, to the dilemma of determinism versus free will, which Kelly considers.

Finally, Kelly's handling of motivation is provocative. There is no concept of motivation or any need for such a concept, since he begins by postulating a process rather than an inert substance that must be put into movement. There is thus no consideration of the aspects of motivation, which are central to so-called dynamic psychology. Kelly's basic postulate has a motivational aspect, however, including a goal or direction of all behavior. This postulate is not too different from the motivational theory of the phenomenology of Combs and Snygg (1959) that a person's basic motivation is the maintenance and enhancement of the phenomenal self.

Similarly, there is no place for the concepts of reward or reinforcement in Kelly's theory. Events are validated by perception of correct anticipation. The scientist is not controlled by reward.

The scientist who attempts only to accumulate a backlog of reinforcements is likely to become rigid, timid, opinionated, and generally inert. The scientist who is inventive, curious, receptive, and progressive is the one who is as happy over negative results and the enlightenment they offer as he is about the positive ones. (Kelly, 1955, vol. 2, p. 1166)

One might quibble over definitions of reward, but the general point is clear. The concept of validation is much broader and thus more useful than the concept of reinforcement.

The psychology of personal constructs presents a view of human behavior that is significant. Bruner (1956) has called it "the single greatest contribution of the past decade to the theory of personality functioning." In a review of *Clinical Psychology and Personality: The Selected Papers of George Kelly,* Appelbaum (1970), while recognizing that Kelly "has been a significant figure in recent psychology," contended that he has given us little that is new, but simply reiterates the phenomenological and humanistic point of view. "His eminence [was] an accident of his time. . . . His point of view will fade away into the limbo of [the history of ideas], and even now its main interest lies more in what it tells us about our professional culture than in its substance."

But Appelbaum was wrong. Kelly's point of view has not faded away. If anything, there appears to be a much renewed, revitalized interest in Kelly and personal construct psychology now (Neimeyer, 1990). This renewed interest can be seen reflected in (a) numerous personal construct psychology books, many of which have appeared in the past 10 to 15 years (Addams-Webber, 1979; Addams-Webber & Mancuso, 1983; Bonarius, Holland, & Rosenberg, 1981; Epting, 1984; Landfield & Epting, 1987; Landfield & Leitner, 1980); (b) the reissuing of Kelly's *The Psychology of Personal Constructs* (Vols. 1 & 2) in 1991; (c) increasingly active personal construct work taking place throughout the world (Neimeyer, 1985; Neimeyer, Baker, & Neimeyer, 1990); (d) the establishment of the *International Journal of Personal Construct Psychology* in 1988, retitled the *Journal of Constructivist Psychology* in 1994; (e) stimulating national and international personal construct conferences (e.g., see Neimeyer & Neimeyer, 1991); and (f) the introduction of a biennial series on advances in personal construct psychology (Neimeyer & Neimeyer, 1990).

Indeed, Kelly's point of view appears to be very much alive and well today. In a recent review of Kelly's reissued volumes, some quotes by Neimeyer (1992) illustrate that. Consider the following.

> Kelly's work . . . has gained increasing force and momentum in contemporary times. (p. 994)
> Kelly's work continues to appear prophetic, revealing an uncommon depth, distance, and clarity of vision. (p. 995)
> Kelly's theory enjoys the irony of becoming increasingly contemporary with age. . . . (p. 995)
> The value of Kelly's treatise remains undiminished in contemporary times, assuring its generative, as well as historical value in the years ahead. (pp. 996–997)

As those quotes show, Neimeyer's review nicely communicates the continuing relevance and value of Kelly's classic work, *The Psychology of Personal Constructs,* for our day and age.

As a therapy approach, Kelly's system, however, has received little testing. "[I]n spite of the relatively extensive clinical literature deriving from personal construct theory, the usual comparative outcome study that characterizes much of psychotherapy research is conspicuous by its rarity" (Neimeyer, 1993, p. 228). But with all this renewed interest and activity taking place in personal construct psychology, perhaps such research will soon follow. Let us hope so.

Last, it may be ultimately true (as Appelbaum, 1970, stated) that Kelly has contributed little beyond what other phenomenologists and humanists have given us; but he has integrated and systematized it. His particular integration and his concepts and terminology may not persist, but the basic substance—the point of view—undoubtedly will, since it appears to be necessary for an adequate understanding of, and therapy with, human beings. In addition, Kelly has stimulated a reexamination of some traditional and current views of human behavior and therapy. He has succeeded in a wish stated in 1963: "If I had to end my life on some final note, I think I would like it to be a question, preferably a basic one, well posed and challenging, and beckoning me to where only others after me may go, rather than a terminal conclusion—no matter how well documented" (Kelly, 1969).

REFERENCES

Addams-Webber, J. R. (1979). *Personal construct theory: Concepts and applications.* New York: Wiley-Interscience.

Addams-Webber, J. R., & Manucuso, J. C. (Eds.). (1983). *Applications of personal construct theory.* New York: Academic Press.

Appelbaum, S. A. (1970). The accidental eminence of George Kelly. [Review of *Clinical psychology and personality: The selected papers of George Kelly,* edited by B. Maher.] *Psychiatry and Social Science Review, 3*(12), 20–25.

Bonarius, H., Holland, R., & Rosenberg, D. (Eds.). (1981). *Personal construct psychology: Recent advances in theory and practice.* London: Macmillan.

Bruner, J. (1956). Review of *The psychology of personal constructs* by G. A. Kelly. *Contemporary Psychology, 1,* 355–357.

Combs, A. W., & Snygg, D. (1959). *Individual behavior: A perceptual approach to human behavior* (rev. ed.). New York: Harper & Row.

Epting, F. R. (1984). *Personal construct counseling and psychotherapy.* New York: Wiley.

Garan, D. G. (1963). *The paradox of pleasure and relativity: The psychological causal law.* New York: Philosophical Library.

Kelly, G. A. (1955). *The psychology of personal constructs.* Vol. 1: *A theory of personality.* Vol. 2: *Clinical diagnosis and psychotherapy.* New York: Norton.

Kelly, G. A. (1969). The autobiography of a theory. In B. Maher (Ed.), *Clinical psychology and personality: The selected papers of George Kelly* (pp. 46–65). New York: Wiley.

Kelly, G. A. (1991). *The psychology of personal constructs.* Vol. 1: *A theory of personality.* Vol. 2: *Clinical diagnosis and psychotherapy.* London: Routledge.

Landfield, A. W., & Epting, F. R. (1987). *Personal construct psychology: Clinical and personality assessment.* New York: Human Sciences Press.

Landfield, A. W., & Leitner, L. M. (Eds.). (1980). *Personal construct psychology: Psychotherapy and personality.* New York: Wiley.

Lecky, P. (1945). *Self consistency.* New York: Island Press.

Maher, B. (1969). *Clinical psychology and personality.* New York: McGraw-Hill.

McCoy, M. M. (1977). A reconstruction of emotion. In D. Bannister (Eds.). *New perspectives in personal construct theory.* New York: Academic Press.

Neimeyer, G. J. (1992). Back to the future with the psychology of personal constructs. [Review of Kelly's *The Psychology of Personal Constructs.*] *Contemporary Psychology 37,* 994–997.

Neimeyer, G. J., & Neimeyer, R. A. (Eds.). (1990). *Advances in personal construct psychology* (vol. 1). Greenwich, CT: JAI Press.

Neimeyer, G. J., & Neimeyer, R. A. (Eds.). (1991). Papers from the Eighth International Congress on Personal Construct Psychology. *International Journal of Personal Construct Psychology, 5,* 223–365.

Neimeyer, R. A. (1980). George Kelly as therapist: A review of his tapes. In A. W. Landfield & L. M. Leitner (Eds.). *Personal construct psychology: Psychotherapy and personality* (pp. 74–101). New York: Wiley.

Neimeyer, R. A. (1985). *The development of personal construct psychology.* Lincoln: University of Nebraska Press.

Neimeyer, R. A. (1990). George A. Kelly: In memoriam. *History of Psychology, 22,* 3–14.

Neimeyer, R. A. (1993). An appraisal of constructivist psychotherapies. *Journal of Consulting and Clinical Psychology, 61,* 221–234.

Neimeyer, R. A., Baker, K. D., & Neimeyer, G. J. (1990). The current status of personal construct theory: Some scientometric data. In G. J. Neimeyer & R. A. Neimeyer (Eds.). *Advances in personal construct psychology* (vol. 1, pp. 3–22). Greenwich, CT: JAI Press.

Rogers, C. R. (1956). Intellectualized psychotherapy. [Review of *The psychology of personal constructs* by G. A. Kelly.] *Contemporary Psychology, 1,* 357–358.

Salter, A. (1949). *Conditioned reflex therapy.* New York: Farrar, Straus.

Wolpe, J. (1990). *The practice of behavior therapy* (4th ed.). New York: Pergamon.

chapter 11

Transactional Analysis: Berne

Eric Lennard Berne (1910–1970) was born in Montreal, Canada (being originally named Eric Lennard Bernstein). He was awarded his M.D. from McGill University in 1935 and served his residency in psychiatry at Yale University from 1936 to 1941. After two years as clinical assistant in psychiatry at Mount Zion Hospital in New York, he entered the armed forces. As did a number of other psychiatrists and psychologists who joined the military, he discovered group therapy and began to develop his own approach. After leaving the service in 1946, he settled in Carmel, California, and returned to the study of psychoanalysis with Erik Erikson at the San Francisco Psychoanalytic Institute. He had begun the study of psychoanalysis at the New York Psychoanalytic Institute, with Paul Federn as his analyst, in 1941. His other teachers included Eugen Kahn and Wilder Penfield. He acknowledges being influenced also by Nathan Ackerman, Martin Grotjahn, and Benjamin Weininger.

In the early 1950s, Berne's ideas diverged from psychoanalysis, and he was denied membership in the San Francisco Psychoanalytic Institute when he applied in 1956. His ideas on transactional analysis, which he developed and put into practice during this period, were first publicized in an address at the meeting of the western region of the American Group Psychotherapy Association in 1957. Entitled "Transactional Analysis: A New and Effective Method of Group Treatment," the paper was published in the *American Journal of Psychotherapy* in 1958. In the 1957 volume of the same journal, his article entitled, "Ego States in Psychotherapy," was published.

Berne's first book, *The Mind in Action* (1947), was republished under the title *A Layman's Guide to Psychiatry and Psychoanalysis* (1968). *Transactional Analysis in Psychotherapy* (1961) was followed by *The Structure and Dynamics of Organizations and Groups* (1963b) and *Principles of Group Treatment* (1966). However, it was his book

Games People Play: The Psychology of Human Relationships (1964) that some time after publication and to Berne's surprise became a best seller and launched transactional analysis on its road to popularity. At the time of his death, two manuscripts were ready for publication: *Sex in Human Loving* (1970) and *What Do You Say After You Say Hello?* (1972). A compilation of selections from his books and articles was assembled by Claude Steiner and Carmen Kerr and published under the title *Beyond Games and Scripts* (1976).

In addition to his private practice, Berne held numerous appointments, including consultant in psychiatry to the Surgeon General, United States Army; attending psychiatrist at the Veterans Administration Mental Hygiene Clinic in San Francisco; lecturer in group therapy at the Langley Porter Neuropsychiatric Institute; visiting lecturer in group therapy at the Stanford-Palo Alto Psychiatric Clinic; and adjunct psychiatrist at Mount Zion Hospital.

In 1962, Berne founded and edited the *Transactional Analysis Bulletin,* which became the *Transactional Analysis Journal* in 1971, published by the International Transactional Analysis Association (ITAA). The association was founded in 1964 and grew out of the San Francisco Social Psychiatry Seminars that Berne began in 1958. It became a society of the ITAA under the name San Francisco Transactional Analysis Seminar (see James, 1977).

A recent book, which considers Berne's life, his theoretical and practical contributions, and his overall influence, has been written by Ian Stewart (1992).

BACKGROUND AND DEVELOPMENT

As noted above, Berne's training was in psychoanalysis. He apparently became dissatisfied with the passivity and length of psychoanalytic treatment: he writes of his "ten years of experience with passive interpretive 'psychoanalytic group therapy,' followed by two years of existential group therapy" and then notes that this was followed by eight years of "active transactional group treatment" (1963b, p. 73). However, he did not reject psychoanalysis but felt that "in many cases, it is clear that the most appropriate treatment is formal orthodox psychoanalysis" or modified psychoanalytic psychotherapy; such treatment is not adapted to the group situation, however (Berne, 1966). Transactional analysis as a broad general approach can be preparation for psychoanalysis or other specific approaches.

Berne's ideas were formulated and tried out in a seminar at Carmel (the Carmel Seminar) during the early 1950s. He reports that he first began to use the ideas "with some regularity" in the autumn of 1954 and that by 1956, "the need for and the principles of transactional and game analysis had emerged with sufficient clarity to indicate a more systematic, ongoing therapeutic program" (1961, p. 244).

Most of Berne's writing, as well as his experience, related to group therapy, or group treatment as he preferred to call it. This was the major reason for not including Berne's transactional analysis in the first edition of this book. The dilution and oversimplification because of its popularization was an additional reason for its absence in the second edition. It is included in this edition in an attempt to present an accurate summary drawn from Berne's own writings for serious students. Berne did work with individual clients, and his basic 1961 book, subtitled *A Systematic Individual and Social Psychiatry,* applies to individual therapy as well as to group therapy. Individual therapy may be useful in preparing an individual for group treatment, or it may be useful or necessary along with or following group treatment.

Although Berne's *Games People Play* became a popular book, Thomas Harris (1969), a psychiatrist, popularized transactional analysis further with his book *I'm OK— You're OK*. Two years later, a further attempt to popularize transactional analysis—*Born to Win: Transactional Analysis with Gestalt Experiments*—was published by Muriel James and Dorothy Jongeward (1971).

PHILOSOPHY AND CONCEPTS

"The transactional theory of personality is also a theory of life." Every individual is born "with the capacity to develop his potentialities to the best advantage of himself and society, to enjoy himself and to be able to work productively and creatively, and to be free of psychological disabilities" (Berne, 1966, p. 259). However, beginning with the first few days of life, the infant may run into difficulties. These and later obstacles may prevent many individuals from developing their full capacities.

Personality Development

The human organism is characterized by the need for various forms of contact and response from others in an interactional process. This need is designated by the term *stimulus hunger.* The first form that this need takes in the infant is *tactile hunger,* or the need for physical closeness and intimacy. The lack of adequate physical contact may lead to susceptibility to disease and resulting death, a condition called *hospitalism* by Rene Spitz (1945), who first recognized it in institutionalized infants.

The need for intimate physical contact continues throughout life, and the individual engages in a perpetual striving for attainment of physical intimacy with others. However, individuals learn early that they cannot have everything they want, so they begin to compromise, accepting other forms of contact. Tactile hunger becomes converted into *recognition hunger,* which includes the simple acknowledgment of existence by others, or "verbal touching." Such evidences of recognition are called *strokes* by analogy with the literal physical strokes or caresses given to infants. The stroke is a basic unit of social interaction; an exchange of strokes constitutes a *transaction.*

A third form of stimulus hunger is *structure hunger,* or the need to organize and fill time in order to avoid boredom. "The question is, what next? In everyday terms, what can people do after they have exchanged greetings?" (Berne, 1964, p. 16). Or, as it is put in the title of one of Berne's (1972) books, "What do you say after you say hello?" "The eternal problem of the human being is how to structure his waking hours. In this existential sense, the function of all social living is to lend mutual assistance for this project" (Berne, 1964, p. 16). (The ways in which people fill time will be considered later under the topic of social intercourse.) *Excitement hunger* is the desire or the preference for structuring time in interesting and exciting ways. A derivative of structure hunger is *leadership hunger.* Leaders provide activities and programs through which people can fill and structure their time.

Personality Structure

Personality structure consists of a tripartite ego system. The three ego states are Parent, Adult, and Child. (Capitalization is used to designate an ego state as distinguished from actual persons.) "The term 'ego state' is intended merely to denote states of mind and their related patterns of behavior as they occur in nature" (Berne, 1961, p. 30). Every individual incorporates all three ego states, which manifest themselves in different—and often inconsistent—sets of behavior patterns. These sets of behavior patterns are referred to as Parent, Adult, and Child.

The Parent Ego State.   The parent ego state derives from the *exteropsyche,* which involves identification activities. All adult individuals have had either actual parents or parent substitutes, who through exteropsychic functioning influence their behavior. Such behaviors are labeled "Parent behaviors," indicating that the individuals are in the state of mind exhibited by one of their parents or parent substitutes in the past and are responding in the same way, for example, in postures, gestures, verbalizations, feelings, and so forth. In the transactional-analysis colloquialism, "We each carry our parents around inside of us."

The Parent is not Freud's superego, although the superego is one aspect of the Parent as the parental influence. The parental influence is not abstract; it is a result of direct, actual transactions with the parents. The parental influence includes not only prohibitions, but also permission, encouragement, nurturing, and commands. The parental influence leads individuals to respond as their parents would want them to respond; as the direct Parent, it responds as their parents actually responded. The Parent functions as the actual parent of children. It also functions by performing many things automatically and thus freeing the Adult of minor decisions.

The Adult Ego State.   "Every human being with sufficient functioning brain tissue is potentially capable of adequate reality testing" (Berne, 1961, p. 35). The Adult ego state represents *neopsychic* functioning. The Adult ego state is focused on data processing and probability estimating. Colloquially, "Everyone has an Adult." The Adult is necessary for survival in the world. It also regulates the activities of the Parent and the Child, mediating between them.

The Child Ego State.   Every adult was once a child, and the relics of childhood exist in later life as the Child ego state, or *archeopsychic* ego state. The Child is under the inhibitory, permissive, or provocative influence of the Parent. It is separate from the Parent, a distinct personality, inconsistent with but not necessarily opposed to the Parent. Colloquially, "Everyone carries a little boy or a little girl around inside of him/her."

The Child is not Freud's id, although it is influenced by the id. In particular, it is not the chaotic or disorganized state of Freud's id, but is well organized. The behavior of the Child is not immature or childish but is *childlike.* The child has three forms: the *natural* Child possesses charm and intuition and is spontaneous and creative; the *adapted* Child's behavior is modified or inhibited by parental influence; the *rebellious* Child resists parental control.

These three ego states are diagrammed as three nonoverlapping but touching circles arranged vertically to indicate their differentiation and usual inconsistency with one another. The Parent, at the top, is the ethical guide; the Adult is concerned with reality; and the Child is a purgatory or sometimes a hell for archaic tendencies. The three form a moral hierarchy. The Parent is the weakest, and the Child is the strongest. This order is shown when a person comes under the influence of alcohol: The Parent is decommissioned first, and soon the Child takes over and is the last to pass out. The same order prevails in falling asleep: The Parent gives way in the hypnogogic state, and the Child takes over during sleep in dreams. They are not, however, topographical parts of the individual, as the superego, id, and ego are often conceived, nor are they concepts, as these Freudian terms are; they are simpler, more scientifically economical and are "experiential and behavioral realities" (Berne, 1966, p. 216).

Parent, Adult, and Child are entitled to equal respect, and each has a place in normal life. It is only when a healthy balance is disturbed that analysis and reorganization are necessary.

Personality Function

The three systems of personality react differently to stimuli. The Parent (exteropsyche) judgmentally attempts to enforce external ("borrowed") standards. The Adult (neopsyche) is concerned with processing and storing information derived from stimuli. The Child (archeopsyche) reacts more impulsively on poorly differentiated perceptions. Each perceives stimuli differently and responds in terms of its perception. The three systems interact with one another, but the Parent and the Child reenact the individual's relationship with the parents.

Psychic energy, or *cathexis,* flows from one to another ego state; the state that is cathected at a particular time has *executive power;* that is, it determines the individual's behavior. The active state is said to be cathected with *unbound energy;* the inactive state is said to be cathected with *bound energy.* There is also a *free cathexis,* which moves from one ego state to another; the feeling of Self resides in the state that is charged with free cathexis. The executive command, or active state, is usually the state that has unbound plus free cathexis.

Each ego state has boundaries that separate it from the other ego states, as indicated by their representation as nonoverlapping circles. Changes in ego state depend on the permeability of the boundaries between the states, the cathectic capacity of each state, and the forces acting on each state. Therapy must recognize these factors in working to induce changes in ego states.

The Four Life Positions

The child is faced, as noted earlier, with the necessity of compromising in satisfying needs, or stimulus hunger. Between the ages of four and seven, the child establishes compromises that affect later relationships. The child makes certain decisions—very specific decisions that can be located and dated—and on the basis of these decisions adopts a position toward the self and others and maintains this position against influences that question or threaten it. The life position is a major determinant of the life script (see below). (In fact, it would appear that they both derive from the same early experiences rather than that one determines the other.)

The four positions involve two polarities: "I–Others" and "OK–not OK." The resulting positions are:

1. I am OK; you are OK.
2. I am OK; you are not OK.
3. I am not OK; you are OK.
4. I am not OK; you are not OK.

"I" may extend to a group—"we." "You" may extend to "they" or may specify groups, such as men or women. "OK" may stand for any specific good, and "not OK" may stand for any specific evil.

Position 1 is the good or healthy success position. Position 2 is the arrogant position, the characteristic of which is dedication to betterment—for example, missionaries, district attorneys, and other "do-gooders." This alternative is called colloquially "getting rid of people." In less healthy individuals, it may lead to homicide and paranoid states. Position 3, the depression position, leads to the individual cutting himself/herself off from other people in some way, such as becoming institutionalized or committing suicide. Colloquially, it is "resigning from the human race." The fourth position is the futility and schizoid position. It leads ultimately to the spiteful or aesthetic suicide. Berne believes that such suicides result from lack of stroking in infancy, leading to depression and despair. Colloquially, this is referred to as "knocking yourself off," and justifications that are presented by patients are called "trading stamps" (see below).

Social Intercourse

Social intercourse provides the opportunity for the satisfaction of structure hunger or structuring time, as well as of stimulus hunger or obtaining recognition or strokes from other persons. The unit of social intercourse is the transaction. It involves a *transactional stimulus* from the person who initiates the transaction by acknowledging the other in some way and the *transactional response*. Transactions are analyzed in terms of the sources of the stimuli and responses, that is, their origination in the Parent, Adult, or Child of the participants. The simplest transactions are Adult-Adult, that is, from the Adult of one to the Adult of the other and from this Adult in return. The next simplest is the Child-Parent transaction, usually a request.

Transactions may be *complementary* or *crossed*. Complementary transactions follow the natural order of healthy relationships. They are of various types: Adult-Adult, Parent-Parent, and Child-Child transactions are complementary; so also are Parent-Child and Child-Parent. Complementary transactions lead to smoothly continuing communication.

Crossed transactions result in the breaking down of communication. The most common and the most disruptive one is an Adult stimulus directed to the Adult of the other, who responds, however, from his/her Child to the Parent of the initiator. A response from the Parent to the Child of the other is a second type of crossed transaction. In the first type, the reply to the question, "Do you know where my cuff links are?" would be, "You always blame me for everything." The response to the second type would be, "Why don't you keep track of your own things? You're not a child any more." There are seventy-two varieties of crossed transactions and only nine types of complementary transactions. Transactions may be further classified as simple or ulterior (involving two ego states and both social and psychological aspects), the latter of which may be either angular (36 types) or duplex (6480 types). Detailed discussion is not possible here. Only about 15 types of transactions occur in ordinary social intercourse.

Transactions occur in series. They may involve *material programming, social programming,* and *individual programming.* Material programming structures time through *activities* or *procedures* and deals with the material external reality. Procedures are simple complementary Adult transactions. These are of interest only insofar as they provide opportunities for recognition and more complex forms of social intercourse. Social programming involves *rituals* and *pastimes.* Activities, rituals, and pastimes are three of the four major ways of structuring time. The fourth is *games,* which arise from individual programming (i.e., individual patterns and sequences of behaving that are "circumscribed by unspoken rules and regulations"; Berne, 1964, p. 17). There are two other limiting cases of social behavior: *withdrawal* at one extreme and *intimacy* at the other.

Rituals.   Rituals are socially prescribed forms for behavior in standard social situations. They are complementary Parent transactions. They meet the need for recognition and strokes. Perhaps the most common ritual is the "Hello-Goodbye" sequence. The withholding of symbols of recognition constitutes rudeness. There are various degrees and types of recognition. Fan letters are a depersonalized form; live applause or the presentation of a bouquet of flowers after a performance is more personal. Verbally, recognition proceeds from a simple "Hello" to "How are you?" The progression is from simple acknowledgment that someone is there, through recognition of feelings, sensations, and personality, to expression of a personal interest. "Mere recognition, however, is not enough, since after the rituals have been exhausted, tension mounts and anxiety begins to appear. The real problem of social intercourse is what happens after the rituals" (Berne, 1961, p. 85).

Pastimes.   Procedures and rituals are stereotyped and thus predictable. Pastimes are less restricted. They involve more time than rituals and may begin and end with rituals. They often fill in time while a person is waiting for a meeting or an activity to begin, or during a cocktail party. Pastimes may facilitate the social-selection process, since they bring together persons who have similar interests or interest in one another, often leading to more complex relationships (games) or friendships. Pastimes are highly varied and are given names such as "PTA," "Man Talk," "Lady Talk," "Do You Know," and so on. They may be classified in various ways. Pastimes are complementary transactions. In addition to having other advantages, such as noted above, pastimes may confirm a person's role and stabilize his/her position (see the four positions above). Pastimes may be enjoyable in themselves or, for neurotic persons especially, simply a way of passing time. They are not particularly exciting, however.

Games.   Pastimes and games are both *engagements;* they fall between *activities* and *rituals,* on the one hand, and *intimacy,* on the other. Whereas pastimes are straightforward transactions, games are dissimulations. Transactions in games are complementary but are ulterior and involve a payoff. "Procedures may be successful, rituals effective, and pastimes profitable, but all of them are by definition candid; they may involve contest but not conflict, and the ending may be sensational, but it is not dramatic. Every game, on the other hand, is basically dishonest, and the outcome has a dramatic, as distinct from a merely exciting, quality" (Berne, 1964, p. 48). Games are not "fun and games"; they are deadly or grimly serious, as gambling may be. Selling involves games and is often referred to as such: the "insurance game," the "real estate game," and so on, up to the "con game"; war is also a game.

Games are given names: one hundred are named and described in *Games People Play* (Berne, 1964), from A ("Addict") to Y ("You've Got to Listen"). Numerous others have been identified since. The most common game between spouses is called "If It Weren't for You," with its social-pastime derivative, "If It Weren't for Him." Several kinds of gains can be obtained by a wife from such a game, including getting out of doing something that she cannot do or is afraid to do, manipulating the husband, and providing a pastime to structure and fill social relationships with other women.

The most common game in social gatherings is "Why Don't You—Yes, But," which can be played by any number. The player who is "it" objects with "Yes, but. . . ." "A good player can stand off the rest of the group indefinitely, until they all give up, whereupon 'it' wins" (Berne, 1961, p. 104). The game is not played for the ostensible purpose of getting help or information but for the ulterior purpose of reassuring and gratifying the Child, who frustrates the Parent.

Games serve a number of functions; they fill up or occupy most of social life. In order to move from the boredom of pastimes without being exposed to the dangers of intimacy, people resort to games for excitement and social reinforcement or stroking. As with pastimes, those who play the same games associate with one another.

Games are also duplex transactions, involving two levels—the social and the psychological—the latter of which is covert. The payoff is at the psychological level, in the form of feelings, which may be good or bad. Repetition of the games leads to the collection of particular feelings or of *"trading stamps,"* which becomes a *"racket."* For some people, certain games are necessary for the maintenance of mental health. "Their dynamic function is to preserve psychic equilibrium, and their frustration leads either to rage or to a state which in transactional analysis is called *despair*" (Berne, 1961, p. 108), which is similar to existential despair rather than depression.

The payoffs of certain games are feelings of guilt, inadequacy, hurt, fear, resentment, and anger, which constitute trading stamps. Self-indulgence in these feelings is the racket. The games manipulate others, so the player is entitled to display these feelings and to take major actions related to his/her life script without feeling guilty. Games, like procedures, rituals, and pastimes, are taught in the family. While the last three are taught by parents directly, games are usually learned indirectly or by imitation. They are passed on for generations.

Intimacy.   "Pastimes and games are substitutes for the real living of real intimacy" (Berne, 1961, p. 86). Intimacy involves highly individual programming at an intense level, which breaks through the restrictions of social patterning and ulterior restrictions. "Society frowns upon candidness, except in privacy" (Berne, 1964, p. 172); intimacy is a private matter. Intimacy involves the natural Child. It is free of games. "Fortunately the rewards of games free of intimacy, which is or should be the most perfect form of human living, are so great that even precariously balanced personalities can safely and joyfully relinquish their games if an appropriate partner can be found for the better relationship" (Berne, 1964, p. 62).

To be able to rise above games and enter into intimacy, a person must have awareness and enough spontaneity to be liberated from the compulsion to play games and, thus, be free to choose and express feelings from the Parent, Adult, or Child. To free the self from games requires an autonomy from the influences of family and parents, from whom games were learned.

Scripts.   Games are organized into scripts. "Operationally, a script is a complex set of transactions, by nature recurrent, but not necessarily recurring, since a complete performance may require a whole lifetime" (Berne, 1961, p. 116). It is the unconscious life plan, originating in a decision made in early childhood. The earliest experience in script formation is called the *protocol* and derives from experiences with and the influence of parents; later it is influenced by the myths and fairy tales to which the child is exposed. It is repressed in later years but reappears in the preconscious as the *script proper*. The script proper is modified as a compromise with reality and becomes the *adaptation,* which is played out in life and in group treatment. All three forms are included in the term *script.* Other refinements include the *operative script,* which is derived from the adaptation, and then a *secondarily adjusted script,* which becomes the *shooting script* of the life production. There is also usually an *antiscript* or *counterscript,* which can be a safer or more constructive plan than the exciting but often *destructive script* and which alternates with the script. The counterscript also may dominate the style of life, while the script determines the ultimate destiny, which may come as a surprise to observers.

Although a script as a life plan requires a lifetime for its performance, it may be reenacted in lesser versions on a yearly or weekly basis, or even in a single group session or a few seconds. Scripts may be constructive or tragic. A common tragic script derives from the childhood belief that there is a kind of Santa Claus who will at some time magically bring success and happiness. When the individual reaches a stage of despair about this coming true, he or she may seek therapy. Scripts are related to the four positions, and the Santa Claus script is related to the "I am not OK; you are OK" position and may lead to the results noted above in the discussion of the four positions.

Scripts are the dominant influences in social intercourse, which is thus influenced by the early experiences that determined the script. Games are selected to fit the script, and transactions are selected to fit the games. Associates are selected on the basis of their participation in transactions: for more stable relationships, they are selected on the basis of willingness to participate in the games; for more intimate relationships, they are selected on the basis of ability to fill the roles in the script. There is an element of fate in a person's life script. A person is the captive of his/her script unless somehow he/she is able to transcend it. Thus, a childhood decision determines a person's life and the way the person faces death.

Psychopathology

The general pathology of psychiatric disorders includes structural and functional pathology. *Structural pathology* involves anomalies of the psychic structure of Parent, Adult, and Child. There are two common types—exclusion and contamination.

In *exclusion,* one of the ego states defensively excludes the others and dominates behavior. In "compensated" schizophrenics, the Parent excludes the archaeopsyche or the Child. In the cold scientist, the Adult is the excluding ego state. In narcissistic, impulsive personalities, the Child excludes the Parent and the Adult. The two ego states that are excluded are said to be *decommissioned.* In *contamination,* one of the adjacent ego states intrudes on the Adult. The contamination of the Adult by the Parent leads to certain kinds of prejudice. The intrusion of the Child on the Adult is present in delusions. Double contamination involves the intrusion of both the Parent and the Child on the Adult.

The second type of psychopathology is *functional.* In functional pathology, the ego boundaries are permeable, which leads to lability (fluctuation) of cathexis from one ego state to another. Lability of cathexis can occur without defect in ego boundaries, however. Sluggish cathexis exists when shifts of cathexis are slow to occur. Ego boundaries can be rigid or highly impermeable; this is necessary for exclusion to take place. The genesis of psychopathology is in the occurrence of traumatic ego states in childhood; the earlier the trauma, the more serious the consequences.

> Symptoms are each exhibitions of a single definite ego state, active or excluded, although they may *result from* conflicts, concerts, or contaminations between different ego states. The first symptomatic task in structural analysis, therefore, is to decide which ego state is actually exhibiting the symptom. (Berne, 1961, p. 61)

Hallucinations generally derive from the Parent. Delusions generally derive from the Child and arise from the area of contamination between the Adult and the Child; they are thus ego-syntonic or experienced as from the Adult. After decontamination, they still may be experienced, but the person recognizes that they do not really exist; they become ego-dystonic. "Boundary symptoms" (feelings of unreality, estrangement, depersonalization, déjà vu, and so on) arise from "lesions of the boundary between the Adult and the Child" (Berne, 1961, p. 63). All these symptoms are schizoid in nature.

> In hypomania there is an exclusion of the Parent by the Child with the cooperation of a contaminated Adult, so that neopsychic (Adult) judgment, impaired though it is, is influential. If mania supervenes, then the Adult as well as the Parent is overpowered by the hypercathected Child, who then has a clear field for his own frantic activity. (Berne, 1961, p. 66)

The symptom in conversion hysteria derives from the Child, which is excluded by the Adult through repression. In general with the neuroses, however, the Parent is the enemy. Character disorders and psychopathies are also exhibitions of the Child with the cooperation of the Adult; impulse neuroses likewise erupt from the Child but without the cooperation of either the Adult or the Parent.

The functional psychoses include all the conditions usually diagnosed as manic-depressive and schizophrenic, but rather than being placed in the usual nosological classifications in terms of structural states, they are classified as *active* or *latent*. "An active psychosis exists when the Child has the executive power and is also experienced as the 'real self,' while the Adult is decommissioned" (Berne, 1961, p. 139). In other conditions such as mild depression, hypomania, character disorders, and paranoia, the Adult is contaminated by the Child and cooperates with the Child but is not decommissioned. These may become active psychoses. In the latent psychoses, which include compensated psychoses, ambulatory psychoses, psychoses in remission, and prepsychotic or borderline conditions, the Adult is the executive and is experienced as the "real self," although it is contaminated and/or temporarily decommissioned.

Diagnosis consists of determining the ego state from which behaviors originate. "Ego states manifest themselves clinically in two forms: either as completely cathected coherent states of mind experienced as 'real self;' or as intrusions usually covert or unconscious, into the activity of the current 'real self'" (Berne, 1961, p. 71). Diagnosis requires acute observation plus intuitive sensitivity to involuntary as well as voluntary and social behavior. Demeanor, for example, "the sternly paternal uprightness" or "the gracious mothering flexion of the neck," betrays the ego attitude, in these instances the Parent. Gestures also, as well as voice and vocabulary, indicate the ego state that is operative.

All ego states have four properties: executive power, adaptability, biological fluidity, and mentality. A complete diagnosis requires that all four be considered and correlated. The *behavioral* diagnosis is based on demeanors, voices, vocabularies, and other characteristics. It is corroborated by the *social* or *operational* diagnosis, which involves the appropriate ego-state behaviors in response to social stimuli. The *historical* diagnosis offers further corroboration; it involves the recall and statement by the individual of the specific origins or prototypes of the behaviors in his/her past. Diagnosis in terms of the standard classification is therapeutically irrelevant. Therapy is based on the structural diagnosis.

THE THERAPY PROCESS

Goals of Therapy

Although made in the context of group treatment, the following statement would appear to apply to individual treatment as well:

> Taking as the most general statement that psychiatric patients are confused, the goal of psychotherapy then becomes to resolve that confusion in a well-planned way by a series of analytic and synthetic operations. Again in the most general form, these operations will consist of decontamination, recathexis, clarification, and reorientation. (Berne, 1966, p. 213)

Transactional analysis is not satisfied with improvement or progress—in making patients more comfortable frogs—but aims for cure and for transformation of schizophrenics into nonschizophrenics, or frogs into princes or princesses (see Berne, 1966, p. 290).

In structural terms, therapy attempts to stabilize and decontaminate the Adult; with the primacy of the Adult, the early decision of the Adult that led to a psychopathological position can be reconsidered, and the Parent can be brought to terms. The position of "I'm OK; You're OK" can then be assumed. However, Berne (1961) seems to accept symptomatic control, symptomatic relief, and social control as goals in the therapy of the neuroses, but "the ultimate aim of transactional analysis is structural readjustment and reintegration" (p. 224).

Stages of Psychotherapy

The therapy process requires, first, restructuring and, second, reorganizing. Restructuring "consists of clarification and definition of ego boundaries by such processes as diagnostic refinement and decontamination." Reorganization is concerned with "redistribution of cathexis through selective planned activation of specific ego states in specific ways with the goal of establishing hegemony of the Adult through social control. Reorganization generally features reclamation of the Child, with emendation or replacement of the Parent. Following this dynamic phase of reorganization, there is a secondary analytic phase which is an attempt to deconfuse the Child" (Berne, 1961, p. 224). There is a series of steps or stages in psychotherapy, and therapy may end with the success of any one of them. Transactional analysis is the name applied to the total process, although it also designates one of the stages.

1. *Structural analysis.* Structural analysis consists of the descriptive study of ego states, along the lines discussed above under psychopathology, to decontaminate the Adult, define ego boundaries, and stabilize Adult control. "The goal of this procedure is to reestablish the predominance of reality-testing ego states [the Adult] and free them from contamination by archaic and foreign elements [of the Child and Parent]" (Berne, 1961, p. 22). Treatment may not need to continue beyond structural analysis. The patient who is treated as though he/she has a perfectly good ego or an Adult ego is likely to respond by activating the Adult ego state and to become more rational and objective, both toward self and toward the world. The result is stabilization, in which the Adult is the executive, and the Parent and Child states can be called on when this is desirable.

2. *Transactional analysis proper.* Following structural analysis, therapy may terminate, the patient may go into psychoanalysis, or transactional analysis may begin. The aim of transactional analysis is social control; "that is, control of the individual's own tendency to manipulate others in destructive and wasteful ways, and of his tendency to respond without insight or option to the manipulations of others" (Berne, 1961, p. 23). The group is the natural medium for transactional analysis. Transactions are analyzed in terms of whether they are complementary or crossed and their implications for the participants. Therapy may terminate here.

3. *Analysis of pastimes and games.* The analysis of extended transactions is done in terms of pastimes, which constitute the initial phases of group therapy, and games. The individual's games are evaluated in terms of primary gains (external and internal), secondary gains, social gains, and biological gains (the removal of isolation by stimulation). The objective of game analysis is freedom from games

in intimate relationships or, more practically in society, the freedom to choose what games to play, how far to go, with whom to play, and when not to play. Transactional group treatment focuses on the analysis of games.

4. *Analysis of scripts.* Scripts are acted out in the group. The object of script analysis is "to close the show and put a better one on the road," or to free the patient from compulsive reliving of the original catastrophe on which the script is based. "Since scripts are so complex and full of idiosyncrasy, however, it is not possible to do adequate script analysis in group therapy alone" (Berne, 1961, p. 118).

   Scripts may not become apparent except in an advanced group or through dreams. To assist in identifying and understanding scripts, the script matrix can also prove useful. "The script matrix is a diagram designed to illustrate and analyze the directives [messages] handed down from parents and grandparents to the current generation. An enormous amount of information can be compressed very elegantly into this relatively simple drawing" (Berne, 1972, p. 279). This can allow the patient to see how parental and grandparental ego states and their directives get transmitted and incorporated into his/her own ego states.

   In patients who come for psychotherapy, life scripts are usually tragic rather than constructive. The object of therapy is for the patient to be able to transcend the script through the control of his/her life by the Adult. This does not mean that the Adult functions in exclusion of appropriate Parent and Child states. It is a stabilized state in which the individual is able to cathect the appropriate ego state at will. The breaking away from the script allows the real person to live in the real world. The most elegant way in which the therapist can get the patient out of his/her script is through the one single intervention that provides the most effective script antitheses. Further work is necessary, however, to achieve a permanent script cure. The intervention is in the form of a permission for the Child to disobey Parental injunctions and provocations.

5. *Analysis of relationships.* Analysis of relationships is mainly in marital relationships and liaisons or impending liaisons. It is used sparingly, since it may be seen by the patient as unwarranted influencing of his/her decisions.

Some cases may require *second-order structural analysis,* which involves the recognition and analysis of complex ego states. The Parent, for example, includes both mother and father elements, with each of these having Parent, Adult, and Child components. The Child ego state includes Parent, Adult, and Child components, the last of which is an archaic ego state within the total Child ego state.

IMPLEMENTATION AND TECHNIQUES

There are three injunctions, or slogans, as Berne calls them, for the therapist, which are taken from the field of medicine.

1. *Primum non nocere:* Above all, the therapist should do no harm. Intervention should be made only when necessary and only to the extent necessary.

2. *Vis medicatrix naturae:* The organism has a built-in drive toward health, which applies to the psychological as well as to the physical realm. The therapist's function is to remove the blocks to natural healing and growth.

3. *Je le pensay, Dieu le guarit:* The therapist treats the patient, but it is God who cures the patient; or, the therapist provides the best treatment possible, avoiding hurting or injuring the patient, and nature does the healing (Berne, 1966, pp. 62–63).

Therapy is preceded by an agreement or a contract. Patients are asked why they have come to the therapist. When patients can express clearly what they want, the therapist states what he/she can offer or suggests that they come for a few sessions to evaluate the therapist and what he/she has to offer. The first goals stated by the patient and accepted by the therapist may be symptomatic relief or social control. The therapist may have another ultimate goal, but this is reserved for the appropriate time when the contract may be amended. The contract is thus not usually agreed on before therapy can start but arises in the process and is changed as therapy progresses.

The methods and techniques of transactional analysis, however, are not very clear. (There is no systematic discussion by Berne.) The method is illustrated by case summaries or brief excerpts, which, however, are not verbatim transcripts but reconstructions after the interview. There is an emphasis on individualization of treatment. Berne (1961) wrote, "It is, unfortunately, difficult to offer more than a few general suggestions as to how to deal with people who are by definition the epitome of individuality" (p. 152).

The general method appears to consist of (1) identifying, pointing out, and labeling the origins of behavior in terms of ego states or their contamination, and decontaminating them through explanation (structural analysis), and (2) identifying, pointing out, and labeling transactions, pastimes, games, and scripts (transactional analysis). This involves teaching: for example, the patient "was educated to distinguish the reactions of his Parent, his Adult, and his Child, respectively, to what the therapist and others said to him" (Berne, 1961, p. 151). Patients are taught the essentials of the theory and concepts of ego states, games, and so on, directly in the early interviews.

Berne provides some therapeutic hints for the beginning therapist, which include the following:

1. First, learn to differentiate the Adult from the Child; the Parent will become clear later.

2. Wait until the patient has provided at least three examples or diagnostic illustrations before introducing the system's concept that is applicable.

3. Later diagnosis of the Parent or the Child must be confirmed by actual historical material.

4. Realize that the three ego states are to be taken literally, as though the patient were three people. The therapist also must recognize *his/her* own three ego states and their influence on the therapy.

5. Every patient is assumed to have an Adult; the problem arises in cathecting it or in "plugging it in."

6. The Child is not childish but childlike and possesses potentially valuable qualities.

7. The patient must experience the Child ego state, not simply recall its experiences (regression analysis).

8. Pastimes and games are not habits, attitudes, or occasional occurrences; they constitute most of the patient's activities.

9. "The ideal intervention is the 'bull's-eye,' one which is meaningful and acceptable to all three aspects of the patient's personality, since all three overhear what is said" (Berne, 1961, p. 237). It is recognized by all three ego states.

10. The beginner is likely to experience a negative reaction toward the terminology, but this is an expected part of learning a new system.

The therapist must be a keen observer, using all the senses, particularly hearing and sight. "Observation is the basis of all good clinical work, and takes precedence even over technique" (Berne, 1966, pp. 65–66). The therapist notes the incipient stages of blushing, palpitation, sweating, tremors, tension, excitement, rage, weeping, laughter, and sexuality by being sensitive to carriage, posture, movements, gestures, facial mimicry, twitches of single muscles, arterial pulsations, local vasomotor and pilomotor phenomena, and swallowing. Facial expressions and gestures may reveal "hidden" thoughts by their inconsistency with verbalization or with one another.

Visual observation should be accompanied by auditory observation, which involves listening to the accompaniments of the content of the patient's talking: coughing, gasping, weeping, or laughing. More subtle auditory observation may require the suspension of visual observation, in order that the therapist be allowed to concentrate on pitch, timbre, rhythm, intonation, and vocabulary. Patients have three voices, depending on whether their Parent, Adult, or Child is talking.

These observations are basic and prior to techniques. In addition, personal interest and concern for the patient and the patient's welfare takes precedence over techniques.

Therapeutic Operations

In his exposition of group treatment, Berne considers eight categories of therapeutic operations or basic techniques of transactional analysis. Each is accompanied by caveats. The first four are classified as simple *interventions*. The others are *interpositions,* which attempt to stabilize the patient's Adult by placing something between it and the Parent and Child to make it more difficult for the patient to slip into Parent or Child activity.

1. *Interrogation.* Interrogation is used to document clinically important points. It should be used when the therapist is confident that the patient's Adult will respond. It should rarely be used to obtain more information than is immediately necessary, or it could lead to the patient playing the game of "psychiatric history."

2. *Specification.* Specification attempts to fix certain things in the patient's mind by the therapist assenting to or reiterating (reflecting on) what the patient has said or informing him/her of it. It is used to help prevent the patient from denying that he/she said or meant something or as preparation for explanation.

3. *Confrontation.* In confrontation, the therapist uses information previously elicited and specified to point out an inconsistency. Its purpose is to cathect the uncontaminated part of the patient's Adult. If it is successful, the patient will respond insightfully. It is used

when the patient is playing "stupid" and when the patient is incapable of recognizing the inconsistency.

4. *Explanation.* Explanation is used in the attempt to recathect (strengthen), decontaminate, or reorient the patient's Adult. It should be used when the patient has been prepared and the Adult is listening; it may be used when the patient is wavering between playing games and facing up to himself or herself. Explanations should be concise, or the game of "psychiatry—transactional type," may develop.

5. *Illustration.* "An illustration is an anecdote, simile, or comparison that follows a successful confrontation for the purpose of reinforcing the confrontation and softening its possible undesirable effects" (Berne, 1966, p. 237). Illustrations may immediately follow a confrontation or may be remote or delayed "from ten minutes to ten weeks" to allow the patient to settle down, so that then he/she can be given an additional push. Illustrations should be light, lively, or humorous and should be intelligible to the Child as well as to the Adult of the patient. Thus, they are used when the Adult is listening and when the Child also will hear and when the therapist is sure that the Parent will not take over. They can also be used to let the patient know that therapy is not always solemn. Caution should be used so that the therapist is not the only one laughing at the joke.

6. *Confirmation.* As the patient's Adult becomes more stabilized, the patient offers material to confirm his/her confrontation, which the therapist then reinforces by confirmation. It should be used only when the patient's Adult is established strongly enough to prevent the Parent from using it against the Child or the Child from using it against the therapist. It should not be used if the previous confrontation and illustration were not successful.

7. *Interpretation.* If the techniques considered so far have been successful in cathecting and decontaminating the Adult so that it is strong and competent, the therapist can enter the terminal phase of pure transactional analysis by crystallizing the situation and providing symptomatic relief and social control for the patient. Even though the Child has not been deconfused, the patient can continue improvement as long as the Adult maintains the executive position, or the therapist can postpone crystallization until the Child is deconfused by the psychodynamic interpretation of orthodox psychoanalysis. Still another alternative is that this may be postponed until the Adult becomes stabilized, and then it can be undertaken. The last may be preferred, since the patient can function well in daily life while bringing up a family. Psychoanalysis postpones improved functioning until it is completed.

Interpretation

deals with the pathology of the Child. The Child presents its past experiences in coded form to the therapist, and the therapist's task is to decode and detoxify them, rectify distortions, and help the patient regroup the experiences. In this an uncontaminated Adult is the most valuable ally. (Berne, 1966, pp. 242–243)

The Child resists, and the Parent also exerts an influence against interpretation as the Child's protector. Interpretation should be used only when the patient's Adult is on the therapist's side, when the Adult is in the executive position, and when the therapist is not directly opposing the Parent and not asking too much of the Child. It must be the therapist's Adult that is talking, and the therapist must be using his/her intelligence instead of intellectualizing.

8. *Crystallization.*

The technical aim of transference analysis is to bring the patient to a point where crystallizing statements from the therapist will be effective. A crystallization is a statement of the patient's position from the Adult of the therapist to the Adult of the patient. (Berne, 1966, p. 245)

In effect, it says to the patient that he/she can stop playing games or function normally if the patient chooses to do so. The choice is still the patient's, however. The Child and the Parent must be prepared. The Child and the Adult are on good terms, so the Child accepts the crystallization. The Parent may resist seeing the Child become healthy, and this resistance must be handled. The patient cannot be pushed; if the patient is pushed, he or she may get well psychologically but develop somatic symptoms or even a broken leg. Transactional analysis is completed with crystallization, whether or not interpretation has been used.

In using all these therapeutic operations, the therapist is advised to stay three steps behind the clinical material and never to get ahead of it. While the therapist should never miss a real chance to forge ahead, he/she should "never push against resistance except for testing purposes based on a well-thought-out concrete hypothesis" (Berne, 1966, p. 248). In addition, in all his/her operations (except in certain types of confrontation), the therapist should avoid crossed transactions; that is, the therapist should direct the intervention at the patient's ego state that is most likely to respond.

With most patients, the therapist functions as his/her Adult, although the patient may perceive or wish the therapist to function as a Parent. The therapist occasionally may function as a Parent in giving the patient permission to engage in desirable activities or in assigning the patient particular tasks, thus freeing the patient from undesirable Parental injunctions or prohibitions. When the therapist functions as an Adult, the patient can accept the therapist in place of his/her own Parent. When the patient can accept his/her own Adult, the patient no longer needs the therapist's Adult, and therapy is completed.

With schizophrenics, modifications of treatment are required. The therapist may have to function as a Parent rather than as an Adult during much, if not most, of the treatment. As a Parent, the therapist will offer *support* (which may be simply stroking), *reassurance, persuasion,* and *exhortation.* Child interventions (where the therapist functions as the patient's Child) are appropriate only in treating children; they should not be used as trickery. "No transactional analyst should allow himself to use any form of deception or dissimulation, for that amounts to deliberately starting a game with the patient" (Berne, 1966, p. 249). In all these situations, whether the therapist is operating from the Adult, the Parent, or the Child, he or she is not playing a role.

If the therapist plays the role of a therapist, he will not get very far with perceptive patients. He has to *be* a therapist. If he decides that a certain patient needs Parental reassurance, he does not play the role of a parent; rather he liberates his Parental ego state. A good test of this is for him to attempt to "show off" his Parentalism in the presence of a colleague, with a patient toward whom he does not feel parental. In this case he is playing a role, and a forthright patient will soon make clear this difference between being a reassuring Parent and playing the role of a reassuring parent. (Berne, 1961, p. 233)

Regression Analysis. In addition to these eight therapeutic operations, regression analysis sometimes may be useful. "The optimal situation for the readjustment and reintegration of the total personality requires an emotional statement from the Child in the presence of the Adult and the Parent" (Berne, 1961, p. 224). This requires that all three ego states be in the state of awareness; thus hypnosis and drugs are ruled out when the therapist obtains the Child's statement. In psychoanalysis, the analyst interprets indirect expressions of the child, which is not satisfactory. In transactional analysis, there is an appeal to the Child in the waking state. "Reasoning and experience leads to the belief that a child expresses himself most freely to another child" (Berne, 1961, p. 225). Regression analysis utilizes this belief. The material produced is then available for detailed examination with the patient.

LENGTH AND LIMITATIONS OF TREATMENT

Length. The length of treatment can be expected to vary, depending on the patient and the severity of his/her condition and issues. In some cases, transactional analysis will be understandably brief, e.g., when a previously treated patient needs a "booster" session; when the issues to be dealt with are relatively minor in nature. In other cases, treatment will understandably be much longer in duration, e.g., where characterological or other such pathologies enter the picture. Transactional analysis can be effectively used in individual therapy, but also lends itself well to group treatment situations.

Limitations. Transactional analysis can be used to treat a wide range of conditions, ranging from couple and family issues to neuroses to personality disorders. Whatever the condition, however, it appears critical that the patient be able to, first, grasp, understand, and make use of transactional analysis concepts and principles. Since transactional analysis is a process that is largely built on teaching by the therapist and learning and application by the patient, it is imperative that patients be able to use and make meaning of their learning. Patients whose ability to learn is much impaired (e.g., because of a debilitating psychological condition or limited intellectual resources) will find treatment to be compromised as well.

It is also important that the patient be willing to enter into a contract—to commit to therapy and fulfill therapeutic responsibilities. Patients who are unwilling to enter into such a contract will most likely not be good candidates for transactional analysis, whatever their problems, issues, or condition might be.

EXAMPLE

The following example is taken from Berne's (1961, pp. 248–261) *Transactional Analysis in Psychotherapy*. The patient, who complained of "depressions" of sudden onset and of difficulty in handling her adolescent son, had had three previous forms of therapy: Alcoholics Anonymous, hypnosis, and psychotherapy combined with Zen and Yoga. "She showed a special aptitude for structural and transactional analysis, and soon began to exert social control over the games which went on between herself and her husband, and herself and her son. The formal diagnosis is best stated as schizo-hysteria." The following material presents Berne's summaries and comments on the therapy sessions. Dr. Q refers to Berne, the therapist.

1. April 1

The patient arrived on time for her initial interview. She stated she had been going to other therapists but had become dissatisfied and had called a municipal clinic, and after some discussion with a social worker had been referred to Dr. Q. She was encouraged to proceed and at relevant points appropriate questions were asked in order to elicit the psychiatric history. She stated that she had been an alcoholic for ten years and had been cured by Alcoholics Anonymous. She dated the onset of her drinking from her mother's psychosis when she was 19. She said that her depressions began at the same time. The nature of her previous psychiatric treatment was discussed. The preliminary demographic information was obtained so that she could be placed as a native-born, 34-year-old, once-married Protestant housewife, a high school graduate, whose husband was a mechanic. Her father's occupation, the length of her marriage, her sibling position in years and months, and ages of her children were noted. A preliminary search for traumatic events elicited that her father drank heavily and that her parents separated when she was 7 years old.

The medical history revealed headaches and numbness of one arm and leg, but no convulsions, allergies, skin afflictions, or other physical disorders with common psychiatric implications. Her age at the time of all operations, injuries, and serious illnesses was noted. Her childhood was explored for gross psychopathology, such as sleep-walking, nail-biting, night terrors, stammering, stuttering, bed wetting, thumb sucking, and other pre-school problems. Her school history was reviewed briefly. Chemical influences such as medications and exposure to noxious substances were also noted. A cautious exploration of her mental status was undertaken, and finally she was asked to relate any dream that she could remember. Recently she dreamed: "They were rescuing my husband from the water. His head was hurt and I started to scream." She mentioned that she often heard inner voices exhorting her to health, and once, two years ago, an "outer" voice. This satisfied the requirements for preliminary history taking, and the patient was then allowed to wander as she pleased.

Discussion

The history taking was carefully planned so that at all times the patient seemed to have the initiative, and the therapist, at most, was curious rather than formal or openly systematic in gathering information. This means that the patient was allowed to structure the interview in her own way as far as possible and was not required to play a game of psychiatric history taking. Because of her complaint of numbness, she was referred to a neurologist for examination.

2. April 8

The neurologist suspected cervical arthritis, but did not recommend any specific treatment. The patient conducted this interview as a kind of psychological survey. She spontaneously mentioned wanting approval and rebelling "like a little girl," as some "grown-up part" of her judged it. She said the "little girl" seemed "childish." It was suggested that she let the "little girl" out, rather than try to clamp down on her. She replied that that seemed brazen, "I like children, though. I know I can't live up to my father's expectations, and I get tired of trying to." This also includes her husband's "expectations." Such expectations were generalized for her as "parental expectations," since she had practically said as much herself. She sees the two most important "parents" in her life as her husband and her father. She is seductive toward her husband and recognized that she was the same with her father. When her father and mother separated she thought (age 7): "I could have kept him." Thus she had not only a conflict about compliance, but also an attitude of seductiveness toward parental figures.

Discussion

The patient's special aptitude for structural analysis is already evident. She herself makes the separation between "the little girl" and "a grown-up part" and recognizes the compliance of "the little girl" toward certain people whom she relates to her parents. It was only necessary, therefore, to reinforce this trichotomy in a nondirective way. With many other patients this might not have been undertaken until the third or fourth session, perhaps even later.

3. April 15

She resents people who tell her what to do, especially women. This is another reaction to "parents." She mentions a feeling of "walking high." It is pointed out that this is the way a very small girl must feel, that this is again the Child. She replied: "Oh, for heaven's sake, that's true! As you said that I could see a little child. . . . [I]t's hard to believe, but that makes sense to me. As you say that, I feel I didn't want to walk: a little girl in rompers. . . . I feel funny now. They pull you up by your right shoulder and you're outraged . . . yet I do the same to my own son. I disapprove while I'm thinking 'I don't disapprove, I know just how he feels.' It's really my mother disapproving. Is *that* the Parent part you mentioned? I'm frightened a little by all this."

It was at this point that it was emphasized that there was no mysterious or metaphysical aspect to these diagnostic judgments.

Discussion

The patient has not experienced some of the phenomenological reality of the Child and has added to the behavioral, social and historical reality she established in the previous interviews. The indications, therefore, are favorable for treatment with transactional analysis.

4. April 22

"This week I've been happy for the first time in fifteen years. I don't have to look far to find the Child, I can see it in my husband and in others too. I have trouble with my son." The game with her son was clarified in an inexact but timely and illustrative way in terms of Parent (her disapproval and determination), Child (her seductiveness and her sulkiness at his recalcitrance), and Adult (her gratification when he finally did his work). It was hinted that an Adult approach (good reason) rather than a Parental approach (sweet reason) might be worth a try.

Discussion

The patient is now involved in transactional analysis proper, and the idea of social control has been suggested.

5. April 28

She reports that things work better with her son. Regression analysis is attempted to find out more about the Child. She relates: "The cat soils the rug and they accuse me and make me wipe it up. I deny that I did it and stammer." In the ensuing discussion she remarks that both Alcoholics Anonymous and the Anglican Church require confession to "messes." For this reason she gave them both up. As the session ends she asks: "Is it all right to be aggressive?" Answer: "You want *me* to tell you?" She understands the implication that she should decide such things on Adult ground rather than asking Parental permission, and replies: "No, I don't."

Discussion

During this session some of the elements of her script are elicited. It can be anticipated that she will try to repeat with the therapist in some well-adapted form the cat situation. Her question "Is it all right to be aggressive?" is perhaps the first move in this adaptation. This gives the therapist an opportunity to decline to play and to reinforce her Adult. The patient has made such good progress in understanding structural and transactional analysis that she is already considered adequately prepared for fairly advanced group therapy. The group she is to enter consists largely of women.

6. May 4

A dream. "I look at myself and say: 'That's not so bad.'" She liked the group but it made her uncomfortable during the rest of the week. She relates some memories, including homosexual play during childhood. "Oh! That's why I didn't like AA. There were two homosexual women there and one of them called me sexy." She complains of vaginal itching. "My mother and I slept together and she bothered me."

Discussion

The manifest content of her dream is taken to be Adult and indicates the possibility of a good prognosis. The experience in the group has activated sexual conflicts, and this is the first indication of their nature.

7. May 11

She felt highly excited on leaving the group meeting. "Things are moving quickly. Why did they make me laugh and blush? Things are better at home. I can kiss my son now and my daughter for the first time came and sat on my lap. I can't be a good lover when things are monotonous."

Discussion

The analysis of her family games . . . has resulted in the establishment of some Adult social control. It is evident that this improved control has been perceived by her children and for the first time in a long while they have the feeling that she can maintain her position and they react accordingly. Her excitement in the group and her statement that she can't be a good lover when things are monotonous indicate that she is involved in a sexual game with her husband.

An experience in the group later this week rather clearly showed her need for parental figures in some of her games. There was a new patient in the group, a male social worker, and she was very much impressed by his occupation. She asked him what they were supposed to do there. It was pointed out that she knew more than he did, since it was his first meeting and her third. She says she resents it when people tell her what to do; yet peasant-like, in spite of her superior experience, she asks a novice for instructions because she appears to be impressed by his education: evidently an attempt to set up a game. This interpretation strikes home. She recognizes how she "cons" a likely candidate into being parental and then complains about it.

8. May 18

She was upset by regression analysis in the group. It made her think of her fear of insanity, and of her mother in the state hospital. Her own production was of some elegant gates leading into a beautiful garden. This is a derivative of a Garden of Eden fantasy from before the age of five. The material indicates that the garden has become adapted to the gates of the state hospital where she visited her mother many years ago. This experience in the group offered a timely opportunity to mention to her that she might want to be hospitalized and so relieved of responsibility.

She has visited her mother only once in the past five or six years and it was suggested that it might be advisable for her to do that again. This suggestion was very carefully worded so as to be Adult rather than Parental. Any implication that she was a bad girl for not visiting her mother had to be avoided. She was able to understand the value of such a visit as an exercise for her Adult and as a means of preventing future difficulties between her Parent and her Child if her mother should die. The good reception of this suggestion was manifested by her bringing up new information. Her husband never washes his hair and always has a good excuse, which she accepts. He has not washed it for many months. She says it doesn't bother her too much. The therapist said she must have known that when she married him. She denied it.

She said she has always been more afraid of sick animals than of sick people. This week her cat was sick, and for the first time she was not afraid of him. Once when she was little her father hit her and her dog jumped on him, whereupon he gave the dog away. She told her children that her mother was dead. Whenever she would think of her mother she would start to drink. One time she was told that when her mother was eight months pregnant, her father tried to poison her. They saved the patient and thought her mother was a goner, but then she was revived. The aunt who told her this story says: "Your life has been a mess since birth."

Discussion

The import of this is not clear. It is evident, however, that she is working through some rather complex conflicts concerning her mother. Her maintenance of social control with the sick cat is evidence that a visit to her mother may be possible in the near future.

10. June 1

"Frankly, the reason I'm afraid to visit my mother is that I might want to stay there myself." She wonders: "Why do I exist? Sometimes I doubted my existence." Her parents' marriage was a shotgun wedding and she has always felt that she was unwanted. The therapist suggested that she get a copy of her birth certificate.

Discussion

The patient is now involved with existential problems. Her Adult has evidently always been shaky because her Child has implanted doubts about her existence, her right to exist, and the form in which she exists. Her birth certificate will be written evidence that she does exist, and should be particularly impressive to her Child. As social control is established and she learns that it is possible for her to exist in a form which she herself chooses, her desire to retreat to the state hospital should diminish.

11. June 8

She described her husband's alcoholic game. At AA she was told she should bless him and comfort him, and that made her sick. She tried something different. "One day I said I would call the ambulance for the hospital, since he didn't appear to be able to take care of himself, so he got up and didn't drink again." He said he was only trying to help her stay sober by drinking himself. This comes up because he was drinking heavily last week and she had pain in her shoulders and wanted to hit him, but told him off instead.

It appears from this that their secret marriage contract is based partly on the assumption that he will drink and she will function as a rescuer. This game was reinforced by AA to her benefit. When she refused to continue as a rescuer and became a persecutor instead, the game was thrown off and he stopped drinking. (Evidently it was reinstituted due to her insecurity of the past week.)

This outline was presented to her. She first said: "It couldn't have been part of our marriage contract, because neither of us drank when we met." A little later in the interview she suddenly said: "You know, I remember I did know when we were married that he didn't wash his hair, but I didn't know that he drank." The therapist said that the unkempt hair was also part of the secret marriage contract. She looked skeptical. Then she thought a minute and said: "By golly, yes, I did know he drank. When we were in high school we used to drink together all the time."

It now appears that in the early years of their marriage, they played a switchable game of alcoholic. If she drank, her husband didn't; and if he drank, she stayed sober. Their relationship was originally based on this game, which they later interrupted, and must have exerted considerable effort to forget about.

Discussion

This session helped to clarify for the patient the structure of her marriage, and also emphasized the amount of time and effort which is required to keep marital games going, and equally, the amount of energy involved in their repression without conscious control.

12. July 6

There has been an interval of a month for summer vacation. The patient returns with a sore shoulder. She has been to the state hospital and her mother sent her away. This made her feel hopeless. She has some olfactory illusions. She thinks she smells gas in the office, but decides it is clean soap. This leads into a discussion of her mental activity. During her recent Yoga training, she developed imagery which was almost eidetic. She would see gardens and wingless angels with sparkling clarity of color and detail. She recalled that she had had the same kind of imagery as a child. She also had images of Christ and her son. Their complexions were clear and lively. She sees animals and flowers. As a matter of fact, when she walks through parks she likes to talk secretly but aloud to trees and flowers. The longings expressed in these activities are discussed with her. The artistic and poetic aspects are pointed out, and she is encouraged therefore to write and to try finger painting. She has seen her birth certificate and her existential doubts are less disturbing.

Discussion

These phenomena and the auditory manifestations she has previously mentioned, are not necessarily alarming. They point to childhood restitutive tendencies related to a deeply disturbed relationship between her and her parents. The conventional approach would be to give her "supportive" treatment and help her repress this psychopathology and live on top of it. Structural analysis offers another possibility which requires some boldness: to allow this disturbed Child to express herself and profit from this resulting constructive experiences.

13. July 13

She went to her internist and he gave her Rauwolfia because her blood pressure was high. She told her husband she was going to finger-paint and he got angry and said: "Use pastels!" When she refused, he started to drink. She recognizes what happened here as a game of "Uproar" and feels some despair at having been drawn into this. She says, however, that if she does not play "Uproar" with him then he will feel despair, and it is a hard choice to make. She also mentions that the gate on the beautiful garden is very similar to the gate on the day nursery where her mother used to send her when she was very small. A problem now arises: How to distinguish the effect of psychotherapy from the effect of Rauwolfia. She is eager to help with this.

14. July 20

She is losing interest and feels tired. She agrees it is possible that this is an effect of the medication. She reveals some family scandals she has never mentioned to anyone before, and states now that her drinking did not begin after her mother became psychotic, but after these scandals.

At this session a decisive move was made. During her therapeutic sessions, the patient habitually sits with her legs in an ungainly exposed position. Now she complains again about the homosexual woman at AA. She complains that the men also made passes at her. She doesn't understand why, since she did nothing to bring this on. She was informed of her exposed position and expressed considerable surprise. It was then pointed out to her that she must have been sitting in a similar provocative way for many years, and what she attributed to the aggressiveness of others is probably the result of her own rather crudely seductive posture. At the subsequent group meeting she was silent most of the time, and when questioned she mentioned what the doctor had said and how this had upset her.

Discussion

This is a crucial session. At the price of sacrificing the possibilities of a normal family life, the patient has obtained a multitude of gains, primary and secondary, by playing games with her husband and other men and women. The primary external gain is the avoidance of pleasurable sexual intercourse. If she can relinquish these gains, she may be ready to undertake a normal marital relationship whose satisfactions should more than repay her for her abdication. The schizoid elements in her Child are clear from her symptomatology. The hysterical elements are most clearly manifested in her socially acceptable game of "Rapo." Hence the diagnosis of schizo-hysteria.

In her case, the naming of the game is avoided since she is still too softboiled to tolerate such bluntness. It is simply described to her without giving it a name. In very sophisticated groups, however, it is known technically as "First-degree Rapo." It is the classical game of hysterics: crude, "inadvertent," seductive exhibitionism, followed by protestations of surprise and injured innocence when a response is forthcoming. (As previously noted, "Third-degree Rapo," the most vicious form, ends in the courtroom or the morgue.) The therapeutic problem at the moment is whether her preparation has been adequate and the relationship between her Child and the therapist sufficiently well-understood to make this confrontation effective. In a sense, her life and those of her children hinge on the therapist's judgment in these matters. If she should decide to become angry and withdraw from treatment, psychiatry might be lost to her for a long time afterward, perhaps permanently. If she accepts it, the effect could be decisive, since this particular game is her chief barrier to marital happiness. The therapist, naturally, has not ventured to bring the matter up without considerable confidence of success.

15. August 10

The therapist returns after a two-week vacation. The confrontation has been successful. The patient now describes an assault by her father in early puberty while her stepmother pretended to be asleep. He also molested other children, but her stepmother used to defend him. She relates this "assault" to her own seductiveness. This situation she discusses at some length, eliciting her feeling that sex is dirty or vulgar. She says she has always been very careful sexually with her husband because of this feeling and has tried to avoid sex with him for this reason. She understands that the games she plays with him are an attempt to avoid sex, as she feels she cannot let go enough to enjoy it and it is merely a burden to her.

Discussion

The patient is evidently shocked at the therapist's directness, but is gratified because it lays bare still further the structure of her marriage and indicates what could be done about it.

16. August 17 (Terminal Interview)

The patient announces that this is her last session. She no longer fears that her husband will think she is dirty or vulgar if she acts lusty. She never asked him if he thought so but just assumed that he did. During the week, she approached him differently and he responded with gratified surprise. For the last few days he has come home whistling for the first time in years.

She also realizes something else. She has always felt sorry for herself and tried to elicit sympathy and admiration because she is a recovered alcoholic. She recognizes this now as a game of "Wooden Leg." She feels ready at this point to try it on her own. She also feels different about her father. Maybe she contributed even more than she thought to the seduction. The remark about her skirts being too short shocked her but helped her. "I would never admit I wanted sex. I always thought I wanted 'attention.' Now I can admit I want sex." During the week she visited her father who was ill in another city in a hospital. She was able to observe her visit with considerable objectivity. Now she feels that she has divorced him and doesn't want him any more. That is why she was able to proceed sexually with her husband. She feels the transfer was accomplished through the intermediary of the therapist, who took her father's place for a while at first; but now she doesn't need him any more. She can talk freely to her husband about sexual repression causing her symptoms, and about her sexual feelings for him. He said he agreed with her and reciprocated her feelings. After she thought all this out, following the last visit, she had a dream that night in which there was a beautiful, feminine, peaceful woman, and it made her feel really good inside. The children are different too; they are happy, relaxed and helpful.

Her blood pressure is down and her itching is gone. The therapist thought the improvement might be due to the medicine. She replied: "No, I don't think so, I would know the difference, I've taken it before. The medicine makes me feel tired and nervous when it's taking hold, but this is an entirely new feeling."

She reports that she is drawing instead of finger-painting, doing what she wants. She feels this isn't wrong, it's like learning to live. "I don't feel sorry for people any more, I feel they ought to be able to do this too if they went about it right. I no longer feel I'm below everyone although that feeling isn't completely gone. I don't want to come to the group any more, I'd rather spend the time with my husband. It's like we're starting to go with each other again when he comes home whistling, it's wonderful. I'll try it for three months and if I feel bad I'll call you. I don't feel so 'neurotic,' either: I mean having psychosomatic symptoms and guilt feelings and my fear of talking about sex, and like that. It's a miracle, is all I can say. I can't explain my feeling of being happy, but I feel we [you and I] worked together on it. There's more closeness and harmony with my husband and he's even taking over the children like he's becoming the man of the house. I even feel a little guilty about AA because I used them in my game of 'Wooden Leg.'"

She was asked directly whether structural analysis helped and whether game analysis helped, and in each case replied: "Oh, yes!" She added: "Also the script. For example, I said my husband had no sense of humor and you said 'Wait a minute, you don't know him and he doesn't know you because you've been playing games and acting out your scripts, you don't know what either of you is really like.' You were right because now I've discovered that he really has a sense of humor and that not having it was part of the game. I'm interested in my home and I'm grateful for that. I can write poetry again and express my love for my husband. I used to keep it in." At this point the hour was drawing to a close. The therapist asked: "Would you like a cup of coffee?" She replied: "No thanks, I've just had some. I've told you now how I feel, that's it, that's all, it's been a great pleasure to come here and I enjoyed it."

General Discussion

There is no need to regard this gratifying improvement with either skepticism, alarm, or pursed lips, in spite of the apparent raggedness of the above extracts. The patient herself has already answered many of the questions which might occur to an experienced reader.

A few days short of the three-month trial period she had suggested, the patient wrote the therapist as follows: "I feel fine. I don't have to take any pills and have been off those blood pressure pills for a month now. Last week we celebrated my thirty-fifth birthday. My husband and myself went away without the children. The water was beautiful, and the trees. Gosh, if only I could paint them. We saw a huge porpoise, the first time I have ever seen one, and it was beautiful to watch, so graceful in movements. . . . My husband and I are getting along so nicely. Night and day such a difference. We have become closer, more attentive, and I can be me. That's what seemed to stump me most of the time. I always had to be polite, etc. He still comes whistling up the stairs. That does more good for me than anything. I am so glad you suggested drawing. You have no idea what that alone has done for me. I am getting better and I might try paints soon. The children think they are very good and have suggested that I exhibit some of them. Next month I am going to take swimming lessons, no fooling, something I would never have been able to do. As the time gets closer I am a little afraid but I have made up my mind I am going to learn. If I can learn to put my head under water, that alone will be a great thrill for me. My garden looks so nice. That's another thing you helped me with. By golly, I go out there at least twice a week now for several hours and no one objects. You know I think they like me better this way.

"I didn't intend to ramble on this way but it seemed I had so much to tell you. I'll write and let you know how my swimming progresses. Love from all of us in Salinas."

This letter reassured the therapist of two things:

1. That the patient's improvement persisted even after the medication for her blood pressure was discontinued.
2. That the improvement in the patient's husband and children persisted even after psychotherapy was discontinued. It should be added that the husband now washes his hair.

The most pessimistic thing which can be said about this case so far is that it represents a flight into a healthy family life. The only clinical demand that can legitimately be placed on transactional analysis is that it should produce results which are as good as or better than those produced by any other psychotherapeutic approach, for a given investment of time and effort. The improvement was still maintained on a one-year follow-up.

SUMMARY AND EVALUATION

Summary.   Transactional analysis divides the personality into three ego states: the Parent, the Adult, and the Child. The Child is derived from actual experiences in childhood, and the Parent represents the actual parents—their behaviors and their influence, in terms of both prohibitions and encouragements. The Adult represents reality testing and regulates and mediates between the Parent and the Child. All behavior can be related to one of these ego states. Early in life, the child solves certain problem situations in a way that leads to a decision about the self and a position toward life. The Child's life becomes a process of justifying or defending this position and warding off influences that threaten it. There are four major positions involving the individual and others:

1. I am OK; you are OK.
2. I am OK; you are not OK.
3. I am not OK; you are OK.
4. I am not OK; you are not OK.

The individual, unless he/she withdraws from social contact, uses social intercourse to satisfy stimulus hunger, including the need for contact, recognition, and structure to occupy and organize the use of time. These contacts involve activities, rituals, simple transactions, pastimes, and games. All are influenced by the individual's position and life script or plan, which derives from a decision made as a child under the influence of the parents. The autonomous individual is able to rise above games and live in intimacy with others.

Psychopathology involves disorders in ego states and their interrelations, which are derived from a tragic life script. Psychotherapy or transactional analysis attempts to resolve these disorders and free the individual from this tragic script by structural analysis (analysis of ego states), transactional analysis, game analysis, and script analysis.

This summary suggests that transactional analysis is quite simple. Berne emphasized its simplicity and its specialized vocabulary of only five terms—*Parent, Adult, Child, games,* and *scripts*—which can be taught to patients in two or three sessions.

Evaluation.   This apparent simplicity is, however, the biggest problem and handicap in transactional analysis achieving recognition as a serious professional method of psychotherapy. Its presumed simplicity has led to its wide popularity. Literally hundreds of practitioners have been spawned from short-term workshops and training courses that teach the simplified terminology and concepts, but their understanding of Berne's actual theory and practice may be quite limited. The simplistic form of transactional analysis has become to many a therapy for the masses, who can easily acquire its terminology.

While this is viewed by many as a desirable situation, it is unfortunate in at least two respects. First, some of its practitioners, who apparently lack a real understanding of Berne, can be highly controlling and manipulative in their activities. In effect, transactional analysis can become the biggest game on the street, whose stakes or payoffs are financial returns to the practitioner or the consultant. Perls (1969) wrote, "The real game they play, the compulsive pigeonholing of each sentence as belonging to parent and child, remained unnamed." Second, in popular practice, some practitioners may be teaching subjects how to play the game of "Psychiatry—Transactional Analysis Type," which consists of labeling their own and other people's behavior in terms of Parent, Adult, or Child and in terms of the games that it involves. This labeling process can be a handicap to or even preclude any real understanding or therapeutic gain.

This popularization of transactional analysis has resulted in its rejection by many professionals. Carson (1977), for example, in a brief review of a collection of papers presented at an international conference on transactional analysis wrote,

> The curious mixture of pop psychology, autistic argot, intellectual superficiality, graphic overkill, and fun-and-games ambience that has characterized this "movement" from its inception is again displayed here. . . . One can only wonder at the success of an organization now claiming 12,000 members and replete with various ranks and certifications that stands on such flimsy and amateurish foundations. (p. 531)

This is perhaps an unfair and unjustified criticism of transactional analysis as it was developed by Berne. Berne's system is highly complex, so much so that it is one of the most difficult theories to summarize adequately in a limited space. His theory and practice are difficult to master. It is not a quick and easy approach, as it may appear from its popular practice. Berne (1966) cautioned against oversimplification:

> Transactional theory is simpler and more scientifically economical than many other psychotherapeutic theories, but its clinical use requires conscientious study, and in the advanced stages where it begins to overlap with psychoanalytic and existential therapies it takes on increased complexity. (pp. 216–217)

Berne's lack of attention to specification of techniques has no doubt been in part responsible for the proliferation of techniques used by individuals who claim to practice transactional analysis, particularly those who may be lacking in a thorough knowledge of Berne's theory. It is also true that those who have had training with Berne have departed from his methods or added to them, so that there is a great variety of techniques now being used by those who identify themselves with transactional analysis, ranging from some psychoanalytic techniques to psychodrama and Gestalt techniques.

Berne had the benefit of years of training in and practice of psychoanalysis as a basis for his work with patients. He was obviously cautious and careful in his interventions (although his clinical intuition led him to interventions that would appear to be rash if done by others). He was genuine and authentic in his relations with his patients, and he was clearly concerned and caring. He observed, listened, and followed the productions of his patients, responding to them perhaps more frequently than initiating interventions and directing them; as he gained experience, however, he apparently became more active.

Yet Berne's penchant for popular terminology and his use of myths and metaphors, along with his claim for simplicity, opened the way for abuse and misuse of his approach through oversimplification and the use of its terminology as jargon. Its terminology actually goes far beyond the five words listed above. In his book on group treatment, Berne includes a glossary of 127 terms (there are almost 100 listed in *What Do You Say After You Say Hello?*), many of which are common words but with other than their standard meanings. There are numerous terms or phrases, often metaphors, which are called "colloquialisms." All of this, plus the catchy names given to games, leads to the development of a whole language that has meaning only to the initiates who have mastered it. Thus, while it can be claimed that there is no technical terminology, there is an extensive jargon, which is used to replace technical (often psychoanalytic) and sometimes common terms.

Because of this, it is difficult to evaluate Berne's contribution. Is transactional analysis anything more than psychoanalysis clothed in a new terminology? Does the new terminology contribute to understanding? And does the terminology aid or improve the practice of psychotherapy? Each of these questions will now be addressed.

1. Berne acknowledges his agreement with the basic theories and concepts of psychoanalysis. His system, however, is not simply a translation of psychoanalysis into a new terminology. There is a relationship between Parent, Adult, and Child ego states and Freud's superego, ego, and id, but they are not the same. Although Freud recognized the importance of early experiences in infancy and childhood on later life, he does not detail the mechanisms of the influence. Berne does this. His concept of the life script also goes beyond psychoanalysis. Also, Berne's concern with interpersonal behavior rather than only intrapersonal factors is an addition to psychoanalysis.

2. The use of a new vocabulary and terminology to apply to old concepts has both advantages and disadvantages. Berne's writing is easier to understand than much of Freud's and other psychoanalysts', and it is certainly more interesting as indicated by its popularity. The use of myths, metaphors, and analogies can be enlightening. The analysis of social behavior in terms of rituals, pastimes, and games is helpful for an understanding of much that goes on in social intercourse. The comparison of a life plan and its implementation to a script is also useful. His dramatic and theatrical vocabulary often throws light on the behaviors with which he was concerned.

    However, analogies and metaphors may come to be accepted for what they stand for, and labels and classifications of behavior have a way of becoming substitutes for the understanding of the specific and unique aspects of individual behavior and of leading to stereotypes. Much of current practice in transactional analysis appears to consist of the use of the terminology as jargon. The clothing of valid, significant, and important ideas in simple language is desirable, but when this language is a newly created, popular language, it may become a substitute for ideas and concepts. Individuals and their behaviors are forced into the Procrustean bed that has been prepared for them. Berne was perhaps too successful with his terminology, maybe in part because his metaphors and analogies were so good; he notes how closely "real" games parallel the social games. Yet there is a difference between the map, no matter how perfect it is, and the territory it depicts.

    Berne was convinced that he had a contribution to make. He placed particular importance on the concept of the life script and the script matrix, which diagrammatically illustrate the origins of an individual's script in his/her forbears.

Even if the origins . . . of the script directives vary in individual cases, the script matrix nevertheless remains one of the most useful and cogent diagrams in the history of science, compressing as it does, the whole plan for a human life and its ultimate destiny into a simple, easily understood, and easily checked design, which also indicates how to change it. (Berne, 1966, p. 302)

Further, "Script analysis is then the answer to the problem of human destiny, and tells us (alas!) that our fates are predetermined for the most part, and that free will is for most people an illusion" (Berne, 1972, p. 295). (He does note, however, that the script is more flexible than the genetic apparatus, is influenced by outside factors and life experiences, and can be changed by psychotherapy.) Yet he admits that "since psychiatric script analysis is itself only a few years old, there is in fact not a single example of clinical observation of a complete life script" (Berne, 1972, p. 296).

3. Berne appears to have been an effective therapist, but there is no way to demonstrate that this was because of his theory. He claimed that on the basis of a brief diagnostic evaluation, and in utilizing his theoretical concepts, he could predict future behaviors of his patients. "Some apparently trivial incident," he writes, "lasting only a few seconds, may reveal to a perceptive therapist the whole story of the patient's life" (1972, p. 301). Perhaps this is true. Berne was a perceptive and highly intuitive therapist. Too often, however, predictions come true or are "verified" by patients because they are made to come true, through the way therapists perceive and interpret what they see and hear and through suggestion.

Transactional analysis teaches patients how to label, analyze, and interpret their behavior and that of others by using the vocabulary and concepts of the system. It is perhaps not surprising that they support the expectations of the therapist. How much is validation of the theory and how much is getting out what is put in is thus questionable. Patients of therapists of any persuasion have a way of supporting their therapists' theories. Berne makes a point of the everyday language of his system, but it is not the everyday language of people who have not been exposed to the system.

And what of research and Berne's approach? Research that examines ego states and their implications for personality functioning can be readily found in the transactional analysis literature (e.g., Heyer, 1987). As Dusay and Dusay (1984) have pointed out, "the greatest research interest has been in the evaluation of the basic concepts of TA" (p. 431). "Ego states and egograms [profiles of ego state functioning] especially lend themselves to research" (Dusay & Dusay, 1989, p. 439).

By comparison, however, research on transactional analysis as a form of therapy has been quite limited. Berne (1961) provided what appear to be the first data-based results. He reported that, from September 1954 to September 1956, 75 patients were treated, 23 of whom were prepsychotic, psychotic, or postpsychotic. Of these, 2 (9 percent) were failures, voluntarily entering a hospital; 3 (13 percent) showed little or no change; and 18 (78 percent) improved. Of 42 other patients, none were failures; 14 (33 percent) showed little or no change; and 28 (67 percent) improved. From 1956 to 1960, about 100 people gave the treatment a fair trial (at least 7 consecutive weeks, and up to 2 to 3 years), of whom 20 were prepsychotic, postpsychotic, or psychotic. "In the majority of cases the treatment ended with the patients, their families, and the therapist all feeling better. Three cases were outright failures, being hospitalized voluntarily. All had had previous hospitalizations" (Berne, 1961, p. 337). Berne considered these results to compare favorably with those of other approaches.

Since Berne's initial report, other research on transactional analysis has been conducted. Some positive results have been forthcoming (see Dusay & Dusay, 1989, for a brief summary of important studies). But as mentioned above, treatment research has been very limited (to a mere handful of studies), most research work instead has focused on other aspects of transactional analysis, and the efficacy of transactional analysis as treatment still remains an issue much in need of empirical attention and verification.

While this empirical side is sorely lacking, interest in transactional analysis, however, is not. The International Transactional Analysis Association continues to have a large membership. The European Association of Transactional Analysis well represents the approach in Europe. The *Transactional Analysis Journal,* which has been in existence for over two decades now, continues to be the primary journal source for learning about transactional analysis research, theory, and practice. Some interesting work on egograms (Dusay, 1986), integrating transactional analysis and Gestalt therapy (Goulding, 1987, 1992; Goulding & Goulding, 1978), as well as integrating transactional analysis with other systems (such as psychodrama) techniques can be found in the current literature. There appears to be much vigor in all of this, with transactional analysis maintaining a recognizable presence on the contemporary psychotherapy scene.

As for the future of transactional analysis, Dusay & Dusay (1984) made the following statement over a decade ago.

> The future of TA seems to be moving in the direction of action, emotive, and energy models to correct overconcentration upon "understanding," resulting in a balance between affect and cognition. The history of TA is a history of rapid change to new and more effective techniques rather than adherence to earlier models. The structural concepts of ego states, the transaction (the unit of social action), and the script or games theory will not be discarded; however, the techniques employed to bring about change have and will be shifted from the major reliance upon understanding and insight (which is still thought to be important) to an approach that is more experiential and emotive. (p. 443)

That statement appears to nicely capture some of what has happened in transactional analysis in the past decade and, also, appears to reflect some of what will continue to happen in the years ahead.

In concluding, let us again say that transactional analysis differs from—and has an advantage over—most other theories in that it openly teaches its concepts and labels. In its simplest form, it is also perhaps clearer and thus more appealing and useful, at least for temporary results. Serious students, as well as practitioners of psychotherapy, will find Berne's writings of value. Berne had a scholarly and highly productive mind. He was a keen observer of people and their behaviors and possessed a strong clinical intuition. Many of his observations are not couched in the terminology of the system but in ordinary language. Whether he employed the terminology or not, what he had to say is well worth reading.

REFERENCES

Berne, E. (1947). *The mind in action.* New York: Simon & Schuster.

Berne, E. (1958). Transactional analysis: A new and effective method of group treatments. *American Journal of Psychotherapy, 12,* 237–248.

Berne, E. (1961). *Transactional analysis in psychotherapy: A systematic individual and social psychiatry.* New York: Grove Press.

Berne, E. (1963a). Group therapy vs. group treatment. *Transactional Analysis Bulletin, 2,* 73.

Berne. E. (1963b). *The structure and dynamics of organizations and groups.* Philadelphia: Lippincott.

Berne, E. (1964). *Games people play: The psychology of human relationships.* New York: Grove Press.

Berne, E. (1966). *Principles of group treatment.* New York: Oxford University Press.

Berne, E. (1968). *A layman's guide to psychiatry and psychoanalysis* (3rd ed.). New York: Simon & Schuster.

Berne, E. (1970). *Sex in human loving.* New York: Simon & Schuster.

Berne, E. (1972). *What do you say after you say hello? The psychology of human destiny.* New York: Grove Press.

Carson, R. C. (1977). Review of *Current issues in transactional analysis: The first international transactional analysis association European conference,* edited by R. N. Blakeney. *Contemporary Psychology, 22,* 531.

Dusay, J. M. (1986). Transactional analysis. In I. L. Kutash & A. Wolf (Eds.). *Psychotherapist's casebook* (pp. 413–423). San Francisco: Jossey-Bass.

Dusay, J. M., & Dusay, K. M. (1984). Transactional analysis. In R. J. Corsini (Ed.). *Current psychotherapies* (3rd ed., pp. 392–446). Itasca, IL: F. E. Peacock.

Dusay, J. M., & Dusay, K. M. (1989). Transactional analysis. In R. J. Corsini & D. Wedding (Eds.). *Current psychotherapies* (4th ed., pp. 405–453). Itasca, IL: F. E. Peacock.

Goulding, M. M. (1987). Transactional analysis and redecision therapy. In J. K. Zeig (Ed.). *The evolution of psychotherapy* (pp. 285–299). New York: Brunner/Mazel.

Goulding, M. M. (1992). Short-term redecision therapy in the treatment of clients who suffered childhood abuse. In J. K. Zeig (Ed.). *The evolution of psychotherapy: The second conference* (pp. 239–246). New York: Brunner/Mazel.

Goulding, R., & Goulding, M. M. (1978). *The power is in the patient: The TA/Gestalt approach to psychotherapy.* San Francisco: TA Press.

Harris, T. A. (1969). *I'm OK—you're OK.* New York: Harper & Row.

Heyer, R. (1987). Empirical research on ego state theory. *Transactional Analysis Journal, 17,* 286–293.

James, M. (1977). Eric Berne, the development of TA, and the ITAA. In M. James and Contributors, *Techniques in transactional analysis for psychotherapists and counselors* (pp. 19–32). Reading, MA: Addison-Wesley.

James, M., & Jongeward, D. (1971). *Born to win: Transactional analysis with Gestalt experiments.* Reading, MA: Addison-Wesley.

Perls, F. S. (1969). *In and out of the garbage pail.* Lafayette, CA: Real People Press.

Spitz, R. A. (1945). Hospitalism: An inquiry into the genesis of psychiatric conditions in early childhood. *The Psychoanalytic Study of the Child, 1,* 53–74.

Steiner, C., & Kerr, C. (Eds.). (1976). *Beyond games and scripts.* New York: Grove Press.

Stewart, I. (1992). *Eric Berne.* London: Sage.

chapter 12

Gestalt Therapy: Perls

Friedrich (Frederick or Fritz, as he was called) Salomon Perls (1893–1970) is credited with having been the founder and developer of Gestalt therapy. He was born in Berlin and educated in Germany, and he obtained his M.D. degree from Frederich Wilhelm University in 1920. (His publications include the title Ph.D. as well as M.D. after his name. However, he never earned a Ph.D.; it was an honorary award, which he received in 1950 from an unrecognized school, the Western College of Psychoanalysis in Los Angeles.) He studied at the Vienna and Berlin Institutes of Psychoanalysis. His training analyst was Wilhelm Reich, and he knew and was influenced by a number of well-known psychoanalysts, including Helene Deutsch, Otto Fenichel, and Karen Horney, and he knew or met many others, including Adler, Jung, Federn, Schilder, and Freud. He also knew or was influenced by a number of Gestalt psychologists—Wolfgang Kohler, Max Wertheimer, and Kurt Lewin— and in 1926 was an assistant to A. Gelb and Kurt Goldstein at the Goldstein Institute for Brain Damaged Soldiers in Frankfurt.

After the rise to power of Hitler, Perls went to South Africa in 1934 and established the South African Institute for Psychoanalysis in 1935. In South Africa, he met Jan Smuts, who had coined the term *holism* in a book (*Holism and Evolution*) that was published in 1926. With Smuts' death and the rise of apartheid, Perls left South Africa for the United States (1946). In New York, he met Paul Goodman, and together with Goodman and his wife, Laura Perls, he founded the New York Institute for Gestalt Therapy in 1952. He was also involved in the founding of the Cleveland Institute for Gestalt Therapy in 1954. In 1964, shortly after the founding of the Esalen Institute at Big Sur, California, Perls joined the staff as resident associate psychiatrist. He remained there until 1969, when he moved to Cowichan on Vancouver Island in British Columbia, where he was attempting to establish a

Gestalt community when he died in March 1970. Perls was one of the three therapists to appear in the film series, *Three Approaches to Psychotherapy* (1966), which was produced by Everett Shostrom.

While he was in South Africa in the early 1940s, Perls wrote *Ego, Hunger and Aggression,* which was first published in South Africa in 1942 and then in England in 1947 with the subtitle *A Revision of Freud's Theory and Method;* the book was dedicated to Max Wertheimer. The American edition (1947) carried the subtitle *The Beginning of Gestalt Therapy.* His book *Gestalt Therapy: Excitement and Growth in Personality* (1951) was written in collaboration with Ralph F. Hefferline (b. 1910) and Paul Goodman (1911–1972). Hefferline has spent his entire student and professional life at Columbia University, where he became chairman of the Department of Psychology. Goodman, with a Ph.D. from the University of Chicago, taught at the University of Chicago, New York University, Black Mountain College, the University of Wisconsin, and the Institutes for Gestalt Therapy in New York and Cleveland. He was perhaps best known for his more popular books, including *Growing Up Absurd* (1956) and *Compulsory Mis-education* (1964).

In 1969, Perls published *Gestalt Therapy Verbatim* and *In and Out of the Garbage Pail,* the latter of which is autobiographical. At the time of his death, Perls was working on two books: the first was to be devoted to theory and the second to practice. Perls felt that the two earlier books (*Ego, Hunger and Aggression,* 1947 and *Gestalt Therapy: Excitement and Growth in Personality,* 1960) were difficult to read and rather outdated. He was concerned about the increasing emphasis on technique and the neglect of theory by many practitioners and wanted to provide a current and clearer statement of theory. After Perls' death, Robert Spitzer, editor in chief of Science and Behavior Books, to whom Perls had entrusted his materials, published the two books. *The Gestalt Approach and Eyewitness to Therapy* (1973) includes 114 pages of theoretical material and 88 pages of excerpts from film transcripts with some comments. Other materials and additional excerpts from film transcripts were published as the second part of *Legacy from Fritz* (Baumgardner & Perls, 1975). In the first part, Patricia Baumgardner discusses clinical aspects of Gestalt therapy and memories of and experiences with Perls. Although it is clearly written, the theoretical material in the first book is poorly organized, unsystematic, and brief. Digressions occur, and material on a single subject is scattered (for example, descriptions of the neurotic person) with no integration into a unified statement. It therefore does not render obsolete or replace Perls' earlier writings. It is not all new material but incorporates material written during the previous ten years.

Following Perls' death, there was a flurry of activity. There was no heir designated for Perls' mantle; he was unique and irreplaceable. A flood of publications appeared, many of which consisted of repetitions and individual elaborations and embellishments of Perls' writings. In addition to journal publications, many collections of articles and papers also appeared (Fagan & Shepherd, 1970; Hatcher & Himmelstein, 1976; Latner, 1973; Simkin, 1974; Smith, 1976; Stephenson, 1975; Zinker, 1977). None of these seemed to provide the comprehensive, systematic textbook that was necessary if students were to obtain an adequate understanding of Gestalt therapy. This is perhaps an unintentional (or intentional) result of the frequently stated dictum that the only way to understand Gestalt therapy is to experience it and of the approach to training through institutes and workshops. Nevertheless, two of the leading practitioners and teachers, who were for

many years at the Cleveland Institute before they moved to California and the codirector-
ship of the San Diego Gestalt Training Center, Erving Polster and Miriam Polster, have
provided a systematic treatment in *Gestalt Therapy Integrated* (1973). The summary we
provide here attempts to integrate the earlier and the later Perls in a clear, systematic presentation.

A recent book (Clarkson & MacKewn, 1993), part of the Key Figures in Counselling
and Psychotherapy book series, examines Perls' life, his theory and practice contributions,
and his overall influence. The Fall 1993 issue of *The Gestalt Journal* was devoted to the
centennial celebration of Fritz Perls' birth.

BACKGROUND AND DEVELOPMENT

Perls' exposure to a wide variety of influences is reflected in his development of Gestalt
therapy. His basic training was in psychoanalysis. He credited psychoanalysis and Freud
with having provided the foundation on which he could build, although mainly by reacting
to and changing psychoanalytic theory. He replaced the sex instinct with the hunger instinct as the major instinct, for example. While still a psychoanalyst, he was influenced
greatly by Wilhelm Reich's views, including Reich's emphasis on affect, body involvement
in neurosis, form rather than content (including the nonverbal in behavior), confrontation
as a method in treatment, and techniques tailored to the individual patient. He was influenced by the existential emphasis on individual responsibility for thoughts, feelings, and
actions and on the immediate experience—the now, the I-Thou relationship, and the what
and how, rather than the why, of experience and behavior.

Perls declares that Gestalt therapy is one of the three existential therapies, together with Frankl's logotherapy and Binswanger's daseinanalysis. Again, before Perls'
rejection of psychoanalysis, Gestalt psychology exerted its influence through his experiences with Goldstein and his reading of Lewin. The meaning of the German word
Gestalt as "whole, configuration, integration, pattern, or form" occupies a central place
in Perls' theory. The Gestalt figure-ground concept is basic also to Perls' theory of
needs and their satisfaction in the drive toward self-actualization, a term first used by
Goldstein. The idea of organismic regulation derives from Gestalt psychology, as does
the concept of closure or completion in Gestalt formation, which Perls used in his concept of unfinished business. Gestalt, in Perls' view, thus refers to the wholeness of completed acts, as well as to the integration of split-off parts of the personality into a self-
actualizing whole. Perls extended the Gestalt treatment of perception to include not
only perception of the external world, but also perception of bodily processes and of
feeling and emotions.

Perls was also influenced by the general semantics of I. A. Richards and A. Korzyb-
ski, in relation to the clear and explicit use of language. Finally, there was the influence of
Zen Buddhism and Taoism, with regard to the principle of opposites (the Yin and the Yang)
and the recognition that human beings can transcend themselves only by becoming what
they are—their true nature.

All of these and other concepts were incorporated into Gestalt therapy by Perls.
While the theory has not yet been developed or stated in a clear, systematic form, the work
of Perls provides the basis for such an integrated statement.

PHILOSOPHY AND CONCEPTS

Perls was more interested in action and experience than in philosophy. He recognized the importance of philosophy, but he was ambivalent about developing a systematic philosophy, one "that hopefully will encompass the human *and* the all" (1969b). Yet, whether they are explicit or implicit, there are assumptions about the nature of humanity and experience in Gestalt therapy as in every other therapy; many of its concepts are philosophical.

Perls rejected the belief that human beings are determined and controlled by external and/or internal factors; this was one of his differences with psychoanalysis. This rejection is reflected in two of his basic ideas: (1) that human beings are responsible for themselves and their lives and living, and (2) that the important question about human experience and behavior is not "Why?" but "How?" Implicit in these assumptions is the belief that human beings are free and have the potential for change. In agreement with Gestalt principles, Perls rejected the dualities of mind and body, body and soul, thinking and feeling, thinking and action, and feeling and action. This rejection of dualities is inherent in the concept of holism.

Nature of the Organism

Holistic Principle.   Perls quotes Wertheimer's formulation of Gestalt theory: "There are wholes, the behavior of which is not determined by that of their individual elements, but where the part-processes are themselves determined by the intrinsic nature of the whole" (1947, p. 27). Human beings are unified organisms and always function as wholes. There is not an *I,* which *has* a body, a mind, and a soul, but *we* who exist *as* organisms. The healthy organism is a feeling, thinking, and acting being. Emotions have thinking and acting (physiological) as well as feeling aspects.

> Mental activity seems to be activity of the whole person carried on at a lower energy level than those activities we call physical . . . the mental and physical sides of human behavior [are] not . . . independent entities which could have their existence apart from human or from one another. (Perls, 1973, pp. 13–14)

Body, mind, and soul are aspects of the whole organism.

Dialectic Principle of Homeostasis.   Perls was influenced by the philosopher Sigmund Friedlander, whose book *Creative Indifference* develops the concept of differential thinking, or thinking in opposites (dialectics). Opposites (polarities) come into being by differentiation from a zero point of undifferentiation.

> [E]very event is related to a zero-point from which a differentiation into opposites takes place. These *opposites* show *in their specific context* a great affinity for each other. By remaining alert in the center, we can acquire a creative ability of seeing both sides of an occurrence and complete an incomplete half. By avoiding a one-sided outlook we gain a much deeper insight into the structure and function of the organism. (Perls, 1947, p. 15)

Opposites relate to each other more than to any other concepts (compare with Kelly). "Thinking in opposites is deeply rooted in the human organism. Differentiation into opposites is an essential of our mentality and of life itself" (Perls, 1947, p. 18).

A specific case of the general concept of opposites is the concept of *organismic balance* or *homeostasis*. The basic tendency of every organism is to strive for balance. The organism is faced at every moment with factors that disturb this balance, either external (a demand from the environment) or internal (a need). A countertendency arises to restore the balance; the process of restoration of the balance constitutes organismic self-regulation. In the process, the organism creates an image or a reality of the satisfaction of the need; in effect, it selects its world or creates a figure-ground situation. The satisfaction of the need decreases tension, restores the balance, and completes the situation. Homeostasis is thus the process by which the organism satisfies its needs. It is a continuous process, since the balance or equilibrium is constantly being upset. The process applies in the satisfaction of psychological needs as well as of physiological needs; indeed, the two processes cannot be separated. In relation to the external environment, the individual may adjust his/her behavior to the environment (autoplastic behavior) or may adjust (adapt) the environment to his/her (alloplastic) behavior.

In terms of Gestalt psychology, the awareness of a need becomes the figure against the background. The unmet need constitutes an incomplete Gestalt that demands completion. Sensorimotor activity is stimulated, and the environment is contacted to meet the need. "When a need is met, the gestalt it organized becomes complete, and it no longer exerts an influence—the organism is free to form new gestalten" (Perls, 1948). Balance is achieved, and the situation is changed. "[T]he dominant need of the organism, at any time, becomes the foreground figure, and the other needs recede, at least temporarily, into the background" (Perls, 1973, p. 8).

Consciousness is not the searching for or the finding of the problem or the imbalance; it is identical with the problem or the disequilibrium; that is, the dominant need's development into the figure or the foreground, and its organization of the functions of contact with the environment to achieve reduction of tension constitute consciousness. What determines which need becomes dominant is the need's relevance to the organism's need for self-preservation and its need to grow or to actualize its potential. "Every individual, every plant, every animal has only one inborn goal—to actualize itself as it is" (Perls, 1973, p. 31).

Instincts.   Freud rightly recognized the importance of the sex instinct, which is necessary for the preservation of the human race, but he overlooked the existence of another instinct, which is necessary for the preservation of the individual. This is the hunger instinct. The numerous specific instincts may all be classified under these two basic instincts.

The stages of the hunger instinct are the prenatal, the predental (suckling), the incisor (biting), and the molar (biting and chewing). The understanding of these stages in their normal and abnormal aspects leads to an understanding of behavior that the sex instinct does not clearly or easily provide. These stages are related to psychological characteristics: the predental to impatience, the incisor to destruction and aggression, and the molar to assimilation. The vicissitudes of hunger and its satisfaction appear to be an analog for all psychological behaviors, as will become apparent later. In his later writings, Perls does not emphasize this parallel, as he does in his earlier writings, although allusions are made to it.

Aggression and Defense.   *Aggression* is an important concept in Perls's early theory. Aggression is neither an instinct nor an energy, although it is a biological function. It is the organism's means of contacting its environment to satisfy its needs and of meeting resistance to the satisfaction of its needs. Its function is not destruction but overcoming the resistance, leaving the object as intact as possible so it can be used for satisfaction. Aggression is similar or analogous to the biting and chewing of food to satisfy hunger: "The use of the teeth is the foremost biological representation of aggression" (Perls, 1947, p. 114). Destruction does not leave the object intact but destructures it—as in biting and chewing—so that a new structure or intactness develops in its assimilation. "Mankind suffers from suppressed individual aggression and has become the executor and victim of tremendous amounts of released collective aggression. . . . *The re-establishment of the biological function of aggression* is, and remains, the solution to the *aggression problem*" (Perls, 1947, p. 112).

Sublimation (letting off steam in aggressive sports and physical work) provides helpful outlets. "But they will never equal dental aggression, the application of which will serve several purposes: one rids oneself of irritability and does not punish oneself by sulking and starving—one develops intelligence, and has a good conscience, because one has done something 'good for one's health'" (Perls, 1947, pp. 116–117). (This statement appears to be inconsistent with the previous contention that aggression is not an instinct or an energy that seeks discharge.)

Defense is an instinctive self-preservation activity. Defenses are mechanical (shells in animals, character-armor [Reich] in humans) and dynamic, either motoric (flight), secretoric (snake poison), or sensoric (scenting.)

Reality.   Since the organism is not self-sufficient, it is continuously interacting with its environment. In the process of striving for a balance in relation to environmental demands, the organism is not a passive receptor or simply a reactor but an active perceiver and organizer of its perception.

> For our purposes we assume that there is an objective world from which the individual creates his subjective world; parts of the absolute world are selected according to our interest, but this selection is limited by our tools of perception, and by social and neurotic inhibitions. . . . [T]he reality which matters is the reality of interests—the *internal* and not the *external* reality. (Perls, 1947, pp. 38–40)

Reality thus changes with the changing interests and needs of the organism.

Through interests and needs, the environment is organized into figure and ground as they emerge and are satisfied, as noted above. An important aspect of this organization of the environment is that individuals cannot perceive or respond to their entire environment at the same time but only to one aspect of it, the figure, which relates to current interests and needs.

The Contact Boundary.   The organism and the environment exist in a mutual, or dialectic, relationship. The organism must find the satisfaction of its needs in the environment. It reaches out toward the world to do so, through the sensory process of orientation and the motor process of manipulation. The point of interaction between the individual and the environment is the *contact boundary*.

The study of the way the human being functions in his environment is the study of what goes on at the contact boundary between the individual and his environment. It is at this contact boundary that the psychological events take place. Our thoughts, our actions, our behavior, our emotions are our way of experiencing and meeting these boundary events. (Perls, 1973, p. 16)

Objects or persons in the environment that provide satisfaction of needs acquire a *positive cathexis* (Freud's term), while those that hinder or threaten satisfaction acquire a *negative cathexis.* The individual seeks contact with the first kind of objects and persons and withdraws from the second. When the first kind of object is appropriated (assimilated), the Gestalt is closed. Similarly, when the second kind of object is annihilated (avoided or rejected), the Gestalt is closed. The individual is in a situation in which he/she can concentrate on another need as it comes to figure. We live by the dialectical process of contacting and withdrawing from objects and persons in the environment as they are discriminated as positive or negative. Activity is energized by the basic excitement inherent in the living organism, which is transformed into specific emotions according to the situation.

The Ego. "The ego is neither an instinct, nor has it instincts; it is an organismic function" (Perls, 1947, p. 36). It is not a substance with either finite or even changing boundaries. Rather, the boundaries, the places of contact, constitute the ego. "Only where the self meets the 'foreign' does the ego start functioning, come into existence, determine the boundary between the personal and impersonal 'field'" (Perls, 1947, p. 143). It is thus the system of responses or contacts of the organism with the environment, involving identification or alienation. Awareness of the self and the nonself constitutes the ego.

The ego performs an integrative or administrative function in relating the actions of the organism to its needs: "it calls, so to speak, upon those functions of the organism which are necessary for the satisfaction of the *most urgent* need" (Perls, 1947, p. 146). It identifies with the organism and its needs and alienates itself from other needs or demands to which it is hostile. It then structures the environment (the field) in terms of the organism's need. If the organism is hungry, food becomes the figure in the Gestalt, but if the food can be obtained only by stealing, and the person would rather die than steal, the ego alienates the taking of the food.

Growth and Maturity

Growth occurs through assimilation from the environment, both physically and mentally. The organism experiences a need, contacts its environment, and satisfies the need by assimilating energy from the environment. The healthy organism is in a continuous process of need → disequilibrium → aggressive contact with the environment → need satisfaction through assimilation → equilibrium, and so forth. "Life is practically nothing but an infinite number of unfinished situations—incomplete gestalts. No sooner have we finished one situation than another develops" (Perls, 1969a, p. 15). The healthy individual successfully finishes each situation, completes each incomplete Gestalt, and, in the process, grows.

Psychological growth is not an unconscious process but occurs through awareness. Sensing, excitement, Gestalt formation, and contact are accompanied by or characterized by awareness in the normal individual.

> Contact as such is possible without awareness, but for awareness contact is indispensable. . . . Sensing determines the nature of awareness, whether distant (e.g., acoustic), close (e.g., tactile) or within the skin (proprioceptive). . . . Excitement . . . covers the physiological excitation as well as the undifferentiated emotions. . . . Gestalt formation always accompanies awareness. . . . The formation of complete and comprehensive Gestalten is the condition for mental health and growth. (Perls et al., 1951, pp. viii–ix)

The normal organism functions as a whole. Its behavior is in tune with its organismic needs, not with external demands or "shoulds." The total organism is involved, with no parts isolated or cut off. The ego—self-awareness—incorporates all organismic needs and functions.

Frustration, rather than preventing growth, fosters it. Frustration challenges the individual and enables the individual to discover his/her potential and to learn to cope with the world. "Without frustrations there is no need, no reason, to mobilize your resources, to discover that you might be able to do something on your own, and in order not to be frustrated, which is a pretty painful experience, the child learns to manipulate the environment" (Perls, 1969a, p. 32).

Through growth, the child matures. Maturation is the transformation from environmental support to self-support. The child becomes independent rather than remaining dependent on others. The child who does not learn to overcome frustration, perhaps because he/she is spoiled or overprotected by the parents, does not grow up. Dependent on others, the child manipulates the environment for support by being helpless, stupid, or compliant. The point at which the child starts to manipulate the environment is when the child cannot get support and cannot yet provide his/her own support; it is called the "impasse."

Normal growth and development is not without problems, as the difficulty of achieving maturity illustrates. *Anxiety* is also an accompaniment of learning. It is "the gap between the now and the later. Whenever you leave the sure basis of the now and become preoccupied with the future, you experience anxiety" (Perls, 1969a, p. 30). It is like stage fright, which when the action begins becomes the excitement that stimulates a good performance. In his later formulation, Perls (1973) appears to use *dread* as a synonym for *anxiety;* dread is a vague, undifferentiated sense of danger, which becomes fear when there is an object with which to cope.

There are also other problems related to or analogous to the hunger instinct. Although in his later writings, Perls discusses these under the topic of neurosis, the earlier recognition that they are present to some extent in normal development also seems to continue to be accepted. They are, therefore, considered here rather than in the discussion of neurosis.

The process of assimilation does not always proceed smoothly but encounters certain kinds of difficulty. There is a similarity or parallel in physiological and mental functioning.

> Our attitude towards food has a tremendous influence upon intelligence, upon the ability to understand things, to get a grip on life and to put one's teeth into the task at hand. Anyone not using his teeth will cripple his ability to use his destructive functions for his own benefit. (Perls, 1947, pp. 114–115)

Such people are excessively modest and lack backbone but there is a greed behind their apparent lack of interest in food. Another character type of a similar parasitic nature is the person who lives in permanent unconscious fear of starvation and seeks financial security in life. These represent disturbances in the contact boundary between the individual and the environment.

Another form of such disturbance consists of *resistances* related to oral development, including the hunger strike in the form of lack of appetite: "I just can't swallow a bite." Analogous is the inability to swallow unpalatable information. *Disgust,* the nonacceptance or emotional refusal of food, is another resistance. Disgust at an object is a reaction to it as though it were in the stomach. There are four other major boundary disturbances: introjection, projection, confluence, and retroflection.

"*Introjection* means preserving the structure of things taken in, whilst the organism requires their destruction" (Perls, 1947, p. 129) for assimilation to occur. The introject, not having been "chewed" but having been "gulped down," remains intact as a foreign body in the system. Introjection is the natural form of eating in the suckling stage. Its persistence relates to disturbances in the development of the biting and the chewing stages. Oral aggression (biting) has been blocked, but food is forced into the child. The oral aggression becomes displaced, in part against other persons. Forced feeding also leads to disgust with food, which is repressed, and the food is swallowed whole or in chunks. In introjection, the organism reacts to an object or situations as it does to food by "swallowing it whole" but then being unable to "stomach it."

Psychologically, introjection is the uncritical acceptance on authority of concepts, standards of behavior, and values. The person who habitually introjects does not develop his/her own personality. The introjection of conflicting or incompatible concepts or values results in personality disintegration. In introjection, the boundary between the self and the world is so far inside the self that there is little real self left.

Projection is the placing in the outside world of those parts of one's personality with which one refuses (or is unable) to identify oneself (or to express). "The projecting person cannot satisfactorily distinguish between the inside and outside world" (Perls, 1947, p. 157). Feelings of guilt lead to the projection of blame onto someone or something else. Projections are usually onto the outside world but can take place within the personality— for example, onto the conscience. Projection gives temporary relief but prevents contact, identification, and responsibility.

In projection, the boundary between the self and the world is extended into the world, so that aspects of the self that are unacceptable are displaced outside the self into the world. The projected aspects are unacceptable because they are inconsistent with introjected attitudes and values.

Confluence exists when the individual feels no boundary between the self and the environment. This condition is present in the newborn infant and in adults in moments of ecstasy or extreme concentration and on ritualistic occasions. A continuous state of confluence, when the individual cannot distinguish between the self and others, is pathological. In states of confluence, the person cannot tolerate differences; everyone must be alike.

"*Retroflection means that some function which originally is directed from the individual towards the world, changes its direction and is bent back towards the originator*" (Perls, 1947, pp. 119–120). Narcissism is an example. Suicide, a substitute for murder, is another. Aggression and hatred are reversed and directed toward the self. Such behavior is a reaction against meeting hostility and frustration. Inhibiting or suppressing emotions and behavior is sometimes necessary, but it can become habitual and lead to neurotic repression. There is a resulting split in the personality between the self as doer and the self as receiver.

The person who retroflects treats his/her self as he/she wants to treat others. Energies are directed inward toward the self, which is substituted for the environment, rather than outward toward the environment to satisfy needs.

The retroflector knows how to draw a boundary line between himself and the environment, and he draws a neat and clean one right down the middle—but he draws it down the middle of himself. The introjector does as others would like him to do, the projector does unto others what he accuses them of doing to him, the man in pathological confluence doesn't know who is doing what to whom, and the retroflector does to himself what he would like to do to others. (Perls, 1973, pp. 40–41)

Introjection, projection, confluence, and retroflection function

to interrupt mounting excitement of a kind and degree with which the person cannot cope. . . . These mechanisms constitute neurosis only when they are inappropriate and chronic. All of them are useful and healthy when they are employed temporarily in particular circumstances. (Perls et al., 1951, pp. 211–212)

Neurosis

Neurosis is an interruption or a stagnation of growth; it is thus a "growth disorder" or a "disturbance in development" (Perls, 1969a, p. 28). This disturbance involves the individual's relation to society, which is a conflict between the needs and the demands of the individual and those of society. The individual is caught in the conflict between the biological needs of humanity and the social (ethical and moralistic) requirements of society, which may be against the biological laws of self-regulation. "Often enough, however, the socially required self-control can only be achieved at the cost of devitalizing and impairing the functions of large parts of the human personality—at the cost of creating collective and individual neurosis" (Perls, 1947, p. 61). Yet there is no inherent conflict between the individual, with his/her basic drives, and society. The individual is not antisocial but has a need for social contact. The difficulties are those of growing up, maturing, and realizing one's nature and potentialities in the face of deprivations and frustrations.

Neither the individual nor the society can be blamed; each is part of a whole, and a causal relationship cannot exist between parts of a whole. Both are ill or disturbed. Yet

man seems to be born with a sense of social and psychological balance as acute as his sense of physical balance. Every movement he makes on the social or psychological level is a movement in the direction of finding that balance, of establishing equilibrium between his personal needs and the demands of his society. His difficulties spring not from a desire to reject such equilibrium, but from misguided movements aimed towards finding and maintaining it. (Perls, 1973, p. 27)

When, in the search for the contact boundary, the individual impinges too heavily on society, the individual becomes a delinquent or a criminal. When the search leads the individual to draw back, so that society impinges too heavily on her/him, neurosis develops. The neurosis is a defensive maneuver against the threat of an overwhelming world. It is an effort to maintain balance and self-regulation in a situation in which the odds are very much against the individual.

Thus, the neurotic person is unable to satisfy any needs and to organize his/her behavior in accordance with a hierarchy of needs. The neurotic person cannot see his/her needs clearly, cannot separate and order them so that they can be dealt with one at a time. There is no continuous sequence in which needs come clearly into awareness in order of urgency and the environment is searched for relevant satisfaction, so that the Gestalt is completed and destructed to make way for the next higher need. The neurotic person is unable to distinguish between objects or persons that have a positive cathexis and those that have a negative cathexis; the neurotic person does not know whether to contact or to withdraw. The latter tendency is stronger. As a result, the neurotic is characterized by avoidance of contact.

The mechanisms of introjection, projection, confluence, and retroflection in extreme or pathological forms are characteristic of the neurotic person's defenses. In whichever of these forms the neurosis is primarily shown, it is a confusion of identification between the self and the other, resulting in disintegration of the personality and incoordination of thought and action. Behavior is rigid and compulsive rather than spontaneous. The neurotic person's efforts are deflected from the actualization of the self to the actualization of a self-image that is the neurotic person's (unrealistic) concept of what he/she should be like. The neurotic is not whole, since parts of the self that are inconsistent with the self-image are disowned or alienated. These (missing) parts are "holes."

Neurotic anxiety is the basic, common symptom of all neuroses. It is exemplified in anxiety attacks, and in individuals in whom it may not be felt, it is manifested by excitement or restlessness and difficulty in breathing. The physiological concomitants of excitement are increased metabolism, increased heart activity, quickened pulse, and increased breathing. If the excitement is inhibited or its expression is suppressed by the restricting of breathing, the insufficiency of oxygen leads to difficulty in breathing. "In a state of anxiety an acute conflict takes place between the urge to breathe (to overcome the feeling of choking), and the opposing self-control. . . . *Anxiety equals excitement plus inadequate supply of oxygen*" (Perls, 1947, p. 77). The neurotic person inhibits or suppresses excitement and suffers anxiety.

Guilt develops when, instead of contacts with others by means of interacting at the boundaries, there is a confluence between persons, "with no appreciation of a boundary between them" and "no discrimination of the points of difference or otherness that distinguishes them" (Perls et al., 1951, p. 118). There is, then, no figure-ground distinction, no awareness, and no contact. Confluence as a result of contact is healthy. It is unhealthy when it prevents contact. A healthy confluence can exist between persons who are close, as in marriage and old friendships. When a confluence is interrupted, guilt or resentment arises—guilt if the person feels responsible for the interruption and resentment if the person believes that the other is responsible (Perls et al., 1951). Guilt is also aroused when people feel unable to question what they have been told to believe and what they feel compelled to accept as what they ought to do but are unable to assimilate and accept. Guilt is thus projected resentment (Perls, 1969a).

Imbalance in the organism-environment field leads to neurosis (Perls, 1973).

> It seems to me that the imbalance arises when, simultaneously, the individual and the group experience differing needs, and when the individual is incapable of distinguishing which one is dominant. The group can mean the family, the state, the social-circle, co-workers—any or all combinations of persons who have a particular functional relationship with one another at a given time. The individual, who is part of this group, experiences the need for contact with it as one of his primary psychological impulses. . . . But when, at the same time, he experiences a personal need, the satisfaction of which

requires withdrawal from the group, trouble can begin. In the situation of conflict of needs, the individual has to be able to make a clear-cut decision. If he does this . . . neither he nor the environment suffers any severe consequences. But when he cannot discriminate . . . he can neither make a good contact nor a good withdrawal, and both he and the environment are affected. (p. 28)

Psychosis

Neurosis is a disturbance in the self-function, or the ego, while psychosis is a disturbance of the id functions (Perls et al., 1951). In neurosis, there is conflict within the self or between individual needs and social demands; in psychosis, the individual is out of touch with reality and is incapable of distinguishing fantasy from reality and thus hallucinates or is deluded.

The manic-depressive cycle involves aggression. "In the manic period the unsublimated, but dentally inhibited aggression is not retroflected as in melancholia but is directed in all its greediness and with most violent outbursts against the world. A frequent symptom of cyclothymia is dipsomania which is on the one hand a sticking to the 'bottle' and on the other a means of self-destruction" (Perls, 1947, p. 133).

In the paranoiac character, *"repressed disgust plays an essential part"* (Perls, 1947, p. 113). In *paranoiac aggression,* there is "an attempt to re-digest projections," which is experienced "not as dental aggression, as belonging to the alimentary sphere, but is directed as personal aggression against another person or against a collection of individuals, acting as screens for the projections" (Perls, 1947, p. 116). Introjection is a part of a *paranoiac pseudometabolism.*

"The healthy character expresses his emotions and ideas, the *paranoid character projects them"* (Perls, 1947, p. 157). "The paranoiac character exhibits what is called 'pseudo-metabolism.'" Material is introjected rather than assimilated, is felt as something strange to the self (as indeed it is), and then projected. The introjection represents the "swallowing" without tasting to avoid disgust. The material cannot be brought up to be rechewed because this would involve vomiting (disgust). It is, therefore, ejected (projected). The paranoiac thus treats as outside material, with attack and aggression, what is really a part of the self. Reintrojection may occur, and the total process may repeat itself.

Every paranoid person exhibits the megalomania-outcast or the superiority-inferiority complex. *"In the period of introjection—of identification with the faeces—the paranoid character feels himself as dirt; in times of projection—of alienation—he thinks himself superior and looks upon the world as dirt"* (Perls, 1947, p. 170). The obsessional neurosis has a psychotic or paranoid nucleus. The continual washing attempts to undo the feeling of being dirty.

THE THERAPY PROCESS

Goals

The man who can live in concernful contact with his society, neither being swallowed up by it nor withdrawing from it completely, is the well-integrated man. . . . He is the man who recognizes the contact boundary between himself and his society, who renders unto Caesar the things that are Caesar's and retains for himself those things which are its own. The goal of psychotherapy is to create just such men. (Perls, 1973, p. 26)

If pathology is the disturbance of the organismic balance, "the object of every treatment, psychotherapeutic or otherwise, is to facilitate organismic balance, to reestablish optimal function" (Perls, 1947, p. 69). Persistent imbalance is characterized by avoidance of various kinds, including avoidance of emotions and excitement, often under the inhibiting influence of shame. Thus, therapy must deal with these avoidances by bringing them to awareness. *"The awareness of, and the ability to endure, unwanted emotions are the conditio sine qua non for a successful cure"* (Perls, 1947, p. 179).

In terms of the relationship of the organism to its environment, the purpose of therapy is to reestablish contact and normal interaction and to replace abnormal retroflection, introjection, projection, and confluence by assimilation. "Only by re-establishing the destructive tendency towards food as well as toward anything that represents an obstacle to the individual's wholeness, by re-instating a successful aggression, the re-integration of an obsessional, and even a paranoid, personality takes place" (Perls, 1947, p. 136).

From the point of view of pathology as a disturbance in the ego function, then, restoration of the integrative function of the ego is the object of therapy. "So what we are trying to do in therapy is step-by-step to *re-own* the disowned parts of the personality until the person becomes strong enough to facilitate his own growth" (Perls, 1969a, p. 38). The wholeness of the organism must be restored.

As neurosis is an arrest or a stagnation of growth, so therapy fosters growth. The focus on organismic control makes it possible for the individual to actualize the *self* rather than to attempt to actualize a *self-image*. Because the neurotic person is immature and dependent on others, therapy fosters maturation, independence, and the transition from environmental support to self-support.

Basic to all these objectives is the attainment of awareness: *"awareness per se—by and of itself—can be curative"* (Perls, 1969a, p. 16). The healthy person "is completely in touch with himself and with reality" (Perls, 1969a, p. 46). Awareness leads to organismic self-regulation based on "the wisdom of the organism" in contrast to "the whole pathology of self-manipulation, environmental control and so on, that interferes with this subtle organismic control" (Perls, 1969a, p. 17). When awareness is present, "the organism can work on the healthy gestalt principle: that the most important unfinished situation will always emerge and can be dealt with" (Perls, 1969a, p. 51). This occurs in therapy, so the therapist does not have to dig because unfinished situations will come to the surface.

Therapy, like living, is in the here and now. "Nothing exists except in the here and now" (Perls, 1969a, p. 41). The past exists only as it is represented in present memory, and the future exists only in present expectation and anticipation. The past affects the individual and persists as unfinished situations.

Process

The patient seeks therapy because he or she is in an existential crisis: psychological needs are not being met. The patient is thus motivated but comes with certain expectations and with neurotic—and unsuccessful—ways of attempting to get the environment to do the work for her/him. The patient expects the therapist to provide environmental support and uses techniques in an attempt to manipulate the therapist to do so by "putting on the appearance of the good child."

Although Gestalt therapy gives the patient much of what he/she wants (exclusive attention, for example), it does not give the patient all that he/she expects (answers that the patient thinks are necessary, admiration, and praise). Thus, while the patient does get some satisfaction, he/she is also frustrated.

Gestalt therapy is not concerned with the whys of the patient's behavior, derived from the patient's history, unconscious, or dreams. It rejects the doctrine of single causes. In addition, the whys explain very little and can lead to projection of responsibility. Gestalt therapy focuses on present characteristics of the patient's behavior of which he/she is unaware. The unaware is broader than the unconscious, including not only material that has been repressed, but also material that has never come into awareness, that has faded, or that has not been assimilated; it "includes skills, patterns of behavior, motoric and verbal habits, blind spots, etc" (Perls, 1973, p. 54). Thus, awareness and unawareness are both mental activities and sensory and motor activities.

Dreams are useful because they represent an attempt to find a solution to an apparent paradox. They are not interpreted by the therapist. Rather, the therapist uses them to help the patient discover the paradox, represented by two inconsistent strivings. All the parts of the dream—objects as well as persons—represent projected and disowned parts of the personality, which must be reowned and integrated.

The neurotic person's problems are not in the past but in the present. Therapy must, therefore, deal with present behaviors and concerns through the development of here-and-now awareness. The solving of present difficulties will resolve any residual past problems, which are also current problems. Through therapy, the patient learns how to live in the present by living in the here-and-now therapy situation.

Since it focuses on present problems and concerns, Gestalt therapy is an experiential therapy. The patient is asked and forced to experience as much of himself/herself as possible—gestures, breathing, voice, and so on. As the patient experiences the ways in which he/she has blocked or "interrupted" the self, the patient becomes more aware of what that self really is. The focus on the *I* as the self, or person who experiences or is aware, places the responsibility on the patient for feelings, thoughts, and actions. The patient becomes aware of relationships between feeling and behavior in different areas, is thus able to integrate the dissociated parts of his/her personality, and can establish an adequate balance and appropriate boundaries between the self and the environment.

The patient's unfinished or interrupted past business must be experienced or relived, not simply recounted, so that it can be resolved in the here and now. An intellectual explanation or understanding (insight) is not enough. The therapist requires the patient to focus or concentrate on each specific area of unfinished business. In contrast to the free-association method of psychoanalysis, Gestalt therapy emphasizes concentration. (Perls called his method "concentration therapy" before adopting the name *Gestalt therapy*.) Free association leads to avoidance, to a flight of ideas, or to "dissociation." Concentration involves focusing on the figure rather than the ground.

Even though the patient is disturbed and confused, there is always something in the foreground—some Gestalt formation—however muddy or fragmental it may be. Whatever is there appears because it represents the most important need for survival at that time. It usually represents a need for security and support from the therapist, accompanied by resistance to being self-supporting. In the "safe emergency" of therapy, unfinished situations (or problems) can emerge into clearer figure. Concentration is necessary in order to overcome resistances. As each piece of unfinished business is resolved or completed, a Gestalt is completed and then destroyed, so that the patient is then ready to go on to another piece of unfinished business. A point is reached at which the patient no longer interrupts himself or herself and the process of assimilating and destructuring.

Therapy, then, by focusing on the recognition and awareness of interests and needs, attempts to reinstate the normal process by which these interests and needs can come to figure and be dealt with, either by seeking and obtaining satisfaction from them in the environment or by effecting a clear, deliberate withdrawal that closes the Gestalt. Thus, the homeostasis or self-regulation process can continue without interruption and accumulation of unfinished business or incomplete Gestalts. Since the goal of therapy is not to solve the patient's problems but to help the patient learn to solve his/her own problems, therapy is not a problem-solving process. Following therapy, the patient should be in a position to solve his/her own current problems and to prevent, minimize, or resolve future problems alone.

IMPLEMENTATION AND TECHNIQUES

There is no systematic presentation of the methods and techniques of Gestalt therapy. Specific exercises are presented in *Ego, Hunger and Aggression* (Perls, 1947) and more systematically in *Gestalt Therapy* (Perls et al., 1951). However, since neurosis is a symptom of growth stagnation, the remedy is not therapy but a method of reinstating growth. This is what the exercises accomplish. The object is to discover the self, which is achieved not through introspection but through action.

Even the average person is lacking in awareness. The first half of *Gestalt Therapy* consists of exercises that help the individual develop awareness of his/her functioning as an organism and as a person. The first set of exercises is for everyone and is directed toward

1. contacting the environment by becoming aware of present feelings, sensing opposed forces, attending and concentrating, and differentiating and unifying;
2. developing awareness of self through remembering, sharpening the body sense, experiencing the continuity of emotion, listening to one's verbalizing, and integrating awareness;
3. directing awareness by converting confluence into contact and changing anxiety into excitement.

Another set of exercises deals with processes that are chronic in organismic malfunctioning and is directed toward changing malfunctioning processes through

1. retroflection, by investigating misdirected behavior, mobilizing the muscles, and executing the re-reversed act;
2. introjection, by introjecting and eating, and dislodging and digesting introjects;
3. projection, by discovering projections and assimilating projections.

These exercises are aspects of therapy.

The emphasis is on the unique ways in which patients attempt to manipulate their environments (and the therapist as well) to gain environmental support. Thus, therapy is improvised as it develops. Methods vary with each patient and with each session by means of techniques invented to meet each situation. "Anything goes if it contributes to the patient's awareness" (Enright, 1975). Yet there are some consistencies among therapists, although therapists may vary in methods as well as style. "Gestalt therapy is done in as many ways as there are Gestalt therapists" (Latner, 1973). Still, there are some common, if not standard, techniques. They focus on developing the patient's awareness.

Much, if not most, Gestalt therapy takes place in groups, either of the workshop type, which Perls developed, in which the therapist works with an individual in the group setting, or of the somewhat more traditional group-therapy type, in which the therapist usually focuses on one individual at a time. In his 1969 introduction to *Ego, Hunger and Aggression*, Perls states his conviction that individual and long-term therapy is obsolete, with individual sessions being the exception rather than the rule. The group format has led to the development of techniques that are called "games" (see p. 370 for examples).

Role of the Therapist

Paradoxically, the therapist is not a helper. But the patient wants to depend on the therapist for support. The therapist who provides help is driven by the patient to give more and more help, or if the therapist does not or cannot help, the therapist is made to feel inadequate by the patient. Helping means providing support, and the patient's demand for support is his or her problem. Goodman phrased it well: "The very worst thing you can do for people is to help them" (Glasgow, 1971). To provide help is not helpful.

Rather, the function of the therapist is to frustrate the demands for support and help from the patient so that the patient can learn that the resources for resolving problems are in himself or herself.

> [W]e frustrate the patient in such a way that he is forced to develop his potential. We apply enough skillful frustration so that the patient is forced to find his own way, discover his own possibilities, his own potential, and discover that *what he expects from the therapist, he can do just as well himself.* (Perls, 1969a, p. 37)

The energy that is misdirected toward attempting to obtain environmental support can be used to actualize the self rather than to try to actualize a self-image. The patient has to learn this alone; teaching, conditioning, information giving, and interpreting cannot do it for him/her.

The patient resists this frustration and avoids facing the "holes" and the disowned parts of his/her personality. The patient is phobic and develops a scotoma; he/she cannot see the obvious. The therapist frustrates the patient "until he is face to face with his blocks, with his inhibitions, with his way of avoiding having eyes, having ears, having muscles, having authority, having security in himself" (Perls, 1969a, p. 39).

At the point at which the patient is unable to manipulate the environment (the therapist) into helping her/him and at which the patient does not feel capable of self-support is the patient at the *impasse*. He/she is stuck. The awareness of *how* he/she is stuck can lead to recovery. The patient discovers that the impasse is mostly a matter of fantasy, that he/she has the resources to get through it but only believed that he/she could not or was prevented from using these resources by imagining catastrophic outcomes.

The therapist must, however, provide a situation in which the patient feels accepted and not threatened. Frustration is not of a hostile, sadistic kind. The therapist is sympathetic, concerned, and caring about the patient and frustrates the patient in the context of this sympathy because it is the only way the therapist can really help the patient.

The therapist provides a "safe emergency," in which the patient can engage in the process of becoming self-supporting. The therapist is the facilitator. The therapist is an expert at directing the process by which the patient comes to the impasse, breaks it, and then achieves awareness and independence. The therapist must be sensitive, aware, and able to experience the patient's total communication, especially the nonverbal communication, since "verbal communication is usually a lie" (Perls, 1969a, p. 53).

Here-and-Now Awareness

The slogan for Gestalt therapy is "I and Thou, Here-and-Now." "Now" is the zero point between the past and the future, neither of which exists; only the now exists. The neurotic person is not one who had a problem in the past but one who has a problem now, which may also have been a problem in the past. The past influences behavior only as it is represented in the present. If the patient

> can become *truly aware* at every instant of himself and his actions on whatever level—fantasy, verbal or physical—he can see how he is producing his difficulties, he can see what his present difficulties are, and he can help himself to solve them in the present in the here and now. (Perls, 1973, p. 62)

Any past problems will also be taken care of, since they are part of the present problems.

The present, the here and now, is the therapy situation itself. The patient lives the problem in the interview. It is not necessary that the therapist probe or get a personal history. It is not even necessary that the patient verbalize the problem, because it will express itself in nonverbal behavior. The patient is not allowed to talk "about" problems in the past tense or in terms of memories; the patient is asked to reexperience them now. More generally, the patient is asked to experience now as much and as fully as possible his/her breathing, gestures, feelings, emotions, and voice. The manner of expression, not the content or the words, is what is important.

> [L]isten to what the voice tells you, what the posture tells you, what the image tells you. If you have ears, then you know all about the other person. You don't have to listen to *what* the person says: listen to the sounds. . . . [T]he voice is there, the gesture, the posture, the facial expression, the psychosomatic language. . . . [I]f you use your eyes and ears, then you can see that everyone expresses himself in one way or another. (Perls, 1969a, pp. 53–54)

The basic sentence that the patient is required to repeat is "Now I am aware." The present tense is required. Variations of this request are "What are you aware of now?"

"Where are you now?" "What are you seeing? feeling?" "What are you doing with your hand? foot?" or "Are you aware of what you are doing with your. . . ?" "What do you want?" "What do you expect?"

The function of the therapist is to call the patient's attention to his/her behavior, feelings, and experiencing, not to interpret them. The purpose is not to discover why but how—how the patient is preventing awareness of interrupted or unfinished business, of the "holes" or missing parts of the personality, or the rejected or dissociated aspects of it. Awareness cannot be forced; the formation of Gestalts is an autonomous process. Thus, if the patient resists dealing with material that the therapist calls the patient's attention to, the therapist does not push it. There will be other times when the patient may be ready to work on it.

Awareness itself can be curative, since it leads to contact with the unfinished business, which can then go to completion. The objective of all the techniques of Gestalt therapy, not only the here-and-now method, is to create awareness in the patient, so that the patient can integrate the disowned parts of his or her personality.

Making the Patient Responsible

The responses of the patient to awareness questions, both verbal and nonverbal, provide indications of the total personality; they are all expressions of the self. The therapist observes these responses and asks further questions. The patient's responses often are avoidance responses or questions to the therapist, or they contain other indications of an attempt to shirk responsibility for behavior. "To him responsibility is blame, and as he is afraid of being blamed, so is he ready to blame. 'I'm not responsible for my attitudes, it's my neurosis that's at fault,' he seems to say" (Perls, 1973, p. 78). Or the patient projects responsibility onto other people—parents—or early experiences. Patients also may dissociate themselves from nonverbal responses, referring to their body or its parts as "it" or to their actions as "they."

The therapist requires the patient to restate questions as statements, thus making the patient responsible for these statements. The therapist requires the patient to use *I* instead of *it* when referring to body parts and activities. "The therapist's primary responsibility is not to let go unchallenged any statement or behavior which is not representative of the self, which is evidence of the patient's lack of self-responsibility" (Perls, 1973, p. 79). The patient is thus led to take responsibility for his/her self and behavior, here and now, and becomes more aware of what and who he/she is.

Drama and Fantasy Work

Although the awareness technique alone is curative, it is slow. The therapist can speed up the process by initiating a number of other techniques that involve dramatic activity (role taking) and fantasy by the patient. The therapist can work with the patient's behavior and experience in fantasy as well as in actuality. This approach is particularly useful if the patient is blocked in dealing with reality. Fantasy, through the use of symbols, reproduces reality on a diminished scale, although it is still meaningfully related to reality. Fantasy can be verbalized, written down, or acted out in various forms with the therapist, with other members of a group, or in *monotherapy*. In monotherapy, the patient creates and directs the entire production, playing all the parts. Fantasy involves acting out in therapy the neurotic tendencies, which then can be handled. Fantasy work may involve a number of different dramatic techniques.

Perls was influenced in the use of drama both by his early interest and some experience in the theater and by Jacob Moreno, who developed psychodrama as a method of treatment for hospitalized patients. However, unlike Moreno, Perls did not involve others in the dramatic production. Rather, he had the patient play all the parts alone. He used various techniques or situations to facilitate the role playing on the part of the patient.

Shuttle Technique.   This involves directing the patient's attention back and forth from one activity or experience to another. In one form, the patient shuttles between talking and listening to himself/herself. The therapist may facilitate the process by calling the patient's attention to what has been said or how it has been said, for example, by asking "Are you aware of this sentence?"

The patient also may shuttle between reliving a past experience in fantasy and in the here and now. The reliving evokes proprioceptions, which when brought to awareness lead to filling in of blanks related to the experience and to completion of the unfinished business that it represents. The shuttle technique is also involved in other techniques, such as the topdog-underdog dialogues and the empty-chair technique.

Top Dog-Underdog Dialogue.   Neurotic conflicts involve opposite or opposing traits or aspects of the personality. When the therapist becomes aware of such a split in the personality, the patient is asked to experiment by taking each part of the conflict in turn by means of a dialogue. The most common split is between two aspects or two selves in the personality, the *top dog* and the *underdog*. The top dog is the equivalent of Freud's superego. It represents the "shoulds" that are introjected by the individual, usually from the parents. It is righteous, perfectionistic, authoritarian, bullying, and punishing. The underdog represents the id, or the *infraego,* to use Perls's term. It is primitive, evasive, "yes but," excusing, passively sabotaging the demands of the top dog and usually succeeding. This success, however, does not resolve the conflict; the conflict can be resolved only by an integration of the two aspects of the personality by the patient. The process of integration is achieved when the patient becomes aware of both the top dog and the underdog by entering into a dialogue in which he/she alternately takes the part of both.

The Empty Chair.   One of the most widely used Gestalt techniques is the *empty chair.* Essentially, it is a method of facilitating the role-taking dialogue between the patient and others or between parts of the patient's personality. It is usually used in a group situation. Two chairs are placed facing each other: one represents the patient or one aspect of the patient's personality (for example, the top dog), and the other represents another person or the opposing part of the personality (for example, the underdog). As the patient alternates the roles, he/she sits in one or the other chair.

The therapist may simply observe as the dialogue progresses or may instruct the patient when to change chairs, suggest sentences to say, call the patient's attention to what has been said or how it has been said, or ask the patient to repeat or exaggerate words or actions. In the process, emotions and conflicts are evoked, impasses may be brought about and resolved, and awareness and integration of polarities may develop—polarities or splits within the patient, between the patient and other persons, or between the patient's wants (underdog) and social norms (represented by top dog).

The empty-chair technique is frequently used in a group situation, in which the therapist works with a member of the group on a one-to-one basis. The person being worked with occupies the "hot seat" and faces the empty chair in front of the group.

Confusion

In *The Gestalt Approach and Eyewitness to Therapy,* Perls (1973) introduced the technique of dealing with confusion without giving it a designation. All patients demonstrate confusion, which is manifested in hesitation between contact and withdrawal, the latter representing the neurotic person's real need. Since confusion is unpleasant, the patient attempts to get rid of it by avoidance, blanking out, verbalism, and fantasy. All of this shows as "faded motoric behavior" in the therapy situation. The therapist must help the patient to become aware of, to tolerate, and to stay with this confusion. When it is not avoided or interrupted and is allowed to develop, it will be transformed into a feeling that can be experienced and can lead to appropriate action. An attempt to develop an intellectual understanding of it, on the contrary, does not resolve it, but constitutes an interruption—a premature arresting of development.

Blankness is a correlate of confusion. The patient cannot visualize anything clearly when asked; his/her fantasy images are hazy, as in a fog. If the patient can stay with it, it will clear up, and an image will form. A complete blank or blackness, like a black velvet curtain, may be another manifestation of confusion. The patient can be asked in fantasy to open the curtain, often revealing what he or she was hiding. Confusion also may be dealt with by the patient's "withdrawal into a fertile void," which is an eerie experience similar to a hypnogogic hallucination before falling asleep. This can lead to an "aha!" experience, in which confusion is transformed into clarity.

Dream Work

Freud referred to the dream as the royal road to the unconscious. Perls stated that it is the royal road to integration. Whereas the psychoanalyst works with associations to the individual elements of the dream and interprets them, the Gestalt therapist attempts to have the patient relive the dream in the present, in the therapy situation, including acting it out. Interpretation is avoided, as it leads only to intellectual insight. The interpretation is left to the patient. "The more you refrain from interfering and telling the patient what he is like or what he feels like, the more chance you give him to discover himself and not to be misled by your concepts and projections" (In Fagan and Shepherd, 1970, p. 29).

The dream represents or contains in some form an unfinished, unassimilated situation.

The dream is an existential message. It is more than an unfinished situation; it is more than an unfulfilled wish, it is more than a prophecy. It is a message of yourself to yourself, to whatever part of you is listening. The dream is possibly the most spontaneous expression of the human being. (*ibid.,* p. 27)

The different parts are projections of different and conflicting sides of the self. In principle, the dream contains all that is essential for the cure, if all its parts are understood and assimilated. "Everything is there. . . . We find all we need in the dream. . . . Understanding the dream means realizing when you are avoiding the obvious" (Perls, 1969a, p. 70). The forms change, but everything is in every dream. "A dream is a condensed reflection of our existence" (*ibid.,* p. 147).

Dreams reveal missing personality parts and the methods of avoidance used by the patient. Patients who do not remember dreams (everyone dreams) are refusing to face what is wrong with their existence; they "*think* that they have come to terms with life" (Perls, 1969a, p. 120). Such patients are asked to talk to the missing dreams: "Dreams, where are you?"

In dream work, the patient is asked to play the part of the various persons and objects. In doing so, the patient identifies with the alienated parts of the self and integrates them. Difficulty in or resistance to playing the alienated parts indicates that the patient does not want to reown or take back rejected parts of the self. The use of the empty-chair technique, in which the patient changes his/her seat during interaction with a dream person, object, or part of the self, facilitates the process.

Homework

"We ask all of our patients to try doing some homework and many are capable of speeding up their therapy in this way" (Perls, 1973, p. 82). Not all patients are able to carry out their assignments, however, and they may go to great lengths to avoid doing so. The homework involves the patient's reviewing the session by imagining himself/herself back in it. If there are blocks in reexperiencing it, the patient must try to find out if something disturbing occurred, such as something that could not be expressed in the therapy. If so, can the patient now say it? The focus is on becoming aware of avoidance and interruption of total expression.

Integration

These techniques (awareness, responsibility giving, drama and fantasy work, confusion, dreamwork, and homework) do not operate in isolation, by focusing on specific actions, feelings, experiences, or awareness per se. All are directed toward integration into a whole person. In Gestalt therapy, the focus is on integrating rather than, as in psychoanalysis, on analyzing. Things that are projected and resisted must be reowned, reassimilated.

Everything the person disowns can be recovered, and the means of this recovery is understanding, playing, becoming these disowned parts. And by letting him play and discover that he already has all this (which he thinks only others can give him) we increase his potential. . . . So what we are trying to do in therapy is step-by-step to *re-own* the disowned parts of the personality until the person becomes strong enough to facilitate his own growth. (Perls, 1969a, pp. 37–38)

The achievement of integration can be fostered by having the patient deal with any of the parts of the total person (the body, emotion, thinking, or speech) and the physical and social environment since all are related and exist in a functional unity. However, if any one is dealt with exclusively,

the effects will not spread sufficiently to those areas which the particular method neglects. If any partial approach is pursued, in isolation from the others, the unaware resistances in other components of the functioning will increase to such a degree as either to make further progress in the selected approach impossible unless or until other kinds of material are admitted or else to achieve a "cure" in terms of a new, arbitrary pattern. (Perls et al., 1951, pp. 112–113)

The basic rule of psychoanalysis—that the patient should say everything that comes to mind—is broadened. In addition to expressing thoughts and emotions, the patient is expected to express everything that is felt in his/her body, including not only major physical symptoms, but also unobtrusive sensations. Also, since the patient is forced to say everything, the patient suppresses embarrassment by

either wording the embarrassing material in a noncommittal manner, or by bracing himself and deadening his emotions. . . . [W]e have to impress upon the patient that he must neither suppress nor force anything, and that he must not forget to convey to the analyst every bit of conscious resistance such as embarrassment, shame, etc. (Perls, 1947, p. 74)

Shame and embarrassment

are the primary tools of repressions. . . . Endurance of embarrassment brings the repressed material to the surface . . . and helps the patient to accept previously refused material via the amazingly relieving discovery that the fact behind the embarrassment may not be so incriminating after all, and may even be accepted with interest by the analyst. . . . The *awareness of, and the ability to endure, unwanted emotions are the sine qua non for a successful cure;* these emotions will be discharged once they have become Ego-functions. This process, and not the process of remembering, forms the *via regia* to health. (Perls, 1947, pp. 178–179)

Thus, therapy is not a pleasant or an easy experience for the patient. The facing and dealing with avoidance is not painless. As a result, most of those who begin therapy do not continue or complete it. The patient who persists, however,

learns that the hard work is not mere drudgery. However far removed it may at first seem from what he thinks is urgent and therefore the place to start, he gradually gains orientation and perspective. He comes to see particular symptoms as merely surface manifestations of a more general and complicated system of malfunctioning which underlies and supports them. Though now, in a way, the job looks bigger and will obviously take longer than originally supposed, it does begin to make sense. (Perls et al., 1951, p. 141)

The therapist is more considerate than relatives or friends in leading the patient to face what the patient wishes to avoid. Nevertheless, the patient, usually following a "honeymoon" period at the beginning of therapy, becomes critical of therapy and the therapist or enters into what the Freudians call a "negative transference" period. If the patient can openly express and discuss this resentment, therapy continues and is accelerated; if the patient cannot or does not discuss it, therapy slows down and is likely to be terminated by the patient.

The development of awareness is directed toward repression. However, unlike psychoanalysis, which focuses on recovering what is repressed, Gestalt therapy emphasizes awareness of the existence of repression or avoidance and how it is being done. The blocked impulse will come out by itself. In *retroflection,* the impulse whose expression is being directed against the self instead of toward the environment is expressed toward its natural object in the environment. This is not easy or rapid. There is a long process in which the patient must first become aware of the retroflection, the repression, the repressed impulse, its acceptance, its redirection (possibly after modification), and its appropriate expression. The reintegration of dissociated parts is painful; "it always involves conflict, destroying and suffering" (Perls et al., 1951, p. 166).

In contrast to the treatment of retroflection, which involves the acceptance and integration of dissociated parts of the self, the treatment of *introjection* involves becoming "aware of what is not truly yours, to acquire a selective and critical attitude towards what is offered you, and, above all, to develop the ability to 'bite off' and 'chew' experience so as to extract its healthy nourishment" (Perls et al., 1951, p. 191).

Introjection leads to the formation of an ego that is a collection of unassimilated traits and qualities taken over from authorities without understanding. Becoming aware of eating habits of gulping, swallowing whole, greed, and disgust is the first step. The next step is to remobilize or reinstate the experience of disgust in eating by chewing a bite of food until it is fully liquefied; then a bit of reading matter or a difficult sentence is thoroughly analyzed and "chewed up." In therapy, that which has been swallowed whole must be brought back up to be rejected or chewed, so it can be assimilated. Catharsis is not enough; the patient must learn not to introject. The "working through" of psychoanalysis does this, but with only limited aspects of behavior.

If projections are to be dealt with, they must be discovered or recognized. Projections are encouraged by our language, which attributes our behavior to external causes. The process of alienation must be reversed by changing our language and thinking from *it* (or id) language to the responsible *I.* "The aim is to come to realize again that you are creative in your environment and are responsible for your reality—not to blame, but responsible in the sense that it is you who lets it stand or changes it" (Perls et al., 1951, p. 216). Once projections are recognized, they must be accepted as aspects of oneself and assimilated or modified.

Rules and Games.   The rules and games of Gestalt therapy have been collected by Levitsky and Perls (1970). The rules include the *principle of the now* (using the present tense), the *I and thou* (addressing the other person directly rather than talking about the person to the therapist), *using I language* (substituting *I* for *it* in talking about the body and its acts and behaviors), *using the awareness continuum* (focusing on the *how* and *what* of experience rather than on the *why*), *no gossiping* (addressing the person directly when he/she is present rather than making statements about the person), and *asking the patient to convert questions into statements.*

The games are mainly techniques used in groups. They are defined briefly as follows:

1. *Games of dialogue.* The patient takes the parts of aspects of the split personality and carries on a dialogue between them. These parts include the top dog (super-ego or shoulds) versus the underdog (passive resistant), aggressive versus passive, nice guy versus scoundrel, masculine versus feminine, and so forth.

2. *Making the rounds.* The patient extends a general statement or a theme (for example, "I can't stand anyone in this room") to each person individually, with additions pertinent to each.

3. *"I take responsibility."* The patient is asked to follow each statement about himself/herself or feelings with "and I take responsibility for it."

4. *"I have a secret."* Each person thinks of a personal secret involving guilt or shame and, without sharing it, imagines how he/she feels others would react to it.

5. *Playing the projection.* When a patient expresses a perception that is a projection, the patient is asked to play the role of the person involved in the projection to discover his/her conflict in this area.

6. *Reversals.* The patient is asked to play a role opposite to his/her overt or expressed behavior (for example, to be aggressive rather than passive) and to recognize and make contact with the submerged or latent aspect of himself/herself.

7. *The rhythm of contact and withdrawal.* The natural inclination toward withdrawal is recognized and accepted, and the patient is permitted to experience the security of withdrawing temporarily.

8. *Rehearsal.* Since much of thinking is rehearsal in preparation for playing a social role, group members share rehearsals with one another.

9. *Exaggeration.* Exaggeration is also a repetition game. When the patient makes an important statement in a casual way, indicating that he/she does not recognize its importance, the patient is required to repeat it again and again with increasing loudness and emphasis.

10. *"May I feed you a sentence?"* The therapist suggests a sentence for the patient to repeat that the therapist feels represents something significant to the patient, so that the patient can try it on for size. This often involves interpretation.

LENGTH AND LIMITATIONS OF TREATMENT

Length.   Gestalt therapy can be used as a form of individual treatment. It also can be used in groups—in workshops or group therapy. In individual therapy, sessions often occur once a week; in group therapy, sessions often last for two hours (again occurring once a week); in the workshop setting, the treatment may last for an entire day or over a weekend (Simkin

& Yontef, 1984). With Gestalt therapy, it is not uncommon for individual and group forms of treatment to both be used in helping patients.

Limitations.   Gestalt therapy has been used in the treatment of a wide range of problems and conditions, including couple issues, psychosomatic disorders, neuroses, even character disorders and psychoses. However, "work with psychotic, disorganized or other severely disturbed people is more difficult and calls for 'caution, sensitivity, and patience'" (Yontef & Simkin, 1989, p. 346). Furthermore, since increasing awareness is so critical to therapeutic progress, "Those who want symptom relief without doing awareness work may be better candidates for behavior modification, medication, biofeedback, and so on" (Yontef & Simkin, 1989, p. 338).

EXAMPLES

These examples are from demonstration workshops, which were Perls's major activity in therapy. These workshops were not therapy groups; they were used for training professionals. Participants volunteered to "work with" Perls on an individual basis. The group was involved only when a volunteer came to a therapeutic realization and was asked to express it in interaction with other participants in the procedure or game called "making the rounds." The cases that follow are taken from *Gestalt Therapy Verbatim* (Perls, 1992, pp. 101–103, 298–306).

LINDA: I dreamed that I watch . . . a lake . . . drying up, and there is a small island in the middle of the lake, and a circle of . . . porpoises—they're like porpoises except that they can stand up. So they're like porpoises that are like people, and they're in a circle, sort of like a religious ceremony, and it's very sad—I feel very sad because they can breathe. They are sort of dancing around the circle, but the water, their element, is drying up. So it's like a dying—like watching a race of people, or a race of creatures, dying. And they are mostly females, but a few of them have a small male organ, so there are a few males there, but they won't live long enough to reproduce, and their element is drying up. And there is one that is sitting over here near me and I'm talking to this porpoise and he has prickles on his tummy, sort of like a porcupine, and they don't seem to be a part of him. And I think that there's one good point about the water drying up, I think—well, at least at the bottom, when all the water dries up, there will probably be some sort of treasure there, because at the bottom of the lake there should be things that have fallen in, like coins or something. But I look carefully and all that I can find is an old license plate. . . . That's the dream.

FRITZ: Will you please play the license plate?

L: I am an old license plate, thrown in the bottom of a lake. I have no use because I'm no value—although I'm not rusted—I'm outdated, so I can't be used as a license plate . . . and I'm just thrown on the rubbish heap. That's what I did with a license plate, I threw it on a rubbish heap.

F: Well, how do you feel about this?

L: (quietly) I don't like it. I don't like being a license plate—useless.

F: Could you talk about this? That was such a long dream until you come to find a license plate. I'm sure this must be of great importance.

L: (sighs) Useless. Outdated. . . . The use of a license plate is to allow—give a car permission to go . . . and I can't give anyone permission to do anything because I'm outdated. . . . In California, they just paste a little—you buy a sticker—and stick it on the car, or the old license plate. So maybe someone could put me on their car and stick this sticker on me, I don't know. . . .

F: Okeh, now play the lake.

L: I'm a lake. . . . I'm drying up, and disappearing, soaking into the earth . . . (with a touch of surprise) *dying.*. . . But when I soak into the earth, I become a part of the earth—so maybe I water the surrounding area, so . . . even in the lake, even in my bed, flowers can grow (sighs).. . . New life can grow . . . from me (cries).. . .

F: You get the existential message?

L: Yes (sadly, but with conviction) I can paint—I can create—I can create beauty. I can no longer reproduce, I'm like the porpoise . . . but I . . . I'm . . . I . . . keep wanting to say I'm *food* . . . I . . . As water becomes . . . I water the earth, and give life-growing things. The water—they need both the earth and water, and the . . . and the air and the sun, but as the water from the lake, I can play a part in something, and producing—feeding.

F: You see the contrast: On the surface, you find something, some artifact—the license plate, the artificial you—but then when you go deeper, you find the apparent death of the lake is actually fertility. . . .

L: And I don't need a license plate, or a permission, a license in order to. . . .

F: (gently) Nature doesn't need a license plate to grow. You don't have to be useless if you are organismically creative, which means if you are involved.

L: And I don't need permission to be creative. . . . Thank you.

Jane

JANE: The dream I started on, the last time I worked, I never finished it, and I think the last part is as important as the first part. Where I left off, I was in the Tunnel of Love—

FRITZ: What are you picking on? (Jane has been scratching her leg)

J: Hmmm. (clears throat) I'm just sitting here, for a minute, so I can really be here. It's hard to stay with this feeling, and talk at the same time. . . . Now I'm in the intermediate zone, and I'm—I'm thinking about two things: Should I work on the dream, or should I work on the picking thing, because that's something that I do a lot. I pick my face, and . . . I'll go back to the dream. I'm in the Tunnel of Love, and my brother's gone in the—somewhere—and to the left of me, there's a big room and it's painted the color of . . . the color that my schoolrooms used to be painted, kind of a drab green, and to the left of me there are bleachers. I look over and there are all people sitting there. It looks as though they are waiting to get on the ride. There's a big crowd around one person, Raymond. (fiancé) He's talking to them and he's explaining something to them and they're all listening to him. And he's moving his finger like this, and making gestures. I'm surprised to see him. I go up to him, and it's very obvious that he doesn't want to talk to me. He's interested in being with all these people, entertaining all these people. So I tell him that I'll wait for him. I sit three . . . three bleachers up and look down, and watch this going on. I get irritated and I'm pissed off, so I say, "Raymond, I'm leaving. I'm not gonna wait for you any more." I walk outside the door. I stand outside the door for awhile. I get anxious. I can feel anxious in my dream. I feel anxious now, because I don't really want to be out here. I want to be inside, with Raymond. So I'm going inside. I go back through the door. . . .

F: Are you telling us a dream, or are you doing a job?

J: Am I telling a dream. . . .

F: Or are you doing a job?

J: I'm telling a dream, but it's still . . . I'm not telling a dream.

F: Hm. Definitely not.

J: I'm doing a job.

F: I gave you only the two alternatives.

J: I can't say that I'm really aware of what I'm doing, except physically. I'm aware of what's happening physically to me but, I don't really know what I'm doing. I'm not asking you to tell me what I'm doing . . . just saying I don't know.

F: I noticed one thing: When you come up to the hot seat, you stop playing the silly goose.

J: Hm. I get frightened, when I'm up here.

F: You get dead.

J: Whew. . . . If I close my eyes and go into my body, I know I'm not dead. If I open my eyes and "do that job," then I'm dead. . . . I'm in the intermediate zone now, I'm wondering whether or not I'm dead. I notice that my legs are cold and my feet are cold. My hands are cold. I feel . . . I feel strange. . . . I'm in the middle, now. I'm . . . I'm neither with my body nor with the group. I notice that my attention is concentrated on that little matchbook on the floor.

F: Okeh. Have an encounter with the match box.

J: Right now, I'm taking a break from looking at you, 'cause it's . . . it's a . . . 'cause I don't know what's going on, and I don't know what I'm doing. I don't even know if I'm telling the truth.

F: What does the matchbook answer?

J: I don't care if you tell the truth or not. It doesn't matter to me. I'm just a match box.

F: Let's try this for size. Tell us, "I'm just a match box."

J: I'm just a match box. And I feel silly saying that. I feel, kind of dumb, being a match box.

F: Uhhm.

J: A little bit useful, but not very useful. There's a millon like me. And you can look at me, and can like me, and then when I'm all used up, you can throw me away. I never liked being a match box. . . . I don't . . . I don't know if that's the truth, when I say I don't know what I'm doing. I know there's one part of me that knows what I'm doing. And I feel suspended, I feel . . . steady. I don't feel relaxed. Now I'm trying to understand why in the two seconds it takes me to move from the group to the hot seat, my whole . . . my whole *persona* changes. . . . Maybe because of . . . I want to talk to the Jane in *that* chair.

She would be saying, (with authority) well, *you* know where you're at. You're playing dumb. You're playing stupid. You're doing this, and you're doing that, and you're sucking people in, and you're (louder) not telling the truth! And you're stuck, and you're dead. . . .

And when I'm *here,* I immediately . . . the Jane here would say, (small, quavering voice) well, that's . . . I feel on the defensive in this chair right now. I feel defensive. I feel like for some reason I have to defend myself. And I know it's not true. . . . So who's picking on you? It's *that* Jane over there that's picking on me.

F: Yah.

J: She's saying . . . She's saying, (briskly) now when you get in the chair, you have to be in the here and now, you have to do it *right,* you have to be turned on, you have to know everything.

F: "You have to do your job."

J: You have to do your job, and you have to do it *right.* And you have to . . . On top of all that, you have to become totally self-actualized, and you have to get rid of all your hangups, and along with that . . . it's not . . . it's not mandatory that you do this, but it's nice if you can be entertaining along the way, while you're doing all that. Try to spice it up a little bit, so that people won't get bored and go to sleep, because that makes you anxious. And you have to *know* why you're in the chair. You can't just go there and not know why you're there. You have to know *everything,* Jane.

    You really make it hard for me. You really make it hard. You're really putting a lot of demands on me. . . . I don't know everything. And that's hard to say. I don't know everything, and on top of that, I don't know what I'm doing half the time. . . . I don't know. I don't know if that's the truth or not. I don't even know if that's a lie.

F: So be your topdog again.

J: Is that. . . ?

F: Your topdog. That's the famous topdog. The righteous topdog. This is where your power is.

J: Yeah. Well . . . uh . . . I'm your topdog. You can't live without me. I'm the one that . . . I keep you noticed, Jane. I keep you noticed. If it weren't for me, nobody would notice you. So you'd better be a little more grateful that I exist.

    Well, I don't want to be noticed, *you* do. You want to be noticed. I don't want to be noticed. I don't want . . . I don't really want to be noticed, as much as you do.

F: I would like you to attack the righteous side of that topdog.

J: Attack . . . the righteous side.

F: The topdog is always righteous. Topdog *knows* what you've got to do, has all the right to criticize, and so on. The topdog nags, picks, puts you on the defensive.

J: Yeah . . . You're a bitch! You're like my mother. You know what's good for me. You . . . you make life *hard* for me. You tell me to do things. You tell me to be . . . *real.* You tell me to be self-actualized. You tell me to . . . uh, tell the truth.

F: Now please don't change what your hands are doing, but tell us what's going on in your hands.

J: My left hand. . . .

F: Let them talk to each other.

J: My left hand. I'm shaking, and I'm in a fist, straining forward, and (voice begins to break) that's kind of . . . the fist is very tight, pushing . . . pushing my fingernails into my hand. It doesn't feel good, but I do it all the time. I feel tight.

F: And the right hand?

J: I'm holding you back around the wrist.

F: Tell it why you hold it back.

J: If I let you go you're . . . then you're gonna hit something. I don't know what you're gonna hit, but I have to . . . I have to hold you back 'cause you can't do that. Can't go around hitting things.

F: Now hit your topdog.

J: (short harsh yell) Aaaarkh! Aarkkh!

F: Now talk to your topdog. "Stop nagging."

J: (loud, pained) Leave me alone!

F: Yah, again.

J: Leave me alone!

F: Again.

J: (screaming it and crying) *Leave me alone!*

F: Again.

J: (she screams it, a real blast) **LEAVE ME ALONE! I DON'T HAVE TO DO WHAT YOU SAY!** (still crying) I don't have to be that good! . . . I don't have to be in this chair! I don't *have* to. *You* make me. You make me come here! (screams) Aarkkh! You make me pick my face, (crying) that's what you do. (screams and cries) Aarkkh! I'd like to kill you.

F: Say this again.

J: I'd like to kill you.

F: Again.

J: I'd like to *kill* you.

F: Can you squash it in your left hand?

J: It's as big as me. . . . I'm strangling it.

F: Okeh. Say this, "I'm strangling. . . ."

J: (quietly) I'm gonna strangle you . . . take your neck. Grrummmm. (Fritz gives her a pillow which she strangles while making noises) Arrghh. Unghhh. How do you like *that!* (sounds of choked-off cries and screams)

F: Make more noises.

J: Hrugghhh! Aachh! Arrgrughhh! (she continues to pound the pillow, cry and scream)

F: Okeh. Relax, close your eyes . . . (long silence) (softly) Okeh. Come back to us. Are you ready? . . . Now be that topdog again. . . .

J: (faintly) You shouldn't have done that. I'm gonna punish you for that. . . . I'm gonna punish you for that, Jane. You'll be sorry you did that. Better watch out.

F: Now talk like this to each one of us. . . . Be vindictive with each one of us. Pick out something we have done. . . . Start with me. As this topdog, for what are you going to punish me?

J: I'm gonna punish you for making me feel so stupid.

F: How are you going to punish me?

J: (promptly) By being stupid. Even stupider than I am.

F: Okeh. Do this some more.

J: Raymond, I'm gonna punish you for being so dumb. I'll make you feel like an ass. . . . I'll make you think I'm smarter than you are, and you'll feel dumber and I'll feel smart. . . . I'm really scared. I shouldn't be doing this. (cries) It isn't nice.

F: Say this to him. Turn it around, "You should not. . . ."

J: You sh- . . . you shouldn't . . . you shouldn't . . . you shouldn't be doing . . . hooo . . . you shouldn't be doing . . . you shouldn't be so dumb. You shouldn't play so dumb. Because it isn't nice.

F: You're doing a job again.

J: Yeah, I know. I don't wanna do it. (crying) I . . . I know how I punish you. (sigh) I'll punish you by being helpless.

RAYMOND: What are you punishing me for?

JANE: I'll punish you for loving me. That's what I'll punish you for. I'll make it *hard* for you to love me. I won't let you know if I'm coming or going.

FRITZ: "How can you be so low as to love somebody like me?" Yah?

J: *I* do that.

F: I know. How can you love a match box?

J: Fergus, I'm gonna punish you for being so slow . . . in your body, but so quick in your mind, The way I'm gonna do that . . . I'm gonna excite you, try to excite you, and it's the truth. I'll punish you for being sexually inhibited. I'll make you think I'm very sexy. I'll make you feel bad around me. . . . And I'll punish you for pretending to know more than you do.

F: What do you experience when you are meting out the punishment?

J: (more alert, alive) It's a very strange experience. I don't know that I've ever had it before, for such a long time. It's kind of . . . it's a feeling I used to get when I . . . when I got back at my brothers for being mean to me. I'd just grit my teeth and think of the *worst* thing I could do and kind of enjoy it.

F: Yah. This is my impression; you didn't enjoy this here.

J: Mm.

F: Okeh. Go back and be the topdog again, and *enjoy* punishing Jane. Pick on her, torture her.

J: You're the only one I enjoy punishing. . . . When you're too loud, when you're too loud, I'll punish you for being too loud. (no sound of enjoyment) When you're not loud enough, I'll tell you that you're too inhibited. When you dance too much, when you dance too much, I'll tell you that you're trying to sexually arouse people. When you don't dance enough, I'll tell you that you're dead.

F: Can you tell Jane, "I'm driving you crazy?"

J: (cries) I'm driving you crazy.

F: Again.

J: I'm driving you crazy.

F: Again.

J: I'm driving you *crazy*. . . . I used to drive everybody else crazy, and now I'm driving *you* crazy. . . . (voice drops, becomes very faint) But it's for your own good. That's what my mother would say. "For your own good." I'll make you feel *guilty* when you've done bad things, so you won't do it again. And pat you on the back when you do something good, so you'll remember to do it again. And I'll keep you out of the moment. I'll . . . I'll keep you planning and I'll keep you programmed, and I won't let you live . . . in the moment. I won't let you enjoy your life.

F: I would like you to use this: "I am relentless."

J: I . . . I *am* relentless.

F: Again.

J: I am relentless. I'll do anything—especially if somebody dares me to do something. Then I've gotta tell you to do it, Jane, so you can prove it, so you can prove yourself. You've *gotta* prove yourself in this world.

F: Let's try this. "You've got a job to do."

J: (laughs) You've gotta job to do. You're gonna quit fuckin' around, and . . . you've been doin' nothin' for a long time.

F: Yah. Now, don't change your posture. The right arm goes to the left and the left arm goes to the right. Say the same thing again and stay aware of this.

J: You've been doing nothing for a long time. You gotta do something, Jane. You've gotta *be* something. . . . You've gotta make people proud of you. You've got to grow up, you have to be a woman, and you gotta keep everything that's bad about you hidden away so nobody can see it, so they'll think you're perfect, just perfect. You have to lie. I make you lie.

F: Now take Jane's place again.

J: You're . . . you're (cries) you are driving me crazy. You're picking on me. I'd really like to strangle you . . . uh . . . then you'll punish me more. You'll come back . . . and give me hell for that. So, why don't you just go away? I won't . . . I won't cross you up any more. Just go away and leave me alone . . . and I'm not begging you! Just go away!

F: Again.

J: Just go away!

F: Again.

J: *Go away!*

F: Change seats.

J: You'll be just a half if I go away! You'll be half a person if I leave. Then you'll really be fucked up. You can't send me away. You'll have to figure out something to *do* with me, you'll have to *use* me. . . . Well then . . . then I . . . I would change your mind about a lot of things if I had to.

F: Ah!

J: And tell you that there's nothing I could do that's bad. . . . I mean, if you'd leave me alone, I wouldn't do anything bad. . . .

F: Okeh. Take another rest.

J: (closes eyes) I can't rest.

F: So come back to us. Tell us about your restlessness.

J: I keep wondering what to do with that. When I had my eyes closed, I was saying, "Tell her to just relax."

F: Okeh. Play *her* topdog, now.

J: Just relax.

F: Make her the underdog and you're the topdog.

J: And you don't have to do anything, you don't have to prove anything. (cries) You're only twenty years old! You don't have to be the queen. . . .

　　　She says, O.K. I understand that. I know that. I'm just in a *hurry.* I'm in a *big* hurry. We've got so many things to do . . . and now, I know, when I'm in a hurry you can't be now, you can't . . . when I'm in a hurry, you can't stay in the minute you're in. You have to keep . . . you have to keep hurrying, and the days slip by and you think you're losing time, or something. I'm *much* too hard on you. I have to . . . I have to leave you alone.

F: Well, I would like to interfere. Let your topdog say, "I'll be a bit more patient with you."

J: Uh. I'll be . . . I'll be a bit more patient with you.

F: Say this again.

J: (softly) It's very hard for me to be patient. You know that. You know how impatient I am. But I'll . . . I'll try to be a bit more patient with you. "I'll try". . . I'll *be* a bit more patient with you. As I say that, I'm stomping my foot, and shaking my head.

F: Okeh. Say, "I *won't* be patient with you."

J: (easily) I *won't* be patient with you, Jane! I won't be patient with you.

F: Again.

J: I won't be patient with you.

F: Again.

J: I won't be patient with you.

F: Now say this to us. Pick a few.

J: Jan, I won't be patient with you. Claire, I won't be patient with you. . . . Dick, I won't be patient with you. Muriel, I won't be patient with you. Ginny, I won't be patient with you. And June, I won't be patient with you, either.

F: Okeh. How do you feel, now?

J: O.K.

F: You understand, topdog and underdog are not yet together. But at least the conflict is clear, in the open, maybe a *little* bit less violent.

J: I felt, when I worked before, on the dream, and the dream thing, that I worked this out. I felt *good.* I keep . . . I keep . . . it keeps . . . I keep going back to it.

F: Yah. This is the famous self-torture game.

J: I do it so *well.*

F: Everybody does it. You don't do it better than the rest of us. Everybody thinks, "I am the worst."

SUMMARY AND EVALUATION

Summary.   There are two basic principles underlying Gestalt therapy as it was developed by Perls: the holistic principle that persons are organized wholes, and the dialectic principle of opposites, including the principle of homeostasis. The experiencing of a need leads to an imbalance, or disequilibrium, in the organism. The organism as a whole responds in an attempt to restore the balance by satisfying the need. In Gestalt terms, the need emerges out of the background and becomes the figure. The organism engages in sensory and motor behavior in interaction with its environment to obtain satisfaction for the need. When the need is met, completing the Gestalt, the Gestalt dissolves or destructs, leaving the organism ready for the emergence of another dominant need. The continuing process of awareness of emerging needs causes disequilibrium, is followed by aggressive contact with the environment and need satisfaction through assimilation from the environment with resulting momentary equilibrium, and then leads to growth and development.

The disturbance of this process constitutes neurosis or psychosis. The disturbed individual is not aware of any needs, is unable to organize his/her needs into a hierarchy, or is unable to obtain need satisfaction and resorts to a pathological degree of introjection, projection, confluence, and/or retroflection.

Therapy consists of reinstating the growth process by enabling the patient to become aware of unmet needs—unfinished business, or incomplete Gestalts—so that the patient can resolve or complete them and then begin to satisfy current needs. Gestalt therapy does not attempt to recover the past by analysis. The unfinished business of the past manifests itself in the present, particularly in nonverbal behavior and dreams. Therapy focuses, then, on behavior in the here and now, which leads to awareness of unresolved conflicts with others and within the self. With awareness, the patient is then able to resolve the conflicts or reintegrate alienated parts of the self.

Evaluation.   The Gestalt approach offers a provocative theory. It overcomes the restriction of psychoanalysis to the individual and the intrapersonal and of Sullivan's interpersonal theory, with its neglect of the individual. It goes beyond those theories that concentrate on reason and the intellect to the neglect of affect and emotion and beyond those theories that may include both but neglect the body and motor activity. It does not, however, limit itself to the latter, as do some approaches, such as Reichian therapy and Lowen's bioenergetics. The concept of the whole organism in the environment incorporates all of these.

The Gestalt concept of the self as the system of and the awareness of the contact boundary with the environment is a major addition to the psychoanalytic concept of the ego. The distinction between the actualization of the self rather than the actualization of a self-image is useful. The Gestalt concept of motivation is a unitary concept, almost identical with that of Combs and Snygg (1959) and of Rogers (1951). Its recognition that needs emerge as they take priority in the process of self-actualization overcomes the problem posed by Maslow's (1969) hierarchy in the same way as that proposed by Patterson (1964). Like the client-centered approach, Gestalt therapy is phenomenological in its orientation. It recognizes that the individual creates a subjective (and effectively real) world according to interests and needs. Internal, not external, reality is the only reality that matters.

A further similarity to the client-centered approach is the parallel between organismic self-regulation and Roger's concept of the organism as a whole reacting to the phenomenal field. There is also a parallel with Rogers's concept of the fully functioning person as one who is open to all experiences, able to symbolize those experiences in awareness, and able to experience himself/herself as the locus of evaluation, with the valuing process being organismically based rather than environmentally based. Perls's concept of introjection of values (the top dog of the ego) is similar to Roger's concept of incongruence as a result of the change in the locus of evaluation from the self in infancy to outside the self with the imposition by others (parents) of conditions of worth. Finally, there appears to be a close similarity between client-centered therapy and Gestalt therapy in their goals: awareness in the client leading to the process of self-actualization.

The theory is appealing; there is little in it that one can reject or greatly disagree with. Questions that arise have to do with the application of the theory: Are the methods and techniques of Gestalt therapy necessary derivations from the theory, and are they the necessary and the most effective and efficient methods for achieving the goals of Gestalt therapy without undesirable side effects? There is considerable doubt that this is the case.

Much of the problem is inherent in the fact that systematic discussion of Gestalt therapy is limited, particularly as it derives from theory. Therefore, a person must depend on description of methods and on excerpts and examples for better understanding. Much of this material derives from workshops conducted by Perls. However, as the Polsters (1973) note: "When the master works, it is hard to discriminate between what is his *style* and what is the theory which supports his style" (p. 286). It becomes difficult, if not impossible, to separate the method from the man, the essence from the style. Perls was, as he admitted, a showman. In his autobiographical book, he wrote, "I feel best when I can be a prima donna and can show off my skill of getting rapidly in touch with the essence of a person and his plight" (Perls, 1969b). Perls (1969b) was superbly egotistical: "I believe I am the best therapist for any type of neurosis in the States, maybe in the world. How is that for megalomania. The fact is that I am wishing and willing to put my work to any research test."

Unfortunately, there is little more than testimonials to support the claims of Perls. His brief demonstrations are often impressive. They, as well as brief examples given by others, sometimes seem little short of miraculous, but there is no validating evidence of the value or any lasting effects of the high emotional experience or insights felt by the subjects. Those who knew Perls and saw him operate acknowledge that he was effective. Kempler (1973), for example, wrote that "his skill consisted of a remarkable ability to perceive and influence behavior. His own behavior was provocative, evocative, and inspiring. To meet him and come away feeling more complete in oneself was not at all unusual." Yet Perls himself apparently had some doubts about his effectiveness. Immediately following the statement about his effectiveness as a therapist, he says, "At the same time I have to admit that I cannot cure anybody, that those so-called miracle cures are spectacular but don't mean much from the existential point of view" (Perls, 1969b).

Shepherd (1970) cautioned against assuming that Gestalt therapy offers "instant cure" on the basis of the sometimes dramatic effects observed in the short time of the demonstrations. It is also not clear what the source is of the effects that are achieved. The combination of Perls' personality, reputation, self-assurance, and techniques, together with the attitudes and expectations of his subjects, or "patients," as he called them, makes for a powerful placebo effect. Kempler (1973), who knew Perls, wrote,

> In no way could Perls' behavior be called "I" [in the I and Thou context]. He was the puppeteer, the manipulator, the director, and that was how it had to be. Any remark inviting Perls to look at his own behavior met with the invitation for the subject to look at *his* own motives in making the suggestion. There is no doubt that Perls did his job well but there was always something missing. And it was the personal Perls. (p. 280)

It must also be remembered that the "patients" with whom he worked in his demonstrations were often professional people. They represent perhaps the kind of persons for whom Gestalt therapy is claimed to be most effective: "overly socialized, restrained, constricted individuals—often described as neurotic, phobic, perfectionistic, ineffective, depressed, etc.—whose functioning is limited or inconsistent, primarily due to their internal restrictions, and whose enjoyment is minimal" (Shepherd, 1970, p. 235); in other words, essentially "normal" but inhibited, intellectually controlled individuals.

In many instances, results seem to be provoked or created by the therapist—in part by suggestion—rather than produced spontaneously by the patient. There is a sense of artificiality, of a forced nature, of patients attempting to divine what Perls wanted and then complying. Perls sometimes does not appear to be listening to the patient but to be waiting for the patient or maneuvering the patient to manifest a split so that an empty-chair dialogue can be set up. This tends to give an aura of technique to the performance. Perls eschewed "gimmicks" and games, yet his demonstrations come dangerously close to these. In his review of the collection of papers published under the title *Gestalt Therapy Now,* Stone (1971) noted that "the most unappealing aspect of Perls' therapy is that he and his followers sometimes seem to be playing games on people rather than with them." While we would not go as far as that, it does appear in many cases that the therapist is playing games—often a guessing game—with the patient.

Perls was justified in his concern about the trend toward techniques without adequate grounding in theory. It is the Gestalt techniques that have spread, picked up by those with no particular theoretical orientation or added to another theoretical orientation, especially Berne's transactional analysis. Kempler (1973) noted that "the greatest hazard to the movement is the gimmick therapist, the tactician. . . . [M]any disciples, eager to learn and clever with mental gymnastics, became enamored of the tactics, learn to confront people by using the tactics initiated by Perls and consider themselves Gestalt therapists."

In one of Perls' seminars, one of the participants raised this question:

> Dr. Perls, will you—as you've been formulating and experiencing what has come out as Gestalt Therapy, I want to be reassured. I want to hear you say it, it seems like a

process of discovery. Yet I think that people can arrange themselves to fit the expectations of the therapist, like, I sit here and watch person after person have a polarity, a conflict of forces, and I think I can do it too. But I don't know how spontaneous it would be, although I think I would feel spontaneous. You've experienced people over a long time; are we fitting you or have you discovered us? [To which Perls (1969a) replied] I don't know. (pp. 214–215)

While our critique thus far has focused on Perls, it seems important to add that Gestalt theory and therapy is bigger than Perls alone, that Gestalt therapists can be quite varied in how they practice Gestalt therapy, and that Gestalt therapy itself has certainly evolved over the years. Simkin and Yontef (1984), for example, stated that

there has been a movement toward more softness in Gestalt therapy practice, more direct self-expression by the therapist, more of a dialogic emphasis, decreased use of stereotypic techniques. . . , and increased use of group process. . . . a patient is more likely to encounter . . . a softer demeanor by the therapist, more trust of the patient's phenomenology, and more explicit work with psychodynamic themes. (p. 287)

This view has been more recently reflected by Rice and Greenberg (1992):

Interestingly, Gestalt therapy is also undergoing a change, one in which the I-Thou relationship is being emphasized more than the use of technique. In addition, a growing interest in self psychology and in the importance of empathy in providing a healing environment has become manifest (Yontef, 1981). The development of a more . . . relational perspective in Gestalt therapy represents an interesting expansion. (p. 217)

So it seems that some of the inattention given to the relationship in earlier Gestalt therapy thinking has now given way to a more relationship focus. This seems to be the most prominent modification in Gestalt therapy in recent years. In our opinion, that change is good.

The Gestalt view today is kept very much alive throughout the United States and Europe by means of major training institutes. For example, such institutes can be found in New York, Los Angeles, Cleveland, and Atlanta, among other cities, and they offer training to many people interested in learning how to do Gestalt work. *The Gestalt Journal* has long been a major outlet for articles about Gestalt therapy. The *British Gestalt Journal* began publication in 1991. Such individuals as Erving Polster (1987, 1992), Miriam Polster (1987), Joseph Zinker (1977), and others (e.g., Edwin Nevis, 1987) continue to advance and serve as vibrant representatives of the Gestalt approach.

And what of research and Gestalt therapy? Perls himself made no broad claims for the success of Gestalt therapy. To the question "Where is your proof?" Perls replied in 1951:

Our standard answer will be that we present nothing that you cannot *verify for yourself in terms of your own behavior,* but if your psychological make-up is that of an experimentalist. . . , this will not satisfy you and you will clamor for "objective evidence" of a verbal sort, prior to trying out a single non-verbal step of the procedure. (Perls et al., 1951, p. 7)

Decades later, some of the same sentiment seems to be expressed by Yontef and Simkin (1989): "Gestalt therapists are singularly unimpressed with . . . nomothetic research methodology. No statistical approach can tell the individual patient or therapist what works for him or her. What is shown to work for most does not always work for a particular individual" (p. 347).

Still, some interesting Gestalt therapy research has been conducted, and we would like to mention some of that here. Specifically, it appears that the most systematic, programmatic attempt to study Gestalt therapy has been carried out by Greenberg, one of our foremost contemporary psychotherapy researchers. In a series of studies (Greenberg, 1979, 1980; Greenberg & Clarke, 1979; Greenberg & Dompierre, 1981; Greenberg & Higgins, 1980; Greenberg & Rice, 1981; Greenberg & Webster, 1982; cf. Greenberg, Rice, Rennie, & Toukmanian, 1991), he examined the effects of the two-chair dialogue on conflict resolution. "These studies showed that two-chair dialogue was more effective than the use of empathic reflection in facilitating the resolution of specific conflicts as measured by in-session depth of experiencing and postsession client report and goal attainment" (Greenberg, 1984, pp. 102–103).

Greenberg (Paivio & Greenberg, 1992; Singh & Greenberg, 1992) and others (e.g., Beutler et al., 1987) have also studied the effects of the empty-chair dialogue on dealing with unfinished business. "Although further research is needed, [data collected thus far suggest that] the use of the expressive empty-chair method . . . [is] promising, at least for depression and resolution of lingering bad feelings toward a significant other" (Greenberg, Elliott, & Lietaer, 1994, p. 529). These studies were all well done, interesting, and show the value that both the two-chair and empty-chair dialogue can have in therapy.

With the exception of Greenberg, however, we are not aware of any other such systematic efforts underway to research Gestalt therapy. For that matter, we are not aware of much other research activity at all having taken place or now taking place on the process and outcome of Gestalt therapy in general. Perhaps, building on the work of Greenberg, more such research will soon be forthcoming.

As for Gestalt therapy's future, what can we expect? As mentioned earlier, an increasing emphasis on relationship has evolved in Gestalt therapy and we suspect that emphasis will continue. Efforts in stretching out, adding to, and complementing Gestalt theory will no doubt continue (e.g., Polster, 1992; Wheeler, 1991), as will efforts to further stretch out, add to, and complement Gestalt therapy (see Rice & Greenberg, 1992). We foresee no diminution of interest in the Gestalt approach. The approach over the last 10 to 15 years seems to have settled into a good rhythm, with Gestalt training institutes continuing to train, with Gestalt books continuing to appear periodically, and with attempts continuing to be made to further refine the work of therapy. While not nearly as popular as it was in the 1960s and 1970s, Gestalt therapy now seems more settled and stable in its foundation and operation. If the last 10 to 15 years provide us with any indication of the future, then we imagine that Gestalt therapy will keep its momentum pushing forward in the years to come.

REFERENCES

Baumgardner, P., & Perls, F. S. (1975). *Legacy from Fritz. Book One: Gifts from Lake Cowichan; Book Two: Legacy from Fritz.* Palo Alto, CA: Science and Behavior Books.

Beutler, L. E., Daldrup, R. J., Engle, D., Oro'-Beutler, M. E., Meredith, K., & Boyer, J. T. (1987). Effects of therapeutically induced affect arousal on depressive symptoms, pain, and beta-endorphins among rheumatoid arthritis patients. *Pain, 29,* 325–334.

Clarkson, P., & MacKewn, J. (1993). *Fritz Perls.* London: Sage.

Combs, A. W., & Snygg, D. (1959). *Individual behavior: A perceptual approach to behavior* (rev. ed.). New York: Harper & Row.

Enright, J. B. (1975). An introduction to Gestalt therapy. In F. D. Stephenson (Ed.). *Gestalt therapy primer.* Springfield, IL: Charles C Thomas.

Fagan, J., & Shepherd, I. L. (Eds). (1970). *Gestalt therapy now.* Palo Alto, CA: Science & Behavior Books. (Republished in two volumes, *What is Gestalt therapy?* and *Life techniques in Gestalt therapy.* New York: Harper & Row, 1971).

Friedländer, S. (1918). *Schöpferische indifferenz.* Munich: Georg Muller.

Glasgow, R. (1971). Paul Goodman: A conversation. *Psychology Today,* November.

Goodman, P. (1960). *Growing up absurd.* New York: Random House.

Goodman, P. (1964). *Compulsory mis-education.* New York: Random House.

Greenberg, L. S. (1979). Resolving splits: The two-chair technique. *Psychotherapy: Theory, Research, and Practice, 16,* 310–318.

Greenberg, L. S. (1980). An intensive analysis of recurring events from the practice of Gestalt therapy. *Psychotherapy: Theory, Research, and Practice, 17,* 143–152.

Greenberg, L. S. (1984). A task analysis of intrapersonal conflict resolution. In L. N. Rice & L. S. Greenberg (Eds). *Patterns of change: Intensive analysis of psychotherapy process* (pp. 67–123). New York: Guilford.

Greenberg, L. S., & Clarke, D. (1979). The differential effects of two-chair experiment and empathic reflection at a conflict marker. *Journal of Counseling Psychology, 26,* 1–8.

Greenberg, L. S., & Dompierre, L. (1981). Differential effects of Gestalt two-chair dialogue and empathic reflection at a split in counseling. *Journal of Counseling Psychology, 28,* 288–294.

Greenberg, L. S., Elliott, R., & Lietaer, G. (1994). Research on experiential psychotherapies. In A. E. Bergin & S. L. Garfield (Eds). *Handbook of psychotherapy and behavior change* (4th ed., pp. 509–539). New York: Wiley.

Greenberg, L. S., & Higgins, H. (1980). The differential effects of two-chair dialogue and focusing on conflict resolution. *Journal of Counseling Psychology, 27,* 221–225.

Greenberg, L. S., & Rice, L. N. (1981). The specific effects of Gestalt intervention. *Psychotherapy: Theory, Research, and Practice, 18,* 31–37.

Greenberg, L. S., Rice, L. N., Rennie, D. L., & Toukmanian, S. G. (1991). York University psychotherapy research program. In L. E. Beutler & M. Crago (Eds). *Psychotherapy research: An international review of programmatic studies* (pp. 175–181). Washington, DC: American Psychological Association.

Greenberg, L. S., & Webster, M. (1982). Resolving decisional conflict by means of two-chair dialogue: Relating process to outcome. *Journal of Counseling Psychology, 29,* 468–477.

Hatcher C., & Himmelstein, P. (Eds). (1976). *The handbook of Gestalt therapy.* New York: Aronson.

Kempler, W., (1973). Gestalt therapy. In R. Corsini (Ed.). *Current psychotherapies* (pp. 251–286). Itasca, IL: F. E. Peacock.

Latner, J. (1973). *The Gestalt therapy book.* New York: Julian Press.

Levitsky, A., & Perls, F. S. (1970). The rules and games of Gestalt therapy. In J. Fagan & I. L. Shepherd (Eds). *Gestalt therapy now* (pp. 140–149). Palo Alto, CA: Science and Behavior Books.

Maslow, A. H. (1969). *Motivation and personality* (2nd ed.). New York: Harper & Row.

Nevis, E. C. (1987). *Organizational consulting: A Gestalt approach.* New York: Garden Press.

Paivio, S., & Greenberg, L. S. (1992). *Resolving unfinished business: A study of effects.* Paper presented at the annual meeting of the Society for Psychotherapy Research, Berkeley, CA.

Patterson, C. H. (1964). A unitary theory of motivation and its counseling implications. *Journal of Individual Psychology, 20,* 17–31.

Perls, F. S. (1947). *Ego, hunger and aggression: The beginning of Gestalt therapy.* New York: Random House. (Paperback published by Orbit Graphic Arts, 1966.)

Perls, F. S. (1948). Theory and technique of personality integration. *American Journal of Psychotherapy, 2,* 565–586.

Perls, F. W. (1969a). *Gestalt therapy verbatim.* Lafayette, CA: Real People Press.

Perls, F. S. (1969b). *In and out of the garbage pail.* Lafayette, CA: Real People Press.

Perls, F. S. (1973). *The Gestalt approach and eyewitness to therapy.* Palo Alto, CA: Science & Behavior Books.

Perls, F. S. (1992). *Gestalt therapy verbatim.* Highland, NY: The Gestalt Journal Press.

Perls, F. S., Hefferline, R. F., & Goodman, P. (1951). *Gestalt therapy: Excitement and growth in personality.* New York: Julian Press. (Paperback published by Dell, 1965)

Polster, E. (1987). Escape from the present: Transition and storyline. In J. K. Zeig (Ed.). *The evolution of psychotherapy* (pp. 326–340). New York: Brunner/Mazel.

Polster, E. (1992). The self in action: A Gestalt outlook. In J. K. Zeig (Ed.). *The evolution of psychotherapy: The second conference* (pp. 143–151). New York: Brunner/Mazel.

Polster, M. (1987). Gestalt therapy: Evolution and application. In J. K. Zeig (Ed.). *The evolution of psychotherapy* (pp. 312–325). New York: Brunner/Mazel.

Polster, E., & Polster, M. (1973). *Gestalt therapy integrated: Contours of theory and practice.* New York: Brunner/Mazel.

Rice, L. N., & Greenberg, L. S. (1992). Humanistic approaches to psychotherapy. In D. K. Freedheim (Ed.). *History of psychotherapy* (pp. 197–224). Washington, DC: American Psychological Association.

Rogers, C. R. (1951). *Client-centered therapy.* Boston: Houghton Mifflin.

Shepherd, I. L. (1970). Limitations and cautions in the Gestalt approach. In J. Fagan & I. L. Shepherd (Eds.). *Gestalt therapy now* (pp. 234–238). Palo Alto, CA: Science & Behavior Books.

Simkin, J. S. (1974). *Gestalt therapy mini-lectures.* New York: Brunner/Mazel.

Simkin, J. S., & Yontef, G. M. (1984). Gestalt therapy. In R. J. Corsini (Ed.). *Current psychotherapies* (3rd ed.) (pp. 279–319). Itasca, IL: F. E. Peacock.

Singh, M., & Greenberg, L. S. (1992). *Development and validation of a measure of the resolution of unfinished business: Relating session change to outcome.* Paper presented at the annual meeting of the Society for Psychotherapy Research, Berkeley, CA.

Smith, W. L. (Ed.). (1976). *The growing edge of Gestalt therapy.* New York: Brunner/Mazel.

Smuts, J. (1926). *Holism and evolution.* New York: Macmillan.

Stephenson, F. D. (Ed.). (1975). *Gestalt therapy primer: Introductory readings in Gestalt therapy.* Springfield, IL: Thomas.

Stone, A. A. (1971). Play: The "now" therapy. [Review of *Gestalt therapy now,* edited by J. Fagan & I. L. Shepherd]. *Psychiatry and Social Science Review, 5,* 12–16.

Wheeler, G. (1991). *Gestalt reconsidered: A new approach to contact and resistance.* New York: Gardner Press.

Yontef, G. M. (1981). The future of Gestalt therapy: A symposium with L. Perls, M. Polster, J. Zinker, and M. V. Miller. *The Gestalt Journal, 4,* 7–11.

Yontef, G. M., & Simkin, J. S. (1989). Gestalt therapy. In R. J. Corsini & D. Wedding (Eds.). *Current psychotherapies* (4th ed.) (pp. 323–361). Itasca, IL: F. E. Peacock.

Zinker, J. (1977). *Creative process in Gestalt therapy.* New York: Brunner/ Mazel.

chapter *13*

Client-Centered Therapy: Rogers

The approach to therapy that was at first called "nondirective" but is now called "client-centered" is still best represented by the writing of its originator or first expositor, Carl Ransom Rogers (1902–1987). Rogers received his B.A. from the University of Wisconsin in 1924 and his M.A. and Ph.D. from Columbia University in 1928 and 1931, respectively. From 1928 to 1938, he was a psychologist at the Child Study Department of the Society for the Prevention of Cruelty to Children in Rochester, New York, and from 1931 on he was the department's director. The department became the Rochester Guidance Center in 1939; Rogers remained as director for a year and then went to Ohio State University, where he was professor of clinical psychology from 1940 to 1945. During 1944 and 1945, he served as director of counseling services of the United Service Organization.

In 1945, Rogers became professor of psychology and executive secretary of the Counseling Center at the University of Chicago. He left Chicago in 1957 to become professor of psychology and psychiatry at the University of Wisconsin. In 1962–1963, he was a Fellow at the Center for Advanced Study in the Behavioral Sciences at Stanford, and in 1964, he joined the staff of the Western Behavioral Sciences Institute (WBSI) at La Jolla, California, as a Resident Fellow. In 1968, he joined with others in forming the Center for Studies of the Person in La Jolla, where he was a Resident Fellow until his death. He was a Diplomate in Clinical Psychology of the American Board of Professional Psychology.

Rogers is the author of *The Clinical Treatment of the Problem Child* (1939); *Counseling and Psychotherapy* (1942); *Client-Centered Therapy* (1951); *On Becoming a Person* (1961a); *Freedom to Learn: A View of What Education Might Become* (1969, revised edition 1983); *Carl Rogers on Encounter Groups* (1970); *Becoming Partners: Marriage and its Alternatives* (1972); *Carl Rogers on Personal Power* (1977); and *A Way of Being* (1980).

He is co-author with Stevens of *Person to Person* (1967). He has edited, with Dymond, *Psychotherapy and Personality Change* (1954); with Gendlin, Kiesler, and Truax, *The Therapeutic Relationship and Its Impact* (1967); and with Coulson, *Man and the Science of Man* (1968). *A Chronological Bibliography of the Works of Carl R. Rogers 1930–1985*, was published in the *Person-Centered Review* (1986).

During the period at WBSI, Rogers became involved in the group movement and extended his theory to the basic encounter group. He also became interested in the application of his theory to education. *Becoming Partners: Marriage and Its Alternatives* (1972) was the result of his interest in the marriage relationship. *Carl Rogers on Personal Power* (1977) extended his theory to interpersonal relationships in general.

At the 1977 Convention of the American Psychological Association in San Francisco, Roger's seventy-fifth year was recognized with three programs of special papers. His work had been recognized earlier by the American Psychological Association, of which he was president in 1946, when in 1956, he was the recipient of one of the first three Distinguished Scientific Awards. In 1972 he received its first Distinguished Professional Contribution Award. A biography of Rogers has been published by Kirschenbaum (1979). Kirschenbaum and Henderson have edited a collection of Rogers' papers (1989a) and the dialogues of Rogers with Paul Tillich, B. F. Skinner, Gregory Bateson, Michael Polanyi, Rollo May, and others (1989b). A recent book in the Key Figures in Counselling and Psychotherapy book series has also given attention to Rogers' life, his contributions, and his overall influence (Thorne, 1992).

BACKGROUND AND DEVELOPMENT

During the period spent in Rochester, Rogers became dissatisfied with the commonly accepted approaches to psychotherapy and began to develop an approach of his own. The traditional, highly diagnostically oriented, probing, and interpretive methods did not appear to be very effective. His own experience in practicing therapy led to a recognition of an orderliness in the experience. The views of Rank, brought into the Rochester group by individuals whose training was influenced by them, had an impact on the development of Rogers' therapeutic methods.

The emerging principles of therapy were subjected to critically minded graduate students in clinical psychology at Ohio State University, and it was recognized that rather than being a distillation of generally accepted principles, as Rogers at first considered them, they constituted a new development. *Counseling and Psychotherapy* (Rogers, 1942) represented the attempt to present the new approach.

The stimulation of teaching and research at Ohio State and then at the University of Chicago, and the continuing experience in practicing psychotherapy, resulted in the development of Rogers' approach, in theoretical formulations of the nature of therapy, and in a tentative theory of personality. In 1951, in *Client-Centered Therapy* (Rogers, 1951), a current view was presented, together with its application in play therapy (by Elaine Dorfman), group-centered psychotherapy (by Nicholas Hobbs), group-centered leadership and administration (by Thomas Gordon), and student-centered teaching. Also included was a theory of personality and behavior. The point of view continued to be developed in many papers and articles, some of which were brought together in *On Becoming a Person* (Rogers,

1961a). The theory of personality was revised and expanded and was presented in 1959 in *Psychology: A Study of Science* (see Rogers, 1959).

Certain basic convictions and attitudes underlie the theoretical formulations (Rogers, 1959):

1. Research and theory are directed toward the satisfaction of the need to order significant experience.
2. Science is acute observation and careful and creative thinking on the basis of such observation, not simply laboratory research involving instruments and computing machines.
3. Science begins with gross observations, crude measurements, and speculative hypotheses, and progresses toward more refined hypotheses and measurements.
4. The language of independent-intervening-dependent variables, while applicable to advanced stages of scientific endeavor, is not adapted to the beginning and developing stages.
5. In the early stages of investigation and theory construction, inductive rather than hypothetico-deductive methods are more appropriate.
6. Every theory has a greater or a lesser degree of error; a theory only approaches the truth, and it requires constant change and modification.
7. Truth is unitary, so that "any theory, derived from almost any segment of experience, if it were complete and completely accurate, could be extended indefinitely to provide meaning for other very remote areas of experience" (p. 191). However, any error in a theory, if projected in a remote area, may lead to completely false inferences.
8. Although there may be such a thing as objective truth, people live in their own personal and subjective worlds. "Thus there is no such thing as Scientific Knowledge, there are only individual perceptions of what appears to each person to be such knowledge" (p. 192).

PHILOSOPHY AND CONCEPTS

The Nature of Human Beings and of the Individual

The common concept of human beings is that they are by nature irrational, unsocialized, and destructive to themselves and others. The client-centered point of view sees human beings, on the contrary, as basically rational, socialized, forward-moving, and realistic (Rogers, 1961a, pp. 90–92, 194–195). This is a point of view developing from experience in therapy rather than preceding it. Antisocial emotions—jealousy, hostility, and so on—exist and are evident in therapy, but they are not spontaneous impulses that must be controlled. Rather, they are reactions to the frustration of more basic impulses—love, belonging, security, and so on. Human beings are basically cooperative, constructive, and trustworthy, and when they are free from defensiveness, their reactions are positive, forward-moving, and constructive. There is, then, no need to be concerned about controlling their aggressive, antisocial impulses; they will become self-regulatory, balancing their needs against one another. The need for affection or companionship, for example, will balance any aggressive reaction or extreme need for sex or for other needs that would interfere with the satisfactions of other persons.

As individuals, human beings possess the capacity to experience, in awareness, the factors in their psychological maladjustment, and have the capacity and the tendency to move away from a state of maladjustment toward a state of psychological adjustment. These capacities and this tendency will be released in a relationship that has the characteristics of a therapeutic relationship. The tendency toward adjustment is the tendency toward self-actualization. Psychotherapy is thus the liberating of an already existing capacity in the individual. Philosophically, the individual "has the capacity to guide, regulate, and control himself, providing only that certain definable conditions exist. Only in the absence of these conditions, and not in any basic sense, is it necessary to provide external control and regulation of the individual" (Rogers, 1959, p. 221). When the individual is provided with reasonable conditions for growth, the individual will develop his/her potential constructively, as a seed grows and becomes its potential.

Philosophical Orientation of the Therapist

The basic philosophy of the therapist is represented by an attitude of respect for the individual, for the individual's capacity and right to self-direction, and for the worth and significance of each individual (Rogers, 1951, pp. 20–22). The orientation follows from these concepts of the nature of humanity.

Definitions of Constructs

The theory of therapy and personality makes use of a number of concepts, or constructs. These are briefly defined prior to their use in the theory (Rogers, 1959, pp. 195–212).

Actualizing Tendency: "The inherent tendency of the organism to develop all its capacities in ways which serve to maintain or enhance the organism."

Tendency toward Self-Actualization: The expression of the general tendency toward actualization in "that portion of experience of the organism which is symbolized in the self."

Experience (Noun): All that is going on in the organism at a given time, whether in awareness or potentially available to awareness, of a psychological nature; the "experiential field" or the "phenomenal field" of Combs and Snygg (1959).

Experience (Verb): The receiving "in the organism of the impact of sensory or physiological events which are happening at the moment."

Feeling, Experiencing a Feeling: "An emotionally tinged experience, together with its personal meaning."

Awareness, Symbolization, Consciousness: The representation of some portion of experience.

Availability to Awareness: The capability of being symbolized freely, without denial or distortion.

Accurate Symbolization: The potential correspondence of symbolization in awareness to the results of the testing of the transitional hypothesis that it represents.

Perceive, Perception: "A hypothesis or prognosis for action which comes into awareness when stimuli impinge on the organism." Perception and awareness are synonymous, the former emphasizing the stimulus in the process. Perceiving is becoming aware of stimuli.

Subceive, Subception: "Discrimination without awareness."

Self-Experience: "Any event or entity in the phenomenal field discriminated by the individual as 'self,' 'me,' 'I,'" or related thereto."

Self, Concept of Self, Self-Structure: "The organized, consistent conceptual gestalt composed of perceptions of the characteristics of the 'I' or 'me' and the perceptions of the relationships of the 'I' or 'me' to others and the various aspects of life, together with the values attached to these perceptions."

Ideal Self: "The self-concept which the individual would most like to possess."

Incongruence between Self and Experience: A discrepancy between the perceived self and actual experience, accompanied by tension, internal confusion, and discordant or incomprehensible (that is, neurotic) behavior resulting from conflict between the actualizing and the self-actualizing tendencies.

Vulnerability: "The state of incongruence between self and experience," with emphasis on "the potentialities of this state for creating psychological disorganization."

Anxiety: "Phenomenologically a state of uneasiness or tension whose cause is unknown. From an external frame of reference, anxiety is a state in which the incongruence between the concept of the self and the total experience of the individual is approaching symbolization in awareness."

Threat: "The state which exists when an experience is perceived or anticipated (subceived) as incongruent with the structure of the self"; an external view of what is phenomenologically anxiety.

Psychological Maladjustment: The state that exists when the organism denies or distorts significant experience in awareness, resulting in incongruence between the self and experience; incongruence viewed from a social standpoint.

Defense, Defensiveness: "The behavioral response of the organism to threat, the goal of which is the maintenance of the current structure of the self."

Distortion in Awareness, Denial of Awareness: Denial or distortion of experience that is inconsistent with the self-concept, by means of which the goal of defense is achieved; the mechanisms of defense.

Intensionality: The characteristics of the behavior of the individual who is in a defensive state—rigidity, overgeneralization, abstraction from reality, absolute and unconditional evaluation of experience, and so on.

Congruence, Congruence of Self and Experience: The state in which self-experiences are accurately symbolized in the self-concept—integrated, whole, genuine.

Openness to Experience: Absence of threat; the opposite of defensiveness.

Psychological Adjustment: Complete congruence; complete openness to experience.

Extensionality: Perception that is differentiated, dominated by facts rather than concepts, with awareness both of the space-time anchorage of facts and of different levels of abstraction.

Mature, Maturity: An individual is mature "when he perceives realistically and in an extensional manner, is not defensive, accepts the responsibility of being different from others, accepts the responsibility for his own behavior, evaluates experience in terms of the evidence coming from his own senses, changes his evaluation of experience only on the basis of new experience, accepts others as unique individuals different from himself, and prizes others;" the behavior exhibited by an individual who is congruent.

Contact: The minimal essential of a relationship, in which each of two individuals "makes a perceived or subceived difference in the experiential field of the other."

Positive Regard: perception of some self-experience of another that makes a positive difference in one's experiential field, resulting in a feeling of warmth, liking, respect, sympathy, and acceptance toward the other.

Need for Positive Regard: A secondary or learned need for love, affection, and so on.

Unconditional Positive Regard: Perception of the self-experiences of another without discrimination as to greater or lesser worthiness; prizing, acceptance.

Regard Complex: "All those self-experiences, together with their interrelationships, which the individual discriminates as being related to the positive regard of a particular social other."

Positive Self-Regard: "A positive attitude toward the self which is no longer directly dependent on the attitudes of others."

Need for Self-Regard: A secondary or learned need for positive self-regard.

Unconditional Self-Regard: Perception of the self "in such a way that no self-experience can be discriminated as more or less worthy of positive regard than any other."

Conditions of Worth: The valuing of an experience by an individual positively or negatively "solely because of . . . conditions of worth which he has taken over from others, not because the experience enhances or fails to enhance his organism."

Locus of Evaluation: The source of evidence for values—internal or external.

Organismic Valuing Process: "An on-going process in which values are never fixed or rigid, but experiences are being accurately symbolized and continually and freshly valued in terms of the satisfactions organismically experienced"; the actualizing tendency is the criterion.

Internal Frame of Reference: "All of the realm of experience which is available to the awareness of the individual at a given moment"; the subjective world of the individual.

Empathy: The state of perceiving "the internal frame of reference of another with accuracy, and with the emotional components and meanings which pertain thereto, as if one were the other person, but without ever losing the 'as if' condition."

External Frame of Reference: Perceiving "solely from one's own subjective frame of reference without empathizing with the observed person or object."

Theory of Personality (Rogers, 1959)

Characteristics of the Human Infant.   The infant perceives experience as reality; for the infant, experience *is* reality. The infant is endowed with an inherent tendency toward actualizing his/her organism. The infant's behavior is goal directed, or directed toward satisfying the need for actualization in interaction with his/her perceived reality. In this interaction, the infant behaves as an organized whole. Experiences are valued positively or negatively in an organismic valuing process in terms of whether they do or do not maintain this actualizing tendency. The infant is adient toward (approaches) positively valued experiences and is abient toward (avoids) negatively valued experiences.

Development of the Self.   As a result of the tendency toward differentiation (which is an aspect of the actualizing tendency), part of the individual's experience becomes symbolized in awareness as self-experience. Through interaction with significant others in the environment, this self-experience leads to a concept of self, a perceptual object in the experiential field.

Need for Positive Regard.   With awareness of the self, the need for positive regard from others develops. The satisfaction of this need is dependent on inferences regarding the experiential fields of others. Satisfaction is reciprocal in human beings in that the individual's positive regard is satisfied when the individual perceives himself/herself as satisfying another's need. The positive regard of a significant social other can be more powerful than the individual's organismic valuing process.

Development of Need for Self-Regard.   A need for self-regard develops from the association of the satisfaction or frustration of the need for positive regard with self-experiences. The experience of loss of positive regard thus becomes independent of transactions with any social other.

Development of Conditions of Worth.   Self-regard becomes selective as significant others distinguish the self-experiences of the individual as more or less worthy of positive regard. The evaluation of a self-experience as more or less worthy of self-regard constitutes a condition of worth. The experience of only unconditional positive regard would eliminate the development of conditions of worth and lead to unconditional self-regard, to congruence of the needs for positive regard and self-regard with organismic evaluation, and to the maintenance of psychological adjustment.

Development of Incongruence between Self and Experience.   The need for self-regard leads to selective perception of experiences in terms of conditions of worth, so that experiences in accord with the individual's conditions of worth are perceived and symbolized accurately in awareness, but experiences contrary to the conditions of worth are perceived selectively or distortedly or are denied to awareness. This presence of self-experiences that are not organized into the self-structure in accurately symbolized form results in the existence of some degree of incongruence between the self and experience, in vulnerability, and in psychological maladjustment.

Development of Discrepancies in Behavior.   Incongruence between the self and experience leads to incongruence in behavior, so that some behaviors are consistent with the self-concept and are accurately symbolized in awareness, while other behaviors actualize the experiences of the organism that are not assimilated into the self-structure and have thus not been recognized or have been distorted to make them congruent with the self.

Experience of Threat and Process of Defense.   An experience that is incongruent with the self-structure is subceived as threatening. If this experience were accurately symbolized in awareness, it would introduce inconsistency, and a state of anxiety would exist. The process of defense prevents this because it keeps the total perception of the experience consistent with the self-structure and the conditions of worth. The consequences of defense are rigidity in perception, an inaccurate perception of reality, and intensionality.

Process of Breakdown and Disorganization.   In a situation in which a significant experience demonstrates the presence of a large or significant incongruence between the self and experience, the process of defense is unable to operate successfully. Anxiety is then experienced to a degree depending on the extent of the self-structure that is threatened. The experience becomes accurately symbolized in awareness, and a state of disorganization results. The organism behaves at times in ways consistent with the experiences that have been distorted or denied and at times in ways consistent with the concept of the self, with its distorted or denied experiences.

Process of Reintegration.   For an increase in congruence to occur, there must be a decrease in conditions of worth and an increase in unconditional self-regard. The communicated unconditional positive regard of a significant other is one way of meeting these conditions. In order to be communicated, unconditional positive regard must exist in a context of empathic understanding. When this regard is perceived by the individual, it leads to the weakening or dissolving of existing conditions of worth. The individual's own unconditional positive regard is then increased, while threat is reduced and congruence develops. The individual is then less susceptible to perceiving threat, less defensive, more congruent, has increased self-regard and positive regard for others, and is more psychologically adjusted. The organismic valuing process becomes increasingly the basis of regulating behavior, and the individual becomes more nearly fully functioning. The occurrence of these conditions and their results constitutes psychotherapy.

Theory of Interpersonal Relationships (Rogers, 1959, pp. 226–240)

Conditions of a Deteriorating Relationship.

A person, Y, is willing to be in contact with person X, and to receive communications from him. Person X desires (at least to a minimal degree) to communicate to and be in contact with Y. Marked incongruence exists in X among the following three elements: his experience of the subject of communication with Y; the symbolization of this experience in his awareness, in its relation to his self-concept; his conscious communicated expression (verbal and/or motor) of this experience.

The Process of a Deteriorating Relationship.   Under the above conditions, the following process occurs:

The communication of X to Y is contradictory and/or ambiguous, containing expressive behaviors which are consistent with X's awareness of the experience to be communicated [and] expressive behaviors which are consistent with those aspects of the experience not accurately symbolized in X's awareness. Y experiences these contradictions and ambiguities. He tends to be aware only of X's conscious communication. Hence this experience of X's communication tends also to be incongruent with his awareness of same [and] . . . his response tends also to be contradictory and/or ambiguous. . . . Since X is vulnerable, he tends to perceive Y's responses as potentially threatening.

Thus, X tends to perceive Y's responses in a distorted way, congruent with his/her own self-structure. He/she also perceives Y's internal frame of reference inaccurately and therefore is not empathic. As a result, he/she cannot and does not experience unconditional positive regard for Y. Y thus experiences the receipt of, at most, a selective positive regard and an absence of understanding and empathy. He/she is thus less free to express his/her feelings, to be extensional, to express incongruence between self and experience, and to reorganize the self-concept. As a result, X is, in turn, even less likely to empathize and more likely to have defensive reactions. "Those aspects of experience which are not accurately symbolized by X in his awareness tend, by defensive distortion of perception, to be perceived in Y": Y then tends to be threatened and to show defensive behaviors.

Outcome of a Deteriorating Relationship.   The process of deterioration leads to increased defensiveness on the part of X and Y. Communication becomes increasingly superficial. Perceptions of self and others become organized more tightly. Thus, the incongruence of self and experience remains in status quo or is increased. Psychological maladjustment is to some degree facilitated in both X and Y.

Conditions of an Improving Relationship.   "A person, Y', is willing to be in contact with Person X', and to receive communication from him. Person X' desires to communicate to and be in contact with Y.' A high degree of congruence exists in X' between the three following elements: (a) his experience of the subject of communication with Y'; (b) the symbolization of this experience in awareness in its relation to his self-concept; [and] (c) his communicative expression of this experience."

Process of an Improving Relationship.   "The communication of X' to Y' is characterized by congruence of experience, awareness, and communication. Y' experiences this congruence as a clear communication. Hence his response is more likely to express a congruence of his own experience and awareness." X', congruent and not vulnerable, is able to perceive the response of Y' accurately and extensionally, with empathy. Y' feels understood and experiences satisfaction of his/her need for positive regard. "X' experiences himself as having made a positive difference in the experiential field of Y'." X' reciprocally tends to increase in feeling of positive regard for Y', and this positive regard tends to be unconditional. The relationship Y' experiences has the characteristics of the process of therapy. "Hence communication in both directions becomes increasingly congruent, is increasingly accurately perceived and contains more reciprocal positive regard."

Outcome of an Improving Relationship.   An improving relationship may result in all the outcomes of therapy within the limitations of the area of the relationship.

Tentative Law of Interpersonal Relationships

> Assuming a minimum mutual willingness to be in contact and to receive communications, we may say that the greater the communicated congruence of experience, awareness, and behavior on the part of the individual, the more the ensuing relationship will involve a tendency toward reciprocal communication with the same qualities, mutually accurate understanding of the communications, improved psychological adjustment and functioning in both parties, and mutual satisfaction in the relationship. (p. 240)

The concept of congruence is important. Congruence is the accurate matching of physiological experiencing with awareness and the matching of these with what is communicated. When congruence is lacking, there is ambiguity in communication: words do not match nonverbal communication. When there is incongruence between experiencing and awareness, the incongruent individual does not recognize this. For example, a person may be unaware that his/her bodily actions and tone of voice communicate anger, while his/her words claim that he/she is cool, rational, and logical in an argument. An incongruence between awareness and communication may also be deliberate, however, when a person is deceitful and insincere. When a person is congruent, we know where he/she stands, but we do not know what an incongruent person really means or feels, and we have difficulty relating to or interacting with him/her. When two persons who are congruent interact, they are able to listen to each other without defensiveness, to understand each other empathically, to develop respect for each other—in short, to be therapeutic for each other. Each will benefit in improved psychological adjustment, becoming more unified and integrated, less in conflict, more mature, and more satisfied in the relationship. In the case of each person, the receiver of the communication must perceive the communication of the other as it is or is intended without distortion or misunderstanding. To the extent that each is congruent and to the extent that each does not feel threatened, this is more likely to occur.

Theory of Therapy and Personality Change (Rogers, 1959)

Conditions of the Therapeutic Process.   For therapy to occur, the following conditions must be present:

1. Two persons are in contact.
2. One person, the client, is in a state of incongruence, being vulnerable or anxious.
3. The other person, the therapist, is congruent in the relationship.
4. The therapist experiences unconditional positive regard toward the client.
5. The therapist experiences an empathic understanding of the client's internal frame of reference.
6. The client perceives, at least to a minimal degree, conditions 4 and 5.

Process of Therapy.   The existence of the conditions listed above results in a process with the following characteristics:

1. The client is increasingly free in expressing his feelings, through verbal and/or motor channels.
2. His expressed feelings increasingly have reference to the self, rather than nonself.
3. He increasingly differentiates and discriminates the objects of his feelings and perceptions . . . his experiences are more accurately symbolized.
4. His expressed feelings increasingly have reference to the incongruity between certain of his experiences and his concept of self.
5. He comes to experience in awareness the threat of such incongruence . . . because of the continued unconditional positive regard of the therapist . . .
6. He experiences fully, in awareness, feelings which have in the past been denied to awareness, or distorted in awareness.

7. His concept of self becomes reorganized to assimilate and include these experiences, which have previously been distorted or denied in awareness.

8. As reorganization of the self-structure continues, his concept of self becomes increasingly congruent with his experiences . . . defensiveness is decreased.

9. He becomes increasingly able to experience, without a feeling of threat, the therapist's unconditional positive regard.

10. He increasingly feels an unconditional positive self-regard.

11. He increasingly experiences himself as the locus of evaluation.

12. He reacts to experience less in terms of his conditions of worth and more in terms of an organismic valuing process (Rogers, 1959, p. 216).

Outcomes in Personality and Behavior.   The process of therapy leads to the following results:

1. The client is more congruent, more open to his experiences, less defensive.

2. He is consequently more realistic, objective, extensional in his perceptions.

3. He is consequently more effective in problem-solving.

4. His psychological adjustment is improved, being closer to the optimum . . .

5. As a result of the increased congruence of self and experience . . . his vulnerability to threat is reduced.

6. As a consequence of (2) above, his perception of his ideal self is more realistic, more achievable.

7. As a consequence of the changes in (4) and (5) his self is more congruent with his idealized self.

8. As a consequence [of this and (4)], tension of all types is reduced . . .

9. He has an increased degree of positive self-regard.

10. He perceives the locus of evaluation and the locus of choice as residing with himself . . . he feels more confident and more self-directing . . . his values are determined by an organismic valuing process.

11. As a consequence of (1) and (2), he perceives others more realistically and accurately.

12. He experiences more acceptance of others, as a consequence of less need for distortion of his perceptions of them.

13. His behavior changes in various ways:
    a.   . . . the proportion of behaviors which can be "owned" as belonging to self is increased.
    b.   . . . the proportion of behavior . . . felt to be "not myself" is decreased.
    c.   . . . Hence his behavior is perceived as being more within his control.

14. As a consequence of (1), (2), (3), his behavior is more creative, more uniquely adaptive . . . more fully expressive of his own purposes and values (Rogers, 1959, pp. 218–219).

This theory of therapy is an if-then theory, involving no intervening variables. Although there are speculations as to why the relationships between the conditions and the events that follow them occur, the why is not a part of the theory.

Theory of the Fully Functioning Person (Rogers, 1969, pp. 279–297)

Each individual possesses an inherent tendency toward self-actualization. Each individual has the tendency and the capacity to symbolize experiences accurately in awareness. The individual has a need for positive regard from others and for positive self-regard. When these needs are met, the tendencies toward actualizing his/her organism and accurately symbolizing experiences are most fully realized. When these conditions are met to a maximum degree, the individual will be a *fully functioning person.* The full functioning of a person is synonymous with optimal psychological adjustment, optimal psychological maturity, complete congruence, complete openness to experience, and complete extensionality. It is the goal, or end point, of optimal psychotherapy.

There are three characteristic or aspects of the fully functioning person, although they integrate in a unitary organization or whole:

1. *Openness to experience.* Having positive regard from others and positive self-regard, the fully functioning person is free from threat and thus free from defensiveness. The person is open to all his or her experiences, and stimuli are received and processed through the nervous system without selectivity or distortion. Although there is not necessarily a self-conscious awareness of organismic experiences, there is availability to awareness, and there are no barriers or inhibitions to prevent the full experiencing of whatever is organismically present.

2. *An existential mode of living.* Openness to experience means that there is a newness to each moment of living, since the same situation of inner and outer stimuli has never existed before. There is a fluidity of experiencing in which the self and the personality emerge from experience; since each experience is new, the person cannot predict specifically what he or she will do in advance. There is a participation in experience without complete control of it. Living is characterized by flexibility and adaptability, rather than rigidity. The personality and the self are in flux; openness to experience is the most stable personality characteristic.

3. *The organism as a trustworthy guide to satisfying behavior.* The fully functioning person does what "feels right" and finds that this results in adequate or satisfying behavior. This is so because, being open to all experience, she or he has all relevant data available, without denial or distortion of any elements. These data include social demands, as well as the person's own complex system of needs. The total organism, including the person's consciousness, processes these data like a complex computer. The total organism is often wiser than consciousness alone. The organism is not infallible, since data may be missing or unavailable, but any resulting unsatisfying behavior provides corrective feedback.

These characteristics of the fully functioning person have relevance to values and the valuing process. The locus of evaluation in the organismic valuing process is internal, that is, within the individual. This is characteristic of the infant's approach to valuing, but in the process of socialization, the locus of evaluation usually becomes externalized as the individual seeks love, acceptance, and social approval from significant others in his or her environment. Value patterns are thus introjected, rather than being the result of the person's own organismic valuing processes or experiencing. They are rigid, and although they often include contradictory values, they are rarely examined. They are often at variance with experiences, and this discrepancy is the basis of insecurity and alienation within the individual. In a therapeutic climate in life or in therapy, some individuals achieve the openness to their experiences and the maturity that return the locus of evaluation to themselves. Although their valuing process is like that of the infant, it is more complex, involving all the individual's past experiences, including the effects or consequences of resulting behaviors on the self and others. The criterion of the valuing process, as in the infant, is the degree to which behaviors lead to self-enhancement or self-actualization.

The value directions that develop in persons as they become more fully functioning are not idiosyncratic or unique but have a commonality that extends through different cultures, suggesting that they are related to the human species; they enhance the development of the individual and others, and they contribute to the survival and evolution of the species. These directions include being real rather than presenting a facade, valuing one's self and self-direction, valuing being a process rather than having fixed goals, valuing sensitivity to and acceptance of others, valuing deep relationships with others, and, perhaps most important, valuing an openness to all one's inner and outer experiences, including the reactions and feelings of others. In other words, the older values of sincerity, independence, self-direction, self-knowledge, social responsivity, social responsibility, and loving interpersonal relationships appear to have a universality arising out of the nature of human beings as they become, under conditions that have been found to be effective in psychotherapy, fully functioning persons. The characteristics of the fully functioning or self-actualizing person include the conditions for the development of such persons.

Several implications of this concept are of interest:

1. *The fully functioning person is a creative person.* Such a person could be one of Maslow's "self-actualizing people," one of whose characteristics is creativeness. His or her sensitive openness and existential living would foster creativeness through allowing awareness of relationships not observed by others. He or she is not a conformist and perhaps not always "adjusted" to the culture but is able to live constructively and to satisfy basic needs. "Such a person would, I believe, be recognized by the student of evolution as the type most likely to adapt and survive under changing environmental conditions. He would be able creatively to make sound adjustments to new as well as old conditions. He would be a fit vanguard of human evolution" (Rogers, 1969, p. 290).

2. *The fully functioning person is constructive and trustworthy.* The basic nature of individuals is good, individually and socially, when they are functioning freely.

> When we are able to free the individual from defensiveness, so that he is open to the wide range of his own needs, as well as the wide range of environmental and social demands, his reactions may be trusted to be positive, forward-moving, and constructive. We do not need to ask who will socialize him, for one of his own deepest needs is for affiliation with and communication with others. When he is fully himself, he cannot help but be realistically socialized. We do not need to ask who will control his aggressive impulses, for when he is open to all of his impulses, his need to be liked by others and his tendency to give affection are as strong as his impulses to strike out and seize for himself. He will be aggressive in situations in which aggression is realistically appropriate, but there will be no runaway need for aggression. His total behavior, in these and other areas, when he is open to all his experience, is balanced and realistic, behavior which is appropriate to the survival and enhancement of a highly social animal. (Rogers, 1969, pp. 290–291)

3. *The fully functioning person's behavior is dependable but not predictable.* Since the particular pattern of inner and outer stimuli at each moment is unique, fully functioning

people are not able to predict their behavior in a new situation, but they appear dependable to themselves and are confident that their behavior is appropriate. On later analysis by another person, a scientist, for example, the fully functioning person's behavior will appear lawful; the scientist can postdict but not predict it. Science cannot collect and analyze all the necessary data, even with a computer, before the behavior has occurred. This suggests that the science of psychology, when it deals with the fully functioning person, will be characterized by understanding (of the lawfulness of behavior that has occurred) rather than by prediction and control.

4. *The fully functioning person is free and not determined.* Science has shown that we live in a world in which cause and effect operate. Behavior can be controlled by external, or environmental, conditions and events. Yet the individual can be free to choose how to act. Clients in therapy have made decisions and choices that have changed their behaviors and their lives. "I would be at a loss to explain the positive change which can occur in psychotherapy if I had to omit the importance of the sense of the free and responsible choice on the part of my clients. I believe that this experience of freedom to choose is one of the deepest elements underlying change" (Rogers, 1969, p. 268).

This freedom is an inner freedom, an attitude or a realization that people have of an ability to think their own thoughts and to live their own lives, choosing what they want to be and being responsible for themselves. Such freedom is phenomenological rather than external. It is not a contradiction to the cause and effect apparent in the psychological universe but a complement to such a universe. "Freedom rightly understood is a fulfillment by the person of the ordered sequence of his life. The free man moves out voluntarily, freely, responsibly, to play his significant part in a world whose determined events move through him and through his spontaneous choice and will" (Rogers, 1969, p. 269). It exists in a different dimension from external cause and effect.

Individuals differ in the extent to which they are free from influence and control by others and external events. In several studies subjects who yielded or conformed or were susceptible to control in psychological experiments differed from those who did not conform. They panicked under stress, showed feelings of inadequacy and personal inferiority, were lacking in openness and freedom in emotional processes and in spontaneity, and were emotionally restricted and inhibited. The nonconformists, on the other hand, were able to cope effectively with stress, were more self-contained and autonomous in their thinking, had a sense of competence and personal adequacy, and were more open, free, and spontaneous. Thus, the sense of personal freedom and responsibility makes a difference in behavior (Rogers, 1969, pp. 271–272).

The ideal fully functioning person does not exist. There are persons who can be observed moving toward this goal in therapy, in the best family and group relationships, and in good educational experiences.

THE THERAPY PROCESS

The therapy process is outlined in the theory of therapy discussed above. More detailed consideration of the process may be approached from two frames of reference: the phenomenological frame of reference, or the client's frame of reference; and the external frame of reference, or an observer's frame of reference.

The Process as Experienced by the Client (Rogers, 1951, Chapter 3; Rogers, 1961a, Chapters 5 and 6)

The client's perception of the process is important, since it is on his/her perceptions of the experience and of the therapist's personality, attitudes, and techniques that therapeutic change depends. The client's perceptions are initially influenced by what the client expects of the therapist and the therapy situation. These expectations vary and include feelings ranging from fear to eager anticipation, but an ambivalent, fearful feeling seems most characteristic. Progress is facilitated when both client and therapist perceive the relationship in the same way. Verbal structuring of the relationship by the therapist, which was earlier considered desirable, does not necessarily lead to a common perception of the relationship, however.

When the therapist is perceived favorably as helpful, it is as someone with warmth, interest, and understanding. At first, client-centered methods often appear frustrating to the client, but they are later perceived as leading to self-exploration and understanding. The therapy hour becomes a stable, accepting experience in an otherwise unstable life and is thus experienced as supportive, although the therapist is not supportive in the usual sense of the term.

Experiencing of Responsibility.   The client soon discovers that he or she is responsible for himself/herself in the relationship, and this may lead to various feelings, including a sense of being alone, annoyance, or anger, and a growing sense of acceptance of responsibility.

Discovery of Denied Attitudes.   As a result of exploration, attitudes that have been experienced but denied to awareness are discovered. Both positive and negative attitudes arise. Experiences inconsistent with the self-concept, formerly denied or distorted, become symbolized in awareness.

Experiencing of Reorganizing the Self.   The bringing of denied experiences into awareness necessitates the reorganization of the self, which begins with a change in perception of and attitude toward the self. The client views himself/herself more positively, as a more adequate person; the client's acceptance of himself/herself increases. This changed perception of the self must begin before the client can become aware of and accept denied experiences. The permitting of more experiential data to enter awareness leads to a more realistic appraisal of the self, of relationships, and of the environment, and to an acknowledgment of the basis of standards within himself/herself. The change in the self may be great or small, with more or less accompanying pain and confusion. More or less disorganization may precede the final organization, and the process may fluctuate up or down. The emotions that accompany the process, although fluctuating, appear to be mainly those of fearfulness, unhappiness, and depression; they are not consistent with actual progress, so a deep insight may be followed by strong despair.

The process of reorganizing the self, of becoming oneself, or becoming a person, includes various aspects. A person may be seen as "getting behind the mask." In the atmosphere of freedom of the therapeutic relationship, the client begins to drop false fronts, roles, or masks and tries to discover something that is more truly himself/herself. The client is able to explore the self and its experience, facing the contradictions that he/she discovers and the facades and fronts behind which he/she has been hiding. The client may discover that he/she seems to have no individual self but exists only in relation to the values and demands of others. There is, however, a compelling need to search for and become oneself.

A part of being one's real self is experiencing feelings to their limits, so that the person *is* his/her fear, anger, love, and so on. There is a

> free experiencing of the actual sensory and visceral reactions of the organism without too much of an attempt to relate these experiences to the self. This is usually accompanied by the conviction that this material does not belong to, and cannot be organized into, the self. The end point of the process is that the client discovers that he can *be* his experience with all of its variety and surface contradiction; that he can formulate himself out of his experience instead of trying to impose a formulation of self upon his experience, denying to awareness these elements which do not fit. (Rogers, 1961a, p. 80)

In the experiencing of these elements of the self, a unit, harmony, or pattern emerges. All these experiences are a part of the potential self, which is being discovered.

The result of the reorganization of the self is not merely acceptance of the self, but also a liking of the self. It is not a bragging, self-assertive liking but a "quiet joy in being one's self, together with the apologetic attitude that, in our culture, one feels it is necessary to take toward such an experience" (Rogers, 1961a, p. 87). It is a satisfying, enjoyable appreciation of oneself as a whole and functioning person.

The process of therapy is not the solving of problems; it is the experiencing of feelings, leading to the being of oneself. It "is a process whereby man becomes his organism—without self-deception, without distortion" (Rogers, 1961a, p. 103). Rather than acting in terms of the expectations of others, a person acts in terms of his/her own experiences. It is the full awareness of these experiences, achieved in therapy, that makes it possible for the person to come to *be* (in awareness) what he/she *is* (in experience)—a complete and fully functioning human organism.

Experiencing of Progress.   Almost from the beginning, the client feels that progress is being made. This progress is felt even when confusion and depression are present. The facing and resolving of some issues and the reconstructing of a segment of personality represent progress and give the client confidence in continuing to explore himself/herself, even though the exploration continues to be upsetting.

Experiencing of Ending.   The client determines when to end the therapy. Sometimes the end is preceded by a period during which the time between interviews is lengthened. Often it is accompanied by feelings of fear, a sense of loss, or a reluctance to give up therapy, so that the ending may be postponed for an interview or two.

Process Conception of Psychotherapy

On the basis of listening to many therapy interviews, abstractions of the therapy process were made (Rogers, 1961a, Chapter 7). A continuum emerged, not from fixity to flux, but from stasis to process. Seven stages of the process were discriminated. At any one time, the client, taken as a whole, falls within a relatively narrow range on this continuum of person-ality change, although in given areas of personal meaning, the client may be at different stages. However, for any specific area, there is a regularity of progression through the stages, although there are some retreats along with the general advance.

First Stage.   In the first stage, there is

> an unwillingness to communicate self. Communication is only about externals. Feel-ings and personal meanings are neither recognized nor owned. . . . Close and com-municative relationships are construed as dangerous. No problems are recognized or perceived at this stage. There is no desire to change. (Rogers, 1961a, p. 132)

Individuals at this stage do not come voluntarily for therapy.

Second Stage.   If the individual in the first stage can be reached through the providing of optimal conditions for facilitating change, then "expression begins to flow in regard to non-self topics" (Rogers, 1961a, p. 133). However, problems are seen as external, and the client accepts no personal responsibility. Feelings may be shown, but they are not recognized or owned. Experiencing is of the past. There is little differentiation of personal meanings and little recognition of contradictions. Clients may come for therapy voluntarily at this stage, but they often do not continue or make progress.

Third Stage.   In the third stage, loosening continues, with freer expression about the self, about self-related experiences as objects, and "about the self as a reflected object existing primarily in others" (Rogers, 1961a, p. 135). Past feelings and personal meanings—usually negative—are expressed, but with little acceptance of them. Differentiation of feelings is less global, and there is recognition of contradictions in experience. Many clients begin therapy at this stage.

Fourth Stage.   Acceptance, understanding, and empathy in the third stage enable the client to move to the fourth stage, in which feelings that are more intense, although not cur-rent, are expressed, as well as some present feelings and experiences, but with some reluc-tance, fear, or distrust. Some acceptance of feeling is present. "There is a loosening of the way experience is construed. There are some discoveries of personal constructs [Chapter 10]; there is the definite recognition of these as constructs; and there is a beginning ques-tioning of their validity" (Rogers, 1961a, p. 138). Differentiation of feelings is increased, and contradictions are of concern. Feelings of self-responsibility in problems occur. There is the beginning of a relationship with the therapist on a feeling basis. These characteristics are very common in much of psychotherapy, as are those of the next stage.

Fifth Stage.   In the fifth stage, present feelings are freely expressed but with surprise and fright. They are close to being fully experienced, although fear, distrust, and lack of clarity are still present. Feelings and meanings are differentiated with more exactness. Self-feel-ings are increasingly owned and accepted. Experiencing is loosened and current, and con-tradictions are clearly faced. Responsibility for problems is accepted. In this stage, the client is close to his or her organismic being, to the flow of his/her feelings. Experience is differentiated.

Sixth Stage.   The sixth stage tends to be distinctive and dramatic. A feeling that has been "stuck" previously is experienced with immediacy, or a feeling is directly experienced with richness or flows to its full result. An experience and its accompanying feeling are accepted as something that *is,* not something to be feared, denied, or resisted. An experience is lived, not felt about. The self as an object disappears. Incongruence becomes congruence. "Differentiation of experiencing is sharp and basic. In this stage, there are no longer 'problems,' external or internal. The client is living, subjectively, a phase of his problem. It is not an object" (Rogers, 1961a, p. 150). Physiological concomitants of a loosening, relaxing nature are present—tears, sighs, muscular relaxation, and, it is hypothesized, improved circulation and improved conduction of nervous impulses. This stage is a highly crucial one and seems to be irreversible.

Seventh Stage.   In the seventh stage, the client seems to continue on his/her own momentum; this stage may occur outside the therapy hour and be reported in therapy. The client experiences new feelings with immediacy and richness and uses them as referents for knowing who he/she is, what he/she wants, and what his/her attitudes are. Changing feelings are accepted and owned; there is a trust in the total organismic process. Experiencing is spontaneous, with an emerging process aspect, and "the self becomes increasingly simply the subjective and reflexive awareness of experiencing. The self is much less frequently a perceived object and much more frequently something confidently felt in process" (Rogers, 1961a, p. 153). Since all the elements of experience are available to awareness, there is the experiencing of real and effective choice. This stage, which relatively few clients reach, is characterized by an openness to experience that leads to a quality of flow, motion, and change. Internal and external communication is free.

   To summarize, the process involves:

1. a loosening of feeling
2. a change in the manner of experiencing
3. a shift from incongruence to congruence
4. a change in the manner in which and the extent to which the individual is willing and able to communicate himself/herself in a receptive climate
5. a loosening of the cognitive maps of experience
6. a change in the individual's relationship to his/her problems
7. a change in the individual's manner of relating.

IMPLEMENTATION

While early presentations of client-centered therapy stressed techniques, the emphasis is now on the therapist's philosophy and attitudes rather than techniques and on the therapy relationship rather than the therapist's words and behavior. "Our concern has shifted from counselor technique to counselor attitude and philosophy, with a new recognition of the importance of technique from a more sophisticated level" (Rogers, 1951, p. 14). Techniques represent implementations of the philosophy and attitudes and thus must be consistent with them. With the development of this emphasis on philosophy and attitudes, there have been some changes in the relative frequency of use of various techniques. Questioning, reassuring, encouraging, interpreting, and suggesting, although never widely used, are now used even less so. But there has been a search for a wider variety of techniques, with the goal of better implementing the basic philosophy and attitudes.

Techniques, then, are ways of expressing and communicating acceptance, respect, and understanding and of letting the client know that the therapist is attempting to develop the internal frame of reference by thinking, feeling, and exploring with the client. They are ways of establishing and maintaining a therapeutic relationship. Techniques cannot be used self-consciously, since the result will be that the therapist is not genuine, not himself/herself.

Whereas the process of psychotherapy was viewed from the standpoint of the client—the client's perceptions and the changes occurring in the client—the technique or implementation aspect may be this process viewed from the standpoint of the therapist, in terms of the therapist's behavior and participation in the relationship. Thus, the therapy process may be regarded as the facilitation of personal growth in the client (Rogers, 1961a, Chapter 2), as the characteristics of the helping relationships (Rogers, 1961a, Chapter 3), or as the necessary and sufficient conditions of therapeutic personality change as provided by the therapist (Rogers, 1957, pp. 95–103).

The Therapy Relationship

The relationship that the therapist provides for the client is not an intellectual one. The therapist cannot help the client by his/her knowledge. Explaining the client's personality and behavior to the client and prescribing actions that the client should take are of little lasting value. The relationship that is helpful to the client and that enables him/her to discover within himself/herself the capacity to use that relationship to change and grow is not a cognitive, intellectual one.

The therapist in the therapy relationship has, or should have, a number of characteristics. No therapist has these characteristics to their ultimate degree, of course. Thus, they are stated essentially as desirable goals or ideal characteristics.

Acceptance.   The therapist should be accepting of the client as an individual, as the client is, with his/her conflicts and inconsistencies and good and bad points. Such an attitude is more than a neutral acceptance; it is a positive respect for the client as a person of worth. It also involves a liking for and warmth toward the client, a "prizing" of her/him. There is no evaluation or judgment, either positive or negative. The client is accepted unconditionally, that is, without any conditions attached to the acceptance. The therapist manifests unconditional positive regard for the client.

Congruence.   The ideal therapist is characterized by congruence in the therapy relationship. The therapist is unified, integrated, and consistent; there is no contradiction between what the therapist is and what the therapist says. He/she is aware of and accepts his/her own feelings, with a willingness to be and express these feelings and attitudes in words or behavior when appropriate. The therapist is real, genuine; he/she is not playing a role.

Understanding.   Understanding means that the therapist experiences "an accurate, empathic understanding of the client's world as seen from the inside. To sense the client's private world as if it were your own, but without losing the 'as if' quality—this is empathy and this seems essential to therapy" (Rogers, 1961a, p. 284). Such understanding enables the client to explore freely and deeply and thus to develop a better comprehension of himself/herself. This understanding does not involve diagnosis or evaluation, which are external. Complete understanding is, of course, impossible and, fortunately, unnecessary. The *desire* of the therapist to understand is accepted by the client as understanding and enables the client to make progress.

Communicating Acceptance, Congruence, and Understanding. It is of no value for the therapist to be accepting, congruent, and understanding if the client does not perceive or experience the therapist as such. It is thus important that acceptance, congruence, and understanding be communicated to the client. The therapist who has these attitudes or characteristics will express them naturally and spontaneously in many ways, both verbally and nonverbally. The ways in which the therapist does so may be considered techniques in a narrow sense. Such techniques are not artificial, forced, or studied, but are genuine and spontaneous expressions of the therapist's attitudes.

The Resulting Relationship. If the therapist has the characteristics and attitudes discussed above, at least to a minimal degree, and if they are communicated to the client, a relationship develops that is experienced by the client as safe, secure, free from threat, and supporting but not supportive. The therapist is perceived as dependable, trustworthy, and consistent. This is a relationship in which change can occur. "When I hold in myself the kind of attitudes I have described, and when the other person can to some degree experience these attitudes, then I believe that change and constructive personal development will *invariably occur*" (Rogers, 1961a, p. 35).

This presentation of the therapeutic process and its implementation is rather abstract and impersonal. Rogers, after reading it, suggested (in personal correspondence, November 13, 1964) that a section of his article "The Process Equation of Psychotherapy" (1961b) would give the reader a better notion of the process as one dealing with warm living people who are dealt with by warm living counselors. Therefore, with his permission, the following material from this article is included (Rogers, 1961b, pp. 27–45):

So then what is the process of counseling and therapy? I have spoken of it objectively, marshaling the facts we have, writing it as a crude equation in which we can at least tentatively put down the specific terms. But let me now try to approach it from the inside, and without ignoring this factual knowledge, present this equation as it occurs subjectively in both therapist and client.

To the therapist, it is a new venture in relating. He feels, "Here is this other person, my client. I'm a little afraid of him, afraid of the depths in him as I am a little afraid of the depths of myself. Yet as he speaks, I begin to feel a respect for him, to feel my kinship to him. I sense how frightening his world is for him, how tightly he tries to hold it in place. I would like to sense his feelings, and I would like him to know that I stand with him in his tight, constricted little world, and that I can look upon it unafraid. Perhaps I can make it a safer world for him. I would like my feelings in this relationship with him to be as clear and transparent as possible, so that they are a discernible reality for him, to which he can return again. I would like to go with him on the fearful journey into himself, into the buried fear, and hate, and love which he has never been able to let flow in him. I recognize that this is a very human and unpredictable journey for me, as well as for him, and that I may, without even knowing my fear, shrink away within myself from some of the feelings he discovers. To this extent I know I will be limited in my ability to help him. I realize that at times his own fears may make him perceive me as uncaring, as rejecting, as an intruder, as one who does not understand. I want fully to accept these feelings in him, and yet I hope also that my own real feelings will show through so clearly that in time he cannot fail to perceive them. Most of all I want him to encounter in me a real person. I do not need to be uneasy as to whether my own feelings are 'therapeutic.' What I am and what I feel are good enough to be a basis for therapy, if I can transparently be what I am and what I feel in relationship to him. Then perhaps he can be what he is, openly and without fear."

And the client, for his part, goes through far more complex sequences, which can only be suggested. Perhaps schematically his feelings change in some of these ways. "I'm afraid of him. I want help, but I don't know whether to trust him. He might see things which I don't know in myself—frightening and bad elements. He seems not to be judging me, but I'm sure he is. I can't tell him what really concerns me, but I can tell him about some past experiences which are related to my concern. He seems to understand those, so I can reveal a bit more of myself.

"But now that I've shared with him some of this bad side of me, he despises me. I'm sure of it, but it's strange I can find little evidence of it. Do you suppose that what I've told him isn't so bad? Is it possible that I need not be ashamed of it as a part of me? I no longer feel that he despises me. It makes me feel that I want to go further, exploring *me,* perhaps expressing more of myself. I find him a sort of companion as I do this—he seems really to understand.

"But now I'm getting frightened again, and this time deeply frightened. I didn't realize that exploring the unknown recesses of myself would make me feel feelings I've never experienced before. It's very strange because in one way these aren't new feelings. I sense that they've always been there. But they seem so bad and disturbing I've never dared to let them flow in me. And now as I live these feelings in the hours with him, I feel terribly shaky, as though my world is falling apart. It used to be sure and firm. Now it is loose, permeable, and vulnerable. It isn't pleasant to feel things I've always been frightened of before. It's his fault. Yet curiously I'm eager to see him and I feel more safe when I'm with him.

"I don't know who I am anymore, but sometimes when I *feel* things I seem solid and real for a moment. I'm troubled by the contradictions I find in myself—I act one way and feel another—I think one thing and feel another. It is very disconcerting. It's also sometimes adventurous and exhilarating to be trying to discover who I am. Sometimes I catch myself feeling that perhaps the person I am is worth being, whatever that means.

"I'm beginning to find it very satisfying, though often painful, to share just what it is I'm feeling at this moment. You know, it is really helpful to try to listen to myself, to hear what is going on in me. I'm not so frightened anymore of what is going on in me. It seems pretty trustworthy. I use some of my hours with him to dig deep into myself to know what I *am* feeling. It's scary work, but I want to *know.* And I do trust him most of the time, and that helps. I feel pretty vulnerable and raw, but I know he doesn't want to hurt me, and I even believe he cares. It occurs to me as I try to let myself down and down, deep into myself, that maybe if I could sense what is going on in me, and could realize its meaning, I would know who I am, and I would also know what to do. At least I feel this knowing sometimes with him.

"I can even tell him just how I'm feeling toward him at any given moment and instead of this killing the relationship, as I used to fear, it seems to deepen it. Do you suppose I could be sharing my feelings with other people also? Perhaps that wouldn't be too dangerous either.

"You know, I feel as if I'm floating along on the current of life, very adventurously, being me. I get defeated sometimes, I get hurt sometimes, but I'm learning that those experiences are not fatal. I don't know exactly *who* I am, but I can feel my reactions at any given moment, and they seem to work out pretty well as a basis for my behavior from moment to moment. Maybe this is what it *means* to be *me.* But of course I can only do this because I feel safe in the relationship with my therapist. Or could I be myself this way outside of this relationship? I wonder. I wonder. Perhaps I could."

What I have just presented does not happen rapidly. It may take years. It may not, for reasons we do not understand very well, happen at all. But at least this may suggest an inside view of the factual picture I have tried to present of the process of psychotherapy as it occurs in both the therapist and his client.

LENGTH AND LIMITATIONS OF TREATMENT

Length.   Sessions are usually scheduled once a week, although they may be more or less frequent. The duration of therapy is determined by the client. Near the ending of therapy, sessions may be less frequent—once every two weeks, for example. Client-centered therapy is sometimes criticized as prolonging therapy by leaving the decision to terminate to the client. However, it appears that client-centered therapy is not interminable; in fact it is relatively short term therapy.

Limitations.   It has been widely believed that client-centered therapy is limited to clients with above average intelligence, such as college students, with relatively simple problems. However, the method has been successful with a wide variety of clients with a wide variety of problems, including mental hospital patients (Gendlin, 1962a; Rogers et al., 1967).

Truax and Mitchell (1971) concluded their review of research on therapist interpersonal skills as follows:

> Therapists and counselors who are accurately empathic, non-possessively warm in attitude and genuine are indeed effective. Also, these findings seem to hold with a wide variety of therapists and counselors, regardless of their training or theoretic orientation, and with a wide variety of clients or patients, including college underachievers, juvenile delinquents, hospitalized schizophrenics, college counselees, mild to severe outpatient neurotics, and a mixed variety of hospitalized patients. Further, the evidence suggests that these findings hold in a variety of therapeutic contexts and in both individual and group psychotherapy or counseling. (p. 310)

EXAMPLES

Experiencing the Potential Self (Rogers, 1961a, pp. 77–78)

CLIENT: It all comes pretty vague. But you know I keep, keep having the thought occur to me that this whole process for me is kind of like examining pieces of a jigsaw puzzle. It seems to me I, I'm in the process now of examining the individual pieces which really don't have too much meaning. Probably handling them, not even beginning to think of a pattern. That keeps coming to me. And it's interesting to me because I, I really don't like jigsaw puzzles. They've always irritated me. But that's my feeling. And I mean I pick up little pieces (*she gestures throughout this conversation to illustrate her statements*) with absolutely no meaning except, I mean, the the feeling that you get from simply handling them without seeing them as a pattern, but just from the touch, I probably feel, well, it is going to fit someplace here.

THERAPIST: And that at the moment that that's the process, just getting the feel and the shape and the configuration of the different pieces with a little bit of background feeling of, yeah, they'll probably fit somewhere, but most of the attention's focused right on, "What does this feel like? And what's its texture?"

CL: That's right. There's almost something physical in it. A, a. . . .

TH: You can't quite describe it without using your hands. A real, almost a sensuous sense in. . . .

CL: That's right. Again it's, it's a feeling of being very objective, and yet I've never been quite so close to myself.

TH: Almost at one and the same time standing off and looking at yourself and yet somehow being closer to yourself that way than. . . .

CL: Um-hum. And yet for the first time in months I am not thinking about my problems. I'm not actually, I'm not working on them.

TH: I get the impression you don't sort of sit down to work on "my problems." It isn't that feeling at all.

CL: That's right. That's right. I suppose what I, I mean actually is that I'm not sitting down to put this puzzle together as, as something I've got to see the picture. It, it may be that, it may be that I am actually enjoying this feeling process. Or I'm certainly learning something.

TH: At least there's a sense of the immediate goal of getting that feel as being the thing, not that you're doing this in order to see a picture, but that it's a, a satisfaction of really getting acquainted with each piece. Is that. . . .

CL: That's it. That's it. And it still becomes that sort of sensuousness, that touching. It's quite interesting. Sometimes not entirely pleasant, I'm sure, but. . . .

TH: A rather different sort of experience.

CL: Yes, Quite.

Experiencing an Affectional Relationship (Rogers, 1961a, pp. 81, 82–84, 84–85, 85–86)

CL: Well, I made a very remarkable discovery. I know it's . . . (laughs) I found out that you actually care how this thing goes. (Both laugh) It gave me the feeling, it's sort of well . . . "maybe I'll let you get in the act," sort of thing. It's . . . again, you see, on an examination sheet, I would have had the correct answer, I mean . . . but it suddenly dawned on me that in the . . . client-counselor kind of thing you *actually care* what happens to this thing. And it was a revelation, a . . . not that. That doesn't describe it. It was a . . . well, the closest I can come to it is a kind of relaxation, a . . . not a letting down, but a . . . (pause) more of a straightening out without tension, if that means anything. I don't know.

TH: Sounds as though it isn't as though this was a new idea, but it was a new experience of really feeling that I did care, and if I get the rest of that, sort of a willingness on your part to let me care.

CL: Yes.

CL: The next thing that occurred to me that I found myself thinking and still thinking, is somehow—and I'm not clear why—the same kind of a caring that I get when I say "I don't love humanity." Which has always sort of . . . I mean I was always

CL: convinced of it. So I mean, it doesn't . . . I knew that it was a good thing, see. And I think I clarified it within myself . . . what it has to do with this situation. I don't know. But I found out, no, I don't love, but I do *care* terribly.

TH: Um-hum. Um-hum. I see. . . .

CL: It might be expressed better in saying I care terribly what happens. But the caring is a . . . takes form . . . its structure is in understanding and not wanting to be taken in, or to contribute to those things which I feel are false and . . . it seems to me that in . . . in loving, there's a kind of *final* factor. If you do that, you've sort of done *enough.* It's a. . . .

TH: That's *it,* sort of.

CL: Yeah. It seems to me this other thing, this caring, which isn't a good term. . . . I mean, probably we need something else to describe this kind of thing. To say it's an impersonal thing doesn't mean anything, because it isn't impersonal. I mean, I feel its very much a part of a whole. But it's something that somehow doesn't stop. . . . It seems to me you could have this feeling of loving humanity, loving people, and at the same time . . . go on contributing to the factors that make people neurotic, make them ill . . . where, what I feel is a resistance to those things.

TH: You care enough to want to understand and to want to avoid contributing to anything that would make for more neuroticism, or more of that aspect in human life.

CL: Yes, And it's . . . (Pause) Yes, it's something along those lines. . . . Well, again I have to go back to how I feel about this other thing. It's . . . I'm not really called upon to give of myself in a . . . sort of on the auction block. There's nothing final. . . . It sometimes bothered me when I . . . I would have to say to myself, "I don't love humanity," and yet, I always knew that there was something positive. That I was probably right. And . . . I may be all off the beam now, but it seems to me that, that is somehow tied up in the . . . this feeling that I . . . I have now, into how the therapeutic value can carry through. Now, I couldn't tie it up, I couldn't tie it in, but it's as close as I can come to explaining to myself, my . . . well, shall I say the learning process, the follow-through on my realization that . . . yes, you *do care* in a given situation. It's just that simple. And I hadn't been aware of it before. I might have closed this door and walked out, and in discussing therapy, said, yes, the counselor must feel thus and so, but, I mean, I hadn't had the dynamic experience.

CL: I have a feeling . . . that you have to do it pretty much yourself, but that somehow you ought to be able to do that with other people. *(She mentions that there have been "countless" times when she might have accepted personal warmth and kindness from others.)* I get the feeling that I just was afraid I would be devastated. *(She returns to talking about the counseling itself and her feelings toward it.)* I mean there's been this tearing through the thing myself. Almost to . . . I felt it . . . I mean I tried to verbalize it on occasion . . . a kind of . . . at times almost not wanting you to restate, nor wanting you to reflect, the thing is *mine.* Course all right, I can say resistance. But that doesn't mean a damn thing to me now. . . . The . . . I think in . . . relationship to this particular thing, I mean, the . . . probably at times, the strongest feeling was, it's *mine.* I've got to cut it down myself. See?

TH: It's an experience that's awfully hard to put down accurately into words, and yet I get a sense of difference here in this relationship, that from the feeling that "this is mine," "I've got to do it," "I am doing it," and so on, to a somewhat different feeling that . . . "I could let you in."

CL: Yeah. Now. I mean, that's . . . that's that it's . . . well, it's sort of, shall we say, volume two. It's . . . it's a . . . well, sort of, well, I'm still in the thing alone, but I'm not . . . see . . . I'm. . . .

TH: Uh-hum. Yes, that paradox sort of sums it up, doesn't it?

CL: Yeah.

TH: In all of this, there is a feeling, it's still—every aspect of my experience is mine and that's kind of inevitable and necessary and so on. And yet that isn't the whole picture either. Somehow it can be shared or another's interest can come in and in some ways it is new.

CL: Yeah. And it's . . . it's as though, that's how it should be. I mean, that's how it . . . has to be. There's a . . . there's a feeling, "and this is good." I mean, it expresses, it clarifies it for me. There's a feeling . . . in caring, as though . . . you were sort of standing back . . . standing off, and if I want to sort of cut through to the thing, it's a . . . a slashing of . . . oh, tall weeds, that I can do it, and you can. . . . I mean, you're not going to be disturbed by having to walk through it, too. I don't know. And it doesn't make sense. I mean. . . .

TH: Except there's a very real sense of rightness about this feeling that you have, hm?

CL: Um-hum.

CL: I'm experiencing a new type, a . . . probably the only worthwhile kind of learning, a . . . I know I've . . . I've often said what I know doesn't help me here. What I meant is, my acquired knowledge doesn't help me. But it seems to me that the learning process here has been . . . so dynamic, I mean, so much a part of the . . . of everything, I mean, of me, that if I just get that out of it, it's something, which, I mean . . . I'm wondering if I'll ever be able to straighten out into a sort of acquired knowledge what I have experienced here.

TH: In other words, the kind of learning that has gone on here has been something of quite a different sort and quite a different depth; very vital, very real. And quite worthwhile to you in and of itself, but the question you're asking is: Will I ever have a clear intellectual picture of what has gone on at this somehow deeper kind of learning level?

CL: Um-hum. Something like that.

Liking Oneself (Rogers, 1961a, pp. 87–88)

CL: One thing worries me—and I'll hurry because I can always go back to it—a feeling that occasionally I can't turn out. Feeling of being quite pleased with myself. Again the Q technique. I walked out of here one time, and impulsively I threw my first care, "I am an attractive personality"; looked at it sort of aghast but left it there, I mean, because honestly, I mean, that is exactly how it felt . . . a—well, that bothered me and I catch that now. Every once in a while a sort of pleased feeling, nothing superior, but just . . . I don't know, sort of pleased. A neatly turned way. And it bothered me. And yet—I wondered—I rarely remember things I say here, I mean I wondered why it was that I was convinced, and something about what I've felt about being hurt that I suspected in . . . my feelings when I would hear someone say to a child, "Don't cry." I mean, I always felt, but it isn't right; I mean, if he's hurt, let him cry. Well, then, now this pleased feeling that I have. I've recently come to feel, it's . . . there's something almost the same there. It's . . . We don't object when *children* feel pleased with themselves. It's . . . I mean, there really isn't anything vain. It's maybe that's how people *should* feel.

TH: You've been inclined almost to look askance at yourself for this feeling, and yet as you think about it more, maybe it comes close to the two sides of the picture, that if a child wants to cry, why shouldn't he cry? And if he wants to feel pleased with himself, doesn't he have a perfect right to feel pleased with himself? And that sort of ties in with this, what I would see as an appreciation of yourself that you've experienced every now and again.

CL: Yes. Yes.

TH: "I'm really a pretty rich and interesting person."

CL: Something like that. And then I say to myself. "Our society pushes us around and we've lost it." And I keep going back to my feelings about children. Well, maybe they're richer than we are. Maybe we . . . it's something we've lost in the process of growing.

TH: Could be that they have a wisdom about that that we've lost.

CL: That's right. My time's up.

Discovering That the Core of Personality is Positive (Rogers, 1961a, pp. 100–101)

CL: I think I'm awfully glad I found myself or brought myself or wanted to talk about self. I mean, it's a very personal, private kind of thing that you just don't talk about. I mean, I can understand my feeling of, oh, probably slight apprehension now. It's . . . well, sort of as though I was just rejecting, I mean, all of the things that western civilization stands for, you see. And wondering whether I was right, I mean, whether it was quite the right path, and still of course, feeling how right the thing was, you see. And so there's bound to be a conflict. And then this, and I mean, now I'm feeling, well, of course that's how I feel. I mean, there's a . . . this thing that I term a kind of a lack of hate, I mean is very real. It carried over onto the things I do, I believe in. . . . I think it's all right. It's sort of maybe my saying to myself, well, you've been bashing me all over the head, I mean, sort of from the beginning, with superstitions and taboos and misinterpreted doctrines and laws and your science, your refrigerators, your atomic bombs. But I'm just not buying, you see, I'm just, you just haven't quite succeeded. I think what I'm saying is that, well, I mean, just not conforming, and it's . . . well, it's just that way.

TH: Your feeling at the present time is that you have been very much aware of all the cultural pressures—not always very much aware, but "there have been so many of those in my life—and now I'm going down more deeply into myself to find out what I really feel"—and it seems very much at the present time as though that somehow separates you a long ways from your culture, and that's a little frightening, but feels basically good. Is that. . . ?

CL: Yeah. Well, I have the feeling now that it's okay, really. . . . Then there's something else—a feeling that's starting to grow, well, to be almost formed, as I say. This kind of conclusion, that I'm going to stop looking for something terribly wrong. Now I don't know why. But I mean just . . . it's this kind of thing. I'm sort of saying to myself now, well, in view of what I know, what I've found . . . I'm pretty sure I've ruled out fear, and I'm positive I'm not afraid of shock. . . . I mean, I sort of would have welcomed it. But . . . in view of the places I've been, what I learned there, then also kind of, well taking into consideration what I don't know, sort of, maybe this is one of the things that I'll have to date and say, well, now, I've just . . . I can't find it. See? And now without any, without, I should say, any sense of apology or covering up, just sort of simple statement that I can't find what at this time appears to be bad.

TH: Does this catch it? That as you've gone more and more deeply into yourself, and as you think about the kind of things that you've discovered and learned and so on, the conviction grows very, very strong that no matter how far you go, the things that you're going to find are not dire and awful. They have a very different character.

CL: Yes, something like that.

Openness to Experience (Rogers, 1961a, pp. 116–117)

CL: It doesn't seem to me that it would be possible for anybody to relate all the changes that you feel. But I certainly have felt recently that I have more respect for, more objectivity toward my physical makeup. I don't expect too much of myself. This is how it works out: It feels to me that in the past I used to fight a certain tiredness that I felt after supper. Well, now I feel pretty sure that I really *am tired*—that I am not making myself tired—that I am just physiologically lower. It seemed that I was just constantly criticizing my tiredness.

TH: So you can let yourself be tired, instead of feeling along with it a kind of criticism of it.

CL: Yes, that I shouldn't be tired or something. And it seems in a way to be pretty profound that I can just not fight this tiredness, and along with it goes a real feeling of I've got to slow down, too, so that being tired isn't such an awful thing. I think I can also kind of pick up a thread here of why I should be that way in the way my father is and the way he looks at some of these things. For instance, say that I was sick, and I would report this, and it would seem that overtly he would want to do something about it, but he would also communicate, "Oh, my gosh, more trouble." You know, something like that.

TH: As though there were something quite annoying really about being physically ill.

CL: Yeah, I'm sure that my father has the same disrespect for his own physiology that I have had. Now, last summer I twisted my back, I wrenched it, I heard it snap and everything. There was real pain there all the time at first, real sharp. And I had the doctor look at it and he said it wasn't serious, it should heal by itself as long as I didn't bend too much. Well this was months ago . . . and I have been noticing recently that . . . hell, this is a real pain and it's still there—and it's not my fault.

TH: It doesn't prove something bad about you. . . .

CL: No—and one of the reasons I seem to get more tired than I should maybe is because of this constant strain, and so . . . I have already made an appointment with one of the doctors at the hospital that he would look at it and take an X ray or something. In a way I guess you could say that I am just more accurately sensitive—or objectively sensitive to this kind of thing. . . . And this is really a profound change, as I say, and of course my relationship with my wife and two children is . . . well, you just wouldn't recognize it if you could see me inside—as you have—I mean . . . there just doesn't seem to be anything more wonderful than really and genuinely . . . really *feeling* love for your own children and at the same time receiving it. I don't know how to put this. We have such an increased respect—both of us—for Judy and we've noticed just—as we partici- pated in this—we have noticed such a tremendous change in her . . . it seems to be a pretty deep kind of thing.

TH: It seems to me you are saying that you can listen more accurately to yourself. If your body says it's tired, you listen to it and believe it, instead of criticizing it; if it's in pain, you can listen to that; if the feeling is really loving your wife and chil- dren, you can feel that, and it seems to show up in the differences in them too.

An Internal Locus of Evaluation (Rogers, 1961a, pp. 120–122)

CL: Well, now, I wonder if I've been going around doing that, getting smatterings of things, and not getting hold, not really getting down to things.

TH: Maybe you've been getting just spoonfuls here and there rather than really dig- ging in somewhere rather deeply.

CL: Um-hum. That's why I say . . . *(slowly and very thoughtfully)* well, with that sort of foundation, well, it's really up to me. I mean, it seems to be really apparent to me that I can't depend on someone else to give me an education. *(very softly)* I'll really have to get it myself.

TH: It really begins to come home—there's only one person that can educate you— a realization that perhaps nobody else can give you an education.

CL: Um-hum *(long pause—while she sits thinking)* I have all the symptoms of fright. *(laughs softly)*

TH: Fright: That this is a scary thing, is that what you mean?

CL: Um-hum. *(very long pause—obviously struggling with feelings in herself)*

TH: Do you want to say any more about what you mean by that? That it really does give you the symptoms of fright?

CL: *(laughs)* I, uh . . . I don't know whether I quite know. I mean . . . well, it really seems like I'm cut loose (pause), and it seems that I'm very—I don't know—in a vulnerable position, but I, uh, I brought this up and it, uh, somehow it almost came out without saying it. It seems to be . . . it's something I let out.

TH: Hardly a part of you.

CL: Well, I felt surprised.

TH: As though, "Well for goodness sake, did I say that?" (both chuckle)

CL: Really, I don't think I've had that feeling before. I've . . . uh, well, this really feels like I'm saying something that, uh, is a part of me really. (pause) Or, uh, *(quite perplexed)* it feels like I sort of have, uh, I don't know. I have a feeling of *strength,* and yet I have a feeling of . . . realizing it's so sort of fearful, of fright.

TH: That is, do you mean that saying something of that sort gives you at the same time a feeling of, of strength in saying it, and yet at the same time a frightened feeling of what you have said, is that it?

CL: Um-hum. I am feeling that. For instance, I'm feeling it internally now—a sort of surging up, or force, or outlet. As if that's something really big and strong. And yet, us, well, at first it was almost a physical feeling of just being out alone, and sort of cut off from a . . . a support I had been carrying around.

TH: You feel that it's something deep and strong, and surging forth, and at the same time, you feel as though you'd cut yourself loose from any support when you say it.

CL: Um-hum. Maybe that's . . . I don't know . . . it's a disturbance of a kind of pattern I've been carrying around, I think.

TH: It sort of shakes a rather significant pattern, jars it loose.

CL: Um-hum. *(pause, then cautiously, but with conviction)* I, think . . . I don't know, but I have the feeling that then I am going to begin to do more things that I know I should do. . . . There are so many things that I need to do. It seems in so many avenues of my living I have to work out new ways of behavior, but—maybe—I can see myself doing a little better in some things.

SUMMARY AND EVALUATION

Summary. Client-centered therapy hypothesizes that human beings are rational, socialized, constructive, and forward-moving and that each individual has the potential for growth and self-actualization. Psychotherapy releases the potentials and capacities of the individual.

The maladjusted or disturbed individual is characterized by incongruence between the self and experiences, which are threatening. This individual reacts defensively, denying or distorting experiences that are inconsistent with the self-concept. Psychotherapy offers a relationship in which incongruous experiences can be recognized, expressed, differentiated, and assimilated, or integrated into the self. The individual becomes more congruent, less defensive, more realistic and objective in his/her perceptions, more effective in problem solving, and more accepting of others—in short, the individual's psychological adjustment is closer to the optimum.

This process and these outcomes are facilitated when the therapist manifests unconditional positive regard for the client, evidences empathic understanding of the client, and is successful in communicating these attitudes to the client in a relationship in which the therapist is congruent, or genuine. The relationship is one in which threat is reduced, thereby freeing the client for experiencing, expressing, and exploring his/her feelings.

Client-centered therapy developed out of Rogers' experience as he engaged in counseling or psychotherapy with many clients over more than 40 years. The theory grew out of experience, the results of which were not anticipated; indeed, Rogers' experience led to radical changes in the theoretical point of view that he had held early in his professional life.

Rogers' development of a theory of therapy preceded the development of a theory of personality. The theory of therapy emerged as a way of giving order to the phenomena experienced in therapy. This experience involved personality change, which led to the evolution of a theory of personality that deals with the nature of normal and abnormal personality and its development.

The theory of personality has been called self-theory because of the central importance of the self, or self-concept, in it. More broadly, however, both the theory of therapy and the theory of personality constitute a perceptual theory, or, more specifically, a phenomenological theory. The phenomenological nature of this theory is clearly represented by Combs and Snygg (1959) in *Individual Behavior: A Perceptual Approach to Behavior.*

Phenomenology assumes that although a real world may exist, its existence cannot be known or experienced directly. Its existence is inferred on the basis of perceptions of the world. These perceptions constitute the phenomenal field, or the phenomenal world, of the individual. Human beings can know only their phenomenal worlds, never any real world. Therefore, they can behave only in terms of how they perceive things, or how things appear to them.

Rogers thus accepts or adopts a phenomenological point of view when he uses the internal frame of reference, or the subjective world of the individual, as a basis for empathizing with and understanding the individual. It is also apparent in his theory of personality when he postulates that the individual perceives his/her experience as reality—that, indeed, the individual's experience *is* his/her reality—and when he defines experience as the phenomenal field of the individual. In therapy, it is the *perception* that the client has of the therapist that is important, not what the therapist actually is or may be trying to be. The process of therapy is seen as a reorganization of the client's perceptions about himself/herself and his/her world. "The essential point about therapy . . . is that the way the client perceives the objects in his phenomenal field—his experiences, his feelings, his self, other persons, his environment—undergoes changes" (Rogers, 1951, p. 142). Rogers quotes, with approval, Snygg and Combs (1949): "We might, therefore, define psychotherapy from a phenomenological point of view as: the provision of experience whereby the individual is enabled to make more adequate differentiation of the phenomenal self and its relationship to external reality" (Rogers, 1951, p. 146).

The outcomes of therapy also include self-direction and the perception of the locus of evaluation and of choice as being in the self. The individual is conceived as a free agent, capable of making choices and decisions and with the right to do so. "There is the experiencing of effective choice of new ways of being" (Rogers, 1961a, p. 154). There is the assumption that the individual is capable of changing—an assumption common to most other theories of psychotherapy. The client-centered view, however, assumes that the individual is able to change by himself/herself, in ways that he/she chooses, without the direction or manipulation of the therapist.

Evaluation.   Phenomenology, however, is deterministic. Combs and Snygg stated (1959): "All behavior, without exception is completely determined by, and pertinent to, the perceptual field of the behaving organism" (p. 20). If all behavior is completely determined, then freedom and choice cannot exist. Beck (1963, pp. 66–67) quoted Snygg and Combs (1949, pp. 130–131) as saying that choice does not exist. This passage apparently was deleted from the second edition of their book (Combs & Snygg, 1959), and there appears to be no reference to choice or freedom; neither word appears in the index. Nevertheless, as Beck noted, phenomenology is deterministic, and thus it appears to be inconsistent with the assumption of client-centered therapy and the theory of personality on which client-centered therapy is based.

It might be argued that the self influences the phenomenal field, but it could also be argued that the self is itself determined. Therefore, it would not be possible to contend that the client, by restructuring the phenomenal field, controls his/her behavior. The behavior leading to the restructuring is itself determined by the phenomenal field at that moment, and so on, with infinite regress. There seems to be no way philosophically to reconcile freedom and determination. Malcolm, (1964), a philosopher, stated that "freedom and determination really are incompatible and will remain so" (p. 107).

How, then, did Rogers deal with the apparent deterministic requirement of science and the assumption of freedom and choice underlying his system? He apparently did not recognize the conflict between the assumption of phenomenology and that of his system with regard to freedom and choice, but he did recognize the difference between the determination of science and the assumption of his system. In research, Rogers accepted the world as a determined world, since the assumption of a cause-and-effect sequence is necessary. "There would be nothing to study scientifically if that were not a part of your assumption" (Rogers, 1964, p. 135).

However, he stated that this "is not the whole of the truth about life. . . . The experiencing of choice, of freedom of choice . . . is not only a profound truth, but is a very important element in therapy" (Rogers, 1964, p. 135). The two assumptions seem to be irreconcilable, but they exist in different dimensions, analogous to the wave and particle theories of light. They constitute a paradox that Rogers accepted as insoluble. However, he attempted to see the dilemma in a new perspective.

> We could say that in the optimum of therapy, the person rightfully experiences the most complete and absolute freedom. He wills or chooses to follow the course of action which is the most economical vector in relationship to all the internal and external stimuli, because it is that behavior which will be most deeply satisfying. But this is the same course of action which from another vantage point may be said to be determined by all the factors in the existential situation. Let us contrast this with the picture of the person who is defensively organized. He wills or chooses to follow a given course of action, but finds that he *cannot* behave in the fashion he chooses. He is determined by the factors in the existential situation, but these factors include his defensiveness, his denial or distortion of some of the relevant data. Hence it is certain that his behavior will be less than fully satisfying. His behavior is determined, but he is not free to make an effective choice. The fully functioning person, on the other hand, not only experiences, but utilizes, the most absolute freedom when he spontaneously, freely, and voluntarily chooses and wills that which is absolutely determined. (Rogers, 1961a, p. 193)

Rogers did not claim that this resolves the issue. Certainly, it is not very satisfying or convincing. That what is determined is what is willed or chosen in the case of the fully functioning person but not in the case of the defensively organized person seems a little forced, if not moralistic. One might also note that what constitutes determinism is determined by the nature of the person and inquire as to what produced this nature. However, it does appear that during therapy, a defensively organized person may become a fully functioning person, but one might contend that the change also was determined in the particular case.

This difficulty seems inherent in the assumptions. What one assumes to exist or to be true does exist or is true by virtue of its being assumed. Determinism is assumed by science and by phenomenology. This assumption was accepted by Rogers in the former instance but not in the latter. Perhaps one need not assume it in either case in order to allow for the existence of science or phenomenology. Paradoxically, human beings choose to accept determinism; there is little convincing proof for it. Indeterminism and probability are accepted in many areas of science itself. Rogers pointed out the paradox of the behaviorist, committed to determinism and the denial of the existence of choice, making choices about the goals and methods of science and of human life (Rogers, 1961a, p. 392). Choice seems to be as much a "fact" as is determination.

It might also be noted that Rogers' position is not entirely inconsistent with phenomenology. Although he seemed to imply at times that freedom and choice exist in some reality, he usually spoke of the *experiencing* or *perceiving* of freedom and choice. This experiencing or perceiving is clearly phenomenological, and, phenomenologically, what is experienced or perceived is reality for the individual. The recognition that what is important is the client's perception of the therapist, rather than the therapist's personality or techniques as seen by others, is also clearly phenomenological. Studies of this phenomenological variable have demonstrated its significance.

It may be worth noting also that the situation is not necessarily an either-or dilemma. Freedom could not exist without determinism, and vice versa. Either concept is meaningless without the other, and both constitute a construct (as contrasts), in Kelly's terms.

While Rogers did not introduce as many new concepts or new definitions of traditional terms as did Kelly, for example, there are a number of rather abstract concepts in his work. Ford and Urban (1963) pointed to the level of abstraction of concepts, such as organismic experience, as a difficulty in the theory. They also criticized the inclusion of subjective concepts, such as unconditional positive regard. They note that operational definitions of these concepts have been developed for research and suggest that such definitions are needed for the therapist as well.

This point appears to be well taken. The concepts of unconditional positive regard, empathic understanding, and congruence have been developed into measurable variables, and their relationship to the client's progress and change have been demonstrated. However, the descriptions of these concepts are broad and general, with little, if any, consideration of how they are manifested by the therapist in the therapeutic process. This lack of specification is an example of the increasing emphasis on attitudes, with consequent deemphasis or neglect of techniques.

Rogers stated: "I believe the quality of my encounter is more important in the long run than is my scholarly knowledge, my professional training, my counseling orientation, the techniques I use in the interview" (Rogers, 1962). While this may be so, the quality of the relationship is not independent of the other factors, including techniques. The beginning therapist, especially, needs some help in going about the process of implementing the basic attitudes, but the impression is sometimes given that techniques are entirely incidental. Gendlin, for example, stated that "many different orientations, techniques, and modes of therapist response could manifest these attitudes. . . . An unlimited range of therapist *behavior* might implement and communicate these *attitudes*" (Gendlin, 1962b). This, of course, cannot literally be true; there are some limits—some techniques are inconsistent with the attitudes. Other client-centered writers have given more attention to techniques, however, including Porter (1950) and Patterson (1959, 1974, 1985).

An important question concerning the client-centered approach is whether the conditions presented by Rogers are the necessary and sufficient conditions for psychotherapy. Rogers stated that when these conditions are present, therapeutic personality change invariably and inevitably occurs. However, the conditions are presented, not as final, but as a theory, a "series of hypotheses which are open to proof or disproof, thereby clarifying and extending our knowledge of the field" (Rogers, 1957).

Ellis (1959) has challenged these conditions, questioning whether they are necessary or sufficient, although he conceded that they may be desirable. He noted that personality change does occur without psychological contact with another through experiences of reading or listening. It may be questioned, of course, whether, although there is no direct *personal* contact, there is not *psychological* contact, even though certain experiences may not involve any individual. Ellis also noted that individuals who were not incongruent, but basically congruent and unanxious, have improved their personalities significantly through life experiences and reading. He pointed out that he has seen clients helped by therapists who were emotionally disturbed and incongruent. However, Ellis did not discuss whether such therapists were congruent in the therapy relationship, which was Rogers' point.

Commenting on unconditional positive regard, Ellis stated that he has seen at least one client who benefited appreciably when treated by therapists who "do not have any real positive regard for their patients, but who deliberately try to regulate the lives and philosophies of these patients for the satisfaction of the therapist's own desires" (Ellis, 1959). Ellis felt that the presence of empathic understanding is the most plausible condition, but he contended that clients whom he has helped by pointing out their self-defeating behavior and showing them alternative methods of behavior—after seeing their problems from their own frame of reference—have then helped friends and relatives by dogmatically and arbitrarily indoctrinating them without any empathic understanding. Finally, Ellis claimed that he has disproved in his own therapy the necessity for the client's perceiving the therapist's acceptance and empathy, in the case of paranoid patients who insisted that they were not understood but who finally accepted the therapist's frame of reference.

Ellis concluded, therefore, that while very few individuals significantly restructure their personalities when all six of the conditions listed by Rogers (1957) are absent, some do. He felt that there is probably no single condition that is absolutely necessary for constructive personality change. There are a number of alternative conditions that might lead to this same result. It might be pointed out that, as has been indicated several times in this chapter, it is not the presence of these conditions as perceived by an external observer that is necessary, but their presence as perceived by the client. Nevertheless, Ellis raises some question as to whether any one or all of the conditions are necessary.

A possible solution of this issue, which appears to be consistent with the general client-centered approach, is that the only necessary—but not sufficient—condition of constructive personality change is that the individual's potential for growth, as manifested in the drive for maintenance and enhancement of the self, is operating and has not been destroyed by severe organic or psychological trauma. The degree of this motivation varies, of course. When it is strong, the conditions that Rogers listed need be present in only very minimal degrees, perhaps hardly observable by an external observer but present from the viewpoint of the client. When the basic motivation for change is weak or when it is inhibited or threatened, the external conditions must be present in greater degrees. They may vary in the degree to which they are present, and it may be possible that not all the conditions need be present, although there appears to be a positive relationship among the conditions that relate to the therapist, so that if one is present, the others are likely to be present, at least to some extent. Or it may be that the only other necessary condition, which, with the client's motivation, constitutes the sufficient conditions, is the perception by the client of congruence, empathy, and unconditional positive regard in the therapist.

Thus, whether the conditions posited by Rogers are necessary is not yet known. However, that they can be sufficient for positive personality and behavior change appears to have been demonstrated in the extensive research that was carried out over some 40 years and that involved a wide variety of clients with a wide variety of problems.

After his move to California, Rogers wrote little in the area of individual counseling or psychotherapy. The approach has become so firmly established, however, that it has continued to be one of the major methods of psychotherapy. For a time, it claimed more adherents than any other school, but with the proliferation of numerous methods and techniques (including behavior therapy), the number of practitioners who identify themselves as eclectic or as combining two or more approaches has increased.

The literature on client-centered therapy is voluminous, beginning shortly after the publication of Rogers' 1942 book. In 1947 Snyder edited a book of cases. Porter (1950) published a useful book for the education of therapists. Patterson (1959, 1974, 1985) has published extensively on client-centered therapy. In 1961 Snyder and Snyder published a book on the psychotherapy relationship. Boy and Pine have published extensively, most recently in 1990. In England, Mearns and Thorne (1988) have published a primer in client-centered therapy. Most of those publishing on client-centered therapy have been students of Rogers at one time or another.

A number of publications have included materials for use in the education of therapists. Porter (1950) included pretests and posttests for instructional use. Patterson (1967; also see Nelson-Jones & Patterson, 1974, 1976; Patterson & Nelson-Jones, 1975) developed a Counselor Attitude Scale, based on an earlier instrument by Stewart (1958). A widely used instrument to measure the perception of therapist attitudes by clients was developed by Barrett-Lennard (1962), the *Barrett-Lennard Relationship Inventory*. Truax and Carkhuff (1967; Carkhuff, 1969) developed scales for rating interviews on a number of therapist variables. Carkhuff's revised scales include those for empathic understanding, respect, genuineness, concreteness or specificity, confrontation, self-disclosure, and immediacy in the relationship. The first four are considered by Carkhuff to be responsive dimensions, and the remaining three to be action dimensions in psychotherapy. Truax also developed a scale to measure client depth of self-exploration, revised by Carkhuff. These scales are reproduced and discussed by Patterson (1985).

Two edited volumes, which bring together papers representing developments in client-centered theory and practice, have appeared. In 1970, Hart and Tomlinson edited *New Directions in Client-Centered Therapy*. Of the 21 authors of papers, 1 was Rogers (5 papers), 10 had received their degrees from the University of Chicago, and 5 others, including the editors, were associated with Rogers at some time. Of the 30 articles, 11 had not been previously published; the remainder had been published during the 1960s. They were grouped into sections, including theory, research, and new directions in practice. In the foreword, Rogers noted that practitioners of client-centered therapy always have had a willingness to change, an openness to experiential and research data. Yet under the fluidity and change are some continuous themes: (1) the reliance on the individual drive toward growth and health, or self-actualization; (2) the greater emphasis on the feeling than on the intellectual aspects of experience; (3) the stress on the immediate situation rather than on the past; (4) the emphasis on the therapeutic relationship itself as a growth experience; (5) the focus on the unique, subjective inner person as the core of human life (a view that is in strong opposition to the major trend of American psychology, which adopts a mechanistic, atomistic, deterministic frame of reference); (6) the recognition of the strong need of people for a human relationship that is a deep, real, and nondefensive person-to-person relationship; and (7) the conviction that the training or preparation of counselors or psychotherapists must be primarily experiential and not only cognitive.

In 1974, Wexler and Rice (1974) published a collection of original papers under the title *Innovations in Client-Centered Therapy*. Fifteen of its authors had received their Ph.D.s from the University of Chicago, one had been a staff member there, and the seventeenth was Rogers, whose chapter was entitled "Remarks on the Future of Client-Centered Therapy." The papers were grouped in sections—one on theory, a second on practice, and a third entitled "Beyond Individual Psychotherapy." The editors stated that although the theory derived from Rogerian theory, the papers represent a "marked departure" from that theory. A notable aspect of this departure was an emphasis on cognitive and information-processing concepts and language in descriptions and analyses of the internal processes that occur within the client as he/she explores and reorganizes his/her experience or, in Wexler's information-processing terms, as he/she differentiates and integrates meanings, thus creating reorganizations.

"The essence of successful therapy is seen to involve a *change in the characteristic style in which information is processed*" (Wexler, 1974). The client-centered therapist, in his/her empathic responding, serves as a surrogate information processor to help the client overcome deficiencies in the style in which the client elaborates and organizes information. Viewing the therapy process in information-processing terms provides a detailed and more specific description and analysis that can help clarify the process and suggest new approaches to study and research. It also makes it clear that, contrary to some critics, client-centered therapy is not an anticognitive or noncognitive therapy.

Rice (1974) also used an information approach in her method of evocative reflection or responding. An evocative reflection is one that re-evokes the client's reaction or experience by giving back (reflecting) the experience, or part of it, vividly, concretely, and accurately. This allows the client to focus on it, to reexperience and reprocess it, so the client can form more accurate constructions of his/her experience. This leads to the substitution of a better method or "schema" (from Piaget) for inadequate or distorting schemas for dealing with or processing similar experiences.

Wexler viewed feelings as products of cognitive activity that arise from certain ways of processing and organizing information. While recognizing their existence, he did not actually deal with them. Butler (1974), in his iconic mode of psychotherapy, came to terms with feelings. For Butler, feelings are neurophysiological processes that are aroused by external and internal stimuli. To be understood and dealt with, particularly in the case of self-generated feelings, they must be rendered or depicted in some form. This is achieved by the development of icons (objectified images). The client expresses (renders or depicts) his/her feelings symbolically in poetic, metaphoric, and figurative language and in dramatic gestures. The empathic therapist experiences these objectified feelings of the client, subjectifies them so that they become his/her own feelings, and then reobjectifies them and gives them back to the client. Thus, by cognitive processes of elaboration and differentiation, they lead to the client's realization or self-actualization of himself/herself in the world. However, the process is not one of literal, discursive, propositional, analytical conceptualization or logic. The self-knowledge involved is symbolic but not logically organized.

An additional development in client-centered therapy, even less cognitive in nature, is Gendlin's experiential psychotherapy (Gendlin, 1962b, 1970a, 1970b, 1974, 1981; Gendlin & Tomlison, 1967). Experiential psychotherapy focuses on the present experiencing of the client and attempts to help the client experience more intensely so that he/she can become more accurate, concrete, and specific in exploring the "felt meanings" involved. The therapist helps the client to verbalize, conceptualize, and symbolize the felt meanings of his/her experiencing. This involves cognitive activity, but words, concepts, or symbols cannot explicate all the felt meanings of experiencing. Thus, although there are cognitive aspects in Gendlin's method, experiential therapy is essentially an intensely affective, or feeling, process. Feelings are not things or something added to experience; they are an essential or inherent part of the experience. Symbolizing or conceptualizing felt experience is not a substitute for a complete representation of the experience but constitutes a further experiencing. Although he used a new term to designate his approach, Gendlin recognized that it involves the essence of client-centered therapy, that is, a relationship focusing on reflective listening, which enables the therapist to participate in the client's experiencing. Gendlin views his experiential approach as a development in, or extension of, client-centered therapy. Brodley (1990), however, argued cogently that it goes beyond client-centered therapy in its methods, which violate some of the basic assumptions of client-centered therapy.

Both the cognitive and the experiential developments retain some of the basic elements of traditional client-centered therapy. Both require that the therapist enter and remain in the (internal) frame of reference of the client. The therapist responds to the client's experiencing and does not react to it, deflect it, or direct it from his/her (the therapist's) frame of reference. This is required by information-processing theory. Thus, the empathic response is the major—indeed the only—therapist activity. The practice of client-centered therapy remains the same. The cognitive (information-processing) and experiential developments focus on the activity of the client, providing detailed descriptions and explanations of the process of the client's self-exploration and demonstrating how the therapist's empathic responses facilitate this process. Wexler's empathic responding or surrogate information processing, Rice's evocative reflection or responding, Butler's iconic reflection, and Gendlin's empathic reflection all have the same objective: To provide responses that open up and facilitate continued feeling, experiencing, and exploring by the client and to avoid responses that would close up this experiencing or take the initiative from the client. Gendlin's methods, however, appear to go beyond responding to the client to direct the experiencing process (Brodley, 1990).

The focus on empathic responding corresponds to Rogers' suggestion that while in some areas of interpersonal relationships, congruence or unconditional positive regard may be the most significant condition, in therapy, empathy has the highest priority (Rogers, 1975). (This represents a change from his 1959 position that congruence or genuineness is primary [Rogers, 1959.]) This agreement on the central importance of empathy is significant in light of the choice of many therapists, including some client-centered therapists, to place congruence or genuineness first. Wexler noted that the introduction of the reactions of the therapist into the relationship departs from the client-centered orientation, because it introduces material from an external frame of reference, which is inconsistent with empathic responding (Wexler, 1974).

These developments in client-centered theory can be useful in clarifying the therapy process and in opening up new approaches to study and research. The cognitive analysis of the nature of the client's experiencing and self-exploration is relevant to practitioners, since many client-centered therapists doubtless have been led to think of feelings as things in themselves, apart from experience and cognition.

Research in client-centered therapy is extensive, beginning in the 1940s and continuing through the 1950s, 1960s, and 1970s, though slowing down in the 1970s. Rogers appeared to be equally devoted to research and practice in the earlier years. He was the first to use electronic recordings of therapy interviews and to analyze the transcribed protocols. His students at Ohio State University and the University of Chicago participated in the research through their doctoral dissertations.

A large section of his 1942 book (Rogers, 1942) consists of eight interviews with "Herbert Bryan." A series of studies done in the late 1940s was published as a complete issue of the *Journal of Consulting Psychology* (Rogers, Raskin, Seeman, Sheerer, Stock, Haigh, Hoffman, & Carr, 1949). Rogers and Dymond (1954) edited a book consisting of later studies, including those by J. M. Butler, Desmond Cartwright, Thomas Gordon, Donald Grummon, Gerard Haigh, Eve S. John, Esselyn Rudikoff, Julius Seeman, Rolland Tongas and Manuel Vargus. Rogers has summarized this research (Rogers, 1961a, Chapters 11 and 12).

A number of reviews of later studies have been published. The review of Truax and Carkhuff (1967) listed 439 references. The review of Truax and Mitchell (1971) covering 92 studies was positive. Later reviews have been rather negative. Mitchell, Bozarth, and Krauft (1977) question, but do not refute, the conclusion of Truax and Mitchell (see Patterson, 1984, for an evaluation of this review). Parloff, Waskow, and Wolfe (1978) stated that

> it must be concluded that the unqualified claim that "high" levels (absolute or relative) of accurate empathy, warmth, and genuineness (independent of the source of rating or the nature of the instrument) represent "the necessary and sufficient" conditions for effective therapy (independent of the outcome measures or conditions) is not supported. (p. 249)

Parenthetically, no one makes an unqualified claim; also, their review found that studies with positive findings outnumbered those with negative findings.

Orlinsky and Howard (1978) reviewed some of the same studies included in the two previous reviews. In addition they evaluated studies involving the client's perceptions of the therapist conditions, and found these studies provided evidence that client perceptions are consistently related to successful outcomes; their conclusion is weakly stated, however. These findings agree with the earlier conclusion of Gurman's (1977) review that "there exists substantial, if not overwhelming evidence in support of the hypothesized relationship between patient-perceived conditions and outcome in individual psychotherapy and counseling" (p. 523).

Lambert, DeJulio, and Stein (1978) selected for review eighteen studies done prior to 1977 as the best in the field. They concluded that "despite more than 20 years of research and some improvements in methodology, only a modest relationship between the so-called facilitative conditions and therapeutic outcomes has been found. Contrary to frequent claims for the potency of these therapist-offered relationship variables, experimental evidence suggests that neither a clear test nor unequivocal support for the Rogerian hypothesis has appeared" (p. 486). Of course, if there has not been a clear test, one could not expect to find unequivocal support. They note the numerous problems involved in the research studies.

Bergin and Suinn (1975), in a review of research reported during 1971, 1972 and 1973, concluded that "it is clearer now that these [therapist] variables are not as prepotent as once believed; but their presence and influence is ubiquitous, even showing up in behavior therapies."

In an interesting review by Gomes-Schwartz, Hadley, and Strupp (1978), Gomes-Schwartz, who authored part of the review, perpetuated the negative evaluation: "Earlier assertions of strong empirical support for the relationship between therapist's facilitative 'conditions' and therapy outcome [by Truax & Mitchell] have been challenged by recent findings" [citing Bergin's review]. Yet she also equivocated: "This does not imply that the quality of the therapeutic relationship is not of major importance in determining the effectiveness of psychotherapy" (p. 440).

In a later section of the review on the therapeutic relationship it is stated that

> in a relationship marked by warmth, closeness, and a sense that the therapist was involved and cared about the patient, patients were more likely to remain in therapy than terminate [four studies cited], to be satisfied with the ongoing therapy process [two studies], and to show greater improvement [three studies]. The therapeutic relationship characterized by relaxed rapport and open communication was likely to promote continuation in therapy [two studies] and better outcome [two studies]. (p. 442)

Although the tone of these reviews is negative, some positive statements appear, as they should considering the preponderance of the evidence. Orlinsky and Howard's (1978) statement warrants attention: "If study after flawed study seemed to point in the same general direction, we could not help believing that somewhere in all that variance there must be a reliable effect" (pp. 288–289). They later (Orlinsky & Howard, 1986) noted that "generally 50–80 percent of the substantial number of studies in this area were significantly positive, indicating that the dimensions were consistently related to patient outcome" (p. 365). The more recent review by Orlinsky, Grawe, and Parks (1994) also provided strong support for the therapeutic bond, which incorporates such elements as empathy and congruence.

In the recent review of research accumulated since 1985, Beutler, Machado, and Neufeldt (1994) introduced their review in part with the following statement:

> Roger's (1957) conceptualizations of the "necessary and sufficient" conditions for effective psychotherapy formed the foundation for the preponderance of research on the psychotherapy relationship over three decades. Most contemporary investigators would probably agree that these facilitative qualities play a central role in therapeutic change. In clinical practice, they are equally well accepted and have been assimilated into much of contemporary theory. These variables are the ones most often considered when the topic of "common" or "shared" psychotherapy characteristics comes up. These are the qualities of the therapy relationship to which much of the therapeutic change is attributed. (p. 243)

Beutler, Machado, and Neufeldt (1994), concluded that "consistent evidence exists to support the assertion (now nearly a 'truism') that a warm and supportive therapeutic relationship facilitates therapeutic success. . . . Research in this area continues to be strong" (p. 259). The conclusion must be reached that there is considerable, if not compelling, research support for the effectiveness of therapy involving the conditions proposed as hypotheses by Rogers (1957) (see Stubbs & Bozarth, 1994).

Patterson (1984) pointed out the influence of bias in many earlier reviewers, whose conclusions are often inconsistent and do not always clearly follow the results of the research reviewed. He also noted other factors involved in the research that must be considered. Relevant to the Orlinsky and Howard statement is the fact that all the flaws in the research studies cited by the reviewers would militate *against* positive findings; yet the majority of findings are positive.

What of the future of client-centered therapy? In the 1950s and 1960s, even into the 1970s, many if not most counselor education programs (as distinguished from programs in counseling and clinical psychology) identified themselves as client-centered. Now there are few if any programs that would do so. Students are no longer exposed to the writings of Carl Rogers.

It has been suggested that much of the client-centered approach has been absorbed into psychotherapy in general. For example, the importance, even the necessity, of a good relationship between the therapist and the client is universally accepted. Yet techniques rather than the relationship are the focus in the education of therapists. And it may be questioned whether the philosophy and assumptions of client-centered therapy are clearly understood, accepted, and implemented (Patterson, 1990). The extent of the influence of client-centered theory or principles on other therapies or therapists may be questioned. At the 1985 Phoenix Conference on the Evolution of Psychotherapy, Rogers was given a five-minute standing ovation, the only one so honored. Yet one looks in vain in the papers presented by the other participants (Zeig, 1987) for evidence of his influence. In 1986, David Cain, supported by Carl Rogers, initiated the publication of the *Person-Centered Review*—a journal devoted to person-centered theory, research, and practice. It ceased publication after five years for lack of subscribers. (Interestingly enough, two similar journals—*The Person-Centered Journal* and *Person-Centered Quarterly*—began publication in 1994; it will be interesting to see if they fare any better.)

Perhaps we are overly pessimistic, but the immediate future of client-centered therapy in our view does not appear to be promising, particularly in the current climate of emphasis on short-term, directive, cognitively oriented, problem-solving therapy. Yet one cannot help but be convinced that in the long run the philosophy and theory, and the practice as well, of client-centered therapy will prevail.

REFERENCES

Barrett-Lennard, G. T. (1962). Dimensions of therapist response as causal factors in therapeutic change. *Psychological Monographs, 76,* no. 43 (whole no. 362).

Beck, C. E. (1963). *Philosophical foundations of guidance.* Englewood Cliffs, NJ: Prentice-Hall.

Bergin, A. E., & Suinn, R. M. (1975). Individual psychotherapy and behavior therapy. *Annual Review of Psychology, 26,* 509–556.

Beutler, L. E., Machado, P. P. P., & Neufeldt, S. A. (1994). Therapist variables. In A. E. Bergin & S. L. Garfield (Eds.). *Handbook of psychotherapy and behavior change* (4th ed., pp. 229–269). New York: Wiley.

Boy, A. V., & Pine, G. J. (1990). *A person-centered foundation for counseling and psychotherapy,* Springfield, IL: Charles C Thomas.

Brodley, B. T. (1990). Client-centered therapy and experiential: Two different therapies. In G. Lietaer, J. Rombauts, & R. Van Balen (Eds.). *Client-centered and experiential therapy in the nineties* (pp. 87–108). Leuven, Belgium: Leuven University Press.

Butler, J. M. (1974). The iconic mode in psychotherapy. In D. N. Wexler & L. N. Rice (Eds.). *Innovations in client-centered therapy* (pp. 171–203). New York: Wiley.

Carkhuff, R. R. (1969). *Helping and human relations.* Vol. 1: *Selection and training.* Vol. 2: *Practice and research.* New York: Holt, Rinehart and Winston.

Chronological Bibliography of the Works of Carl R. Rogers, 1930–1985 Inclusive (1986). *Person-Centered Review, 1,* 83–99.

Combs, A. W., & Snygg, D. (1959). *Individual behavior: A perceptual approach to behavior* (rev. ed.). New York: Harper & Row.

Ellis, A. (1959). Requisite conditions of therapeutic personality change. *Journal of Consulting Psychology, 23,* 538–549.

Ford, D. H., & Urban, H. B. (1963). *Systems of psychotherapy.* New York: Wiley.

Gendlin, E. T. (1962a). Client-centered development in work with schizophrenics. *Journal of Counseling Psychology, 9,* 205–212.

Gendlin, E. T. (1962b). *Experiencing and the creation of meaning.* New York: Free Press.

Gendlin, E. T. (1970a). Existentialism and experiential psychotherapy. In J. T. Hart & T. M. Tomlison (Eds.). *New directions in client-centered therapy* (pp. 70–94). Boston: Houghton Mifflin. (Originally published in C. Moustakas (Ed.). *Existential child therapy.* New York: Basic Books, 1966.)

Gendlin, E. T. (1970b). A theory of personality change. In J. T. Hart & T. M. Tomlinson (Eds.). *New directions in client-centered therapy* (pp. 129–173). (Originally published in P. Worchel & D. Byrne (Eds.). *Personality change.* New York: Wiley, 1964.)

Gendlin, E. T. (1974). Client-centered and experiential psychotherapy. In D. A. Wexler & L. N. Rice (Eds.). *Innovations in client-centered therapy* (pp. 221–246). New York: Wiley.

Gendlin, E. T. (1981). *Focusing.* New York: Everett House. (Rev. ed. 1984. New York: Bantam Books.)

Gendlin, E. T., & Tomlinson, T. M. (1967). A scale for the rating of experiencing. In C. R. Rogers, E. T. Gendlin, D. J. Kiesler, & C. B. Truax (Eds.). *The therapeutic relation and its impact: A study of psychotherapy with schizophrenics* (pp. 589–592). Madison: University of Wisconsin Press.

Gomes-Schwartz, B., Hadley, S. W., & Strupp, H. H. (1978). Individual psychotherapy and behavior therapy. *Annual Review of Psychology, 29,* 435–471.

Gurman, A. S. (1977). The patient's perception of the therapeutic relationship. In A. S. Gurman & A. M. Razin (Eds.). *Effective psychotherapy.* New York: Pergamon Press.

Hart, J. T., & Tomlinson, T. M. (Eds.) (1970). *New directions in client-centered therapy.* Boston: Houghton Mifflin.

Kirschenbaum, H. (1979). *On becoming Carl Rogers.* New York: Dell.

Kirschenbaum, H., & Henderson, V. L. (Ed.) (1989a). *The Carl Rogers reader.* Boston: Houghton Mifflin.

Kirschenbaum, H., & Henderson, V. L. (Eds.) (1989b). *Carl Rogers: Dialogues.* Boston: Houghton Mifflin.

Lambert, M. J., DeJulio, S. S., & Stein, D. (1978). Therapist interpersonal skills. *Psychological Bulletin, 85,* 467–489.

Malcolm, N. (1964). Behaviorism as a philosophy of psychology. In T. W. Wann (Ed.). *Behaviorism and phenomenology.* Chicago: University of Chicago Press.

Mearns, D., & Thorne, R. (1988). *Person-centered counseling in action.* London & Beverly Hills, CA: Sage.

Mitchell, K. M., Bozarth, J. D., & Krauft, C. C. (1977). A reappraisal of the therapeutic effectiveness of accurate empathy, non-possessive warmth, and genuineness. In A. S. Gurman & A. M. Razin (Eds.). *Effective psychotherapy* (pp. 482–502). New York: Pergamon Press.

Nelson-Jones, R., & Patterson, C. H. (1974). Some effects of counselor training. *British Journal of Guidance and Counseling, 2,* 2–14.

Nelson-Jones, R., & Patterson, C. H. (1976). Effects of counselor training: Further findings. *British Journal of Guidance and Counseling, 4,* 66–73.

Orlinsky, D. E., Grawe, K., & Parks, B. K. (1994). Process and outcome in psychotherapy—noch eminal. In A. E. Bergin & S. L. Garfield (Eds.). *Handbook of psychotherapy and behavior change* (4th ed., pp. 270–376). New York: Wiley.

Orlinsky, D. E., & Howard, K. I. (1978). The relation of process to outcome in psychotherapy. In S. L. Garfield & A. E. Bergin (Eds.). *Handbook of psychotherapy and behavior change* (2nd ed.) (pp. 283–330). New York: Wiley.

Orlinsky, D. E., & Howard, K. I. (1986). Process and outcome in psychotherapy. In S. L. Garfield & A. E. Bergin (Eds.). *Handbook of psychotherapy and behavior change* (3rd ed., pp. 311–384). New York: Wiley.

Parloff, M. B., Waskow, I. E., & Wolfe, R. E. (1978). Research on therapist variables in relation to process and outcome. In S. L. Garfield & A. E. Bergin (Eds.). *Handbook of psychotherapy and behavior change* (2nd ed.) (pp. 233–282). New York: Wiley.

Patterson, C. H. (1959). *Counseling and psychotherapy: Theory and practice.* New York: Harper & Row.

Patterson, C. H. (1967). Effects of counselor education on personality. *Journal of Counseling Psychology, 14,* 444–448.

Patterson, C. H. (1974). *Relationship counseling and psychotherapy.* New York: Harper & Row.

Patterson, C. H. (1984). Empathy, warmth and genuineness in psychotherapy: A review of reviews. *Psychotherapy, 21,* 431–438.

Patterson, C. H. (1985). *The therapeutic relationship.* Pacific Grove, CA: Brooks/Cole.

Patterson, C. H. (1990). On being client-centered. *Person-Centered Review, 5,* 425–442.

Patterson, C. H., & Nelson-Jones, R. (1975). Measuring client-centered attitudes. *British Journal of Guidance and Counseling, 3,* 228–236.

Porter, E. H., Jr. (1950). *An introduction to therapeutic counseling.* Boston: Houghton Mifflin.

Rice, L. N. (1974). The evocative function of the therapist. In D. A. Wexler & L. N. Rice (Eds.). *Innovations in client-centered therapy* (pp. 289–311). New York: Wiley.

Rogers, C. R. (1939). *The clinical treatment of the problem child.* Boston: Houghton Mifflin.

Rogers, C. R. (1942). *Counseling and psychotherapy: Newer concepts in practice.* Boston: Houghton Mifflin.

Rogers, C. R. (1951). *Client-centered therapy: Its current practices, implications, and theory.* Boston: Houghton Mifflin.

Rogers, C. R. (1957). The necessary and sufficient conditions of therapeutic personality change. *Journal of Consulting Psychology, 21,* 95–103.

Rogers, C. R. (1959). A theory of therapy, personality, and interpersonal relationships, as developed in the client-centered framework. In S. Koch (Ed.). *Psychology: A study of science. Study I: Conceptual and systematic. Vol. 3: Formulations of the person and the social context* (pp. 184–256). New York: McGraw-Hill.

Rogers, C. R. (1961a). *On becoming a person.* Boston: Houghton Mifflin.

Rogers, C. R. (1961b). The process equation of psychotherapy. *American Journal of Psychotherapy, 15,* 27–45.

Rogers, C. R. (1962). The interpersonal relationship: The core of guidance. *Harvard Educational Review, 32,* 416–429.

Rogers, C. R. (1964). Toward a science of the person. In T. W. Wann (Ed.). *Behaviorism and phenomenology.* Chicago: University of Chicago Press.

Rogers, C. R. (1969). *Freedom to learn: A view of what education might become.* Columbus, OH: Merrill.

Rogers, C. R. (1970). *Carl Rogers on encounter groups.* New York: Harper & Row.

Rogers, C. R. (1972). *Becoming partners: Marriage and its alternatives.* New York: Delacorte.

Rogers, C. R. (1975). Empathic: An unappreciated way of being. *The Counseling Psychologist, 5* (2), 2–10.

Rogers, C. R. (1977). *Carl Rogers on personal power.* New York: Delacorte.

Rogers, C. R. (1980). *A way of being.* Boston: Houghton Mifflin.

Rogers, C. R. (1983). *Freedom to learn for the 80s.* Columbus, OH: Merrill.

Rogers, C. R., & Coulson, W. (Eds.). (1968). *Man and the science of man.* Columbus, OH: Merrill.

Rogers C. R., & Dymond, R. (Eds.). (1954). *Psychotherapy and personality change.* Chicago: University of Chicago Press.

Rogers, C. R., Gendlin, E. T., Kiesler, D. J., & Truax, C. B. (Eds.). (1967). *The therapeutic relationship and its impact.* Madison: University of Wisconsin Press.

Rogers, C. R., Raskin, N. J., Seeman, J., Sheerer, E., Stock, D., Haigh, G., Hoffman, A., & Carr, A. (1949). A coordinated research in psychotherapy. *Journal of Consulting Psychology, 13,* 149–220.

Rogers, C. R., & Stevens, B. (1967). *Person to person.* Moab, UT: Real People Press.

Snyder, W. U. (Ed.) (1947). *Casebook of nondirective counseling.* Boston: Houghton Mifflin.

Snyder, W. U., & Snyder, B. J. (1961). *The psychotherapy relationship.* New York: Macmillan.

Snygg, D., & Combs, D. (1949). *Individual behavior: A new frame of reference for psychology.* New York: Harper & Bros.

Stewart, C. C. (1958). Attitude change following a counseling seminar. *Personnel and Guidance Journal, 37,* 273–275.

Stubbs, J. P., & Bozarth, J. D. (1994). The Dodo Bird revisted: A qualitative study of psychotherapy efficacy research. *Applied and Preventive Psychology, 3,* 109–120.

Thorne, B. (1992). *Carl Rogers.* London: Sage.

Truax, C. B., & Carkhuff, R. R. (1967). *Toward effective counseling and psychotherapy.* Chicago: Aldine.

Truax, C. B., & Mitchell, K. M. (1971). Research on certain therapist interpersonal skills in relation to process and outcome. In A. E. Bergin & S. L. Garfield (Eds.). *Handbook of psychotherapy and behavior change* (pp. 299–344). New York: Wiley.

Wexler, D. A. (1974). A cognitive theory of experiencing, self-actualization and therapeutic process. In D. A. Wexler & L. N. Rice (Eds.). *Innovations in client-centered therapy* (pp. 49–116). New York: Wiley.

Wexler, D. A., & Rice, L. N. (Eds.) (1974). *Innovations in client-centered therapy.* New York: Wiley.

Zeig, J. K. (Ed.) (1987). *The evolution of psychotherapy.* New York: Brunner/Mazel.

part five

EXISTENTIAL PSYCHOTHERAPY

Chapter 14 Logotherapy: Frankl

In our presentations thus far, we have considered several different conceptions of therapy, with some approaches adopting more of a rational or mainly cognitive problem-solving process and others focusing more on attitudes, feelings, and affects. Concomitant changes in methods and techniques have accompanied these different foci. The concern with understanding the client as he/she exists in the world is at the basis of yet another approach (or approaches) to psychotherapy. The adjective *existential* has been attached to such a view, with the general name *existential psychotherapy* being applied to the therapeutic approach. The general approach was developed independently in various parts of Europe (May & Yalom, 1989). A number of psychiatrists, many of whom were trained in Freudian psychoanalysis, have been concerned with the relation of existential concepts to psychotherapy. They include Binswanger (1956), Boss (1957), Frankl (1965), Marcel (1948), and Sonneman (1954). In this country, Rollo May (1961), James Bugental (1976, 1978, 1981, 1987), and Irvin Yalom (1980) have been perhaps the foremost exponents of an existential approach to psychotherapy, although others such as Lefabre (1963) and van Kaam (1961, 1962) have contributed.

The development of existentialism has been sketched by May (1958b). It is in part an outgrowth of the phenomenological movement in philosophy (Spiegelberg, 1960b), with Husserl's (1929) phenomenology influencing it particularly (Spiegelberg, 1960a). Mainly, phenomenology contributed the method of approach to the person and his/her world. Existential philosophy, the second major contributor, had its origins in the work of Kierkegaard (1944, 1954a, 1954b) and Jaspers (1955). Later existential philosophers, such as Heidegger (1949, 1962), Marcel (1948), and Sartre (1953), were influenced by the phenomenology of Husserl. Existential philosophy is concerned with the nature of humanity, with its existence in the modern world, and with the meaning of this existence to the individual. Its focus is on the individual's most immediate experience, his/her own existence and the experiencing of this existence.

Existentialism is defined by May (1958b) as

the endeavor to understand man by cutting below the cleavage between subject and object which has bedeviled Western thought and science since shortly after the Renaissance. . . . It arose specifically just over a hundred years ago in Kierkegaard's violent protest against the reigning rationalism of his day, Hegel's "totalitariansim of reason," to use Maritain's phrase. (p. 11)

The individual is not a substance or a mechanism but an emerging, becoming, or *existing* being, and *exist* means literally "to stand out; to emerge." Existence has been opposed to essence, which is an abstraction and which has been the concern of traditional science. However, this opposition has been reconciled unwittingly, as Tillich (1961) notes, by Sartre's denial of it in his statement, "Man's essence is his existence"; that is, the essence of a human being is the power to create oneself.

The human being as the subject can never be separated from the object that the human being observes. The meaning of objective fact depends on the subject's relationship to it. Human beings exist in a world of which they are a part—beings-in-the world. Existentialism focuses on the individual's experience—particularly the nonintellectual modes of experience—and on existence in its total involvement in a situation within a world. It makes an individual's experience the center of things; its "frame of reference is in man as he exists inside, in the full range of his fears, hopes, anxieties, and terrors. . . . The fundamental contribution of existential therapy is its understanding of man as being. . . . The fundamental character of existential analysis is, thus, that it is concerned with *ontology,* the science of being, and with *Dasein,* the existence of this particular being sitting opposite the psychotherapist" (Van Dusen, 1957).

Nor is there a single existential psychotherapy; rather, there are numerous approaches, often unsystematic and with little attention given to techniques. Sartre's analysis is a philosophy rather than a clinical practice. Binswanger's (1958) analyses are, as van Kaam (1961) notes, not examples of how to do therapy but only suggestions that "the therapist has to foster a participation of the whole human existence of the patient in the existence of others in order to overcome his anxiety."

Just as there is no one existential psychotherapy, there is no one school of existentialist philosophy either. There are differences and conficts among schools. Van Dusen (1957) sees them on a continuum, with some, such as Sartre, emphasizing the nonbeing end and with others such as Marcel emphasizing the being end of the range of human experiences. One end is characterized by pessimism—darkness and death—and the other by optimism—light and life.

While there is thus no single theory or approach, there are perhaps some common aspects or elements basic to all existential approaches to psychotherapy. These may include the following themes (Braaten, 1961; May, 1958b; van Kaam, 1961).

1. The distinctive character of human existence is *Dasein,* the being who is there, who has a there in that the being knows he/she is there and can take a stand with reference to that fact. Human beings differ from all other animals in their capac-

ity for being aware of (conscious of) themselves, as well as of the events that influence them and of the past, present, and future as a continuum. This makes possible choices and decisions. A person is thus responsible because he/she can choose. "Self-consciousness itself—the person's potential for awareness that the vast complex, protean flow of experience is his experience—brings in inescapably the element of decision at every moment" (May & van Kaam, 1963, p. 78).

Persons are thus free and are what they make of themselves; heredity, environment, upbringing, and culture are alibis. External influences are limiting but not determining.

Man is the being who can be conscious of, and therefore responsible for, his existence. It is this capacity to become aware of his own being which distinguishes the human being from other beings. The existential therapists think of man not only as "being-for-itself." Binswanger and other authors . . . speak of Dasein choosing this or that, meaning "the person who-is-responsible-for-his-existence choosing." (May, 1958a, p. 41)

2. Existentialists share the "conviction that it is impossible to think of the subject and the world as separate from each other" (van Kaam, 1961). Terms such as *participation, encounter, presence,* and *Dasein* express this conviction. Human beings live in three worlds simultaneously, the *Umwelt,* or the biological world, without self-awareness; the *Mitwelt,* or the world of interrelationships or encounters with other persons, involving mutual awareness; and the *Eigenwelt,* or the world of self-identity or being-in-itself (May & Yalom, 1989).

3. Thus, the human being is not a static entity but is in a constant state of transition, emerging, becoming, evolving, that is, *being.* The human being actualizes himself/herself, or fulfills inner potentialities by continuous participation in a world of things and events and always in encounters or dialogue with other people. Some qualities of being can be distinctly developed only in relation to another person. Therapy is an encounter or a dialogue in which the client is enabled to develop certain human qualities. Being is thus not something given once and for all but is constantly developing. The future is, therefore, the significant tense for human beings.

4. Human beings also know that at some future time, they will not be. Being implies the fact of nonbeing, and the meaning of existence involves the fact of nonexistence. Existentialism holds that death gives life reality; it is the one absolute fact of life. Human beings are aware of the fact that they must die; and they must confront this fact. They are also capable of choosing not to be at any instant. They are conscious of isolation, nothingness, loss of individual significance or identity, alienation, or emptiness (see Yalom, 1980).

5. The threat of nonbeing is the source of "normal" anxiety, hostility, and aggression—normal because the threat is always present in all individuals. This anxiety (sometimes called "existential anxiety") is "an ontological characteristic of man, rooted in his very existence as such" (May, 1958a, p. 50). Anxiety strikes at the core of the individual's self-esteem—the sense of value as a self; it is the threat of dissolution of the self, the loss of existence itself. It involves a conflict

between being and nonbeing, between the emerging potentiality of being, on the one hand, and the loss of present security on the other. It is a concomitant of freedom. Guilt accompanies the failure to fulfill one's potentialities.

6. Being is not reducible to the introjection of social and ethical norms. The self-esteem based on a sense of being is not simply the reflection of others' views of the individual. Although it involves social relatedness, it presupposes *Eigenwelt,* the "own world" of a sense of self-identity or being-in-itself. Each individual, then, is not a carbon copy cut from social pressures and norms but is unique, singular, and irreplaceable—and thus significant.

7. Human beings have the capacity to transcend the immediate situation, to rise above the past, to transcend themselves. This capacity is inherent in the term *exist.* Human beings exemplify transcendence in their concept of the possible, in bringing the past and the future to bear on the present, in thinking in symbols, in seeing themselves as others see them, and perhaps most characteristically in the capacity to be aware that they are the ones who are acting—to see themselves as both subject and object at the same time. "Self-conscious implies self-transcendence" (May, 1958a, p. 74). The capacity for transcendence is the basis of freedom, since it opens up possibilities for choice. There are, however, limits to life and to being that must be accepted.

8. The modern person, "normal" as well as neurotic, is characterized by alienation from the world and from the community. Psychiatrists and other therapists are no longer presented with the symptoms with which they were presented while Freud was developing his theories. Increasingly, the symptoms or complaints are loneliness, isolation, depersonalization, and detachment. The person has lost his/her world, is homeless and a stranger in a world that he/she not only did not make, but also is no longer a part of.

Ellenberger (1958) selects three concepts of existential psychotherapy as especially significant: (1) the concept of *existential neurosis,* according to which emotional disturbances are a result of an inability to see meaning in life rather than of repressed drives or trauma, a weak ego, or life stress; (2) the concept of the therapeutic relationship as an encounter or a new relationship opening up new horizons, rather than a transference relationship repeating the past; and (3) the concept of *kairos,* critical points when the patient is ready for therapy and when rapid change and improvement are possible.

While these elements and concepts seem to characterize most, if not all, existential therapies, they are not sufficient to develop *an* existential psychotherapy. May (1963) feels that it would be a mistake for a special school of existential psychotherapy to be developed. Indeed,

> there cannot be any special existential psychiatry. . . . Existentialism is an *attitude,* an approach to human beings, rather than a school or group. Like philosophy, it has to do with *presuppositions* underlying psychiatric and psychoanalytic techniques. The existential approach is not a system of therapy—though it makes highly important contributions to therapy. It is not a set of techniques—though it may give birth to them. It is rather a concern with understanding the structure of the human being and his experience, which to a greater or lesser extent should underlie *all* technique. (p. 8)

May also feels that concern about techniques is undesirable, since "it is precisely the overemphasis upon techniques, an overemphasis which goes along with the tendency to see the human being as an object to be calculated, managed, 'analyzed,'" that blocks the understanding that existentialism seeks. "The central task and responsibility of the therapist is to seek to understand the patient as a being and as being in his world." Technique follows rather than precedes understanding.

Many existential therapists, particularly those who have been influenced by Binswanger, appear to use the techniques of psychoanalysis. Binswanger (1958) essentially sees existential analysis as an "anthropological type of scientific investigation," rather than as a method of psychotherapy for which psychoanalysis is indispensable. His discussions are concerned with the analysis of cases in terms of existential concepts instead of being discussions of a therapeutic approach.

While existential therapists appear to use many of the techniques common to other approaches, particularly psychoanalysis, certain aspects or emphases seem to characterize existential therapies and to distinguish them as a group from other approaches. May (1958a; cf. May & Yalom, 1989) discusses six characteristics:

1. Existential therapists evidence considerabale variability of technique. They are flexible and versatile, "varying from patient to patient and from one phase to another in the treatment of the same patient," depending on what appears to be necessary "to best reveal the existence of this particular patient at this moment of his history" and "what will best illuminate his being-in-the-world" (May, 1958a, p. 78).

2. Existential therapists, particularly those with a psychoanalytic background, use psychological dynamisms such as transference, repression, and resistance but always in terms of their meaning for the existential situation of the patient's own immediate life.

3. Emphasis is placed on *presence,* or the reality of the therapist-patient relationship, in which the therapist is "concerned not with his own problems but with understanding and experiencing so far as possible the being of the patient" (May, 1958a, p. 80) by entering and participating in the patient's field. This emphasis is shared by therapists of other schools who see the patient as a being to be understood rather than as an object to be analyzed. "Any therapist is existential to the extent that, with all his technical training and his knowledge of transference and dynamisms, he is still able to relate to the patient, as 'one existence communicating to another,' to use Binswanger's phrase" (May, 1958a, p. 81). The patient is not a subject but an "existential partner," and the relationship is an encounter or "being-together" with each other in genuine presence (Binswanger, 1958). The concern of the therapist is to provide a meaningful relationship as a mutual experience, not a relationship in which the therapist influences the patient.

4. The therapist attempts to avoid behavior that would impede or destroy the existence of full presence in the relationship. Since full encounter with another person can produce anxiety, the therapist may tend to protect himself/herself by treating the other person as "only a patient" or as an object or by focusing on behavior mechanisms. Technique may be used as a way of blocking presence.

5. "The aim of therapy is that the patient *experience* his existence as real. The purpose is that he become aware of his existence fully, which includes becoming aware of his potentialities and becoming able to act on the basis of them" (May, 1958a, p. 85). Interpretation of mechanisms or dynamisms, as a part of existential therapy, will "always be in the context of this person's becoming aware of his existence" (May, 1958a, p. 86). Therapy "proceeds *not* merely by showing the patient where, when and to what extent he has failed to realize the fullness of his humanity, but tries to make him *experience* this as radically as possible" (Binswanger, 1958). This is important because it is one of the characteristics of the neurotic process in our day that individuals have lost a sense of being and, in an attempt to be objective about themselves, have come to view themselves as objects or mechanisms. Simply to give the individual new ways of thinking of himself/herself as a mechanism structures the neurosis, and therapy that does this only reflects and continues the fragmentation of the culture that leads to neurosis. Such therapy may result in the loss of symptoms and of anxiety, but it does so because the patient conforms to the culture and constricts his/her existence, giving up freedom.

6. Existential therapy helps the patient develop the attitude or orientation of commitment. Such an attitude involves decisions and actions but not decisions and actions for their own sake. It is, rather, commitment to some point in the patient's own existence. Such commitment is necessary before knowledge is possible. "The patient cannot permit himself to get insight or knowledge until he is ready to decide, takes a definite orientation to life, and has made the preliminary decisions along the way" (May, 1958a, p. 87).

A seventh characteristic might be added: In the therapeutic situation, existential psychotherapy focuses on the here and now. The past and future are involved insofar as they enter into the present experience. The here and now includes not only the patient's experiences outside therapy, but also the patient's relationship with the therapist. The patient's life history may be investigated, but not in order to explain it in terms of any school of psychotherapy. Instead, it is understood as a modification of the total structuring of the patient as being-in-the-world (Binswanger, 1958).

These aspects or emphases of existential psychotherapy are hardly enough on which to base a practice. The underlying concepts are, of course, of first importance, and it is significant that the object of concern or focus of existential therapy—existence as it is experienced rather than symptoms—differs from that of most conventional therapies. However, it is necessary that the concepts be implemented by methods, and it would be supposed that a theory such as existentialism differs enough from other theories in its concepts and principles that it would lead to somewhat different methods. However, there is nowhere a thorough, systematic statement of the nature and procedures of existential psychotherapy, particularly as the procedures may differ from those of other approaches to psychotherapy. Lyons (1961) suggested that there is little that is new or different from other therapies. However, he agrees that the approach has had an influence on the field of psychotherapy as a corrective to psychoanalysis and, as Alexander (1959) stated it, as a counterbalance to the psychoanalytic trend toward concentration on techniques.

We must still ask how the existential therapist operates, how the therapist interacts with clients, and how the therapist participates in the therapeutic relationship. If the therapist uses essentially psychoanalytic techniques, how does he/she use them, and how, then, does existential therapy differ from psychoanalytic therapy or psychoanalysis? If the therapeutic relationship is defined as an encounter, what does this mean? What does it mean to say that the therapist is authentic? If the therapist is concerned with the mode of being-in-the-world of the client, how does he/she gain access to this world? When the therapist understands the client's mode of being-in-the-world, what does he/she do with this understanding? Does the therapist interpret in terms of existential concepts? Is existential therapy an interpretive psychotherapy, then, that uses another theoretical system as a basis for approaching, understanding, and finally interpreting the experiences of the client? Hora (1961) contends that special interpretations are not required in existential psychotherapy, since "that which is speaks for itself, provided it is understood phenomenologically rather than interpreted in accordance with certain theoretical presuppositions. That which is understood needs no interpretation. That which is interpreted is seldom understood."

Binswanger (1958) appears to reject any attempt to systematize the approach. He rejects theory because he feels that it leads therapists to try to make the client's behavior fit their theories and that it may result in therapists' attending only to the behavioral phenomena that fit their categories of analysis, thus obstructing a full understanding of the client. However, can therapists enter into client relationships without being influenced by their own concepts, ideas, hypotheses, theories, or values? If therapists are to be authentic, does not their own view of the world, and their own being-in-the-world enter into the relationship? Can a person enter the world of another person and view it from that individual's point of view? Can a person view things as they are or as they manifest themselves without bias or without a prior assumption (Husserl's method of pure phenomenology)?

It remains true that those who profess to engage in a form of psychotherapy that has been influenced by existentialism have not faced the problem of methods. If they feel that techniques must be subordinated and must not interfere with the authenticity of the relationship, they should be concerned with avoiding involvement with techniques and with defining how they function in order to do so. They not only have not dealt with this problem as a problem, but also have not provided illustrations or demonstrations of how they function so that a person could attempt to understand or learn their methods and procedures. These methods and procedures must exist and, therefore, must be given attention, unless the approach is to be considered entirely intuitive.

Although, as Lyons (1961) pointed out, a number of existential therapists have published articles or books on existential therapy, "as a full scale exposition of theory and practice, there is next to nothing from any of the major European figures in this movement." Such a situation poses a problem in terms of the presentation of this approach. However, as Lyons also noted, there is one exception—Viktor Frankl. Frankl is possibly not typical (if anyone is) of the existential approach. While earlier he used the term *existenzanalysis,* he later adopted the word *logotherapy* to distinguish his approach from Binswanger's existential analysis, or daseinsanalysis, and its related approach to psychotherapy. Frankl's work is more accessible to students and is less obtuse than that of most other existential writers. For these reasons, his approach has been selected for inclusion here.

May and van Kaam (1963) noted that a number of American psychiatrists and psychologists have held existential viewpoints (including Wiliam James, Adolph Meyer, Harry

Stack Sullivan, Gordon Allport, Carl Rogers, Henry Murray, and Abraham Maslow). They go on to say that "what has been lacking . . . has been a consistent underlying structure which would give unity to the work of these psychiatrists and psychologists who are concerned with man and his immediate existence." They continue: "We propose here that the existential approach, recast and re-born into our American language and thought forms, can and will give this underlying structure." This recasting, though, has not yet occurred.

May, Yalom, and Bugental are perhaps the best-known American representatives of existential therapy. Bugental (1976, 1978, 1981, 1987) has developed an existential approach that is built on a psychoanalytic base. He has described his methods in a series of case studies. A wide range of techniques is included, appearing to be used on an intuitive basis.

It might be argued that this is the nature of existential therapy—that it is, on the one hand, the technique of no technique and, on the other hand, the use of any and all techniques—but this is not necessarily the case. There is an increasing similarity between existential concepts and client-centered therapy (cf. Rice & Greenberg, 1992). It must have been evident to the reader that many, if not most, of the concepts discussed above characterize client-centered therapy, which emphasizes the immediate experiencing of the psychotherapist. The phenomenology represented in existentialism is fundamental to and is implemented in client-centered therapy—with its focus on the client's perceptions and the necessity of the therapist's entering into the client's frame of reference. It would appear that client-centered therapy has been moving toward existentialism; van Kaam (1962), in "Counseling from the Viewpoint of Existential Psychology," differs very little from exponents of the client-centered approach. May (1958a) recognizes the existential nature of client-centered therapy, and Wolf (1950) notes its similarity to existentialism.

Therefore, it should not be too surprising that a therapist trained in the client-centered approach should have also developed an existential approach. Gendlin (1962a, 1962b), for example, has focused on the immediate felt experiencing of the client. He writes that "psychotherapy generally, with any type of population seems to involve not only verbalization, but more fundamentally, the client's inward data, concretely felt, seem to be the actual stuff of psychotherapy, not the words." The therapist, however, must be able to understand and respond to the client's felt experiencing. Gendlin has come to grips with this in the development of what he calls experiential psychotherapy, which is essentially an extension or an elaboration of client-centered therapy in an existential direction. However, Gendlin's experiential therapy goes beyond client-centered therapy in its directive focusing upon the client's felt experiencing (see Chapter 13). As noted in Chapter 13, experiential psychotherapy focuses on the basic method of client-centered therapy—the empathic response—as the way of encountering the felt experiencing of the client. Gendlin's systematic formulation of this approach may well become *the* American existential psychotherapy (see Gendlin, 1970a, 1970b, 1973, 1974, 1984).

REFERENCES

Alexander, F. (1959). Impressions from the Fourth International Congress of Psychotherapy. *Psychiatry, 22,* 89–95.

Binswanger, L. (1956). Existential analysis and psychotherapy. In F. Fromm-Reichmann & J. L. Moreno (Eds.). *Progress in psychotherapy: 1956* (pp. 144–148). New York: Grune & Stratton.

Binswanger, L. (1958). The existential analysis school of thought. In R. May, E. Angel, & H. F. Ellenberger (Eds.). *Existence* (pp. 191–213). New York: Basic Books.

Boss, M. (1957). "Daseinsanalysis" and psychotherapy. In J. H. Masserman & J. L. Moreno (Eds.). *Progress in psychotherapy: 1957* (pp. 156–161). New York: Grune & Stratton.

Braaten, L. J. (1961). The main themes of existentialism from the viewpoint of a psychotherapist. *Mental Hygiene, 45,* 10–17.

Bugental, J. F. T. (1976). *The search for existential identity: Patient-therapist dialogues in humanistic psychology.* San Francisco: Jossey-Bass.

Bugental, J. F. T. (1978). *Psychotherapy and process: The fundamentals of an existential-humanistic approach.* Reading, MA: Addison-Wesley.

Bugental, J. F. T. (1981). *The search for authenticity: An existential-analytic approach to psychotherapy.* New York: Irvington.

Bugental, J. F. T. (1987). *The art of the psychotherapist.* New York: Norton.

Ellenberger, H. F. (1958). A clinical introduction to psychiatric phenomenology and existential analysis. In R. May, E. Angel, & H. F. Ellenberger (Eds.). *Existence* (pp. 92–124). New York: Basic Books.

Frankl, V. E. (1965). *The doctor and the soul* (2nd ed.). New York: Knopf.

Gendlin, E. T. (1962a). Client-centered developments and work with schizophrenics. *Journal of Counseling Psychology, 9,* 205–212.

Gendlin, E. T. (1962b). *Experiencing and the creation of meaning.* New York: Free Press.

Gendlin, E. T. (1970a). Existentialism and experiential psychotherapy. In J. T. Hart & T. M. Tomlinson (Eds.). *New directions in client-centered therapy* (pp. 70–94). Boston: Houghton Mifflin. [Originally published in C. Moustakas (Ed.). *Existential child therapy.* New York: Basic Books, 1966.]

Gendlin, E. T. (1970b). A theory of personality change. In J. T. Hart & T. M. Tomlison (Eds.). *New directions in client-centered therapy* (pp. 129–173). Boston: Houghton Mifflin. [Originally published in P. Worchel & D. Byrne (Eds.). *Personality change.* New York: Wiley, 1964.]

Gendlin, E. T. (1973). Experiential psychotherapy. In R. Corsini (Ed.). *Current psychotherapies.* Itasca, IL: F. E. Peacock.

Gendlin, E. T. (1974). Client-centered and experiential psychotherapy. In D. A. Wexler & L. N. Rice (Eds.). *Innovations in client-centered therapy.* New York: Wiley.

Gendlin, E. T. (1984). *Focusing.* New York: Bantam Books.

Heidegger, M. (1949). *Existence and being.* Chicago: Regnery.

Heidegger, M. (1962). *Being and time.* London: SCM Press.

Hora, T. (1961). Existential psychiatry and group psychotherapy. *American Journal of Psychoanalysis, 21,* 58–70.

Husserl, E. (1929). Phenomenology. In *Encyclopaedia Britannica* (vol. 17, 14th ed.). (pp. 699–702).

Jaspers, K. (1955). *Reason and existence.* New York: Noonday.

Kierkegaard, S. A. (1944). *Either/or: A fragment of life.* Princeton, NJ: Princeton University Press.

Kierkegaard, S. A. (1954a). *Fear and trembling.* New York: Doubleday.

Kierkegaard, S. A. (1954b). *The sickness unto death.* New York: Doubleday.

Lefabre, L. B. (1963). Existentialism and psychotherapy. *Review of Existential Psychology and Psychiatry, 3,* 271–285.

Lyons, J. (1961). Existential psychotherapy: Fact, hope, fiction. *Journal of Abnormal Social Psychology, 62,* 242–249.

Marcel, G. (1948). *The philosophy of existence.* London: Harvill.

Marcel, F. (1951). *Homo Victor.* Chicago: Regnery.

May, R. (1958a). Contributions of existential psychotherapy. In R. May, E. Angel, & H. F. Ellenberger (Eds.). *Existence* (pp. 37–91). New York: Basic Books.

May, R. (1958b). The origins and significance of the existential movement in psychology. In R. May, E. Angel, & H. F. Ellenberger (Eds.). *Existence* (pp. 3–36). New York: Basic Books.

May, R. (1961). The emergence of existential psychology. In R. May (Ed.). *Existential psychology* (pp. 11–51). New York: Random House.

May, R. (1963). Dangers in the relation of existentialism to psychotherapy. *Review of Existential Psychology and Psychiatry, 3,* 5–10.

May, R., & van Kaam, A. (1963). Existential theory and therapy. In J. H. Masserman (Ed.). *Current psychiatric therapies* (vol. 3). (pp. 74–81). New York: Grune & Stratton.

May, R., & Yalom, I. D. (1989). Existential therapy. In R. J. Corsini & D. Wedding (Eds.). *Current psychotherapies* (4th ed., pp. 363–402). Itasca, IL: F. E. Peacock.

Rice, L. N., & Greenberg, L. S. (1992). Humanistic approaches to psychotherapy. In D. K. Freedheim (Ed.). *History of psychotherapy* (pp. 197–224). Washington, DC: American Psychological Association.

Sartre, J. P. (1953). *Existential psychoanalysis.* New York: Philosophical Library.

Sonneman, U. (1954). *Existence and therapy.* New York: Grune & Stratton.

Spiegelberg, H. (1960a). Husserl's phenomenology and existentialism. *Journal of Philosophy, 57,* 62–74.

Spiegelberg, H. (1960b). *The phenomenological movement: A historical introduction* (2 vols). The Hague: Martinus Nijhoff.

Tillich, P. (1961). Existentialism and psychotherapy. *Review of Existential Psychology and Psychiatry, 1,* 8–16.

Van Dusen, W. (1957). The theory and practice of existential analysis. *American Journal of Psychotherapy, 11,* 310–322.

van Kaam, A. (1961). The impact of existential phenomenology on the psychological literature of western Europe. *Review of Existential Psychology and Psychiatry, 1,* 62–91.

van Kaam, A. (1962). Counseling from the viewpoint of existential psychology. *Harvard Educational Review, 32,* 403–415.

Wolf, W. (1950). *Values and personality.* New York: Grune & Stratton.

Yalom, I. D. (1980). *Existential psychotherapy.* New York: Basic Books.

chapter *14*

Logotherapy: Frankl

Viktor E. Frankl was born (1905) and educated in Vienna and received his M.D. (1930) and Ph.D. (1949) from the University of Vienna. He founded the Youth Advisement Centers in Vienna in 1928 and headed them until 1938. From 1936 to 1942, he was specialist in neurology and psychiatry and then head of the Neurological Department at Rothschild Hospital in Vienna. He became head of the Neurological Policlinic Hospital (in Vienna) in 1946. In 1947, he was appointed associate professor of neurology and psychiatry at the University of Vienna and became professor in 1955. He has been a visiting professor at Harvard University, Southern Methodist University, Stanford University, Duquesne University, and the Chicago Psychiatric Foundation, among others. From 1942 to 1945, he was imprisoned in German concentration camps, including Auschwitz and Dachau. His mother, father, brother, and wife died in the camps or gas chambers.

Frankl has written a number of books in German, some of which have been translated into Polish, Japanese, Dutch, Spanish, Portuguese, Italian, Swedish, and English. He has made many lecture tours in South America, India, Australia, Japan, the United States, and Europe.

BACKGROUND AND DEVELOPMENT

Frankl began his professional career in psychiatry with a psychoanalytic orientation, having been a student of Freud. However, he became influenced by the writings of existential philosophers, including Heidegger, Scheler, and Jaspers, and began developing his own existential philosophy as well as an existential psychotherapy. In 1938, he first used the terms *existenzanalysis* and *logotherapy* in his writings. In order to avoid confusion with Binswanger's existential analysis, Frankl has concentrated on the term *logotherapy.* The name existential analysis has continued to be used, however, and appears to refer to a different aspect of Frankl's theory and method than does logotherapy.

Tweedie (1961), who attempted to summarize Frankl's approach, noted that "these terms are nearly synonymous and refer to two facets of the same theory. While Existential Analysis is more indicative of the anthropological direction in which this theory is developed, Logotherapy is more descriptive of the actual therapeutic theory and method" (p. 27). He went on to say that "Logotherapy proceeds from the spiritual, while Existential Analysis proceeds toward the spiritual" (p. 30). Later he wrote that "Logotherapy . . . seeks to bring to awareness the unconscious spiritual factors of the patient's personality, while Existential Analysis is the endeavor to enable the patient to become conscious of his responsibility" and quotes Frankl: "By definition Existential Analysis aims at 'being conscious of having responsibility' (*Bewusstsein des Verantworkunghabens*)" (p. 129). He then gives another quotation from Frankl: "Beyond this it is the task of logotherapeutic endeavor to stimulate concrete meaning possibilities; this, however, requires an analysis of the concrete human existence (Dasein), the personal existence of the patient in question, in a word, existential analysis" (p. 129). It appears that existential analysis refers to the analysis of the individual's existence, while logotherapy refers to the actual treatment. The name *logotherapy* seems to be more generally used, however, to include both aspects, and will be so used in this chapter.

This philosophy and therapy, developed in clinical practice and teaching, was tested and strengthened in Frankl's concentration camp experiences. He saw the truth so often expressed by poets and writers, that love is the ultimate and highest goal of human beings and that *"the salvation of man is through love and in love"* (Frankl, 1985a, p. 57). He became convinced that there was one ultimate purpose to existence.

Frankl recorded his experiences in a book published in German in 1946 and in English in 1959 under the title *From Death Camp to Existentialism.* A revised edition, with the added section "Basic Concepts of Logotherapy," is called *Man's Search for Meaning* (1963b). A revised paperback edition appeared in 1968, another in 1985. This little book is one of the main sources for this chapter. Another source is *The Doctor and the Soul,* a translation of *Ärztliche Seelsorge* (1946a). A second, expanded edition, with revisions and an added chapter, was published in 1965. A third revision was published in 1986. This book brought together materials published in German prior to 1946, some of which had been published in the 1930s. Some other books of Frankl's include *Psychotherapy and Existentialism* (1967, 1985b), *The Will to Meaning* (1981), *The Unconscious God* (1985c), and *The Unheard Cry for Meaning: Psychotherapy and Humanism* (1985d).

PHILOSOPHY AND CONCEPTS

In spite of the apathy of the prisoners in concentration camps, which resulted from both physical and psychological causes, Frankl (1985a) found that "man *can* preserve a vestige of spiritual freedom, of independence of mind, even in such terrible conditions of psychic and physical stress" (p. 86). Opportunities for choice were many, and there were examples of heroic choices to help others rather than to preserve oneself.

[T]he sort of person the prisoner became was the result of an inner decision, and not the result of camp influences alone. Fundamentally, therefore, any man can, even under such circumstances decide what shall become of him—mentally and spiritually. He may retain his human dignity even in a concentration camp. . . . It is this spiritual freedom—which cannot be taken away—that makes life meaningful and purposeful. (p. 87)

If there is a meaning to life, there is a meaning to suffering, since suffering, like death, is an ineradicable part of life; without them, life cannot be complete.

Only a few prisoners resisted falling victim to the prison camp's degenerating influences. The lack of any future goal or hope caused many to overlook existing opportunities to make something positive of camp life. Unusually bad external situations can also give a person the opportunity to grow beyond himself/herself spiritually. To do this, however, the person must have faith in the future. Without it, he/she gives up and has no will to live. With no aim, no purpose, no sense or meaning in life, there is no point in carrying on. Frankl (1986) asked his fellow prisoners—who said that they expected nothing more from life—"whether the question was really what we expected from life. Was it not, rather, what life was expecting from us?" (p. xvii). Life sets tasks for each person, and in meeting them, the person defines the meaning of his/her life. The tasks are different for each, and each situation is different, requiring a unique response. Sometimes a person is required to accept fate or to suffer. Each person's suffering is unique, and opportunity for growth lies in the way the person bears it.

Nature of the Person

An individual is a unity with three aspects or dimensions: the somatic, or physical; the mental, or psychological; and the spiritual. (It must be emphasized that by "spiritual" Frankl does not necessarily mean "religious.") The first two are closely related and together constitute the "psychophysicum." They include inherited and constitutional factors, such as the innate drives. Psychoanalysis, through Freud, Adler, and Jung, has contributed to the understanding of these dimensions, particularly the psychological, but has neglected the spiritual, the distinctively human dimension.

Logotherapy emphasizes the third dimension, the spiritual. Spirituality is the first of three characteristics of human existence that distinguish people from animals. Spirituality is revealed phenomenologically in immediate self-consciousness, but it is derived from the "spiritual unconscious."

Unconscious spirituality is the origin and root of all consciousness. In other words, we know and acknowledge, not only an instinctive unconscious, but rather also a *spiritual unconscious,* and in it we see the supporting ground of all conscious spirituality. The ego is not *governed* by the id, but the spirit is *borne by the unconscious.* (Frankl, 1957, p. 674)

Spirituality is the chief attribute of the individual, and from it derives conscience, love, and aesthetic conscience.

The second characteristic of human existence is freedom. "But what is man? He is the essence which always decides. And he again and again decides what he will be in the next instant" (Frankl, 1951, p. 39). Freedom means freedom in the face of the instincts, inherited disposition, and environment. Although human beings are influenced by all of these, they still have freedom to accept or reject and to take a stand on these conditions. Thus, human beings do not simply exist; they decide what their existence will be. Since they can rise above biological, psychological, and sociological conditions, on which predictions can be based, they are individually unpredictable (Frankl, 1963a).

The third factor in the individual's existence is responsibility. The individual's freedom is not only freedom *from,* but also freedom *to* something, which, according to Frankl, is the individual's responsibilities. The individual is responsible to himself/herself, to his/her conscience, or to God. "Logotherapy tries to make the patient fully aware of his own responsibilities; therefore, it must leave to him the option for what, to what or to whom, he understands himself to be responsible" (Frankl, 1985a, p. 132).

Psychoanalysis is concerned with individuals becoming conscious of their repressed experiences or drives. Adler's individual psychology is concerned with persons accepting responsibility for their symptoms. Each is one-sided and complements the other. "One might in fact state it as a basic theorem that *being human means being conscious and being responsible.* Both psychoanalysis and individual psychology err in that each sees only one aspect of humanity, one factor in human existence—whereas the two aspects must be taken jointly to yield a true picture of man" (Frankl, 1986, p. 5). Logotherapy goes beyond both to add the realm of the spiritual (*Geistig*). Responsibility is related to consciousness through conscience.

Although each individual is unique, he/she would have no meaning alone. "The significance of such individuality, the meaning of human personality, is, however, always related to community" (Frankl, 1986, p. 70). In the community, each individual, because he or she is unique, is irreplaceable. This is the difference between the community and the "mass," which is composed of identical units. "The community needs the individual existence in order for itself to have meaning" (p. 70), but also "the meaning of individuality comes to fulfillment in the community. To this extent, then, the value of the individual is dependent upon the community" (p. 71). The mass, however, submerges the individual: "by escape into the mass, man loses his most intrinsic quality: responsibility" (p. 72). But by becoming a part of the community, which is in itself a choice, the individual adds to his/her responsibility.

Motivation

Homeostasis, tension reduction, or the psychoanalytic pleasure principle cannot adequately account for human behavior. The status drive of Adler's individual psychology is also an insufficient explanation, as are self-expression, self-fulfillment, and self-actualization. These, according to Frankl, are effects rather than intentions, and the same is true for pleasure. In fact,

only when the primary objective orientation is lacking and has foundered, does that interest in one's self arise, as it is so strikingly manifested in neurotic existence. Therefore the striving for self-fulfillment is in no way something primary, rather, we see in it a deficient mode and a reduced level of human existence. (Frankl, 1958, p. 31)

The primary motivation in the individual is not the will to pleasure or the will to power, but the will to meaning. It is this that "most deeply inspires man," that is "the most human phenomenon of all, since an animal certainly never worries about the meaning of its existence" (Frankl, 1986, p. xvi).

Meaning is not invented by human beings, as Sartre claims, but is "discovered" by them.

> Men can give meaning to their lives by realizing what I call *creative values,* by achieving tasks. But they can also give meaning to their lives by realizing *experiential values,* by experiencing the Good, the True, and the Beautiful, or by knowing one single human being in all his uniqueness. And to experience one human being as unique means to love him. (Frankl, 1986, p. xix)

Even when these experiences are impossible, "a man can still give his life a meaning by the way he faces his fate, his distress" (p. xix). Human beings realize values by their attitude toward their destined, or inescapable, suffering. These are *attitudinal values* and the possibility for their realization exists until the last moment of life. Suffering thus has meaning.

The will to meaning is not a driving force in the psychodynamic sense. "Values do not drive a man; they do not *push* him, but rather *pull* him" (Frankl, 1963b, p. 157). They involve choices or decisions. "Man is never driven to moral behavior; in each instance he decides to behave morally." He does so, not to satisfy a moral drive or to have a good conscience, but "for the sake of a cause to which he commits himself, or for a person whom he loves, or for the sake of his God" (p. 158).

The meaning of life is not an abstraction.

> Ultimately, man should not ask what the meaning of life is, but rather he must recognize that it is *he* who is asked. In a word, each man is questioned by life; and he can only answer to life by *answering for* his own life; to life he can only respond by being responsible. . . . This emphasis on responsibleness is reflected in the categorical imperative of logotherapy, which is: "Live as if you were living already for the second time and as if you had acted the first time as wrongly as you are about to act now!" (Frankl, 1985a, pp. 131–132)

The meaning of life is thus unique for each individual and varies with time.

Existence is transitory, but on its transitoriness hinges its responsibleness, since individuals are constantly faced with choices among the current potentialities. Humankind constantly makes choices about "the mass of present potentialities." Once

> we have used an opportunity and have actualized a potential meaning we have done so once and for all. We have rescued it into the past, wherein it has been safely delivered and deposited. In the past, nothing is irretrievably lost, but rather, on the contrary everything is irrevocably stored and treasured. (Frankl, 1985a, p. 175)

Potentialities that are not chosen, however, are lost.

Existential Vacuum and Existential Frustration

A common complaint of patients today is that their lives are meaningless. "They lack the awareness of a meaning worth living for. They are haunted by the experience of their inner emptiness, a void within themselves; they are caught in that situation which I have called the 'existential vacuum'" (Frankl, 1985a, p. 128). With no instincts to guide their behavior and with the disappearance of traditions to guide their choices but faced with the necessity of making choices, people do not know what to do or what they want to do. "This existential vacuum manifests itself mainly in a state of boredom. . . . In actual fact, boredom is now causing, and certainly bringing to psychiatrists, more problems to solve than distress" (Frankl, 1985a, p. 129). One manifestation is the "Sunday neurosis," which is "that kind of depression which afflicts people who become aware of the lack of content in their lives when the rush of the busy week is over and the void within themselves becomes manifest" (Frankl, 1985a, p. 129).

The frustration of the will to meaning is "existential frustration." This frustration is sometimes

> vicariously compensated for by a will to power. . . . In other cases, the place of frustrated will to meaning is taken by the will to pleasure. That is why existential frustration often eventuates in sexual compensation. We can observe, in such cases, that the sexual libido becomes rampant in the existential vacuum. (Frankl, 1985a, pp. 129–130)

Existential frustration is not pathological or pathogenic per se.

> Not every conflict is necessarily neurotic . . . suffering is not always a pathological phenomenon. . . . I would strictly deny that one's search for a meaning to his existence, or even his doubt of it, in every case is derived from, or results in, any disease. . . . A man's concern, even his despair, over the worthwhileness of life is an *existential distress* but by no means a *mental disease*. (Frankl, 1985a, pp. 124–125)

Philosophical conflicts and problems involving a person's view of the world are psychologically, biologically, and sociologically "conditioned but not caused." It is the fallacy of psychologism "to analyze every act for its psychic origin, and on that basis to decree whether its content is valid or invalid" (Frankl, 1986, p. 15). Even if there is pathology in the individual, his/her philosophy or world view cannot necessarily be labeled as pathological. Psychologism, however, tends to devaluate; "It is always trying to unmask," is forever bent on debunking, is constantly hunting down extrinsic—that is, neurotic or culturopathological motivations. "Everywhere, psychologism sees nothing but masks, insists that only neurotic motives lie behind these masks" (Frankl, 1986, pp. 18–19).

The search for meaning may lead to tension rather than to equilibrium, but such tension is not pathological; it is, rather, "an indispensable prerequisite of mental health . . . mental health is based on a certain degree of tension, the tension between what one has already achieved and what one still ought to accomplish, or the gap between what one is and what one should become" (Frankl, 1985a, pp. 126–127). What the individual needs in the first place is not the discharge of tension—a homeostasis, or equilibrium—but "'noödynamics,' i.e., the existential dynamics in a polar field of tension where one pole is represented by a meaning that is to be fulfilled and the other pole by the man who has to fulfill it" (Frankl, 1985a, p. 127).

Nature of Neuroses and Psychoses

Although existential conflicts may exist without neurosis, every neurosis has an existential aspect. Neuroses are "grounded in the four basically different layers (or 'dimensions') of man's being" (Frankl, 1986, pp. 176–177)—the physical; the psychological; the societal; and the existential, or spiritual. The physiological bases are the constitutional (including neuropathy and psychopathy) and the conditioned (for example, the shock of a traumatic experience). The conditioned bases are probably precipitating factors. The various types of neuroses differ in terms of the relative importance of each of the four dimensions. The physiological bases cannot be reached by psychotherapy but only by drugs, and when the physiological component is great, there is little that psychotherapy can do (Frankl, 1986).

Noögenic Neuroses. *Noetic* refers to the spiritual dimension. "Noögenic neuroses do not emerge from conflicts between drives and instincts but rather from existential problems. Among such problems, the frustration of the will to meaning plays a large role" (Frankl, 1985a, p. 123). The disturbance is not in the spiritual dimension as such but is manifested in the psychophysicum. "Noögenic neuroses are illnesses 'out of spirit' (*aus dem Geist*), but they are not illnesses 'in the spirit' (*im Geist*)" (Frankl, 1956, p. 125).

Collective Neurosis. Although our age has been called the age of anxiety, it is doubtful that anxiety is more prevalent now than in other times. There are, however, certain characteristics of the modern person that are "similar to neurosis" and may be designated as the collective neurosis. "First, there is the planless, day-to-day attitude toward life," with no long-term planning, which seems to be related to the uncertainty of life since the Second World War and the development of the atomic bomb. "The second symptom is the fatalist attitude toward life. This, again, is a product of the last war" (Frankl, 1986, p. xxii). It is the attitude that it is not possible to plan one's life.

The third symptom is collective thinking. "Man would like to submerge himself in the masses. Actually, he is only drowned in the masses; he abandons himself as a free and responsible being" (Frankl, 1986, p. xxii). Then comes the fourth symptom, fanaticism. "While the collectivist ignores his own personality, the fanatic ignores that of the other man. . . . Only his own opinion is valid. . . . Ultimately, all these four symptoms can be traced back to man's fear of responsibility and his escape from freedom" (Frankl, 1986, pp. xxii–xxiii). Education and mental hygiene, rather than psychotherapy, are required to cure the collective neuroses.

Neuroses. Noögenic neuroses and the collective neuroses are included under the neuroses in the broad sense of the term. In a more restricted sense, neurosis involves primarily the psychic dimension of the person. "Neurosis is no noetic, no spiritual illness, no illness of man merely in his spirituality. Much more it is always an illness of man in his unity and wholeness" (Frankl, 1956, p. 125). Psychological complexes, conflicts, and traumatic experiences, however, are manifestations rather than causes of neurosis, which is more closely related to a developmental defect in the personality structure. Anxiety is a common factor, although it is not the cause of neurosis; however, it sustains the neurotic circle. Anticipatory anxiety is a more basic element. A fleeting symptom or a momentary failure in functioning may become the focus of attention. A fear of the recurrence of the symptom arises, which reinforces the symptom, beginning a neurotic circle that includes anticipatory anxiety. There are two major types of neurosis: Anxiety neurosis and obsessional neurosis.

Anxiety neurosis involves a malfunctioning of the vasomotor system, a disturbance of endocrine function, or a constitutional element. Traumatic experiences act as precipitating agents by focusing attention on the symptoms, but behind neurotic anxiety is an existential anxiety. This existential anxiety is the "fear of death and simultaneously the fear of life as a whole" (Frankl, 1986, p. 180). It is the result of a guilty conscience toward life, a sense of not having realized one's own value potentials. This fear becomes focused on a particular organ of the body or becomes concentrated on a symbolic concrete situation in the form of a phobia. A patient suffering from fear of open places described her anxiety as "a feeling like hanging in the air," which aptly described her whole spiritual situation, of which her neurosis was an expression (Frankl, 1986, p. 180). The neurosis, existentially, is a mode of existence.

Obsessional neurosis, like all other neuroses, includes a constitutional, dispositional factor as well as a psychogenic factor. However, there is also an existential factor, represented by the choice or decision of the individual to go on to a fully developed obsessional neurosis. "The patient is not responsible for his obsessional ideas," but "he certainly is responsible for his attitude toward these ideas" (Frankl, 1986, p. 188). The obsessional neurotic is not able to tolerate uncertainty, the tension between what is and what ought to be. His or her world view is that of "hundred-percentness," or a search for the absolute, a striving for "absolute certainty in cognition and decision" (Frankl, 1986, p. 191). Since it is impossible for this person to achieve his/her total demands on life, he/she concentrates on a specific area; but even so, the person can succeed "only partially . . . and always at the price of his naturalness, his 'creaturalness.' Thus all his strivings have an inhuman quality" (Frankl, 1986, p. 193).

Psychoses.   In the neuroses, both the symptoms and the etiology are psychological. In the psychoses—melancholia and schizophrenia—the etiology is physical and the symptoms are psychological.

Melancholia, or endogenous psychosis, also involves psychogenetic and existential aspects, or a "pathoplastic" factor, which refers to the freedom to shape one's destiny and to determine one's mental attitude toward the disease. Thus, "even psychosis is at bottom a kind of test of a human being, of the humanity of a psychotic patient" (Frankl, 1986, p. 200). With freedom of mental attitude goes responsibility. The anxiety present in melancholia has a physiological basis, but this does not explain the anxiety or the guilt, which are caused primarily by fear of death and of conscience and represent a mode of existence or of experiencing. "Conscientious anxiety can be understood only . . . *as the anxiety of a human being as such: as existential anxiety*" (Frankl, 1986, p. 201), not in physiological terms. Although an animal can suffer from anxiety, human psychoses involve a crucial element of humanity—of existentiality—above and beyond the organic condition.

In melancholia, the physiological basis or "psychophysical insufficiency is experienced in uniquely human fashion as tension between what the person is and what he ought to be," between "the need and the possibility of fulfillment" (Frankl, 1986, p. 202). This insufficiency is felt as inadequacy and appears in various forms, bringing out fears that were present in the premorbid condition: fears of inability to earn sufficient money, of inability to attain one's life goals, of "Judgment Day." The melancholiac "becomes blind to the values inherent in his own being" and later to the values outside himself; first "he feels himself as worthless and his own life as meaningless" (Frankl, 1986, p. 204) and then the world itself is seen in the same light. Guilt arising from the individual's feeling of insufficiency and "resulting from his intensified existential tension can swell to such a point that he feels his guilt to be ineradicable" (Frankl, 1986, p. 205). Life then assumes colossal dimensions.

In schizophrenia, the phenomena of feelings of being influenced, observed, or persecuted are all forms of the "'experience of pure objectness.' . . . The schizophrenic experiences himself as the object of the observing or persecuting intentions of his fellow men" (Frankl, 1986, pp. 208–209). Schizophrenics experience themselves as though they were transformed from a subject into an object. An "experiential passivity" is evidenced in the language of schizophrenics by their use of the passive mood. "The schizophrenic person experiences himself as so limited in his full humanity that he can no longer feel himself as really 'existent'" (Frankl, 1986, p. 210). Both consciousness and responsibility are affected.

THE THERAPY PROCESS

Patients repeatedly present problems concerning the meaning of their lives, that is, philosophical or spiritual problems. These problems may or may not be a sign of disease or neurosis. Neuroses and psychoses, including the organic psychotic processes, have an existential aspect as well as constitutional and psychogenetic aspects. They involve both a freedom of spiritual attitude toward the constitutional and psychological factors and a mode of existence. Therefore, treatment must be more than medical and more than psychological; it must include consideration of the existential aspects, too.

Logotherapy is directed toward such problems. The word *logos* has the twofold definition of "the meaning" and "the spiritual." Logotherapy thus deals with the existential and spiritual nature of the person.

Diagnosis

Proper diagnosis is the first step in psychotherapy, and an important one. All emotional disturbance or mental illness involves physical, psychological, and spiritual factors: "there are really no pure somatogenic, psychogenic, or noögenic neuroses. There are merely mixed cases, cases in which, respectively, a somatogenic, psychogenic, or noögenic moment moves into the foreground of the theoretical object and the therapeutic objective" (Frankl, 1956, see Foreword). The purpose of diagnosis is to determine the nature of each factor and which is the primary factor. When the physical factor is the primary one, it is a psychosis: when the psychological factor is primary, it is a neurosis; and when the spiritual factor is the primary one, it is a noögenic neurosis.

Therapy involves the whole person, however, and may include physical (or medical) treatment, psychotherapy, and logotherapy, together or consecutively. It is "not the aim of logotherapy to take the place of existing psychotherapy, but only to complement it, thus forming a picture of man in his wholeness—which includes the spiritual dimension

(Frankl, 1986, p. xvii). It focuses explicitly on meanings and values. A psychotherapy "that is blind to values"—for "there is no such thing as a psychotherapy unconcerned with values" (Frankl, 1986, p. xvii)—is inadequate to deal with these problems.

General Nature of Logotherapy

Whereas the aim of psychoanalysis is to make the unconscious conscious and the aim of individual psychological therapy (Adler) is to make the neurotic accept responsibility for his/her symptoms, the aim of logotherapy is to make the person consciously accept responsibility for oneself. "For the aim of the psychotherapist should be to bring out the ultimate possibilities of the patient, to realize his latent values" (Frankl, 1986, p. 8). Logotherapy fills a gap in psychotherapy; it "operates, as it were, beyond the fields of the Oedipus complex and the inferiority complex." It is "a form of psychotherapy which gets underneath the psychic malaise of the neurotic to his spiritual struggles" (Frankl, 1986, p. 11).

Philosophical and existential, or spiritual, problems cannot be avoided, nor can they be disposed of by focusing on their pathological roots or consequences—physical or psychological.

> What is needed here is to meet the patient squarely. We must not dodge the discussion, but enter into it sincerely. We must attack these questions on their own terms, at face value. Our patient has a right to demand that the ideas he advances be treated on the philosophical level. . . . A philosophical question cannot be dealt with by turning the discussion toward the pathological roots from which the question stemmed, or by hinting at the morbid consequences of philosophical pondering. . . . If only for the sake of philosophical fairness, we ought to fight with the same weapons. (Frankl, 1986, pp. 11–12)

Psychotherapy cannot deal with philosophical questions. The neurotic person's world view may be wrong, but correcting it is the function of logotherapy rather than of psychotherapy. If the neurotic person's world view were right, psychotherapy would be unnecessary. Philosophical questions cannot be reduced to psychological terms. "[P]sychotherapy as such is exceeding its scope in dealing with philosophical questions. . . . Logotherapy must *supplement* psychotherapy" (Frankl, 1986, p. 17).

In actual practice, however, psychotherapy and logotherapy cannot be separated, since the psychological and the philosophical or spiritual aspects of the individual are indissolubly joined and can be separated only logically. Nevertheless, in principle, they represent different realms. Psychotherapy uncovers the psychological background of an ideology, while logotherapy reveals the flaws in the improper bases for a world view. With some patients, it is wise to begin with the spiritual level, even though the genesis of the problem may be in the lower layers. With others, logotherapy follows psychotherapy of psychoses or neuroses.

Therapy and the Noögenic Neuroses

Logotherapy is the specific therapy for existential frustration, existential vacuum, or the frustration of the will to meaning. These conditions, when they result in neurotic symptomatology, are called *noögenic neuroses.*

Logotherapy is concerned with making people conscious of their responsibility, since being responsible is an essential basis of human existence. Responsibility implies obligation, and obligation can be understood only in terms of meaning—the meaning of human life. The question of meaning is an intrinsically human one and arises in dealing with patients suffering from existential frustration or conflicts (Frankl, 1986, see p. 26). Thus, logotherapy is concerned with problems that involve meaning in its various aspects and realms.

Meaning of Life and Death.   The normal individual can escape from a responsible life only in situations such as festivals and intoxication. The neurotic person seeks a permanent refuge from everyday society. The melancholic person seeks it through suicide. If questioned, the melancholic person will deny such thoughts.

> Whereupon we ask him . . . why he does not have (or no longer has) ideas of committing suicide. A melancholiac who really is not harboring such intentions, or has overcome them, will answer without hesitation that he must consider his family, or think of his work, or something of the sort. The man who is trying to fool his analyst, however, will immediately fall into a typical state of embarrassment. He is actually at a loss for arguments supporting his "phony" affirmation of life. Characteristically, such dissimulating patients will try to change the subject, and will usually bring up their naked demand to be released from confinement. People are psychologically incapable of making up counterfeit arguments in favor of life, or arguments for their continuing to live, when thoughts of suicide are surging up within them. (Frankl, 1986, pp. 30–31)

We can grasp the meaning of the universe best in the form of a "supermeaning" to indicate that the meaning of the whole goes beyond what is comprehensible. However, "belief in a supermeaning—whether as a metaphysical concept or in the religious sense of Providence—is of foremost psychotherapeutic and psychohygienic importance. . . . To such a faith there is, ultimately, nothing that is meaningless" (Frankl, 1986, p. 33).

The individual, of course, is not only, or perhaps even primarily, concerned with the meaning of the universe, but also is concerned with the meaning of his/her own life. Patients often assert that the meaning of life is pleasure,

> that all human activity is governed by the striving for happiness, that all psychic processes are determined exclusively by the pleasure principle. . . . Now, to our mind the pleasure principle is an artificial creation of psychology. Pleasure is not the goal of our aspirations, but the consequence of attaining them. (Frankl, 1986, pp. 34–35)

Pleasure cannot give meaning to life. If pleasure were the source of meaning, life would have little to offer, since unpleasant sensations outnumber pleasant sensations in life. "In reality, life is little concerned with pleasure or unpleasure. . . . Life itself teaches most people that 'we are not here to enjoy ourselves'" (Frankl, 1986, pp. 36–38). Those who are bent on the search for pleasure and happiness fail to find them, because of their concentration on them.

The basic skepticism and nihilism of these patients has to be countered. "But it often becomes necessary in addition to disclose the full richness of the world of values, and to make clear the extent of its domain" (Frankl, 1986, p. 42). If the patient bewails his life for its lack of meaning, "since his activities are without any higher value . . . this is the point at which we must reason with him, showing him that it is a matter of indifference what a person's occupation is, or at what job he works. The crucial thing is how he works, whether he in fact fills the place in which he happens to have landed" (Frankl, 1986, pp. 42–43).

In the case of a would-be suicide, "the question is . . . whether the sum of such a balance sheet can ever turn out so negative that living on appears incontrovertibly without value" (Frankl, 1986, p. 50). Such a conviction is subjective and may be unjustified.

> We can therefore risk the generalization that suicide is never ethically justified. . . . [I]t is our duty to convince the would-be suicide that taking one's own life is categorically contrary to reason, that life is meaningful to every human being under any circumstances. We believe this can be done by objective argument and analysis of the problem on its own terms—by the methods of logotherapy, that is . . . [w]here no psychopathological basis of motivation can be shown, and where, therefore, psychotherapy in the narrower sense of the word can find no point of departure, logotherapy is the indicated method. (Frankl, 1986, pp. 51–52)

Even in suicide "man cannot escape his sense of responsibility. For he commits the act of suicide in freedom (assuming, of course, that he is still sane)" (Frankl, 1986, p. 53).

The aim of logotherapy is to help patients "find an aim and a purpose in their existence" and to help them "achieve the highest possible activation" of their lives (Frankl, 1986, p. 54). In addition to being led to experience existence as a constant effort to actualize values, patients must be shown the value of the conviction of responsibility for a task—a specific task.

> The conviction that one has a task before him has enormous psychotherapeutic and psychohygienic value. We venture to say that nothing is more likely to help a person overcome or endure objective difficulties or subjective troubles than the consciousness of having a task in life. (Frankl, 1986, p. 54)

"[T]he factors of uniqueness and singularity are essential constituents of the meaningfulness of human existence" (Frankl, 1986, p. 55). The patient must be shown that every life has a unique goal, which is reached by a single course. If the patient does not know his/her unique potentialities, then his/her primary task is to discover them. "Existential analysis accordingly is designed to help the individual comprehend his responsibility to accomplish each of his tasks" (Frankl, 1986, p. 58); the fulfillment of these assignments gives meaning to life.

The finiteness of existence also gives meaning to life. Death does not render life meaningless; rather, the temporality of life gives it meaning. If life were not finite, everything could be postponed; there would be no need for action, choice, or decisions, and thus no responsibility. "The meaning of human existence is based upon its irreversible quality" (Frankl, 1986, p. 64). In logotherapy, this aspect of life must be put before the patient to bring him/her to consciousness of his/her responsibility. The patient may be encouraged to imagine that he/she is reviewing his/her "own biography in the declining days of . . . life" and in coming to the

> chapter dealing with the present phase of his life . . . by a miracle he has the power to decide what the contents of the next chapter shall be. He is to imagine, that is, that it still lies within his capacity to make corrections, as it were, in a crucial chapter of his unwritten inner life story. (Frankl, 1986, p. 64)

The categorical imperative of logotherapy applies here: "live as if you were living for the second time and had acted as wrongly the first time as you are about to act now" (Frankl, 1986, p. 64). Once a patient does this, he/she will realize the great responsibility for the next hour and the next day.

Every person has a unique destiny, which, like death, is a part of life. "For what we call destiny is that which is essentially exempt from human freedom, that which lies neither within the scope of man's power nor his responsibility" (Frankl, 1986, p. 78). Destiny has meaning, and to quarrel with it is to overlook its meaning. Without the restrictions imposed by destiny, freedom would have no meaning.

> Freedom without destiny is impossible; freedom can only be freedom in the face of a destiny, a free stand toward destiny. . . . Freedom presupposes restrictions, is contingent upon restrictions. . . . If we wanted to define man, we would have to call him that entity which has freed itself from whatever has determined it (determined it as biological-psychological-sociological type); that entity, in other words, that transcends all these determinants either by conquering them and shaping them, or by deliberately submitting to them. (Frankl, 1986, pp. 75–76)

The past is part of a person's destiny, since it is unalterable, but the future is not exclusively determined by the past. The mistakes of the past can serve as lessons for shaping the future. A person's disposition, or biological endowment, is part of the destiny, as is the person's situation, or external environment, and psychic attitude, to the extent that it is unfree. The constant struggle between the person's inward and outward destiny and his/her freedom is the intrinsic nature of life.

Logotherapy sees destiny as "the ultimate testing ground for human freedom" (Frankl, 1986, p. 82). Biological, psychological, and sociological destiny obstruct human freedom, but the way in which the same handicaps and barriers are meaningfully incorporated into a person's life varies widely among individuals, as does the attitude or position taken toward them. Neurotic persons exhibit a morbid acceptance of fate and destiny, but such neurotic fatalism is only a disguised form of escape from responsibility. Patients cannot be allowed to blame childhood educational and environmental influences for what they are or for determining their destinies. This practice and that of blaming their neuroticism for their faults are ways of avoiding responsibility. Even the patient with an organic disorder is responsible for his/her spiritual attitude toward his/her condition.

Meaning of Suffering

A person's responsibility is to actualize values. The three categories of values (already mentioned) are those that are actualized by doing; those that are realized by experiencing the world; and attitudinal values, which

> are actualized wherever the individual is faced with something unalterable, something imposed by destiny. From the manner in which a person takes these things upon himself, assimilates these difficulties into his own psyche, there flows an incalculable multitude of value-potentialities. This means that *human life can be fulfilled not only in creating and enjoying, but also in suffering.* (Frankl, 1986, pp. 105–106)

Life can obtain its ultimate meaning not only in sacrificing it, as a hero, but in the very process of facing death. Trouble and suffering guard a person from apathy and boredom; they result in activity, thus leading to growth and maturity.

The destiny a person suffers is "to be shaped where possible, and to be endured where necessary" (Frankl, 1986, p. 111). Only when a person

> no longer has any possibility of actualizing creative values, when there is really no means at hand for shaping fate—then is the time for attitudinal values to be actualized. . . . The very essence of an attitudinal value inheres in the manner in which a person resigns himself to the inevitable; in order therefore for attitudinal values to be truly actualized, it is important that the fate he resigns himself to must be actually inevitable. (Frankl, 1986, p. 112)

Thus, every situation offers the opportunity for the actualization of values, if not for creative or experiential values, then for attitudinal values.

> Consequently, cases may arise where existential analysis is called upon to make a person capable of suffering—whereas psychoanalysis, for instance, aims only at making him capable of pleasure or capable of doing. For there are situations in which man can fulfill himself only in genuine suffering, and in no other way. (Frankl, 1986, pp. 113–114)

Meaning of Work

Responsibility to life is assumed by responding to the situations that it presents. "[T]he response should be given not in words but in acting, by doing" (Frankl, 1986, p. 117). Consciousness of responsibility arises out of awareness of a unique concrete personal task, a "mission." The realization of creative values usually coincides with a person's work, which generally represents the area in which the person's uniqueness can be seen in relation to society. This work as a contribution to society is the source of the meaning and the value of the person's uniqueness. It is not the particular occupation on which fulfillment depends. "[T]he job at which one works is not what counts, but rather the manner in which one does the work" (Frankl, 1986, p. 118). Neurotic persons who complain that a different occupation would offer fulfillment must be shown this. It is not the occupation itself but the expression of the person's uniqueness and singularity in the work or beyond the required duties that gives meaning to the occupation.

For some, work seems to be only a means to the end of obtaining money to live, and life seems only to begin with leisure. There are also those whose work is so exhausting that there is no time for leisure, but only for sleep. Some devote all their time to the pursuit of wealth as an end in itself. Work can be misused as a means to a neurotic end. The neurotic person also may sometimes attempt to escape from life in general by taking refuge in work. When the neurotic person is not working, he/she feels at a loss, and the poverty of meaning in the neurotic person's life is revealed.

> [T]hese people who know no goal in life are running the course of life at the highest possible speed so that they will not notice the aimlessness of it. They are at the

same time trying to run away from themselves—but in vain. On Sunday, when the frantic race pauses for twenty-four hours, all the aimlessness, meaninglessness, and emptiness of their existence rises up before them once more. (Frankl, 1986, pp. 127–128)

Commercialized entertainment provides a refuge for these people with Sunday neurosis.

The existential importance of work is seen in what Frankl calls the "unemployment neurosis." The most prominent symptom in the unemployed person is apathy, the feeling of uselessness and emptiness. "He feels useless because he is unoccupied. Having no work, he thinks life has no meaning" (Frankl, 1986, p. 121). In neurotic persons, unemployment becomes an alibi for all their failures and wipes out all responsibility to others and to themselves, as well as to life. However, the unemployment may be a result of the neurosis rather than the neurosis being a result of unemployment.

Unemployment is not an unconditional fate to which a person must succumb by developing an unemployment neurosis. There is an alternative to surrendering physically to the forces of social destiny. It is possible to engage in various other activities, to use time constructively, and to take an affirmative attitude toward life. Work is not the only way to give life meaning. The individual can decide what his/her attitude will be, whether positive and hopeful or apathetic.

Unemployment neurosis can be treated psychotherapeutically, but only by logotherapy, since it is a problem related to the meaning of existence. Logotherapy "shows the jobless person the way to inner freedom in spite of his unfortunate situation and teaches him that consciousness or responsibility through which he can still give some content to his hard life and wrest meaning from it" (Frankl, 1986, p. 126).

Meaning of Love

The community is a rich field of human experience. The intimate community of the self with another is the area in which experiential values are especially realizable.

Love is living the experience of another person in all his uniqueness and singularity. . . . In love the beloved person is comprehended in his very essence, as the unique and singular being that he is; he is comprehended as a Thou, and as such is taken into the self. As a human person he becomes for the one who loves him indispensable and irreplaceable without having done anything to bring this about. . . . Love is not deserved, is unmerited—it is simply grace. . . . [I]t is also enchantment. (Frankl, 1986, pp. 132–133)

Enchantment reflects on the world and on a person's values. There is a third factor that enters into love—"the miracle of love," that is, the entrance into life of a new person, a child.

The individual as lover can react differently to the three layers of the human person—the physical, the psychic, and the spiritual. The most primitive attitude is the sexual, which is directed toward the physical layer. The erotic attitude (commonly called "infatuation") is directed toward the psychic layer. Love is the third attitude, directed toward the loved one's spiritual layer. This layer constitutes the uniqueness of the loved one, which unlike the physical and psychological states, is irreplaceable and permanent.

> Love is only one of the possible ways to fill life with meaning, and is not even the best way. Our existences would have come to a sad pass and our lives would be poor indeed if their meaning depended upon whether or not we experienced happiness in love. . . . The individual who neither loves nor is loved can still shape his life in a highly meaningful manner. (Frankl, 1986, p. 141)

The absence of love may be due to a neurotic failure rather than to destiny. Outward physical attractiveness is relatively unimportant, and its lack is not sufficient reason for being resigned to renunciation of love. Renouncing love engenders resentment, since it implies either overvaluing or devaluing love.

Emphasis on appearance or external beauty leads to devaluation of the person as such. Sex appeal is impersonal. Relationships based on sex are superficial; they are not love. Nor do those involved in such relationships want love, which includes responsibility. True love is experienced as valid forever. A person can mistake infatuation for love, but it can turn out to be error only later on.

Neurotic persons may fear the tensions of unhappy, unrequited love and so avoid opportunities for love. Such persons must be reeducated to be ready and receptive, to wait for the single happy love affair that may follow nine unhappy ones. Psychotherapy must bring the flight tendency into the open.

Psychosexual maturing, which begins in puberty, is subject to three kinds of disturbance, resulting in different sexual neuroses. One type occurs at the final stage of sexual maturing, when the physical sexual urge is becoming an erotic tendency directed toward a person. It may happen, perhaps after some disappointment in love, that a young person believes that he/she will never find someone that he/she can at the same time respect and desire sexually. This person then plunges into sexuality without emotion or love, reverting to a lower level of psychosexual development. This is the "resentment type."

The second type is represented by persons who have never progressed beyond sexuality to an erotic attitude and do not expect to experience love. This is the "resignation type." Such individuals maintain that love is an illusion; they include the Don Juan. The third type, the "inactive type," shuns the other sex entirely. The sexual instinct is expressed only in masturbation. This group also includes young people who suffer from sexual frustration, which is the expression of a more general psychological distress. Such sexual frustration in a young person is "an indication that his sex instinct is not yet (or is no longer) subordinated to an erotic tendency and so integrated into the total system of his personal strivings" (Frankl, 1986, p. 170).

The so-called sexual frustration of youth is not solved by sexual activity but by maturation to love. "The therapy is of the simplest. It suffices to introduce the young person in question into a mixed company of people of his age. There the young man will sooner or later fall in love—that is, he will find a partner—in the erotic and not in the sexual sense" (Frankl, 1986, pp. 170—171) and will progress to the erotic stage of development. Crude sexuality and frustration will disapper. The person meanwhile matures, so that if and when a serious sexual relationship does develop, its sexuality will assume the appropriate form, as an expression of love.

> Now, under the dominance of the erotic tendency, he can build up an erotic relationship within the framework of which sexual relations can then be considered. . . . The young man's sense of responsibility has meanwhile matured to the point where he

can decide on his own and his partner's behalf whether and when he ought to enter into a serous sexual relationship with her. (Frankl, 1986, p. 172)

The therapist's position on sexual intercourse between young people is that he/she must veto it if possible whenever it is not a part of real love. In no case, however, can the therapist recommend it, since this is a personal moral problem and it is the responsibility of the person to decide. The therapist's task is to teach the person to be responsible.

Logotherapy is the specific therapy for the noögenic neuroses because it directs itself toward the primary problem—their basic nature, the existential frustration or vacuum, or the lack of meaning in life and its various aspects. The therapeutic goal is to eliminate the frustration by filling the vacuum, by helping the patient achieve meaning in life. This is accomplished by helping the patient to understand and accept the existential or spiritual nature of life and to assume responsibility for himself/herself and for the actualization of values by responding to the demands or tasks that life presents.

Logotherapy as a Nonspecific Therapy of Neuroses

In the treatment of psychogenic neurotic reactions, logotherapy directs itself neither to the symptoms nor to their psychogenesis, but to the patient's attitudes toward the symptoms. Logotherapy has developed two specific techniques for dealing with neuroses. These are described below. In addition, general logotherapy, as applied in the noögenic neuroses, is applicable to the treatment not only of the specific neuroses, but also of psychoses, in relation to the existential or spiritual problems that are present.

In dealing with neurotic persons, logotherapy is not a symptomatic treatment. It is concerned instead with the patient's attitude toward his/her symptoms. "Insofar as logotherapy does not treat the symptom directly, but rather attempts to bring about a change of attitude, a personal reversal of attitude toward the symptom, it is truly a personalistic psychotherapy" (Frankl, 1947, p. 34).

IMPLEMENTATION: TECHNIQUES OF LOGOTHERAPY

Logotherapy places emphasis on the relationship between the patient and the therapist. "This relationship between two persons is what seems to be the most significant aspect of the psychotherapeutic process, a more important factor than any method or technique" (Frankl, 1967, p. 144). With the diversity of patients and therapists, "the psychotherapeutic process consists of a continuous chain of improvisations" (ibid., p. 144). The relationship requires a balance between the extremes of human closeness and scientific detachment. "This means that the therapist must neither be guided by mere sympathy, by his desire to help his patient, nor, conversely, repress his human interest in the other human being by dealing with him in terms of technique" (ibid., p. 144).

Because it is concerned with existential, spiritual, or philosophical problems, logotherapy engages in discussion of these problems. The method is not an intellectual or strictly rational one, however. "Logotherapy is as far removed from being a process of 'logical' reasoning as from being merely moral exhortation. Above all, a psychotherapist—and the logotherapist included—is neither a teacher nor a preacher." The maieutic dialogue in the Socratic sense may be used; "it is not necessary, however, to enter into sophisticated debates with the patients" (Frankl, 1967, pp. 57–58; cf. Frankl, 1961a).

The concern with existential or spiritual questions is "fraught with intricate problems, for it then becomes necessary for the doctor to take a stand on the question of values. The moment the doctor commits himself to such a 'psychotherapy' . . . his own philosophy necessarily comes to the fore—whereas previously his outlook remained hidden behind his role as doctor" (Frankl, 1986, p. 11). The logotherapist must "beware of forcing his philosophy on the patient. There must be no transference (or, rather, countertransference) of a personal philosophy, of a personal concept of values, to the patient" (Frankl, 1986, pp. xxi–xxii). This is because the concept of responsibility implies that the patient is responsible for himself/herself. The logotherapist only brings the patient to experience this responsibility; the logotherapist does not tell the patient to what—conscience, society, God or another higher power—or for what—the realization of values, the fulfillment of personal tasks, the particular meaning of life—he/she is responsible.

Two logotherapeutic techniques, paradoxical intention and dereflection, are designed to deal with conditions met in cases of the anxiety, obsessive-compulsive, and sexual neuroses (Frankl, 1975, 1991). Anxiety neuroses and phobic conditions are characterized by anticipatory anxiety, which produces exactly the condition that the patient fears. The occurrence of the condition then reinforces the anticipatory anxiety, creating a vicious circle, until the patient avoids or withdraws from situations in which he or she expects the fear to recur. This withdrawal is "wrong passivity" (Frankl, 1960), which is one of the "four patterns of response." The patient suffering from obsessive-compulsive neuroses engages in "wrong activity" when he/she fights obsessive ideas and compulsions. "Wrong activity" also occurs in sexual neuroses, in which the patient, striving for competent sexual performance, which the patient feels is demanded of him/her, engages in responses that are inappropriate to the situation. "Excessive intention" makes the performance of the desired function impossible. In such cases, there is also frequently an "excessive attention" and a compulsive self-observation.

In cases involving anticipatory anxiety, and obsessive-compulsive and phobic conditions, the logotherapeutic technique called *paradoxical intention* is useful (e.g., Gerz, 1962, 1966, 1980). This technique, first described by Frankl in 1939, requires or encourages the patient to intend, if only momentarily, that which is anticipated with fear. The obsessive-compulsive patient stops resisting obsessions and compulsions, and the phobic patient stops fighting fears, breaking the vicious circle of anticipatory anxiety. This is a reversal of the patient's attitude toward the situation. In addition,

> it is carried out in as humorous a setting as possible. This brings about a change of attitude toward the symptom which enables the patient to place himself at a distance from the symptom, to detach himself from his neurosis. . . . [I]f we succeed in bringing the patient to the point where he ceases to flee from or to fight his symptoms, but on the contrary, even exaggerates them, then we may observe that the symptoms diminish and that the patient is no longer haunted by them. . . .
>
> "Paradoxical intention is effective irrespective of the underlying etiologic basis: in other words it is an intrinsically nonspecific method. . . . This is not to say that it is a symptomatic therapy, however, for the logotherapist, when applying paradoxical intention, is concerned not so much with the symptom in itself but, with the patient's *atti-*

tude toward his neurosis and its symptomatic manifestations." (Frankl, 1967, pp. 147, 152–153)

Paradoxical intention is sometimes successful in severe and longstanding cases. It is particularly effective in short-term treatment of phobias with underlying anticipatory anxiety. Seventy-five percent of the patients treated have been cured or have improved. It is not a superficial method; it appears to affect deeper levels. It is "essentially more than a change of behavior patterns; rather, it is an existential reorientation (*existentielle Umstellung*)" (Frankl, 1967, pp. 156–157). It is logotherapy in the truest sense of the word, "based on what is called in logotherapeutic terms psychonoetic antagonism . . . which refers to the specifically human capacity to detach oneself, not only from the world but also from oneself" (Frankl, 1967, p. 157).

Excesses of attention, intention, and self-observation are treated by another logotherapeutic technique, called *dereflection*. Dereflection is particularly useful in cases of male sexual impotence and female inability to reach a climax. Hyperintention and hyperreflection inhibit performance. Dereflection diverts attention from the act and from the self to the partner, and removes the demand for performance.

> Such ignoring, or de-reflection, however, can only be attained to the degree to which the patient's awareness is directed toward positive aspects. De-reflection, in itself, contains both a negative and a positive aspect. The patient must be de-reflected from his anticipatory anxiety to something else. . . . Through de-reflection, the patient is enabled to ignore his neurosis by focusing his attention away from himself. He is directed to a life full of potential meanings and values that have a specific appeal to his personal potentialities. (Frankl, 1967, pp. 160–162)

Paradoxical intention substitutes "right passivity" for "wrong passivity." Dereflection substitutes "right activity" for "wrong activity" (cf. Kocourek, 1980).

LENGTH AND LIMITATIONS

Length. There appears to be no approximate length to a logotherapeutic treatment. For instance, in the case examples that follow, treatment typically lasted for only a few months. But, as Gerz (1962) has said,

> the number of therapy sessions depends largely on how long the patient has been sick. When the illness is acute . . . most patients respond to this [paradoxical intention] therapy within about four to twelve sessions. Those who have been sick for several years . . . need six to twelve months of biweekly sessions to bring about recovery. (p. 375)

While that may be applicable for paradoxical intention, how long would treatment last if therapy's goal was to help the patient find meaning? to develop a logophilosophy? It seems more difficult to pinpoint an approximate number of sessions for such treatment.

Limitations.   "For whom logotherapy?. . . [E]veryone can benefit from it. People in all walks of life, those with or without problems, the mentally ill or well, all can avail themselves of the advantages offered by logotherapy" (Sahakian, 1980, p. 3). But with logotherapy there are also limitations or contraindications to be mindful of. "Paradoxical intention is strictly contraindicated in psychotic depressions. . . . As for schizophrenic patients, logotherapy is far from yielding a causal treatment" (Frankl, 1986, p . 264). For schizophrenic patients, dereflection can be used as a "psychotherapeutic adjunct"—serving "to support other forms of therapy" (Frankl, 1986, p. 264). Logotherapy, thus, appears best directed at dealing with neurotic conditions—collective, noögenic, phobic, obsessive.

EXAMPLES

The following case is reported by Frankl (1967) in his book of selected papers (pp. 153–154).

> Paradoxical intention is also applicable in cases more complex than those involving monosymptomatic neurosis. The following will demonstrate that even instances of severe obsessive-compulsive character neurosis (in German clinical terminology referred to as anankastic psychopathic character structure) may be appropriately and beneficially treated by means of paradoxical intention.
>
> The patient was a sixty-five-year-old woman who had suffered for sixty years from a washing compulsion of such severity that she was admitted to our clinic for a period of observation in order that I might certify her for a leucotomy (which I expected to be the only available procedure for bringing relief in this severe case). Her symptoms began when she was four years of age. When she was prevented from indulging her washing compulsion, she would even lick her hands. Later on she was continually afraid of being infected by people with skin diseases. She would never touch a doorknob. She also insisted that her husband stick to a very complicated prophylactic ritual. For a long time the patient had been unable to do any housework, and finally she remained in bed all day. Nevertheless, even there she persisted in scrubbing things with a cloth for hours, up to three hundred times or more, and having her husband repeatedly rinse out the cloth. "Life was hell for me," she confessed.
>
> In the hope of avoiding brain surgery, my assistant, Dr. Eva Niebauer, started logotherapeutic treatment by means of paradoxical intention. The result was that nine days after admission the patient began to help in the ward by mending the stockings of her fellow patients, assisting the nurses by cleaning the instrument tables and washing syringes, and finally even emptying pails of bloody and putrid waste materials! Thirteen days after admission she went home for a few hours and upon her return to the clinic, she triumphantly reported having eaten a roll with soiled hands. Two months later she was able to lead a normal life.
>
> It would not be accurate to say that she is completely symptom-free, for frequently obsessive-compulsive ideas come to her mind. However, she has been able to get relief by ceasing to fight her symptoms (fighting only serves to reinforce them) and, instead, by being ironical about them; in short, by applying paradoxical intention. She is even able to joke about her pathologic thoughts. This patient still kept in contact with the outpatient clinic, for she continued to need supportive logotherapy. The improvement in her condition persisted however, and thus the leucotomy, which previously had seemed unavoidable, had now become unnecessary.

The following case report is taken from a report (Frankl, 1961b) of seven cases by an American psychiatrist who applied the method of paradoxical intention to twenty-four cases with successful results.

A.V., aged forty-five, married mother of one sixteen-year-old son, has a twenty-four-year history of a grave phobic neurosis consisting of severe claustrophobia such as fear of riding in cars. She had fear of heights, of riding in elevators, of crossing bridges, of collapsing, of leaving the house (when forced to do so, she would hang on to trees, bushes, anything). She also had a fear of open spaces, being alone, and becoming paralyzed. She was treated for her phobic neurosis over the past twenty-four years by various psychiatrists and received, repeatedly, long-term psychoanalytically oriented psychotherapy. In addition, the patient was hospitalized several times, received several series of electroconvulsive treatments (ECT), and finally lobotomy was suggested. During the four years before I saw her, she had been hospitalized continuously on a disturbed ward in a state hospital. There she received ECT and intensive drug therapy with barbiturates, phenothiazines, monoamine oxidase inhibitors, and amphetamine compounds—all to no avail. She had become so paralyzed by her numerous phobias that she was unable to leave a certain part of the ward which surrounded her bed. She was constantly in acute distress in spite of receiving large doses of tranquilizers. Her tension was so great that her muscles hurt intensely. She tried constantly "not to collapse," "not to get nervous," and "not to become panicky." Diagnoses of her illness, made by private psychiatrists, ranged from psychoneurosis to schizophrenic reaction, schizo-affective type, with phobic anxiety and depressive manifestations. While in the hospital, she had been treated for a year and a half with "intensive analytically oriented psychotherapy" by an experienced clinical psychologist.

On March 1, 1959, all medication was discontinued and I began treatment with Paradoxical Intention. The technique was fully explained to her and we worked together, symptom by symptom and fear by fear. We started off first with removing the smaller fears, such as the one of not being able to sleep. The patient was removed from the disturbed ward and was instructed to "try to pass out and become as panicky as possible." At first, she said angrily, "I don't have to be afraid! I am afraid! This is ridiculous. You are making me worse!" After a few weeks of struggle, the patient was able to remain on a ward located on the third floor and "unsuccessfully" tried hard to pass out and become paralyzed. Both the patient and I went to the elevator to ride to the fifth floor. The patient was instructed to walk into the elevator and ride up with the strong intention of passing out and showing me "how wonderfully she can become panicky and paralyzed." While on the elevator, I commanded her to pass out, but at this she laughed and replied: "I am trying so hard—I can't do it. I don't know what is the matter with me—I can't be afraid anymore. I guess I'm trying hard enough to be afraid!" Upon reaching the fifth floor, the patient was proud and overjoyed as well. This seemed to be the turning point in the treatment. From then on, she used Paradoxical Intention any time she needed it. For the first time in many years, the patient walked outside alone around the hospital without fear, but "constantly trying hard to become panicky and paralyzed." After five months of this therapy, she was symptom-free. She returned home for a week-end visit and enjoyed her stay without any phobias for the first time in twenty-four years. When she returned to the hospital from this trip, she was contented and stated that there was only one fear left, namely that of crossing bridges. The same day we went together in my car and crossed a bridge. While crossing, I ordered her to pass out and become panicky, but she only laughed and said, "I can't! I can't!" Shortly thereafter, she was released from the hospital. Since then she has seen me every two to three months for a check-up "because of gratefulness." It is important for me to emphasize that quite purposefully I did not familiarize myself with her past history, nor with the underlying psychodynamics.

Two months ago she wanted a special appointment. When I saw her, she was quite tense, expressing anticipatory anxiety about getting sick again. Her husband had been out of work for several months and also had been suffering from a neurological disorder which was in the process of clearing. At the same time the patient was menstruating. This pressure caused her to become anxious and she was just beginning to slide back into the vicious cycle of her previous illness. In one session, however, she was able to understand what had happened and to avoid a re-establishment of the destructive pattern of her phobias. This patient has been out of the hospital and living a full and happy life with her family for two and a half years. Recovery was brought about with no attempt on my part to "understand" the patient's symptoms in terms of psychoanalytic theory and "depth psychology."

The question might well be asked: what really goes on in the sessions? Therapy is begun with taking the case history, recording symptomatology, etc., explaining to the patient the basic principles of Paradoxical Intention, and discussing case histories of my own and some of the typical cases reported by Frankl, Niebauer, and Kocourek. This usually takes between one and a half and two hours. This will do two things for the patient: he will learn to understand what we are trying to do and he will gain confidence that this therapy is effective. I have, for instance, found it very valuable to have a patient who has been cured with this type of treatment meet with the one who is starting in therapy, both in hospital and private practice. This can be done very well individually, and also is valuable in the group psychotherapy setting. I do not deny that this sort of thing has suggestive value, but, may I ask, what doctor or psychiatrist can treat his patients without this factor? As far as the technique itself is concerned, it must not be confused with suggestion. In fact, Paradoxical Intention represents just the opposite. It does not tell the patient as Coué did, "everything will get better and better," but it instructs the patient to *try intentionally to get worse.* The logotherapist asks the patient himself to wish that the feared thing will happen to him. Frankl says very specifically that "Paradoxical Intention is most genuine logotherapy. The patient shall objectivize his neurosis by distancing himself from his symptoms. The spiritual in man shall detach itself from the psychic within him, and the patient shall call on the *Trotzmacht des Geistes,* man's spiritual capacity to resist, and by his inner freedom choose a specific attitude in any given situation."

The following comments are from a practitioner of logotherapy in America (Gerz, 1962; also in Frankl, 1967).

When I feel that the patient thoroughly understands the mechanism involved in the technique, we apply and practice it together in my office. For instance, the patient who is afraid he might lose consciousness is asked to get up and try to "pass out." To evoke humor in the patient I always exaggerate by saying, for example, "Come on; let's have it; let's pass out all over the place. Show me what a wonderful 'passer-out' you are." And, when the patient tries to pass out and finds he cannot, he starts to laugh. Then I tell him "If you cannot pass out here on purpose, intentionally, then you cannot pass out any other place if you try." So together we practice Paradoxical Intention in the office over and over again; but also, if necessary, in the patient's home or wherever his neurotic symptoms appear. Once the patient has successfully used Paradoxical Intention on one of his phobias, he enthusiastically applies the technique to his other symptoms. The number of therapy sessions depends largely on how long the patient has been sick. When the illness is acute, and duration has been of only a few weeks or months, most patients respond to this therapy within about four to twelve sessions. Those who have been sick for several years, even as long as twenty years or more (in my experience I had six such cases, although more have been reported in the literature), need six to twelve months of biweekly sessions to bring about recovery. It is necessary during the course of treatment to repeatedly teach and encourage the patient to use the technique according to his specific symptoms. Since the nervous system in itself is well known for its repetitious qualities, and since our feelings are carried and expressed through nerve tissue, namely the autonomic nervous system, a once-established neurotic feeling pattern will tend to repeat itself and become a sort of reflex, even when the causes of the neurotic symptoms have been resolved and removed. Because of this repetitous quality of the nervous system, it is also absolutely essential in therapy to repeat the application of Paradoxical Intention over and over. . . .

Initially, patients show very good response to Paradoxical Intention but during the course of therapy, particularly in chronic cases, patients will repeatedly suffer little setbacks. This is caused by the fact that as soon as patients *try to get better,* they enter the vicious cycle again, trying for health and providing the neurosis with new fuel. In other words, they "forget" to apply Paradoxical Intention and become worse by Coué's method of suggestion. This failure of the patient to continue to practice the technique is precisely because of the above-mentioned repetitive neurotic behavior patterns. ("I have tried to fight my neurosis for so many years the wrong way. It is hard to re-learn.") But there is another element involved here: the therapist demands from the patient tremendous courage, namely to do the things he so much fears. For instance, the patient who has the fear of blushing when in a group, is asked to do just that. Here, we appeal to the personal pride of the patient and his inner freedom in his spiritual dimension, and thus practice logotherapy in its true meaning. For all these reasons the therapist must never tire of encouraging the patient to continue to use Paradoxical Intention over and over—just as his neurosis produces the symptoms over and over. Then, finally, the neurotic symptoms will "become discouraged" and disappear. Only too often "they try to come back" but then Paradoxical Intention strangles them. "When they saw that they could not get anywhere with me anymore, they gave up completely."

SUMMARY AND EVALUATION

Summary.   Logotherapy is an existential approach to aiding the individual with problems of a philosophical or a spiritual nature. These are problems of the meaning of life—the meaning of death, of suffering, of work, and of love. Problems in these areas result in existential frustration or a sense of meaninglessness in life.

The meaning of life is not found by questioning the purpose of existence. It arises from the responses that a person makes to life, to the situations and tasks with which life confronts the person. Although biological, psychological, and societal factors influence a person's responses, there is always an element of freedom of choice. The person cannot always control the conditions with which he/she is confronted, but the person can control his/her responses to them. The person is thus responsible for his/her responses, choices, and actions.

Existential frustration may exist without neurosis or psychosis, but it may lead to neurosis, and neuroses and psychoses always have existential aspects. Logotherapy is directed toward existential frustration and the existential aspects of neurosis and psychosis. Thus, it is not a substitute for but is complementary to psychotherapy. Logotherapy is not concerned with psychodynamics or psychogenesis, but deals with the patient's philosophical and spiritual problems. Its aim is to bring out the ultimate possibilities of the patient, to realize the patient's latent values, not to lay bare his/her deepest secrets. Self-actualization is not accepted as an end in itself. Fulfillment of the self is possible only to the extent that the person has fulfilled the concrete meaning of his/her personal existence. Self-actualization is thus a byproduct.

Two specific techniques are described: paradoxical intention and dereflection. The former appears to be quite similar to Knight Dunlap's (1933) negative practice. Some other aspects of Frankl's method also resemble deconditioning. However, Frankl relates these techniques to existentialism and emphasizes effects beyond symptom removal. Nevertheless, there appear to be some similarities and parallels between the cases described by Frankl and those presented by Salter and by Wolpe. Paradoxical intention deals with symptoms. The method encourages the patient to enter or expose himself/herself to feared situations but without the expected results occurring, thus breaking the vicious cycle and leading to extinction of the fear or the anticipatory anxiety. Frankl, however, emphasizes the attitudinal aspects of the situation. It is the patient's attitude rather than the command, urging, or encouragement of the therapist that leads the patient to put himself/herself in a situation in which extinction can take place. It may be that at the bottom, it is the changing of the patient's attitudes that is also the effective or necessary condition of other methods that lead to deconditioning or extinction, such as those of Salter and of Wolpe.

Evaluation.   For Frankl, the spiritual aspect is a separate dimension of the individual, different from the psychological. This is probably a result of the lack of concern for, or even rejection of, meanings and values by psychology. However, it should not be necessary to consider meanings and values as constituting an independent aspect of the individual; they should be included as part of his/her psychological aspect. Nevertheless, Frankl has recognized and dealt with the concerns and the distress of the modern person by admitting them into psychotherapy as legitimate objects of treatment, rather than ignoring them or treating them as symptoms of unconscious or repressed intrapsychological impulse conflicts. His concept of attitudinal values is also a contribution. Ungersma (1961) said that with this concept Frankl "has made a profound and unique contribution to psychotherapy of all orientations . . . an insight that transcends the profoundest of Freud's contributions" (p. 28).

While other approaches to psychotherapy emphasize self-actualization, self-fulfillment, or self-enhancement as the goal of therapy, Frankl subordinates this goal to that of the achievement of meaning. One might argue that it is the significance of events, situations, tasks, values, attitudes, and so on for self-realization that gives them meaning; they have no meaning in and of themselves but only as they relate to the development of the individual.

It is probably unfair to judge logotherapy (or existential psychotherapy) on the basis of the techniques of paradoxical intention and dereflection. They appear to be specific techniques for rather specific symptoms or neurotic conditions. They would hardly be generally applicable for the other major disturbances with which existential psychotherapy is concerned—existential frustration and loss or lack of meaning in life.

Logotherapy does deal with these philosophical or spiritual problems. The discussion of methods is inadequate and disappointing, however. Logotherapy often appears to be combined with general psychotherapy and to use common techniques. Frankl denies that his approach involves teaching or preaching or that it is an intellectual or a rational approach. Yet it often appears to be essentially a discussion of philosophical or spiritual problems with just these characteristics. Terms such as *reasoning, convincing, instructing, training, leading,* and so forth occur in the discussion of cases. Suggestion, persuasion, and reasoning appear to be part of the process.

Weisskopf-Joelson (1975) made the relevant point that logotherapy is a faith, a philosophy of life, or a secular religion, rather than a science or a school of psychotherapy in the usual sense. Frankl's writings are not limited to the preparation of logotherapists but are useful to clients as well. Weisskopf-Joelson suggests that therapy sessions are essentially devoted to teaching the values and philosophy of logotherapy rather than using techniques. It has only one technique—paradoxical intention. The first part of the technique, the accepting rather than the fighting of neurotic symptoms, is consistent with the philosophy. The second part, the magnification of symptoms, she regards as a gimmick. It is this that she feels is overemphasized by those therapists who are seeking for techniques, although it is inconsistent with the philosophy. Frankl, she said, is

> a mixture of prophet, guru and preacher disguised as a psychiatrist who disseminates his message in a language to which men and women of the twentieth century are likely to listen, the language of psychology. But the world, and perhaps the man himself, has taken the disguise too seriously and has become oblivious to the prophetic person who stands behind the psychiatric cloak. (p. 240)

There seems to be no question about Frankl's concern, sincerity, and dedication. He neither prescribes the meanings of life for nor specifies the responsibilities of his clients, but he does appear to exert considerable influence in leading them to define and analyze their problems and to accept responsibility.

What, then, is the value of logotherapy? Perhaps its major value is the frank and open acceptance of philosophical problems involving goals and values as being of concern to the therapist. There is increasing evidence that the modern person is troubled by problems of values and goals, the meaning of existence, and questions about freedom and responsibility. While other therapists show some peripheral concern about this area of human experience, Frankl makes it the center of his approach. This is the general center of interest of existentialism as manifested in the work of other existentialists, but Frankl's work has some advantages for students of psychotherapy. It is not as obscure and as difficult to read as are most of the writings in existentialism. It is not as abstract or as mystical in its orientation, nor is it characterized by the morbidity or pessimism of other existentialist approaches. While Frankl uses the word *spiritual* as a key concept, he is not using it as a synonym for *religious.* In addition, although he seems to use *spiritual* interchangeably with *intellectual* or *mental,* it goes beyond these, or beyond their rational aspects. Perhaps *philosophical* is the closest synonym.

While the approach of logotherapy is rather vague, and neither the theory nor the technique has been systematically developed or presented, it is of value to the student as an indication of the growing concern with aspects of life that are not considered or not emphasized in most other approaches to psychotherapy. It is possible that these aspects—related to values, goals, and the meaning of life—are today more frequently the source of problems and so-called neuroses than was true in the past. Contemporary civilization and society perhaps have changed the nature of the problems of people. If so, psychotherapy should reflect this changing or differing content. Changing conditions have brought to light a different view of the individual that should be considered by those interested in psychotherapy.

In terms of research, "logotherapy's basic concepts—the will to meaning, the existential vacuum, and the noögenic neurosis—have been validated empirically" (Fabry, 1980, p. 15). That may be true to some extent, but what about logotherapy as treatment? What does the research have to say there? Rice and Greenberg (1992) have pointed out that "within the Existential therapy approach, there has been little empirical research" (p. 216). While they were speaking about existential therapies in general, their words also have application to logotherapy. The one exception, however, appears to be in regard to paradoxical intention—where an increasing amount of empirical work has been forthcoming.

Early on, most testaments to the efficacy of paradoxical intention came through case studies (e.g., see Frankl, 1981, 1985a, 1986; Gerz, 1962, 1966; Victor & Krug, 1967). According to Frankl (1986), the first actual experimental studies to investigate paradoxical intention came about in the 1970s (Ascher & Turner, 1979; Solyam, Garza-Perez, Ledwidge, & Solyam, 1972). In the 1980s, empirical attention to paradoxical intention, and to paradoxical strategies in general, was increasingly in evidence (see Ascher, 1989; DeBord, 1989; Dowd & Milne, 1986; Greenberg & Pies, 1983; Katz, 1984; Hill, 1987; Seltzer, 1986; Shoham-Salomon & Rosenthal, 1987; Strong, 1984). That attention has continued on into the 1990s as well (e.g., Betts & Remer, 1993; Hampton & Hulgus, 1993; Weeks, 1991).

But is paradoxical intention effective? In some studies, paradoxical intention has shown promise. But the results have not been uniformly positive (see Turner & Ascher, 1982), and what stands out most about this body of work is that it is still very much in its infancy. Much of the current status of paradoxical intention research seems best summed up by Kim, Poling, & Ascher (1991), who pointed out that, while empirical examination of paradoxical intention is on the increase, most studies thus far have focused exclusively on insomnia or agoraphobia with other problem areas receiving only minimal attention. "Based on the lack of available studies, [they concluded that] a definitive statement on the efficacy of paradoxical techniques would be premature" (p. 244). And further still, they stated: "There are many criticisms that one can lodge against even the best controlled studies and there are not sufficient data, even in the case of insomnia and agoraphobia, to resolve conflicts and support useful conclusions" (p. 244). Their statements, though first appearing several years ago, still seem applicable today and point to the fact that continued rigorous experimental work is sorely needed in this area.

And what can we say of logotherapy's future? Logotherapy appears to have much appeal and to have rather broad applications—as a philosophy, as a form of psychotherapy, in confronting death and disease, and in medicine and even dentistry (Fabry, Bulka, & Sahakian, 1980). The Victor Frankl Institute is located in Vienna. There are logotherapy courses, societies, and centers throughout the world (e.g., in Japan, Rio De Janeiro); there is an Institute of Logotherapy located in California, which was founded in the late 1970s. There is *The International Forum for Logotherapy,* which began publication then, too. The *Journal Des Viktor-Frankl-Instituts,* an international journal devoted to the study and explication of logotherapy and existential analysis, began publicaton in 1993. The First World Congress of Logotherapy was held in 1980. Those avenues of disseminating information about and furthering logotherapy continue on.

Frankl's therapy is a "meaning therapy" (Mahoney, 1991), and meaninglessness and finding meaning will always be problems that humans confront; so for that reason alone, we would suspect logotherapy to remain a viable form of treatment on the psychotherapy scene. Furthermore, the continuing relevance of Frankl's message also seems reflected in the following: (a) he was a keynote speaker at the second Evolution of Psychotherapy Conference in 1990, (b) the book resulting from that conference (Zeig, 1992) was dedicated to him (and his wife) "for his monumental contributions to humanity and for being an affirming flame, illuminating possibilities, for discovering meaning in life," and (c) Frankl was the key speaker at the 1994 Evolution of Psychotherapy Conference, which was held in Hamburg, Germany.

But Frankl has never been one to view himself as the "be-all and end-all" in logotherapy. By calling for a "degurufication of logtherapy," he has in his own way given encouragement to logotherapy's future: "My interest does not lie in raising parrots that just rehash 'their master's voice,' but rather in passing the torch to 'independent and inventive, innovative and creative spirits'" (Frankl, 1985a, p. 178). Some of that "independent and inventive, innovative and creative spirit" can be found in Fabry et al.'s (1980) volume, as well as in other more recent works. Such creative spirit and commitment will no doubt contribute to making logotherapy's future a brighter, more enduring one.

REFERENCES

Ascher, L. M. (Ed.). (1989). *Therapeutic paradox.* New York: Guilford.

Ascher, L. M., & Turner, R. M. (1979). Controlled comparison of progressive relaxation, stimulus control, and paradoxical intention therapies for insomnia. *Journal of Consulting and Clinical Psychology, 47,* 500–508.

Betts, G. R., & Remer, R. (1993). The impact of paradoxical interventions on perceptions of the therapist and ratings of treatment acceptability. *Professional Psychology: Research and Practice, 24,* 164–170.

DeBord, J. B. (1989). Paradoxical interventions: A review of the recent literature. *Journal of Counseling and Development, 67,* 394–398.

Dowd, E. T., & Milne, C. R. (1986). Paradoxical interventions in counseling psychology. *The Counseling Psychologist, 14,* 237–282.

Dunlap, K. (1933). *Habits: Their making and unmaking.* New York: Liveright.

Fabry, J. B. (1980). Logotherapy in action: An overview. In J. B. Fabry, R. P. Bulka, & W. S. Sahakian (Eds.). *Logotherapy in action* (pp. 12–21). New York: Jason Aronson.

Fabry, J. B., Bulka, R. P., & Sahakian, W. S. (Eds.). (1980). *Logotherapy in action.* New York: Jason Aronson.

Frankl, V. E. (1939). Zur medikamentösen unterstützung der Psychotherapie bei Neurosen. *Schweizer Archiv für Neurologie und Psychiatrie, 43,* 26–31.

Frankl, V. E. (1946a). *Ärztliche seelsorge.* Vienna: Verlag Franz Deuticke.

Frankl, V. E. (1946b). *Ein psycholog erlebt das Konzentrationslager.* Vienna: Verlag Franz Deuticke.

Frankl, V. E. (1947). *Der Unbedingte Mensch.* Vienna: Verlag Franz Deuticke.

Frankl, V. E. (1951). *Logos und Existenze.* Vienna: Amandus-Verlag.

Frankl, V. E. (1956). *Theorie und Therapie der Neurosen.* Vienna: Urban & Schwarzenberg.

Frankl, V. E. (1957). *Handbuch der Neurosenlehre und Psychotherapie.* Vienna: Urban & Schwarzenberg.

Frankl, V. E. (1958). On logotherapy and existence analysis. *American Journal of Psychoanalysis, 18,* 28–37.

Frankl, V. E. (1959). *From death camp to existentialism.* Boston: Beacon Press.

Frankl, V. E. (1960). Paradoxical intention: A logotherapeutic technique. *American Journal of Psychotherapy, 14,* 520–535.

Frankl, V. E. (1961a). Logotherapy and the challenge of suffering. *Review of Existential Psychology and Psychiatry, 1,* 3–7.

Frankl, V. E. (1961b). *Seminar on logotherapy.* Conducted at Harvard University Summer School, Cambridge, MA.

Frankl, V. E. (1963a). Existential dynamics and neurotic escapism. *Journal of Existential Psychiatry, 4,* 27–42.

Frankl, V. E. (1963b). *Man's search for meaning* (rev. ed.). New York: Washington Square Press.

Frankl, V. E. (1965). *The doctor and the soul* (2nd ed.). New York: Knopf.

Frankl, V. E. (1967). *Psychotherapy and existentialism: Selected papers on logotherapy.* New York: Washington Square Press.

Frankl, V. E. (1975). Paradoxical intention and dereflection. *Psychotherapy: Theory, Research, and Practice, 12,* 226–237.

Frankl, V. E. (1981). *The will to meaning: Foundations and applications of logotherapy.* New York: New American Library.

Frankl, V. E. (1985a). *Man's search for meaning.* New York: Washington Square Press.

Frankl, V. E. (1985b). *Psychotherapy and existentialism: Selected papers on logotherapy.* New York: Washington Square Press.

Frankl, V. E. (1985c). *The unconscious God: Psychotherapy and theology.* New York: Simon & Schuster.

Frankl, V. E. (1985d). *The unheard cry for meaning: Psychotherapy and humanism.* New York: Simon & Schuster.

Frankl, V. E. (1986). *The doctor and the soul: From psychotherapy to logotherapy.* New York: Vintage Books.

Frankl, V. E. (1991). Paradoxical intention. In G. R. Weeks (Ed.). *Promoting change through paradoxical therapy* (2nd ed.; pp. 99–110). New York: Brunner/Mazel.

Gerz, H. O. (1962). The treatment of the phobic and the obsessive-compulsive patient using paradoxical intention sec. Viktor E. Frankl. *Journal of Neuropsychiatry, 3,* 375–387.

Gerz, H. O. (1966). Experience with the logo-therapeutic technique of paradoxical intention in the treatment of phobic and obsessive-compulsive patients. *American Journal of Psychiatry, 123,* 548–553.

Gerz, H. O. (1980). Paradoxical intention. In J. B. Fabry, R. P. Bulka, & W. S. Sahakian (Eds.). *Logotherapy in action* (pp. 75–86). New York: Jason Aronson.

Greenberg, R. P., & Pies, R. (1983). Is paradoxical intention risk-free? A review and case report. *Journal of Clinical Psychiatry, 44,* 66–69.

Hampton, B. R., & Hulgus, Y. F. (1993). The efficacy of paradoxical strategies: A quantitative review of the research. *Psychotherapy in Private Practice, 12,* 53–71.

Hill, K. A. (1987). Meta-analysis of paradoxical interventions. *Psychotherapy, 24,* 266–270.

Katz, J. (1984). Symptom prescription: A review of the clinical outcome literature. *Clinical Psychology Review, 4,* 703–717.

Kim, R. S., Poling, J., & Ascher, L. M. (1991). An introduction to research on the clinical efficacy of paradoxical intention. In G. R. Weeks (Ed.). *Promoting change through paradoxical therapy* (2nd ed., pp. 216–150). New York: Brunner/Mazel.

Kocourek, K. (1980). Dereflection. In J. B. Fabry, R. P. Bulka, & W. S. Sahakian (Eds.). *Logotherapy in action* (pp. 87–94). New York: Jason Aronson.

Mahoney, M. (1991). *Human change processes: The scientific foundations of psychotherapy.* New York: Basic Books.

Rice, L. N., & Greenberg, L. S. (1992). Humanistic approaches to psychotherapy. In D. K. Freedheim (Ed.). *History of psychotherapy: A century of change* (pp. 197–224). Washington, DC: American Psychological Association.

Sahakian, W. S. (1980). Logotherapy—for whom? In J. B. Fabry, R. P. Bulka, & W. S. Sahakian (Eds.). *Logotherapy in action* (pp. 3–9). New York: Jason Aronson.

Seltzer, L. (1986). *Paradoxical strategies in psychotherapy: A comprehensive overview and guidebook.* New York: Wiley.

Shoham-Salomon, V., & Rosenthal, R. (1987). Paradoxical intervention: A meta-analysis. *Journal of Consulting and Clinical Psychology, 55,* 22–28.

Solyam, L., Garza-Perez, J., Ledwidge, B. L., & Solyam, C. (1972). Paradoxical intention in the treatment of obsessive thoughts: A pilot study. *Comprehensive Psychiatry, 13,* 291–297.

Strong, S. R. (1984). Experimental studies in explicitly paradoxical interventions: Results and implications. *Journal of Behavior Therapy and Experimental Psychiatry, 15,* 189–194.

Turner, R. M., & Ascher, L. M. (1982). Therapist factors in the treatment of insomnia. *Behavior Research and Therapy, 20,* 33–40.

Tweedie, D. F., Jr. (1961). *Logo-therapy and the Christian faith.* Grand Rapids, MI: Baker Book House.

Ungersma, A. J. (1961). *The search for meaning.* Philadelphia: Westminister.

Victor, R. G., & Krug, C. M. (1967). Paradoxical intention in the treatment of compulsive gambling. *American Journal of Psychotherapy, 21,* 808–814.

Weeks, G. R. (Ed.). (1991). *Promoting change through paradoxical therapy* (2nd ed.). New York: Brunner/Mazel.

Weisskopf-Joelson, E. (1961). Logotherapy: Science or faith? *Psychotherapy: Theory, Research, and Practice, 12,* 238–240.

Zeig, J. K. (Ed.). (1992). *The evolution of psychotherapy: The second conference.* New York: Brunner/Mazel.

part six

CONCLUSION: DIVERGENCE AND CONVERGENCE IN PSYCHOTHERAPY

This book has summarized a number of theories of psychotherapy. Many more could have been included—enough for at least another volume. The picture, at least on the surface, is one of extreme diversity. The theories appear to differ from one another in philosophy, in basic concepts, in goals, and in methods and techniques.

Frank (1982), noting this emphasis on differences, attributes it to a pluralistic, competitive American society.

> Since the prestige and the financial security of psychotherapists depend to a considerable extent on their being able to show that their particular theory and method is more successful than that of their rivals, they inevitably emphasize their differences; and each therapist attributes his or her successes to those conceptual and procedural features that distinguish that theory and method from its competitors rather than to the features that they all share. (p. 22)

This attempt to be different results in schools within schools of psychotherapy, and the proliferation of new methods and techniques. In addition there are differences among individual practitioners: Every psychotherapist is different or unique in some respects.

Chapter 15 considers the diversity among the various theories in terms of three sources: (1) a basic philosophical difference in views of the nature of human beings, (2) the specific treatment for specific conditions paradigm, and (3) the multicultural movement.

Chapter 16 considers attempts to integrate the diverse approaches to psychotherapy. Since all approaches derive from the experience of capable and honest people dealing with the same population—disturbed human beings—we should expect some agreement in their observations, even though they may be expressed in differing language or terminology. Or differing observers may, like the blind men describing an elephant, be dealing with somewhat different elements of the same process. Moreover, since it has been widely observed that the differing theories are apparently equally successful or effective, they must all share something in common.

A historical survey of the literature representing attempts to integrate varying approaches to psychotherapy has been provided by Goldfried (1982) and Goldfried and Newman (1986, 1992). The major focus on integration has been the eclecticism movement. The emphasis in Chapter 16, however, will be on a second, less popular approach to integration—the common elements solution.

REFERENCES

Frank, J. D. (1982). Therapeutic components shared by all psychotherapies. In J. H. Harvey & M. M. Parks (Eds.). *Psychotherapy research and behavior change* (pp. 5–38). Washington, DC: American Psychological Association.

Goldfried, M. A. (1982). On the history of therapeutic integration. *Behavior Therapy, 13,* 572–593.

Goldfried, M. R., & Newman, C. (1986). Psychotherapy integration: An historical perspective. In J. C. Norcross (Ed.). *Handbook of eclectic psychotherapy* (pp. 25–61). New York: Brunner/Mazel.

Goldfried, M. R., & Newman, C. (1992). A history of psychotherapy integration. In J. C. Norcross & M. R. Goldfried (Eds.). *Handbook of psychotherapy integration* (pp. 46–93). New York: Basic Books.

chapter 15

Divergence

Over thirty years ago, Rogers (1963) wrote, "The field of psychotherapy is in a state of chaos." He earlier had felt that therapists were talking about the same experiences but using different words and labels to describe them. By the time he wrote these words, he had come to believe that therapists differed at the basic level of personal experiences.

At about the same time, Ungersma (1961) wrote:

> The present situation in psychotherapy is not unlike that of the man who mounted his horse and rode off in all directions. The theoretical orientation of therapists is based upon widely divergent hypotheses, theories and ideologies. . . . Individual practitioners of any art are expected to vary, but some well-organized schools of therapy also seem to be working at cross-purposes with other equally well-organized schools. Nevertheless, all schools, given favorable conditions, achieve favorable results: the patient or client gets relief and is often enough cured of his difficulties. (p. 55)

A few years later Colby (1964) opened his review of the previous three years in psychotherapy with the words: "Chaos prevails." Five years later Kanfer and Phillips (1969) noted that not only do clinicians disagree in the theories they hold, but also "their practices and beliefs reflect even deeper inconsistencies and contradictions." Another five years later Singer (1974) called the training of psychotherapists a "Tower of Babel."

Almost thirty years ago, the cover of an issue of the *Saturday Review*—containing an article by Parloff (1976) whose lead-in referred to 130 schools of psychotherapy (not enumerated in the article)—had the headline "The Psychotherapy Jungle." Shortly thereafter came *The Psychotherapeutic Handbook* by Hebrink (1980), listing 255 methods of psychotherapy. (Many were simply techniques, while others were not actually psychotherapy methods.) Going along with all this, again consider the quote from Frank (1982)—cited in the introduction to this section.

In 1985 the Phoenix Conference on the Evolution of Psychotherapy brought together the world's leading theorists and therapists. Lee (1985), reporting on the conference for *Time* magazine, quoted one participant as saying: "All the experts are here and none of them agree." In his presentation, Wolpe (1987) referred to psychotherapy as "a babel of conflicting voices" (p. 144), and continued: "psychotherapy presents the prescientific spectacle of viewpoints that differ on fundamentals, schisms within viewpoints and the frequent blossoming of new viewpoints . . ." (p. 134). Prochaska (1988) titled his review of the book containing the papers presented at the conference "The Devolution of Psychotherapy," and quotes from the introduction by Zeig (1987): "Here were the reigning experts on psychotherapy and I could see no way they could agree on defining the territory. Can anyone dispute, then, that the field is in disarray!" That quote also seems equally applicable to the second Evolution of Psychotherapy conference, which was held in Phoenix in 1990 (see Zeig, 1992).

It is no wonder then that the student of psychotherapy is confused, and indeed develops the feeling of being in a jungle. Here we attempt to cut away some of the tangle of underbrush. In the following sections of this chapter, three major sources of disagreement are elaborated upon. In the next chapter we shall present a possible path out of the jungle.

A BASIC PHILOSOPHICAL DIFFERENCE

Some 30 years ago Gordon Allport (1962) delineated what he referred to as three images of the nature of man. The first is the image of humans as reactive beings. People are viewed as biological organisms reacting to stimuli from their environment. Human beings are determined by their experiences, by past learning and by conditioning, and by potential reconditioning. The concepts representing this point of view include the following: reaction, reinforcement, reflex, respondent, reintegration, reconditioning.

Allport's second image viewed humans as reactive beings in depth. Rather than being conceived as an organism reacting to its environment, the human is viewed as reacting to innate drives, motives, and needs, and is influenced by past satisfactions and frustrations of these internal forces. Concepts include repression, regression, resistance, abreaction, reaction formation, and recall and recovery of the past.

These two images are similar in basic respects. Humans are viewed as reacting to forces or stimuli, in one case from without, and in the other case from within. In one case persons are the victims of their environment, and in the other case of their innate needs and drives.

In contrast to these two images is Allport's third image. Allport designated this person as proactive, a being in the process of becoming. Persons are viewed as personal, conscious, future-oriented. Concepts include tentativeness and commitment.

It is easy to classify theories of psychotherapy under these three images, or philosophies, of human nature. Behaviorists and psychotherapists who take a traditional learning theory approach to therapy fall into the first category. Psychoanalysis and psychoanalytic approaches or the so-called dynamic theories fall under the second category. These two categories share one thing in common. Both view human beings as controlled rather than controlling, as objects rather than subjects, as passive rather than active.

In contrast to these theories are those commonly designated as humanistic or existential, of which client-centered therapy is the clearest example. Rogers has explicated his philosophy in many places. He viewed human beings as having certain characteristics inherent in their species, described by such terms as *positive, forward-moving, constructive, realistic,* and *trustworthy* (Rogers, 1957a, 1957b, 1961).

Freud, also, was clear about his view of human beings: "[T]here are present in all men destructive, and therefore anti-social and anti-cultural tendencies, and [that] with a great number of people these are strong enough to determine their behavior in human society" (Freud, 1949, p. 11). "Civilized society is perpetually menaced with disintegration through this primary hostility of men towards one another. . . . Culture . . . has to erect barriers against the aggressive instinct of men" (Freud, 1930, pp. 86–97).

The behaviorist philosophy is implicit rather than explicit. Skinner, for example, proposed no assumptions or presuppositions about the nature of the human being (Skinner, 1974). Wolpe (see Chapter 6) is not concerned about philosophy. The philosophy is implicit in such statements as Watson's:

> Give me a dozen healthy infants, well-formed, and my own specified world to bring them up in and I'll guarantee to take any one at random and train them to be any type of specialist I might select—doctor, lawyer, merchant-chief, and, yes, even beggarman and thief regardless of his talents, penchants, tendencies, abilities, vocations and race of his ancestors. (1930, p. 104)

Many years later Skinner (1948) stated it succinctly: "Give me the specifications and I'll give you the man!" (p. 343).

These two major views of human beings lead to two entirely different ways to practice psychotherapy. The first, the humanistic, leads to a practice characterized by the term *facilitating,* that is, freeing the individual to develop his/her potentialities. As Rogers (1961) has stated it:

> We have established by external control conditions which we predict will be followed by internal control by the individual, in pursuit of internally chosen goals. We have set the conditions which predict various classes of behaviors—self-directing behaviors, sensitivities to realities within and without, flexible adaptiveness—which are by their nature *unpredictable* in their specifics. The conditions we have established predict behavior which is essentially "free." . . . The conditions we have chosen to establish predict such behavioral consequences as these: that the client will become more self-directing, less rigid, more open to the evidence of his senses, better organized and integrated, more similar to the ideal which he has chosen for himself. (pp. 397–398)

The locus of control is with the client. The therapist facilitates the therapy process through empathic understanding, genuineness, and acceptance of the client.

The second view, represented mainly by the behavior therapists but including the cognitive therapists, leads to a practice of psychotherapy that focuses on more specific (and limited) goals—changes in concrete behaviors. Its therapy is more active, with the therapist being an expert in controlling and directing the client toward the specific goals. London

(1964) labeled these "action therapies": "The therapist assumes a much greater influence over the detailed conduct of treatment sessions, and possibly over the outside life of the patient" and "The therapist is much more responsible for the outcome of the treatment, that is for whatever changes take place in the patient" (p. 78).

These two approaches have sometimes been designated by the terms *facilitators* and *manipulators* (Patterson, 1958, 1959). Margo Adler (a granddaughter of Alfred Adler), reporting on the Phoenix conference for PBS radio, said that there were two kinds of therapists present: the manipulators and the enablers. Manipulation has been objected to because of its pejorative element, yet one of its dictionary definitions is relevant: "To treat or manage with the intellect. To control the action of, by management" (Webster, 1941, p. 609). It may be that the terms directive and nondirective as used earlier in psychotherapy are appropriate here.

It would appear to be clear that until we can reach agreement on the nature of human beings, no agreement on a philosophy and theory of psychotherapy is possible. And until some agreement on philosophy and theory is achieved, no agreement on the practice of psychotherapy is possible (Patterson, 1989a),

THE SPECIFIC TREATMENTS PARADIGM

A second source of diversity is the current effort to match treatments to specific problems or diagnoses. The most frequently cited statement of this paradigm is that of Paul (1969): "*What* treatment, by *whom,* is most effective for *this* individual with *that* specific problem, and under *which* set of circumstances?" (p. 44; cf. Paul, 1967). Krumboltz (1966) phrased it similarly: "What we need to know is which procedures and techniques, when used to accomplish which kinds of behavior change, are most effective with what kind of client when applied by what kind of counselor [or therapist]." Blocher (1968) also wrote that the appropriate questions are "Which treatment in the hands of which counselors can offer what benefit to particular clients?" (p. 16). Strupp and Bergin (1969) and later Bergin and Strupp (1972), following their review of research in psychotherapy, wrote: "the problem of psychotherapy research in its most general terms, should be reformulated as a standard scientific question: What specific therapeutic interventions produce what specific changes in specific patients under specific conditions?" (p. 8). Urban and Ford (1971) wrote that the task of the field of psychotherapy is "to articulate the conditions under which specific tactics are appropriate for particular sets of problems. . . . The discovery of which set of procedures is effective for what kinds of patients under which set of problems and practiced by which set of people," (p. 20). And Goldfried, Greenberg, and Marmor (1990) reiterated the paradigm: "Research must be able to demonstrate that for *this* determinant, *this* intervention produces *this* type of change process, resulting in *this* type of outcome" (p. 669).

This is an appealing position, cast in scientific form. It is however, purely empirical, unguided by theory. And it is impractical, if not impossible, to carry out the necessary research. It would require

1. a taxonomy of client problems or of psychological disorders (a reliable and valid diagnostic system);
2. a taxonomy of therapeutic interventions or techniques;

3. a taxonomy of therapist personalities;
4. a taxonomy of circumstances, conditions, situations or environments in which therapy is provided;
5. principles or rules for matching all these variables.

It is apparent that a research matrix including measures of all the variables would require a prohibitive number of cells. Kish and Kroll (1980) wrote: "The compelling question of what aspects of therapy work for what kinds of patients is probably empirically unanswerable because it is methodologically unsolvable" (p. 406). Parloff (1982) pointed out that "a systematic approach to dealing with a matrix of 250 psychosocial therapies and 150 classes of disorders would require approximately 4.7 million separate comparisons" (p. 723).

Stiles, Shapiro, and Elliott (1986) noted that such a design "renders the specificity schema unrealistic as a basis for progress. In principle, to evaluate 10 types each of client, therapist, technique, and setting, a matrix of 10,000 cells must be used!" (p. 168). These authors concluded that "after 20 years' work in the paradigm, researchers have yet to deliver many clear prescriptions" (p. 169). And Arkowitz's (1992) comments, though written in the context of technical eclecticism, apply:

> If the number of variables is limitless, the number of interactions among them is also limitless. In simple terms, the task seems overwhelming unless we have some coherent framework to guide the selection of relevant variables and to help in understanding the interactions among variables. It is here that theory is helpful, and perhaps even essential. (p. 288–289)

This complexity of the problem may be why there has been so little research following this paradigm in the more than 25 years since it was proposed. Behavior therapists have presented some research to support the claim that behavior therapy techniques are differentially effective (e.g., Kazdin & Wilson, 1978; Rachman & Wilson, 1980). The great majority of the studies are analogue studies. Hersen and Bellack (1985) wrote: "In summary, the core of the research supporting the efficacy of behavioral treatments lies in analog studies whose generalizability is questionable" (p. 16).

Lazarus (1990) responded to Strupp's (1989) statement that "research has made relatively little headway in demonstrating that specific techniques are uniquely effective in treating particular disorders (Lambert, Shapiro, & Bergin, 1986)" (p. 717). Lazarus stated that "in fact, research *has* produced a wide array of specific treatments for specific strategies for specific syndromes" (1990, p. 670). That may be true, but there is little research support for the specific effects of the treatments and strategies.

Lazarus refered to Bandura's (1986) work on the effectiveness of modeling in phobia disorders. But before Bandura's work, systematic desensitization was believed to be the specific treatment for phobias. Moreover, modeling involves a personal relationship; the therapist—even the experimenter—is a model for the client or subject. Lazarus cited a number of studies; he recognized the presence of relationship variables, but insisted they were not sufficient (though necessary). However, it is not possible to eliminate the relationship variables, which confound all research attempting to demonstrate the effectiveness of behavioral or cognitive techniques.

An interesting study attempting to control the relationship was reported by Lang, Malamed, and Hart (1970), a laboratory study of fear modification using an automated desensitization procedure. Instructions to the subjects were taped; subjects listened to tapes instead of having personal contact with a therapist. But the tapes were of a human voice, and the experimental situation involved relationship elements—the subjects were introduced to the experiment by persons. The possibility that the subjects related personally to the taped voice—and the machine—was present: The machine was designated as DAD (device for automatic desensitization).

The attempt to apply the specific treatments paradigm in practice has led to numerous prescriptive statements of specific treatments for specific conditions, often with little or no research support. Beutler and Clarkin (1990) have developed the most elaborate system of matching clients and treatments. The system is not based on the *Diagnostic and Statistical Manual of Mental Disorders* (American Psychiatric Association, 1994), but on their classification of client personal characteristics and environments and circumstances. In addition to the patient and environmental variables, there are dimensions of therapists and therapies, and specific therapy interventions. Their elaborate system, incorporating research, is a complex process, "perhaps too complex to hold the reader's interest" (Beutler & Clarkin, 1990, p. xii); it is perhaps too complex to put into actual practice. While presented as a systematic model, it contributes to the plethora of treatment techniques selected on an empirical basis with no theoretical foundation.

To date the specific-treatment paradigm appears to have contributed to the diversity of methods and techniques being used on an empirical or trial-and-error basis. Strupp's (1982) prediction may well be borne out: "The quest for specific psychotherapeutic techniques for specific disorders (analogous to a drug) may turn out to be futile" (p. 44). Seven years later he concluded that "research has made relatively little headway in demonstrating that specific techniques are uniquely effective in treating particular disorders (Lambert, Shapiro, & Bergin, 1986)" (Strupp, 1989, p. 717). Stubbs and Bozarth (1994), after evaluating the literature on the specific-treatment paradigm, concluded that "the research concerning specificity of treatment, dysfunction, therapist variables, and client variables is characterized by fragmentation, few replications, and lack of generalizability. . . . [S]pecificity research . . . has yielded inconclusive and misleading findings" (p. 109).

THE MULTICULTURAL MOVEMENT

The multicultural movement in psychotherapy has been a third major influence toward diversity. The movement began some thirty years ago. An early statement was Wrenn's (1962) article on "The Culturally Encapsulated Counselor." But the movement gained momentum from observations that "minority-group clients receive unequal and poor mental health services" (S. Sue, 1977, p. 116). They were, it was claimed, underserved and poorly served. Sue cited as examples reports by Yamamoto, James, and Palley (1968) and others. He later (S. Sue, 1988) referred to the report of the President's Commission on Mental Health (1978), as had others before this. It appeared in Sue's study that minority clients were more likely to receive supportive treatment than white clients. Sue found, however, that black clients and native Americans "were heavily overrepresented" in the community mental health centers he studied in Seattle, while Chicanos and Asian American clients were heavily underrepresented (Sue & McKinney, 1974, 1975; Sue, McKinney, Allen, & Hall, 1974). The failure-to-return rate (after the first session) was over 50 percent for blacks, native Americans and Asian Americans; the Chicano rate was 42 percent, while the white rate was 30 percent. Blacks were the only group who received differential treatment, more often becoming inpatients and less often provided group and marital therapy (see also Wu & Windle, 1980).

Mays and Albee (1992) summarized as follows:

> Members of ethnic minority groups are neither users of traditional psychotherapy nor purveyors of psychotherapy in anything like their proportion in the population. . . . The pattern of usage should not be confused with levels of need or helpseeking for emotional problems. In general, ethnic minorities experience a higher proportion of poverty and social stressors typically regarded as antecedents of psychiatric and psychological disorders than Whites. . . . Yet, in spite of the preponderance of these events in their lives, ethnic minorities are often underserved by high quality mental health resources (Wu & Windle, 1980). (pp. 552–553)

Early concern focused on minority groups in the United States (D. W. Sue, 1978). Publications on these groups mushroomed. D. W. Sue's book (1981a) contained chapters on Asian Americans, Black Americans (by Elsie Smith), Hispanics (by R. Ruiz), and American Indians (by E. H. Richardson). A special issue of the journal *Psychotherapy,* on psychotherapy with ethnic minorities (Dudley & Rawlins, Eds., 1985), included papers on these groups. (See also Atkinson, Morten & Sue, 1993.) Sue and Sue (1990) include chapters on American Indians, Asian Americans, Black Americans, and Hispanic Americans.

But multiculturism expanded to include other groups: various subcultures, racial groups, gender groups, age groups, and socioeconomic groups, including the poor (see Goldstein, 1973). Curiously, little has been written about therapy in other cultures outside the United States. The book edited by Pedersen, Lonner, and Draguns (1976) does include some material on this topic.

The assumption was quickly made that a psychotherapy developed in the United States (and other Western countries) for upper middle class white clients was inappropriate for other groups, even within the same general culture. Pedersen (1976), in an early review, wrote that "each cultural group requires a different set of skills, unique areas of emphasis, and specific insights for effective counseling [or therapy] to occur" (p. 26).

Many reasons have been advanced for the inadequacies of mental health services for ethnic minority groups: Lack of bilingual therapists and therapists who are members of the minority groups; discrimination; prejudice in therapists from the majority group. S. Sue (1988) cited as one of the most frequent criticisms of psychotherapy with minority clients "the lack of bilingual and bicultural therapists who can communicate and can understand the values, lifestyles, and backgrounds of these clients" (p. 302). Sue and Zane (1987) wrote that "the most important explanation for the problem in service delivery involves the inability of therapists to provide culturally responsive forms of treatment. The assumption, and a fairly good one, is that most therapists are not familiar with the cultural background and styles of the various ethnic-minority groups and have received training primarily developed for Anglo, or mainstream, Americans (Bernal & Padillo, 1982; Chunn, Dunston, & Ross-Sheriff, 1983; Wyatt & Parham, 1985)" (p. 37).

In his early review Pedersen (1976) wrote: "There is increasing evidence that the trained counselor [or therapist] is not prepared to deal with individuals who come from different racial, ethnic, or socio-economic groups whose values, attitudes, and general life styles are different from and threatening to his own (Padilla, Boxley, & Wagner, 1972)" (p. 35). And Mays and Albee (1992) referred to "the cultural insensitivity" of traditional psychotherapy and "a failure of the profession of psychology to develop and promote relevant and adequate mental health services for this population" (p. 554; cf. Lopez et al., 1989; Sue, Zane, & Young, 1994).

Since every client belongs to numerous groups, it does not take much imagination to recognize that the number of combinations and permutations of these groups is staggering. How different theories, methods, and techniques could be developed for each of these groups would be an insurmountable problem. Yet attempts have been made, limited to a few of the major ethnic-cultural groups.

There are numerous publications attempting to remedy the lack of knowledge about ethnic, racial, and cultural groups. The literature is replete with the characteristics of these groups and how to treat or not to treat them (e.g., D. W. Sue, 1981a; Sue & Sue, 1990; Vontress, 1981).

Pedersen (1976) in his early review reported that:

Native American Indian culture presents its own unique requirements for effective counseling. When counseling Native American Indian youth, the counselor is likely to be confronted by passively nonverbal clients who listen and absorb knowledge selectively. A counselor who expects counselees to verbalize their feelings is not likely to have much success with Native American clients. The Native American is more likely to withdraw and using the advice he has received, work out the problems by himself. The Native American is very conscious of having to make his own decisions and is likely to resent being pushed in a particular direction by persons seeking to motivate him or her. (p. 30)

Ridley (1984) stated that black clients distrust whites and do not self-disclose. "Thus both the clinical and research evidence converge in portraying a black client who, as a therapeutic participant, is generally reluctant to disclose intimately to a white therapist" (p. 1236). Ridley's statement on self-disclosure in blacks applies to other groups as well, including Asian Americans. Yet not all blacks are non-self-disclosing, nor are all Asian Americans. Sue and Zane (1987) noted that "many Asian American clients who were unacculturated seemed quite willing to talk about their emotions and to work with little structure" (p. 39). Trimble (1976) noted that "The Indian is not accustomed to self-analysis nor is there a familiarity with the process of discussing with a non-Indian one's emotional conflicts" (p. 79). Meadow (1982) recommended that therapists deemphasize the necessity for self-disclosure with Hispanic clients. D. W. Sue (1981a) wrote that counselors or therapists who "value verbal, emotional and behavioral expressiveness as goals in counseling are transmitting their own values" (p. 38; cf. Sue & Sue, 1990, p. 38). It appears that lack of self-disclosure is not necessarily an inability to do so, but a reluctance to do so in certain situations with certain persons.

A second characteristic of certain (many) ethnic minority groups is the desire for a structured relationship in which the therapist is cast as an expert, giving advice and solutions to problems (e.g. Sue & Morishima, 1982; Sue & Sue, 1990; Szapocznik, Santisteban, Kurtines, Hervis, & Spencer, 1982; Vontress, 1976, 1981). Many clients from ethnic-minority groups are dependent, desiring a therapist who is active, authoritative, directive, and concrete (Atkinson, Maruyama, & Matsui, 1978; Leong, 1986; D. W. Sue, 1981b; Sue & Zane, 1987; Trimble, 1976, 1981). It is usually stated that such clients *need* therapists who provide these conditions. However, it would be more accurate to say that they *want* or prefer such therapists. Virtually all of the research on the preferences of minority groups toward counseling or psychotherapy involves subjects from small, unrepresentative samples, not actual clients, involving statements about the kind of counselor or therapist the subjects would like if they were to go to a counselor or therapist.

Yet, the almost universal recommendation is that therapists use techniques that "fit" the presumed characteristics of clients. Basic to this is "the assumption that different cultural and subcultural groups require different approaches" (Sue & Sue, 1990, p. 161). S. Sue (1988), listing five publications (including Ridley, 1984), states:

> All seem to endorse the *notion* that various racial groups may require approaches or techniques that differ from white Anglo-Saxon middle-class clients. Indeed, the *belief* held by many cross-cultural scholars is that minority clients tend to prefer and respond better to directive rather than nondirective approaches, that counseling approaches which are active rather than passive are more effective, that a structured, explicit approach may be more effective than an unstructured, ambiguous one, and that minority clients may desire a counselor who self-discloses his/her thoughts or feelings (Atkinson, Maruyama, & Matsui, 1978; Berman, 1979; Dauphinais et al., 1981; Ivey, 1986; D. W. Sue, 1978; Szapocznik, et al., 1982). (Also in Sue & Sue, 1990, p. 160.) (Italics added.)

There has been a plethora of publications recommending that "culturally sensitive," "culturally relevant" and "culturally appropriate" techniques be developed (e.g., D. W. Sue, 1991; Sue, Bernier, Durran, Feinberg, Pedersen, Smith, & Velasquez-Nuttall, 1982; Sue & Sue, 1990, Chapter 8, The Culturally Skilled Counselor). There are a number of problems with the attempt to provide information and knowledge about ethnic-minority groups, and to recommend specific methods or techniques to fit these characteristics, as discussed below.

1. First, descriptions of the various groups are generalizations, describing the modal (abstract average) person. The result is the proliferation of stereotypes, a danger that a number of writers recognize. S. Sue (1983) cites Campbell (1967) who "warned that the finding of actual differences between groups often leads to exaggerated stereotyped images of these differences" (p. 585). S. Sue (1983) was one of the first to point out the existence of wide individual differences within each group. In statistics when within-group variance is great as compared with between-group variance, it becomes difficult, if not impossible, to assign individuals to groups or to differentiate among groups.

A note about the emphasis on value differences among cultures is relevant here. There are, to be sure, some value differences. But it needs to be pointed out that the word *values* is used indiscriminately. Many so-called value differences among groups are actually customs, lifestyles, social norms or habits, and preferences. There are many values that are common to many different groups, and some universal values (Patterson, 1989c). Brown (1991) wrote that "universals exist, they are numerous. . . . [I]t will be irresponsible to continue shunting these questions to the side, fraud to deny that they exist" (see pp. 142–156).

2. The assumptions regarding the characteristics of ethnic-minority groups lead to the self-fulfillment prophecy. If clients from other cultural groups are believed to be non-self-disclosing, dependent, in need of structure, direction, advice, etc., then they will be treated as if these things are true, and they will respond to confirm the therapist's beliefs. It is thus ensured that standard or traditional therapy will not be effective.

3. The assumption that the therapist's knowledge of the culture of his/her client will lead to more appropriate and effective therapy has not been borne out. Sue and Zane (1987) stated "Recommendations that admonish therapists to be culturally sensitive and to know the culture of the client have not been very helpful" (p. 37). They continued:

> The major problem with approaches emphasizing either cultural knowledge or culture-specific techniques is that neither is linked to particular processes that result in effective psychotherapy. . . . [R]ecommendations for knowledge of culture are necessary but not sufficient for effective treatment. . . . [T]he knowledge must be transformed into concrete operations and strategies. (p. 39)

4. Perhaps the greatest difficulty with accepting assumptions about the characteristics and so-called needs about clients from differing cultures is that they will lead to failure, or lack of success in psychotherapy. While some therapists may adopt an active, problem-solving role, overly controlling or dominating therapeutic stances are usually counterproductive. To provide this kind of treatment (it would not be called therapy) to clients from other cultures would be providing poor or second-class treatment.

D. W. Sue (1981a, p. 38) and Sue and Sue (1990, p. 40) referred to "the belief in the desirability of self-disclosure." But client self-disclosure is more than desirable—it is necessary for client progress. Sue and Sue (1990) appear to recognize its importance, referring to self-disclosure as an "essential" condition, "particularly crucial to the process and goals of counseling, because it is the most direct means by which an individual makes himself/herself known to another (Greene, 1985; Mays, 1985)" (p. 77). Vontress (1976, 1981) recognized it as "basic to the counseling process" (p. 53). Ridley (1984) wrote that "nondisclosure means that a client forfeits an opportunity to engage in therapeutic self-exploration. . . . [T]he result will most surely be nontherapeutic" (p. 1237).

Modifying or adapting therapy to the presumed needs, or desires of ethnic minority clients cannot lead to abandoning the things that are essential for therapeutic progress. Ho (1985) recognized this: "there is a limit on the degree to which the fundamental psychological-therapeutic orientation [the Western model] can be compromised" (p. 1214). To attempt to apply all the techniques that have been suggested in working with ethnic-minority clients is to water down the therapy process until it is no longer effective in any meaningful sense of psychotherapy. While clients may be pleased or satisfied with such treatment, and even receive some immediate, temporary help, therapy that includes goals such as client independence, responsibility, and ability to resolve his/her own problems is not achieved.

Culture-specific techniques for all the innumerable groups that may appeal to a therapist for help have not been clearly specified, described, or matched with the groups to which they apply. More important, there is little if any research support for the effectiveness of the theorized differential techniques or methods.

S. Sue (1988) noted that

> considerable controversy exists over the effectiveness of psychotherapy for ethnic minority groups. . . . Despite the strongly held opinions over the problems ethnic clients

> encounter in receiving effective services, empirical evidence has failed to consistently demonstrate differential outcomes for ethnic and White clients. . . . Most treatment studies have failed to show differential outcomes on the basis of race or ethnicity of clients (pp. 301–302)

once clients enter and continue in treatment.

What then, is the solution to the problem of psychotherapy with members of minority groups? It is certainly not that traditional therapy should be abandoned.

Early on, before the emphasis on specific techniques for different groups, a number of writers listed a number of therapist characteristics or attitudes as being necessary. Wohl (1976, p. 187) noted that McNeill (1965, p. vii) emphasized that the healing function includes a caring and concern on the part of the healer. And discussing Pande (1968), Wohl wrote that "therapy provides a special, close, love relationship" (Wohl, 1976, p. 189). Stewart (1976), at the same time, emphasized the importance of warmth, genuineness, and especially empathy. Torrey (1970, 1972), according to Pedersen (1976) "identified the expectations of troubled contrast-culture clients and the personal qualities of a counselor as being closely related to the healthy change, accurate empathy, and nonpossessive warmth and genuineness that are essential to effective mental health care" (p. 30). Vontress (1976) emphasized the importance of rapport as "the emotional bridge between the counselor and the counselee. . . . Simply defined rapport constitutes a comfortable and unconstrained mutual trust and confidence between two persons" (p. 45). He appeared to include empathy in rapport. Richardson (1981) listed the following among the ways of working with American Indian clients: listen, be accepting, respect their culture, be natural, be honest, honor their presence, do not be condescending. Vontress (1976) also commented on counselor training that "what is needed most are affective experiences designed to humanize counselors. . . . Few counselors ever ask what they can do to change themselves; few want to know how they can become better human beings in order to relate more effectively with other human beings who, through the accident of birth, are racially and ethnically different" (p. 62).

Unfortunately, the emphasis on techniques overshadowed attention to the nature of the relationship between the counselor and the client. It now appears that this preoccupation with techniques is fading, and that it is being recognized that therapist competence inheres in the personal qualities of the therapist. The competent therapist is one who provides an effective therapeutic relationship. The nature of this relationship has long been known, and is the same regardless of the group to which the client belongs.

There are four basic therapist and client essentials for all effective therapy (Rogers, 1957b).

1. *Respect for the client.* This includes trust in the client, assumes that the client is capable of taking responsibility for him/herself, including during the therapy process, of making choices and decisions, of resolving problems—and moreover, should be allowed to do so, as a right.

2. *Therapeutic genuineness.* Therapy is a real relationship. The therapist does not assume a role as an all knowing expert, operating on the client with a battery of techniques. The therapist is not an impersonal, cold, objective professional, but a real person.

3. *Empathic understanding.* Empathic understanding is more than a knowledge of the client based on knowledge of the groups to which he/she belongs. It requires that the therapist be able to use this knowledge as it applies or relates to the unique client, which involves entering into the client's world and seeing it as he/she does. "The ability to convey

empathy in a culturally consistent and meaningful manner may be the crucial variable to engage the client" (Ibrahim, 1991, p. 18).

The only way in which the therapist can enter the world of the client is with the permission of the client, who communicates the nature of his/her world to the therapist through self-disclosure. Thus, client self-disclosure is the *sine qua non* for therapy. Therapist respect and genuineness facilitate client self-disclosure.

4. *Communication of empathy, respect, and genuineness to the client.* The conditions must be perceived, recognized and felt by the client if they are to be effective. This becomes difficult with clients who differ from the therapist in culture, race, socioeconomic class, age, and gender. Understanding of cultural differences in verbal and nonverbal behaviors (Sue, 1989; Sue & Sue, 1990) can be very helpful here. However, the therapist is not always successful in communicating these qualities, not only to clients from a different culture or class, but to clients such as psychotic individuals, who may be unable to or refuse to accept the conditions.

Sue and Sue (1990) conceded that "qualities such as respect and acceptance of the individual, unconditional positive regard, understanding the problem from the individual's perspective, allowing the client to explore his or her own values, and arriving at an individual solution are core qualities that may transcend culture" (p. 187). These therapist qualities are not only essential for effective therapy, they are also elements of all facilitative interpersonal relationships. They are neither time bound nor culture-bound.

In addition to these four, there is another element in all therapy that is of particular importance in intercultural therapy: Structuring. It appears to have been recognized by few writers. Vontress (1976) is one who has, and his statement bears repeating:

> On the whole, disadvantaged minority group members have had limited experiences with counselors and related therapeutic professionals. Their contacts have been mainly with people who tell them what they must and should do. . . . Relationships with professionals who place major responsibility upon the individual for solving his own problems are few. Therefore, the counselor working within such a context should structure and define his role to clients; that is he should indicate what, how, and why he intends to do what he will do. . . . Failure to structure early and adequately in counseling can result in unfortunate and unnecessary misunderstanding. (p. 47) (see also Sue & Zane, 1987, pp. 41–43)

These misunderstandings may contribute to the failure of the client to continue therapy. Structuring is necessary whenever a client does not know what is involved in the therapeutic relationship—how the therapist will function and what is expected of the client—or holds misconceptions about the process.

There appears to have been the beginning of a change in the literature on multicultural therapy that could portend a return to a recognition of the basic nature of therapy as an interpersonal relationship. Patterson (1978) earlier had proposed such a view of multicultural therapy or counseling. Change has been introduced by the statement of Pedersen (1990) that "to some extent all mental health counseling is multicultural" (p. 94). This was followed by his statement that "we are moving toward a generic theory of multiculturalism" (Pedersen, 1991, p. 6). He continued: "The obvious differences in behavior across cultures are typically over-emphasized, whereas the more difficult to discover similarities of expectations are typically underemphasized" (p. 9). Vontress (1988) earlier had emphasized the common humanness of all clients. Ibraham (1991) also accepts multicultural counseling as generic. Speight, Myers, Cox, and Highlen (1991) stated it clearly: "All counseling is cross-cultural or multicultural because all humans differ in terms of cultural background, values, or lifestyle. . . . [M]ulticultural counseling is redefined as basic to all forms of helping relationships. All counseling is multicultural in nature" (pp. 29, 31). Unfortunately, the Statement of Standards of the Association for Multicultural Counseling and Development (D. W. Sue, Arredondo, & McDavic, 1992) does not adequately recognize this core of counselor competence.

All clients, as previously noted, belong to multiple groups, all of which influence the client's perceptions, beliefs, feelings, thoughts, and behavior. The therapist must be aware of these influences, and of their unique blending or fusion in the client if therapy is to be successful.

The current (over)emphasis on cultural diversity and culture-specific therapy leads to (a) a focus on specific techniques (or skills as they are now called), with the therapist becoming a chameleon, changing styles, techniques, and methods to meet the presumed characteristics of clients from varying cultures and groups, and (b) an emphasis on differences among cultures and their contrasting world views. This approach ignores the fact that we are rapidly becoming one world, with rapid communication and increasing interrelations among persons from varying cultures, leading to increasing homogeniety and a world view representing the common humanity that binds all human beings together as one species.

Vontress (1979) proposed an existentialist philosophical view of cross-cultural counseling, a "philosophical orientation that transcends culture" (p. 117). Freeman (1993), citing Pedersen's (1991) proposal for a search for a framework that recognizes the complex diversity of a plural society while, at the same time, suggesting bridges of shared concern that bind culturally different persons to one another, develops such a framework that includes the universal and the specific in therapy. Though she does not make this point, the universal is the process, while the specific deals with the content in therapy.

Finally, in view of these observations, and if all therapy is multicultural, then it is possible to develop a universal system of psychotherapy (Patterson, 1989b). This will be developed in the next chapter.

CONCLUSION

In this chapter, we have considered three main sources of diversity in the theory and practice of psychotherapy. The first is a philosophical difference concerning the nature of human beings. On the one hand, they are viewed as reactive beings, responding to inner and outer forces and stimuli. On the other hand humans are perceived as proactive beings capable of exerting considerable control over their lives. The second source of divergence is the specific treatments for specific problems paradigm. The third source has been the multiculturalism movement, which has advocated specific treatments or techniques for clients from different ethnic, racial, cultural, socioeconomic, age, and gender groups. Recently, however, this approach has moved toward the view that all therapy is multicultural, and that the crucial problem is the competence of the therapist as a person. This leads to the possibility of a universal system of psychotherapy. The next chapter will propose a resolution of the first two sources of divergence and propose a universal system of psychotherapy.

REFERENCES

Allport, G. W. (1962). Psychological models for guidance. *Harvard Educational Review, 32,* 373–381.

American Psychiatric Association (1994). *Diagnostic and statistical manual of mental disorders* (4th ed.). Washington, DC: American Psychiatric Association.

Arkowitz, H. (1992). Integrative theories of psychotherapy. In D. K. Freedheim (Ed.). *History of psychotherapy: A century of change* (pp. 261–303). Washington, DC: American Psychological Association.

Atkinson, D. R., Maruyama, M., & Matsui, S. (1978). Effects of counselor race and counseling approach on Asian American's perceptions of counselor credibility and utility. *Journal of Counseling Psychology, 25,* 76–83.

Atkinson, D. R., Morten, G., & Sue, D. W. (1993). *Counseling American minorities: A cross-cultural perspective* (4th ed.). Dubuque, IA: W. C. Brown.

Bandura, A. (1986). *Social foundations of thought and action: A social cognitive theory.* Englewood Cliffs, NJ: Prentice-Hall.

Bergin, A. E., & Strupp, H. H. (1972). *Changing frontiers in the science of psychotherapy.* Chicago: Aldine.

Berman, J. (1979). Counselor skills used by Black and White male and female counselors. *Journal of Counseling Psychology, 26,* 81–84.

Bernal, M. E., & Padilla, A. M. (1982). Status of minority curricula and training in clinical psychology. *American Psychologist, 37,* 780–787.

Beutler, L. E., & Clarkin, J. F. (1990). *Systematic treatment selection.* New York: Brunner/Mazel.

Blocher, D. (1968). What can counseling offer clients? In J. M. Whiteley (Ed.), *Research in counseling* (pp. 5–29). Columbus, OH: Merrill.

Brown, D. E. (1991). *Human universals.* Philadelphia, PA: Temple University Press.

Campbell, D. T. (1967). Stereotypes and the perception of group differences. *American Psychologist, 22,* 817–829.

Chunn, J. C., Dunston, P. J., & Ross-Sheriff, F. (1983). (Eds.). *Mental health and people of color: Curriculum development and change.* Washington, DC: Howard University Press.

Colby, K. M. (1964). Psychotherapeutic processes. *Annual Review of Psychology, 15,* 347–370.

Dauphinais, R., Dauphinais, L., & Rowe, W. (1981). Effects of race and communication style on Indian perceptions of counselor effectiveness. *Counselor Education and Supervision, 21,* 72–80.

Dudley, G. R., & Rawlins, M. L. (Eds.) (1985). Psychotherapy with ethnic minorities. *Psychotherapy, 22,* 308–477.

Frank, J. D. (1982). Therapeutic components shared by all psychotherapists. In J. H. Harvey & M. M. Peaks (Eds.). *Psychotherapy research and behavior change* (pp. 5–37). Washington, DC: American Psychological Association.

Freeman, S. (1993). Client-centered therapy and diverse populations. *Journal of Multicultural Counseling and Development, 21,* 248–254.

Freud, S. (1930). *Civilization and its discontents.* New York: Jonathan Cape & Harrison Smith.

Freud, S. (1949). *The future of an illusion.* London: Hogarth Press.

Goldfried, M. R., Greenberg, L. S., & Marmor, C. (1990). Individual psychotherapy: Process and outcome. *Annual Review of Psychology, 41,* 659–688.

Goldstein, A. P. (1973). *Structured learning therapy: Toward a psychotherapy for the poor.* New York: Academic.

Greene, B. A. (1985). Considerations in the treatment of Black patients by white therapists. *Psychotherapy, 22,* 389–393.

Hebrink, R. (1980). *The psychotherapy handbook.* New York: American Library.

Hersen, B., & Bellack, A. S. (1985). (Eds.) *Handbook of clinical behavior therapy with adults.* New York: Plenum.

Ho, D. Y. F. (1985). Cultural values and professional issues in clinical psychology: The Hong Kong experience. *American Psychologist, 40,* 1212–1218.

Ibraham, F. A. (1991). Contribution of cultural worldview to generic counseling and development. *Journal of Counseling and Development, 70,* 13–19.

Ivey, A. E. (1986). *Developmental therapy.* San Francisco: Jossey-Bass.

Kanfer, F. H., & Phillips, J. A. (1969). A survey of current behavior therapies and a proposal for clarification. In C. M. Franks (Ed.). *Behavior therapy: Appraisal and status* (pp. 445–475). New York: McGraw-Hill.

Kazdin, A. E., & Wilson, G. T. (1978). *Evaluation of behavior therapy: Issues, evidence and research.* Cambridge, MA: Ballinger.

Kish, J., & Kroll, J. (1980). Meaningfulness versus effectiveness: Paradoxical implications in the evaluation of psychotherapy. *Psychotherapy: Theory, Research, and Practice, 17,* 401–413.

Krumboltz, J. D. (1966). Promoting adaptive behavior: New answers to familiar questions. In J. D. Krumboltz (Ed.), *Revolution in counseling* (pp. 1–26). Boston: Houghton Mifflin.

Lambert, M. J., Shapiro, D. A., & Bergin, A. E. (1986). The effectiveness of psychotherapy. In S. L. Garfield & A. E. Bergin (Eds.). *Handbook of psychotherapy and behavior change* (3rd ed., pp. 157–211). New York: Wiley.

Lang, P. J., Malamed, B. G., & Hart, J. (1970). A psychophysical analysis of fear modification using an automated desensitization procedure. *Journal of Abnormal Psychology, 76,* 220–234.

Lazarus, A. A. (1990). If this be research. . . . [Comment] *American Psychologist, 45,* 670–671.

Lee, J. (1985). A therapist in every corner. *Time,* December 23, 59.

Leong, F. T. (1986). Counseling and psychotherapy with Asian-Americans. *Journal of Counseling Psychology, 33,* 196–206.

London, P. (1964). *The modes and morals of psychotherapy.* New York: Holt, Rinehart & Winston.

Lopez, S. R., Grover, K. P., Holland, D., Johnson, M. J., Kain, C. D., Kanel, K., Mellins, C. A., & Rhyne, M. C. (1989). Development of culturally sensitive psychotherapists. *Professional Psychology: Research and Practice, 20,* 369–376.

Mays, V. M. (1985). The Black American and psychotherapy: The dilemma. *Psychotherapy, 22,* 379–388.

Mays, V. M., & Albee, G. W. (1992). Psychotherapy and ethnic minorities. In D. K. Freedheim (Ed.). *History of psychotherapy,* (pp. 552–570). Washington, DC: American Psychological Association.

McNeill, J. T. (1965). *A history of souls.* New York: Harper & Row.

Meadow, A. (1982). Psychopathology, psychotherapy, and the Mexican-American patient. In E. E. Jones & S. J. Korchin (Eds.). *Minority mental health* (pp. 331–361). New York: Praeger.

Padilla, E., Boxley, A., & Wagner, N. (1972). *The desegregation of clinical psychology training.* Unpublished manuscript.

Pande, S. (1968). The mystique of Western psychotherapy: An Eastern interpretation. *Journal of Nervous and Mental Diseases, 146,* 425–432.

Parloff, M. (1976). Shopping for the right therapy. *Saturday Review,* February 21.

Parloff, M. B. (1982). Psychotherapy evidence and reimbursement decisions: Bambi meets Godzilla. *American Journal of Psychiatry, 139,* 718–729.

Patterson, C. H. (1958). Two approaches to human relations. *American Journal of Psychotherapy, 12,* 691–708.

Patterson, C. H. (1959). *Counseling and psychotherapy: Theory and practice.* New York: Harper & Row.

Patterson, C. H. (1978). Cross-cultural or intercultural counseling or psychotherapy. *International Journal for the Advancement of Counseling, 1,* 231–247.

Patterson, C. H. (1989a). Eclecticism in psychotherapy: Is integration possible? *Psychotherapy, 26,* 157–161.

Patterson, C. H. (1989b). *A universal system of psychotherapy.* Keynote speech, Southeast Asian Symposium on Counseling and Guidance in the 21st Century. Taipei, Taiwan, December, 1989.

Patterson, C. H. (1989c). Values in counseling and psychotherapy. *Counseling and Values, 33,* 164–176.

Paul, G. L. (1967). Strategy of outcome research in psychotherapy. *Journal of Consulting Psychology, 31,* 109–118.

Paul, G. (1969). Behavior modification research: Design and tactics. In C. M. Franks (Ed.). *Behavior therapy: Appraisal and status* (pp. 29–62). New York: McGraw-Hill.

Pedersen, P. (1976). The field of intercultural counseling. In P. Pedersen, W. J. Lonner, & J. G. Draguns (Eds.). *Counseling across cultures* (pp. 17–41). Honolulu: University Press of Hawaii.

Pedersen, P. B. (1990). The multicultural perspective as a fourth force in counseling. *Journal of Mental Health Counseling, 12,* 93–95.

Pedersen, P. B. (1991). Multiculturalism as a generic approach to counseling. *Journal of Counseling and Development, 70,* 6–12.

Pedersen, P. B., Lonner, W., & Draguns (1976). (Eds.). *Counseling across cultures.* Honolulu: University Press of Hawaii. (See also, 3rd ed., 1989.)

President's Commission on Mental Health (1978). *Report to the President.* Washington, DC: United States Government Printing Office.

Prochaska, J. O. (1988). The devolution of psychotherapy. [Review of J. K. Zeig (Ed.). "The evolution of psychotherapy."] *Contemporary Psychology, 33,* 305.

Rachman, S. J., & Wilson, G. T. (1980). *The effects of psychological therapy* (2nd ed.). New York: Pergamon Press.

Richardson, E. H. (1981). Cultural and historical perspectives in counseling American Indians. In D. W. Sue (Ed.). *Counseling the culturally different: Theory and practice* (pp. 216–255). New York: Wiley.

Ridley, C. R. (1984). Clinical treatment of the non-disclosing black client. *American Psychologist, 39,* 1234–1244.

Rogers, C. R. (1957a). A note on "The nature of man." *Journal of Counseling Psychology, 4,* 199–203.

Rogers, C. R. (1957b). The necessary and sufficient conditions of therapeutic personality change. *Journal of Consulting Psychology, 21,* 95–103.

Rogers, C. R. (1961). *On becoming a person.* Boston: Houghton Mifflin.

Rogers, C. R. (1963). Psychotherapy today or where do we go from here? *American Journal of Psychotherapy, 17,* 5–16.

Singer, J. (1974). *Imagery and daydream methods in psychotherapy and behavior modification.* New York: Academic Press.

Skinner, B. F. (1948). *Walden two.* New York: Macmillan.

Skinner, B. F. (1974). *About behaviorism.* New York: Knopf.

Speight, S. L., Myers, L. J., Cox, C. I., & Highlen, P. S. (1991). A redefinition of multicultural counseling. *Journal of Counseling and Development, 70,* 29–36.

Stewart, E. C. (1976). Cultural sensitivities in counseling. In P. Pedersen, W. J. Lonner, & J. Draguns (Eds.). *Counseling across cultures* (pp. 98–122). Honolulu: University of Hawaii Press.

Stiles, W. B., Shapiro, D. A., & Elliott, R. (1986). "Are all psychotherapies equal?" *American Psychologist, 41,* 165–180.

Strupp, H. H. (1982). The outcome problem in psychotherapy: Contemporary perspectives. In J. H. Harvey & M. M. Peaks (Eds.). *Psychotherapy research and behavior change* (pp. 43–71). Washington, DC: American Psychological Association.

Strupp, H. H. (1989). Psychotherapy: Can the practitioner learn from the research? *American Psychologist, 44,* 717–724.

Strupp, H. H., & Bergin, A. E. (1969). Some empirical and conceptual bases for coordinated research in psychotherapy. *International Journal of Psychiatry, 7,* 18–90.

Stubbs, J. B., & Bozarth, J. (1994). The Dodo Bird revisted: A qualitative study of psychotherapy efficacy research. *Applied and Preventive Psychology, 3,* 109–120.

Sue, D. W. (1978). Eliminating cultural oppression in counseling: Toward a general theory. *Journal of Counseling Psychology, 25,* 419–428.

Sue, D. W. (1981a) (with chapter contributions by E. H. Richardson, R. A. Ruiz, & E. J. Smith). *Counseling the culturally different: Theory and practice.* New York: Wiley.

Sue, D. W. (1981b). Evaluating process variables in cross-cultural counseling and psychotherapy. In A. J. Marshall & P. Pedersen (Eds.). *Cross-cultural counseling and psychotherapy.* New York: Pergamon.

Sue, D. W. (1989). *Cultural specific techniques in counseling: A counseling framework.* Paper presented at the Southeast Asia Symposium on Counseling and Guidance in the 21st Century. Taipei, Taiwan, December, 1989.

Sue, D. W. (1991). A model for cultural diversity training. *Journal of Counseling and Development, 70,* 99–105.

Sue, D. W., Arredondo, P., & McDavic, R. J. (1992). Multicultural counseling competencies and standards: A call to the profession. *Journal of Counseling and Development, 70,* 477–488.

Sue, D. W., Bernier, J. E., Durran, A., Feinberg, L., Pedersen, P., Smith, E. J., & Velasquez-Nuttall, E. (1982). Position paper: Cross-cultural counseling competencies. *The Counseling Psychologist, 10*(2), 45–52.

Sue, D. W., & Sue, D. (1990). *Counseling the culturally different* (2nd ed.). New York: Wiley.

Sue, S. (1977). Community mental health services to minority groups: Some optimism, some pessimism. *American Psychologist, 32,* 616–624.

Sue, S. (1983). Ethnic minorities in psychology: A reexamination. *American Psychologist, 38,* 583–592.

Sue, S. (1988). Psychotherapeutic services for minorities: Two decades of research findings. *American Psychologist, 43,* 301–308.

Sue, S., & McKinney, H. (1975). Asian Americans in the community mental health system. *American Journal of Orthopsychiatry, 45,* 111–118.

Sue, S., McKinney, H., Allen, D., & Hale, J. (1974). Delivery of community mental health services to black and white clients. *Journal of Consulting and Clinical Psychology, 42,* 794–801.

Sue, S., & Morishima, J. K. (1982). *The mental health of Asian Americans.* San Francisco: Jossey-Bass.

Sue, S., & Zane, N. (1987). The role of culture and cultural techniques in psychotherapy. *American Psychologist, 42,* 37–45.

Sue, S., Zane, N., & Young, K. (1994). Research on psychotherapy with culturally diverse populations. In A. E. Bergin & S. L. Garfield (Eds.). *Handbook of psychotherapy and behavior change* (4th ed., pp. 783–817). New York: Wiley.

Szapocznik, J., Santisteban, D., Kurtines, W. M., Hervis, O. E., & Spencer, F. (1982). Life enhancement counseling: A psychosocial model of services for Cuban elders. In E. E. Jones & S. J. Korchin (Eds.). *Minority mental health.* New York: Praeger.

Torrey, E. F. (March, 1970). *The irrelevancy of traditional mental health services for urban Mexican-Americans.* Paper presented to the American Orthopsychiatric Association, San Francisco, CA.

Torrey, E. F. (1972). *The mind game: Witch doctors and psychiatrists.* New York: Emerson Hall.

Trimble, J. E. (1976). Value differences among American Indians: Concerns for the concerned counselor. In P. Pedersen (Ed.). *Counseling across cultures* (pp. 65–81). Honolulu: University Press of Hawaii.

Trimble, J. E. (1981). Value differences and their importance in counseling American Indians. In P. Pedersen, J. G. Draguns, W. J. Lonnor, & J. E. Trimble (Eds.). *Counseling across cultures* (2nd ed.). Honolulu: University Press of Hawaii.

Ungersma, A. J. (1961). *The search for meaning.* Philadelphia: Westminster.

Urban, H. B., & Ford, D. H. (1971). Some historical and conceptual perspectives on psychotherapy and behavior change. In A. E. Bergin & S. L. Garfield (Eds.). *Handbook of psychotherapy and behavior change: An empirical analysis.* New York: Wiley.

Vontress, C. E. (1976). Racial and ethnic barriers in counseling. In P. Pedersen, W. J. Lonner, & J. Draguns (Eds.). *Counseling across cultures* (pp. 42–64). Honolulu: University of Hawaii Press.

Vontress, C. E. (1979). Cross-cultural counseling: An existential approach. *Personnel and Guidance Journal, 58,* 117–122.

Vontress, C. E. (1981). Racial and ethnic barriers in counseling. In P. Pedersen, J. S. Draguns, W. J. Lonner, & J. E. Trimble (Eds.). *Counseling across cultures* (2nd ed.). Honolulu: University of Hawaii Press.

Vontress, C. E. (1988). An existential approach to cross-cultural counseling. *Journal of Multicultural Counseling and Development, 16,* 73–83.

Watson, J. B. (1930). *Behaviorism* (rev. ed.). New York: Norton.

Webster's Collegiate Dictionary (5th ed.) (1941). Springfield, MA: G. C. Merriam.

Wohl, J. (1976). Intercultural psychotherapy: Issues, questions, and reflections. In P. Pedersen, W. J. Lonner, & J. Draguns (Eds.). *Counseling across cultures* (pp. 184–207). Honolulu: University of Hawaii Press.

Wolpe, J. (1987). The promotion of a scientific psychotherapy: A long voyage. In J. K. Zeig (Ed.). *The evolution of psychotherapy* (pp. 133–142). New York: Brunner/Mazel.

Wrenn, C. G. (1962). The culturally encapsulated counselor. *Harvard Educational Review, 32,* 444–449.

Wu, I. H. & Windle, C. (1980). Ethnic specificity in the relative minority use and staffing of community mental health services. *Community Mental Health Journal, 16,* 156–168.

Wyatt, G. E., & Parham, W. D. (1985). The inclusion of culturally sensitive issue materials in graduate school and training programs. *Psychotherapy, 22,* 461–468.

Yamamoto, J., James, T. C., & Palley, N. (1968). Clinical problems in psychiatric therapy. *Archives of General Psychiatry, 19,* 45–49.

Zeig, J. K. (Ed.). (1987). *The evolution of psychotherapy.* New York: Brunner/Mazel.

Zeig, J. K. (Ed.). (1992). *The evolution of psychotherapy: The second conference.* New York: Brunner/Mazel.

chapter 16

Convergence

The objective of every science is to arrive at, or develop, an integration of all the evidence, or facts, in a field, to resolve apparently opposed or conflicting facts. For example, Stephen Hawking is devoting his life to discover or develop a principle or law that will reconcile Einstein's unified field theory (the theory of relativity) and quantum mechanics. It would appear that the objective of the field of psychotherapy would be to develop a universal theory or system. However, this does not seem to be the case. Few would agree that such an objective is possible, or even desirable. Yet there is an interest in attempting to integrate differing methods, if not theories.

THE MOVEMENT TOWARD INTEGRATION

Early attempts to relate learning theory to psychotherapy occurred in the 1930s and 1940s (see Introduction to Part II). The book by Dollard and Miller (1950) was the first major attempt to integrate behavior theory and psychoanalytic theory. Wachtel's (1977) book was the next major attempt at integration of these two approaches and was continued in a series of papers. In 1984 Arkowitz and Messer (1984) edited a book titled *Psychoanalytic Therapy and Behavior Therapy: Is Integration Possible?*

During the 1980s interest in integration broadened beyond the psychoanalytic-behavioral focus. In 1979 Marvin Goldfried, Paul Wachtel, and Hans Strupp initiated an association of those interested in integration in psychotherapy, which circulated a newsletter. The group became the Society for the Exploration of Psychotherapy Integration (SEPI). The *International Journal of Eclectic Psychotherapy,* which began publication in 1982, became the *Journal of Integrative and Eclectic Psychotherapy.* The *Journal of Psychotherapy Integration* began publication in 1991 as the journal for SEPI. Norcross (1986) wrote that: "The psychotherapy Zeitgeist of the 1980s is rapprochement, convergence, integration" (p. ix).

The movement toward integration in psychotherapy does not have the development of a single, universal system of psychotherapy as its goal. It does not agree with the statement that "The objective of any movement toward eclecticism or integration in psychotherapy must be the development of a single comprehensive system of psychotherapy, including philosophical and theoretical foundations" (Patterson, 1989). Although Norcross (1986) earlier noted that "the promise of eclecticism is the development of a comprehensive psychotherapy based on a unified body of empirical work," he called Patterson's statement "patently false" (Norcross, 1990). Others are also in disagreement with this as an objective of integration. Arkowitz (1992), in his review and evaluation of integrative theories, expressed concern that "the integration of today may become the single-school approach of tomorrow. . . . Such a path takes us full circle back to where we started" (p. 273). Yet the development of numerous differing integrations or integrative therapies poses the same problem: "whether there will be competition among specific schools of integrative therapy. . ." (Arnkoff & Glass, 1992, p. 684).

It does appear that the integration movement is not likely to move in the direction of a universal theory or system in the near future. Lazarus and Beutler (1993) have even said that integration is not desirable: "We believe that integrationist views, as opposed to the technical eclectic approaches, may retard progress and lead in unproductive future directions" (p. 382). Goldfried and Castonguay (1992) in an article titled "The Future of Psychotherapy Integration" wrote:

> It is doubtful that the integration movement will provide the field with one grand theoretical integration. Given the epistemological differences . . . it is hardly likely that this is possible. Moreover, we would maintain that as long as there exist theoreticians, it is likely that there will always be competing theories. (p. 8)

Norcross (1986) wrote: "The ideal of integrating *all* available psychotherapy systems is not likely to be met" (p. 6).

THE PHILOSOPHICAL ISSUE

It would appear that the two views of the nature of human beings (Chapter 15) are irreconcilable. But Allport (1962) pointed the way to a reconciliation: "The trouble with our current theories of learning is not so much that they are wrong but that they are partial. . . . The plain fact is that man is more than a reactive being" (pp. 379, 380). The reactive model is a limited model, applying to a limited range of human behavior. Compared to animals, relatively little of the behavior of adult humans is the result of classical or operant conditioning; such behavior occurs mainly in highly controlled, restricted situations such as experiments in a laboratory or an institution such as a mental hospital. Nor is adult behavior determined by uncontrolled internal drives or motives.

Psychotherapy is concerned with the total individual, with current perceptions, thoughts, feelings and emotions, future goals, as well as innate drives and conditioned behaviors. While this would appear to be a reasonable philosophy on which a theory of therapy could be based, it does not appear to have led to an integrative system of therapy. The two differing images of humans as reacting to the environment or to internal drives are involved in the attempt to integrate behavior therapies and psychoanalytic therapies. Messer and Winokur (1984) felt that this difference was important at not only a philosophical level, but at a clinical level, preventing a real integration. Franks (1984) also felt that this difference precluded integration at a conceptual level.

THE ECLECTIC SOLUTION

Eclecticism in psychotherapy is not a new development, although it has gained increasing attention in the past ten to twenty years. Most therapists were probably eclectic in the first half of the century, before the rise of the numerous current theories. Psychoanalysis and its derivatives were the first theories to develop and most of those therapists who were not eclectic adhered to some form of psychoanalysis or psychoanalytic (dynamic) psychotherapy. The so-called Minnesota point of view of E. G. Williamson (see Patterson, 1966b, 1973, 1980) was an eclectic position. Frederick Thorne's system of clinical practice (see Patterson, 1966b, 1973, 1980, 1986) was perhaps the first to adopt the term *eclecticism*, and is still the most comprehensive and detailed system.

The numbers, or percentages, of psychologists-therapists who considered themselves eclectic during the 1940s and 1950s are not clear. Frederick Thorne (personal communication, June 2, 1967) stated that there were no members of the American Psychological Association (APA) who identified themselves as eclectics in 1945. (The source of this figure is not known.) Shaffer (1953), as part of an extensive study of clinical psychologists, noted that 35 percent of those who practiced therapy identified themselves as eclectic when required to limit their choice to analytic, nondirective, or eclectic. In 1961, Kelly reported a survey of APA clinical psychologists (Fellows and Members, with a 40 percent return) in which 40 percent identified themselves as eclectic. Since then numerous surveys of varying groups of psychologists have found percentages from 30 to 65 percent, fluctuating around 50 percent (Fee, Elkins, & Boyd, 1982; Garfield & Kurtz, 1974, 1976; Jensen, Bergin, & Greaves, 1990; Kelly, Goldberg, Fiske, & Kilkowski, 1978; Larson, 1980; Norcross & Prochaska, 1982; Norcross, Prochaska, & Gallagher, 1989; Prochaska & Norcross, 1983; Smith, 1982; Swan & MacDonald, 1978; Watkins, Lopez, Campbell, & Himmel, 1986; Watkins & Watts, 1995). Though eclectism is the most frequently chosen label, the statement by Lambert and Bergin (1994; cf. Lambert, Shapiro, & Bergin, 1986) that "the vast majority of therapists have become eclectic in orientation" (p. 181) is an overstatement.

Eclecticism in psychotherapy has been subjected to extensive criticism, falling into disrepute among many writers and theorists who hold to a particular school of thought. Rogers (1951, p. 8) referred to this attempt to reconcile various schools as "a superficial eclecticism which does not increase objectivity, and which leads nowhere," and referred to a "confused eclecticism," which "has blocked scientific progress in the field" of psychotherapy (Rogers, 1956). Snygg and Combs (1949) wrote that "an eclectic system leads directly to inconsistency and contradiction, for techniques derived from conflicting frames of reference are bound to be conflicting" (p. 82). Thus, from the point of view of research and of practice, eclecticism has been considered undesirable. In research, "it is only by acting consistently upon a well-selected hypothesis that its elements of truth and untruth can become known" (Rogers, 1956, p. 24). In practice, a consistent frame of reference is desirable.

A problem with eclecticism is defining what it is, or what it consists of in specific terms. Garfield and Bergin (1986) stated that "there is no single or precise definition of an eclectic orientation. . . . [I]t is exceedingly difficult to characterize an approach in terms of either theory or procedures" (p. 8; cf. Garfield & Bergin, 1994, p. 7). Garfield's (1982) earlier characterization still holds: "Eclecticism is perceived as the adherence to a nonsystematic and rather haphazard clinical approach" (p. 612). Strupp and Binder (1984) made a similar statement: "The term *eclectic*, which many therapists use to describe their orientation and practices, is so fuzzy it defies definition" (p. xii). Arkowitz (1992) stated that "Eclectism is a strategy of selecting whatever seems best from a variety of alternatives . . . on the basis of what they think will work for the particular person or problem" (p. 284). Lazarus, Beutler, and Norcross (1992) stated that "the term frequently conveys nothing of substance—it simply implies that concepts from two or more of the more than 400 separate 'schools' of psychotherapy (Karasu, 1986) have been blended, often in an arbitrary, subjective, if not capricious manner (Franks, 1984; Lazarus, 1988)" (p. 11).

Norcross's edited book (Norcross, 1986) includes chapters by authors of the major eclectic positions, including Beutler (1983, 1986), Garfield (1980, 1986b), Hart (1983, 1986), Lazarus (1981a, 1986), and Prochaska and DiClementi (1984, 1986). Goldfried and Newman (1986) provide a historical background, and Dryden (1986), Goldfried and Safran (1986), Messer (1986), and Murray (1986) provide critical comments. More recently we have related efforts by Norcross and Goldfried (1992) and Stricker and Gold (1993). In effect, there are as many eclectic approaches as there are eclectic therapists. While there is a verbal commitment to empirically valid techniques, in fact each therapist operates out of his/her unique bag of techniques, on the basis of his/her particular training, experiences, biases, and intuition on a case-by-case basis, with no general theory or set of principles as guides. Thus, there is no single eclectic therapy. Goldfried and Safran (1986) note that "there exists a real danger that . . . we may ultimately end up with as many eclectic models as we currently have schools of psychotherapy" (p. 464).

Various kinds of eclecticism have been proposed; theoretical eclectism, prescriptive eclectism (Dimond, Havens, & Jones 1978), strategic eclectism (Held, 1984), radical eclectism (Robertson, 1979), and probably others. The lack of theoretical foundations has been acknowledged. Prochaska and Norcross (1983) noted

> The need for theoretical orientation has been frequently recognized, but few, if any, adequate models of systematic eclecticism have been created. . . . Beyond its conceptual relativity and personal appeal, eclecticism in its current state may not possess adequate clinical utility or validity for increasing numbers of therapists. (p. 171)
>
> The real challenge for synthetic eclectic therapists and theorists alike is to construct models of systematic eclecticism that have both empirical validity and clinical utility. (p. 168)

Murray (1986), discussing the contributions to Norcross (1986), said: "In the contributions of the eclectic therapists in this volume, theoretical orientations play a relatively small role" (p. 405). He continued: "However, true integration requires a coherent theoretical structure, which does not exist. We are still waiting for our theoretical integration" (p. 413). London (1988) recognized that "Integration involving continuity across all techniques is still missing, and it is missing for a good reason, I think. It may not be possible" (p. 10).

A true eclecticism is neither nontheoretical nor haphazard. English and English (1958) defined it as follows:

> *Eclecticism.* n. In theoretical system building, the selection and *orderly combination* of compatible features from diverse sources, sometimes from incompatible theories and systems; the effort to find valid elements in all doctrines or theories and to combine them into *a harmonious whole.* . . . Eclecticism is to be distinguished from unsystematic and uncritical combination, for which the name is syncretism. (p. 168, italics added)

As a matter of fact, most of what is currently called "eclecticism" is actually syncretism.

There have been attempts to develop a systematic—though not theory based—eclectic psychotherapy. Foremost among these have been Lazarus and Beutler. Lazarus (1967) proposed the term *technical eclecticism* to apply to "procedures drawn from different sources without necessarily subscribing to the theories that spawned them" (Lazarus, Beutler, & Norcross, 1992, p. 12). "To attempt a theoretical rapprochement is as futile as trying to picture the edge of the universe. But to read through the vast amount of literature on psychotherapy, in search of techniques, can be clinically enriching and therapeutically rewarding" (Lazarus, 1967, p. 416). Lazarus developed his approach in a number of later publications (Lazarus, 1971, 1976, 1981a, 1981b, 1986).

Lazarus began as a behavior therapist and was associated with Wolpe for several years. He abandoned behavior therapy and became critical of it (Lazarus, 1971, 1976) when a follow-up of his patients found that many of them had not continued the improvement seen at the conclusion of treatment. He did not, however, give up all behavioristic techniques. He also adopted some cognitive therapy techniques. He first referred to his approach as multimodal behavior therapy (Lazarus, 1976) but later left out the "behavior" (Lazarus, 1981a). He also uses many other techniques, including imagery and fantasy, Gestalt exercises, and client-centered reflection. He coined the acronym *BASIC I.D.* to indicate the breadth or comprehensiveness of his approach: behavior, affect, sensation, imagery, cognition, interpersonal relationships, biological functioning, or drugs. The patient is assessed in all these areas, and then each is dealt with in order of judged importance.

Beutler's systematic eclectic therapy (Beutler, 1983, 1986; Beutler & Clarkin, 1990) is, as noted in the last chapter, based on the specific treatments for specific conditions paradigm. There is an attempt to support treatment choices with empirical research, but no attempt to provide an overall theory position. The matching of pertinent variables with techniques is broadened to include therapist variables, the therapist-patient relationship, and their interactions. These variables, according to Beutler, are more important than specific techniques (Beutler, 1989). In terms of theory, Beutler (1986) advocated the development of a functional theory. The main theoretical bases for his current position were social psychological theories of persuasion, since he views psychotherapy as a process of persuasion (Beutler, 1978).

Arkowitz (1992), in his evaluation of Lazarus and Beutler, wrote:

> At the very heart of modern eclecticism is an actuarial approach that uses data from past cases to predict what will work best for new cases. This actuarial approach requires a search for relations among variables, rather than for an overall theory to fit

these data. . . . One problem is the enormous number of possible variables that may correlate with the enormous number of outcome variables. . . . If the number of variables is limitless, the number of interactions among them is also limitless. . . . The task seems overwhelming unless we have some coherent framework to guide the selection of relevant variables and to help in understanding the interactions among variables. (pp. 288–289)

Lazarus, Beutler, and Norcross (1992) joined in a prediction of the future of technical eclecticism. Some of their predictions included the following: (1) *"Technical eclecticism will represent the psychotherapeutic Zeitgeist well into the 21st century"*; (2) *"Limitations of theoretical integration will be more fully realized"*; (3) *"Treatments of choice for selected clinical disorders will become standard practice"*; (5) *"The meaning of technical eclecticism will be broadened to denote . . . therapist relationship stances"*; (6) *"Common therapeutic factors will be concretely operationalized and prescriptively employed"*; (10) *"Technical eclecticism, as one thrust of the psychotherapy integration movement, will become 'institutionalized'"* (pp. 13–17).

Paradoxically, eclecticism as an integrating force, based on the specific treatment paradigm, actually appears to be fostering divergence. But Norcross (1986) wrote that "a truly eclectic psychotherapy may begin with and be based on an operationalization of common variables that play an important role in most therapies (Garfield, 1973, 1980; Goldfried, 1980, 1982; Prochaska & DiClementi, 1984)" (p. 15).

THE COMMON ELEMENTS SOLUTION

For nearly sixty years (Rosenzweig, 1936) it has been recognized that there are basic common elements or factors in the diverse approaches to psychotherapy. Following Rosenzweig, other writers include Oberndorf (1946), Hathaway (1948), Wyatt (1948), Ziskind (1949), Collier (1950), Rioch (1951), Black (1952), Cottle (1953), and Patterson (1959, Chapter 13). As Arkowitz (1992, p. 278) noted, there was a drop in "common factors" publications in the 1960s and 1970s. Exceptions were Goldstein (1962), Hobbs (1962), Garfield (1980), and especially Frank (1961, 1971, 1973, 1974, 1982), and Marmor (1976).

The common factors suggested have been numerous and varied, from the general to the specific. All therapies, at a very general level, involve an interaction or communication between therapist and client (Rioch, 1951). Rapport and transference are other general factors (Black, 1952; Hathaway, 1948; Ziskind, 1949). Rosenzweig (1936) listed three factors: (1) therapist personality; (2) interpretations (whether right or wrong they provide explanations of client behavior); and (3) theoretical orientation (though different, they have a synergistic effect on various areas of functioning). More specific factors have included advice, encouragement, explanations, therapist attention, warmth, persuasiveness, support, reassurance, and suggestion (see Lambert & Bergin, 1994).

Implicit Commonalities

Frank, who has been writing about common elements for over 30 years, has focused on a group of components more specific than those considered above (Frank, 1959, 1961, 1971, 1973, 1974, 1976, 1982; Frank & Frank, 1991). They center on his concept of therapy as "a means of directly or indirectly combating demoralization" (1982, p. 10), which is the source of emotional disturbances. His first component is "an emotionally charged confiding relationship with a helping person," involving the therapist's status or reputation but also including the communication of caring, competence, and the absence of ulterior motives (p. 19). Second, is a healing setting that heightens the client's expectation of help from a healer and that provides safety. Third, is "a rational, conceptual scheme or myth that provides a plausible explanation for the patient's symptoms and prescribes a ritual or procedure for resolving them" (p. 20). The fourth is "a ritual that requires active participation of both patient and therapist and that is believed by both to be the means of restoring the patient's health" (p. 20). Though developed in detail over a period of time, Frank's elements are abstract and not operationalized. Yet they have apparently had wide acceptance. They bear a striking resemblance to Fish's (1973) delineation of placebo therapy.

A number of characteristics of psychotherapy appear to be present in all theories or approaches but are seldom explicitly noted.

1. All approaches and all therapists agree that human beings are capable of change or of being changed; disagreement is on how best to bring about change. Human beings are not predetermined; at any stage of development, they are still pliable. Learning theory approaches are based on this assumption. Skinner (1958) expressed it as follows:

> It is dangerous to assert that an organism of a given species or age can not solve a given problem. As a result of careful scheduling, pigeons, rats, and monkeys have done things in the last five years which members of their species have never done before. It is not that their forebears were incapable of such behavior; nature had simply never arranged effective sequences of schedules. (p. 96)

Other approaches may not be so optimistic about the changeability of personality or of behavior, but they clearly assume the possibility of change; otherwise there would be no point to engaging in psychotherapy.

2. There is agreement that some kinds of behavior are undesirable, inadequate, and harmful or result in dissatisfaction, unhappiness, or limitation of a person's potential and, therefore, warrant attempts at change. These behaviors may include cognitive or emotional disturbances or disorders, conflicts, unresolved problems, or behaviors designated as neurotic or psychotic.

3. All therapies and therapists expect their clients or patients to change as a result of their particular techniques. This expectation may vary in its degree; in some instances, it approaches a highly optimistic or even enthusiastic expectation, while in others, it may be minimal, or minimal changes may be expected.

4. Every therapist believes in or has confidence in the theory and method that he/she uses. If the therapist did not believe that this approach was the best method, it would not be used; some other method would replace it. As in the case of belief in the ability of clients to change, therapists would not be engaged in the practice of therapy if they did not expect their clients to change and did not believe that their methods would lead to change. It might be hypothesized that success (or at least therapists' and perhaps clients' reports of success) bears a strong relationship to the degree of confidence that the therapist has in his/her approach. A common aspect of therapy thus appears to be the therapist's commitment to a particular theory or at least a particular method or set of techniques. The effect of this commitment, or the interaction of commitment and effectiveness of a method, is one of the

problems in attempting to evaluate the effectiveness of a method apart from the therapist who uses it.

5. Individuals who enter and continue in therapy feel the need for help. They "hurt," they are suffering or are unhappy because of conflicts, symptoms, negative feelings or emotions, interpersonal problems or conflicts, inadequate or unsatisfying behaviors, and so on. Therefore, they are motivated to change. Therapists are not particularly interested in working with unmotivated or "involuntary" clients, even though such clients may obviously have problems. Persons who do not recognize their problems or do not feel any need for help do not often enter therapy, or if they do, they usually do not continue.

6. Clients also believe that change is possible and expect to change. Frank (1959, 1961) has emphasized the universality of this factor in clients. Cartwright and Cartwright (1958) indicated that this is a complex factor: there may be a belief that improvement will occur, a belief in the therapist as the major source of help, or a belief in himself/herself as the major source of help. Cartwright and Cartwright felt that it is only the last belief that leads to improvement in a positive, linear manner. The other beliefs are probably present to some extent in all clients, however. If the client did not feel that he/she would improve and that the therapist and the therapist's methods could effect such improvement, the client would not enter or continue in treatment.

7. All therapists appear to expect and insist that the client be an active participant in the process. The client is not a passive recipient, as is the physically ill patient who is being treated by a physician, even in the approaches that are most directive and active. All learning (behavior change) appears to require some activity, whether motor, verbal, or intellectual, on the part of the client.

These characteristics of a therapy relationship form the background for therapy itself. They are accepted as given by all approaches.

The Therapist in the Relationship

A set of elements even more specific deal with therapist variables in the therapy relationship.

In 1967 Truax and Carkhuff, after reviewing the major theoretical approaches to psychotherapy, in a chapter titled "Central Therapeutic Ingredients: Theoretic Convergence," found three sets of characteristics: (1) "the therapist's ability to be integrated, mature, genuine or congruent," (2) "the therapist's ability to provide a non-threatening, trusting, safe or secure atmosphere by his acceptance, nonpossessive warmth, unconditional positive regard, or love," and (3) "the therapist's ability to be accurately empathic, be with the client, be understanding, or grasp the patient's meaning" (Truax & Carkhuff, 1967, p. 25). Accurate empathy, respect or nonpossessive warmth, and genuineness are "aspects of the therapist's behavior that cut across virtually all theories of psychotherapy and appear to be common elements in a wide variety of approaches to psychotherapy and counseling" (p. 25). These are the conditions specified (as assumptions) by Rogers (1957) as the necessary and sufficient therapist conditions for therapeutic personality change.

1. All therapists manifest a real concern for their clients. They are interested in their clients, care for them, and want to help them. Rogers used the phrase *unconditional posi-*

tive regard. Others have referred to warmth or nonpossessive warmth, respect, prizing, valuing, and accepting. While client-centered therapists would include a respect for the client's potential to take responsibility for self and to resolve his/her own problems, some therapists would not include this. The client-centered nonevaluative, nonjudgmental attitudes also might not be shared by others, but a basic interest, concern, and desire to help another human being are common to all therapists and are a powerful aspect of the therapeutic relationship.

2. A second characteristic of all effective therapists is honesty, or a genuineness and openness. Rogers referred to it as therapist congruence—a consistency between the thoughts and feelings of the therapist and the therapist's expressions to the client. Therapists are sincere, authentic, transparent, and real persons. They are not engaged in trickery or deceit in their relations with their clients.

3. Empathic understanding is a third aspect of a therapeutic relationship. In some form or other, although it varies in terminology, all the major writers on psychotherapy refer to this characteristic of therapists as being important. Theorists vary in the degree of emphasis they place on empathic understanding, and therapists of different persuasions vary in the degree to which they provide it, but no one seems to deny its desirability, if not its importance. There appears to be general agreement on the importance, even the necessity of a good relationship fostered by the therapist.

The most widely known studies on the nature of the relationship as viewed by therapists are those of Fiedler (1950a, 1950b, 1951), who found that therapists from different schools of psychotherapy agreed on the nature of the ideal therapeutic relationship. Factor analysis yielded one common factor of "goodness," whose items were concerned with empathy or understanding. Fiedler also concluded that a good therapeutic relationship as viewed by these therapists is similar to a good interpersonal relationship.

There is currently widespread, if not universal, agreement among theorists and therapists on the influence of the relationship in therapy or behavior change. Goldstein (1962), reviewing the literature on therapist and patient expectations in psychotherapy, concluded: "There can no longer be any doubt as to the primary status which must be accorded the therapeutic transaction" (p. 12).

Menninger and Holzman (1973), in the second edition of *Theory of Psychoanalytic Techniques,* viewed the relationship as the "central focus of the therapeutic process." Goodstein (1977), reviewing a collection of papers published under the title *What Makes Behavior Change Possible?,* stated that "among virtually all of the contributors there is an awareness of and attention to the therapeutic relationship as an essential ingredient of behavior change." The fourteen contributors included Frank, Strupp, Burton, Ellis, Raimy, the Polsters, Bandura, and Wolpe.

There is an extensive literature on the therapeutic relationship, now frequently called the "therapeutic alliance," including research studies and reviews. Beutler, Crago, and Arizmendi (1986) writing in the third edition of Garfield and Bergin's *Handbook of Psychotherapy and Behavior Change,* stated: "The importance of such [therapist] qualities have subsequently been almost universally accepted by all psychotherapies, with varying levels of emphasis" (p. 276). Lambert and Bergin (1994) stated that

> Virtually all schools of psychotherapy accept the notion that these [accurate empathy, positive regard, nonpossessive warmth, and congruence or genuineness] or related

therapist relationship variables are important for significant progress in psychotherapy and, in fact, fundamental in the formation of a working alliance. (p. 164)

"These and related factors common across therapies seem to make up a significant portion of the effective ingredients of psychotherapy" (Lambert, Shapiro, & Bergin, 1986, p. 171). And Emmelkamp (1994), reviewing behavior therapy, concluded that "it is . . . becoming increasingly clear that the quality of the therapeutic relationship may be influential in determining success or failure of the behavior therapies." (p. 417, cf. Emmelkamp, 1986).

The Client in the Relationship

The literature on the therapeutic relationship has focused almost entirely on the therapist's contribution, but the client must also be considered. The therapy relationship cannot exist without the participation of the client. In fact, the client's contribution is considered more important than that of the therapist in determining the outcome of therapy. Frank (1974), after twenty-five years of research, concluded that "the most important determinants of long-term improvement lie in the patient" (p. 39). Norcross (1986) wrote that "experts estimate that about one-third of treatment outcome is due to the therapist, and two-thirds to the client. Less than 10% of outcome variance is generally added for techniques" (p. 15). These experts presumably include Strupp (in Bergin & Strupp, 1972): "In my judgment, by far the greatest proportion of variance in therapeutic outcomes is accounted for by patient variables" (p. 410), and Bergin and Lambert (1978) who wrote: "We believe . . . that the largest variation in therapy outcome is accounted for by preexisting client factors such as motivation for change, and the like. Therapist personal factors account for the second largest proportion of change, with techniques coming in a distant third" (p. 180). Bergin still held this belief when he and his associates (Lambert, Shapiro, & Bergin, 1986) wrote: "It is becoming increasingly clear that the attributes of the patient, as well as the therapist, play an important part in creating the quality of the relationship and the outcome of psychotherapy" (p. 171). These views have been more recently echoed in Lambert (1991), in Lambert and Bergin (1992), as well as in Bergin and Garfield's (1994) most recent *Handbook of Psychotherapy and Behavior Change.*

It is not clear what client variables other than motivation are involved—they are not specified. Research on client demographic and personal variables provides no basis for predicting outcome from these client variables (Garfield, 1986a).

Rogers, in his 1957 article, listed two client conditions as being necessary, and sufficient, for positive therapy outcome.

> 1. [T]he client is in a state of incongruence, being vulnerable and anxious (p. 96). [Incongruence] refers to a discrepancy between the actual experience of the organism and the self-picture of the individual insofar as it represents that experience. . . . [T]here is a fundamental discrepancy between the expressed meaning of the situation as it registers in his organism and the symbolic representation of that experience in awareness in such a way that it does not conflict with the picture he has of himself. . . . When the individual has no awareness of such incongruence, then he is merely vulnerable to the possibility of anxiety and disorganization. . . . If the individual dimly per-

ceives such an incongruence in himself, then a tension state occurs which is known as anxiety. (pp. 96–97)

Simply put, the individual is anxious, confused, in conflict—he/she hurts and needs and wants help. In other words he/she is motivated. It is objective evidence of motivation that clients present for and continue in therapy.

2. The second condition states that "the communication to the client of the therapist's empathic understanding and unconditional positive regard is to a minimal degree achieved" (Rogers, 1957, p. 96). "Unless some communication of these attitudes has been achieved, then such attitudes do not exist in the relationship as far as the client is concerned, and the therapeutic process could not . . . be initiated. Since attitudes cannot be directly perceived it might be somewhat more accurate to state that the therapist behaviors and words are perceived by the client as meaning that to some degree the therapist accepts and understands him. (Rogers, 1957, p. 99)

The research evidence (Orlinsky & Howard, 1986) indicates that, in relating therapist qualities and outcome, "the proportion of positive findings is highest across all outcome categories when therapist warmth and acceptance are observed from the client's perspective. Here, again, the most decisive aspect of therapeutic process seems to be the patient's experience of it" (p. 348; cf. Orlinsky, Grawe, & Parks, 1994, pp. 326, 339, 360–361).

There is an additional client condition that Rogers does not include, though it is necessary. That is that the client must be able to engage in the process of self-exploration, including self-disclosure—the verbal expression of feelings, attitudes, thoughts and experiences. In Rogers' conditions, it is assumed that when the therapist and the other client conditions are present, at least to a minimal degree, then the client is enabled to engage in the process of self-exploration.

THE RELATIONSHIP AS A NONSPECIFIC ELEMENT

Many writers of diverse theoretical orientations view the total psychotherapeutic relationship as nonspecific. Frank (1973, 1982) has long maintained this position. Bergin and Lambert (1978) and Strupp (1978, 1986b) also have emphasized the nonspecific nature of the relationship, repeatedly emphasizing the necessity of specific techniques in addition to the nonspecific relationship.

Behaviorists view the therapeutic relationship as nonspecific, in contrast to the specific techniques of behavior therapy. Wolpe, for example, has claimed that his method of reciprocal inhibition, as well as other behavioristic techniques, increases the improvement rate over that of the relationship alone, stating that "the procedures of behavior therapy have effects additional to those relational effects that are common to all forms of psychotherapy" (Wolpe, 1973, p. 9). Such claims have been disputed and are not supported by any research that has controlled for the relationship.

Those who regard the relationship as nonspecific hold that it is not related directly to the treatment of any of the client's specific problems. It is the substrate from which the therapist operates, the setting or environment in which specific methods are used; some therapists view it as rapport or as the basis of the client's trust in the therapist, providing a power base for influencing the client in some way.

There are two arguments against this view. First, if it is assumed that the source of many, if not most, of the problems of clients involves disturbed interpersonal relationships, then a therapeutic relationship that includes the characteristics of a good human relationship is a relevant, and specific, method of treatment. The therapist is a model for the client from whom the client can learn how to maintain a good relationship with others, and, at the same time, the client is helped by experiencing the relationship offered by the therapist. It is being increasingly recognized that good interpersonal relationships are characterized by understanding, honesty, openness, sincerity, and spontaneity. Psychotherapy is an interpersonal relationship that includes these characteristics. Indeed, therapy would be limited if it attempted to help the client develop better interpersonal relationships in the context of a different kind of relationship.

It is pervasive and generally acknowledged that the evidence that the source of much, if not most, emotional disturbance is the absence of good human relationships. Ford and Urban (1963) in evaluating the theories or systems of psychotherapy presented in their book, stated that "all of these theorists seem to agree that the situational conditions necessary for the development of behavior disorder are the ways other people behave toward the growing person" (p. 649). Spitz's (1945) classic studies of institutionalized infants indicate that deprivation of attention, handling, and personal contact is deleterious not only psychologically, but also physiologically. Love, which is the essence of a good human relationship, is necessary for survival. Burton (1972) wrote that "the basic pathogen is, for me, a disordered maternal or care-taking environment rather than any specific trauma as such" (p. 14). Many other writers and therapists have suggested that emotional disturbances or neuroses and psychoses are the result of lack of or inadequate love and acceptance (or unconditional positive regard) in childhood (Glasser, 1965; Patterson, 1985a; Walsh, 1991). Burton (1967) noted that "after all research in psychotherapy is accounted for, psychotherapy still resolves itself into a relationship best subsumed by the word 'love'" (p. 102–103).

The second argument against the view that the relationship is nonspecific is the research on relationship (nonspecific) variables. There is evidence that the providing of the relationship as defined here, without any additional techniques, is effective with many clients who have many kinds of social-psychological or interpersonal problems (see references to this research in Chapter 13).

THE UBIQUITOUS PLACEBO

Related to the argument that relationship factors are nonspecific is the contention that such factors are placebos. Rosenthal and Frank (1956) took this position, as did Krasner and Ullmann (1965) and Wolpe (1973).

Shapiro (who probably has engaged in more intensive study of placebos than anyone else) and Morris (1978) gave the following definitions:

> A *placebo* is defined as any therapy or component of therapy that is deliberately used for its nonspecific, psychologic, or psychophysiological, effect, or that is used for its presumed specific effect, but is without specific activity for the condition being treated.

The *placebo effect* is defined as the nonspecific, psychologic, or physiologic effect produced by placebos.

A *placebo,* when used as a control in experimental studies, is defined as a substance or procedure that is without specific activity for the condition being evaluated.

The *placebo effect* is defined as the psychological or psychophysiological effect produced by placebos. (p. 369)

Shapiro and Morris (1978) considered placebo effects in both medical treatment and psychotherapy, which are quite different situations. They noted that "the placebo effect may have greater implications for psychotherapy than any other form of treatment because both psychotherapy and the placebo effect function primarily through psychological mechanisms. . . . *The placebo effect is an important component and perhaps the entire basis for the existence, popularity, and effectiveness of numerous methods of psychotherapy*" (p. 369).

The placebo as an inert substance does not exist in psychotherapy. All the variables in the therapeutic relationship are psychological and active, having some specific or direct effects on the client (see Patterson, 1985b).

In an earlier discussion of the placebo effect, Shapiro (1971) stated that he was presenting "an examination of psychotherapy as a placebo effect," thus suggesting that psychotherapy is nothing more than a placebo. However, Shapiro and Morris (1978) viewed the total psychotherapy *relationship* as a placebo. They referred to a review by Luborsky, Singer, and Luborsky (1975) (see also Smith & Glass, 1977, and Smith, Glass, & Miller, 1980) that found several types of psychotherapy to be about equally effective. Shapiro and Morris concluded that this equal effectiveness was related to the common therapist-patient relationship and pointed to this relationship as a demonstration of the placebo effect.

Rosenthal and Frank (1956) much earlier came to the same conclusion. Referring to the placebo effect as a nonspecific form of psychotherapy, they wrote, "The similarity of the forces operating in psychotherapy and the placebo effect may account for the high consistency of improvement rates found with various therapies, from that conducted by physicians to intensive psychoanalysis" (p. 298). More recently, Pentony (1981) in his extensive analysis of the placebo as a model of psychotherapy, suggests that "the placebo effect constitutes the most parsimonious explanation that would account for the apparently equal success achieved by each of the diverse collection of therapies practiced" (p. 56).

This statement assumes that the total therapeutic relationship is a placebo. It is proposed here, however, that the relationship consists of two major classes of variables: specific variables and nonspecific, or placebo variables. We have already enumerated the major specific variables: empathic understanding, respect or warmth, and genuineness.

The nonspecific, or placebo, variables are the social-influence variables (Strong, 1978)—perceived therapist expertness or credibility, trustworthiness, attractiveness, and therapist expectations. These variables are among those listed by Shapiro and Morris (1978) as variables through which the placebo operates. Indeed, they are the essence of what Fish (1973) boldly called "placebo therapy."

Recognizing that "the social influence process has been considered the active ingredient in the placebo," Fish stated that placebo therapy "denotes a broad frame of reference for considering all forms of human interaction, especially psychotherapy, in terms of social influence process" (Fish, 1973, p. xi). The therapist does everything possible to establish

himself/herself as an expert and an authority in the eyes of the client. The client's susceptibility to influence and persuasion is assessed. The impression is created that "once I know
what is wrong with you I can cure you."

A treatment strategy is then formulated and communicated to the client in a plausible
manner, tailored to the client's belief system. The major techniques used are those of behavior modification, together with suggestion and hypnosis. "Placebo therapy is a strategy
for getting the maximum impact from such techniques regardless of their validity" (Fish,
1973, p. vii). Placebo communications are used not because they are true, but because of
their effects. The validity of the techniques, or the "therapeutic ritual," to use Fish's term, is
important only as it enhances the patient's faith—that is, how believable, impressive, or
persuasive the technique is to the patient. The therapist "says things for the effect they will
have rather than for his belief that they are true. Instead of speaking empathically because
he believes that empathy cures, he does so because he sees that such statements add to
credibility in the patient's eyes" (Fish, 1973, p. 32). Further, "lying to a patient is desirable
if the lie furthers the therapeutic goals, is unlikely to be discovered (and hence backfire)
and is likely to be more effective than any other strategy" (Fish, 1973, p. 39).

Pentony provided a critical evaluation of Fish's placebo therapy. He stated that "it
seems questionable whether a treatment based on suggestion [or persuasion] alone will be
universally applicable," given the existence of strong resistance to change. He raised three
other questions about placebo therapy:

> 1. Is it ethical to mislead the client in regard to the therapeutic strategy? 2. Will the
> therapist be convincing when he is not a true believer in the ritual he is carrying
> through? 3. If placebo therapy becomes general and clients become aware of its na-
> ture, will they lose faith in the healing rituals and hence render these ineffective?
> (Pentony, 1981, pp. 63–64)

Fish's attempts to answer these questions are less than convincing. No attention is given to
the problem of therapist genuineness and the client's detection of its absence in the therapist.

There are other problems with placebo therapy. Fish, who claimed that it works,
urged that the reasons be researched. There is probably no question that placebo therapy
works with some clients some of the time. It is the basis for the success of charlatans and
charismatics, who produce satisfied clients and testimonials.

There are three problems with the placebo as therapy, however. First, it is uncertain,
or unreliable. Not all subjects are placebo reactors, and it is not possible to identify those
who will respond positively to placebos. Fish attempted to determine who among his
clients will be positive reactors. Although he noted that many are called but few are chosen,
he did not tell how many or what proportion are chosen. He referred to the problem client
who expects and desires a different relationship with the therapist. Second, placebo effects
are not dependable; that is, when they do exist, they usually are not durable, but tend to be
transitory. None of the research on the social-influence variables has included long-term, or
even short-term, follow-up of results. Third, the possible side effects of placebo therapy are
undesirable, including the fostering of dependence.

The social-influence variables and the specific-relationship variables probably are
not completely independent. LaCrosse (1977) found significant correlations between the

Counselor Rating Form, which measures client perceptions of counselor expertness, attractiveness, and trustworthiness, and the Barrett-Lennard Relationship Inventory, which measures client perceptions of counselor empathic understanding, congruence, level of regard, and unconditional positive regard. Observer ratings were also highly correlated, although ratings by the counselors themselves were not, which raises some question about the presence of an artifact, such as the halo effect, in the client and observer ratings.

The presence of correlations between these two sets of relationship variables poses the question of which is primary, or which causes or leads to the others. That the core conditions are primary is suggested by studies that have shown them to be related to various therapy outcomes, while this has not been shown for the social-influence variables. Krumboltz, Becker-Haven, and Burnett (1979) have indicated the direction of the relationship when they suggested, after reviewing the research, that therapists "who want to be seen as attractive should be empathic, warm and active." It also would appear, from LaCrosse's research, that therapists who want to be regarded as experts also should be empathic, respectful, warm, and genuine. Similarly, it might be suggested that therapists who want to be perceived as trustworthy should demonstrate the same qualities.

It appears that the complex therapeutic relationship cannot be prevented from being "contaminated" by placebo elements. Clients perceive therapists, to some extent at least, as authoritative and expert—regardless of the therapists' behavior. Clients normally trust their therapists. Therapists' belief in their theory is inextricable from their methods. If they did not have confidence in them, they would use other methods in which they did have confidence.

If placebo elements cannot be entirely eliminated from psychotherapy, they can be either maximized or minimized. If they are maximized, the therapist is engaging in placebo therapy, with the possibility that results may be limited, superficial, or temporary. Research on the social-influence variables has attempted to maximize the placebo effect in various ways, including favorable introductions of therapists to clients, display of degrees and diplomas and of professional books and journals, wearing of a white coat by the therapist, luxurious office furnishings, and cultivation of a self-confident, charismatic manner by the therapist. In spite of this, the research does not demonstrate the effectiveness of the variables. If, on the contrary, placebo elements are minimized and specific-relationship variables are maximized, therapy is effective.

TOWARD A UNIVERSAL SYSTEM OF PSYCHOTHERAPY (PATTERSON AND HIDORE, IN PRESS)

It would appear that any attempt at integration in psychotherapy, or the development of a single universal system, must be based on the common elements of the major existing theories or systems. The following is an attempt to do this.

There are three major elements of psychotherapy: (1) goals or objectives; (2) the process in the client; and (3) the therapist and client conditions necessary for client progress. Mahrer's (1967) edited book, *The Goals of Psychotherapy,* revealed the almost endless number and variety of goals considered by the contributors. Parloff's (1967) contribution suggested a way of dealing with the problem. He proposed two levels of goals—mediating and ultimate. He notes that while there may be great differences in mediating goals, "differences in the stated ultimate goals will in all likelihood be small" (p. 9).

Parloff's suggestion is the basis for the present discussion. Three, rather than two, levels of goals are considered, and the definitions of ultimate and mediating goals are different. The three levels are (1) the ultimate goal, (2) mediate or mediating goals, and (3) the immediate goal. The last consists of the therapist and client conditions necessary for therapy to occur.

Goals

The Ultimate Goal.   The ultimate goal concerns the kind of person we want the client to become as a result of psychotherapy. It should be apparent that the kind of person we want the client to be is the kind of person we would like all persons to be. It is related to the question of what is the purpose of life, a question with which philosophers have been concerned since Aristotle.

There have been many suggested goals. Jahoda (1958) proposed the concept of positive mental health, but it has been impossible to define it clearly. Concepts of adjustment raise the question of Adjustment to what? White's (1959) concept of competence raises the question of Competence for what? Psychological effectiveness involves the same problem. All require a higher-level criterion.

There are a number of terms or concepts that appear to transcend this limitation and to constitute an acceptable criterion. These include *self-realization, self-enhancement,* the *fully-functioning person* of Rogers, and *self-actualization.* This last term appears to be widely and commonly used, and is adopted here.

The definition of the self-actualizing person derives from the work of Maslow (1956). He formulated a general definition of self-actualizing people as being characterized by

the full use and exploitation of talents, capacities, potentialities, etc. Such people seem to be fulfilling themselves and to be doing the best that they are capable of doing. They are people who have developed or are developing the full stature of which they are capable. (pp. 161–162)

Selecting a group of people, living and dead, who seemed to represent self-actualizing people, he attempted to find what these people had in common and that differentiated them from ordinary people. Fourteen characteristics emerged:

1. More efficient perception of reality and more comfortable relations with it.
2. Acceptance of self, others, and nature.
3. Spontaneity; lack of rigid conformity.
4. Problem-centeredness: sense of duty, responsibility.
5. Detachment; need for privacy.
6. Autonomy, independence of culture and environment.
7. Continued freshness of appreciation.
8. Mystic experiences; oceanic feelings.
9. *Gemeinshaftsgefuhl;* empathy, sympathy, compassion for all human beings.
10. Deep interpersonal relations with others.
11. Democratic character structure; respect for others.
12. Discernment of means and ends.

13. Philosophical, unhostile sense of humor.

14. Creativeness. (For more detail, see Maslow [1956] and Patterson [1985a].)

There have been some objections to the concept of self-actualization. These derive, it appears, from misconceptions or misunderstandings of the nature of self-actualization and of self-actualizing persons. One such objection is that self-actualization consists of a collection of traits that are the same for all persons, resulting in standard, identical behaviors. But what is actualized are varying individual potentials. As Maslow (1956) noted, "self-actualization is actualization of a self, and no two selves are altogether alike" (p. 192).

A second, and opposite, misconception is that a self-actualizing person is antisocial, or at least, asocial. Maddi (1973a, 1973b) took this position. Williamson (1950, 1958, 1963, 1965) also made this criticism. Smith (1973) appeared to see self-actualization as including undesirable, or antisocial behaviors, and thus unacceptable. And White (1973) appeared to view self-actualization as selfish: "I ask readers," he wrote, "to observe carefully whether or not self-actualization, in its current use by psychological counselors and others, is being made to imply anything more than adolescent preoccupation with oneself and one's impulses" (White, 1973, p. 69). And Janet Spence, in her presidential address to the American Psychological Association (Spence, 1985) spoke as follows of the youth of the 1960s and early 1970s:

> Although some were led to careers that were expressions of idealism, others turned their backs on the work ethic or substituted as a goal for material success self-actualization and "doing your own thing." . . . Although the pursuit of self-actualization was stimulated by rejection of materialistic goals, it represents another facet of unbridled materialism. (pp. 1289–1290)

These criticisms appear to confuse the concept of self-actualization with selfishness and self-centeredness, and identify it with the characteristics of the "me" generation of the 1970s, the "culture of narcissism" (cf. Amitai Etzioni [1982], Christopher Lasch [1979] and Tom Wolfe [1976]). It is also perhaps influenced by the human potential movement, which no doubt, in many of its manifestations, promoted extreme individualism and self-centeredness.

Rogers answered these criticisms when he noted that individuals live in a society of others, and can become actualized only in interaction with others. They need others, and the affiliation, communication, and positive regard of others (Rogers, 1959, 1961).

Self-actualization as the goal of psychotherapy has some significant implications, as discussed below.

1. Self-actualization constitutes a criterion in the sense that it is not vulnerable to the question: For what? Self-actualization avoids the problems of an adjustment model, which include in addition to the question Adjustment to what? the questions of conformity and social control (Halleck, 1971).

2. Self-actualization as a goal avoids the problems of the medical model and its illness-health dilemma. The goal involves more than the elimination of pathology and the achievement of some undefined (and undefinable) level of mental health or "normality." It is not a negative concept, such as the absence of disturbance, disorder, or "mental illness." It is a positive goal.

3. Self-actualization eliminates the conflict or dichotomy between intrapersonal and interpersonal. It includes the whole person in a society of other persons.

4. The goal is a process, not a static condition to be achieved once and for all. It is the development of *self-actualizing persons,* a continuing process. An adequate goal for persons must be an ideal that is ever more closely approximated but never completely achieved.

5. Self-actualization as a goal is not limited to psychotherapy, or to the treatment of disturbed individuals. It is the goal of life, for all persons, all of whom are, to some degree, dissatisfied with themselves, unhappy, unfulfilled, and not fully using their capabilities or potentials. Thus, self-actualization should be the goal of society and all of its institutions—education, marriage and the family, political, social and economic systems—all of which exist for the benefit of individuals. As a matter of fact, psychotherapy has come into existence as a way in which society provides special assistance to those whose progress toward self-actualization has been blocked, interrupted, or impeded in some way, mainly by the lack of good human relationships.

6. There is another aspect of self-actualization that is particularly significant. Goals are related to—or are the obverse of—drives or motives. Thus, when we talk about the goal of life, we become involved in purpose, needs, drives or motives, since goals are influenced by, indeed determined by, needs. Self-actualization is the basic motivation of all human beings, indeed of all living organisms. Goldstein (1939), one of the earliest writers to adopt the term *self-actualization,* stated that "an organism is governed by a tendency to actualize, as much as possible, its nature in the world" (p. 196). The goal, then, is not an abstract, theoretical, philosophical, ethical, or religious goal, but derives from the biological nature of the organism.

7. Since the drive toward self-actualization is biologically based, it is neither time-bound nor culture-bound. It is thus a universal goal. And as a universal goal, not only for psychotherapy but for life, it provides a criterion for the evaluation of cultures. Maslow (1971), influenced by the anthropologist Ruth Benedict, wrote: "I proceed on the assumption that the . . . immediate goal of any society which is trying to improve itself, is the self-actualization of all individuals" (p. 213). [More extended discussion can be found in Patterson (1985a).]

8. This formulation of the ultimate goal of psychotherapy resolves the problem of who selects the goal—the therapist or the client. Neither the therapist nor the client chooses this goal. It is a given; it is implicit in the nature of the individual as a living organism. It is the nature of the organism, a characteristic of Rogers' actualizing tendency, to grow, to develop, to strive to actualize its potentials, to become what it is capable of becoming —to be more self-actualizing.

9. Finally, the concept of self-actualization provides a solution to the problem of organizing needs in some hierarchy. All specific drives, including those in Maslow's (1970) hierarchy, are subservient to the drive toward self-actualization. All specific needs are organized and assume temporary priority in terms of their relevance to the basic drive toward self-actualization (Patterson, 1985a).

Mediate Goals.   Mediate goals are the usual goals considered by psychotherapists. They include the specific and concrete goals of behavior therapists. Contributors to Mahrer's (1967) book focused on this level of goals, including such things as reduction of symptoms; reduction of anxiety, of psychological pain and suffering, and of hostility; and elimination of unadaptive habits and acquisition of adaptive habits. Other mediate goals include good marital and family relationships; vocational and career success and satisfaction; educational achievement, including study skills and good study habits; and development of potentials in art, music, athletics, etc.

The ultimate goal is a common goal, applicable to all individuals. Mediate goals provide for, or allow for, individual differences. People have differing, and multiple, potentials; they actualize themselves in differing ways.

A number of implications of the separation of goals into ultimate and mediate become apparent:

1. While the ultimate goal is universal, applying across time and cultures, mediate goals vary with individuals, time and cultures. It is here that client choices and decisions operate.

2. Mediate goals may be considered as mediating goals, between the immediate goal and the ultimate goal. That is, they are steps toward the ultimate goal. In some instances they may overlap with aspects of the ultimate goal—the development of self-understanding, self-esteem, or self-acceptance, for example.

3. The ultimate goal provides a criterion for the acceptability of mediate goals, something that is lacking, or implicit, in behavior therapy.

4. While mediate goals may be considered as subgoals, or steps toward the ultimate goal, they may also be seen as byproducts of the ultimate goal. Self-actualizing persons normally and naturally seek to achieve the mediate goals on their own, or seek and obtain the necessary assistance, such as tutoring, instruction, information, education and training, or reeducation, to achieve them. As byproducts, they are not necessarily goals to be directly achieved or specifically sought. Thus, in psychotherapy, they need not be determined or defined in advance, but are developed by the client during, or even following, the therapy process. It appears that it may be sufficient, in some cases, to provide the conditions leading to the development of self-actualizing persons; thus, as individuals become more self-actualizing, they develop, pursue, and achieve their own more-specific goals.

5. It is apparent that many of the mediate goals are the objectives of other helping processes, of education, reeducation, and skill training.

The Immediate Goal. The mediating goals of Parloff (1967) are aspects of the psychotherapy process, the initiating and continuing of which is the immediate goal in the present model or system. The therapy process and its elements have been described in many ways, in the various theories of psychotherapy. Parloff (1967) included the following specific goals: making the unconscious conscious; recall of the repressed; deconditioning; counterconditioning; strengthening or weakening of the superego; development and analysis of the transference neurosis; promoting increased insight; and increasing self-acceptance. There is little, if any, evidence that many of these goals lead to desirable therapy outcomes, particularly to increased self-actualization.

Essential to the therapy process is client activity of some sort. The client activity involving self-exploration, or intrapersonal exploration, appears to be universally present in successful psychotherapy. It includes some of the mediating goals mentioned by Parloff, such as developing awareness of unconscious (or preconscious) material (self-awareness).

The process of self-exploration is complex, involving several aspects or stages, as discussed below.

1. *Self-disclosure.* Before clients can explore themselves, they must disclose, or reveal, themselves, including their negative thoughts, feelings, problems, failures, inadequacies, etc. These are the reasons clients come for therapy, their "problems," and it is

necessary to state or define the "problem" before it can be dealt with. Self-disclosure, or self-exposure, requires that clients be open and honest, or genuine.

2. *Self-exploration* consists of clients working with the disclosed material, exploring what and who they really are. The process may be slow, and not a smooth or continuous one. There is resistance to looking at and facing up to one's undesirable aspects.

3. Self-exploration leads to client *self-discovery,* an awareness of what one is really like.

4. With self-discovery comes *self-understanding* and *self-acceptance.* Clients become aware of failures to actualize themselves and their potentials. They see the discrepancies between their actual selves and their ideal selves. They begin to reduce the discrepancies, modifying their actual or ideal selves, or both. A realistic *self-concept* is developed, a self-concept more congruent with experience. Clients are able to accept themselves as they are, and to commit themselves to becoming more like they want to be. [See Patterson (1985a) and Rogers (1961), for fuller discussions of the therapy process in the client.]

Questions have been raised about self-disclosure and self-exploration by writers about cross-cultural therapy. Persons in other cultures (as well as the poor in our own culture [Goldstein, 1973]), it is said, cannot, or do not, engage in self-disclosure or self-exploration (or "introspection"). Pedersen, for example, referring to American Indian clients, wrote: "A counselor who expects clients to verbalize their feelings is not likely to have much success with Native American clients" (Pedersen, 1976, p. 26). Sue (1981) referred to "certain groups (Asian Americans, Native Americans, etc.) that dictate against self-disclosure to strangers" (p. 48). He noted "the belief in the desirability of self-disclosure by many mental health practitioners" (p. 38). Yet, paradoxically, he also referred to self-disclosure as an "essential" condition that is "particularly crucial to the process and goals of counseling" (Sue, 1981, p. 48).

That is the problem. If self-exploration is essential for progress in psychotherapy (and this is supported by the research), then it cannot be abandoned, as some suggest, with the therapist taking an active, directing, leading, or structured approach. But client reluctance or difficulty in self-disclosure is a social, not a purely cultural, characteristic. People (in general, not only Asians) do not disclose to strangers, social superiors, or experts, including professionals. Yet, paradoxically, people sometimes tell things to strangers (as well as to therapists) that they would not tell to families or friends. Chinese persons with whom the senior author has talked make it clear that they self-disclose among their families and friends. The reluctance or difficulty in self-disclosing among certain clients is not a reason for abandoning psychotherapy (for which it is a necessary condition), but for providing the conditions which make client self-disclosure possible.

The Conditions

Therapist Conditions.   How does the therapist make it possible for the client to engage in activities necessary for therapeutic progress? He/she does so by providing certain conditions. Three major conditions have been identified and defined (Rogers, 1957) and are now supported by considerable research (Patterson, 1984, 1985a).

1. *Empathic understanding* is more than a knowledge of the client based on information about the client. It is an understanding of the client from his/her frame of reference. The therapist enters the client's world and views things as he/she does. Rogers (1961) de-

fined empathy as "an accurate, empathic understanding of the client's world as seen from the inside. To sense the client's private world as if it were your own, but without losing the 'as if' quality—this is empathy" (p. 284). The client permits the therapist to enter his/her world by engaging in self-disclosure.

2. *Respect* includes the unconditional positive regard of Rogers. It involves a genuine interest in the client, a warmth, caring, and concern, even compassion. It involves a trust in the client, a confidence that the client is capable of taking responsibility for him/herself, including during the therapy process, and can make choices and decisions, and resolve problems. It involves recognizing that these are rights of the client.

3. *Therapeutic genuineness,* or *congruence,* to use Rogers' term, includes authenticity, transparency (to use existentialist terms), and honesty. Therapy is a real relationship; the therapist is not playing a role, maintaining a professional facade, or operating as an objective expert. Genuineness must be a therapeutic genuineness. Without this modifier, genuineness can become an excuse for therapists to engage in behaviors that are harmful to clients.

4. There is another element, that may be more at the technique level than a condition, that we believe has the status of a necessary element in the therapist's behavior: Concreteness or specificity in responding to client productions. This is the opposite of abstractions, labels, generalizations or interpretations, all of which, rather than encouraging client self-exploration, stifle or extinguish it.

These conditions may be summed up, we think, in the concept of love, in the sense of agape. They are part of all the great world religions and philosophies. Lao Tzu, a Chinese philosopher of the fifth century B.C. wrote a poem titled *Leader,* which applies when *therapist* is substituted for *Leader* and *clients* is substituted for *people.*

A Leader (Therapist)

A leader is best when people hardly know he exists;
Not so good when people obey and acclaim him;
Worst when they despise him.
But of a good leader who talks little,
When his work is done, his aim fulfilled,
They will say, "We did it ourselves."

The less a leader does and says,
The happier his people;
The more he struts and brags,
The sorrier his people.

[Therefore] a sensible man says:
If I keep from meddling with people, they take care of themselves.
If I keep from preaching at people they improve themselves.
If I keep from imposing on people, they become themselves.

Client Conditions. Psychotherapy is, of course, a two-way process, a relationship, and it takes two to form a relationship. There are two conditions that must be present in the client before the process of therapy can begin; these were considered earlier (see pp. 498–499).

Characteristics of the System

The characteristics of this system—therapist conditions, client conditions, and goals—are presented in Table 1. Some characteristics of this system of psychotherapy that are worth noting include the following.

I. Note the similarities in the Conditions, the Process, and the Goals. All include empathy, respect, and genuineness or honesty. *The conditions are also the goal.*

II. The client, in becoming more self-actualizing becomes a therapeutic influence on others, contributing to their self-actualizing progress.

III. The conditions operate in a number of ways, consistent with our understanding of the learning or change process.

(1) The conditions create a nonthreatening environment, in which the client can feel safe in self-disclosing and self-exploring. Threat, as is well known, is inimical to learning. The warm, accepting atmosphere provided by the therapist contributes to desensitizing the client's anxieties and fears in human relating and to lowering inhibitions about self-disclosure.

(2) The process is not a straight-line progression, but is like the typical learning process or curve, with plateaus or even regressions. The client evidences the approach-avoidance conflict, progressing up to the point at which internal threat or anxiety becomes too great, then retreating or "resting" until the anxiety is reduced. Nor is the process one in which separate problems are worked on until each is resolved. All problems interrelate, and the client grapples with one for a while, then may move on to another, and another, and then return to each in an alternating or spiraling process.

(3) The conditions provide an environment for self-discovery learning. While discovery learning is not always possible or desirable in other areas, it is the most relevant and most effective method for learning about oneself.

(4) The conditions are the most effective reinforcers of the desired client behavior, or self-exploration. More broadly, love is the most potent reinforcer of desirable human behavior.

(5) The conditions also operate through modeling. The client becomes more like the therapist in the therapy process. It follows that the therapist, to be a model, must be at a higher level of the conditions, and of the self-actualizing process, than the client.

(6) The conditions, when offered at a high level by the therapist, include the expectation by the therapist of change in the client. Expectations have a powerful effect on the behavior of others.

(7) The therapist conditions free the actualizing tendency in the client, so that he/she can become a more self-actualizing person.

IV. The conditions are the specific treatment for the lack or inadequacy of the conditions in the past and/or present life of the client. This lack is the source of most functional emotional disturbances, and of failures in the self-actualizing of human beings.

V. The conditions constitute, or include, the major basic, general, enduring, and universal values of life. They are necessary for the survival of a society or cul-

Table 16.1
A UNIVERSAL SYSTEM OF PSYCHOTHERAPY

	Goals		
Conditions	*Immediate*	*Mediate*	*Ultimate*
Therapist conditions	**Client Process**	**Individual**	**Self-Actualizing Person**
Empathic understanding, listening, communicating	Self-Exploration Self-disclosure Openness	Academic achievement— study skills and habits	Acceptance of self Acceptance of others
Respect, warmth, caring, compassion	Genuineness Self-revelation	Development of talents— art, music, athletics, etc.	Empathy
Therapeutic genuineness, congruence, honesty	Intrapersonal exploration Self-discovery Self-awareness	Vocation-work achievement and satisfaction	Genuineness Autonomy, independence
Concreteness, specificity	Self-acceptance Self-understanding	Personal relationships— family	Responsibility
Client Conditions Voluntary, motivated, vulnerable		Reduction of symptoms— anxiety, phobias, pain, etc.	Democraticness
Client perception of therapist conditions			Openness to experience Self-esteem

ture. Society could not exist if these conditions were not present in its members at a minimal level. They are the conditions necessary for human beings to live together and to survive as a society. Skinner (1953) wrote: "If a science of behavior can discover those conditions of life which make for the ultimate strength of men, it may provide a set of 'moral values' which, because they are independent of the history and culture of any one group, may be generally accepted" (p. 445). We have those values (Patterson, 1966a).

VI. Thus, this system of psychotherapy, incorporating the goal of living, and the conditions for achieving this goal, is a universal system, neither time- nor culture-bound. It is the *process* that is universal; the *content* will vary not only with society, culture, race, sex, age, etc., but with each individual client.

CONCLUSION

In Chapter 15, we came to the conclusion that over the past decade or two, divergent approaches to psychotherapy have been developed. One stream, or extreme, was earlier represented by behavior therapy but now appears to be represented by cognitive therapy. In both approaches, the therapist is an expert who controls and directs the therapy process, ideally in a planned manner toward preconceived specific goals; the attitude is that the therapist knows best. The other stream, in its extreme form, is represented by existential psychotherapy. With its lack of structure or techniques, it tends to be rather vague and mysterious. The therapist is hardly an expert; rather, the therapist is a fellow traveler on a road for which neither he/she nor the client has a map or even a clear idea of the destination.

In this chapter, we have presented an alternative, somewhat middle-ground approach. It is based on the convergence of many theorists, researchers, and practitioners toward recognizing that the essence of psychotherapy is the relationship between the therapist and the client. If the therapist is an expert, he/she is an expert in human relationships—an expertise that the therapist does not and cannot retain for himself/herself but shares with nonprofessionals. Indeed, the therapist's goal, in effect, is to help the client become more expert in interpersonal relationships, which usually is the source of the client's difficulties. It is a sad commentary on our society that so many people must seek and pay for a good personal relationship, designated as psychotherapy, and that other people have to be educated and trained to provide such a relationship. The development of psychotherapy as a means of meeting the need of a large number of people for a good relationship institutionalizes the process as a profession, but with the recognition that psychotherapists do not have a monopoly on facilitative interpersonal relationships, psychotherapy will no longer be recognized as a profession. It may be that for some time the direct teaching of good interpersonal relationships may continue as a professional activity.

The nature of the placebo in psychotherapy is considered. While it probably cannot be eliminated from the therapy relationship, the therapist variables can be either maximized, as in placebo therapy, or minimized.

Discussing integration in psychotherapy, Garfield (1982) wrote that

one important step in the desired direction [toward integration in psychotherapy] is to delineate and to operationalize clearly some of the common variables which seem to play a role in most psychotherapies, and, perhaps, to regard them as a basis for a clearer delineation of psychotherapeutic principles and procedures. This may not be popular, but I think it will be worth the effort. (p. 620)

This chapter is an effort in that direction, closing with a proposal for a universal system of psychotherapy. The focus is on three variables that, although recognized by many writers as common elements, have not been given the importance they deserve, for reasons that have been suggested. Empathic understanding, respect or warmth, and therapeutic genuineness are specific variables whose effectiveness has been overwhelmingly demonstrated in hundreds of research studies. They cannot be ignored; they constitute the heart of any systematic approach to psychotherapy. We are still far from the recognition that a universal system of psychotherapy is either possible or desirable and from the days of schools of psychotherapy.

REFERENCES

Allport, G. W. (1962). Psychological models for guidance. *Harvard Educational Review, 32,* 373–381.

Arkowitz, H. (1992). Integrative theories of therapy. In D. K. Freedheim (Ed.). *History of psychotherapy: A century of change* (pp. 261–303). Washington, DC: American Psychological Association.

Arkowitz, H., & Messer, S. B. (Eds.). (1984). *Psychoanalytic therapy and behavior therapy: Is integration possible?* New York: Plenum.

Arnkoff, D. B., & Glass, C. R. (1992). Cognitive therapy and psychotherapy integration. In D. K. Freedheim (Ed.). *History of psychotherapy* (pp. 657–694). Washington, DC: American Psychological Association.

Bergin, A. E., & Garfield, S. L. (Eds.). (1994). *Handbook of psychotherapy and behavior change* (4th ed.). New York: Wiley.

Bergin, A. E., & Lambert, M. J. (1978). The evaluation of therapeutic outcomes. In S. L. Garfield & A. E. Bergin (Eds.). *Handbook of psychotherapy and personality change* (2nd ed.; pp. 139–189). New York: Wiley.

Bergin, A. E., & Strupp, H. H. (1972). *Changing frontiers in the science of psychotherapy.* Chicago: Aldine-Atherton.

Beutler, L. E. (1978). Psychotherapy and persuasion. In L. E. Beutler & R. Greene (Eds.). *Special problems in child and adolescent behavior* (pp. 119–159). Westport, CT: Technomic Publishing.

Beutler, L. E. (1983). *Eclectic psychotherapy: A systematic approach.* Elmsford, NY: Pergamon Press.

Beutler, L. E. (1986). Systematic eclectic psychotherapy. In J. C. Norcross (Ed.). *Handbook of eclectic psychotherapy* (pp. 94–131). New York: Brunner/Mazel.

Beutler, L. E. (1989). Differential treatment selection: The role of diagnosis in psychotherapy. *Psychotherapy, 26,* 271–281.

Beutler, L. E., & Clarkin, J. F. (1990). *Systematic treatment selection: Toward targeted therapeutic interventions.* New York: Brunner/Mazel.

Beutler, L. E., Crago, M., & Arizmendi, T. G. (1986). Therapist variables in psychotherapy process and outcome. In S. L. Garfield & A. E. Bergin (Eds.). *Handbook of psychotherapy and behavior change* (3rd ed., pp. 257–310). New York: Wiley.

Black, J. D. (1952). Common factors of the patient-therapist relationship. *Journal of Clinical Psychology, 8,* 302–306.

Burton, A. (1967). *Modern humanistic psychotherapy.* San Francisco: Jossey-Bass.

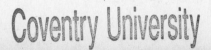

Burton, A. (1972). *Interpersonal psychotherapy.* Englewood Cliffs, NJ: Prentice-Hall.

Cartwright, D. S., & Cartwright, R. D. (1958). Faith and improvement in psychotherapy. *Journal of Counseling Psychology, 5,* 174–177.

Collier, E. M. (1950). A basis for integration rather than fragmentation in psychotherapy. *Journal of Consulting Psychology, 14,* 199–205.

Cottle, W. C. (1953). Some common elements in counseling. *Personnel and Guidance Journal, 32,* 4–8.

Dimond, R. E., Havens, R. A., & Jones, A. C. (1978). A conceptual framework for the practice of prescriptive eclecticism in psychotherapy. *American Psychologist, 33,* 239–248.

Dollard, J., & Miller, N. E. (1950). *Personality and psychotherapy: An analysis in terms of learning, thinking, and culture.* New York: McGraw-Hill.

Dryden, W. (1986). Eclectic psychotherapies: A critique of leading approaches. In J. C. Norcross (Ed.). *Handbook of eclectic psychotherapy* (pp. 353–375). New York: Brunner/Mazel.

Emmelkamp, P. M. G. (1986). Behavior therapy with adults. In S. L. Garfield and A. E. Bergin (Eds.). *Handbook of psychotherapy and behavior change* (3rd ed., pp. 385–442). New York: Wiley.

Emmelkamp, P. M. G. (1994). Behavior therapy with adults. In A. E. Bergin & S. L. Garfield (Eds.). *Handbook of psychotherapy and behavior change* (4th ed., pp. 379–427). New York: Wiley.

English, H. B., & English, A. C. (1958). *A comprehensive dictionary of psychological and psychoanalytic terms.* New York: McKay.

Etzioni, A. (1982). *An immodest agenda: Rebuilding America before the 21st century.* New York: McGraw-Hill.

Fee, A. F., Elkins, G. R., & Boyd, L. (1982). Testing and counseling psychologists: Current practices and implications for training. *Journal of Personality Assessment, 46,* 116–118.

Fiedler, F. (1950a). The concept of an ideal therapeutic relationship. *Journal of Consulting Psychology, 14,* 235–245.

Fiedler, F. (1950b). A comparison of therapeutic relationships in psychoanalytic, nondirective and Adlerian therapeutic relationships. *Journal of Consulting Psychology, 14,* 436–445.

Fiedler, F. (1951). Factor analyses of psychoanalytic, nondirective and Adlerian therapeutic relationships. *Journal of Consulting Psychology, 15,* 32–38.

Fish, J. M. (1973). *Placebo therapy.* San Francisco: Jossey-Bass.

Ford, D. H., & Urban, H. B. (1963). *Systems of psychotherapy.* New York: Wiley.

Frank, J. D. (1959). The dynamics of the psychotherapy relationship. *Psychiatry, 22,* 17–29.

Frank, J. D. (1961). *Persuasion and healing.* Baltimore: Johns Hopkins University Press.

Frank, J. D. (1971). Therapeutic factors in psychotherapy. *American Journal of Psychotherapy, 25,* 350–361.

Frank, J. D. (1973). *Persuasion and healing* (2nd ed.). Baltimore: Johns Hopkins University Press.

Frank, J. D. (1974). Psychotherapy: The restoration of morale. *American Journal of Psychiatry, 131,* 271–274.

Frank, J. D. (1976). Restoration of morale and behavior change. In A. Burton (Ed.). *What makes behavior change possible?* (pp. 73–95). New York: Brunner/Mazel.

Frank, J. D. (1982). Therapeutic components shared by all psychotherapies. In J. H. Harvey & M. M. Peeks (Eds.). *Psychotherapy research and behavior change* (pp. 9–37). Washington, DC: American Psychological Association.

Frank, J. D., & Frank, J. B. (1991). *Persuasion and healing* (3rd ed.). Baltimore: Johns Hopkins University Press.

Franks, C. M. (1984). On conceptual and technical integrity in psychoanalysis and behavior therapy: Two fundamentally incompatible systems. In H. Arkowitz, & S. B. Messer (Eds.). *Psychoanalytic therapy and behavior therapy: Is integration possible?* (pp. 223–247). New York: Plenum.

Garfield, S. L. (1973). Basic ingredients or common factors in psychotherapy? *Journal of Consulting and Clinical Psychology, 41,* 9–12.

Garfield, S. L. (1980). *Psychotherapy: An eclectic approach.* New York: John Wiley.

Garfield, S. L. (1982). Eclecticism and integration in psychotherapy. *Behavior Therapy, 13,* 610–623.

Garfield, S. L. (1986a). Research on client variables in psychotherapy. In S. L. Garfield & A. E. Bergin (Eds.). *Handbook of psychotherapy and behavior change* (3rd ed., pp. 213–256). New York: Wiley.

Garfield, S. L. (1986b). An eclectic psychotherapy. In J. C. Norcross (Eds.). *Handbook of eclectic psychotherapy* (pp. 132–162). New York: Brunner/Mazel.

Garfield, S. L., & Bergin, A. E. (1986). Introduction and historical overview. In S. L. Garfield & A. E. Bergin (Eds.). *Handbook of psychotherapy and behavior change* (3rd ed., pp. 3–22). New York: Wiley.

Garfield, S. L., & Bergin, A. E. (1994). Introduction and historical overview. In A. E. Bergin & S. L. Garfield (Eds.). *Handbook of psychotherapy and behavior change* (4th ed.; pp. 3–18). New York: Wiley.

Garfield, S. L., & Kurtz, R. N. (1974). A survey of clinical psychologists: Characteristics, activities and orientations. *The Clinical Psychologist, 28*(1), 7–10.

Garfield, S. L., & Kurtz, R. N. (1976). Clinical psychologists in the 1970's. *American Psychologist, 31,* 1–9.

Garfield, S. L., & Kurtz, R. N. (1977). A study of eclectic views. *Journal of Consulting and Clinical Psychology, 45,* 78–83.

Glasser, W. (1965). *Reality therapy.* New York: Harper & Row.

Goldfried, M. R. (1980). Toward the delineation of therapeutic change principles. *American Psychologist, 36,* 991–999.

Goldfried, M. R. (Ed.). (1982). *Converging themes in psychotherapy.* New York: Springer.

Goldfried, M. R., & Castonguay, L. G. (1992). The future of psychotherapy integration. *Psychotherapy, 29,* 4–10.

Goldfried, M. R., & Newman, C. (1986). Psychotherapy integration: An historical perspective. In J. C. Norcross (Ed.). *Handbook of eclectic psychotherapy* (pp. 25–61). New York: Brunner/Mazel.

Goldfried, M. R., & Safran, J. D. (1986). Future directions in psychotherapy integration. In J. C. Norcross (Ed.). *Handbook of eclectic psychotherapy* (pp. 463–483). New York: Brunner/Mazel.

Goldstein, A. P. (1962). *Therapist-patient expectations in psychotherapy.* New York: MacMillan.

Goldstein, A. P. (1973). *Structured learning therapy: Toward a psychotherapy for the poor.* New York: Wiley.

Goldstein, K. (1939). *The organism.* New York: Harcourt Brace Jovanovich.

Goodstein, L. D. (1977). Dialect in psychotherapy. [Review of *What makes behavior change possible?* A. Burton (Ed.).] *Contemporary Psychology, 22,* 578–579.

Halleck, S. L. (1971). *The politics of therapy.* New York: Science House.

Hart, J. (1983). *Modern eclectic therapy: A functional orientation to counseling and psychotherapy.* New York: Plenum.

Hart, J. T. (1986). Functional eclectic therapy. In J. C. Norcross (Ed.). *Handbook of eclectic psychotherapy* (pp. 201–225). New York: Brunner/Mazel.

Hathaway, S. R. (1948). Some considerations relative to nondirective counseling as therapy. *Journal of Clinical Psychology, 4,* 226–235.

Held, B. S. (1984). Toward a strategic eclecticism: A proposal. *Psychotherapy, 21,* 232–241.

Hobbs, N. (1962). Sources of gain in psychotherapy. *American Psychologist, 17,* 740–747.

Jahoda, M. (1958). *Current concepts of mental health.* New York: Basic Books.

Jensen, J. P., Bergin, A. E., & Greaves, D. W. (1990). The meaning of eclecticism: New survey and analysis of components. *Professional Psychology: Research and Practice, 21,* 124–130.

Karasu, T. B. (1986). The specificity versus nonspecificity dilemma: Toward identifying therapeutic change agents. *American Journal of Psychiatry, 143,* 687–695.

Kelly, E. L. (1961). Clinical psychology—1960. Report of survey findings. *Newsletter: Division of Clinical Psychology of the American Psychological Association, 14,* 1–11.

Kelly, E. L., Goldberg, L. R., Fiske, D. W., & Kilkowski, J. M. (1978). Twenty-five years later: A follow-up study of graduate students in clinical psychology assessed in the VA Selectron Research Project. *American Psychologist, 33,* 746–755.

Krasner, L., & Ullmann, L. P. (Eds.). (1965). *Research in behavior therapy.* New York: Holt, Rinehart & Winston.

Krumboltz, J. D., Becker-Haven, J. F., & Burnett, K. F. (1979). Counseling psychology. *Annual Review of Psychology, 30,* 555–602.

LaCrosse, M. B. (1977). Comparative perceptions of counselor behavior: A replication and an extension. *Journal of Counseling Psychology, 24,* 464–471.

Lambert, M. J. (1991). Introduction to psychotherapy research. In L. E. Beutler & M. Crago (Eds.). *Psychotherapy research: An international review of programmatic studies* (pp. 1–11). Washington, DC: American Psychological Association.

Lambert, M. J., & Bergin, A. E. (1992). Achievements and limitations of psychotherapy research. In D. K. Freedheim (Ed.). *History of psychotherapy: A century of change* (pp. 360–390). Washington, DC: American Psychological Association.

Lambert, M. J., & Bergin, A. E. (1994). The effectiveness of psychotherapy. In A. E. Bergin & S. L. Garfield (Eds.). *Handbook of psychotherapy and behavior change* (4th ed., pp. 143–189). New York: Wiley.

Lambert, M. J., Shapiro, D. A., & Bergin, A. E. (1986). The effectiveness of psychotherapy. In S. L. Garfield & A. E. Bergin (Eds.). *Handbook of psychotherapy and behavior change* (3rd ed.; pp. 157–211). New York: Wiley.

Larson, D. (1980). Therapeutic schools, styles, and schoolism: A national survey. *Journal of Humanistic Psychology, 20*(3), 1–20.

Lasch, C. (1979). *The culture of narcism: American life in an age of diminishing expectations.* New York: Norton.

Lazarus, A. A. (1967). In support of technical eclecticism. *Psychological Reports, 21,* 415–416.

Lazarus, A. A. (1971). *Behavior therapy and beyond.* New York: McGraw-Hill.

Lazarus, A. A. (1976). *Multimodal behavior therapy.* New York: Springer.

Lazarus, A. A. (1981a). *Multimodal therapy.* New York: McGraw-Hill.

Lazarus, A. A. (1981b). *The practice of multimodal therapy.* New York: McGraw-Hill.

Lazarus, A. A. (1986). Multimodal therapy. In J. C. Norcross (Ed.). *Handbook of eclectic psychotherapy* (pp. 65–93). New York: Brunner/Mazel.

Lazarus, A. A. (1988). Eclectism in behavior therapy. In P. M. G. Emmelkamp, W. T. A. M. Everalrd, F. Kraaimaat, & J. J. M. vanSon (Eds.). *Advances in theory and practice in behavior therapy.* Amsterdam: Swets & Zeitlinger.

Lazarus, A. A., & Beutler, L. E. (1993). On technical eclecticism. *Journal of Counseling and Development, 71,* 381–386.

Lazarus, A. A., Beutler, L. E., & Norcross, J. C. (1992). The future of technical eclecticism. *Psychotherapy, 29,* 11–20.

London, P. (1988). Metamorphosis in psychotherapy: Slouching toward integration. *Journal of Integrative and Eclectic Psychotherapy, 7*(1), 3–12.

Luborsky, L., Singer, B., & Luborsky, L. (1975). Comparative studies of psychotherapy. *Archives of General Psychiatry, 32,* 995–1008.

Maddi, S. (1973a). Ethics and psychotherapy: Remarks stimulated by White's paper. *The Counseling Psychologist, 40*(2), 26–29.

Maddi, S. (1973b). Creativity is strenuous. *The University of Chicago Magazine,* September-October, 18–23.

Mahrer, A. R. (Ed.) (1967). *The goals of psychotherapy.* Englewood Cliffs, NJ: Prentice-Hall.

Marmor, J. (1976). Common operational factors in diverse approaches to behavior change. In A. Burton (Ed.). *What makes behavior change possible?* (pp. 3–12). New York: Brunner/Mazel.

Maslow, A. H. (1956). Self-actualizing people: A study of psychological health. In C. E. Moustakis (Ed.). *The self: Explorations in personal growth,* (pp. 160–194). New York: Harper & Row.

Maslow, A. H. (1970). *Motivation and personality* (2nd ed.). New York: Harper & Row.

Maslow, A. H. (1971). *The farther reaches of human nature.* New York: Viking Press.

Menninger, K. A., & Holzman, P. S. (1973). *Theory of psychoanalytic techniques* (2nd ed.). New York: Basic Books.

Messer, S. B. (1986). Eclecticism in psychotherapy: Underlying assumptions, problems, and trade-offs. In J. C. Norcross (Ed.). *Handbook of eclectic psychotherapy* (pp. 379–397). New York: Brunner/Mazel.

Messer, S. B., & Winokur, M. (1984). Ways of knowing and visions of reality in psychoanalytic therapy and behavior therapy. In H. Arkowitz & S. B. Messer (Eds.). *Psychoanalytic therapy and behavior therapy: Is integration possible?* (pp. 63–100). New York: Plenum.

Murray, E. J. (1986). Possibilities and promises of eclectism. In J. C. Norcross (Ed.). *Handbook of eclectic psychotherapy* (pp. 398–415). New York: Brunner/Mazel.

Norcross, J. C. (Ed.). (1986). *Handbook of eclectic psychotherapy.* New York: Brunner/Mazel.

Norcross, J. C. (1990). Commentary: Eclecticism misrepresented and integration misunderstood. *Psychotherapy, 27,* 297–298.

Norcross, J. C., & Goldfried, M. R. (Eds.). (1992). *Handbook of psychotherapy integration.* New York: Basic Books.

Norcross, J. C., & Prochaska, J. O. (1982). A national survey of clinical psychologists: Affiliations and orientations. *The Clinical Psychologist, 35*(3), 1–6.

Norcross, J. C., Prochaska, J. O., & Gallagher, K. M. (1989). Clinical psychologists in the 1980's: II. Theory, research, and practice. *The Clinical Psychologist, 42,* 45–53.

Oberndorf, C. P. (1946). Constant elements in psychotherapy. *The Psychoanalytic Quarterly, 15,* 435–449.

Orlinsky, D. E., Grawe, K., & Parks, B. K. (1994). Process and outcome in psychotherapy—noch eminal. In A. E. Bergin & S. L. Garfield (Eds.). *Handbook of psychotherapy and behavior change* (4th ed., pp. 270–376). New York: Wiley.

Orlinsky, D. E., & Howard, K. I. (1986). Process and outcome in psychotherapy. In S. L. Garfield & A. E. Bergin (Eds.). *Handbook of psychotherapy and behavior change* (3rd ed., pp. 311–384). New York: Wiley.

Parloff, M. B. (1967). Goals in psychotherapy: Mediating and ultimate. In A. R. Mahrer (Ed.). *The goals of psychotherapy* (pp. 5–19). Englewood Cliffs, NJ: Prentice-Hall.

Patterson, C. H. (1959). *Counseling and psychotherapy: Theory and practice.* New York: Harper & Row.

Patterson, C. H. (1966a). Science, behavior control and values. *Insight, 5* (2), 14–21.

Patterson, C. H. (1966b). *Theories of counseling and psychotherapy.* New York: Harper & Row.

Patterson, C. H. (1973). *Theories of counseling and psychotherapy* (2nd ed.). New York: Harper & Row.

Patterson, C. H. (1980). *Theories of counseling and psychotherapy* (3rd ed.). New York: Harper & Row.

Patterson, C. H. (1984). Empathy, warmth and genuineness in psychotherapy: A review of reviews. *Psychotherapy, 21,* 431–438.

Patterson, C. H. (1985a). *The therapeutic relationship: Foundations for an eclectic psychotherapy.* Pacific Grove, CA: Brooks/Cole.

Patterson, C. H. (1985b). What is the placebo in psychotherapy? *Psychotherapy, 22,* 163–169.

Patterson, C. H. (1986). *Theories of counseling and psychotherapy* (4th ed.). New York: Harper & Row.

Patterson, C. H. (1989). Eclecticism in psychotherapy: Is integration possible? *Psychotherapy, 26,* 157–161.

Patterson, C. H., & Hidore, S. (in press). Northvale, NJ: Jason Aronson.

Pedersen, P. (1976). The field of intercultural counseling. In P. Pedersen, W. J. Lonner, & J. G. Draguns (Eds.). *Counseling across cultures.* Honolulu: University Press of Hawaii.

Pentony, P. (1981). *Models of influence in psychotherapy.* New York: Free Press.

Prochaska, J. O., & DiClementi, C. C. (1984). *The transtheoretical approach: Crossing traditional trends of therapy.* Chicago: Dorsey Press.

Prochaska, J. O., & DiClementi, C. C. (1986). The transtheoretical approach. In J. C. Norcross (Ed.). *Handbook of eclectic psychotherapy* (pp. 163–200). New York: Brunner/Mazel.

Prochaska, J. O., & Norcross, J. C. (1983). Contemporary psychotherapists: A national survey of characteristics, practices, orientations, and attitudes. *Psychotherapy: Theory, Research, and Practice, 20,* 161–173.

Rioch, D. M. K. (1951). Theories of psychotherapy. In W. Dennis (Ed.). *Current trends in psychological theory.* Pittsburgh: University of Pittsburgh Press.

Robertson, M. (1979). Some observations from an eclectic therapist. *Psychotherapy: Theory, Research and Practice, 16,* 18–21.

Rogers, C. R. (1951). *Client-centered therapy: Its current practice, implications and theory.* Boston: Houghton Mifflin.

Rogers, C. R. (1956). Client-centered therapy: A current view. In F. Fromm-Reichmann & J. L. Moreno (Eds.). *Progress in psychotherapy: 1956.* New York: Grune & Stratton.

Rogers, C. R. (1957). The necessary and sufficient conditions of therapeutic personality change. *Journal of Consulting Psychology, 21,* 95–103.

Rogers, C. R. (1959). A theory of therapy, personality and interpersonal relationships, as developed in the client-centered framework. In S. Koch (Ed.). *Psychology: A study of a science. Vol. 3: Formulations of the person and the social context* (pp. 184–256). New York: McGraw-Hill.

Rogers, C. R. (1961). *On becoming a person.* Boston: Houghton Mifflin.

Rosenthal, D., & Frank, J. D. (1956). Psychotherapy and the placebo effect. *Psychological Bulletin, 53,* 294–302.

Rosenzweig, S. (1936). Some implicit common factors in diverse methods of psychotherapy. *American Journal of Orthopsychiatry, 6,* 412–415.

Shaffer, L. F. (1953). Of whose reality I cannot doubt. *American Psychologist, 8,* 608–623.

Shapiro, A. K. (1971). Placebo effects in medicine, psychotherapy, and psychoanalysis. In A. E. Bergin and S. L. Garfield (Eds.). *Handbook of psychotherapy and behavior change* (pp. 439–473). New York: Wiley.

Shapiro, A. K., & Morris, L. A. (1978). The placebo effect in medical and psychological therapies. In S. L. Garfield and A. E. Bergin (Eds.). *Handbook of psychotherapy and behavior change* (2nd ed., pp. 369–410). New York: Wiley.

Skinner, B. F. (1953). *Science and human behavior.* New York: Macmillan.

Skinner, B. F. (1958). Reinforcement today. *American Psychologist, 14,* 94–99.

Smith, D. (1982). Trends in counseling and psychotherapy. *American Psychologist, 37,* 802–809.

Smith, M. B. (1973). Comment on White's paper. *The Counseling Psychologist, 4*(2), 48–50.

Smith, M. L., & Glass, G. V. (1977). Meta-analysis of psychotherapy outcome studies. *American Psychologist, 32,* 752–760.

Smith, M. L., Glass, G. V., & Miller, J. (1980). *The benefits of psychotherapy.* Baltimore: Johns Hopkins University Press.

Snygg, D., & Combs, A. W. (1949). *Individual behavior: A new frame of reference for psychology.* New York: Harper.

Spence, J. T. (1985). Achievement American style: The rewards and costs of individualism. *American Psychologist, 40,* 1285–1295.

Spitz, R. (1945). Hospitalism: Genesis of psychiatric conditions in early childhood. *Psychoanalytic Study of the Child, 1,* 53–74.

Stricker, G., & Gold, J. R. (Eds.). (1993). *Comprehensive handbook of psychotherapy integration.* New York: Plenum.

Strong, S. R. (1978). Social psychological approaches to psychotherapy research. In S. L. Garfield & A. E. Bergin (Eds.). *Handbook of psychotherapy and behavior change* (2nd ed., pp. 101–135). New York: Wiley.

Strupp, H. H. (1978). Psychotherapy research and practice: An overview. In S. L. Garfield and A. E. Bergin (Eds.). *Handbook of psychotherapy and behavior change* (2nd ed., pp. 3–22). New York: Wiley.

Strupp, H. H. (1986a). Psychotherapy: Research, practice and public policy. *American Psychologist, 41,* 120–130.

Strupp, H. H. (1986b). The nonspecific hypothesis of therapeutic effectiveness. *American Journal of Orthopsychiatry, 56,* 513–520.

Strupp, H. H., & Binder, J. L. (1984). *Psychotherapy in a new key: A guide to time limited dynamic psychotherapy.* New York: Basic Books.

Sue, D. W. (1981). *Counseling the culturally different: Theory and practice.* New York: Wiley.

Swan, G. E., & MacDonald, M. L. (1978). Behavior therapists in practice: A national survey of behavior therapists. *Behavior Therapy, 9,* 799–807.

Truax, C. B., & Carkhuff, R. R. (1967). *Toward effective counseling and psychotherapy.* Chicago: Aldine.

Wachtel, P. L. (1977). *Psychoanalysis and behavior therapy: Toward an integration.* New York: Basic Books.

Walsh, A. (1991). *The science of love.* Buffalo: Prometheus Books.

Watkins, C. E., Jr., Lopez, F. G., Campbell, V. L., & Himmell, C. D. (1986). Contemporary counseling psychology: Results of a national survey. *Journal of Counseling Psychology, 33,* 301–309.

Watkins, C. E., Jr., & Watts, R. E. (1995). Psychotherapy survey research studies: Some consistent findings and integrative conclusions. *Psychotherapy in Private Practice, 13,* 49–68.

White, R. W. (1959). Motivation reconsidered: The concept of competence. *Psychological Review, 66,* 297–333.

White, R. W. (1973). The concept of healthy personality: What do we really mean? *The Counseling Psychologist, 4*(2), 3–12.

Williamson, E. G. (1950). A concept of counseling. *Occupations, 29,* 182–189.

Williamson, E. G. (1958). Values orientation in counseling. *Personnel and Guidance Journal, 37,* 520–528.

Williamson, E. G. (1963). The social responsibilities of counselors. *Illinois Guidance and Personnel Association Newsletter,* Winter, 5–13.

Williamson, E. G. (1965). *Vocational counseling.* New York: McGraw-Hill.

Wolfe, T. (1976). The "ME" decade. *New York Magazine,* August 23, pp. 26–40.

Wolpe, J. (1973). *The practice of behavior therapy* (2nd ed.). New York: Pergamon Press.

Wolpe, J. (1982). *The practice of behavior therapy* (3rd ed.). New York: Pergamon Press.

Wyatt, F. (1948). The self-expression of the psychotherapist. *Journal of Consulting Psychology, 12,* 82–87.

Ziskind, E. (1949). How specific is psychotherapy? *American Journal of Psychiatry, 106,* 285–291.

Acknowledgments

CHAPTER 1: Case example from *The Collected Papers, Volume 3* by Sigmund Freud. Authorized translation under the supervision of Alix and James Strachey. Published by Basic Books, Inc. by arrangement with the Hogarth Press, Ltd. and the Institute of Psycho-Analysis, London. Reprinted by permission of Basic Books, a division of HarperCollins Publishers, Inc.

CHAPTER 2: Jung, Carl; *Collected Works (vol. 16), Appendix.* Copyright © 1966 by Princeton University Press. Reprinted by permission of Princeton University Press.

CHAPTER 3: Portion of case example reproduced by permission of the publisher, F. E. Peacock Publishers Inc., Itsaka, Illinois. From J. G. Manaster & R. J. Corsini, *Individual Psychology,* copyright 1982, pp. 261, 278–283.

CHAPTER 4: "Case Example: Withdrawal and Regression" from *Through Pediatrics to Psychoanalysis* by D. W. Winnicott. Copyright © by Basic Books, Inc. Reprinted by permission of BasicBooks, a division of HarperCollins Publishers, Inc.

CHAPTER 5: Case example reprinted with the permission of Simon & Shuster from the Macmillan College textbook *Steps in Psychotherapy* by John Dollard, Frank Auld, and Alice Marsden White. Copyright © 1953 by Macmillan Publishing Company, renewed 1981 by Frank Auld, Jr., and Joan C. Dollard.

CHAPTER 7: Case example from Yankura/Dryden, *Doing RET: Albert Ellis in Action.* Used by permission of Springer Publishing Company, Inc., New York, 10012.

CHAPTER 8: Case example from "Cognitive Therapy of Panic Disorder" by A. T. Beck and Robert Greenberg. In Frances and Hales (Eds.). *American Psychiatric Press Review of Psychiatry, 7,* 571–572, 1988. Reprinted by permission.

CHAPTER 10: Case example from R. A. Neimeyer, "George Kelly as Therapist: A Review of His Tapes." In A. W. Landfield and L. M. Leitner (Eds.). *Personal Construct Philosophy: Psychotherapy and Personality,* © 1980. Reprinted by permission of John Wiley & Sons, Inc.

CHAPTER 11: Case sample from *Transactional Analysis in Psychotherapy* by Eric Berne, M.D. Copyright © 1961 by Eric Berne. Reprinted by permission of Random House, Inc.

CHAPTER 12: Case example from "Gestalt Therapy Verbatim" by F. S. Perls. *The Gestalt Journal, Press xx,* 101–103 and 298–306, 1992. Reprinted with permission.

CHAPTER 13: Case examples from Carl R. Rogers, *On Becoming a Person: A Psychotherapist's View of Psychotherapy.* Copyright © 1961 by Houghton Mifflin Company. Reprinted with permission.

NAME INDEX

SUBJECT INDEX